A Man of Sorrow

Patrick Brontë, shortly after his arrival at Haworth, c.1825

A Man of Sorrow

The Life, Letters and Times of the
Rev. Patrick Brontë
1777-1861

by

John Lock and Canon W. T. Dixon

Foreword by
The Archbishop of York

NELSON

THOMAS NELSON AND SONS LTD
36 Park Street London W1
Parkside Works Edinburgh 9
10 Warehouse Road Apapa Lagos
P.O. Box 25012 Nairobi

Thomas Nelson (Australia) Ltd
597 Little Collins Street Melbourne

Thomas Nelson and Sons (Africa) (Pty) Ltd
P.O. Box 9881 Johannesburg

Thomas Nelson and Sons (Canada) Ltd
81 Curlew Drive Don Mills Ontario

Thomas Nelson and Sons
Copewood and Davis Streets Camden 3, N.J.

First published 1965

©

John Lock
Canon W. T. Dixon
1965

Printed in Great Britain by
Thomas Nelson (Printers) Ltd, London and Edinburgh

Foreword

MY FRIENDS Mr John Lock and Canon W. T. Dixon have given us in this book a fine piece of literary and historical work. It represents the results of long years of painstaking research, and uses a wealth of material contained in letters and diaries which hitherto have been unpublished. The outcome is a self-authenticating portrait of Patrick Brontë.

The typescript pages of this book held me spellbound, as well they might, for they deal with places which to me are more than places of literary interest: most of the places were of parochial and pastoral concern to me when I was Bishop of the Diocese of Bradford. But there was more in it even than this. As I read, I discovered that I was being introduced, as it were person to person, to a *man*. Here was no undiscriminating eulogy, nor indeed a corroboration of a portrait already given to the world. Here was a living person—ambitious and sometimes hot-tempered in his early years, with an avid appetite for books and a capacity to produce some quite atrocious verse. Here was a man who, from a pastoral point of view, was a not unworthy successor to the great William Grimshaw, and one who, from the point of view of the father of a unique family, by no means corresponded to the picture given by Mrs Gaskell. Indeed this book proves to be largely a justification of Patrick Brontë, a man maligned by ill-informed critics, and overshadowed by brilliant daughters who owed far more to him than history has so far allowed.

If Charlotte, for example, owed much to the moors which surrounded the parsonage where she lived—and who can doubt that indebtedness ?—she owed an immense debt to the father who, unbowed as storm after storm swept over him, provided her with an eager mind, a stable home and, it would seem, at least a measure of sympathetic understanding. That is no mean contribution towards the making of books which will for ever retain a place of high honour among our English classics.

It remains for the experts to pronounce a verdict on the thesis of this book. As they do so, they will not only reflect on the wealth of material to which the authors have had access and of which they have made such rich use. They will also recollect that the writers have lived long enough in the Yorkshire moorland village of Haworth to allow its influence to penetrate into their beings in some such way as it did into the Brontës themselves; and that, it may well be, is a factor in the understanding of the Brontës, and perhaps especially of Patrick, the importance of which it is hard to over-estimate. I have referred to the experts. I do not pretend to be among their number. But to one reader of the typescript, at least, there is a clear ring of authenticity and truth about the portrait which emerges from this outstanding book, and he is grateful.

Bishopthorpe, York   DONALD EBOR
December 1962

Preface

THERE is a mass of evidence from which to fill in the details of the Rev. Patrick Brontë's long life. It has never before been collected together; most of it has never been published. Letters, diaries, note-books, by Patrick and about him, some in public hands, many in private, have remained ignored for over a century.

Archbishops' palaces, bishops' registries, Church commissioners, religious societies, Church trustees, Methodist records, a cathedral, churches, chapels, cemeteries, historical research institutes, universities, colleges, schools, museums, libraries, government offices, banks, police records, estate papers, general and district registries, and the Inns of Court, have all yielded up those forgotten truths. From private sources come diaries, and letters which, together with the contemporary news-papers, fill in many scenes from the accounts of eye-witnesses.

Patrick Brontë has been followed closely from the mud-cabin in Ireland until he came to rest in the vaults of Haworth Church—followed even to places which he was hardly known to have visited. His friends and acquaintances have been followed too, and they are numerous: some of them were leaders of the age. Their letters, diaries and note-books have also been examined to provide further information about Patrick's life. Nor have his family and servants, and indeed his various flocks, failed to give a great many further facts.

How the Rev. Patrick Brontë lived, who were his friends, how exciting and how sad was his life, the facts reveal. But he does *not* very much resemble the portrait given by Mrs Gaskell over a century ago, when she first opened the door of Haworth Parsonage to admit the outside world. Her attacks on both Mr Brontë and Haworth were equally unjustified, and the impressions they created are still deeply rooted. It is a great pity that, having been forced to delete whole passages about Mr Brontë from the hurried third edition, the publishers restored them when the original was once more permitted.

Mrs Gaskell met Mr Brontë four times: in September 1853, when he was already seventy-six years old; again in 1855; in 1856; and finally when he was on his death-bed. She knew nothing of his earlier life, indeed it was not her province to examine it. The task in hand was to present Charlotte's nobility to the world, as Patrick Brontë knew when he said little to her of his own long life.

That life when fully known reveals courage, both physical and spiritual, ambition of the better sort, energy, passion, learning, compassion, sincerity, wit, honesty, and a great love of children, animals and, above all, God. Indeed, the stuff of the Brontës was not lacking in the father. He it was who gave his daughters their belief in Eternity, their high moral standards, and, if not the talent for, certainly the love of, artistic things. It is also too seldom recognized that Mr Brontë's sufferings were greater in extent than those of his children. Throughout the great ordeal of losing in turn all those he held dear, he possessed a courage and faith that are an inspiration.

In every case where the originals of published documents or texts exist, they have been consulted and used. In quoting from all documents the original spelling and punctuation are preserved, including the varying accents used in the name Brontë. Where we quote published material, it is invariably from old newspaper files and works long out of print, or not easily available to the public.

Practically all the letters of Patrick Brontë that are extant are included in this volume, most of them in full.

The Brontës have never been fully placed against their ecclesiastical, social, and topographical background. Such a background belongs to the life of the father. We give, therefore, the detailed record of the 103 years covering the Brontë story, from 1776 (the marriage of Patrick's parents) to 1879 (the pulling-down of old St Michael's Church, Haworth).

Having lived at Haworth for many years we possess the invaluable advantage of meeting many amongst the thousands who come here, and have based the book largely on their queries and requests for information. Of Mr Brontë's life as an active clergyman nothing seems known by the general public, and little of his wide interest in public affairs and the inventions of his age. We have therefore stressed in more detail those parts of his life about which there are the most queries.

Over a hundred years ago Patrick Brontë wrote to Mrs Gaskell asking her to undertake the task of placing before the world a true portrait of his daughter Charlotte—a task he was even prepared to attempt himself, had he been unable to procure a worthy biographer. We feel it is time that the long story of Patrick Brontë should also be made known and his real character revealed; indeed a full-scale biography of him is long overdue. If, as a result of the evidence contained

here, Patrick Brontë should be considered in a new and more favourable
light, we shall have done some belated justice to his memory, and that,
we believe, would please the Brontë sisters greatly.

Haworth, 1964

J. L.
W. T. D.

Haworth 1861

ON a June day in 1861 the people of Haworth heard the news that their
old parson had been called to his last rest. They had known for some
months that the end was coming, for Sunday by Sunday they had
missed him from his accustomed place in church. Nevertheless when
his death was announced it came as a great shock to them all, as for over
forty years they had always known Mr Brontë in the parsonage. The
children he had christened in his early days had long since married and
brought their own children to him for christening. A whole generation
had grown up with Mr Brontë and it would be a long time before they
grew accustomed to his passing.

The searchlight of world publicity had not yet focused on the
village of Haworth. Few of the villagers had read Mrs Gaskell's
criticism of their incumbent, though Mr Nicholls had told them about
it. To them he was just their parson, and his daughters very clever
girls whom they had always known and of whom they were justly proud.

Now they stood in silent rows, with heads bowed, as through the
little "gate of the dead" the body of Patrick Brontë was carried. This
was no new experience for them; they had stood there so often in the
last forty years, first for Mrs Brontë, then for each of the children in
turn (save Anne). As a muffled peal rang out from the tower, they
remembered that it was Mr Brontë who had helped to have the bells
put there. As they entered the church it was to the solemn notes of the
great organ swelling into a crescendo of praise, and they remembered
again that he had been largely responsible for the installation of their
organ. As the service drew to its close they sang together *Nunc Dimittis*,
"Lord, now lettest thou thy servant depart in peace", and left their old
parson reunited at last with his family. This was indeed the end of the
chapter, for even the church itself was soon to be pulled down and
re-built, leaving the old tower a silent witness of the past.

But a new chapter was soon to begin, a chapter which still goes on ; the story of the hundreds of thousands of people who from every land have come to stand beside the last resting-place of the Brontë family, to visit their old parsonage home, and to pay their tribute to the genius of the sisters.

The picture of their old parson that the people of Haworth carried away with them that day was summed up perfectly by Nancy Garrs, a faithful servant of the parsonage when she said, "He was the kindest man who ever drew breath." And it is still the same picture which the people of Haworth carry of him, so contrary to the judgment of the world.

What then was he really like, this man of sorrow ?

Contents

List of Plates

xiii

TO ALL THOSE
WHO HAVE WORSHIPPED
AT HAWORTH CHURCH
PAST AND PRESENT

Yet man is born unto trouble, as the sparks fly upward.

Job v. 7

I do not deny that I am somewhat eccentrick. Had I been numbered amongst the calm, sedate, concentric men of the world, I should not have been as I now am, and I should in all probability never have had such children as mine have been.

Rev. Patrick Brontë to Mrs Gaskell,
30th July 1857

CHAPTER I

Ambition

EVEN at its very inception the Brontë story is cloaked in romance. From the obscure mists of eighteenth-century Ireland comes the tale of a runaway marriage between Hugh Brunty and Eleanor McClory—an elopement necessitated mainly by that insuperable Irish obstacle, religious opposition.

Hugh Brunty, at the time a young farm-hand at Donoughmore—a Protestant, if anything—sought the hand of the tall and beautiful Eleanor McClory, a member of a Roman Catholic family of Ballynaskeagh in County Down. There are tales of feuds, fierce opposition to the match, a rival for the lady's hand and runaway rides at night. We even have details of the bride, "a pure Celt, with long golden ringlets, forehead of Parian marble, evenly set teeth like lustrous pearls, rosy cheeks, long dark-brown eyelashes, deep hazel eyes with violet tint and melting expression, lambent fire ready to flash indignation and scorn, a tall and stately figure, with head well poised above a graceful neck, and well-formed bust . . . .".

However the mists begin to lift and the sun of truth illuminates the facts. In 1776 Hugh Brunty married his Eleanor (or Alice, as she was often called) at the Protestant Magherally Church. At her marriage Eleanor McClory renounced her faith and became a Protestant—a most important fact for her Yorkshire-born grandchildren. Hugh seems to have been so indifferent to Church attendance in his youth that it remains surprising that it was not he who transferred his thin allegiance in order to gain his bride. The honeymoon, lasting only a few days, was spent at Warrenpoint on the north side of Carlingford Lough, near the Mourne mountains. After the brief tranquillity of this delightful place Mrs Brunty returned to spend the next few weeks with her presumably angry brother, whilst Hugh made the final preparations for their new home. Alas, these were few enough! Before working as a farm-labourer for James Harshaw of Donoughmore, Hugh Brunty had had little or no chance to save money; his previous employment at Mount Pleasant limekilns near Dundalk earned him only two and sixpence a week and his present wage was very little more. He had no friends from whom he might seek assistance. Indeed, had he not become acquainted with the Rev. William M'Cormick, when the latter was curate at Rathfriland, and who was now in charge of Magherally Established Church, he would have searched long to find anyone prepared to marry him. The religious opposition to his marriage precluded all help or friendship.

Soon, however, Hugh found a home for his bride, one within reach of even his slender pocket, having a rent of only sixpence a week. It was a thatched cabin at Emdale, Loughbrickland, in the parish of Drumballyroney-cum-Drumgooland, County Down. Well isolated from its fellows, the cottage stood on the Banbridge and Warrenpoint road, just where the Newry and Rathfriland road crossed it, about a mile from Ballynaskeagh Manse. This lonely little cottage had a mud floor and walls of loose-fitting stone, the gaps filled in with dried earth ; the roof was thatched. It contained but two tiny rooms : a small bedroom at the back, and the main room which was used as kitchen and corn kiln. Having brought his wife to this cabin, Hugh endeavoured to make a living on the premises—hence the erection of the corn kiln. Strong indeed must the atmosphere have been at times, as the only real source of fresh air was through the cottage door, although the bedroom was provided with a small window. Working ceaselessly day and night, Hugh began to make a little money to provide for the large family that was to come. In the small back room amidst the pungent smell of roasting corn, on St Patrick's Day, Monday, 17th March 1777, his first child was born, Patrick Brunty. Soon there would be another child and then another, ten in all ; but they would be born in two other homes, both larger and more luxurious than this little cabin. Only Patrick was destined to be born in the mud of Ireland, yet only Patrick would shake that mud from his boots and achieve a high place for himself in the wider world.

In 1778 Hugh and his wife and child left the little cabin and rented a small house (yet how large compared to the hovel they had quit) at Lisnacreevy, barely half a mile away. There was a little money now, and room for a growing family. Already a second child was on the way.

Now that he was settled, Hugh Brunty helped occasionally at farms or on fence-repairing or road-making, which together with his corn-roasting brought in enough money to keep a large family well above the starvation level—however simple the fare ; indeed he invited his sister to stay for a time. At the house at Lisnacreevy the Brunty family remained until 1794. Eight more children were born there. William in 1779, Hugh in 1781, James in 1783, Walsh in 1786, Jane in 1789, Mary in 1791 and Rose and Sarah (twins) about 1793. The Drumgooland parish registers began only in 1779, so there is no record of Patrick's baptism. The baptizing of the next six children is fully recorded, but the names of Rose and Sarah do not appear. In one case the father's name is written as Hugh Bruntee and the mother's name varies between Eleanor and Elinor. In 1794 the family moved to a larger house at Ballynaskeagh which had five rooms, including three bedrooms, and there the last child, Alice, was born in 1796. Thus the first five children were boys, followed by five girls.

As the eldest, Patrick was much looked up to by his brothers and sisters. His tall, erect figure, fine features, bright auburn hair, aquiline nose and powerful eyes, which flashed fire at times for all their almost insipid pale blue colour, commanded their early respect. From their youngest days the Brunty children mixed little with others: in some measure this was forced upon them by their neighbours. Their parents were of mixed religion (for the local people would always consider Eleanor Brunty to be a Roman Catholic), therefore the young Bruntys were heathens and not such as decent children could mix with.

The growing family were brought up on the plainest of Irish fare, from the simplicity of which Patrick rarely departed in later life, save for the addition of meat and a few Yorkshire specialities that were irresistible. Breakfast at the Brunty home in Lisnacreevy consisted of coarse porridge and milk served in a wooden noggin and eaten with a wooden spoon. Dinner, taken at about noon, was invariably a platter of potatoes roasted in their skins. "Piece-time" at about four o'clock consisted of home-made bread and a little butter-milk. The bread was made by mashing together Fadge potatoes and oatmeal, a most indigestible mixture that frequently caused heartburn. Thus at an early age Patrick felt the scourge of dyspepsia that was to dog him all his life.

Supper was usually at seven, with more potatoes and boiled milk and occasionally an egg. At least once a year a cow or pig was purchased to be well salted. The only alternative beverage to milk was peppermint tea, which was frequently drunk in order to counteract the ravages of Mrs Brunty's bread.

As with their food, so their clothes were of the simplest. Hugh Brunty preferred woollen garments for his entire family: his great dislike of cotton or linen clothes sprang from a dread of fire. This fear was born with Patrick and remained with him always—woollen or silken garments only were to be allowed his family when he had a home of his own.

As he was a tall and strong lad, young Patrick was expected to help his mother about the house and this he did willingly enough; but of an evening, as the family sat round the fire, there were no words to be got from him. With his back to the fire he would sit in the corner peering at the volume he had taken from his father's shelf, the thin light dancing on the pages. Slowly he spelt the words out to himself. It would take some time for him to read this volume, which was as well, for there were only four books in the house. Both his mother and father were practically illiterate and relied for their amusement on the telling and hearing of the tales of old Ireland.

His mother possessed a small copy of the New Testament, whilst his father had three books—the Bible, Burns's *Poems* and the one that Patrick had decided to read first, *The Pilgrim's Progress*.

He knew that his father was familiar with the book, having had passages read to him and having puzzled out others for himself. Hugh made no attempt to interfere with his eldest son's desire to read and even encouraged him as much as was in his power. This liberty young Patrick never forgot and years later was to extend it freely to his own children to the enrichment of the world. As he falteringly accompanied Christian on his journey Patrick became entranced with Bunyan's visions and there was born within him a hungry desire to read, to travel and to reach some golden, if indefinable, goal.

Soon Patrick would have read and re-read those four volumes many times, learning all his favourite passages by heart and reciting them to himself as he walked alone down the solitary Irish lanes near his home. He was twelve now and would shortly be going out to work to help keep his younger brothers—then there might be no time for books, and he had read so very little. These were pleasant lanes to ramble in during the early summer months. Patrick wondered if the preacher would be along this way soon—he came every other year—up the Rathfriland road from Newry, passing near the old cabin at Emdale, preaching as he went. At first he had come on horseback, but of recent years advancing age and infirmity had forced him to hire a coach. Patrick remembered his coach breaking down nearby and the old man walking to Tanderagee to spend the night with his friend Dr Leslie. There is little doubt that young Patrick heard the preacher as he passed through the district; there is no doubt that he heard the hymns sung by his followers winging upwards towards the distant Mourne mountains. The words reached the heart of the young lad as he stood listening, and were implanted there for ever.

> Ye mountains and vales, in praises abound;
> Ye hills and ye dales, continue the sound:
> Break forth into singing, ye trees of the wood,
> For Jesus is bringing lost sinners to God.

The twelve-year-old Patrick, as he wandered along the lanes in that summer of 1789, would have, however, only one more opportunity of hearing John Wesley preach, but the impression created on his young mind would be lasting. Across the Channel the people of France would revolt against hunger, poverty and want. But in these islands there would be no such outbreak. The promise of glory in the world to come—of mansions in the sky—played a vital part in subduing the people's longing for better conditions. Although the Wesleyans were foremost in providing food for empty bellies it was the Bread of Heaven that proved their most nourishing offering. The people waited for death to bring them their reward, and the crisis passed.

But Patrick could run home happily and tell his parents that he had heard the hymns of the great and good men, John and Charles Wesley, and could ponder their meaning in his heart.

Hugh Brunty deserves some credit for this stirring of Patrick's emotions, for in an unwitting moment of inspiration he had, in defiance of some of his ostracizing neighbours, named his youngest son after Thomas Walsh, that persecuted follower of Wesley. In John Wesley's *Journal* we find this description of Patrick's homeland: "The country was uncommonly pleasant, running between two high ridges of mountains. But it was uphill and down all the way, so that we did not reach Rathfriland till near noon. Mr Barber, the Presbyterian Minister (a princely personage, I believe six feet and a half high), offering me his new spacious preaching-house, the congregation quickly gathered together."

But if many of the poor were dreaming of the joy and bliss that awaited them after death, Patrick was at this time concerned only with the life that stretched before him: yet he little foresaw the vital part that the influence of the travelling preacher was destined to play in his life.

Later that year, 1789, Patrick began work as a part-time assistant to a local blacksmith. He soon learned to blow the bellows, a task which left him free to recite under his breath those well-loved passages from the four precious books at home, or to chant to himself a snatch from one of the hymns of John Wesley. Soon he was put to more skilful tasks and became proficient in the casting of horseshoes and their nails.

One day a gentleman turned his horse into the yard to be shod. He fell into conversation with the blacksmith while Patrick worked on the new shoe. Soon the topic of what constituted "a gentleman" was discussed and the blacksmith opined that according to his view there were "three kinds of gentlemen, the born gentleman, the gentleman by good fortune, and the gentleman by nature". Suddenly he jerked his thumb towards Patrick and raised his voice: "Now, for instance, that boy standing there, though he *is* only between six and seven years of age [*sic*], is what I call a gentleman by nature."

Patrick let go the horse's leg and stiffened. Something indefinable, never to be eradicated, thrilled through his whole being.

"No one could tell what effect those few words had had upon him through life," he informed John Greenwood, the Haworth stationer, just before his eighty-second birthday. Greenwood confided the above incident to his diary, adding: "How true, and how prophetic were the words of this poor blacksmith! How oft have *we* had to remark that he was a real, a thorough Gentleman."

But there was little money to be gained from this employment and by now Patrick had four brothers and a sister—the birth of this sister, Jane, had reduced the family fortunes to a precarious state once more. Hugh Brunty knew a weaver called Robert Donald, who remained on friendly terms with the family despite the local hostility, and he managed to get Patrick apprenticed to him. Patrick worked hard, learning to weave linen and soon attained great skill in his new work. He would take his webs to Banbridge and Newry to be sold and then, having accomplished his business, could spend many hours browsing among the bookstalls. Patrick was in heaven, for to him a book was the most beautiful thing in the world; his hunger for books grew almost intolerable.

One day he was sent to Belfast with a special web he had made; he had some savings in his pocket, and some hours to spare. The result was inevitable: Patrick returned home laden with books and not a penny in his pocket. Now he commenced the habit of weaving with a book propped up before him, certainly to the detriment of his work. Years later his daughter Emily was to emulate him when baking in the kitchen.

Shortly after this raid on the Belfast bookstalls, Patrick left Mr Donald's employment and obtained work in Banbridge with a linen draper named Clibborn.

It was fortunate for Patrick that his webs had attracted Clibborn's attention previously when he brought them to his shop, for his engrossment in his books had lately caused his work to deteriorate to such an extent that his former employer was glad to see him go.

Patrick was now engaged in the making of very fine linen webs and for a time concentrated entirely on his new work. Meanwhile his little library grew slowly but surely. His latest treasure was a small copy of Milton's *Paradise Lost*, a treasure in more senses than one, for this little volume was soon to aid him climb the first rung of the ladder that would lead him out of the Irish bogs.

It was now his custom to take a book with him on his lone wanderings through the lanes and fields, and during the summer days of 1792 Patrick, now fifteen years old, rarely went forth without a book in his pocket. One day he was discovered by the Rev. Andrew Harshaw (a kinsman of James Harshaw, the farmer of Donoughmore for whom his father had once worked) strutting up and down between two trees, throwing his arms wildly about as he read out lines from Milton's epic. As he recited aloud the boy worked himself into a frenzy of excitement, to the complete fascination of the onlooker.

Now Harshaw was a Presbyterian "Stickit" minister—having no living within the Church—who taught at nearby Ballynafern School. A far-sighted, well-educated man, who had, however, failed to make the progress in his Church that he had hoped for, he suffered from a sense of frustration in being reduced to teaching a few peasant children in a tiny village school. He remembered the hopes and dreams of his own youth as he stood watching the enthusiastic youngster in front of him, and a deep chord of sympathy was instinctively struck within him. Only two helping hands were to be necessary to take Patrick Brunty out of Ireland and into the wider world. On that summer's day the first of these was offered, and gladly accepted. Andrew Harshaw had a good library and from it he lent Patrick those books that would best satisfy his hungry craving. There was little rest for Patrick now. He had made his decision: he would be a teacher. To teach meant books, and books meant life itself. Patrick slept little: Ovid, Virgil, Homer, Herodotus were his constant companions until the small hours. Sleep was limited at first to five or six hours a night, then reduced to only four. Every morning Patrick rose before dawn and went to Andrew Harshaw for two hours' schooling in the classics and mathematics. Then, at first light, he would be off to Banbridge, finishing his breakfast during the five-mile walk to the linen draper's, where he would work at his loom until dark, then walk home to supper and Ovid and Virgil and Homer and Herodotus. So it went on week after week, Patrick never flagging, indeed increasing his energies until sleep became almost a stranger. Hour after hour he studied in his room, never lifting his head from the closely printed pages before him: and there was only the sickly glimmer of a feeble rushlight to work by. The pursuit of learning went on month after month, but his eyes were often red and swollen in the morning. His close attention to study under such difficult circumstances, along with his intricate work in making linen webs, was destined to injure his eyesight—a source of much trouble to him in later life. Indeed, even at such an early age he might have caused his eyes to be irreparably damaged had they not been partly relieved of their arduous duties at the beginning of 1793.

After Patrick had worked for Mr Clibborn for a year, his employer died suddenly and he was out of work. Fortunately for the family, his brothers William and Hugh were apprenticed out and it would not be very long before young James followed suit.

Patrick therefore decided to give all his time to study, and there seems to have been no strong objection from his father, so long as it would lead to some better form of employment. The Rev. Andrew Harshaw now gave Patrick all the tuition that his duties at Ballynafern would allow. Freed from the attentions to the loom and the daily ten-mile walk, Patrick made tremendous progress with his education—and gained those precious hours of sleep that saved his eyesight from almost certain destruction.

But these successful studies were soon to be interrupted, and rewarded. Early in the same year, when Patrick was sixteen, there was a vacancy for the position of teacher with the Glascar Hill Presbyterian Church School, and Andrew Harshaw did not hesitate a moment. Patrick had had only a smattering of education until the previous year, but he was now quite ready and able to undertake the required duties. Straight away Harshaw wrote to the Church authorities and strongly recommended Patrick for the position. There would be a short qualifying examination locally before he could become a teacher, but Harshaw had no grounds for fear in that connection. At first, his hopes for his young *protégé* seemed likely to be bitterly disappointed. The minister concerned, the Rev. Alexander Moore, wrote to say that as the young man's mother was a Catholic they could not consider the application and would be engaging someone else. But a few days later it was further announced that the other candidate had found himself unable to accept the post and Patrick Brunty would be appointed as teacher, subject to his proving satisfactory both in character and ability. Patrick soon proved himself acceptable on both heads and with a grateful heart plunged into his new work with tremendous enthusiasm.

Until now the Brunty family had never regularly attended a place of worship, but upon his new appointment Patrick rarely missed the Glascar Presbyterian service and soon assisted in conducting the music there. He continued to study with great assiduity and to enlarge his world of reading. He met and became friendly with the Rev. David Barber, Presbyterian minister of Rathfriland (the giant of John Wesley's *Journal*) and borrowed from him Spenser's *Faerie Queene*, the *Spectator*, Hume's *History of England* and the works of Shakespeare.

Nor did he neglect to add to his own library from his savings, although at this time this consisted, by necessity, of many text-books connected with his teaching. In 1795, for instance, he bought a calico-backed arithmetic book by Vosper, of Dublin, dated 1789. Inside the young teacher wrote his name several times, together with the year of purchase. In view of a later decision on his part regarding his name, it was not surprising that he varied from Pruty, Prunty and Brunty. A geography book printed in the same year was also purchased.

In such a thinly populated area the school at Glascar Hill was not overcrowded, the pupils consisting of the children of local farmers and workpeople. Each pupil paid a penny a week and regularly every Monday morning brought a turf as a contribution towards heating the small stone building. Yet such payments could not always suffice. One parent, John Lindsay of Bangrove, Rathfriland, entered in his account book for November 1793: "Pat Prunty for David's School bill—£1." David, the second son, became an officer in the Down Militia, as did many of Patrick's first pupils.

At this school Patrick was to remain for over five years and prove himself the most enlightened and advanced teacher the district had known. An examination of his methods and the encouragement he gave his young charges shows, thus early in his life, that it was only the mode of expression of his time to which he was to be tied, not the ideas.

From the very start Patrick studied closely the character of his pupils so that he could instruct each one according to his or her ability— a most unusual method in those days, especially in a village school. He scorned to use the whip on young children but troubled himself to find out what each boy could do, or liked best to do, and taught accordingly.

He lent the more eager readers of the class some of his own books so that they could take them home (one at a time) to learn a passage by heart. He visited all the parents and tried to persuade those of the brighter pupils to keep their children at school as long as was financially possible, in order that they might have a better chance in life. Where there was more than one in a family attending the school Patrick would overcome parental opposition to this by suggesting that the duller youngster be kept at home to help, rather than disturb the prospects of his more intelligent brother. He started a night-school—another innovation—for the slower-witted, giving up his own precious time of private study to help the lamer dogs along the path of knowledge. He also introduced some of the classics to the youngsters, often throwing aside the set text-books. He gave time for church singing to improve the soul and introduced gymnastics to benefit the body. But, greatest innovation of all, he shared with his pupils his growing love of nature. Frequent excursions were made into the countryside, where Patrick would point out the lines of the hills, the effects of light and shade, the various flights of birds. Patrick too was learning much on these rambles, and feelings were arising that would stay with him until the grave. During the summer holidays he would put away his books and lead the older boys in exploration of the Mourne mountains. They would climb to some vantage point for Patrick to point out to them all the wonders of their native land that stretched beneath them.

Once in winter he took some of the boys skating, when suddenly there was a low rumbling noise and the ice began to break at several points. The group of skaters were in the very centre of the ice, but with a calm authority that subdued the rising panic, Patrick quietly led the way, steering his pupils to safety through the breaking ice until they reached the shore. It was not the last time he would show courage in his life.

But Patrick came to the Mourne mountains many times, alone. Here, only, he needed no books : he could feast his eyes on the beauty of the hills, the sky, the sea. A love of eternal nature entered his heart ; the first snatches of the poems he would later write came vaguely into his mind, but they were mixed somehow with the hymns of Wesley. The preacher was dead now but his verses were still raised to the glory of God. Patrick stood gazing in rapture at the scene before him, and thanked God that the world could be beautiful. In his heart was born that love and understanding of the hills and the rocks and of beings that are not men, and the glory of it all entered his soul. Nature and God seemed one indivisible truth. Patrick would never forget these joys and when later he gave his daughter Emily life he would give her also this vital part of his heart and soul.

Meanwhile the years were passing and Patrick was growing up in another sense : could a passionate Irish youth of twenty-one think only of learning and hymns and the mountains ? In the summer of 1798 he found it difficult to ignore the growing attractions of a pupil called Helen. The daughter of a local farmer, she was a mature girl with flaming red hair. Report had it that she was discovered with her pockets full of his youthful verses, not all of them of an educational nature, so the attraction would appear to have been mutual. When the gallant Patrick was discovered kissing her among the corn-stacks the fiery Helen came close to upsetting the hopes and plans that Patrick's mentor had conceived for him five years earlier. Although she was fifteen, at that time a marriageable age, her family considered the incident an immoral breach of trust. Her brothers threatened to thrash the school-master, her father forbade all contact with him and the angry Patrick treated Harshaw to the first of those often more justified rages to come. Yet the affair was innocent enough. There was no official complaint

against the teacher and the good opinion of Andrew Harshaw was in
no way forfeited: the second helping hand that was to assist Patrick
on his way was not withdrawn in displeasure but was to be extended
to Patrick that autumn.

The Rev. Thomas Tighe, A.M., of Drumballyroney, rector of
Drumgooland and vicar of the united parishes of Drumgooland and
Drumballyroney was more than a little interested in the young teacher,
indeed he had had his eye quietly fixed on Patrick for some time. Thomas
Tighe, who was fifty-five, had obtained the living of Drumgooland the
year after Patrick was born and was the most important man in the
district. John Wesley had been a great friend of the Tighe family.

He and his preachers had always been welcome at the rectory and
at Rosanna, the mansion in County Wicklow belonging to the rector's
half-brother William Tighe. Here the Methodist teachers found warming shelter as they wandered through Ireland. "At Mrs Tighe's,
Rosanna, the itinerants had richly furnished apartments, were attended
by liveried servants, and met with Senators, Ministers, and ladies of
rank and talent, while within a day or two they stopped in a mud cabin,
with a little straw for a bed." On the very last visit which John Wesley
paid to Ireland he stayed at Rosanna on 25th June 1789 before returning
to England to die in 1791.

There was a vacancy for a teacher at the school connected with the
parish church of Drumballyroney; there was a tutor needed for the
rector's sons; and Thomas Tighe knew the man he wanted. He offered
both posts to Patrick Brunty. Now the Presbyterian minister of Rathfriland was also a friend and follower of Wesley; thus there was no real
change in loyalty for Patrick in his giving up his teaching at the Presbyterian school to enter the rector's house nearby. Patrick accepted at
once and resigned his post as master at Glascar Hill.

Shortly after commencing his new duties at the much larger school
at Drumballyroney he was entrusted with the private education of
Tighe's children, whom the rector would scarcely have committed to
Patrick's charge if he had considered as a serious offence the kiss
bestowed on the youthful Helen. Patrick could indeed be happy at his
promotion. His career as a teacher was progressing well; but a little
over three years at Drumballyroney School and that career would end
for ever.

When Patrick was appointed as master there and, at the same time,
accepted into the family of the Rev. Thomas Tighe, he entered into
the stream of a great religious movement that would soon carry him
across the sea away from his native land. Thomas Tighe had watched
Patrick for a long time and marked him as a most promising recruit for

the service of the Lord. Wesley and his followers were ever eager to add young men to their ranks and constantly on the watch for any shining possibility. The rector of Drumgooland had found a tutor for his children ; with the use of gentle persuasion would he not also find a worthy servant of God ? Patrick found the transfer from the Presbyterian Church to the parish church at Drumballyroney of little consequence at the time : the same praises were sung, for in both services the hymns of Charles and John Wesley played the most prominent part. As for the school, the new master was soon a great favourite and continued the original ideas he had introduced at Glascar Hill. Patrick knew the preacher's hymns by heart now, and under the shade of the beeches and chestnut trees in the large rectory grounds and on the lonely slopes of the mountains would pour out his soul in song. He had written some verses and found he enjoyed writing poetry almost as much as reading. He wanted one day to write poems to the glory of God and the beauty of the hills.

By the end of 1799, after working just over a year for Thomas Tighe, Patrick found he was able to save money. The rector's large library was at his disposal, so there was no need to buy books. Patrick could have wished for a greater selection at the rectory : he was anxious to read of military exploits and exploration. He interested himself closely in world affairs and read the gazettes. His first hero was Nelson, whose exploits he followed and who that year was created Duke of Bronté. Throughout his life Patrick would retain a passionate interest in military matters and political affairs. But Tighe wished his young teacher to read the volumes of theology he possessed and Patrick could hardly refuse. So he read on, agreeing with some of the ideas and convictions he met with and violently disagreeing with others. He pondered on what he had learnt, listened to the hymns in church, wandered along the lanes singing them to himself, and went again to the mountains to see the wonders of nature. When the Rev. Thomas Tighe eventually suggested he should enter the ministry he found that Patrick had already made up his mind to do so, had he but the means to achieve this end. In the classroom he could but impart the knowledge of the world, from the pulpit he could extend the wonder and glory of Christ. Would he not also have a larger audience to whom he could show the joys and marvels of nature ? Patrick had made his decision and thereby, perhaps, the Army lost a gallant commander. Certainly the teaching profession lost an enlightened and wise instructor.

Patrick now saved every penny he could, and whilst he taught the rector's children, Tighe gave him religious instruction. By the spring of 1802 Patrick had saved over £25 and had a thorough grounding in theology. Despite the ridicule of some of the local young men Patrick was confident he could succeed, and it was arranged that he should go to Cambridge in the following October and enter St John's College. The choice of Cambridge was that of Thomas Tighe, who had been at St John's from 1771 to 1775. From the religious point of view no harm was likely to come to his young *protégé*. At King's College Charles Simeon was wielding great influence over the undergraduates, and he had learned his Methodism from Wesley's great friend, John Fletcher. He was at this time anxious to win recruits to the Evangelical banner to save them from falling into the Calvinistic clutch of the Countess of Huntingdon's "Connexion" and to retain a leaven of Methodism within the Church as a balance to the High Churchmen of the Establishment.

This was important for Patrick and many other young men with Methodist training and sympathies; as Dissenters they could enter the university, but were not permitted to proceed to their degree until they had subscribed to the Thirty-nine Articles.

Patrick determined to take the oath and his degree and, like many other Evangelicals within the Church, keep something of Methodism inside the Establishment whilst working closely whenever possible with the independent Wesleyans.

But there were other reasons for choosing St John's; the fees were moderate compared with those of most colleges and, by means of the many scholarships awarded, Patrick could, possibly, be independent of financial assistance. Certainly awards would be necessary to Patrick if his meagre financial resources were to suffice him to remain at Cambridge long enough to succeed. At St John's he would find others who could obtain a university education only by living a frugal life. In addition, "the divinity faculty was more strongly represented in St John's than in any other society". But for Patrick the most important advantage to his future ministry would prove to be that St John's was "noted for its preponderance of Yorkshiremen".

Patrick left the school at Drumballyroney in the summer of 1802 and prepared for his new life. His family were not without means of succour: his four brothers were working and their home at Ballynaskeagh seemed well provided for. Nevertheless Patrick promised his mother that he would send regularly whatever money he could spare, a promise he kept until her death.

Tender were the leave-takings, although his brothers had no interest in books and were perplexed as to why Patrick should wish to go so far from home to learn when he had a good job teaching others at a local school.

In September Patrick sailed for England—he was twenty-five years of age. Something of his feelings in that hour he later bequeathed to Albion, the hero of his tale. He stood at the ship's rail gazing at his native land as it fell away into the distance. He could still make out dimly the mountains where only a day or two ago he had wandered for the last time. The pale blue eyes were moist with tears as he realized the sacrifice always entailed in any ambitious endeavour. Later, as the coach rolled southwards along the dusty roads of England, there was time to remember the days that were now over: the preacher, and the hymns that rose up from the country lanes; Andrew Harshaw, who had taught him so much; Thomas Tighe and the musty books in his library. Yet the greatest influence over his heart were those hills he had seen yesterday dropping into the sea. He had come to England to enter the service of God, that God whose love he had first felt among the Mourne mountains.

On 1st October 1802, the tall, striking young Irishman with his auburn hair and eager pale blue eyes walked through Cambridge with a determined tread and boldly entered the imposing gateway of St John's, wherein lay all his hopes. He entered the Second Court with its red-brick perfection; this part of the College was practically unaltered since it was built by Ralph Symons in 1598-1602. Two centuries had passed since he and his Cambridge partner Gilbert Wigg brought the brick from Stow in Norfolk and the freestone from King's Cliffe in Northamptonshire. The cost had been borne by Mary Cavendish, Countess of Shrewsbury, whose statue looked down from its niche over the gateway to the Court. Patrick thought of the many great men who had passed through this College, as William Wordsworth did some years earlier when he had studied here:

> I could not print
> Ground where the grass had yielded to the steps
> of generations of illustrious men,
> Unmoved.

Leaving the Court Patrick sought the registrar's room to enter himself officially as a sizar. The entry was made: "Patrick Branty, born in Ireland; admitted sizar 1st October, 1802; tutors Wood and Smith". The practice was for the student to give his details verbally and the Irish brogue defeated the registrar with regard to the surname: Patrick feeling, naturally, somewhat diffident, did not correct the error. He returned to his lodgings, as the Michaelmas Term did not commence until 4th October (Monday) and he would not be required to take up residence until the previous evening. He had two days in which to explore the town before beginning the great studies that lay ahead of him. Everything he saw fascinated the young Irishman, although much appeared strange after the village life of his native country. Apart from his visits to Belfast, Patrick had never known life in a town of any size. At night, in his room, he thought about the registrar's error, and remembered experimenting with his own name in the arithmetic book at Glascar Hill long ago.

Two days later Patrick returned to St John's College and reported to the butler who kept the Residence Register. "Sizar Patrick Branty. First day of Residence, 3rd October, 1802." This time Patrick did not allow the error to pass, but gave the butler a correction; the latter erased the name and substituted "Patrick Bronte".

CHAPTER 2

Ordination

NAPOLEON'S army massed at Boulogne; rumours of an invasion current almost weekly, alarm along the English Channel; volunteers drilling regularly in the universities; such was the unsettled atmosphere of Cambridge as Patrick started his new life with a changed name.

He soon joined the volunteers, the only taste of military life he was to know, but otherwise the alarms of the time had no distracting influence on his studies. As for his name, he adhered firmly to the new style as he was to do until the end of his days, although the various accents that would appear on the final letter, culminating in the choice of the famous diaeresis, were still in the future. Whether Patrick's decision in this matter was influenced by the title lately conferred on Lord Nelson is not certain, but it seems quite likely. Perhaps his Celtic imagination was also attracted to the word as it was the Greek for thunder!

Once again there was much burning of the midnight oil, but mercifully the flame was brighter than that of the feeble rushlight at home; far into the night Patrick worked, determined to allow himself no respite from his labours, save that which his enlistment in the patriotic corps of volunteers enforced. He joined with great enthusiasm in the military exercises and became expert in the handling of the latest weapons which were issued to this civilian army so that they might prove an effective body able to aid the regular forces, should the French cross the English Channel. In the corps raised at St John's, and in the same company as Patrick, was a young peer who also took part in the military exercises with an ardent zest. He was seven years younger than Patrick, but almost as tall. Patrick knew him only slightly but noted his great interest in politics in which, like Patrick, he adopted the Tory point of view. They would leave Cambridge in the same year but would be brought together again for a brief time by correspondence. Napoleon's army never came, but Patrick would always remember that he had served in arms with Lord Palmerston.

Before leaving Cambridge Patrick also met the future sixth Duke of Devonshire (Trinity) who was to show him much kindness more than fifty years later. In the matriculation register of St John's for the year 1802, written in a large round hand and next but one to that of

Patrick Bronte appears the name of John Nunn. The latter, who was five years younger than Patrick, was also studying for Holy Orders, and became a great friend of Patrick's, keeping up a correspondence with him after they had left Cambridge. But a year after coming down these two friends were destined to meet again in Nunn's native town of Colchester. Their mutual friend at St John's was Robert Cox, from Wisbech, whom Patrick would also shortly meet again.

However, for all the military junketings and perils of imminent invasion Patrick had his eyes fixed on the immediate goal, the gaining of an exhibition or scholarship that would aid his financial resources. One of his tutors in particular gave him all the encouragement and assistance within his power: this was James Wood, who afterwards became Master of St John's. Patrick was older than most of his companions at Cambridge, but this, coupled with the recollection of his hard struggles in Ireland, acted rather as a spur to greater efforts than as a source of inferiority, and he worked on in a state of fierce enthusiasm. In early February 1803, just four months after entering College, Patrick obtained one of the Hare exhibitions, which he was to hold annually until March 1806. These were founded by Sir Ralph Hare "for thirty of the poorest and best-disposed scholars" and the exhibitioners shared amongst them the annual value of the rectorial tithe of Cherry Marham, Norfolk. The total rent was £200; should the full complement of exhibitioners be successful, the value to Patrick would be £6 13s 4d per annum. Small amount though it was, it was a promising and welcome start for the young Irishman. Towards the end of that year, at Christmas 1803, Patrick won a Duchess of Suffolk exhibition and continued on the Foundation as an exhibitioner until Christmas 1807. This had a value to Patrick of only £1 3s 4d a year and came from the fund left to St John's by the Duchess for the benefit of four poor but promising scholars. Later again, at midsummer 1805, he was elected to a Dr Goodman Exhibition which he held until he left Cambridge. This was worth £1 17s 6d.

Patrick, even with this small addition to his savings, was forced to live a very frugal life. Indeed, there could be no question of his affording a visit home during the long vacations: these were spent in his room at the College continuing the pursuit of learning, save for long walks about the Cambridgeshire countryside. He was fond of walking but found himself longing for the hills of home, and often returned to his chamber sad at heart.

There was so little money to spare, yet Patrick never forgot to send his mother whatever he could afford: many small luxuries, and necessities too, were sacrificed to maintain this regular payment.

During his period at college Patrick attracted the attention of many
men in Cambridge and in particular of Henry Martyn, the great
Cornish Wesleyan missionary. Martyn had a brilliant career as Senior
Wrangler and Smith's Prizeman at the university and then became
curate to Charles Simeon at Holy Trinity. The Methodists at Cambridge, ever on the watch for new recruits to the Church, had received
the signal from Thomas Tighe, and money was always available to aid
such promising newcomers. On 14th February 1804, Martyn wrote to
William Wilberforce regarding the latter's decision that Patrick Bronte
be allowed to draw assistance from his Church Missionary Society's
Fund.

St. John's.   Feb. 14th 1804

My Dear Sir,
        I availed myself as soon as possible of your generous offer to
Mr Bronte and left it without hesitation to himself to fix the limits of his
request.

He says that £20 per annm. will enable him to go on with comfort,
but that he could do with less. He has twice given me some account of
his onset to college, which for it's singularity has hardly been equalled,
I suppose since the days of Bishop Latimer. He left his native Ireland
at the age of 22 [sic] with seven pounds, having been able to lay-by no
more after superintending a school some years. He reached Cambridge
before that was expended, and then received an unexpected supply of
£5 from a distant friend. On this he subsisted some weeks before
entering St John's, and has since had no other assistance than what the
college afforded. There is reason to hope that he will be an instrument
of good to the church, as a desire of usefulness in the ministry seems to
have influenced him hitherto in no small degree. I desire to unite with
him in thanks to yourself and the directors of the Society. I acknowledge
also with gratitude the offer of your continued friendship, and rejoice
to embrace it. I have the honor [sic] to subscribe myself your obliged
friend and servant

H. Martyn

This letter was endorsed in Wilberforce's hand:
    "Martyn about Mr Bronte. Henry Thornton and I to allow him £10
each annually."

Patrick had given generously to his mother from his scant savings
before leaving home. The "distant friend" was Andrew Harshaw.

Thus from the same source that supplied Charles Wesley's widow
with financial relief could Patrick draw the extra money he might need.
He had received patronage before, but never financial assistance in so

direct a form, and was still young enough to have pride in standing on his own two feet. However, for all that he was a sizar or servitor, involving the payment of reduced fees both to the college and university, there was still the probability that his own resources would prove inadequate, despite the small supplementation of the scholarships. As he was determined to continue at Cambridge and to send his mother those little remittances, the knowledge that assistance was his for the asking must have been a great comfort indeed.

Henry Martyn was shortly to make the choice between his beloved Lydia Grenfell and the lonely missionary field in India. Finding her refusal to accompany him quite unshakeable he went alone—as a chaplain to the East India Company. She would not join him and he died a feverish death in Turkish Tokat on 16th October 1812, aged thirty-one, whilst "hasting home to be with her".

Patrick would recall him to mind later when his daughter Charlotte read to him of St John Rivers.

One of Patrick's contemporaries at St John's was the poet Henry Kirke White, who died in 1806 aged twenty-one. White also received financial assistance from the Methodists. On 25th May 1804 he wrote, "I am admitted of St. John's, and I shall certainly reside, if I trust only to my own resources, as there is a man of *that* college, who has only £20 per annum." In a letter to his mother, dated 26th October 1805, mentioning the problems of a sizar, he obviously refers to Patrick. "I have got the bills of Mr —, a Sizar of this college, now before me, and from them, and his own account, I will give you a statement of what my college bills will amount to . . . £12 or £15 a-year at the most. I shall not have any occasion for the whole sum I have a claim upon Mr Simeon for . . . Mr —, whose bills I have borrowed, has been at college three years. He came over from —, with £10 in his pocket, and has no friends, or any income or emolument whatever, except what he receives for his Sizarship ; yet he does support himself, and that, too, very genteelly . . . Our dinners and suppers cost us nothing ; and if a man choose to eat milk-breakfasts, and go without tea, he may live absolutely for nothing . . . and on feast-days, which our fellows take care are pretty frequent, we have wine . . . I sleep on a hair mattress, which I find just as comfortable as a bed ; it only cost me £4, along with blankets, counterpane, and pillows, and etc. I have three rooms—a sitting-room, a bed-room, and a kind of scullery or pantry . . . I must get a supply of sugar from London . . . here, it will cost me 1/6 per pound."

White was sent to St John's by Wilberforce at Simeon's request and was shown much kindness by Martyn. His financial aid came from the Elland Clerical Society (founded at Huddersfield in 1767 by the

Vicar, Henry Venn) which provided an Evangelical Ordination Candidates' fund. Both Henry Thornton and Wilberforce gave generous sums to this "West Riding Charity for catching the colts running wild on Halifax Moor, and cutting their manes and tails, and sending them to college", as Wilberforce described it in 1789.

By the time Patrick reached Cambridge the assistance was widened to include such as Kirke White from Nottingham. One of the qualifications required was "a sound and enquiring mind, capable of the benefit which a literary education is calculated to afford".

There was no disturbance to Patrick's career at Cambridge and on 23rd April 1806 he obtained his degree of Bachelor of Arts. No doubt the Irishman born on St Patrick's Day felt a deeper sense of delight in that the reward for his hard labours should have been granted him on the anniversary of Shakespeare's birthday. His life at Cambridge now drew to a close as he entered Holy Orders. He had joined St John's College in October 1802 and remained for the next eleven succeeding university terms, ending his official residence at the end of the Lent term 1806. Although harassed by pecuniary difficulties his record during the three and a half years he was there as shown in the Register of Scholars and Exhibitioners, culminating in his admittance as *Baccalaureus Artium* fully justified his own hopes and those of the ministers who had placed confidence in him.

But the exhibitions were not the only prizes Patrick won at Cambridge—there were others in the form of books that delighted his heart. Two quarto copies of Homer and Horace in particular he greatly treasured.

"Homeri Ilias. Graece et Latine. Samuel Clarke, S.T.P. Impensis Jacobi et Johannis Knapton, in Coemeterio D. Pauli, mdccxxix." Inside this book, which bore the College arms on the cover, Patrick wrote, "My prize book for always having kept in the first class at St. John's College, Cambridge. P. Brontê, A.B. To be retained semper."

Then there was "Horatius Flaccus, Rich, Bentelii, Amstelodami, 1728."—"Prize obtained by Rev. Patrick Brontê, St. John's College." Patrick also received a copy of Lemprière's *Bibliotheca Classica* (third edition) from a pupil he coached during his latter days at Cambridge— another small source of income. Patrick inscribed it, "The gift of Mr Toulmen pupil—Cambridge. Price 12s/."

At the beginning of July Patrick offered himself to the Bishop of London as a candidate for Holy Orders. Thomas Tighe had sent him a certificate of age and he collected testimonials from Cambridge to enclose with his application to London :

I hereby certify that by the Register of this Parish it appears that William Bronte, Son of Hugh & Elinor Bronte, was baptized on 16th March 1779—& I further certify that Patrick Bronte, now of St. Johns College, Cambridge, is the elder brother of the said William—& that no Register was kept of Baptisms in this Parish for time immemorial till after Sept 1778—when I became minister.

T. Tighe (Div.Johan : Col : Cant :
Olim Alum : postea — Sanc : Pet : Soc :)
30 Decr 1805 Minister of Drumballyroney
Diocese of Dromore

Patrick Bronte B.A. St. Johns Coll. has attended Fortyseven of my lectures. (in Divinity)

J. Fawcett Norr. Prof

Cambridge
22 Mar 1806

Mr. Bronte has attended the whole Course save three, one omission was occasioned by indisposition, two by necessary business in the Country.

WHEREAS our well beloved in Christ Patrick Bronte Bachelor of Arts, hath declared unto us his intention of offering himself a Candidate for the sacred office of a Deacon and for that end hath requested of us Letters Testimonial of his good Morals & Learning ; We the Master and senior Fellows of the College of Saint John the Evangelist in the University of Cambridge according to the ancient and approved custom of this University, do hereby testify that the said Patrick Bronte hath behaved himself studiously & regularly during the time of his residence amongst us which began in October one thousand eight hundred and two and is now with us. Nor do we know that he hath believed or maintained any opinion contrary to the doctrine or discipline of the Church of England. IN WITNESS whereof we have hereunto set our Hands & Seal this second day of July in the Year of our Lord one thousand eight hundred and six.

W. Craven Mr.

J. Wood B.D.
Tutor

J. Pennington M.D.
W. Wood B.D.
Herbert Marsh B.D.
Thos Catton B.D.
R. Boon B.D.
A. Mainwaring B.D.
W. Millers B.D.

Next Patrick's *Si Quis*:

This is to certify that public Notice was given by me, in the Parish Church of All-Saints in the town of Cambridge on Sunday the twenty-ninth day of June last, that Mr. Patrick Brontë intended to offer himself a Candidate for Holy Orders and no impediment was alledged.

Cambridge   Samuel Chilcote . . . Curate
                                        of the Parish of All Saints

Jul. 4 — 1806

To your Lordships Secretary.

Revd Sir,

I beg leave to offer myself a candidate for Holy Orders, at his Lordships next Ordination. If I be admitted by his Lordship, be so kind as to let me know as soon as convenient, when and where his Lordship will hold his Ordination; and (if customary) what books I shall be examined in ; with whatever directions you may judge necessary.

                               Sir, your most
                                 obed^t & humble serv^t

St. Johns College,   P. Brontē
Cambridge,
    July 4th 1806.

Instructions were sent for Patrick to report to the Bishop's secretary in early August in order that he might be ordained deacon in the chapel of the Bishop's Palace at Fulham on the tenth of that month.

Patrick left Cambridge with a heart full of gratitude for the old red-bricked college that had been his home for so long. He had entered it as Patrick Brunty, the hopeful school-teacher from Drumballyroney ; he was leaving soon to be the Rev. Patrick Brontē, A.B., and carrying with him a flood of new hopes. His appetite for books was partially satiated ; now came the new hunger : a desire to see the world and learn of men by mixing with them and understanding their desires and fears, their hopes and disappointments, to ease them in suffering and to correct them in sin. What a refreshing change it would be to earn his keep and not live on meagre savings spun out over the years !

It was August 1806 and if Cambridge had seemed strange to him at first, how much more bewildering appeared the bustle of the busy London streets. Patrick visited St Paul's, and first became acquainted with the Chapter Coffee House in Paternoster Row. This house was often frequented by clergymen passing through London. Patrick found the cost of a lengthy residence beyond his means and the church authorities found him cheaper lodgings.

Patrick reported to the Bishop's secretary and then explored the wonders of the great city.

On Sunday, 10th August 1806, Patrick was ordained deacon at Fulham Chapel and came forth from the ceremony with the honour and the humility of the occasion weighing equally on his shoulders.

Again the influence of the followers of John Wesley was directed in Patrick's favour and before he left the Bishop's Palace he was licensed to his first curacy, at Wethersfield in Essex. It was in the gift of Trinity Hall, Cambridge, and the Vicar was the Rev. Joseph Jowett, Regius Professor of Civil Law at Cambridge, Member of Trinity Hall and friend to Charles Simeon and the other leading Evangelical clergy.

Dr Jowett, a Yorkshireman, and the author of a book of village sermons, was a non-resident vicar of Wethersfield, so that, as much work in the parish would devolve on the assistant curate, Patrick had been favourably recognized in this, his first nomination. His stipend was to be £60 per annum.

His duties were to commence in early October, so there was time for him to visit Ireland, although this entailed the spending of all his remaining money.

As the ship drew near his native land the well-known shapes of the Mourne mountains loomed out of the mist to bring humility and chase away feelings of false pride. Patrick came home—for the last time. Never again would he tread the mud of Ireland, never again see his beloved hills. But there was time surely for one last visit to them, a final glimpse of their splendour, in sight of which he could open his soul. Not to praise God this time, but to pour out the heart in gratitude for His great bounty.

One Sunday he preached his first sermon—at Drumballyroney Church—and his sister Alice, over eighty years later, was still fond of telling how her brother preached to a crowded congregation "and never had anything in his hand the whole time". Patrick was to deliver almost all his sermons *ex tempore* and nearly always scorned the use of a written address or even the aid of notes. The text of this maiden sermon is not known; but some indication of his feeling at the time may be learned from a part of one of his poems written soon after he left Cambridge, entitled "An Epistle to a Young Clergyman", and prefaced by the text, "Study to shew thyself approved unto God, a workman that needeth not to be ashamed, rightly dividing the word of truth." (2 Tim. 2 : 15)

The greatest office, you sustain,
For love of Souls, and not of gain ;
Through your neglect should one be slain,
The Scriptures say,
Your careless hands, his blood will stain,
on the Last Day.

* * *

Dare not, like some, to mince the matter—
Nor dazzling tropes, and figures scatter,
Nor coarsely speak, nor basely flatter,
Nor groveling go :
But let plain truths, as Life's pure water,
Pellucid flow.

Whatever the manner of his sermon, or indeed its matter, the local villagers, even those who had never allowed themselves to mix with the children of parents with different religions, were very impressed by the young man who had returned to preach to them. Doubtless also as they sat listening to Patrick's strong voice, ringing through the little church, the Rev. Andrew Harshaw was extremely pleased and the Rev. Thomas Tighe highly satisfied.

Patrick, as became his cloth, took his vocation seriously and from the very start of his clerical life determined to succour the poor and needy, comfort the sick and dying, protect the oppressed by all the means in his power and see that, as far as possible, justice was rendered to all. He firmly believed that this world was but a preparation for the greater life to come, but that this was no reason why the lot on earth of those who were poor or persecuted should not be alleviated as far as humanly possible. True, poverty prevented those temptations to sin that came to the over-wealthy, but Patrick saw no reason why preparation for life eternal should be made a veritable hell on earth. In his parish it would always be the poor that needed comfort, but Patrick was sure that all could find salvation. He abhorred the selective creed of Calvinism and adhered firmly to the Arminian beliefs. There were always those who, blind and deaf to beauty and tolerance and reason, would plot their own destruction but Patrick felt there was a chance of everlasting life for all mankind. Some might damn and blight their own immortality but God was there to offer it to all.

Happy were those days at home with his parents and brothers, full of boyhood memories the walks along the familiar lanes of County Down. Whilst at home, Patrick gained a little money to launch him on his career by coaching privately some of the brighter youngsters of the district. But their parents could afford little and he was forced to practise again that careful husbanding of his resources. Whilst at home Patrick obtained another certificate of age—needed later for his ordination as priest—and his father signed the affidavit. An applicant over thirty was frowned upon in those days, hence the subtraction of a year from Patrick's age. In the event he was over thirty when he was ordained priest.

County of Down
Ireland.

I Hugh Brontē of Ballynaskeagh Parish of Ahaderg, in said County, do swear, that my son Patrick Brontē late of St. Johns College Cambridge England, is twenty eight years of age,

Hugh Brontē

Sworn before me,

this 25th of Septr 1806   John Fury

Eager as he was to start his work amongst the people of Wethersfield, Patrick's last hours in Ireland must have been clouded by much sadness. He took leave of the large family he would never see again, and set off to serve God in an unknown corner of England.

Until her death, he continued to send his mother that regular payment of money he had started at Cambridge, increasing its sum as his fortunes improved; and at least once a year he wrote to one of his brothers or sisters.

Hugh Brunty died about 1808, not long after his eldest son had paid his visit home, and his wife in 1822. They were buried together in the small churchyard at Ballyroney.

Patrick's eldest sister Jane died in 1819 at the age of thirty, but his other sisters and the four brothers all lived to a great age. The men grew into tall and striking figures, whilst the sisters have been described as tall, red-cheeked, fair-haired, handsome women, with dark eyelashes, strong minds and massive frames. Only three, William, Walsh and Sarah, married. William had at least six sons; Walsh had two, one being drowned at the age of twenty-two whilst fording the Bann; and Sarah was the mother of ten, as her own mother had been: there were four boys and six girls, although one of the former died in infancy. William, known locally as Billy Brunty, was a "United Irishman" and fought at the affray at Ballinahinch, escaping after the skirmish through the bogs he knew so well. Later he kept a public-house on the Knock Hill. Hugh and Walsh gained a great reputation as road-makers and, for a pastime, became expert fiddlers. James became a shoe-maker and carpenter. The great bare-fist fight between Walsh Brunty and Sam

Clark at Ballynafern was long remembered in the district : it is believed the contest lasted many hours before Walsh forced his opponent to retire. Years later the name Brunty was to disappear from the several carts owned by Hugh and Walsh and be replaced by Bronte : and when their nieces in Yorkshire became famous the change was general throughout the family. Even the diaeresis was to find its way to Ireland.

William lived to be 83, Hugh 82, James 87, Walsh 82, Mary 75, Rose 77, Sarah 82, whilst the youngest, Alice, died on Thursday, 15th January 1891, aged 95. She died at Dromorebrague and the following Saturday was buried in the churchyard of Drumballyroney parish, where rested all her family save Patrick. For the last nine years of her life she received an annuity of £20 from Pargeter's Old Maids' Charity Trustees, Birmingham.

But Patrick was now leaving this Irish world behind him for ever. As he again travelled southwards over the dusty English roads he was not thinking of the past, but forward to the future. What it held in store he could not tell, but he would do his utmost to serve God and his fellow-men.

Early in October Patrick reached the small village of Wethersfield to take charge of the parish as curate in the frequent absence of Dr Jowett. At this time, however, the vicar had been doing duty at Wethersfield until his new curate arrived and he was there to greet the newcomer.

Lodgings had been arranged for Patrick in a house opposite the church, occupied by an elderly spinster, Miss Mildred Davy.

Wethersfield was an agricultural village tucked away in the hilly part of Essex. Braintree, the nearest town, was seven miles away and the remote atmosphere of the place appealed to the nature-loving young curate. It was a country of winding lanes, and Patrick saw several windmills dotted about the fields. There were a few cottages, grouped mainly around the small village green, and farther out a number of larger houses and mansions. Facing the village green stood the minister's house, so rarely visited by Dr Jowett, and near it an old manse and meeting-house (Congregationalist, built in 1707. In 1806 the Pastor was the Rev. Thomas Mark).

But Patrick now saw none of these, for, standing before him on rising ground, was the building he was seeking—Wethersfield Church, dedicated to St Mary Magdalene. It was not a large church, yet to the new curate a first charge can appear as huge as a cathedral.

There had been a church at Wethersfield since Saxon times. In 1806 the late twelfth-century tower was surmounted by a shingled belfry. Inside the church were thirteenth-century and fourteenth-century octagonal pillars, a window dating from 1340, a fifteenth-century screen and a Tudor timbered roof. The bells dated from 1623. In the sloping churchyard a son of Rogers the Proto Martyr was buried.

Patrick found his new home clean and comfortable, and Miss Davy a woman of education and good taste. She was seventy years of age, and, having been lame since she was a little girl, led a quiet life of reflection, rarely stirring beyond the village. The new curate was made welcome and felt at ease and at home from the very start.

St George's House with its oak-panelled hall, living-rooms and bedrooms, was a fine dwelling. There was an oak-banistered staircase and many old beams. The house stood higher up the street than the village green, facing the church gates. Four stone steps led up to a tiny enclosed front garden.

Despite the occasional cottage across the fields Wethersfield was a small parish and Patrick quickly became acquainted with his parishioners. At first there was the difficulty of brogue: Patrick still retained a strong Ulster accent and the congregation of Essex villagers found it extremely difficult at times to grasp the meaning of his words. Happily, they soon became used to his diction, and this source of embarrassment to the new curate was removed.

On 12th October 1806 Patrick performed his first marriage and signed the church register for the first time. Here, at Wethersfield, he was to sign himself Patrick Brontë.

He threw all his energy into his responsibilities at Wethersfield. There were not the cottage meetings of his later days, but he was always to be found visiting the poor and aged, lending books to those of the sick who could gain comfort from them, and prepared to walk miles across the fields to visit anyone who needed his comfort and guidance. He was often seen striding along the country roads either on a mission of mercy or for his own pleasure, and rarely failed to take with him the dog of one of his parishioners. It was exercise for the animal and the best of company for the curate. He could not very well keep a pet of his own at Miss Davy's house but if ever he was settled in a living of his own he would make sure that he was so befriended.

Thus the months passed, with Patrick winning the hearts of many of his flock by his unremitting attention to duty and with that extra service that supersedes duty and is the mark of a true man of God. But though the country lanes and cottages of his quiet Essex parish seemed so remote, the eyes of the Church leaders who had sent him there noticed all these things and Patrick Bronte was marked down for greater service in the future.

But the young curate, now thirty years of age, for all his sincerity and enthusiasm as a churchman was still a passionate young Irishman.

He believed what he believed but was no dogmatist. A warm-blooded human being and no ascetic, he liked a pretty face and would never hesitate in saying so. Early in 1807 there came tripping across the fields to Miss Davy's house one who possessed even more charms than young Helen of the corn-stacks. Patrick on entering the kitchen found to his surprise a young girl busy there: a pheasant was on the table before her, and with one sleeve well rolled up she was about to wind the roasting-jack. One glance sufficed for Patrick and he startled her by immediately exclaiming, "Heaven bless thee! Thou hast the sweetest face I ever looked on!" And so she had, or the impulsive young Irishman would not have said so.

But, however startled she may be at the time, no young lady would take offence at such a quick-sighted and penetrating remark, particularly from a tall and handsome new curate. No apology would have been forthcoming in any event, but, happily, none was required and Patrick was soon on terms of warmest friendship with Mary Burder.

Mary Mildred Davy Burder was eighteen, with dark brown curls and blue eyes that could bewitch most men. As her name suggests she was Miss Davy's favourite niece, and her aunt's affection for her was fully returned. Mary's father, John Burder, had been a prosperous man, handsome, cheerful, and much liked and respected by the other farmers in the district. After marrying Miss Davy's sister he had lived at The Broad, a large, many-windowed and comfortable farmhouse nearly three miles across the fields from Wethersfield. Shortly before Patrick's arrival in Essex he had been struck down suddenly by a most painful disease, and died at the early age of forty. He was buried at Finchingfield and all the local farmers attended his funeral on horseback. One of the doctors, on leaving his agonized sick-bed, had been forced to remark, "He is still the strongest and finest man in the whole parish."

His widow and four children were left grief-stricken and for poor Mary, who was the eldest daughter, the pang of sorrow was sharpened when, only three weeks after his death, her father's favourite dog to whom she was devoted also died. Mr Burder's executor was his only brother, who lived at nearby Yeldham. He properly accounted himself the guardian of the children until they should be of age, and of the money to which they would be entitled on reaching the age of twenty-one or in the event of marriage. Unlike his late brother he was not popular in the district, being of a cold, heartless and selfish disposition.

Shortly after her father's death, Mary's brother John came running home from boarding-school, his arm red and black with stripes. "Give him as much on the other arm, and send him back to his master," cried Uncle Burder. "Oh, Mr Burder," appealed the mother, "you have never been a parent, or you wouldn't say so." Mary, remembering her own school blows from the "rod of Madame Fowle" took care that her brother never returned, but it was her last permitted defiance of Uncle Burder! This, then, was the man who was free to play his contemptible but vital part in Patrick's life.

Mrs Burder was a timid woman and, after the death of her husband, found it impossible to oppose his brother's will on any matter: thus Mary turned more and more towards the kind companionship of her aunt at Wethersfield. She would often bring her some farm produce from home and spend the evening with the old lady. On the day of her first meeting with Patrick she had been sent over by her mother with a present of game for her aunt and was preparing the bird for dinner when Patrick surprised her by his sudden entry into the kitchen. Yet it was surely only his words that could cause surprise: Mary knew well that the curate was staying at her aunt's house and her natural curiosity could be restrained no longer.

Although she was not one of his congregation, for she worshipped in the Dissenting meeting-house near the village green, Patrick and Mary were soon very much attracted to each other. He discovered that she was of an inherent God-fearing nature, intelligent, and of a very deep, strong and serious mind not unlike his own, save that hers was calm, whilst his was somewhat prone to gusts of passion.

The attachment grew, and more and more frequent became the errands and messages across the fields to Aunt Davy's house. Mary was surprised and pleased at the curate's mind and conversation. The latter revealed that he had read a great deal and observed much. He lent her books that she wished to read and yet, she noticed, he made no endeavour to question her differing mode of worship or convert her to his own Church. She soon perceived also that he was a man of strong purpose and inflexible will. They took walks together, and sometimes she accompanied him for part of the way on his visits to outlying parishioners, for Patrick never permitted even the fair Mary to distract his attention from parochial duties. But the dogs must have wondered why he came so seldom now to take them for the usual run. So it went on; the pleasant, improving book-reading and talks, the evening strolls taken at some little distance from the uncle's house—and friendship ripened into love, although Patrick would declare hotly that he had loved her at first sight. Sometimes he almost frightened her by the passionate earnestness of his declarations: she shrank from such vehement demonstrations but tried to remember that he was Irish, after all.

In July 1807 Patrick offered himself for ordination as priest.

To your Lordships Secretary.

Wethersfield, near Braintree, Essex, July 1st 1807

Sir,

Be so kind as to inform me, when, and where, his Lordship will hold his next Ordination; and what papers I must send, as a candidate for Priests Orders.

Your most obedient and humble servant P. Brontë

To the Right Revd Father in God Beilby Lord Bishop of London.

These are to certify your Lordship that I Joseph Jowett, Vicar of Wethersfield, in the county of Essex do hereby nominate & appoint Patrick Brontë to perform the office of a Curate in the Church of Wethersfield aforesaid; and do promise to allow him the yearly sum of sixty pounds for his maintenance in the same and to continue him to officiate as Curate in my said Church until he shall be provided with some other place where he may exercise his ministerial function, unless on account of any fault by him committed, he shall be lawfully removed from performing the office of a Curate in my said Church by your Lordship or your successors.

And I hereby solemnly declare that I do not fraudently [*sic*] give this certificate to entitle the said Patrick Bronte to receive the Holy Order of Priest but with a real intention to employ him in my said Church according to what is before expressed.

Witness my hand this fourteenth day of July in the year of our Lord 1807.

Joseph Jowett

To the Right Reverend Father in God, Beilby, by divine permission, Lord Bishop of London, greeting.

Whereas our well beloved in Christ, Patrick Brontë Bachelor of Arts, hath declared to us his intention of offering himself a candidate for the sacred office of a Priest, and for that end hath requested of us letters testimonial of his learning and good behaviour: we therefore, whose names are hereunto subscribed, do testify, that the said Patrick Brontë having been personally known to us, during his residence at Wethersfield, which was nine months; hath during that time lived piously, soberly, and honestly, and diligently applied himself to his studies; nor hath he at any time (as far as we know or have heard) maintained or written any thing contrary to the doctrine or discipline of the Church of England : and moreover we think him a person worthy to be admitted to the sacred Order of Priests.

In witness wereof we subscribe our names.

> Thomas Stevens, Rector of Panfield
> John Thurlow, Vicar of Gosfield
> Thomas Jee, Vicar of Thaxted

At this time Patrick took duty in Colchester for three weeks whilst Dr Jowett was visiting Wethersfield—staying with John Nunn, who was on a visit home.

In Colchester Patrick became friendly with the Vicar of St Peter's, the Rev. Robert Storry who was also an Evangelical. St Peter's, Colchester, was among the first livings to be acquired by Simeon's Trustees in their attempt to preserve an Evangelical tradition in the Establishment.

To Your Lordships Secretary.

Colchester, July 20th 1807

Sir,

Agreeably to your orders I have sent all my papers except my Si Quis, which I cannot possibly get before the next Sunday, at which time I shall send it, hoping that his Lordship will excuse my not sending it sooner. By addressing a few lines to me at Colchester (as I shall reside here for a few weeks) mentioning the time of the Ordination, and his Lordships pleasure respecting my papers, you will very much oblige,

> Sir, your most obedient and humble servant, P. Brontē.

Next, Patrick sent his *Si Quis*.

Whereas the Rev Patrick Brontē is desirous of proceeding to the Holy Order of Priests notice of his intention was given in the Parish Church of Wethersfield on the three following Sundays in the twelfth, the nineteenth & the twenty-sixth of July 1807 and no objections have come to our knowledge why he ought not to be ordained Priest.

> Joseph Jowett, Vicar
> Thomas Fitch ⎱ Church Wardens
> John Legerton ⎰

Again Patrick wrote from Colchester.

To your Lordships Secretary.

Colchester, July 29th 1807

Sir,

I have sent my *Si Quis*, and hope his Lordship will not look upon it as too late. By letting me know, whether this together with my other

papers are satisfactory, and the time and place of his Lordships Ordination you will very much oblige your most obedient and humble servant

P. Bronte

Happy in the knowledge that his papers were indeed in order,
Patrick returned to Wethersfield—and Mary.

Summer days gave way to autumn evenings at St George's House
with Mary and Aunt Davy. In his oak-panelled room Patrick awaited
two answers: from the Bishop and from Mary. But before the growing
romance could reach a safe haven or be suddenly smashed to pieces on
the rocks of life, Patrick received letters dimissory from London, dated
19th December 1807, requesting that he offer himself before the Bishop
of Salisbury two days later, to be ordained priest at the Chapel Royal
of St James.

Patrick hurried up to London, faced with a joyous Christmas: to
preach the Gospel for the first time as an ordained priest of God's
Church.

It would seem a long time since he had left London to start his new
life. He had tried to serve his people well; had brought God's mercy to
many and His Promise of Eternal Life to all. These were matters to
drive even thoughts of Mary out of his mind during the journey.

On Monday, 21st December 1807, in the Chapel Royal of St James,
Westminster, Patrick Brontë was ordained a priest of the Established
Church, for which purpose he had left Ireland for Cambridge over five
years earlier. Many indeed were the rungs of the ladder he had climbed
during that period.

As he approached the communion-table and knelt down before the
Bishop of Salisbury, he offered himself anew to the service of God and
those parishioners whom providence would place in his keeping. As
long as he lived Patrick would never betray his trust to either.

CHAPTER 3

Yorkshire

IT WAS a most happy Christmas for Patrick in 1807 : indeed, the world was well with him. He preached his first sermon as a fully-fledged servant of the Lord, and the joy in his heart must have communicated itself to the listening congregation. It was the very season when hearts turn outward in warmth and kindness : he thought of Mary Burder and was sure he loved her. But in the meeting-house nearby Mary was thinking of Patrick and was not so certain of his love. For all his passionate declarations there seemed to run through him a streak of reticence that chilled her heart. He had promised to walk over to The Broad with her soon and call on her mother, but unless Mamma could be more successful than she herself in gleaning some information about his past life and his family there would be scant chance of Uncle Burder's agreeing to any alliance between them. Happily for Patrick he knew nothing of Mary's thoughts that Christmas morning : no sense of impending storm clouded his untroubled mind and his address came forth lucidly from his tranquil heart.

Mary hoped that Patrick's ordination would soon lead to greater candour on his part, and the romance continued as before. Patrick was writing poetry now, and hoped one day to have some of his verses published. All his poems were of a religious nature and Mary was the recipient of many lines—including "Verses sent to a Lady on her Birth-day". However hackneyed the theme and despite the quite appalling verse it was nevertheless such a poem as a young Nonconformist woman of the early nineteenth century would not feel insulted to receive.

> The joyous day illumes the sky,
> That bids each care and sorrow fly,
>   To shades of endless night :
> E'en frozen age, thawed in the fires
> Of social mirth, feels young desires,
>   And tastes of fresh delight.
> In thoughtful mood, your parents dear,
> Whilst joy smiles through the starting tear,
>   Give approbation due :

4

As each drinks deep, in mirthful wine,
Your rosy health, and looks benign,
     Are sent to heaven for you.
But, let me whisper, lovely fair,
This joy may soon give place to care,
     And sorrow cloud this day;
Full soon, your eyes of sparkling blue,
And velvet lips, of scarlet hue,
     Discoloured, may decay.
As bloody drops, on virgin snows,
So vies the lily with the rose,
     Full on your dimpled cheek;
But, ah! the worm in lazy coil,
May soon prey on this putrid spoil;
     Or leap, in loathsome freak.
Fond wooers come, with flattering tale,
And load with sighs the passing gale,
     And love-distracted rave:
But, hark, fair maid! What e'er they say,
You're but a breathing mass of clay,
     Fast ripening for the grave.
Behold, how thievish time has been!
Full eighteen summers you have seen,
     And yet, they seem a day!
Whole years, collected in time's glass,
     In silent lapse, how soon they pass,
     And steal your life away. . . .

The remaining five verses appeal to the young girl to seek her joy
"where Jesus reigns in boundless love" and remind her that "all
earthly things are vain".

If Mary did read these verses on her eighteenth birthday she must
indeed have been a serious-minded young woman if they were not to
cast a gloom over the entire festivities.

Years later Patrick was to write "Lines addressed to a Lady on her
Birth-day". This poem was in similar vein, although of greater merit
and far less gruesome. But it was addressed to quite another lady.

The months passed and Patrick remained silent about his life in
Ireland. He talked to Mary of Cambridge and of the great men he had
met there: Simeon, Martyn, and many young men of the nobility. He
told her over and over again that he had influential friends who would
help him to rise high in his calling, but about Ireland he said nothing.

Patrick felt bitterly ashamed of his reticence. Was it not rank arrogance to deny his upbringing, to feel his parents and brothers unworthy of discussion and to conceal his hard toil at anvil and loom ? Was it not the height of ingratitude to omit any mention of the help he had received from Andrew Harshaw and Thomas Tighe ? Was it not even unfair to himself to talk about his studies at the university and make no mention of the earlier labours that had gone on far into the night ?

Yet Patrick knew something of the ways of the world. Above all, he knew the attitude of mind of families like the Burders, prosperous and comfortable in their farms. For all their religious convictions they were a part of this world in that they sought only security for their families. Patrick had felt from the beginning that he loved Mary and yet he knew that the vague promise of great achievements in the future would count as nothing in the Burders' eyes : to have revealed his humble start in life would have been fatal. He knew well what kind of man Mary's uncle was and had long realized that only by silence on that score would he retain a chance of gaining her hand. Patrick was aware that within him was the taint of snobbery—it would be there all his days—but his decision to remain deaf to all Mary's questions originated from his recognition of the fatality to his hopes that a true answer would have incurred.

One day he walked with Mary across the fields and paid his first visit to The Broad. He was introduced to Mrs Burder, her other daughter, Sarah, and the two young boys. The afternoon went pleasantly enough and everyone appeared to be at ease, but nevertheless Patrick felt that Mrs Burder was endeavouring all the time to turn the conversation towards the subject of Ireland and his early days. He told them of the beauty of his native land and of the glory of the mountains but then forced the talk back to the present time by comparing County Down with this part of the Essex countryside. Patrick also told them how delighted and honoured he felt that his first curacy should have led him into "such a green and pleasant land". But it was not his wish to remain for too long in the south of England ; he had a desire to reside in Yorkshire, which, he said, was the very centre of the Evangelical revival.

During the summer months Patrick made several visits to The Broad and pleasant were the evening walks back to Wethersfield with Mary walking beside him for a part of the way. He promised her that when he had a little money put by they could be married, and Mary answered that if her feelings were then unchanged it might well be so. For the next few weeks the fate of some of the greatest writing that would appear in the English language, and certainly the greatest novel

hung in the balance, then the storm broke : fate intervened in the shape
of Uncle Burder and an irreparable loss to world literature was narrowly
avoided.

Reports of the visits to The Broad by the young curate reached
Yeldham and brought Mr Burder hurrying over to see his sister-in-law
and Mary. His worst fears were realized : not only was Patrick Brontë
an Irishman, a foreigner, but there was no trace of his family or con-
nections. How could they be sure he had a future, or that he could
carry that brogue into a decent English rectory ? What did it matter
that he had brushed against stripling peers at Cambridge—would his
Bachelor of Arts degree earn bread and butter for a growing family ?
He thundered over to Wethersfield, to the astonishment of poor Miss
Davy, and hurled his questions in Patrick's face. Patrick stood there
white and trembling, not with fear, but with the restraint he imposed on
the flood of blazing anger that surged up within him. How he longed
to pitch the sneering farmer down the stairs ! But the mantle of priest-
hood was still new upon him and overcame his Irish rage. In a calm
voice he told Burder to mind his own business. Alas for poor Patrick, it
was the business of a guardian to make such inquiries respecting his
niece's future, and leaving the angry curate, Burder returned to The
Broad and commenced to make it very much his business.

He informed the widow that the young Irishman was no sort of
companion for Mary, to say nothing of a future husband, and that it
would be best for Mary to return home with him to Yeldham and stay
with her aunt and uncle for an indefinite period. Poor, weak Mrs Burder
agreed and Mary was told to prepare at once for her visit.

Patrick was beside himself with rage and indignation. He called to
see Mary's mother, only to learn that she was away from home, staying
with friends. He divined the truth at once and, returning to his room at
Wethersfield, poured out his heart in a long letter to Mary. He told her
of his great love for her and his shock at the treatment she had received.
He implored an early answer and prayed that God would protect her
and watch over her. The letter, hurriedly written, was soon despatched
and Patrick waited hopefully for an answer. But it never came. Day
followed day and the silence was unbroken. He wrote again, in a calmer
mood, and implored a reply however brief. There was no answer.
Patrick walked along the lanes where he had strolled with Mary so
many times—the dogs welcomed the invitations to accompany him
after they had been sure he had forgotten them. By now the fever of the
last few weeks was over and Patrick was quite calm again. He thought
of the hard struggles of his life, of the many hours of toil he had spent
to reach the position he now held and he thought of Mary Burder.

He remembered again his hopes for the future, his dreams of serving God in one of the vital churches of His Kingdom and of reaching that goal that was the vision of all earnest young clerics of the day—the almost Holy Land that was Yorkshire. And he thought of Mary Burder. Patrick stood gazing across the fields of Essex but saw them not. They were obscured by visions of the Mourne mountains and of the rugged Pennine Chain. He knew what he must do. He went back to his room and wrote again to Mary. The letter began with his expression of grief that she had not deigned to answer his previous letters: even if Mr Burder was determined to prevent a meeting, surely there could be no valid excuse for her silence unless it was that she loved him not. What there had been of passion in their friendship had been entirely his— that he freely admitted to her. She was not of a demonstrative nature but of a more thoughtful, even he might add, of a more calculating, cast of mind. He had offered her his heart and her response had been cool. On the occasion of their walk together she had told him that even if their union never became a reality he would always be welcome at her home as a friend. He now accused her of qualifying her love until it lacked all warmth. How could she dare to mention the cool word "friendship" to one who loved her to distraction? No doubt, at her uncle's house, she could have time for further reflection and might carry her hesitation still further until it resembled her family's point of view. He reminded Mary that he had been grossly insulted by her uncle without ever having given that gentleman any offence whatsoever. It would appear that he was not worthy of her, that the Holy Book was no guarantee of worth and steadfastness and certainly not an adequate substitute for gentility. No doubt had he arrived in Wethersfield, not with the Bible, but with a book of personal pedigree clutched in his hand, his cause would have prospered. He could not credit for a moment that Mr Burder would be such a scoundrel as to withhold his letters from her, therefore he must assume that she willingly acquiesced to instructions that she should not communicate with him again. That she had played him false and broken his heart would, no doubt, be of little moment to her, whilst the possibility of local gossip spreading beyond the confines of Essex, thus prejudicing and damaging his career at the outset, would matter to her even less. But he had been received into Holy Orders and his primary, nay, his only duty was to God, and as he felt that he could render valuable service, however humbly, in the Church, he could not allow any creature, however vaunted her opinions of what life should be, to deter him from the path he had chosen. He would apply almost immediately for a transfer to another parish and would trouble her no more. As he had mentioned to her many times,

he had friends who would be in a position to help him rise in his calling
and he would communicate with them at once. If his circumstances
changed for the better he would, if spared, return one day on a visit to
her neighbourhood. He trusted, and believed, that when that day came
she would keep her promise (nearly the last words he had heard her
utter) to see him, as a friend. He had loved her, and notwithstanding
her harsh treatment of him and the cruel actions of her family, he must
confess he loved her still.

Patrick signed the letter hastily and folded it over without once
reading it through. Perhaps, years later, he would regret his impetuosity
but now there was no hesitation : he handed the epistle to Miss Davy,
requesting that it be delivered to Mary as soon as convenient.

Later Mary Burder's daughter, Mrs Lowe, maintained stoutly that
none of Patrick's letters ever reached her mother, but the evidence does
not bear this out. Certainly their delivery was delayed by Mr Burder
until the curate had left Wethersfield but that Mary eventually received
at least some of them she was to admit to Patrick himself years later.
He continued to write her a short note every few months until 1810—
as he did also to the kindly Miss Davy—and Mary was to refer to these
letters too. The latter were of a cool nature, although Patrick thought
often of Mary after leaving Essex ; but no answers came and he was
forced to place her memory at the back of his mind.

In the autumn of 1808 Patrick went into Leicestershire, having
heard from his Cambridge friend Robert Cox, now rector of St Mary's,
Broughton Astley, that the curacy of St Peter's, Glenfield, was at his
disposal. For a few weeks Patrick took duty at Glenfield, meeting the
Rev. William Campbell who was in charge until there was a new
nomination. But destiny awaited Patrick elsewhere and he did not
accept the curacy ; a letter from John Nunn arrived just in time.

Nunn, who left Cambridge to be ordained shortly before Patrick,
was now curate at St Chad's, Shrewsbury. On 28th June 1806, he
signed the registers of another Shrewsbury church, St Mary's, as
"Deacon". He had been among the first to whom Patrick had written
explaining that he was now anxious for a change of curacy. Nunn
advised Patrick that there was a vacancy for an assistant curate in his
district, at Wellington, Shropshire, and that, as this was much farther
north than Wethersfield and a parish of considerable importance he
would perhaps consider it as appropriate to his wishes. He suggested
that Patrick should apply for the transfer and he would, meantime,
recommend him locally.

Glenfield or Wellington ? There did not seem such an important
difference ; but when Patrick chose the latter and did as Nunn suggested

he could only have known of one of the four people there whom he would meet and who would so powerfully shape his life.

Patrick made his farewells to Cox and Campbell and returned to Wethersfield, without totally giving up the Glenfield idea until he had obtained the Wellington curacy. The reason for his wishing a change had been well explained to both men.

Then came his appointment to Wellington. He at once wrote to Campbell, giving the latest news from Wethersfield.

To The Rev^d Mr. Campbell, Glenfield, near Leicester.
   Wethersfield, near Braintree, Essex. 12th Novr 1808.

Dear Campbell,

 I should not have troubled you so soon, was it not that I expect there is a letter directed to me at Glenfield, if there be I will thank you to redirect it to me at Wethersfield. I will be much obliged to you also to tell Mr. Cox, that I shall not return to Glenfield, if therefore, he wishes to get rid of that Curacy (as I understand he does,) let him keep it only a quarter of a year from this date, and signify the same to Mr. Robinson. Perhaps you may soon see Mr. Robinson, if you do, you will have the goodness to mention this to him. A quarter of a year will be sufficient notice, & any less, would be too little.

 Had I not been circumstanced as I am, I should have kept the Glenfield Curacy, for a year or two at least. Would it not suit Hill of Magdalene ? You might mention this to Mr. Cox. But I fear he could not undergo the Bishop of Lincolns Examination. Since I returned here, I have enjoyed more peace, & contentment than I expected I should have done. The Lady I mentioned, is always in exile ; her guardians can scarcely believe me, that I have given the affair entirely up forever. All along, I violated both the dictates of my conscience and my judgment. "Be not unequally yoked", says the Apostle. But Virgil was not far wrong, when he said, "Omnia vincit Amor" ; & no one can deny Solomons authority, who tells us that "Love is stronger than Death". But for Christs sake we are, to cut off a right hand, or to pluck out a right eye, if requisite. May he by his grace enable me always to conform to his will. I had a letter lately from Ireland, they are all well. Have you heard, since I saw you, from America ? And how are your relations there ? Ah ! "Dulce Domum". When do you intend to revisit Columbia ? Perhaps you intend to live & to rot in old England. In some things, our lots in life are nearly similar ; both as respects our late love affairs, & our voluntary exile from our dear Homes ; though I believe, literally speaking, it is not voluntary. But why should I grieve, ?

who is he that can say he has not a wish unfullfilled [sic]? Oh! that I could make my God and Saviour, my home, my Father, my All! But this happy state is reserved for better men than I. I hope my dear Friend it is your portion. I often wish myself in your place: but Gods will be done; in due time he may bring me nearer to himself, & consequently nearer to heaven and happiness. I heard from Nunn lately, he desired his best respects, to Cox, to Benson & to you; he was not very well owing to too much exertion. When you see your Vicar [sic] & the Curate of St. Mary's, remind me to them in the most affectionate manner. Give my most sincere regards also, to the very good & amiable Mrs Cox, whom I believe to be just such a wife, as I wish both you & I to get, when it pleased God to bestow upon us a peril [sic] of such great price. Can you read this scrawl of mine which I have written in the greatest haste, & which I have no time to revise? I suppose you are now a good deal alone; yet not alone, for God is with you. I hope to hear from you soon. Believe me your sincere though unworthy Friend.

P. Brontè

In quoting "Be not unequally yoked" Patrick was granting to the Burders the "social" superiority.

Patrick's "letter Testimonial"—to be used again in subsequent moves—was sent to the Bishop of London, the subscribers headed by Dr Jowett and Patrick's friend in Colchester, Robert Storry.

It was to be a dismal Christmas this year for Patrick, and to make matters worse there came Miss Davy to say that the family were demanding that he return all Mary's letters. He went up to his room and after some time returned with the little bundle, which he handed over sadly. When Mary came to open the packet she would find a small card with Patrick's face in profile and under it the words, "Mary, you have torn the heart; spare the face."

Patrick made his farewells as cheerfully as he could. How different were his feelings that Christmas from those of a year ago! He had then returned from his ordination full of hopes and tender love. Now, after two years, he was leaving his first parish at his own wish. He had served his people well in Wethersfield, he felt he could honestly say that; but the thought of Mary was an open wound yet and could heal only if he were somewhere far away.

He preached his last sermon in Wethersfield Church and made his last entry in the register—"P. Brontè". His final duty was that of conducting a funeral on 1st January 1809. Then, on Saturday, 7th January, he left the village with mixed feelings of sadness and relief.

Patrick had mnch to occupy his thoughts as he travelled across

country into Shropshire. Despite the tragic end to his work at Wethersfield, his new appointment was in the nature of a promotion : his new
parish was a large one and considered of sufficient importance to carry
with the living a resident minister and two curates. Wellington was at
this time indeed a growing town, with a large mining population. But
although it was far less congenial than Wethersfield, Patrick could find
some consolation in the grandeur of the Wrekin, which crouched above
the town. He was to stay here only eleven months—until the beginning
of December 1809—but there would be time for him to lose a friend
and gain a new one.

His vicar was the Rev. John Eyton, who found lodgings for Patrick
near the vicarage and showed him over the parish church, All Saints,
built in 1790. He started his duties and found at once a great contrast
between this parish and his last. In the small Essex village there had
been much prosperity amongst the farmers and very few of the people
had been in need of financial assistance; but here there was poverty
and, in parts of the town, hunger stalked the streets.

There was much work to be done to bring the hope of God's
Kingdom to these people, but Patrick, as he preached and prayed and
visited the poor, wished in his heart that he could also offer them bread
and butter. Patrick Brontë (he often spelt his name this way) was soon
well known in the town and his tall figure could be seen at the pit-head
if there should be some anxiety for the men. In the event of disaster
Patrick's attitude was to aid the rescue of the trapped and bring succour
to the hurt before uttering a single prayer over the corpses. For all that
men's eyes should be fixed on the Life Eternal, Patrick felt that there
was too little being done for the living. Certainly to waste precious
seconds by praying over a dead man when the living could still be saved
was the height of folly.

But it was pleasant to meet John Nunn again and to talk over the
happy times spent at St John's. Patrick sat for his portrait to present to
his friend. There were walks and scrambles on the Wrekin and much
discussion about their futures. During these talks Nunn informed his
friend that he was shortly to marry Elizabeth Tipton of Shrewsbury
and hoped Patrick would pay him a visit when he and his wife were
settled. But marriage was a sore subject at this stage of Patrick's life
and, remembering his recent experiences, he roundly condemned Nunn
for his folly and abused the state of matrimony in no uncertain terms.
Nunn was astonished at his companion's vehemence and not a little
hurt. He considered that his future wife had been insulted and that
Patrick's remarks ill became his cloth. Shortly afterwards John Nunn
was married and he and Patrick never met again. But when, in the

following year, Patrick's first poem was published, a copy was sent to Nunn, warmly inscribed. Many years later John Nunn's niece, Miss Maria Tipton, wrote to Clement Shorter as follows :

"In 1857 I was staying with Mr. Nunn at Thorndon in Suffolk, of which place he was rector. The good man had never read a novel in his life, and of course had never heard of the famous Brontë books. I was reading Mrs Gaskell's 'Life' with absorbed interest, and one day my uncle said, 'I have heard lately a name mentioned with which I was well familiar, what is it all about?' He was told, when he added, 'Patrick Brontë was once my greatest friend.' Next morning my uncle brought out a thick bundle of letters and said, 'These were written by Patrick Brontë. They refer to his spiritual state. I have read them once more, and now I destroy them.'"

But a new acquaintance had been made, a fresh friend discovered : one who was destined to prove of great importance to Patrick, closely affecting both his career and his personal life.

Shortly after his arrival in Wellington Patrick was introduced to his fellow-curate at All Saints, the Rev. William Morgan, B.D. Morgan, who was five years younger than Patrick, was a Welshman; he was stout, red-faced and very hearty. At first, his apparent determination to be jolly at all costs and his ceaseless flood of words bore heavily upon Patrick, but he soon discovered the true worth of the man hidden behind this gushing exterior and they became firm friends.

William Morgan, who was ordained priest on 22nd September 1805, whilst curate at St Cynog's, Boughrood, Radnorshire, had been assistant curate at Wellington since 1806. He was well in the swim with the Methodist flood. Although lacking the advantage of Nunn's and Patrick's Cambridge acquaintance with Simeon, and the latter's friendship with Martyn, he was nevertheless known to many of the leading Evangelicals and Wesleyans in Yorkshire: the Rev. John Crosse, Vicar of Bradford, John Fennell, the Methodist lay preacher, and even the fanatical Jabez Bunting, who was later to help prepare the way for a corporate Methodist Church, quite separate from the Church of England. But there was patronage much closer at hand than either Cambridge or Yorkshire—at nearby Madeley Vicarage. Here, in 1809, still lived the widow of Wesley's great friend, John Fletcher. Although dying of cancer and barely able to walk, Mary Fletcher of Madeley was nevertheless still bent on God's business and had the ear of all the Church leaders. She had made her own sacrifices to God, spending her fortune on orphan houses at Leytonstone and Birstall, Yorkshire. At the latter place, as Mary Bosanquet, she lived prior to her marriage to John Fletcher. For twenty-five years they had loved each other, but like

Henry Martyn and his Lydia, had placed their work above personal desires. But in 1781, Fletcher relented and Mary joined him at Madely Vicarage. He was soon to die and Mary Fletcher wrote to John Wesley, "*Three years, nine months, and two days*, I have possessed my *heavenly-minded husband*: but now the sun of my earthly joy *is set for ever*, and my soul filled with an anguish, which only finds its consolation in a total *abandonment* and *resignation* to the Will of God." Largely thanks to her influence William Morgan had come into communication with the Rev. John Crosse and John Fennell: the latter, who was born at Madeley, was the godson of her late husband.

Morgan excitedly told Patrick that Mrs Fletcher was still interested in furthering the advancement of young curates who, in her opinion, were worthy to carry Wesley's banner through the land. Fennell was not the only young man she wished to send to Yorkshire—"the Goshen of our land", as her husband had named it—there had been others whom she had recommended for such promotion. Indeed, Morgan was himself one of that fortunate number: he had, it seems, impressed Mrs Fletcher considerably as a most promising new recruit to the Church and one deserving of all possible assistance. The usual word had been sent to high places in Yorkshire, and William Morgan expected at any moment now to be appointed curate to a Yorkshire parish, probably in the Bradford district—the very heart of Wesley's country.

As the summer of 1809 passed, Patrick Brontë and his new companion drew closer and closer in friendship. There were many visits to Morgan's friend, the Rev. Samuel Walter, curate of Madeley; and there in the old Jacobean vicarage Patrick met that "Blessed Mother in Israel", Mary Fletcher.

She watched the Irish curate, listened intently to his speech, and Patrick's spiritual passport to Yorkshire was made out in her mind. All the three curates grouped so eagerly round the lame, short-breathed woman of seventy were destined to reach that county. Patrick was to be first. (In 1815 Samuel Walter became curate, later incumbent, of Slaithwaite, near Huddersfield.) How great the fascination of Yorkshire, how strong the challenge!

Years later when William Morgan wrote the Life of his vicar at Bradford, John Crosse (who was at Madeley for three months in 1781 when he exchanged with John Fletcher to enable the latter to marry Mary Bosanquet at Batley), he paid his tribute to Mary Fletcher.

"I am truly thankful to a gracious providence that I had the privilege of enjoying her friendship and advice as long as she lived . . . it was in a great measure owing to her judicious direction that I became Mr. C's Curate . . . the Rev P. Bronte, on whose judgment I can safely rely,

considered Mr. C. and Mrs. F. as very similar to each other in their
Christian simplicity, zeal, and manner of speaking to their friends, on
the leading subjects of religion."

Another friend to Patrick in Wellington was Joshua Gilpin, Vicar
of Wrockwardine, who had been close to John Fletcher.

But of far greater importance for Patrick was his meeting, both in
Wellington and at Madeley, with John Fennell, then head of a boarding-
school in Wellington where the "strictest vigilance" was exerted to
preserve the pupils' morals "uncorrupted and render them useful members of Society". When Patrick and Morgan entered the Fennells' home
they little guessed that they would eventually join that family circle.

At Nunn's rare circular church of St Chad's in Shrewsbury, Patrick
had also first met John Buckworth, Vicar of Dewsbury—who was
visiting Shropshire for health reasons; thus the stage was almost set for
the Yorkshire scene to follow.

Patrick continued to exert himself at Wellington. He often preached
in place of the Rev. John Eyton, but the text is known of only one
sermon he gave there, "Judge not and ye shall not be judged." It was
a sermon William Morgan was to recall later.

The year drew to a close and Mary Fletcher viewed the Irish curate
with increasing approbation. She added Patrick's name to her select list
of "my precious young men", as she called them. Patrick was the most
favoured of the chosen. It was a blessing straight from John Wesley
himself, who had designated two successors to follow him and his
brother—Grimshaw of Haworth and Fletcher of Madeley. It was
Patrick's unique glory to become successor to the one largely due to the
recommendation of the widow of the other.

At last came the summons to Yorkshire! Patrick was appointed
curate of Dewsbury Parish Church to replace the Rev. Jenkins. Although
he was sorry to leave old parishioners, this was the exciting rung
of the ladder that mattered to him. Patrick's Wellington curacy
ended on 4th December; his "letter Testimonial", stating him to
be "a person worthy of the said cure", included the signatures of
his vicar and Gilpin and was endorsed by the Bishop of Lichfield and
Coventry.

So Patrick left William Morgan behind. But their parting would be
brief, and their reunion would soon lead to an even closer bond between
them. Patrick received from his friend a book of "homilies" or sermons.
In this large brown volume, with red title band, Morgan inscribed on
the fly-leaf:

"The Reverend P. Brontë's Book—Presented to him by his Friend
W. Morgan as a Memorial of the pleasant and agreeable friendship,

which subsisted between them at Wellington, and as a Token of the same Friendship, which, as is hoped, will continue for ever—"

Underneath this he added,

"By this shall all men know that ye are my disciples, if ye love one another—Jesus Christ.

"Let brotherly love continue. St. Paul."

Patrick used this book many times and with his pencil marked or underlined those passages he considered important. "Explain broadly" he wrote against lines likely to be of use in his sermons, and "omit" against others.

Once again Patrick travelled over the dusty English roads, but this time in the right direction—northwards towards the "Promised Land". Many thoughts would crowd his brain on that journey. He knew that Dewsbury, on the banks of the Calder, was a thriving little town with a very fine church. He knew also that the vicar, the Rev. John Buckworth, was much respected in the Church and was considered a splendid preacher and writer of hymns. He was the author of several devotional discourses. All this was a great challenge to Patrick, but there was yet more he had heard. The vicar of Dewsbury enjoyed but indifferent health and frequently travelled in the south of England because of its warmer climate. This time, therefore, in contrast to the Wethersfield position, large responsibilities would be likely to rest on Patrick's shoulders. The thought of Wethersfield reminded him of Mary Burder and he wondered if she would care that he had received such promotion. As the coach rumbled on, Patrick again thought of the land that lay before him, and of the men who had spread the Holy Gospel amongst its hills : John Wesley, whom he had seen as a boy in the lanes at home, Charles Wesley, and old Parson Grimshaw who had driven his flock out of the taverns and into church at the whip's end. Grimshaw ! What tales were told of his ministry in a small Yorkshire moorland village ! He had achieved immortal fame and passed it on in some measure to the village where he had worked. No one could ever think of the Rev. William Grimshaw without conjuring up also the name of Haworth. Until his coming no one had heard of such a place and now for all time the two names, Grimshaw and Haworth, would be linked. How strange and how magnificent that the deeds of one individual could bring fame not only to himself but to a tiny moorland village that had previously lived in silence. There had been reports of pilgrims coming from all over England, not only to visit Grimshaw's grave at Luddenden but even to climb the steep hill to visit his church at Haworth and see the famous pulpit from which he had preached. Patrick wondered what the moorland folk thought of such visitors, for had it not been for William

Grimshaw they would surely have lived out their lives in undiscovered solitude.

Late on a cold winter's day, Tuesday, 5th December 1809, Patrick arrived at Dewsbury. He eagerly sought and found the parish church, on the site of which, it was believed, Paulinus, the Roman missionary, had preached and baptized in A.D. 627. He longed to explore the church, but that would have to wait the morrow: he sought the old vicarage which stood close to the church on the north side and striding firmly up to the thick oak door, he gave a vigorous knock. Patrick Brontë had arrived in Yorkshire—he would reside there for the rest of his days.

CHAPTER 4

Dewsbury

PATRICK remained as curate at Dewsbury for a little over a year but it was a momentous year for him. He would take up both the pen and the sword in no uncertain manner and wield them both in righteous causes. However quiet had been his arrival, on his departure from the town Patrick would leave behind him, in the minds of his parishioners, divers memories of their Irish curate that would linger long in the Calder Valley.

In 1809 Dewsbury was a typical Yorkshire country town surrounded by rural beauty, rich with trees. Under the heights of Crackenedge and Westboro' with their crown of woods were a few scattered farmsteads; below them again meadows with stone cottages, each having its own weaving-shed down in the valley beside the winding Calder. In those days the river was pure and its banks at Dewsbury a favourite place for anglers.

But in Europe the war went on and the growing prosperity of the town was halted. There was already talk of installing labour-saving machines in the mills. The future frame-breakers were gathering their forces to oppose such a measure, and at the time when Patrick came to Dewsbury there was a sullen undertone of discontent in the district. This was to simmer quietly for a year or two yet and then burst forth into the violence of the Luddite Riots.

Lawlessness existed in plenty, however, without the aid of political strife: bull-baiting, badger-baiting, cock-fighting and dog-fighting were common amusements of the working people, ending not infrequently in drunken brawls. The Rev. John Buckworth had felt himself obliged to denounce these lawless activities from the pulpit in sermon after sermon.

In these first days at Dewsbury, however, Patrick had much to excite his interest, without as yet concerning himself with the district, or even the town itself. He was to reside at the vicarage and have rooms of his own there. There was the church to become acquainted with and Patrick, although knowing something of its long story, had to learn more.

The vicarage at Dewsbury stood at right angles to the church, facing

47

the north side and at a distance from it of only some forty yards. Behind the vicarage was a garden hidden from the road by a stone wall and stretching away to the east of the building. On the west side at a little distance stood the thirteenth-century Moot Hall, originally the rectory, but later frequently used as the Court House. The churchyard ran closely beside the south wall of the church, in front of it to the west and continued round between the church and vicarage. Thus the vicarage was contained in the same enclosure as the church, the entrances to the grounds being opposite the main west door and between the Moot Hall and the side of the vicarage.

The old vicarage at Dewsbury was established in 1349, an appropriation having been made to the Dean and College of the Free Chapel in the Palace at Westminster—St Stephen's. In this deed was ordered the erection of a dwelling for successive clergymen holding the living. It was stipulated that the minimum accommodation to be provided was "in one competent mansion-house, well built, consisting of one hall, two chambers at the least, a kitchen, a stable, a granary, and a house cattle, and other necessary purposes of the said vicar"; "likewise for a convenient garden and an enclosure as big as the neighbourhood will allow of". This deed was signed and sealed on 20th June 1349, and, as stated at the foot of the document, "Given at our Manor of Ripon".

The vicarage was to be erected at the expense of the Dean and Chapter and was probably, at the time it was built, the finest building in the locality. Many vicars were to live there, the succession being broken only once when, in Parliamentarian times, the occupant was ejected and a Presbyterian minister installed. The unfortunate vicar died shortly afterwards at Dewsbury in great poverty and never lived to see the Restoration.

A long, low house, with four ground-floor and four first-floor windows, the front was entwined with young creeper when Patrick first gazed at it in 1809. Mr Buckworth conducted him over the old building. From the entrance hall there led off a large drawing-room, as by then it was called, in which Patrick noticed a great Gothic arched stone fireplace with its cosy ingle-nook. There was also a dining-room with a doorway giving access into a smaller apartment, the breakfast-room. Leading out of the entrance hall opposite this and on the west side of the house was the small room allocated to Patrick for his study, and which a generation before had been the butler's pantry. There was room for his small collection of books and his writing desk; ample accommodation also for him to stretch his long legs in walking about whilst composing his sermons—or his poems. The walls were panelled in oak, already dark with age, so that Patrick was grateful for the large window as an aid to his eyesight.

There was a spacious kitchen at the back of the house, with an adjoining scullery. The latter contained a large pump and beneath it was the well from which many of the townspeople fetched their water. They would insist on obtaining their water from the pump room, as the scullery was called, because "it was so good for tea-making". But as the well ran up from one corner of the graveyard Patrick much doubted the wisdom of their preference; and later in life bitter experience would render him even more certain of their folly.

There were two staircases ascending to the upper storey, the main one for the family and guests, and a small back stair for the servants. Patrick's room was again in the west part of the house : he was informed that there was a haunted room upstairs—it had the reputation of being visited by a mysterious lady dressed in green—but that chamber was not for him! At the other end of the house, over the breakfast-room, was Mr Buckworth's study, where the vicar could write his sermons and his magazine articles and compose his hymns undisturbed.

Such was Patrick's first home in Yorkshire. The venerable building was demolished in 1889, to the great regret of many of the people of Dewsbury, for it was the oldest dwelling-house in the parish. When the vicarage was pulled down, the carved lion on the gable end, called the "Stone Dog" by the children of the parish school, was lowered at noon on Shrove Tuesday to fulfil the legend that it jumped to the ground when it heard the pancake bell ring from the church. The site of the old vicarage and its "convenient garden" are now part of the graveyard. The masonry of the large drawing-room fireplace has been preserved and built into the north wall of the churchyard—the only relic of this ancient house. This is flanked by two thirteenth-century doorways which were originally in the church, one on each side of the chancel.

Next Patrick was shown over the church and it was a wonderful moment in his life when he entered this historic building for the first time.

All Saints Church, Dewsbury, was not so large in 1809 as it is today : in 1823 the north and south aisles were rebuilt and an extension eastward was completed in 1887. But what Patrick saw was imposing enough : a long nave with four Norman arches supported on fine pillars, those on the south aisle dating from 1200 and those on the north from about 1250. Running from the back of the church on either side were the usual small galleries, whilst the pews were high-backed in those days. The tower was recent, having been built in 1785. The font was a stone circular basin on an octagonal pillar, with a thirteenth-century floral design under the bowl. The registers were complete and dated from 1538: they were claimed to be the oldest set in the north of England.

Many stones in the church dated from the eighth and ninth centuries. The tradition that Paulinus "preached and celebrated" here in A.D. 627, some thirty years after the landing of St Augustine, seems well founded: the locality was excellently sited for baptism as the river Calder, a wide-running brook, was near at hand and the subsoil showed the land free from possible bogs. Portions of runic crosses have been discovered, dating from Saxon times, and there can be seen the Paulinus Cross with its inscription *Hic Paulinus predicavit et celebravit*. Certain it is that Dewsbury Church was flourishing in Saxon times, and that the parish was of enormous extent, covering 400 square miles. Gradually, in Norman times, separate parishes were formed at Thornhill, Bradford, Halifax and other places until finally in 1261 the parish of Mirfield was formed. But in 1809 the livings of Hartshead-cum-Clifton and Ossett were still included in Dewsbury parish, and even today the benefices of Huddersfield, Bradford and others pay Easter dues to the Vicar of Dewsbury, although the tribute from Halifax ceased long ago.

In Domesday Book is recorded, "In Dewsberia there are three carucates to be taxed, which two ploughs will till. This land belongs to Wakefield, yet King Edward had it in a Manor. It now belongs to the King, and there are six villanes and two bordars, with four ploughs, a priest and a church. The whole Manor is four quarentens long and the same broad. In the time of King Edward the value was ten shillings; it is the same now."

Dewsbury was a rectory until the reign of Edward the Third, the district being given to the Warren family at the time of the Norman Conquest. During the time of Henry the First the advowson of Dewsbury was given to the priors of Lewes. They held it until the reign of Edward the Second, when they sold the patronage to Hugh Dispenser, whose family retained it for twenty-five years. Edward the Third then acquired it, and presented it to the Dean and Canons of St Stephen's, Westminster.

Patrick saw the names of past rectors and vicars. He read at the top of the list: 1189–99 Ketel 1225. Jointly. John de Dewsbury, Odo de Richmond. William de Heton was first vicar in 1349, followed by William de Dewesbury 1362. Finally he noticed immediately above John Buckworth's name that of Matthew Powley, 1st May 1777, and recalled that he had been the great friend of William Cowper, and Mary Unwin's son-in-law.

As Patrick came out of the church, he noticed some of the large slab tombstones. Many dated from the early seventeenth century, some even earlier, and yet, after two hundred years or more, they were as perfectly preserved as, say, the stone inside the church to the memory of John Mowbray, 1610.

As he returned to the vicarage full of the importance of the long history of the parish church and of the men who had served God there, he little thought that one day in the south aisle there would be erected a brass memorial plaque to yet another servant of Dewsbury Church, and one that would attract more attention than even the names of the saints of ancient times:

"In Memory of The Reverend Patrick Brontë B.A. St. John's College, Cambridge. Born at Emdale, County Down, St. Patrick's Day 1777 . . ."

and above these opening words would appear, in relief, a likeness of his own head.

Life at the vicarage was very pleasant for Patrick and from the start he formed a great respect for and deep attachment to his vicar. The Rev. John Buckworth was born at Colsterworth in Lincolnshire in 1779 and completed his education at St Edmund Hall, Oxford. He had been ordained to the curacy of Dewsbury in 1804, serving under the Rev. Matthew Powley until the latter's death in 1806, when he was appointed to succeed him as vicar. He was installed as Vicar of Dewsbury on 23rd January 1807. Thus he was two years younger than Patrick, and the new curate found that fact a great help in dispersing the awe which he might otherwise have felt if called upon to preach in such an important parish under the eye of an older man. John Buckworth's wife, Rachel, was two years younger than her husband; thus there existed in the vicarage an agreeable atmosphere for the thirty-three-year-old curate. But possibly the inhabitant of the vicarage that gained most of Patrick's affection was Mrs Buckworth's beloved dog, Robin Tweed; and the pet could always look to him for support whenever he had incurred the wrath of Esther, the vicarage servant.

A great friendship sprang up between vicar and curate, for besides their duties they shared a common desire to write. In this Buckworth had already been quite successful. He had composed many hymns that achieved a great popularity and there were few schools and nurseries in Yorkshire that did not hear

> Great God, and wilt thou condescend,
> To be my Father and my Friend?

His best known hymns such as "My Bible" and "The Sunday Scholar" were issued in book form soon after Patrick's arrival at the vicarage and printed by F. Inkersley of Bradford, the firm Patrick would later use for some of his printed works. Buckworth's hymns had run to five editions by 1812 and nine years after his death, which occurred on 2nd April 1835, a twelfth edition was issued.

Besides his many tracts published in various magazines of the period, he wrote "A Series of Discourses containing a System of Devotional, Experimental, and Practical Religion, particularly calculated for the Use of Families. Preached at the Parish Church of Dewsbury, Yorkshire, by the Rev. J. Buckworth, A.M., Vicar, Wakefield" and published by E. Waller.

He later presented Patrick with a copy of this work, inscribed, "Revd P. Brontè 1811—A Testimony of Sincere Esteem from the Author".

Whatever the merits or demerits of these discourses Patrick considered himself most fortunate to serve a vicar who had a bent for religious literature and it rekindled his own ambitions in that direction: no doubt Mr Buckworth could be of great assistance to him in his own efforts. John Buckworth was a fine preacher and very much respected in the parish: his favourite motto respecting himself was the humble "A sinner saved by Grace".

Patrick found that he was given every opportunity to study, consistent with his duties. He took most of his meals alone in his room and lived very plainly, as was his custom. Oatmeal porridge and potatoes were his principal diet, with a dumpling as dessert. Mr and Mrs Buckworth teased him about his frugality and urged him to keep a better table but Patrick firmly declined. On Sundays, however, the household dined and supped together. Even then Patrick would hardly enjoy a feast: true there was meat and plenty of it to afford a change for him, but it would always be cold. Patrick understood the reason for this. Indeed he fully shared the strict ideas of Mr and Mrs Buckworth that the Sabbath should be properly observed: a day of rest from all possible secular work and one devoted to religious labours.

Patrick was soon quite at home in the vicarage and felt that here in Dewsbury he would be content to serve for several years. Deeply as he longed for a living of his own, he now felt, for the first time in his life, that ambition could rest its wings a while.

He commenced his duties in the parish church a few days after his arrival and on 11th December 1809 officiated at the wedding of two of his new parishioners: on that day he married John Senior to Ellen Popplewell, and signed the old registers for the first time—"P. Brontê, curate". (He still continued this way of spelling his name, although whilst at Dewsbury he would vary it sometimes, thus "Brontĕ".)

Patrick quickly became well known in Dewsbury and almost universally liked and admired. The tall, erect figure, the almost classical features, the auburn hair and determined expression were such as to create respect. He was well formed and of a good presence. Indeed his parishioners described him as handsome, and being Yorkshire people, they meant it. As yet there was no need for spectacles save at work, but the pale blue eyes were slowly growing weaker.

Patrick mostly wore black but occasionally whilst at Dewsbury he donned a blue linen frock coat. Around his neck was the customary white cravat. Like a true son of his race he obtained a shillelagh and carried it with him everywhere. Soon his way of carrying it was to earn him the nickname "Old Staff". Thus he commenced the habit that would remain with him all his days, for Patrick rarely went forth again without a stick of some kind in his hand. His figure was soon familiar with its long strides and rapid gait as he passed through the streets or walked down by the banks of the Calder.

Patrick made a great impression on his congregation also, although he approached his first sermon with some trepidation, knowing the very high reputation his vicar held as a preacher. John Buckworth was also of the Evangelical School and his addresses, both from the pulpit and in print, commanded the utmost respect.

But Patrick's sermon went down well with his listeners and his gift of speaking without reference to his manuscript won him many admirers. As young Buckworth's health was never robust, Patrick had the opportunity to preach often from the old three-decker pulpit that faced the rows of high pews. Into his sermons he threw all the passionate sincerity and compassionate understanding at his command—not, be it admitted, without some consciousness that now he was in Yorkshire, and in such a parish, nothing but his best endeavours would suffice. The Yorkshire folk came and listened and were impressed. His popularity increased each week ; but as they walked away they still considered him not quite equal to Mr Buckworth, either as a thinker or a speaker. But he spoke plain to them, they admitted that to themselves ; you could understand his meaning better than the vicar's ; but he was not so clever, they were quite sure of that. Some of the older ones among the congregation suggested that neither the vicar nor the Irish curate was a match for young Hammond Roberson when he had been curate under Powley from 1779 to 1785. Patrick knew what was being said and felt that the comparisons were more than fair. Certainly he knew of the reputation of Roberson. Soon he would have occasion to hear the great man speak and, when the Luddite riots sprang up, to meet him.

Once a month Patrick catechized the children in church, the pupils of the Wesleyan Sunday School attending along with the others, and this was work he loved. The old desire to be a teacher re-emerged within him, infused now with a new purpose.

But his growing popularity at this time rested not on his work inside the parish church, but outside it. He was recognized as a truly earnest clergyman who did much good work in the town. Like his vicar, he was fond of holding cottage meetings and would walk miles in order to perform these informal services, often carrying messages from one dweller to another which were quite unconnected with the state of their souls, but saved them from the necessity of going out in inclement weather. "Mr Brontë is here" would be the cry and many would flock into the kitchen or "house" as the living-room was called. Patrick would then hold a short prayer meeting and close with a hymn.

Many at first thought him rather austere but the children were very fond of him, and his friendship with them often led to visits to the parents in their cottages.

Although only the curate, Patrick became quite a force in the town and was soon a friend to the humbler folk. He found himself exceedingly intolerant of assertive ignorance and quickly, if not too gently, put it down, particularly if the person exhibiting it was one of the wealthy people of the town. There were certainly those among the wealthy of Dewsbury who tended to look down on the Irish curate and his meddlesome ways. He was not a favourite with the men whose political views were of either extreme. The bent of his mind politically was distinctly Tory—so had been his training, for the Evangelicals all adhered firmly to the Tory banner—but his sympathies were very much with the working people, particularly at this time. The war in Europe dragged on, dislocating all trade, and the bad laws and Orders in Council at home threatened many with starvation. Patrick's instincts were always for justice and at that time the poor people in Dewsbury were not receiving any. Justice for all was his strongest feeling and Patrick would apply it to every contingency in life. He would always support those in the right whatever their creed or class. Thus, when later the pent-up feelings burst into strife, Patrick judged each incident on its own merit and was found to defend both sides on different occasions. There was much to be done to alleviate the sufferings of the poor and Patrick spent nearly all his time visiting the cottages of the parish, to comfort and relieve. Although he never sought the company of the wealthy people of Dewsbury it was, perhaps, inevitable that he should, through his vicar, become acquainted with the Halliley family and visit them at their home, The Aldams. The heads of this family were long called "The Kings of Dewsbury", partly in derision, by the people of the town.

Many years after he had left, Patrick Brontë would still be remembered by the people of Dewsbury, and their summary of his character seems to have been that he was a very earnest man, but a little peculiar in his manner; that he was brave, impetuous, daring, proud and generous; a good friend and a good enemy where there was a wrongdoing. He was, however, inclined to take offence when none was meant, and to fly into a rage for no apparent reason. He could never abide a supposed taunt or sneer of any kind. Patrick had an adventurous stay amongst these people and was to earn all these opinions in turn.

Meanwhile, however, there were many leading preachers to hear and Patrick went over to Bradford to listen to a sermon by the Rev. John Crosse; news in plenty to give to the impatient William Morgan down in Wellington.

As the spring of 1810 drew on, Patrick spent much of his time in the quiet vicarage garden, where he could study in the fresh air. Sometimes callers would observe him pacing up and down, paper and pencil in hand, and stopping now and then to write something down. The curate was preparing his sermon they thought; but Patrick was doing nothing of the sort. He was trying, oh so very hard, to write poetry. His great obsession to be a writer had been renewed by the successful example of John Buckworth and he was determined to get into print at all costs. Here at Dewsbury he felt more settled than at any previous time in his life and felt sure that, with his vicar's aid, a little touching up here and there, and the addition of a few new verses he could produce a book of poems that would give religious instruction to the simple-minded folk and to the children. Here, in the garden, it was easier to write of God and nature than in his small study: there he could put down a sermon to learn by rote but he needed the fresh air and the smell of the soil to inspire his verse. So he struggled on, wrestling with that most noble ambition. Poor Patrick—although his first poem would soon be published and there would be other little books, of verse and prose, he would know in his heart that they were not good; that with the exception of a very few lines and parts of his "Maid of Killarney", they were very bad indeed. But Patrick was not quite so crushed as he might have been: his disappointment at his lack of ability in imaginative writing was softened by the comforting knowledge that its main purpose was largely achieved. There were many humble people who read his words and derived comfort from them. It is true that they are very much the language of the clergy of his day, that they borrow largely from Wesley, and that there is no brilliant innovation of thought. Yet many poor folk and many children gained solace from his words, and that was what Patrick was seeking to achieve. Pathetic as some of his verse may seem, it must be remembered that he wrote in simple terms for simple people : as in his sermons, he refused to go above their heads. He could have written nothing of greater literary merit—it was not in him. But even if he had, the brilliance would have floated away into thin air, would have been incomprehensible to the majority of his readers, and his message from God would never have reached those for whom he intended it. In his *Poets of Yorkshire* in 1845, Newsam rightly describes some of Patrick's poems as presenting "pious sentiments in a plain garb". He wished to reach the almost illiterate people whom he served, not the educated few : the latter's salvation rested on their own consciences. Patrick had learned well the wise dictum of that great Yorkshire scholar of St John's, Cambridge, Roger Ascham : "We preachers ought to think like great men, but speak like common people." So Patrick struggled on in the vicarage garden, composing his feeble verse, and if the world of letters has a right to decry his work, its purpose should, at least, preclude the ready sneer. There was in Patrick a relentless urge to create : to write, and mirror this world and the next for the comfort of his people. But, although his own pen was feeble and quite unequal to the task, he would live to gain reward. The seed of literary longing within him was too potent to wither in an old man's frame : it would pour forth into his daughters' hearts and the Yorkshire moors would fertilize it into glorious bloom.

During this year of 1810 Patrick's work was first published:

Winter – Evening
Thoughts.
A
Miscellaneous Poem.

Dum, operosa parvus carmina fingo : me quoque, qui facio, judice, digna lini plurima cerno.

London : Printed for Longman, Hurst, Rees, and Orme, and John Hurst, Wakefield. 1810

A copy was sent to John Nunn inscribed : "To my dear Friend Nunn, with my unfeigned love, and christian regards. P. Brontë."

Although the poem was published anonymously Patrick added in ink on this presentation copy : "By P. Brontë. B.A."

Later, Patrick would revise the poem as "Winter-Night Meditations" in his *Cottage Poems*, published the following year. John Drinkwater wrote in 1922 : " . . . It is the author's best poem, and has much of Crabbe's quality." The poem was of 265 lines, covering pages 3 to 23, the pages measuring 6¼″ by 3¾″.

Patrick introduced his poem thus :

In this Miscellaneous Poem, now offered to the Public, which in due time will probably be followed by others of a similar nature, and upon the same plan, the Author's intention is, to "become all things to all men, that he might by all means save some" :

He wishes by a judicious mixture of the *Profitable* and *Agreeable*, to gain access to the libraries of certain characters, who would shut their doors against any thing savouring of *Austerity*.

Should the Author succeed, in being made the happy instrument of adding to the comforts of any individual, or of reclaiming but *one*, from the error of his ways, he will esteem himself amply recompensed for his labours.

E. Waller, Printer, Wakefield.

Patrick attacks those who give to the poor :

> But, to receive as much again ;
> or, from a selfish shallow cause,
> To fan the breath of vain applause.
> Such gifts, may charm the eyes of fools,
> And gain the praise of flatt'ring tools ;
> But wise and good men, pass them by
> Indignant . . .

He condemns the sexual indulgence of the city dwellers, and reminds the land :

> Oh, Britain fair ! thou Queen of Isles !
> Nor hostile arms, nor hostile wiles,
> Could ever shake thy solid throne ;
> But for thy sins.—Thy sins alone,
> Can make thee stoop thy royal head . . .
> In vain, our statesmen plot and scheme,
> In vain, our fields with falchions gleam,
> In vain, our conqu'ring thunders roar
> Terrific, round the Gallic shore ;
> If, all the while, within our breast,
> We foster sin . . .

He reminds men of their frailty against nature : of the wreck at sea which means "The merchant's care, and toils, are vain." Fair Susan (the first Brontë heroine) gazes from the shore to see

If, hanging far, 'twixt sea and sky,
She can a coming sail descry . . .
Then forth she goes, with sidelong glance,
Eyes all the crew, if there perchance,
Her long lost William might appear—
Till all on shore; approaching near,
No William's found . . .

The poem ends with the reminder that wealth without religion is no guarantee of escape from winter's trials.

Oft, Gold, and shining pedigree,
    Prove only splendid misery.
The King who sits upon his throne,
And calls the kneeling world his own;
Has oft, of cares a greater load,
Than he, who feels his iron rod . . .

Religion alone

Brightens our prospect, proves our stay,
December turns to smiling May;
Conveys to us that peaceful shore,
By raging billows lash'd no more,
Where endless happiness remains,
And one eternal Summer reigns.

FINIS

One of Patrick's favourite walks was by the side of the river. Leaving the eastern end of the vicarage garden he would turn down Longcauseway into Sands Lane, a broad path on the banks of the Calder leading towards Horbury: here he would spend many happy hours walking briskly by the stream and pausing, now and again, to watch the anglers.

One day in early spring 1810 Patrick set off for a walk in the afternoon, turning westwards along Water Lane, a reputed Roman road. It was a fine afternoon, but there had been continuous rain for the preceding two or three days, and the river Calder was much swollen. Indeed, Patrick noticed that at places the banks were flooded. He was glad to be out for a long stroll as the weather had kept him indoors recently. He walked along beside the river, enjoying the sudden sunshine and whistling an Irish air to himself. He noticed a group of three or four boys approaching him along the bank from the long weir, which was at the south-western end of Dewsbury.

Before long they stopped and appeared to be attempting to recover some pieces of wood from the river as they floated down stream. One of the boys held a home-made grapnel, consisting of a long cord with a lump of iron attached, and made several unsuccessful attempts to attach it to the moving timber. He eventually threw it into the river in disgust. As Patrick strode past them they appeared to be venting their vexation on a taller, slightly older boy, who, at one glance, he could tell was a simpleton : they were teasing him and nudging him as boys will. Patrick had proceeded only twelve yards or so when he heard a yell and a splash behind him. The lad who had carried the grappling-hook, a boy aged twelve, had pushed too hard, and as Patrick spun round he saw the poor idiot boy battling for his life in mid-stream. There was a scream of horror from the boys and they stood petrified at what had occurred. Patrick never hesitated a second. He ran back and, without pausing to remove his coat, plunged into the icy river. Although he had bathed often in the streams at home he was not much of a swimmer, but there was no thought of that deficiency in his mind as he struggled to reach the frantic youth. He saw a white face. It disappeared, was seen again, nearer this time, and Patrick grabbed the boy under the armpits. For a minute or so he could do no more than tread water, and swallow it. His clothes became heavy, as did those of the lad in his embrace. Patrick gave a great thrust with his legs, and they were clear of the main current. Gradually he fought his way to the bank. There was no fence, just a few bushes by the river brink, but luckily the water was swollen almost bank high and Patrick soon had his heavy burden stretched out safely on the path, about twenty yards below the place where he had been pushed in.

Too frightened to approach, the boys stood back watching Patrick as he attended to the poor creature. Happily there was no damage done —the youth was conscious but too frightened to utter a word. Patrick, dripping with water from head to foot, picked up the lad in his arms and told one of the boys to lead him to the youth's home. Off they went, with the others bringing up the rear, still too scared to approach the new curate. They reached the poor cottage where the unfortunate boy lived with his widowed mother, at Dawgreen. Patrick took him inside and calmed the natural fears of the mother at witnessing such a spectacle. The lad was soon put to bed and was none the worse for his adventure.

After a few words of comfort to the widow and after refusing to listen to her many expressions of thanks, Patrick left the cottage hurriedly to go back to the vicarage and change his clothes. Hatless and shivering, he emerged from the cottage door and saw that the boys were still there, afraid to go home until they had learned how the victim was. Patrick paused in his hurried stride and gave them a severe lecture on their stupid and criminal conduct, reserving his severest censures for the chief culprit, although Patrick was not certain which boy it had been. They had never heard the curate so angry. The guilty one tried to excuse himself: "I only picked [pushed] him to make him wet his shoon." Patrick's stern expression suddenly relaxed and a kind smile softened his features: he was thinking of days long ago when he and his brothers had played by the stream near their home. He told the boys that it was no use their saying to him how sorry they were; *he* needed no apology. But they must step inside the cottage and ask forgiveness from the mother and from her unfortunate son. As they ran towards the cottage he called them back again to remind them that although the youth might appear to the world as a simpleton, even an idiot, in God's eyes that was not so. It was not for us to judge of wisdom: for there were birds in the trees and beasts in the fields with wiser heads than some men. Leaving them to offer their sincere contrition inside the cottage, Patrick, breaking into a brisk trot, ran all the way back to the vicarage. As he changed into dry clothes he was pleased; he had never asked who had done the deed—the culprit had freely admitted the action—and his frankness had done much to soften his anger. As he moved towards the fire, his limbs glowing and tingling as the blood returned to them, there was a great warmth in his heart also, for he had saved the life of a poor fellow-creature.

The story of this incident soon spread throughout the town and Patrick was now something of a hero. One day not long afterwards, John Buckworth informed Patrick that, the weather continuing cold, he proposed to travel to the south of England for a few weeks' rest in a milder climate. His health had not been good and now that Patrick was in full understanding of the work of the parish, and something of a popular hero besides, he felt he could safely leave the curate to take charge.

Mr and Mrs Buckworth were away some weeks and Patrick, for the first time, had the keeping of one of Yorkshire's finest and oldest churches. He happily accepted the new responsibility and his able conduct of parish affairs enhanced his reputation with the people of Dewsbury. But there was time for Patrick to write a poem and send it to his vicar. It consisted of twenty-nine verses and was addressed to Buckworth. Whatever the thoughts of the latter on his curate's friendly poem, it appeared later at the head of Patrick's little volume of *Cottage Poems*. It was entitled "Epistle to the Rev. J— B—, (Vicar of Dewsbury) whilst journeying for the recovery of his health". Patrick informs his vicar that, inadequate as is his rustic muse to express what he feels, he thinks often of him in his absence and pretends that they are together. The poem ends with a wish for the vicar's speedy restoration to good health.

> To all, my heart is kind, and true,
>   But glows with ardent love for you ;
> Though absent, still you rise in view,
>   And talk, and smile,
>   Whilst heavenly themes, for ever new,
>   our cares beguile . . .
> Where rocky mountains prop the skies,
> And, round, the smiling landscape lies,
>   Whilst you look down with tearful eyes,
>   on grovelling man ;
>   My sympathetic fancy flies,
>   The scene to scan . . .
> May rosy health with speed return,
> And all your wonted ardour burn,
>   And sickness buried in her urn,
>   Sleep many years !
>   So, countless friends who loudly mourn,
>   Shall dry their tears !
> Your wailing flock will all rejoice,
>   To hear their much-loved shepherd's voice
>   And long will bless the happy choice
>   Their hearts have made . . .

But during this absence of their vicar, the people of Dewsbury were to be presented with yet another side to the character of their Irish curate.

One Sunday evening, having concluded the church service, Patrick returned to the vicarage and went into his study to rest. He had barely sat down when, to his great astonishment, the bells pealed forth again. He made inquiry of Esther and learned the reason for the ringing. It appeared that, with the vicar away, the bell-ringers thought they would have a practice peal undisturbed, for on the following day there was to be a contest with their rivals from other local church towers. Competitors were entered from other towns and the ringers of Dewsbury were naturally anxious to acquit themselves well. They had never thought to advise the curate. They knew that Mr Buckworth would have granted permission had he been there—that was sufficient for them.

Patrick stood for a moment gazing at the servant after she had told him this. Suddenly Esther backed away with a look of fear. The curate's eyes had become almost bloodshot, and the veins in his forehead had swelled up until they stood out from his head like blue cords. Without a word he turned on his heels and rushed from the kitchen.

Patrick was beside himself with fury : the heathens, he would soon let them know that somebody was in charge of the church—aye, and that included the belfry ! He seized his shillelagh from the study, rushed out of the vicarage and made for the nearby house of Thomas Smith, the parish clerk.

He thundered on the door with his stick and asked Smith why the bells were making that infernal noise. The clerk confirmed the story of the coming competition, and Patrick became more incensed than ever. He shouted that it was a desecration of the Sabbath. How dare they ring his bells for such a purpose ? He would permit it no longer !

Grabbing the keys from the astonished clerk he ran across the churchyard and bounded up the winding steps of the tower. He burst in upon the ringers, brandishing his shillelagh and shouting at them to cease at once their noisy profanity. Immediately the bells were silent. Patrick gave the ringers warning that he would not tolerate such behaviour, shouting that he had not been consulted and that they had destroyed the peace of a Sabbath evening. Still beside himself with uncontrollable rage, he laid about him with his weapon, driving the terrified bell-ringers out of the belfry, down the steps and into the churchyard.

Patrick then returned to the clerk's house and strongly reproved him for conniving at the practice without advising the curate in charge. Smith was too frightened to argue with such an angry man and admitted that, by arrangement, he had locked the men in the tower so that they might be undisturbed.

Patrick returned to his room and sat down. He suddenly felt very tired and his hands were shaking (as the Dewsbury people reported after witnessing some of his furies). But it had been a profanity, he reasoned, to jingle about in such a fashion on the Sabbath ; and besides, the bell-ringers had not sought his permission. Patrick would not know yet which of these two errors on the part of the bell-ringers had enraged him most—the insult to God or to himself. He suspected the latter.

The next morning Patrick found the bell-ringers waiting for him in the vicarage ; they had recovered their courage and were extremely indignant. They informed him that they were in no fit state of prepared-

ness for the coming competition, and that there had been no harm done
as the service was over and the day's public worship at an end. Patrick
repeated, calmly this time, his accusations of the previous evening and
advised the ringers sternly that he would forbid a repetition of such an
occurrence. Tempers began to rise and one ringer declared that he
would never enter the tower again until the curate had made a full
apology for his outrageous and unclerical behaviour. They could
manage without him. But Patrick had decided that, even if his reasons
had been personal, his actions had been fully justified. He therefore
declined to express regret for terminating the practice ring, as it had
taken place on the Sabbath. Without another word the deputation left
the house. As for the outspoken man who had demanded the apology,
he kept his word and never entered the ringing-chamber again. He
resigned his position and shortly afterwards left the church altogether.
But Patrick had winning ways and no lasting enmity was made ; a few
weeks later the man returned to the congregation and became, what he
had scarcely been before, a most devout member of the parish church.
Whatever the fate of the Dewsbury bell-ringers in the local competition,
the curate was soon on good terms again with all his church officers and
the incident was overlooked on both sides ; but the people of the town
would remember it for many years to come.

Soon after this clash in the church tower, Mr and Mrs Buckworth
returned to Dewsbury. The vicar, however, was still far from well and
could undertake only light duties.

John Buckworth's great joy in that year was the erection of the new
Sunday school nearby in which he had been the guiding spirit from the
start. This work was a real labour of love for him and he entered into the
new venture with all the energy his frail strength permitted. There had
been religious instruction for the children in church, and previously
Powley and Buckworth had taught them in the cottages—an innovation
for the north. But now, with a good-sized building of their own, the
children could really have a chance to hear the Holy Scriptures told
them in a way that they could understand. Patrick also entered into
these extra duties with great relish ; they would mean much additional
labour for him owing to the vicar's ill-health, but he was a firm favourite
of the children and possessed a great understanding of the good and bad
that was in all of them. But almost immediately this new work was to
involve him in yet another scene in which he would play the leading
part, albeit a wholly creditable one.

Each year at Whitsuntide the scholars and teachers of the various
Sunday schools connected with Dewsbury parish church walked in
procession through the principal streets of the town before marching

to the village of Earlsheaton for "the sing". Here in an open space in the centre of the village, called the Town's Green, they would raise their young voices in praise of God. This was very much a feature of Yorkshire parishes in those days and, happily, is not unknown even today. All the inhabitants took a great interest in this annual event, and in 1810 the people of Dewsbury were bitterly disappointed that their vicar's health would not permit his leading the procession: it was the harder on John Buckworth in that he had been recently instrumental in obtaining the new Sunday school for the town.

Patrick was asked to lead the march, supported by the churchwardens from Dewsbury and Soothill. As he assembled his young army, placing the girls in the front, Patrick could not suppress some of the old excitement that the thought of a military life had always stimulated in him: he was leading an army at last. But it was no carnal force, seeking spoils on earth, but a host of young innocents searching for salvation under the banner of Jesus Christ. However, the fates were kind to Patrick in his early life, and he would not bring his peaceful troops safely home without being allowed to taste a little of worldly glory.

Whit Tuesday 1810 was a day of bright sunshine and Patrick, with a light heart, led the schoolchildren along the Wakefield road, turning off at Dewsbury Bank and up the lane that led to Earlsheaton. Soon they reached the hill that looked down over the beautiful valley of the Calder. Here he left the head of the column and marched beside the children so that he might take a longer look at the wonderful view below him.

As he gazed at the glittering river winding its way between the fields there were cries of alarm from the front of the procession and the marchers came to a sudden halt. Patrick was some dozen yards from the front and rushed up to learn the cause of the stoppage. It was only too clear!

From amongst a group of men who had been watching the procession from the side of the road, there emerged a tall and well-built man, about forty years of age, obviously drunk. Placing himself in front of the leading girls, he spread out his arms and, with an oath, told them to go back to Dewsbury as he had no intention of allowing them to proceed. Seeing that the fellow was in earnest, and anxious to avoid the continuance of such vile language, Patrick seized the drunkard by the collar and with one heave flung him across the road, where he fell in a heap amongst his companions. He then restarted the scholars on their march and calmly resumed his place at the side of the column as if nothing unusual had occurred.

The man who had caused the interruption soon recovered from the blow he had received in falling, and was a great deal sobered. He was very much surprised at the treatment he had received and had certainly not expected to be made such a fool of by a curate. His pride had been lowered in front of many onlookers and the ridicule of his comrades incensed him further. He swore that upon the return of the procession he would have it out with the parson. Much excitement grew at this part of the route, for the man was known as a local boxer and cock-fighter, and so there should be some sport when the curate returned. The bully, who came from Gawthorpe, near Ossett, now urged his friends to join in settling matters with the parson, and as they were as rough and uncouth as himself and equally addicted to drinking, there promised to be an exciting spectacle for the onlookers later that afternoon.

Meanwhile the children had arrived at Earlsheaton ; but at first they seemed too upset by the occurrence to sing properly. Patrick walked on to the village green and calmed them. As the hymns were sung the usual large crowd gathered to listen. The voices, gaining confidence with every note, were led by two stringed instruments played by the men who officiated in "the singers' loft" at the parish church (there being no organ installed at that time).

When it was time to return home there was much trepidation amongst the children and the churchwardens. The latter grouped themselves around Patrick and suggested they should march back to Dewsbury with him safe in the centre. They were sure he would need protection as the drunkard and his friends would be waiting for him ; they could not permit their curate to be beaten up, either for his own sake or that of the children, who were frightened enough as it was. Patrick smiled and thanked them for their courageous offer, but there would be no alteration in the order of march.

He re-formed the procession, the girls leading as usual, and placed himself alone at its head. Off they went towards Dewsbury where the "afternoon drinkings" awaited them. As they walked along, men and boys from the village of Earlsheaton raced on ahead to secure vantage points for themselves on the hillside so that they could witness the expected conflict.

As the procession approached the place, there was the intruder, standing as before, by the roadside, surrounded by his companions. Patrick marched calmly on, keeping his eyes fixed warily on the man. As the leading girls reached the place where the earlier scuffle had occurred, Patrick left the column and stood aside while the girls filed past him.

He gazed steadily at the braggart but nothing happened. There were scowls in plenty from the latter but he did not move forward one inch, remaining on the causeway as the children trooped past.

Patrick waited until the last of the boys were well out of sight and then hurried after them to take a place at the side of the procession. Thus he returned to Dewsbury in triumph, marching beside his army.

This further incident, coming as it did so shortly after his rescue of the drowning boy from the Calder, won him the hearts of the people of the West Riding. He was much admired ; indeed the youngsters viewed him in the light of a hero. From this time forth he would never lack friends in Dewsbury, or, indeed, in West Yorkshire, for the tales about him soon spread beyond the confines of the town. Years later he would tell the tale of the Sunday school march to his daughters, and although such an occurrence was not unknown in Yorkshire at that time, Charlotte would be thinking of her father when she wrote of Matthewson Helstone leading his "army" out of Briarfield. Many of the young pupils who took part in that Whitsuntide march in 1810 remembered the Irish curate to the end of their days, not only for his prowess on that occasion but for his enlightened teaching in Sunday school. There, secular as well as religious knowledge was given and Patrick had never been happier. Whilst instructing the older pupils in the Scriptures he would teach the others to read and write, and felt that he enjoyed the best of both the professions he had adopted since Andrew Harshaw had found him years ago. He was now teacher and cleric and could not ask more of life. The pupils who were taught by Patrick at Dewsbury Sunday school found him resolute regarding obedience, but very kind and helpful. His great popularity was beyond dispute.

In the early summer of 1810 after spending some very pleasant months in his rooms at the vicarage, Patrick had to make a great sacrifice and leave the comfort of the old place to find lodgings near at hand. John Buckworth informed him that he had been asked by the Church Missionary Society to train a few young men for ordination so that they could go abroad as agents of the Society and spread the Gospel in other lands, especially India. Although one or two of the students would be local men, others would come from farther afield in Yorkshire and, with regret, Buckworth advised Patrick that, in order to accommodate them, he would require his rooms.

Patrick soon found accommodation at an old house in Priest Lane known as the Ancient Well-House because of the discovery made there years before of a well many centuries old. This was a convenient lodging for Patrick as his new quarters were almost opposite the west door of the church and barely forty yards from the vicarage. It was a small room but clean and extremely quiet. Priest Lane was a short street, full of old houses with several narrow passages running between them : names like Fryer's Passage reflected the origin of this part of the town. (Priest Lane is now called Church Street. The Ancient Well-House has long since disappeared but was near the Royal Oak.)

Patrick moved his few belongings over to his new home, reflecting that, at least, the vicarage garden was still at his disposal whenever he wished to use it.

The owner of the Ancient Well-House was Mr Elliot Carrett, a young man studying for the law, who later became an attorney of local repute. Patrick did not see much of his landlord as both men were too busy to be often at home. But the latter saw enough of the curate to describe him later as "clever and goodhearted, but hot-tempered, and in fact, a little queer".

John Buckworth called on Patrick to assist him in the training of the missionary students. He had opened a small college in the vicarage and without the curate's assistance his strength would have been quite insufficient for this large additional task. Among his students were Benjamin Bailey of Dewsbury who remained for a year with Buckworth, Thomas Dawson of Wakefield and Samuel Oates, a former local hat manufacturer. All these young men had a burning desire to serve the heathen in other lands. Many were former Sunday school scholars from the district. After leaving the vicarage they would have a short period of practical work and then would be sent to India and elsewhere. From the inception of the scheme until the end of 1811 no less than four young men and six girls, missionaries' wives, went forth from the congregation of Dewsbury parish church. Among them, although not trained by Buckworth, was William Greenwood, recorded as the first clergyman of the Church of England to be sent as a missionary to India.

Meanwhile Patrick became accustomed to his new and more cramped lodgings. He had recently made a new friend and in a surprising quarter. It was Thomas Smith, the parish clerk, who since the evening of the bell-ringing practice had held the curate in great regard. Smith, previously the sexton, had been appointed clerk in 1802, having in some measure signed the pledge, since his great weakness for drink, excusable in a sexton, would not be tolerated if he was to retain his post as clerk to the parish. Smith therefore had undertaken to "abstain from frequenting ale-houses needlessly, and from tippling and drinking to excess, and other vices connected with such a practice, and that if ever I am drawn in, and overcome, I will submit to reproof from the Minister or Churchwardens". Either his strength of will or his good fortune held out, for he remained clerk at Dewsbury for twenty-eight years. Towards the end of his office he was assisted by his son John, but in 1810 he had only just received an assistant clerk. This was a young man named Joseph Tolson, who lived at Bridge End, Dewsbury. One day Thomas Smith came to Patrick and told him that his new assistant wished to join the choir : would Patrick see him ?

Patrick sent for the young man and listened to his voice : he was immediately satisfied and accepted him into the church choir. He further learned in conversation that young Tolson could both read and write extremely well and was anxious, if his duties would permit, to help at the Sunday school in however humble a capacity.

Patrick questioned the man further and found a good mind, a true heart, and an anxious desire to learn. As he listened Patrick remembered a young man long ago reading *Paradise Lost* in a frenzy of excitement and a kind clergyman who had stood listening, and he could see again the glades of his native land. He, more than most men, could understand the yearning within Tolson's breast ; he knew also what a helping hand could do.

Patrick saw Mr Buckworth and, shortly afterwards, Tolson was admitted not only as a member of the choir but as an under-teacher at the Sunday school. There he taught the very young pupils how to spell and write the simplest words.

Joseph Tolson knew that he owed all this to Patrick and his heart was full of gratitude. Later he married, and became a weaver at York; but as long as Patrick stayed at Dewsbury there was a bond of understanding between them. The love of the younger man for the curate who had understood his feelings became very strong, and there was no duty Patrick called upon him to do that was not carried out with great readiness.

At the time of his Whitsuntide adventure Patrick had had other exciting news. John Buckworth, on the eve of a visit to Oxford, had informed him that the minister at Hartshead-cum-Clifton, the Rev. William Hanwell Lucas, A.B., was gravely ill and forced to resign the living. It was in the gift of the vicar of Dewsbury, and he, as "undoubted Patron", wished to recommend Patrick at once.

The day after Whit Tuesday Patrick wrote to York.

Thos Porteus Esq. Secretary.

Dewsbury, near Leeds, Yorkshire, June 6th 1810.
Sir,

I thank you for your information—I have got certificates for three years of my Ministry, reckoning back from this period.

The living of Hartshett [*sic*] is small : salary only 62£ a year. I am not at present licensed to the curacy of Dewsbury. Will you have the goodness, Sir, to inform me, whether I can get Licensed to this curacy, be inducted into Hartsheath [*sic*] Living, and obtain License for non-residence in time, to give a Title to a Gentleman, who intends to offer himself a candidate for Holy Orders, at his Graces next ordination ?

As my Vicar is at Oxford, taking his Master of Arts Degree, and the journey from this to London so far, it will be a most desirable thing for me if I can get all done without leaving this place. Be so kind, Sir, as to inform me what steps I am to take, and to excuse the trouble I have given you.

I am Sir, Your most obed^t & humble Servt P. Brontè

On 12th June John Buckworth, M.A., back from Oxford, signed Patrick's testimonial together with the ministers of Ossett and Wood-kirk and Matthew Sedgwick, curate of Batley.

On 28th June Patrick again wrote to York.

Jos^h Buckle, Esqr Secretary

Dewsbury, near Leeds, Yorkshire, June 28th 1810.

Sir,

I have sent enclosed in this, and another, which you will receive at the same time, my Nomination to the Perpetual Curacy of Hartshead, and my Testimonial for three years back. My Letters of Order I shall take with me, or send before me, should his Grace require it.

Should my papers prove satisfactory to his Grace & etc, will you have the goodness to tell me, when & where, I may be inducted into the Perpetual Curacy of Hartshead, and to give me such other directions as you may judge necessary.

I am Sir, Your most obedient & humble servant P. Brontè

On 19th July Buckworth sent the Archbishop his nomination of "Patrick Brontè" to Hartshead " . . . now void by the Resignation of Willm Hanwell Lucas the last Incumbent, & doth of right belong to my Nomination . . .".

The Archbishop licensed Patrick on 20th July 1810. But this proved premature. The new Dewsbury curate did not arrive, Buckworth had continually to leave his parish, and Patrick had therefore little time to visit Hartshead—and, in the event, forgot to read himself in ! Thus another cleric took duty at Hartshead and Patrick remained in Dewsbury to participate in further adventures.

Not long after Patrick had taken up his quarters at the Ancient Well-House he was involved in another dispute—one that was not to be confined to Dewsbury. He saw that a most grave injustice was being committed and took up, not his shillelagh, but his pen this time, in defence of the rights of a fellow-man.

CHAPTER 5

Promotion

On 20th September 1810 a party of soldiers hammered impatiently on the house door of Thomas Nowell, of Dawgreen, Dewsbury. Thomas opened it, in some anger at the violent assault on his door, but fell back in great astonishment on observing the military. The corporal in charge demanded to see Thomas's son William or, if he was out, to be given information as to his whereabouts. On hearing the mention of his name the young man in question came out from the kitchen, followed by his mother. To the astonishment of William, the corporal asked him why he had failed to report at Regimental Headquarters in Wakefield. William replied that he did not understand them : they must be at the wrong house. To this the corporal made inquiry : was he not William Nowell, of Dewsbury, cloth weaver ? Did he know a James Thackray of that town ? William assented, adding that he knew Thackray slightly. When did he last meet Thackray ? William could not say exactly : several weeks since, at least. Had he not spent some time with Thackray at Lee Fair two days previously ? He had not been to the Fair that year. That was a lie, was it not ? At this point Thomas Nowell intervened to ask the corporal the meaning of this interrogation and to demand an explanation of these queries. It was given in full and the astonishment and alarm of the family grew with every word.

On 18th September 1810, at Lee Fair, otherwise Woodchurch, in the township of West Ardsley—on the occasion of the great horse fair held there on that day, William Nowell did accept and receive from one James Thackray, recently enlisted in the 30th Regiment, the King's Shilling, thereby freely accepting unto himself enlistment in the same Regiment. That James Thackray had reported such to Headquarters in Wakefield, and as the said William Nowell, cloth weaver, had failed to report for duty it was the orders of the guard now present to inquire the reason for his desertion from the Colours. The corporal ceased speaking and looked steadily at young Nowell. The parents regarded each other in sheer bewilderment. William had not been to the Fair, he must again deny that. True, his mother and father had gone but he had remained in Dewsbury and could account for his movements. The soldier ordered him to stay in the house until further notice and said that he would report what Nowell had answered to his colonel.

From then on events moved rapidly. The colonel at Wakefield expressed his complete dissatisfaction with Nowell's remarks—he was obviously a cowardly deserter—and next day the soldiers returned to Dawgreen and arrested him.

On 25th September William Nowell was taken before Mr Dawson, J.P., at Wakefield and charged with desertion. James Thackray, a recent recruit himself, swore to the enlistment of Nowell; and furthermore, he claimed that there was an acquaintance of his, a girl named Love Webster, who had been with him at the horse fair when he met Nowell. She had seen him give the shilling to Nowell and the latter's acceptance of the coin. No doubt she would be prepared to stand witness to this, if necessary.

For the defence Thomas Nowell called the names of seven Dewsbury men who could testify that his son was in that town at the time mentioned by Thackray. The coroner at Wakefield, a kind, honest man named Brook, joined with Nowell senior in offering to send two postchaises to Dewsbury at once, to collect these important witnesses. But Dawson refused consent and straight away committed the accused to the House of Correction as a deserter.

At Dewsbury the news was soon on everyone's lips and, as the details became known and were detached from idle rumours, a great sense of shock and outrage was felt by the inhabitants. Many offers were made to take the oath that William Nowell had been seen in Dewsbury on the day in question, several from people who had never set eyes on him in their lives or would not have known him if they had.

At The Aldams the younger Halliley was in a fury over such criminal treatment of a townsman of Dewsbury and poured the story angrily into his father's ear before returning to his own home, Grove House, to brood over the matter. The Rev. John Buckworth threw up his arms in horror and rushed to tell his wife. The churchwardens could talk of nothing else, and Thomas Smith found it more difficult than ever to avoid being "drawn in and overcome" at one of the ale-houses in the town.

In no time the news was everywhere and, in his small room at the Ancient Well-House, it reached the ears of Patrick Brontë. He stared out of the window, tapping his long fingers nervously on the desk before him. This time he was icy cool and not a muscle in his face moved, but he was all the more dangerous for that!

On the Friday following Nowell's committal to the House of Correction at Wakefield, Patrick and three of the senior churchwardens called upon Mr Dawson and asked him to revise his decision : they met with a blank refusal.

Patrick returned home and prepared a memorial which was "signed by the Clergymen, the Churchwardens, and the principal inhabitants of Dewsbury". He then wrote a brief accompanying letter demanding a re-trial, and sent it off to the Commander-in-Chief of the Army. The reply came : "the clergyman is requested to state, for the information of the Secretary at War, whether the facts alleged in the memorial were to his own knowledge true, or if they were only believed to be so, and if so, to state the grounds of that belief". Patrick felt heartened at once, for the Secretary at War was his old comrade-in-arms at Cambridge, Lord Palmerston. Of course, Palmerston would not remember him, but if it would help the case, perhaps he could write to remind him of those youthful days.

Patrick, now given a free hand by his vicar, called a vestry meeting at once, and it was proposed that a second memorial be sent. There were a few honest citizens who had indeed seen Nowell in the town that day, and now there was a Wakefield tradesman stating that he had heard Thackray confess that he had not really enlisted Nowell at all ; indeed he had not even seen him at the Fair. These facts were incorporated in the fresh petition and off it went. Back came the answer that the Secretary did not see that he could "with propriety interfere with the decision of the civil magistrate in the case". Patrick felt somewhat dashed, and was glad that he had not made much of his former relationship with Lord Palmerston ; but he was by no means beaten yet. He returned to his room and wrote out the facts of the case in some detail. He sent them to the editor of the *Leeds Mercury* asking that he should bring the matter to the public eye, as an act of duty. He then wrote to Mr Halliley senior, who had recently travelled to London on business, and suggested that he should ask the aid of the county Members of Parliament. The two members concerned were Viscount Milton (later third Earl Fitzwilliam) and William Wilberforce. Patrick was tempted to write personally to the latter—again a reminder of his days at Cambridge—but forbore. Wilberforce had helped him financially in the past, so perhaps it would be better for Halliley to present the case in person.

In the *Leeds Mercury* of 10th November 1810 there appeared a paragraph stating that "a very industrious and respectable young man of the name of William Nowell, of Dewsbury, in the neighbourhood" was lying in the House of Correction at Wakefield, having been committed on 25th September on a charge of deserting from the 30th Regiment, after enlistment "at Lee Fair, about 4 miles from Dewsbury, whereas no such enlistment had taken place, and he had not been at Lee Fair". The editor commented, "This young man's case ought to awaken public sympathy, and we cannot doubt, call forth the humane interference of our County members."

So far so good, thought Patrick; and matters were mending indeed, for Lord Milton and the great Wilberforce were now very much interested in the case.

Halliley and Wilberforce called together at the War Office and asked for a re-hearing of the case. They were granted permission to apply to Dawson at Wakefield.

Without delay they engaged an eminent barrister named Maule, who sent the application to Wakefield. But once again Dawson was obdurate. There could be no re-hearing of the case: it was closed.

Wilberforce was most indignant, and went again to the War Office. This time he persisted and Palmerston gave him an order calling upon the unwilling magistrate to allow the case to be heard again. Furthermore, all the evidence was to be sent to the War Office in detail so that it might be closely examined.

Accordingly, Patrick, Halliley junior, a Mr Hague, and Rylah, a local attorney, arrived at Wakefield and confronted Dawson, bringing with them fifteen witnesses. The magistrate, much chagrined at the trouble he was being put to, remarked that they could have saved themselves a great deal of bother—the youth could easily have been bought off for twenty-five pounds.

This was the moment for Patrick to explode! He informed Dawson that they were not going to buy justice on those terms; that, though an appeal to the proper tribunal was expensive, yet the redress was to be had, and that ten times twenty-five pounds—aye, and much more— would willingly be forthcoming to procure that redress, rather than the smallest sum to purchase Nowell's liberty.

The re-hearing took place and the witnesses "proved a most incontestable alibi". The Wakefield tradesman gave his evidence concerning Thackray's denial of his official statement, and the case against William Nowell on its first full hearing collapsed completely. Five days later, after ten weeks' imprisonment, he was released.

Wilberforce, the great emancipator, beset with problems eternal and worldly, did not omit from his diary this attempted enslavement of a fellow Yorkshireman—as Patrick would later read with satisfaction. ". . . off early to London to the War Office about the boy Nowell, unlawfully recruited . . . Lord Palmerston had not yet read the minutes of the second examination, which decisive . . . after breakfast to the Horse Guards, where talked to Lord Palmerston about the poor boy . . .', and got the necessary "orders sent down for his discharge". A few weeks later he added: ". . . I hear, that I am likely to be popular now amongst the West Riding clothiers about poor Nowell, the boy falsely enlisted. How this shows that God can affect whatever He will, by means the most circuitous, and the least looked for . . ."

However, Patrick had not yet finished with the case. He urged the parents to bring an indictment against Thackray: only by stern measures could a repetition of such a sorry affair be avoided elsewhere.

Almost immediately after Nowell had been acquitted Patrick received the following letter, the text of which was published in the *Leeds Mercury*, with a few words of commendation on the action that had been taken.

War Office, 5th December, 1810

Sir,

Referring to the correspondence relative to William Nowell, I am to acquaint you that I feel so strongly the injury that is likely to arise to the Service from an unfair mode of recruiting, that if by the indictment which the lad's parents are about to prefer against James Thackray they shall establish the fact of his having been guilty of perjury, I shall be ready to indemnify them for the reasonable and proper expenses which they shall bear on the occasion,

I am, sir, Yours, &c, (Signed) Palmerston.

To the Reverend P. Bronte, Dewsbury, near Leeds

No mention of camaraderie at Cambridge, but Patrick was satisfied, as he had every reason to be. Shortly after this, Patrick wrote a long letter to the *Leeds Mercury* which was published on 15th December 1810 under the *nom de plume* "Sydney". The letter was prefaced by the lines from *Measure for Measure*:

> Oh, 'tis excellent
> To have a Giant's strength: but 'tis tyrannous
> To use it like a Giant.

It was fully two columns in length, prominently placed, and gave an extended account of the charge, false imprisonment, and final acquittal of William Nowell. He then mentioned that matters were in train to punish Thackray for his wickedness. He stated that certain clauses in the Mutiny Act operated against the liberty of the subject: it was to be hoped that this fault would be corrected as the result of the publicity that would attend the pending prosecution of Thackray and, he added, the action for false imprisonment that would be brought against the committing magistrate, Dawson. After praising the interest and energy displayed in this matter by Lord Milton and Mr Wilberforce, Patrick closed with these remarks: "It is a proud reflection and a source of consolation in these times that, while the iron hand of despotism is falling heavy on the continent of Europe, we Englishmen still enjoy the pure administration of justice; that we have laws to regulate the conduct of every man, from a beggar to a King; and that no station, however low, no rank, however high, can screen from justice him that doeth wrong."

Patrick was the leading figure in urging that action be taken against both Thackray and Dawson, as he hoped this would avoid a similar occurrence in the future. His letter to the *Leeds Mercury* was also intended to add sufficient publicity to the event as to make a repetition unlikely.

With the publication of Lord Palmerston's letter, and now the one from "Sydney", Patrick felt he had indeed struck a blow for the freedom of mankind. This was the end of his active participation in the affair, although he followed the trial of Thackray, which took place in August of the following year, very closely indeed.

Now that Nowell was a free man the people of Dewsbury had time to reflect on the curious chain of circumstances that had provided him with his firm and unshakable alibi. The witnesses for the defence, from Dewsbury, had all seen Nowell in the town on the day of the horse fair, and most of them had seen him in the graveyard. Patrick himself had been present on that occasion but had been too busily engaged to notice the young cloth weaver. The reason for Nowell's presence there was a morbid one—to attend the exhumation of a body; but it helped save him from false imprisonment. As one witness after another came forward to swear that they had seen Nowell in Dewsbury graveyard on 18th September, the story behind the exhumation was gradually revealed. A tragic tale, although not without amusement for the hearers, it was typical of the West Riding of Yorkshire in those wild days.

It appeared that on Sunday, 2nd August 1810, Samuel Mark Jackson, a druggist in Dewsbury, visited a friend in Rothwell jail where he passed a convivial day, returning in a drunken condition, on horseback. Noticing the church door open, he rode in and trotted his horse up to the pulpit in the midst of the service. He proceeded to shout at the top of his voice at John Buckworth and, in a moment, the entire congregation was in uproar. The churchwardens rushed forward and seized the animal's head, dragging beast and rider out of the church, to the accompaniment of continuous roars from the inebriated druggist.

Jackson was taken into custody and locked up in the local prison known as "Old Towzer". His poor wife had just returned from

Wakefield, after attending her sister's funeral, when she heard of her husband's arrest. The shock was very great, particularly as she was soon to have a child, and she became extremely ill. A few days later she was prematurely confined and died. Word of his wife's death was taken to Jackson in the prison and he was stunned at the news. Almost immediately he had a convulsive fit and died also.

Dewsbury was greatly distressed at this tragic series of events for Jackson had been much respected in the town and had not been an habitual drunkard; so that his one great lapse had led to such a double tragedy was very painful to contemplate. Rumour soon spread that, in his remorse, he had killed himself. His wife, Martha, was buried on 5th August, and he on the 14th. Later the reports became more definite: that he had poisoned himself. As this story persisted, the local authorities applied to the Secretary of State for an order of exhumation. This was granted and the body was disinterred on 18th September, a month after burial. Patrick, in the course of his duties, had conducted the funeral service, and was present at the exhumation. There was no trace of poison whatsoever: death had been from natural causes.

But if Patrick was too busy to scan the faces of the morbid onlookers, there were those present who noticed and spoke to Nowell as he waited for the coffined body of the druggist to be raised from the ground. As he had spent some time there and was also seen in other parts of Dewsbury on that day, the charge that Nowell was at the Lee Fair was completely demolished.

At York Lammas assizes, James Thackray was indicted for perjury. In the *Leeds Mercury* of Saturday, 10th August 1811, there appeared: "James Thackray, the soldier who was indicted for perjury for having falsely sworn that he enlisted William Nowell, of Dewsbury, at Lee Fair, on the 18th September, 1810, took his trial in the criminal court at York, on Thursday last, and was convicted of the offence on the clearest evidence, to the satisfaction of the whole court." The editor remarked, "We envy the feelings of those gentlemen whose public-spirited and persevering conduct has secured to public justice a victory over the advocates and abettors of this profligate delinquent: by their exertions a worthy young man has been restored to his family and friends, and the grey hairs of his aged parents have been rescued from an untimely grave to which the outrage done to their only son was fast hastening them. We have already, at some personal risk, brought the public acquainted with the facts of this nefarious transaction, and we shall not fail to seize the earliest opportunity to give the particulars of the trial."

Such was the appeal to sentiment by the press of those days!

Both the *Mercury* and the *Intelligencer* gave full reports of the trial, at which thirteen witnesses were called for the prosecution and five for the defence. Nowell reported, briefly, that his parents had gone to the Fair about one o'clock and that he "went to warp a chain preparatory to weaving". He placed the chain or warp in his loom and continued in the workshop until 3 o'clock. Then, "there being an outcry that they were going to take up the body of Mr Jackson, buried without a coroner's inquest, he went into the churchyard, amongst many others, to look on, and hearing that the raising was not to take place till 6 o'clock, he went into the market place", then to Halliley's mill; and he was able to account for his movements until late in the day, and provide witnesses to cover that period.

The defence then called George Blackburn, a soldier, who deposed to having seen Nowell at the Fair. This piece of evidence was, however, soon nipped in the bud. Mr Halliley junior was called and told the jury that whilst driving to York to attend this case he had overtaken Blackburn walking along the road; that, as the soldier had complained of fatigue, he had given him a ride in his gig and, during the journey to York, Blackburn had freely confessed that he had not seen Nowell at Lee Fair. So the evidence was mounted against James Thackray; he was found guilty of perjury and sentenced to seven years' transportation. It was a severe punishment, but in keeping with the harsh criminal laws of the period. At the same assize the death penalty was passed on other prisoners for horse-stealing, rape, house-breaking, and the theft of a bill of exchange; however, the next day, these sentences were commuted to transportation for life. There is no evidence that the perjured soldier Blackburn, also from Dewsbury, was punished, but it must be doubted whether he would ever again consider it safe to show himself in his native town.

As for the magistrate, Dawson, he escaped with a slight censure, to the great fury of Patrick. In the latter's opinion, that worthy should have been shipped away with Thackray: had he not shown himself as great an offender against the cause of true justice?

When the matter was over, William Nowell resumed his weaving; later he joined Messrs. Hagues, Cook and Wormald, blanket manufacturers of Dewsbury Mills, as a fuller, and remained with that firm until his death.

Thus there was another human heart that would always beat in gratitude to Patrick Brontë, and the curate's popularity and fame became greater than ever in Dewsbury. In his year there he had won the hearts of his parishioners. They recalled his rescue of the drowning boy, the way he had shown his feelings at the desecration of the Sabbath, the treatment meted out to the drunken bully on the Whitsuntide march, and his strenuous exertions in the recent injustice to an innocent man. Yes, their Patrick was a match for any curate in the three Ridings, aye, or any minister, for that matter ! As the year 1810 drew towards its close, however, Patrick's stay amongst them was nearing its end also. But there would be no quiet stealing away on the part of their curate : he would treat his parishioners to one more scene of blazing defiance and then depart.

But as the year ended, Patrick, in common with many others of his cloth was a puzzled and worried man. More and more defiance was being shown by the extremists among the followers of Wesley. No longer were they content with holding their meetings outside the hours of regular worship. The erection of independent Methodist churches was spreading and soon would come the definite cleavage of the Society of People called Methodists from the Mother Church. Partick, his friend William Morgan, John Fennell and many others of the Evangelical school, were to remain faithful to the establishment. The final break had not yet come, but the murmurings of division were already heard and Patrick had much to ponder over in his room in Priest Lane.

There were other discontented rumblings, too, for those that cared to lend an ear : poverty was still rife, unemployment was on the increase and the condition of many of the working people was going from bad to worse. Dissatisfaction was spreading and brooded as heavily as the smoke over the towns of West Yorkshire. Soon there would be marching feet in plenty, as the militant Methodists walked out of the Established Church, and the hungry poor burst into riot for food and work.

Patrick, popular both as a man and a priest, was not the less liked by the people of Dewsbury because of his political beliefs. That he was a staunch Tory, everybody knew, but the working people of the town were not much upset by that. Most of the mill owners were Whigs, they argued, and there were surely no greater enemies in the land than they. Patrick, apart from his ministering, had a great sympathy for the poor, knowing the terrible conditions under which they were forced to live. True, all his days he would believe that the working people were unfit to play any part in the government of the nation, but, unlike some of his contemporaries, he did not consider that a dirty hovel, starvation and lack of work should be their only stake in the country's wealth. Above all he wanted the children to obtain a good schooling to prepare them for this world and the next. The one aspect of his humble origin he would never forget was the unceasing struggle to gain knowledge for himself.

Very early in 1811 Patrick found himself with additional duties : already, with his vicar's health so precarious, he had many of the services to take in the parish church, as well as looking after the Sunday school and assisting in the training of the young would-be missionaries at the vicarage. Now, John Buckworth advised him that Hartshead would be without a preacher for some time to come and he must ask Patrick to perform much of the duty there.

Hartshead was a little more than four miles from Dewsbury so the extra burden placed on Patrick's shoulders was considerable. He had assisted there before in the previous year, when on 31st March he had helped the minister at a baptism, so the old church was not unfamiliar to him.

Patrick hired two cobs and took young Tolson with him, and many were the journeys to and fro during the next few weeks. Happily for the curate, the services at Hartshead were often very short. There was no surpliced choir in those days and the service often consisted only of the saying of prayers and psalms by the parson and the reading of the responses by the clerk.

To add to Patrick's burdens his vicar was not in good health and was hoping shortly to make another visit to the south of England. Now the curate had visions of conducting the services at both Dewsbury and Hartshead on the same day, and he had not long to wait for his vision to become a reality. One Sunday, as he and Joseph Tolson were preparing to set forth for Hartshead where Patrick was to conduct the morning and afternoon services, John Buckworth came running to ask the curate if he would mind returning in time to take the evening service at Dewsbury. He had meant to take it himself, but had promised to spend the evening at The Aldams. His wife was a daughter of Mr Halliley senior and there was to be a family gathering.

Patrick readily agreed and he and Tolson rode off across the hills to Hartshead. When the afternoon service was over the two men jumped on their horses and made rapidly back for Dewsbury; not because Patrick feared that he would be late for evening worship, but because Tolson, on leaving the church, had pointed to the blue-black storm-clouds piling up over the hills. They rode as quickly as they could but were still a mile from Dewsbury when the storm broke over their heads. In a minute they were drenched to the skin, and the horses slackened their pace in the blinding rain.

As they entered the town, Tolson was surprised to find that Patrick rode direct to The Aldams instead of going immediately to his room to change his soaked clothing. The curate said nothing, however, and the youth, greatly wondering, followed.

Patrick banged on the door of the mansion with his stick. They were admitted and, in a moment, Mr Halliley senior appeared, greatly astonished at sight of the dripping figures standing in the entrance hall.

Patrick asked Halliley if he would be so good as to inform Mr Buckworth that, as he was wet to the skin, he would very much like the vicar to take evening service himself.

The older man laughed loudly on hearing this request. "What! Keep a dog and bark himself!" The smile vanished from Halliley's face the instant he had uttered the words. Patrick's eyes dilated, the veins in his head stood out like whipcord, and the mill owner knew well what that foreboded. For a few seconds the curate stood there ashen-faced—Tolson every moment expecting the shillelagh to be smashed across the other's face—but without a word, Patrick turned on his heels and left the house, followed by a very relieved assistant clerk.

Halliley, even more relieved, went back to report the occurrence to Buckworth. He had meant only to jest, but he realized that his hasty remark was in the nature of an insult, particularly to a curate who was so very much overworked.

Outside in the rain Patrick and Tolson parted in silence, each going home to change into dry clothes. Tolson, as he related in later life, wondered what would be the result of this affair. Would Mr Buckworth come over to the church to take the service after what had occurred?

When Tolson arrived at the church, there was Patrick, seemingly calm and collected. Of the vicar there was no sign. Prayers were gone through, the psalms and the lessons read; then, as the last verse of a hymn was being rendered, Patrick slowly ascended the stairs of the three-decker pulpit to deliver his address. As the last notes of the hymn died away there was silence, and Tolson waited with his eyes shut tight.

Patrick announced straight away that it was not his intention to preach again from that pulpit, after the evening's service. His reason was simple: he had been most grievously insulted; but he could add no particulars.

The astonishment of the congregation was considerable, and a buzz of conversation went round the parish church. Patrick soon silenced this by commencing his address, and proceeded to deliver a sermon of great power. At the end the congregation waited, hoping to learn something from the curate that would explain his opening remarks, but they were disappointed: he turned slowly round and left the pulpit of Dewsbury Church for the last time. Patrick kept his word: he would perform marriages, indeed carry out all his other duties, but he never preached again from there.

PLATE 1   *The cabin at Emdale, Co. Down, birthplace of Patrick Brontë*

PLATE 2   *The Rev. Thomas Tighe's rectory at Drumballyroney, Co. Down*

PLATE 3   *Henry Martyn*

For poor John Buckworth this was an added trial : he would have to postpone his vacation in the south and preach the sermons himself whilst his curate officiated at the little church of Hartshead. But in his heart, despite the vexation and grief the incident had occasioned, the vicar knew that the mill owner's words had been offensive. He felt that any man, even one less hard-working and worthy than Patrick, would have been incensed at such an insolent remark. The friendship between the two clergymen was as warm as ever, and the vicar's desire to recommend the promotion of his curate at the first opportunity unaltered.

As the truth of the matter gradually seeped through the town, all sympathy was for the curate, together with regret at the burden thus placed on the delicate vicar. Even young Mr Halliley continued on friendly terms with Patrick, although the latter could not forget the slight offered by the father.

Long after this incident, Tolson would describe Patrick Brontë as rather reserved in manner and apt to be abrupt in speech when strangers were present, but then he was extremely shy. Nevertheless, he could be chatty and most agreeable with people he knew well. This agreed with the opinion of many who lived in Dewsbury whilst he was curate there. The clash of his impulsive Irish temperament against the rough, out-spoken, practical nature of the West Riding people was remembered with fascination.

But if there were any who thought that he had deeply annoyed his vicar by his outspoken words from the pulpit and by his high-handed refusal to preach from it again, the answer was soon forthcoming. A week or two after Patrick's surprise announcement to the congregation, he was relieved of his double burden. The former incumbent of Harts-head, the Rev. W. H. Lucas, had died. Patrick was freed to take up his first full ministry. He was "again" appointed as incumbent of Harts-head-cum-Clifton. It might have crossed Mr Halliley's mind that the vicar would be only too glad to rid himself of such an irascible assistant at the first opportunity, but that was not the reason for Buckworth's decision. The people of Dewsbury knew their vicar too well to counten-ance such an idea.

John Buckworth informed Patrick of his promotion, adding that until a new curate had been appointed in his stead and had settled in to his duties, he knew he could rely on his continued assistance at Dews-bury whenever his new parish responsibilities allowed.

Patrick walked back to his room : he was now a perpetual curate, an incumbent, a minister. He had a living of his own, at last. He was nearing the top of his ladder ; this surely had been the widest rung of all.

7

In the vicarage he had thanked the vicar with a full heart. In his room he could go down on his knees and allow that heart to overflow with gratitude to God.

He continued for some little time to help at Dewsbury Parish Church after commencing his duties at Hartshead. He signed the registers of Dewsbury Church for the last time on 11th March 1811, as "Patrick Brontë, curate".

But soon the new curate was established and Patrick ceased his double work. Shortly afterwards Mr and Mrs Buckworth were able to travel south leaving the new assistant in charge. Whilst they were away, Patrick walked over occasionally to keep an eye on Robin Tweed : the dog always missed his mistress when left behind and this time there was no kind Patrick to show such an interest in him. He was ailing and Patrick worried about the poor creature : he seemed to be pining for his mistress with great intensity.

Back in Hartshead, Patrick honoured his promise to write and advise Mrs Buckworth how Robin was faring. He was not at all sanguine about the dog's looks and yet had no desire to cause any unnecessary alarm. He took up his pen and wrote, "Tweed's letter to his Mistress".

Ah ! Mistress, dear,
Pray lend an ear,
To simple Robin Tweed ;
I've been to you,
Both kind and true,
In every time of need.
I have no claim,
To rank or name,
Amongst the barking gentry ;
No spaniel neat,
Nor greyhound fleet,
To grace the street, or entry.
But then, you know,
I still can shew,
A bonny spotted skin,
Can watch the house,
Kill rat or mouse,
And give you, "welcome in".
How oft have I,
With watchful eye,
And fondly wagging tail,

And bark, and whine,
And frisk so fine,
Said "Mistress dear, all hail".
Rap! at the door—
I soiled the floor,
With capering, and with jumping,
Whilst on my back,
With lusty thwack
Fierce Esther, was a thumping!
My love for you,
Still bore me through,
Whatever my disaster;
If you said "Tweed"!—
And stroked my head,
Each wound had then a plaster.
Each night I lie
With sleepless eye,
And longing wait the morrow;
And poke my nose,
And smell your clothes,
And howl aloud for sorrow!
The other night,
By clear fire-light,
I saw your gown a drying,
So, on the stones,
I stretched my bones,
And spent the night in sighing!
But all in vain!
I thus complain,
Alas! there's none to heed me,
You have not sent,
As you were went,
To Esther for to feed me.
Hard is my lot!
Since I'm forgot,
By one I'll love forever!—
But mankind change,
As round they range—
A dog, he changes, never!
A long farewell!—
The gloomy knell,
Will soon inform the neighbours,

That Tweed is dead,
And has got rid,
of all his cares and labours.

Your kind, trusty, and humble dog, Robin Tweed, at my kennel
near the Vicarage, Dewsbury, the 11th June 1811.

Patrick addressed the poem as from himself to Mrs Buckworth,
adding "the Dog Tweed's letter to his mistress". In the love he bore
for a dumb creature—the existence of whose soul was uncertain—and in
his desire to prepare Rachel Buckworth against the possibility of a sad
homecoming, Patrick for once forgot to write of Mansions in the Sky.

But before this poem was despatched Patrick had settled down in
his new parish, the first he could call his own. He now devoted all his
time to Hartshead, and on 3rd March 1811 signed the registers for the
first time—"Patrick Brontë"—proudly adding, "Minister".

CHAPTER 6

Hartshead

HARTSHEAD-CUM-CLIFTON, as the larger parish was called in 1811, consisted of two straggling hamlets of those names and was about four miles west-north-west of Dewsbury. Patrick would find little difference either in the type of people or in the district from his former curacy.

It was upland country with fertile valleys and much high shrubland. There were the usual stone farm-cottages dotted over the higher land. Apart from Dewsbury the nearest towns were Huddersfield and Cleckheaton. At some little distance from Hartshead was the old church, dedicated to St Peter. It was beautifully situated, standing alone, crowning a hill overlooking the Calder Valley. To the north and east this high ground ran into soft tableland which swept into the narrow valleys. On this open plateau there was a splendid view westwards towards Kirklees Park with its Hall and ruined Priory, in the grounds of which Robin Hood is supposed to be buried.

St Peter's Church, Hartshead, was the oldest daughter church of Dewsbury parish, Hartshead and Dewsbury being united when the old vicarage at the latter was constituted in 1349. The deed was made by William, Archbishop of York, at his Manor of Ripon on 20th June of that year. At that time Hartshead was only a "Chapell".

St Peter's, Hartshead, was greatly restored in 1881, but at the time Patrick Brontë was minister there the church was in a very dilapidated condition. From the squat tower an old weatherbeaten ash tree thrust forth its sturdy limbs, having its roots in the roof. Parts of the walls were crumbling away and the flaking masonry was everywhere rotten.

For nearly 900 years there has been a place of worship on this site. Even today St Peter's retains its ancient appearance: the old tower survives, although treeless, and there remain Norman arches in the south porch and the chancel. In 1811 there were small, domestic Georgian windows—the present mansard windows did not exist. Inside this little low-roofed church, with its rounded arch and splendid old beams, there still lingers much of the atmosphere that must have existed when Patrick preached his first sermon there.

The registers date from 1612, although there is a blank period of about 100 years in the recording of births, marriages and deaths. Within the church are buried many of the Armytage family from nearby Kirklees Hall. James Armytage was one of Patrick's churchwardens.

In the small churchyard in Patrick's day there were many slab-stones dating from the early seventeenth century, whilst near the church-gates stood the stocks that were still in use when he came to Hartshead. Opposite the gates was the mounting-block and the narrow entrance to a field path descending into the valley. The tower was believed to be Saxon, and not far from the church stood the base of a Saxon cross.

But it was no busy parish with which Patrick had been launched into his first ministry: indeed in 1811 there was but a very small congrega-tion, no Sunday school and no parsonage. True, there was a free grammar school in the district, founded by Sir John Armytage, Baronet, in 1729, whose family usually appointed the master. Sometimes the position would be offered to the minister, but at the time Patrick arrived there was no vacancy and he did not take the office whilst at Harts-head. During the illness of the Rev. W. H. Lucas, the position had been filled by a teacher from the district.

This then was Patrick's first parish and, small as the church was, and for all its state of dilapidation, he loved it with all his soul. At thirty-four years of age there was yet a long life of service to God before him and now that he was a free agent, what better place to commence his lone duties than here at St Peter's? Years later one of his daughters would have Hartshead Church in mind when she mentioned "Nunnely's low-roofed Temple".

As he commenced his work at Hartshead Patrick was sustained and encouraged by the fact that a recent predecessor of his had been the Rev. Hammond Roberson, whose sermons as curate of Dewsbury had impressed his former congregation so much. He had been incumbent of St Peter's from 1795 to 1803.

As there was no parsonage available, Patrick had to find lodgings for himself, and as his salary at this time was only £62 a year, the Church granted him a small allowance to cover this necessity. He found a home with a Mr and Mrs Bedford, who rented a farm at no great distance from the church. This was Thorn Bush Farm, always called in those days "Lousey Thorn". Despite its name, Patrick was most comfortable there. The Bedfords had at one time been the lodge-keepers at Kirklees Hall, and were a kindly couple. Once again Patrick moved his few precious belongings and settled down.

He was soon to fill his church, although not necessarily with his new parishioners. Many of his Sunday school pupils at Dewsbury would make the journey of eight miles or more to Hartshead and back in order to hear their old master preach, some of them bringing their food with them so that they could remain to listen to all the Sunday services. Years after Patrick had left Hartshead and gone farther away, to the other side of Bradford, there was at least one enthusiastic admirer who made the longer pilgrimage to hear his old curate preach on the Sabbath.

Joseph Tolson made frequent visits to Hartshead Church to hear the sermons of the man who had befriended him in the past. In his position as assistant parish clerk of Dewsbury he was sometimes required to give the responses during the service and it was a great joy to the young man that his work with his former curate could continue. He often visited Lousey Thorn to share Patrick's supper before returning home. For many years to come, long after Patrick had left Hartshead-cum-Clifton, the young man would continue to visit him, and they maintained a steady correspondence.

But Patrick's own parishioners were soon impressed by their young and active new minister, and the attendance at the church became larger, even when his former congregation was not represented. The vigour and power of his delivery, the old magic trick of delivering most of his sermons without recourse to notes, the energy with which he continued to hold his cottage meetings, and the eagerness to visit the sick no matter how far off they lived, soon convinced the hard-headed Yorkshire people that they had a good clergyman indeed. Besides all this, there had drifted up to the villages of Hartshead and Clifton many tales of the Dewsbury curate, and the villagers were rather proud that the man who had defied all and sundry and become the talk of that town should now belong to them.

Patrick's tall, athletic figure was soon familiar to all as he strode rapidly down the fields or across the moorland heights to visit some outlying farm where comfort was needed. Not that such walks were all sacrifice for him; as he strode against the winds that blew fiercely across the common, the dog from Lousey Thorn trotting by his side, Patrick was a very happy man. Sometimes there would be such grief and affliction, such suffering and distress awaiting him that the return journey was made in a mood of sorrowful despair. But on all other occasions these were his happiest hours. Here he could compose a sermon in a few minutes : the mind became clear, as if swept clean by the moorland wind, thoughts grew like magic in his brain, and a wild joy filled his heart. The view down over the Calder Valley, the sylvan shades of Kirklees Priory, the winding lanes below him with their tiny cottages, the long grass blown by the wind into a yellow ripple that surged like the sea ; and, barely above his head, the white clouds sweeping across the hills in triumph so that the deep blue patches of the sky were a thousand ever-changing shapes, the scent of sheep, the joyous bark of his companion, the shrill peewit plunging half a mile into the gale without a flap of its wings—all made his senses quicken into a realization that God the Father and Mother Nature were the Parents of us all. Down at the farm, he did not always find it easy to compose a message for the people. Even in the church, he reflected guiltily, inspiration was not always present. But up here the pattern of existence became plain, the words to express it readily available, and he wished that some of his cottagers would walk, like himself, amongst the freedom of the hills. It was Patrick's first full glimpse of the Pennine Moors, and without a passing thought to the Evangelical ministers who had achieved fame there, he thanked his God that fate had brought him to these highlands of Yorkshire.

He was not so reserved now as he had been in the town. Something of the freedom of the moorland parish communicated itself to his tongue and he would be remembered at Hartshead as "something of a talker". One of his congregation would recall, "Mr Brontë was a well-informed man and I always enjoyed his conversation." It was noted that although his learning and knowledge of the world placed him at a great advantage over most of the people he worked among, he was always eager to impart what he knew to others: the spreading of education appeared almost as vital in his eyes as the teaching of the Gospel itself.

Another reason for Patrick's greater inclination to talk with his people was the fact that his Irish brogue had blunted considerably and he was more easily understood, both in the pulpit and outside. In addition, a year at Dewsbury had served to familiarize him with the sharp dialect of the West Riding. In those days it was far broader than it is today—alas, many of the old words have dropped out of usage, save in the hills—and it was some months before Patrick had understood a word said to him by his sexton. He would never quite lose the Ulster lilt to his voice, but by the time he reached Hartshead his brogue had almost vanished.

Thus Patrick conversed freely with anyone he chanced to meet with on his daily rounds, or with the occasional farmer who would pass him as he took his favourite walk over the moors; and he became a great teller of tales. When years afterwards his children were famous, the people of Hartshead remembered Patrick's stories, and had no doubt that the youngsters had listened to his account of his early days in the West Riding. They felt that "he was a greater educator of his girls than he has been given credit for".

Patrick did not omit to visit his old friends at Dewsbury whenever time permitted, and paid more than one call on young Mr Halliley to discuss the pending trial of James Thackray. There were suppers at the old vicarage, when Mr and Mrs Buckworth would chide him about his past adventures, and there would be mutual inquiry regarding the work of the two clergymen and the progress they had made with their various writings. John Buckworth informed Patrick that he and several other local clergymen had hopes of founding a religious magazine and of having the first volume published at the beginning of the following year. It would probably be entitled *The Cottage Magazine*, and he would look to Patrick for some contributions. The latter readily promised : he had already contributed a number of articles to the *Leeds Mercury* and the *Leeds Intelligencer*, and the Nowell case had made his pseudonym "Sydney" famous locally.

Early in April 1811, a few days before Easter, William Morgan arrived in Yorkshire to be curate to John Crosse in Bradford and minister at Bierley Chapel above the town. (Bierley Chapel was something of a private living. Built in 1766 by the Richardsons of Bierley Hall, it was in their gift, and, although licensed, was not consecrated until 1824. No district was assigned to it until 1864. At the time William Morgan was minister, and for the following fifty years, the patron was the Richardsons' heir—Miss Frances Mary Richardson *Currer*.)

Morgan wrote : "In the month of March, in 1811, I was taking the duty at Madeley Church, a very few Sundays before my removal to the curacy of Bradford, when one of the old men came to me after the service, and said to me, 'Sir, you are going to be Curate to that very kind and good man, Mr. Crosse : God bless you, Sir ; and please to give my love to him. We shall never forget his kindness to us at Madeley. He was next to dear Mr. Fletcher' . . . When I communicated the message of these dear old men to Mr. C, it gave him most sincere delight, and he prayed with great fervency for them . . . I was prepared, as I approached his house, on my arrival in Bradford, to meet him with profound reverence. As soon as I saw him, I felt a cheerful confidence that banished every degree of reserve, and I was at once *at home* with him. His kind reception of me, and behaviour on the occasion, made me consider him in the same light as my own father."

Patrick was delighted to see his old friend again and Morgan found time to preach for him in Hartshead Church. About this time John Fennell also came to Bradford with prospect of an important Methodist appointment.

So passed the spring of 1811, and the long summer days replaced it, adding greater beauty to the surrounding countryside. Patrick could indulge his passion for walking to his heart's content and, on every journey, whether on duty or for pleasure, the well-known places attained a new charm. There were plenty of sheep on the moors now and his companion had to be led on the chain.

On 20th July Patrick was officially inducted as minister of St Peter's, Hartshead-cum-Clifton, and there came a strong contingent from Dewsbury to witness the ceremony. After the service was over and Patrick had dedicated himself anew to the service of God and the people in his spiritual charge, there was a warm congratulation from young Tolson.

The latter remembered Patrick walking back across the open heath to his lodgings "reflecting soberly on those who had placed so much confidence in him, so much trust, and recalling the help they had given so freely in their different ways, he had a faith to keep with them also". Back at Lousey Thorn "he received a warm greeting from Mr and Mrs Bedford and his canine friend".

Yet even now Patrick was not quite the minister of Hartshead.

J. Buckle, Esq. Secretary.

Hartshead, near Leeds, Yorkshire, July 31st 1811

Sir,

For want of proper information on the subject, I neglected, reading myself in, in due time, in consequence of which I find that I am not lawfully possessed of this living.

I therefore take the liberty of requesting that you will be so kind as to inform me how I am to proceed, in order to regain right and lawful possession. Though this Living is but small it merits particular attention; as Hartshead Church is the only one for several miles round, and there is an increasing number of people here, who are far from being friendly towards the Establishment.

It is my intention to get a Parsonage-House builded, and to make as far as I can, the necessary improvements, but I cannot proceed, till I get every impediment removed in the way of my retaining the Living. I beg, therefore, that as soon as convenient, you will give me instructions how I am to act. Will it be necessary that I should get another presentation and by his Graces permission, be reinstated? Or will it do, if, through your mediation, I be licensed anew? And can this be done without my going over to York?

Have the goodness to excuse the trouble I am giving you.

I am Sir, Your most obedient, and humble servᵗ P. Brontè

Buckworth sent a further testimonial on 27th August and another nomination on the 30th. Patrick was re-licensed to Hartshead on 27th

September 1811. But he had experienced nothing compared with the troubles awaiting him over a later appointment!

Meanwhile Patrick had conducted his first wedding service at Hartshead. On 25th August he married Henry Taylor to Rachel Kay, both of that parish. They "were married in this church by Banns this 25th August 1811, by me, Patrick Brontë, Minister". Neither could write, so they made their mark in the register; the witnesses were Luke Priestly and George S. Sheard.

One of the sermons Patrick gave in Hartshead Church is preserved and gives an indication of his preaching at that time. In Patrick's hand and written in ink, the sermon covered twenty-four pages, ending with "Sermon = about 1 hour". The text was taken from "The Epistle of Paul to the Romans—the 2nd chapter and the 28th and 29th verses."

"For he is not a Jew, which is one outwardly; neither *is that* circumcision, which is outward in the flesh:

"But he *is* a Jew, which is one inwardly; and circumcision *is that* of the heart, in the spirit, *and* not in the letter; whose praise *is* not of men, but of God."

Patrick elaborated the point that it is no good a Jew's going through the outward signs of his faith if his heart is not true to God, and that the same applied to Christians. ". . . there are at least three descriptions of men, the ignorant—the sympathetic—and the avaricious hearers . . .".

There are those who attend Church and obey the outward form of the ritual ". . . who are almost as unacquainted with the doctrine of the Gospel, as those who live in a heathenish land, where the name of Christ has never been heard . . .". Sympathetic hearers may weep and cry, as they would under an affecting romance whether real or fictional, but they do not feel the load of their sins. ". . . Many embrace religion as the miser hoards up his gold . . ." ". . . To prefer religion to all other sources of enjoyment is certainly right; but to do this without any love to Christ or faith in his holy name, justly entitles a man to be called an avaricious hearer . . ." ". . . When avaricious hearers meet some worldly object, such as riches or honours, and this object seems attainable, they will forsake Christ . . ."

All these people mentioned are Jews outwardly but not of the heart; others could be mentioned ". . . but it is time that we should proceed—to show the nature of *his* state who is *really* converted unto Godliness . . ." To the outward eye the ". . . formal hypocrite and genuine believer appear in many respects alike, but in *his* sight from whom nothing lies hid things are far otherwise . . ." He is not a Jew whose circumcision is outwardly of the flesh but he is a Jew whose circumcision is of the heart in the spirit. ". . . The character of the true

Christian may be divided into two parts—an outward holy conduct—proceeding from an inward and holy principle . . ."

To be a true Christian one must be moral and pure within—not full of outward show. ". . . Reflect I beseech you on the necessity of a change of heart—Let every soul who is in the faith rejoice in the consideration, that however his motives, and actions may be misrepresented by men, he is well pleasing in the sight of God ; and through the mercy of Christ, will be honoured and recompensed on that day when the secrets of all hearts shall be disclosed and every soul shall be consigned over to everlasting happiness, or misery, accordingly as he *has* or *has not* been born again—Now to God & etc."

Such was the tenor of a sermon made by Patrick at an early stage of his life as a minister of the Church. In view of the ignorant and unfair portrait of him left to the world after his death there is an echo to his words ". . . that however his motives, and actions may be misrepresented by men, he is well pleasing in the sight of God. . .".

But Patrick had to be on his mettle regarding his sermons and the purity of religious thought he expressed, for he was ringed by famous preachers : men of experience, young leaders of religious thought, who would not hesitate to rebuke sharply any cleric who swerved from the set course or who betrayed lethargy in his pulpit. There was old John Crosse at Bradford Parish Church, William Atkinson also in Bradford, Thomas Atkinson at the Old Bell Chapel, Thornton, William Margetson Heald at Birstall six miles over the hills, John Buckworth to keep an eye open from Dewsbury, James Charnock up at Grimshaw's Haworth and, not far from Hartshead, although without a church at that time, Hammond Roberson himself. Save for Charnock, Patrick had heard all of them preach and had met them also—sometimes accompanied by William Morgan, at other times alone. Crosse, elderly and almost blind, William Atkinson, giving the appearance of eccentricity as he lashed the Dissenters, Thomas Atkinson, so beloved in Thornton, Heald, whose family had been intimate with Wesley, Buckworth who fought ill-health to serve his parish, and Roberson, in Patrick's view the greatest of them all.

The Rev. Hammond Roberson, A.M., who had been a predecessor of Patrick as curate at Dewsbury and incumbent of Hartshead, was born at Cawston, Norfolk, in 1757, and was a Fellow of Magdalene College, Cambridge. He had been curate at Dewsbury from 1779 until 1785, when he resigned in order to start a boys' school, renting for his purpose Squirrel's Hall on Dewsbury Moor.

In 1795 he purchased Heald's Hall at Liversedge and transferred his school there : this three-storey building, erected in 1766, was the largest

house in the neighbourhood and Roberson soon had a large and flourishing boarding-school. Shortly after buying the Hall, he became incumbent of nearby Hartshead Church, but continued to reside at the
former.

In 1803 he again resigned his curacy to concentrate on teaching,
in which he was so successful that at the time Patrick arrived at Hartshead he had already commenced plans to build a church at Liversedge
out of his savings from the school.

In the pulpit he was a brave and intrepid preacher, with a very
strong personality. He would occasionally give the sermon at some of
the local churches in the capacity of visiting preacher. That was all
Patrick knew about him in the summer of 1811, but it would not be
many months before he learned a very great deal more. Since March of
that year there had been reports of continuous riots in Nottingham, of
workmen endeavouring to smash the stocking and lace frames recently
introduced there. Soon the flames of discontent would spread northwards to lick hungrily at the Calder Valley. Then Patrick would know
Roberson much better.

But, for the present, Patrick had a far more personal matter on his
mind than the fiery addresses of Hammond Roberson or the ugly
disturbances in far-away Nottinghamshire. Encouraged and advised by
John Buckworth, he spent some time revising the verses he had written
with a view to publication. He gave what hours he could to this work,
adding two or three new poems, trying desperately hard to imbue some
magic sense of poetry into his lines, yet endeavouring always to speak
in language comprehensible to his simple readers. At last he felt all was
ready. He had grouped together twelve of his poems under the title
Cottage Poems, and he wrote his "Advertisement" or Introduction.
For this, his second publication, he did not send his work to Buckworth's
printers but to P. K. Holden of Halifax. Whether Patrick made much
profit from this little book is very doubtful. He would probably have
to contribute largely to the cost of printing; but as he wrote in his
Introduction: "The Author must confess, that his labours, have already
rewarded him by the pleasure which he took in them . . .". Years later,
no doubt from his own experiences, he would warn his daughters of the
great expense in having a volume published. But he had spent many a
joyful day writing his verses and enough copies were sold to assure
him that quite a number of his parishioners, both past and present,
were reading his words. It was his earnest prayer that they
would gain comfort thereby, as he had intended. So his poems were
published and another rung of the ladder in his imagination was
scaled.

The title page ran :

Cottage Poems,
By the
Rev. Patrick Brontë, B.A.
Minister
of
Hartshead-cum-Clifton,
near Leeds, Yorkshire.
All you who turn the sturdy soil,
or ply the loom with daily toil,
and lowly on, through life turmoil
For scanty fare :
Attend : and gather richest spoil,
To sooth your care.
Halifax :
Printed and sold by P. K. Holden, for the Author.
Sold also by B. Crosby & Co. Stationers' Court, London ;
F. Houlston and son, Wellington ;
and by the Booksellers of Halifax, Leeds, York, &c.
1811.

The printers anglicized his degree, but in all his future publications it would revert to the form then used, namely A.B.; and here for the first time appeared his name as the world would remember it—Brontë. For years yet Patrick would continue with the acute accent or a variety of dashes, sometimes leaving the final letter unadorned by any mark; but the printers found the diaeresis the only convenient way of spelling his name within the range of their type, and his name continued as Brontë in all his works. Thus, when later Patrick finally decided to spell his name that way, it was the example of these printers that he had in mind. It was their choice that became such an important word in world literature.

The little book was soon printed and Patrick held it proudly in his hands. The size was 12mo., $6\frac{1}{2}''$ by $4''$; there were 152 sheets and the twelve poems ran from pages 1 to 136. Apart from the running headline "Cottage Poems", more than sixteen lines of verse never appeared on any page. The contents were : (1) "Epistle to the Rev. J— B—, whilst journeying for the recovery of his health", referring, as already mentioned, to his vicar at Dewsbury; (2) "The Happy Cottagers", with a mention of a lake that could be Irish ; (3) "The Rainbow", a sign from God that the Deluge will not return; (4) "Winter-Night Meditations" (a revision of his first published poem), the fall of a maiden called Maria, who after seduction turns prostitute. Happily this was printed before he met his future wife of that name! (5) "Verses sent to a Lady on her Birth-day", his dolorous lines to Mary Burder; (6) "The Irish Cabin", a traveller in the snow takes shelter in "the Cabin of Mourne", a description of his humble birthplace:

> Well thatched, had a good earthern floor,
> one chimney in midst of the roof,
> one window, and one latched door.

(7) "To the Rev. J. Gilpin, on his improved edition of the *Pilgrim's Progress* . . ." Joshua Gilpin, Vicar of Wrockwardine, had published in 1811 in Wellington, Shropshire, a re-dressing of Patrick's first favourite; it was a complete failure, but Patrick is not censorious of the friend who had signed his Wellington testimonial; (8) "The Cottage Maid", appalling verses on a maiden who lives alone in religious contemplation; (9) "The Spider and Fly", worldlings on pleasure bent should take warning from the "silly fly"; (10) "Epistle to a young Clergyman" (already mentioned), his ideals regarding his calling when a young man; (11) "Epistle to the labouring Poor", riches are but earthly, and lead to sin: Christ says that all shall be rich and blest in Him. Evangelical comfort for the oppressed written just before the Luddite Riots; (12) "The Cottager's Hymn", no princes or dukes visit the humble cottage but King Jesus is present. If faithful, the cottager will "gain a palace, above".

Patrick's various writings are discussed more fully later on, but as this was his first major publication, here are two short extracts from "Winter-Night Meditations", followed by his Introduction in full.

> . . . Now, pent within the city wall,
> They throng to theatre and hall,
> Where gesture, look and words conspire,
> To stain the mind, the passions fire;
> Whence sin-polluted streams abound,
> That whelm the country all around.
> Ah! Modesty, should you be here,
> Close up the eye, and stop the ear;
> Oppose your fan, nor peep beneath,
> And blushing shun their tainted breath.
> Here, every rake, exerts his art,
> T'ensnare the unsuspecting heart.

The prostitute with faithless smiles,
Remorseless plays her tricks and wiles,
Her gestures bold, and ogling eye,
Obtrusive speech, and pert reply,
And brazen front, and stubborn tone,
Shew all her native virtues flown.
By her, the thoughtless youth is ta'en,
Impoverished, disgraced, or slain :
Through her, the marriage vows are broke,
And Hymen proves a galling yoke.
Diseases come, destructions dealt,
Where'er her poisonous breath is felt,
Whilst she, poor wretch, dies in the flame,
That runs through her polluted frame.
Once she was gentle, fair and kind.
To no seducing schemes inclined,
Would blush to hear a smutty tale. . . .
A blithesome youth, of courtly mien,
Oft called to see this rural queen :
His oily tongue, and wily art,
Soon gained Maria's yielding heart.
The aged pair, too, liked the youth,
And thought him nought but love and truth.
The village feast, at length is come ;
Maria by the youth's undone—
The youth is gone ; so is her fame ;
And with it, all her sense of shame :
And, now, she practices the art,
Which snared her unsuspecting heart ;
And vice, with a progressive sway,
More hardened makes her every day.
Averse to good, and prone to ill,
And dexterous in seducing skill ;
To look, as if her eyes would melt ;
T'affect a love, she never felt ;
To half suppress the rising sigh ;
Mechanically to weep and cry ;
To vow eternal truth, and then
To break her vow, and vow again.
Her ways, are darkness, death and hell ;
Remorse, and shame, and passions fell ;
And short-lived joy, with endless pain. . . .

PLATE 4   *St George's House, Wethersfield*

TE 5   *St Mary Magdalene, Wethersfield*   PLATE 6   *All Saints, Wellington*

PLATE 7   *Mary Fletcher*

PLATE 8   *Madeley Church, Vicarage and Vicarage Barn*

The "Advertisement" went thus:

"Cottage poems, is a title which the Author has prefixed to the following work, because it is chiefly designed for the lower classes of society. For the sake of readers of a different description, into whose hands this little volume might occasionally fall, and to relieve the mind by a little variety, Poems are intermixed, which do not immediately refer to the Cottage, but which, in general, are not above the comprehension of the meanest capacities. For the convenience of the unlearned and poor, the Author has not written much, and has endeavoured not to burthen his subjects with matter, and as much as he well could, has aimed at simplicity, plainess, and perspicuity, both in manner and style.

"As the Author has not seen any work of exactly the same nature, he has been obliged both to think and speak for himself; and has had recourse, for assistance, only to that Book of Books, the Bible, in which the wisest may learn that they know nothing, and fools be made wise; and in which the divine, the philosopher, and the poet, may find a richer magazine, than in the best productions of Greece and Rome.

"It will be seen, that in speaking of the pious Cottager, his piety is not described as a consequence of poverty, but, as a consequence of Grace. As riches cannot, of themselves, make a man wicked, neither can poverty, of itself, make a man righteous. Some circumstances, are certainly more favourable to piety than others, and in this respect, the poor man has generally the advantage. The Author's wish is, not to lead any one, into an error, but to shew to all, that he, who would be truly happy, must be truly religious.

"Some, in reading this work may be ready to say, that it is too religious, others, that it is not religious enough. In answer to both these characters, the Author would just observe, that he had written not only for the good of the pious, but for the good of those who are not so. And as no two characters can be more opposite, than these are, it is generally difficult, and sometimes impossible, in the same thing, to please both. The Great Apostle, says 'I am made all things to all men, that I might by all means, save some': and may not the Author, acting from the same good motive, endeavour to walk in the same steps?

"Should any be disposed to find fault, with a poetical method of illustrating and enforcing sacred truths, it may just be observed, that many portions of the sacred Scriptures, were originally written in verse, and that from the days of Moses, down to the present time, both sacred and profane writers, have considered poetry, as a channel, through which, the warm effusions of the heart, might be poured with delightful facility, and with the most powerful effect.

"It has been erroneously stated by some, that a religious field is not favourable for a poet to range through. As the great mystery of godliness, in the nature and necessity of the atonement, with every other thing, forming a part of, or connected with the plan of salvation, are undoubtedly the most important, interesting and sublime of all subjects, they must certainly afford the amplest scope for the finest imagination, and the most enlarged understanding. If the Author has not succeeded as a poet, he will not blame his subject, but will readily acknowledge the fault to be entirely his own ; nor will he be able to offer, as an excuse, that he was not interested. He certainly was interested, and that in no small degree. His scenes, it is true, generally lay amongst cottagers, but he would willingly hope that he loves souls, and anxiously desires their happiness, and cottagers, as well as princes, have immortal souls, and the manners of the lowly and obscure, though uncultivated, are commonly the most simple, and natural, and when refined by religion, they generally shine, with a peculiar degree of gospel simplicity, which when genuine, has a dignified and becoming majesty, that is wonderfully calculated to disarm prejudice, and to silence, and put infidelity to the blush.

"In the pursuit of his humble task, though the Author, for the most part held mental conversation with the unlearned and poor, he was amply recompensed by the suggestions of an approving conscience, and the pleasing reflection, that his Great Master, was the poorest of the poor, and was always ready, not only to instruct, but to associate with the meanest of his sheep.

"Some licentious writers, may have a transient, unsatisfactory joy, when their labours are extolled as ingenious, but unless such men are awfully hardened, reflection must now and then sting them with remorse, and dash the cup of their pleasures with poison, and gall. Whatever may be the fate of this little work, the Author has the pleasure to reflect that he meant well, and will be amply recompensed by this reflection. It has been said by some, that virtue is its own reward. However this may be, the Author must confess, that his labours, have already rewarded him by the pleasure which he took in them.

"When released from his clerical avocations, he was occupied in writing the Cottage Poems ; from morning till noon, and from noon till night, his employment was full of real, indescribable pleasure, such as he could wish to taste as long as life lasts. His hours glided pleasantly, and almost imperceptibly by : and when night drew on and he retired to rest, ere he closed his eyes in sleep, with sweet calmness and serenity of mind, he often reflected, that though the delicate palate of Criticism might be disgusted, the business of the day, in the prosecution of his humble task, was well-pleasing in the sight of God, and might, by his blessing, be rendered useful to some poor soul, who cared little about critical niceties, who lived unknowing and unknown in some little cottage, and whom, perchance, the Author, might neither see nor hear of, till that day, when the assembled universe, shall stand before the tribunal of the Eternal Judge. The only source of the Author's grief was a consciousness of his depravity and weakness, and a conviction, that the best of his actions, whether it related to their motives or end, could not stand the test of the All-seeing Eye."

CHAPTER 7

Pistols

ONE winter's evening towards the end of 1811, Patrick, who had been working in his small vestry, left the church to walk home for his tea at Lousey Thorn Farm. It was not quite dark, being that period of twilight which the Yorkshire hill-folk call "dimpsy"; there was a severe frost on the ground and the sky was clear with early evening stars. It was bitterly cold and Patrick set off down the lane at a brisk pace. Suddenly he paused to listen. Behind him, at some distance, he clearly heard the sound of horses' hooves as they struck the iron-hard roads. They were approaching rapidly and, as they drew nearer, Patrick realized that there was a considerable number of riders coming that way. He hugged the hedge as he walked down the hill, to allow passage to the travellers. Shortly afterwards a party of red-coated soldiers thundered past him in the fading light and turned down the Huddersfield road. Patrick stood for a moment at the farm gate, peering into the gathering darkness as the sound of the horses died away. He whistled softly to himself: so it was coming to that, was it? Cavalry! No less than twelve of them, and obviously in great haste! He went thoughtfully in to have his tea. Afterwards he tore up the notes he had prepared for Sunday's sermon and memorized another, which was to be very different from the address he had abandoned.

For some months now the disturbances that had commenced in Nottingham during March had spread slowly into Leicestershire, northwards into Derbyshire, then into neighbouring Lancashire. The government had introduced a bill to render frame-breaking a crime punishable by death. Lord Byron (whose property, Newstead Abbey, was near Nottingham), making one of the few speeches he would ever deliver in the House of Lords, bitterly attacked the bill, backing his arguments with much knowledge of the subject and showing great compassion for the sufferings of the working people; but the bill was passed into law. Still the riots continued, still new factory equipment was smashed. The demand for the abolition of all labour-saving machinery was as strong as ever. Indeed, as the price of bread continued to rise, the frame-breakers became more desperate. What was the choice? Death at the hands of the public executioner or starvation! For

100

the workmen knew only too well that the latest equipment would destroy the need for the hand-looms, which were to be found also in many of the artisans' cottages. So the strife spread towards Yorkshire, as the hangings grew in number. The owners of the new machinery were aided in the defence of their property by the military, who, as no police force existed in those days, patrolled the districts where trouble was likely to arise. Thus Patrick on seeing the red-coats galloping along the quiet lanes of Hartshead knew that the sullen resentment which had brooded in the district for such a long time was about to explode into violence.

From the pulpit Patrick expressed again his great sympathy for the sufferings of the many poor mill-hands in the district. Their provocation was indeed great, but violence was Satan's work and no man of the Church could condone it. He reminded his listeners that there was a war on the Continent largely responsible for conditions at home, but that as soon as victory was ours—as it would be—matters would mend. The new machines were needed : they were of vital importance to the developing industry of our country. In time they would lead to greater employment than we had ever known. True, it had been a cruel time to introduce them, when so many men were without work or bread, but he was sure they were necessary. He prayed that some alleviation of the widespread suffering would speedily be forthcoming, but violence could not be tolerated—even if it had to be met with a like use of force.

This was as weak as water, however, compared with the sermons Hammond Roberson was delivering. From every pulpit in the district this little man could climb into, he blasted at the rioters in the neighbouring counties and warned the working people that such anarchy would be dealt with ruthlessly should it break out in the Calder Valley. Property was sacred and he would not hesitate to sanction with arms its defence from destruction by a rabble who were not aware what they were about.

As the year 1812 commenced these two men continued from the pulpit in the same vein—Roberson threatening the mill-workers with damnation if they dared to raise a finger, Patrick Brontë going most of the way with him but still rather pleading than threatening.

The former was a staunch Tory of the old school, hating anything which in his opinion smacked of anarchy. But he was a very sincere man, prepared to make personal sacrifices for his opinions both religious and political, and always ready to give his life for what he believed to be true.

As for Patrick, not only was he a Tory but he had a great love for the authority of the law. He despised the cowardice of the magistrates who were too afraid of the Luddites to dare interfere and prevent the destruction of property. Indeed it seemed the only brave men were the clergy! But there was yet a greater reason why Patrick wished the trouble in that district to be strangled at birth. He knew the poor wretches concerned, as he also knew the mill-owners, and he saw that there could come nothing out of strife but greater misery and privation. Deeply as his Irish blood quickened with excitement at the prospect of a skirmish, he prayed that somehow common sense would prevail.

January came and passed, then February, and the tension grew steadily, especially at Mirfield. There were groups of silent figures to be seen gathering at night at the Dumb Steeple—a monument without an inscription—not far from Hartshead by the Huddersfield road. At the nearby Three Nuns men could be seen coming and going far into the night, and yet remaining very sober. In the fields that slope down from Roe Head to Kirklees Park were many men whispering together and dispersing into the woods at the first sound of horses.

In March a waggon of spare frames destined for a mill near Huddersfield was attacked as it crossed the moorland roads, the guards were tied up, and the machinery was smashed to pieces. The Luddites had struck at last! It was the signal that men on both sides had anxiously awaited. From now on there would be small parties of soldiers available to protect all waggons if they carried equipment for the mills, and if the owners so requested.

Further attacks followed upon the equipment of mill-owners who had not judged it necessary to call in the assistance of the military. There were hundreds of men drilling at night on the lonely moors, men who, goaded into desperation by misery and hunger, imprudently proclaimed open threats against several prominent figures in the district: Parson Roberson received a warning that his life would be forfeit. The threat had not the slightest effect on him, save that he thundered at the Luddites more ferociously than before.

One day Patrick was approached by some well-disposed members of his congregation and informed that threats against his person had been overheard locally. He would appear to be in danger; he had better be on his guard. Patrick thanked them for their kind warning and returned to Lousey Thorn grasping his shillelagh tightly in his hand. This constant companion of his had vastly amused both Roberson and Thomas Atkinson and they rarely called Patrick by any other name than "Old Staff". But stout though it was and powerfully as he had wielded it in the past it was no weapon for these turbulent times; so Patrick went and bought himself two pistols. Thus he commenced the habit,

which would remain with him most of his days, of having a loaded
fire-arm close at hand. Whilst at Hartshead he would, from now on,
always carry at least one pistol with him in his pocket. Thus armed and
with his faithful stick grasped firmly in his hand he sallied forth on his
duties; and if anyone should be fool enough to start a revolution here
such as there had recently been in France, or if any of the frame-breakers
attempted to molest him in the course of his work as minister of the
parish, he would soon show them who could shoot the straightest—and
pray for their souls afterwards!

As the weeks passed matters went from bad to worse. There were
seen in the district many men who were strangers; and it was soon
known that they were some of the rioters from Nottingham and
Lancashire, sent to Huddersfield to agitate the local discontent into
open strife. Women were afraid to venture abroad lest they should meet
with these gangs, who treated with contempt even the fellow-workers
with whom they were supposedly in sympathy, and did not hesitate to
use the foulest language in public.

The arrival of these intruders was the signal for open conflict.
Towards the end of March many lonely farms and other dwellings
were entered at night by these bands, and the pistols and bludgeons that
the poor frightened citizens had procured towards their self-defence
were forcibly taken from them. Before the military could be deployed
to afford protection for the farmers, there were attacks on two or three
mills in the district, and the soldiers had to give primary protection to
these, in accordance with their main purpose in the district.

These mills had been broken into at dead of night by small groups
of local men, who hunted the premises for the hated shears that would
be used to dress the wool. If they found none they quietly stole away
without committing any damage, but should any of the new equipment
be discovered, they smashed everything in sight.

Two or three small mill-owners were suddenly attacked whilst
returning home from work and had narrow escapes from death; one
arrived at his house bleeding from a bullet wound in the shoulder. At
once the military were dispersed so as to provide a guard for every mill
in the district, whilst a force was held in reserve ready to gallop to the
assistance of any owner whose premises were under severe attack. This
so dissipated their strength that barely more than half-a-dozen soldiers
could be spared for each defensive position, and the mill-owners were
thus forced to recruit what loyal employees they could find to remain
at the mill, day and night, armed for its defence.

As April began it became more and more certain that a full-scale
assault on one of the large local mills would not be delayed much

longer, and the authorities had little doubt that the target chosen would be Rawfolds Mill at Liversedge, near Cleckheaton.

This large stone building was situated on the road between Heckmondwike and Cleckheaton, only some two miles from Hartshead and not far distant from Hammond Roberson's Heald's Hall. The owner of Rawfolds was William Cartwright (or, to be precise, he held it on a long lease as a finishing cloth mill). It did not need the inflaming influence of the agitators from Nottingham to inculcate into the hearts and minds of the Yorkshire mill-hands a bitter hatred of this man. Of all the employers in the district Cartwright was chosen as the main enemy by the Luddites : even Parson Roberson was considered by some as a saint in comparison. He was a tall, extremely handsome man of thirty-seven, with dark eyes and a sallow complexion. He had lived abroad a great deal, spoke French well and had most polished manners —additional reasons why he was unpopular with the natives of the West Riding.

Long before the riots had even started in far-off Nottingham, Cartwright had been detested by the local mill-workers and his decision to stock Rawfolds fully with the new machinery was the last straw for them. Many of the smaller owners of factories had held their hand, or only partially introduced the new shears, in fear of the Luddites. Cartwright was fully aware of his unpopularity and of the dangerous consequences likely to result from his decision. But he was a determined man and a brave one : if up to this time only the clergy had shown any courage, the head of Rawfolds Mill would soon show his mettle also. The poor wretched workpeople had chosen rightly when they nominated him as their chief enemy, for William Cartwright would prove to be the rock against which their vessel of hopes would dash itself to pieces.

It was reported that he had foreign blood in his veins—this certainly accorded with his dark appearance—but then any man who was not a local might be so termed. He would be remembered as "more of a foreigner nor an Englishman. A quiet man with a cutting tongue. Had ne'er a civil word for a man, an' down on him in a jiffy if he looked at a pot o' beer. Drank nowt himself . . . was sacking the old hands and stocking Rawfolds with machines; and Parson Roberson was worse nor him".

Even if Cartwright had not been so very unpopular, there was only one alternative mill the Luddites could attack if they wished to gain a major triumph in the neighbourhood—only one other mill-owner of comparable stature who had also stocked the new shears on a large scale, and that was William Horsfall of Marsden, nearer to Huddersfield. But so far the attacks had been made on that side of Hartshead, and now the authorities considered it more likely that the area of assault would be extended to Liversedge. Reports soon reached the military, and, indeed, Cartwright himself, that an assault on a large scale was to be made upon Rawfolds. Cartwright was immediately offered reinforcements. These he bravely refused, as he had no desire to gain a greater protection at the expense of his fellow-employers, and he felt that if soldiers were drawn off from the defence of other mills in order to be quartered at Rawfolds, then the assault could easily be switched to Horsfall's or one of the smaller mills. He was anxious for the rioters to attack him as he felt certain he could speedily crush their endeavour. He prepared the mill for a siege, barricading the doors and windows and taking up his lodgings there. To assist him were four loyal workmen and five soldiers. In addition to these ten men within the premises, two armed sentinels took up watch outside the mill at night. Thus there were only twelve men in all to defend the large building.

Meanwhile the Rev. Hammond Roberson had thrown open his school for the billeting of the soldiers ; and at Heald's Hall were posted some of the reserve, ready to reinforce any point that was hard pressed. Roberson was confident that Rawfolds would bear the brunt of the next attack. He therefore armed himself and his household and arranged with Cartwright that in the event of the mill's being in dire peril a signal should be given, and if the soldiers were otherwise engaged he would himself gallop over to the rescue.

Two soldiers, all that could be spared, were despatched to Cartwright's home for the protection of his wife and two young children. Thus matters stood on Thursday, 9th April 1812 : the defenders were all in position awaiting the coming assault, no matter where it might fall. Cartwright hoped the attack would be on Rawfolds—so far no one had stood up to the rioters and they had been encouraged to commit further excesses. He felt that one severe defeat in the field would be far more salutary than the continual hanging of stray, and generally almost guiltless, offenders. Roberson waited for the signal as night drew on, anxious also that Cartwright's mill should be the target for the frame-breakers' wrath. At Lousey Thorn Patrick sat with his loaded pistols on the table before him, praying one minute that common sense would prevail even yet and that there would be no violence, the next minute cursing his fortune that Rawfolds mill was just outside his area of watchfulness.

Meanwhile the Luddites had made their decision : it *was* to be Cartwright's place ! There is an old story that it was decided on the toss of a coin. Most of the local men were more favourably disposed towards Horsfall of Marsden : at least he was a Yorkshireman out and out !

However, heads for Horsfall, tails for Cartwright. Down came the coin
—heads! The man who had tossed it hurriedly picked it up and took it
to the light of the fire as if to see better the result, turning it over as he
did so. " 'I'm glad it fell on Cartwright,' I said to my cousin, as we
doffed our things that night. 'Aw thought tha would be,' said George.
'It wer' a weight off me when it fell tails,' I added. 'But it were a head,'
said George, with a quiet smile. 'A head !' 'Aye, a head. But I knew tha
wanted tails, so I turned it i' my palm when I stooped o'er th' fire.' "

But whatever was the real mode of selection, it is surely ironical that
it was Horsfall who would lose his life.

On the night of 9th April a sentinel at Rawfolds mill noticed several
signals and a flashing of lights : the attack seemed imminent. He gave the
alarm to William Cartwright, but the hours passed and dawn came :
there had been no assault. The next night came and went—all was still
quiet.

Early the next evening, Saturday, 11th April 1812, soon after dark,
scores of cloth-dressers slipped quietly away from their homes and
melted into the night. One by one the dim figures reappeared in the
large field above Kirklees Priory that sloped down from Roe Head.
There, not far below that mansion, which years later three of Patrick
Brontë's daughters would know, the Luddite army grew stealthily and
steadily until there were well over a hundred men assembled. The
leaders, including some men from Nottingham, went amongst them
handing out pistols, muskets, hatchets and bludgeons to those who
possessed no arms. When all was ready, and the plan of campaign
understood, there was a pause : it would not do to attack too early, the
defenders would be too much on the alert.

About half an hour before midnight the order to march was given,
and silently the sullen army moved forward in the direction of Rawfolds
Mill. They branched off at some distance from Lousey Thorn and
Patrick, with his pistols at the ready, was not destined to see action that
night.

At half-past twelve the defenders of Rawfolds were fired at from all
directions and the attackers flung themselves on the two sentinels,
capturing them without resistance. The infuriated rebels, having tasted
an early success, hurled themselves upon the mill, smashing the window-
frames and firing into the building. There was a heavy return fire of
musketry and several of the assailants fell.

There was then a desperate attempt to force an entrance, but in vain.
The steady fire from within caused further casualties and drove the
rioters back time and time again. One attacker, John Walker, clung
tenaciously to a window-frame until his hand was shot off. After twenty

minutes of fruitless endeavour, the attackers gave up the attempt and fled in disorder, leaving their wounded to make the best escape they could. Their defeat was complete, for although the defenders had certainly had the advantage of cover, not one of them was hurt: ten men had routed well over a hundred.

As the unhappy mill-hands fled for their lives they were without hope. The great attack had failed miserably. Yet perhaps it was not entirely a failure, for the authorities of Britain had received a severe fright by these riots and would be forced to take some heed of the conditions of the working man. The recent revolution in France was still on their minds, for all that it had led to an equal danger—Napoleon. But the victory was William Cartwright's for no one before had dared stand up to the Luddites as he had done—certainly no mill-owner had gained such a triumph. Never again would the present riots frighten the authorities; only the fear remained that, in the future, they might turn into something far more powerful and dangerous.

There appeared a more detailed account of the attack on Rawfolds Mill in the *Leeds Mercury* of Saturday, 18th April 1812, a week after the event, under the heading "Riots. Fatal conflict": "We have made it our business to collect a faithful narrative of the sanguinary contest that last Saturday night took place at Rawfolds, between the men calling themselves the army of General Ludd and the persons employed in guarding the property of Mr Cartwright, in order to place upon record the particulars of an event that will survive in local remembrance the present generation; and we can undertake to say, that the following narrative may be implicitly relied upon:—

"It is known to our readers that the use of machinery for raising and dressing woollen-cloth has of late become very unpopular amongst the shearmen in this part of the country; and that all mills where machinery of this kind is in use have been marked out for destruction, and that in several of them the obnoxious machines have been destroyed.

"At Rawfolds, near Cleckheaton, a place at an equal distance from Huddersfield and Leeds, from each of which it is about eight miles, a gentleman of the name of William Cartwright has a mill used for the purpose of dressing cloth in the way objected to by the men; at this mill it was understood that an attempt was to be made, and on Thursday night, the 9th inst, the sentinel at the mill observed several signals that were supposed to indicate an approaching attack, though both that and the following night passed over without molestation. On Saturday night, about half-past twelve o'clock, there was a firing heard from the north, which was answered from the south, and again from west to east; this firing was accompanied by other signals and in a few minutes a number of armed men surprised the two sentinels without the mill, and having secured both their arms and their persons, made a violent attack upon the mill, broke in the window-frames, and discharged a volley into the premises at the same instant. Roused by this assault, the guard within the mill flew to arms, and discharged a heavy fire of musketry upon the assailants; this fire was returned and repeated without intermission during the conflict, the mob attempting all the time to force an entrance, but without success, a number of voices crying continually 'Bang up !' 'Murder them !' 'Pull down the door !'— and mixing these exclamations with the most horrid imprecations. Again and again the attempts to make a breach were repeated, with a firmness and constancy worthy a better cause ; but every renewed attempt ended in disappointment, while the flashes from the fire-arms of the insurgents served to direct the guards in their aim. For about 20 minutes this engagement continued with undiminished fury, till at length, finding all their efforts to enter the mill fruitless, the firing and hammering without began to abate, and soon after the whole body of the assailants retreated with precipitation, leaving on the field such of their wounded as could not join in the retreat. An attempt was made to rally their scattered forces, to carry off their wounded, but it was in vain ; the fire from within had been kept up with so much steadiness and perseverance as to produce universal dismay ; during this spirited eng agement 140 balls were discharged from the mill ; what number of shots were fired by the mob, it is impossible to say, but the doors and windows were perforated with a vast number of pistol and musket balls, though none of them took effect, not one of the guards having sustained the least personal injury. During the principal part of the engagement the alarm-bell was rung, and a quantity of large stones were hurled from the roof, which had an instantaneous effect, otherwise a quantity of oil of Vitriol, in reserve, would have been poured down.

"On the cessation of the firing, the ears of the guard were assailed with the cries of two unfortunate men, weltering in their blood, and writhing under the torture of mortal wounds ; 'For God's sake,' cried one of them, 'shoot me—put me out of my misery !'—'Oh !' cried the other, 'help ! help !—I know all, and I will tell all.' On the arrival of a detachment of the Queen's Bays, which took place about an hour after the attack commenced, these ill-fated men were removed on litters from the field to the Star Inn, at Roberttown, and medical aid was called in with all possible despatch. One of them proved to be a cropper, of the name of Samuel Hartley, formerly in the employment of Mr. Cartwright ; a fine-looking young unmarried man, about 24 years of age, and a private in the Halifax Local Militia, in which regiment Mr. Cartwright is a Captain. The other was John Booth, a youth about 19 years of age, son of a clergyman in Craven, and an apprentice to Mr. Wright, of Huddersfield, tinner. Hartley had received a shot in his left breast, apparently while making a blow at some part of the mill, which, passing through his body, lodged beneath the skin at the left shoulder, from whence it was extracted with a portion of bone. In this situation he languished till about three o'clock on Monday morning, when he expired. Booth's wound was in his leg, which was shattered almost to atoms; it was found necessary that he should submit to have the leg amputated, but owing to the extreme loss of blood before the surgeons arrived, spasms came on during the operation, and he died about six o'clock on Sunday morning; having previously observed, that if he should recover, 'he would never be brought into such a scrape again'. It was observed that neither of these victims of lawless violence manifested any sense of religion. On Monday, a Coroner's Inquest assembled upon the dead bodies, and returned a Verdict of 'Justifiable Homicide'. None of the wounded men except Hartley and Booth have yet been discovered.

"On the morning after the engagement a number of hammers, axes, false-keys and picklocks, with two masks, a powder-horn, and a bullet mould were found upon the field, which was stained in several places with blood; and it is evident that many others besides those left in the field were wounded, as traces of gore were distinctly marked in almost every direction, and in one place to the distance of four miles. The assailants have much reason to rejoice that they did not succeed in entering the building, for we speak from our own observation when we say, that had they effected an entrance, the death of vast numbers of them from a raking fire which they could neither have returned nor controlled, would have been inevitable. It is unnecessary to speak of the heroism of the little band that guarded these premises; there is not perhaps upon record a more distinguished instance of manly courage and cool intrepidity; but it may be proper to add, that though the assailants exceeded a hundred, the number opposed to them was very inconsiderable, and of that number one of the military conducted himself in so unsoldierlike a manner, that he was on the following morning placed in confinement, and now awaits the issue of a Regimental Court Martial."

The *Leeds Mercury* records a week later the sentence of 300 lashes which was passed upon the soldier referred to, for refusing or neglecting to defend the mill in the proper manner, as his orders required. The private declared that he had refused to fire for fear of hitting his brothers who were actively engaged in the assault. At the earnest entreaty of William Cartwright, the sentence was reduced to twenty-five lashes; these were inflicted at Rawfolds Mill itself, the victim being escorted there by a party of Dragoons.

Now the newspaper had stated, "None of the wounded men except Hartley and Booth have yet been discovered", but there was one man at least who knew where some of them could be found, and that was the Rev. Patrick Brontë.

After the attack had been broken off, several of the insurgents, grievously wounded, had crawled and limped away from Rawfolds as best they could. They were no longer an organised force and with the authorities determined to apprehend every man who had taken part in the attack, their position was desperate : they knew only too well that, now their power was broken, they would be crushed without pity. How many died of their injuries that night in the woods and on the slopes of Liversedge is not known, but more than one perished in that fashion. Others reached friendly cottages, where those not badly wounded could find succour and hiding, and where the more gravely hurt could die in peace.

Meanwhile the hunt was on, with the red-coats searching every thicket, every cottage, in their quest for the fugitives, wounded or otherwise. Foremost in the chase were Parson Roberson and William Horsfall, the latter, whose mill had so narrowly escaped attack, being the most zealous in tracing the ringleaders of the Luddite rising.

Some few nights after the affray at Rawfolds, Patrick was walking near Hartshead Church, when through the darkness he heard the sound of muffled footsteps approaching the church from the direction of Hightown and could dimly discern the outline of several men who appeared to be carrying something large and bulky on their shoulders. The dark shapes grew in number as further figures loomed up, each group with its indefinable burden. Patrick's pistol was in his hand in a moment. He grasped his stick like a cudgel and kept to the shelter of the wall at some distance from the church gates.

As he watched, the leading figures noiselessly opened the gates and some score of men passed into the churchyard. So it was to be *his church* this time, was it. Patrick moved forward quickly, determined to send to their account as many of the sacrilegious scoundrels as possible before they were well aware of his presence. But even as he came forward he suddenly realized what they were doing there, knew the meaning of those dark loads they carried, and silently turned on his heels and strode off through the night back to Lousey Thorn.

At the farm he "paced up and down his room" faced with two

conflicting conceptions of duty. These men were wanted by the
magistrates and hunted by the military. They had broken the peace in a
savage fashion, defied the law, and heeded not the advice of their
church. It was his bounden duty as a responsible law-abiding subject
of King George to advise the authorities immediately and have them
send a posse of soldiers to Hartshead churchyard to arrest the fugitives.
Yet, they had but come to bury their dead. Was it not also his duty as
minister of the parish to permit that any man, however great a sinner,
should rest at last in hallowed ground ? Perhaps not, according to the
law, but in this matter he wished to obey only the authority of the
merciful Christ. What of the cottagers who had probably sheltered those
unhappy wretches in their last hours ? If he informed the military, they
would soon be discovered and punished severely for aiding the fugitives.
Should innocent men and women be made victims of their own
humanity ? This last consideration decided him. They were his flock,
they had suffered much already for their folly ; and it would ill become
his cloth to betray them, when all they wished for was a decent burial
for their fallen comrades-in-arms.

Putting his pistols to one side, Patrick went to bed determined to
turn a blind eye on all that was happening in the churchyard that night.
Undisturbed and in silence could the graves be dug, and the bodies
gently lowered into the ground. There was no religious ceremony but
over each resting-place a friend whispered a short, simple prayer. The
men quietly trod the disturbed ground as flat as possible, and then, in
the small hours, dispersed without a sound.

In the morning it was obvious what had taken place. Near the
south-east corner of the graveyard and contiguous to the road, the soil
lay loosely on the surface and the fresh imprints of many boots were to
be seen. Nothing was ever said to Patrick on the matter, although both
sides admitted, when they discovered the truth, that "knowing more
than his flock gave him credit for, he wisely held his peace". He had the
soil smoothed over and left the dead to sleep, unmarked, in that corner
of the churchyard.

But the dead were the lucky ones, for the survivors knew no peace
as they fled from shelter to shelter. The noose was drawn tighter and
tighter and most of them were soon captured. Those that remained at
liberty were crazed with desperation. They knew well that they would
soon be taken, and revenge, no matter in what form, was their only
consideration.

On the afternoon of Saturday, 18th April, a week after his routing
of the Luddite forces, William Cartwright was returning home by way
of Bradley Wood, near Huddersfield, when two men hiding on either

side of the lane opened fire simultaneously upon him ; but both shots
went astray and the rioters' arch-enemy escaped unhurt.

In the *Leeds Mercury* of 25th April 1812 the incident was described
thus : "On Saturday last, an attempt was made to assassinate Mr. Cartwright, the intrepid defender of Rawfolds Mill, by two villians who
fired at him from behind a hedge, as he was returning from Huddersfield. The shots were discharged at nearly the same moment from
opposite sides of the road, but happily without effect. This diabolical
attempt upon the life of this gentleman, took place in open day, between
the hours of four and five in the afternoon, about a mile at this side of
Huddersfield."

But if Cartwright seemed immune from the rioters' bullets, revenge
of a kind would soon be theirs. William Horsfall also had by now
incurred the bitter hatred of the Luddites by the energetic way in
which he had tracked down all the ringleaders known to him ; and on
Tuesday, 28th April 1812, on Crossland Moor, not far from the Warren
House Inn, four men waiting in ambush shot him down. He was
mortally injured and died the following day. One of the assassins was
George Mellor, a ringleader of the local rioters. But Cartwright was not
forgotten, as this further extract from the *Leeds Mercury* shows. It is
from the issue of 16th May 1812. "Yesterday se'nnight, 11 pair of
shears belonging to Mr. Cartwright, which had been sent to Wakefield
to grind and two pairs belonging to another person, were taken from
the grinders to a field at a distance and broken." This, however, was the
last fling of the rioters ; the murderers of Horsfall were soon apprehended
and, by the beginning of May, most of the Luddite leaders had been
captured.

There would continue sporadic outbreaks of petty violence, but the
terror of civil war was over—although on 11th May Spencer Perceval,
the Prime Minister and Chancellor of the Exchequer, was shot dead in
the lobby of the House of Commons by a lunatic, John Bellingham.
On 18th June 1812, the hated Orders in Council were repealed, the
blockaded ports were thrown open and all over Yorkshire and Lancashire
the bells rang out to celebrate this mercantile victory. True, the joy
would be somewhat premature, but there was a boom in trade, more
work for the people and, at last, wages began to rise and keep pace with
the increasing cost of bread. Even the new machinery would, in time,
be accepted as more of it was brought into the rapidly expanding mills
and men were needed to handle it. Not in 1812 would all this happen,
but the beginnings would be seen. At the end of that year Napoleon
would reel out of Russia, no longer the omnipotent power he had been,
and three years later Wellington would destroy his forces at Waterloo.

So ended the Luddite risings in the Calder Valley, with the courageous and faithful villagers smuggling out their kin, both living and dead, as the loyal Scottish Highlanders had done in 1746.

Many were the stories that would come to light about the battle at Rawfolds Mill, some true, others invented. Of the former kind the most interesting concerned Mrs Cartwright. During the attack some of the extremists among the Luddites had warned Cartwright that if he did not surrender his mill they would go and murder his wife and children —an added source of worry to the harassed mill-owner. On that night Mrs Cartwright, hearing, as she imagined, approaching footsteps, had put her infants in a basket and thrust it up the great chimney, where it rested on a ledge. Happily she had heard only the steps of the patrolling sentry. One of the children, when a grown woman, would point out with pride the marks of musket shots in the walls of her father's mill.

William Cartwright had so earned the goodwill of all the neighbouring manufacturers by his resolute stand against the Luddites, that they presented him with a testimonial, written on parchment, and dated 17th May 1813. In addition a subscription for his benefit realized £3,000.

These then were the scenes, and these the characters Charlotte Brontë would use so vividly in her great novel *Shirley*. Whilst at Roe Head she would visit all the places connected with those troublesome times, and Margaret Wooler would be an informative guide. Her father would relate all his stories of those exciting days, and with the files of the *Leeds Mercury* before her, she had enough material around which to weave her tale. Thus Cartwright would become Robert Moore, and Hammond Roberson and Patrick Brontë would merge into Matthewson Helstone.

At the beginning of 1813, sixty-six of the poor Luddites were arraigned at a special commission held in York Castle and seventeen were sentenced to death : three of these had been concerned in the murder of William Horsfall, the fourth man, Benjamin Walker, turning "King's Evidence". These three were hanged on 8th January. The others were executed on 16th January 1813 and their corpses carried in carts through the streets of York. (But Yorkshiremen have tenacious memories and years later, after Walker's natural death, his body was secretly dug up by night and given for medical research.) In addition, transportation for a period of seven years was imposed on six other men. Years later Mrs Abraham Hirst, who was in service with the Rev. Thomas Atkinson, said that after the executions at York some of the bodies were brought to Hightown at dead of night and buried in the churchyard at Hartshead. But in view of the complete lack of a need for secrecy at that time, together with the fact that all the hanged men were from Huddersfield, it appears likely that she was mistaken in her timing of the event and that what she really remembered were the furtive funerals after the fight at Rawfolds mill.

Hammond Roberson, the "Duke Ecclesiastic" as he had been called, continued to build his church at Liversedge; it was finally consecrated on 29th August 1816. Christ Church, Liversedge, was beautifully situated on a knoll on the opposite side of the valley from Heald's Hall. It was erected entirely at Roberson's own expense and, from his detailed statement, was known to cost £7,474 11s 10¾d. He became, naturally, its first incumbent, and died on 9th August 1841, aged eighty-four years. Roberson, who was instrumental in building many other local churches, was appointed Canon of York in 1830. It was said that whilst vicar of Liversedge he noticed that one parishioner had been buried with a headstone larger than the others; this was very much against his principle of one small stone per person, and all stones to be uniform. Roberson had the offending gravestone torn out of the ground and hurled into the hollow at the bottom of the churchyard. When he died his headstone conformed with his ruling: it was half a yard high, and gave just his name, age and date of burial.

It is appropriate that not far from his gravestone in Liversedge churchyard is another bearing the simple inscription "William Cart-wright of Rawfolds, died 15th April, 1839, aged 64 years." Thus the two men who between them destroyed the Luddites in the West Riding of Yorkshire, were laid at rest, almost side by side, within a space of two years or so.

As happens when men adhere firmly to the unpopular side, many exaggerations of Roberson's character would linger as the truth in the minds of the local people. Mrs Gaskell tells the reported tales of his refusing to give water to the wounded Luddites left in the mill-yard, when he rode in on the morning after the attack to congratulate Cart-wright on his great victory; yet, as is known, there were no wounded there by that time. He is reported to have discovered that his servant Betty had a follower called Richard, and finding him in the kitchen, to have ordered the boys of his school to set him under the pump until he promised never to visit her again. It was also reported that he forced his refractory pupils to stand on one leg in a corner of the class-room, holding heavy books in their hands; or if they played truant, that he followed them on horseback, bringing them back tied to the stirrup by a rope. He was reported to have shot his wife's favourite horse and buried it in a quarry whilst in a passion; but the truth is that it was old and in pain and he destroyed it to put the animal out of its misery. He was even seen "dancing, in a strange red light, with black demons all whirling and eddying round him". Such were the fantastic stories aroused by the political hatred in which he was held.

Yet he was a man who never courted esteem. Indeed in his young days at Dewsbury he had thrown away much popularity by first summoning, and when that failed, indicting at York the ringleaders of the cruel bull-baiting in that town. He obtained a verdict against them and was hooted all the way home.

At the advanced age of eighty, he still delighted in breaking in wild horses, and he was long remembered on his strong white horse, his shovel hat fixed firmly on his bald head, as he rode to church each Sunday, determined to die, if possible, in the pulpit. He had an eagle eye, and his bearing to the end was proud and dignified.

Charlotte's friend Mary Taylor wrote to Mrs Gaskell thus: ". . . old Roberson said he would wade to the knees in blood rather than the then state of things should be altered. . . ". But the final, most impartial, word comes from *Shirley*: "He was not diabolical at all. The evil simply was—he had missed his vocation: he should have been a soldier, and circumstances had made him a priest. For the rest he was a conscientious, hard-headed, hard-handed, brave, stern, implacable, faithful little man: a man almost without sympathy, ungentle, prejudiced, and rigid: but a man true to principle—honourable, sagacious, and sincere."

Meanwhile Patrick was heartily glad the strife was over: it had, like most violent uprisings, done a little good, but had brought with it untold suffering. Although matters seemed quiet enough for the present, Patrick did not throw away his pistols. Since his first arrival in Yorkshire he had seen enough of violence to convince him that they might prove useful at any time.

But whilst the embers of revolt were still faintly flickering, and had not yet been quite extinguished, William Morgan came rushing excitedly to Patrick with news that John Fennell, now headmaster of the new Wesleyan Academy at Woodhouse Grove, wished him, Patrick Brontë, to accept the appointment as school examiner there.

This was wonderful news for Patrick—a chance to work with the famous lay-preacher who was a godson of Fletcher of Madeley; it was also, although he could not know it, an opportunity to meet Maria Branwell.

CHAPTER 8

Maria

THE Wesleyan Academy at Woodhouse Grove, Apperley Bridge, near Bradford, was opened on 8th January 1812. It was intended for the education of the sons of Wesleyan ministers and, at its inception, had eight pupils. But after only a year this number had risen rapidly to seventy boys, whose ages ranged from eight to nearly fourteen, at which time they would leave the school. They were recruited, for it was no less, from manses all over the country, although the majority were from the north of England—from Hull, Leeds, Huddersfield and like places. The school uniform was soon recognizable everywhere in that part of the land: a dark blue cloth jacket, corduroy trousers and a large, flat cap of red and yellow with slanting peak. Thus attired the boys were soon well known on the roads, and local Methodists in every village or town through which they passed would wish them God speed.

A pupil, John Stamp, wrote to his father on 11th April 1812 giving, in detail, the crowded hours of their Sabbath: ". . . We rise at six o'clock in the morning, and to half-past, washing etc.; to seven, a public prayer meeting; to eight, private prayer and reading; from eight to nine, family prayer and breakfast; from nine to half-past ten, reading; from half-past ten to twelve, preaching; from twelve to half-past one, private bands, dinner; from half-past one to two, the chapter to be read from which the morning's text has been taken and each boy to remember a verse; from two to half-past four, preaching and reading; from half-past four to six, public prayer meeting; from six to eight, supper and family prayer and go to bed."

This on a diet of three meals a day of which two consisted of bread and milk! Had Patrick Brontë been more than the examiner there, and had not his heart and mind been otherwise engaged during his visits to the Academy, he would, perhaps, have made a note of these things and the future tragedy of Cowan Bridge might not have occurred. (In 1814 when Fennell was gone and Jonathan Crowther was headmaster, the discipline at Woodhouse Grove became severe indeed, with thrashings very much a part of the syllabus; the Rev. Dr Waddy remembered: 'When I was a boy at the Grove, I was thrashed *every day*. I have no doubt that I generally deserved it; but it was too much—it did no good.")

In 1812, John Fennell, the first headmaster, writes: "I am happy to inform you that God has begun a most blessed work among the children. I preached yesterday from Proverbs iv, 3, 4 (For I was a son unto my father, tender and only beloved in the sight of my mother, and he taught me and said unto me 'Let thine heart retain my words. Keep my commandments and live'). In the evening many of them were deeply affected and sighs and tears were on all sides. To-day the work seems spreading among them and while I am now writing this, I hear the voice of prayer and praise in the higher part of the chapel, where several of them are assembled for that purpose. Blessed be God that out of the mouths of these babes, Woodhouse Grove is, this moment, resounding with His praise. In the morning at seven we assembled again and it would have gladdened your heart to have seen and heard what I then witnessed. The very grove echoed with the voice of praise and thanksgiving. Indeed to have heard the sweet warbling of the birds in the wood, and the melting strains of the boys in the chapel, uniting in one blessed, heavenly chorus to God, was enough to have moved a heart of stone. How often did we sing with hearts full of gratitude, and eyes full of tears,

> " 'Ye mountains and vales, in praises abound;
> Ye hills and ye dales, continue the sound:
> Break forth into singing, ye trees of the wood,
> For Jesus is bringing lost sinners to God.' "

Charles Wesley's lines, that Patrick had heard sung in the lanes of Ireland, were not inappropriate to Woodhouse Grove, for it was a most beautiful place.

In the *Morning Chronicle* of 25th July 1811 there had appeared the following advertisement: "Yorkshire. Elegant Mansion House, Woodhouse Grove, delightfully situate in Aire Dale. To be sold or let, the elegant mansion called Woodhouse Grove, near Apperley Bridge, about eight miles from Leeds, four from Bradford, and five from Otley, adapted for the residence of a large genteel family. The house consists of drawing and dining rooms of large dimensions, with breakfast room, study, butler's pantry, housekeeper's room, servants' hall, kitchens and every other convenience on the ground floor, twelve lodging rooms, dressing room and accommodation for servants, wash-house, laundry, brew-house and other offices, fitted up in a complete manner. Out buildings comprise stabling for twelve horses, double coach-house, harness-room etc. : Conveniently detached is a farm-yard, with large barn, cow house, pigging house. The whole of the buildings are of free-stone, and in the best repair. The pleasure ground and gardens contain about seven acres, well planted, and laid out with much taste and beauty, with hot house, greenhouse, an excellent bath, a fish pond well-stocked and supplied by a never-failing spring of soft water. The country for many miles round is beautifully ornamented by the seats of many families of distinction, and the picturesque scenery of this part of Aire Dale is equal to any in the country. In front of the house is eight acres of rich land, ornamented with large oaks, and other fine timbers. The river Aire winds in front and the stream affords fine trout fishing ; the country also abounds in game that altogether renders this a complete residence for a gentleman.

"—Application by letter, post paid to Mr. Teale, Surgeon or Mr. James Holdforth, Leeds."

However, Woodhouse Grove was not destined for the use of a worldly gentleman, but for higher things. The Methodist Conference urged by the energetic Jabez Bunting, moved speedily and acquired the mansion, so admirably situated for the purpose of educating the sons of their preachers. Until then they had made do with Wesley's own school at Kingswood, Bristol.

The Conference paid £4,575 for the estate, of which £1,377 was contributed by their preachers. (A Methodist preacher and his wife received only 15s a week board, £4 4s a quarter wage, £6 per annum for a Servant and 10s 6d a quarter for postage.)

Soon, however, the house would present a faded appearance, for the Methodists had no money to spare for the upkeep of the building, being concerned only with what went on inside. So the trout and game went largely unmolested, save by poachers, and in view of the regimen of bread and milk, it is to be surmised that the brew-house was made to serve another purpose.

The mansion, one storey high, with a balustraded roof, stood on high ground on the north bank of the Aire, commanding a fine view overlooking Bradford. It was approached by a circular drive, overhung by tall, gnarled sycamores and beeches. The path wound round a wooded knoll surmounted by a square watch-tower, successor to the temple or summer-house built by a former owner, Robert Elam, a Quaker.

John Fennell, the first governor, was to be the only layman who would occupy that post. He was appointed headmaster, and his wife governess or matron of the establishment, being responsible for the household arrangements. Their joint salary was £100 a year. Fennell was born at Madeley near Wellington, Shropshire, on 19th June 1762 and became a schoolmaster and class-leader among the Wesleyans at Penzance in Cornwall. In December 1790 at Madron Church (the Mother Church of Penzance) he married Jane Branwell, who was some nine years older than himself, having been born on 10th November 1753. Their only child, Jane Branwell Fennell, was born at Penzance on 9th October 1791.

Fennell had written for the *Wesleyan Methodist Magazine*: in 1801 there appeared a letter in which he discussed the character of his god-father, the Rev. John Fletcher of Madeley. He also contributed replies to mathematical questions in *The Ladies' Diary*. Schoolmaster, lay preacher, and friend of many of the leading Methodists, he never became a fully-fledged Methodist minister, although he was described as such in *The Dictionary of National Biography*. One of his closest friends was the Rev. John Crosse, Vicar of Bradford, with whom he was in complete agreement on all matters of Evangelical theology. At the time of Patrick's first passing through the gates of Woodhouse Grove, Fennell was fifty years of age, his wife fifty-nine, and his daughter Jane, twenty-one.

At first Fennell had a tremendous enthusiasm for his new and honoured appointment. The Wesleyan influence was strongest in Cornwall and Yorkshire, and he would have served faithfully in both counties. Shortly after his appointment he wrote: "After supper they gathered round me like bees, telling me how the Lord had been amongst them, and earnestly entreating that they might be permitted to spend a few hours more before bed-time in prayer. Love for their souls, and a desire to indulge them in anything that might do their souls good, on the one hand, and feeling the indispensable necessity for keeping all things in order and mixing prudence with piety on the other, caused such a struggle in my mind that I was at my wits' end while surrounded with the loud clamour of 'Do, Sir, do, Sir, let us, if it be but one hour.' " Among early scholars entreating for time to pray were Rayner Stephens, leader of the Chartists, Atherton, who was legal adviser to the government during the American Civil War, and Morley, who applied his discoveries of the properties of strychnine to the study of its use in crime.

But John Fennell's tenure of his office was to be brief. For a year he would bestride two worlds—that of the old Evangelical school of Methodism and that of the new, more militant kind that no longer wanted men like himself, Crosse, Morgan and the others. The Methodists now intended to fend for themselves, to recruit from the sons of their own ministers, and they no longer looked to the bosom of the Church to supply their needs. Chapels, schools and ministry quite separate from the Church of England had sprung up everywhere with mushroom growth. Fennell would have to make his decision; and he was to choose the Established Church.

As Patrick walked up the winding drive of Woodhouse Grove for the first time, on a spring day in 1812, William Morgan, who had travelled over from Hartshead with him, would have to get his own news off his chest before they entered the house, and risk Patrick's wrath. Morgan, "a great talker", was much excited: it was a wonderful chance for Patrick; how far they had both come since their Wellington days; he was still in charge of Bierley Chapel but there was likely to be promotion for him in the not too distant future; poor Crosse was failing somewhat and there was talk of Morgan's being sent into Bradford as his permanent assistant at the parish church; should the old vicar be translated to Glory he might even get the parish church. He must speak, he could keep it back no longer, Patrick could say what he liked, but he must inform him that he was engaged to be married— to young Jane Fennell.

But the scars of Wethersfield had healed a good deal and Patrick, when such a subject was now mentioned, "could smile". It must have been a relief to Morgan, for he remembered the fate of John Nunn when he had imparted similar news to Patrick at Wellington. Morgan announced that he and Jane intended to be married before the year's end, and was thankful for Patrick's heartiest good wishes.

Patrick was "re-introduced" to Mrs Fennell and the blushing young lady. His "introduction" to John Fennell had been made spiritually years ago, by Mary Fletcher. He was shown the barn, newly converted into a schoolroom, with its small double desks into which two fervent young Methodists could barely squeeze, and the long upper room over the stables that served as the chapel. He was informed that the boys were granted only one holiday a year—the month of May; that as inspector of the school he would be required to examine the boys at the end of the summer term, in the Scriptures, Latin, and so on; that it was an appointment for that year only, as there would probably be a different minister chosen for the purpose each year. He was then advised as to the small fee that would be his for this extra duty and, without hesitation, he accepted with gratitude Mr Fennell's offer. Mrs Fennell then insisted on showing him the kitchens, remarking that it was a difficult task to feed so many mouths and, in addition, to manage all the divers household responsibilities. In a few weeks' time one of her nieces from Penzance was coming up for a time to give assistance in the needlework department; she was most adept at sewing and would be an invaluable help.

Patrick, in the pleasure at his new appointment, barely listened to the harassed matron and soon made his escape. As he walked back to Hartshead that night Patrick, fond of walking though he was, was not sorry that his duty required only an occasional visit to Woodhouse Grove—lovely as it was—for the distance from Lousey Thorn to Apperley Bridge was considerable. But before long he would make the journey almost daily and consider it the merest stroll.

So the boys of Woodhouse Grove Academy went on their first holiday in May 1812 and Patrick continued his efforts to heal the wounds that the recent riots had caused in his parish. He was thirty-five years of age now, and anxious that his income should be supplemented as far as possible : his fee for examining at Woodhouse Grove, in addition to his extra allowance for board and lodging, had brought his income from all sources to £75 per annum. Thus the allowance to his widowed mother continued, however much he would shortly need money for himself.

Meanwhile Patrick kept his promise to John Buckworth by sending short papers for his *Cottage Magazine*. In the first volume, in 1812, appeared extracts from Patrick's *Cottage Poems*, together with a collection of articles under the pseudonym "A Cottage Writer", believed to be his also. These included "Moses Humble", "Abraham Faithful", "Nathaniel Upright" and "A Dream". In the next year would appear "Hints for Cottage Writers" and "The Faithful Pastor"—the latter of interest as the author gives the turning-point in his religious experiences from formalism to evangelicalism. Later, in November 1816 and in 1825, there were "Labouring Poor" and two short articles on the "Harvest Home".

Patrick was not required at Woodhouse Grove on official duty until the beginning of August but there came a social invitation to spend an evening with the Fennells and friend Morgan shortly after his acceptance of the post there. In June he again walked up that winding drive, and with a most confident step. He had every reason to be pleased : he was minister of his own parish, had emerged from the recent violence with respect from both sides, was the inspector of the new academy here, had published his first books of poems and had a ready publisher of his articles in John Buckworth. He was still in this most satisfied frame of mind as he entered the large drawing-room and saw Maria Branwell sitting there.

At first he noticed how very pale and delicate she looked, then how small she was, and again, how unlike her cousin Jane in appearance. As the evening went on there was much teasing of William Morgan and Jane Fennell, with the former having plenty to say on the subject of their forthcoming marriage, and on the religious and political questions of the day. Maria Branwell had her own views to put forward and produced them quietly yet without shyness or embarrassment; and when the others were twitting poor Morgan, Patrick saw the amused smile that softly showed itself in the corners of her mouth. She was not pretty, with her light brown hair, hazel eyes and small chin, yet there was something elegant about her as she sat there, for all the quiet simplicity of her silk dress and the stillness of her manner. It was as if she knew of matters that no one else present could even guess at, as if she possessed some secret source of knowledge denied to the rest, yet which she dare not reveal. That slightly knowing smile bewitched Patrick's every thought.

How many times Patrick walked the ten miles or so from Hartshead to Apperley Bridge, on the other side of Bradford, during the months of June and July is not known, nor how often he would dream the ten miles back to his farm lodgings. But there were always matters to discuss with Fennell on the coming examination of the boys, it would be as well to keep in close touch with the headmaster on all points; and if William Morgan had to take a funeral in Bradford, well, it was the least a friend could do to walk over to the Grove and advise Jane Fennell that her lover was thus prevented from seeing her until later.

Such a short walk it was really, he was not in any way fatigued, and would be only too happy to show Miss Branwell something of the Yorkshire countryside, if her aunt could spare her for a few hours. So in the sunshine of long summer days Patrick and Maria walked together down the meadows to the banks of the swift flowing stream in the scented Calverley Woods, and to the romantic ruins of Kirkstall Abbey. There were also picnics with Morgan and Cousin Jane but, as August came, they were more often alone together: it was quite remarkable how often Morgan would lead Jane off to visit a place she had seen a score of times before.

It was an idyllic time for the new-found friends: Patrick soon knew that he loved Maria and was certain of the answering light in those brown eyes. They talked of religion and all the subjects they could think of to test the views of the other and find out a little more of their hearts; then as the realization of their mutual affection, although unspoken, became apparent to them both, there was that shy silence that is the plainest of confessions. Patrick, even at this time, would remember Mary Burder and determined that no delay should be encountered again; so he wrote Maria a letter and decided that, should the answer be favourably disposed, he would ask her to be his wife on the very next visit they made to the old abbey.

Maria Branwell was twenty-nine years of age, having been born on Tuesday, 15th April 1783, at Penzance. She was the fifth daughter of Thomas Branwell and his wife Anne (née Carne), Mrs Fennell being the former's sister. She was one of eleven children—three boys and eight girls, of whom four had died before 1812. Her parents had died only a few years previously, her father on 5th April 1808 and her mother on 19th December 1809, and were buried in the churchyard at St Mary's Church, Penzance.

Thomas Branwell, who was married on 28th November 1768, had been a prosperous merchant there, and also a councillor in the town. His son, Benjamin, had been Mayor of Penzance in 1809. The Branwells were a much respected family in this old Cornish town, the more so as tradition had it that their forebears were pirates : even in Maria's young days there would be plenty of smuggling in the Mount's Bay parish. The Branwells were a strong Methodist family, although all were baptized and married at Madron Church.

Maria had been left an annuity of £50, a not inconsiderable sum for a lady of those days. At the time her Aunt Fennell suggested she should come to Yorkshire to assist in the running of Woodhouse Grove School and be a companion for her cousin Jane, Maria had been living in Penzance with her elder sister Elizabeth and the youngest one, Charlotte. There she had led a quiet but happy life reading books from the Ladies' Book Club and doing much work for the poor. But it had been rather dull. Elizabeth, who according to her own statements had been a *belle* with many conquests, was no longer young (thirty-six), and Charlotte had but recently become engaged to her cousin, Joseph Branwell.

So Maria did not hesitate to accept her aunt's offer of a protracted stay in Yorkshire, making the long journey with a happy heart. She found, however, that Cousin Jane was in little need of company after all, but that poor Mrs Fennell was very much in need of assistance.

Patrick had decided on a lightning courtship, if possible. What could there be against such a match ? From the financial aspect, his salary added to Maria's annuity would be sufficient for their needs. They had found in discussion that neither of them was a religious bigot. True, Maria had been bred a Wesleyan Methodist but had a most open mind ; and was not he, an Evangelical minister of the Established Church, examining the boys at a Wesleyan Methodist Academy ? This time, surely, there would be no objection from a relative. He felt sure that John Fennell was sufficiently well disposed towards him to forward the strongest possible references to Maria's brother in Cornwall. But for all this, he sent off his letter to Maria with great anxiety and awaited her answer with much nervousness.

Unhappily, Patrick's letters to Maria Branwell have never come to light, but nine of hers to him are extant; and the first one was the reply for which he waited so anxiously.

To Rev. Patrick Bronte, A.B., Hartshead.

Wood House Grove, August 26th, 1812.

My Dear Friend, This address is sufficient to convince you that I not only permit, but approve of yours to me—I do indeed consider you as my *friend*; yet, when I consider how short a time I have had the pleasure of knowing you, I start at my own rashness, my heart fails, and did I not think that you would be disappointed and grieved, I believe I should be ready to spare myself the task of writing. Do not think that I am so wavering as to repent of what I have already said. No, believe me, this will never be the case, unless you give me cause for it.

You need not fear that you have been mistaken in my character. If I know anything of myself, I am incapable of making an ungenerous return to the smallest degree of kindness, much less to you whose attentions and conduct have been so particularly obliging. I will frankly confess that your behaviour and what I have seen and heard of your character has excited my warmest esteem and regard, and be assured you shall never have cause to repent of any confidence you may think proper to place in me, and that it will always be my endeavour to deserve the good opinion which you have formed, although human weakness may in some instances cause me to fall short. In giving you these assurances I do not depend upon my own strength, but I look to Him who has been my unerring guide through life, and in whose continued protection and assistance I confidently trust.

I thought on you much on Sunday, and feared you would not escape the rain. I hope you do not feel any bad effects from it? My cousin wrote you on Monday and expects this afternoon to be favoured with an answer. Your letter has caused me some foolish embarrassment, tho' in pity to my feelings they have been very sparing of their raillery.

I will now candidly answer your questions. The *politeness of others* can never make me forget your kind attentions, neither can I *walk our accustomed rounds* without thinking on you, and, why should I be ashamed to add, wishing for your presence. If you knew what were my feelings whilst writing this you would pity me. I wish to write the truth and give you satisfaction, yet fear to go too far, and exceed the bounds of propriety. But whatever I may say or write I will *never deceive* you, or *exceed the truth*. If you think I have not placed the *utmost confidence* in you, consider my situation, and ask yourself if I have not confided in you sufficiently, perhaps too much. I am very sorry that you will not have this till after to-morrow, but it was out of my power to write sooner. I rely on your goodness to pardon everything in this which may appear either too free or too stiff, and beg that you will consider me as a warm and faithful friend.

My uncle, aunt, and cousin unite in kind regards.

I must now conclude with again declaring myself to be

Yours sincerely, Maria Branwell.

It was more than Patrick had dared to hope and, as he folded the letter over again, he could have wept for very joy.

Two or three days afterwards, at the end of August 1812, Patrick and Maria went again to Kirkstall. There under an ivy-covered arch amidst the ruins of the old abbey he asked her to become his wife, his companion through this life and the next, the mother of his children. Maria said yes.

Here, faith may stretch her wings and fly,
To regions far beyond the sky,
    And dwell with God above ;
Whilst each celestial flame will play
Around the heart, with melting sway,
    And all the soul, be love.

For those who love literature more than the men and women who dream it, this moment was a consummation of great importance, but they were simply two young people in love and Patrick would remember the scene in those lines.

As they walked slowly back to Woodhouse Grove School, their arms lovingly entwined, Patrick could not help but reflect what an exciting and eventful year 1812 had been, and how happy he felt at the course of his life. There would be some years yet in which the tempo of his existence would be speedy before it finally slowed down under the crushing weight of continual grief.

There was nothing said on either side upon their return, and shortly afterwards Patrick left for his lodgings. Here he was forced to break the news to the Bedfords, as he wished to give them plenty of notice that he would be leaving them shortly. It was his desire to rent a house not too far from the church, large enough for his bride and himself and a potential family. By this time he had completed his examination of the scholars of Woodhouse Grove Academy and given his report to John Fennell.

But it was most difficult for Patrick to keep his own counsel for very long on such an exciting event, however much Maria might wish to accustom herself to the idea of marriage before informing her relatives, and he soon gave the news to some of his Hartshead friends, to Maria's slight dismay.

To Rev. Patrick Bronte, A.B., Hartshead.

         Wood House Grove, September 5th, 1812.

My Dearest Friend, I have just received your affectionate and very welcome letter, and although I shall not be able to send this until Monday, yet I cannot deny myself the pleasure of writing a few lines this evening, no longer considering it a task, but a pleasure, next to that of reading yours. I had the pleasure of hearing from Mr. Fennell, who was at Bradford on Thursday afternoon, that you had rested there all night. Had you proceeded, I am sure the walk would have been too much for you; such excessive fatigue, often repeated, must injure the strongest constitution. I am rejoiced to find that our forebodings were without cause. I had yesterday a letter from a very dear friend of mine, and had the satisfaction to learn by it that all at home are well. I feel with you the unspeakable obligations I am under to a merciful Providence—my heart swells with gratitude, and I feel an earnest desire that I may be enabled to make some suitable return to the Author of all my blessings. In general, I think I am enabled to cast my care upon Him, and then I experience a calm and peaceful serenity of mind which few things can destroy. In all my addresses to the throne of grace I never ask a blessing for myself but I beg the same for you, and considering the important station which you are called to fill, my prayers are proportionately fervent that you may be favoured with all the gifts and graces requisite for such a calling. O my dear friend, let us pray much that we may live lives holy and useful to each other and all around us!

Monday morn.—My cousin and I were yesterday at Calverley Church, where we heard Mr. Watman preach a very excellent sermon from "learn of Me, for I am meek and lowly of heart". He displayed the character of our Saviour in a most affecting and amiable light. I scarcely ever felt more charmed with his excellences, more grateful for his condescension, or more abased at my own unworthiness; but I lament that my heart is so little retentive of those pleasing and profitable impressions.

I pitied you in your solitude, and felt sorry that it was not in my power to enliven it. Have you not been too hasty in informing your friends of a certain event? Why did you not leave them to guess a little longer? I shrink from the idea of its being known to everybody. I do,

indeed, *sometimes* think of you, but I will not say how often, lest I raise
your vanity; and we sometimes talk of you and the doctor. But I believe
I should seldom mention your name myself were it not now and then
introduced by my cousin. I have never mentioned a word of what is past
to anybody. Had I thought this necessary I should have requested you
to do it. But I think there is no need, as by some means or other they
seem to have a pretty correct notion how matters stand betwixt us;
and as their hints, etc., meet with no contradiction from me, my silence
passes for confirmation. Mr. Fennell has not neglected to give me some
serious and encouraging advice, and my aunt takes frequent opportunities of dropping little sentences which I may turn to some advantage.
I have long had reason to know that the present state of things would
give pleasure to all parties. Your ludicrous account of the scene at the
Hermitage was highly diverting, we laughed heartily at it; but I fear it
will not produce all that compassion in Miss Fennell's breast which you
seem to wish. I will now tell you what I was thinking about and doing
at the time you mention. I was then toiling up the hill with Jane and
Mrs Clapham to take our tea at Mr. Tatham's, thinking on the evening
when I first took the same walk with you, and on the change which had
taken place in my circumstances and views since then—not wholly
without a wish that I had your arm to assist me, and your conversation
to shorten the walk. Indeed, all our walks have now an insipidity in
them which I never thought they would have possessed. When I work,
if I wish to get *forward* I may be glad that you are at a distance. Jane
begs me to assure you of her kind regards. Mr. Morgan is expected to
be here this evening. I must assume a bold and steady countenance to
meet his attacks!

I have now written a pretty long letter without reserve or caution,
and if all the sentiments of my heart are not laid open to you believe me
it is not because I wish them to be concealed, for, I hope there is nothing
there that would give you pain or displeasure. My most sincere and
earnest wishes are for your happiness and welfare, for this includes my
own. Pray much for me that I may be made a blessing and not a
hindrance to you. Let me not interrupt your studies nor intrude on that
time which ought to be dedicated to better purposes. Forgive my
freedom, my dearest friend, and rest assured that you are and ever will
be dear to

Maria Branwell.

Write very soon.

It was an autumn of delight for Patrick. The news was received with
great pleasure by the Fennells, whilst William Morgan, not without

much raillery, was most effusive in his congratulations; as he told Patrick, it had been all his doing anyway. There was an air of jollification at the prospect of the approaching double wedding, with gay picnic parties in the surrounding countryside, laughter and teasing by the drawing-room fire, and the old man who came for the letters was run off his feet in seeing they were delivered at Bierley and Hartshead. But in another part of the building the more sober-minded scholars begged for but one extra hour of prayer!

Patrick took his Maria back to Kirkstall Abbey many times and there, as lovers do, they planned their future, as if the writing of Destiny was in their power alone. Back at his lodgings he lived again the happy hours, remembering every detail of the scene, and his beloved's face. When his next volume of poems was published it included "Kirkstall Abbey, a fragment of a Romantic Tale". Some lines from this poem have already been quoted. Here is a further short extract:

> . . . Hail ruined tower! that like a learned sage,
> With lofty brow, looks thoughtful on the night;
>   The sable ebony, and silver white,
>   Thy ragged sides from age to age,
>   With charming art inlays,
>   When Luna's lovely rays,
>   Fall trembling on the night,
> And round the smiling landscape, throw,
> And on the ruined walls below,
>   Their mild uncertain light.
> How heavenly fair, the arches ivy-crowned,
>   Look forth on all around!
> Enchant the heart, and charm the sight,
> And give the soul serene delight! . . .

But long before Maria saw this poem she admitted shyly to her lover that some time ago she had written a short religious essay, which she hoped to revise and send to one of the periodicals for publication. It was "The Advantages of Poverty in Religious Concerns" and nearly a hundred years would pass before it was published; but Patrick was to keep it all his life and endorse it thus: "The above was written by my dear wife, and sent for insertion in one of the periodical publications. Keep it as a memorial of her."

Whilst full of compassion for the poor, although under the conviction that ". . . a wretched extremity of poverty is seldom experienced in this land of general benevolence . . ." it is the familiar argument that the poor are less prone to temptation than the rich and, if they are religious, have therefore a greater chance of salvation. In a word it was the usual Methodist palliative of the day, intended to sooth the needy and warn the wealthy. For the poor man ". . . free from the pride and prejudice of learning and philosophy, his mind is prepared to receive the truths that the Bible inculcates . . .". It ends, ". . . Taking this view of Poverty, where are the evils attending it ? Do they not appear to be imaginary ? But O, what words can express the great misery of those who suffer all the evils of poverty here, and that, too, by their own bad conduct, and have no hope of happiness hereafter, but rather have cause to fear that the end of this miserable life will be the beginning of another, infinitely more miserable, never, never to have an end !

"It surely is the duty of all Christians to exert themselves in every possible way to promote the instruction and conversion of the poor, and, above all, to pray with all the ardour of Christian faith and love that every poor man may be a religious man. M."

Meanwhile, Patrick's desire for a speedy end to the period of engagement was to be fulfilled. John Fennell advised Maria's family of the romance and no opposition was encountered from Cornwall. The weddings would have to take place soon, for the convenience of all concerned. Fennell had made his decision. As the Methodists became more and more independent of the Establishment his position as governor and headmaster of Woodhouse Grove became more untenable. He decided to take Holy Orders in the Established Church, and this being known, the Methodist Conference had no alternative but to ask for his immediate resignation. As he would therefore be leaving Woodhouse Grove at the beginning of the New Year, it was considered the more convenient that his daughter and niece should be married before the removal, and 29th December was the date chosen. As soon as this news reached Cornwall Charlotte Branwell and her cousin Joseph Branwell arranged for their wedding to take place on the same day and hour at Madron, the parish church of Penzance.

It was decided that the double wedding should take place at Guiseley Church, only three miles from Woodhouse Grove of which it was the parish church, and much nearer to William Morgan's Bierley than Hartshead. As Mr Fennell was not yet a minister of the Church, and in any case was to give both the brides away, Patrick and Morgan agreed that the simplest thing was for them to marry each other whilst Maria and Jane could act as bridesmaids to each other.

So it was arranged and Patrick concentrated his energies on renting a house suitable for his bride. He soon discovered an ideal three-storey house opposite the top of Clough Lane, at Hightown near Liversedge, about one mile from Hartshead Church.

Thus passed that time of waiting, beguiled for him by many visits to Woodhouse Grove, and many letters from Maria. This period is charmingly described in her own words.

To Rev. Patrick Bronte, A.B., Hartshead.

Wood House Grove, September 11th, 1812.

My Dearest Friend, Having spent the day yesterday at Miry Shay, a place near Bradford, I had not got your letter till my return in the evening, and consequently have only a short time this morning to write if I send it by this post. You surely do not think you *trouble* me by writing? No, I think I may venture to say if such were your opinion you would *trouble* me no more. Be assured, your letters are and I hope always will be received with extreme pleasure and read with delight. May our Gracious Father mercifully grant the fulfillment of your prayers! Whilst we depend entirely on Him for happiness, and receive each other and all our blessings as from His hands, what can harm us or make us miserable? Nothing temporal or spiritual.

Jane had a note from Mr. Morgan last evening, and she desires me to tell you that the Methodists' service in church hours is to commence next Sunday week. You may expect frowns and hard words from her when you make your appearance here again, for, if you recollect, she gave you a note to carry to the Doctor, and he has never received it. What have you done with it? If you can give a good account of it you may come to see us as soon as you please and be sure of a hearty welcome from all parties. Next Wednesday we have some thoughts, if the weather be fine, of going to Kirkstall Abbey once more, and I suppose your presence will not make the walk less agreeable to any of us.

The old man is come and waits for my letter. In expectation of seeing you on Monday or Tuesday next,—I remain, Yours faithfully and affectionately,

M.B.

Miry Shay was a fine old Jacobean building in Barkerend Road, Bradford.

To Rev. Patrick Bronte, A.B., Hartshead.

Wood House Grove, September 18th, 1812.

How readily do I comply with my dear Mr. B.'s request! You see, you have only to express your wishes, and as far as my power extends

I hesitate not to fulfil them. My heart tells me that it will always be my pride and pleasure to contribute to your happiness, nor do I fear that this will ever be inconsistent with my duty as a Christian. My esteem for you and my confidence in you is so great, that I firmly believe you will never exact anything from me which I could not conscientiously perform. I shall in future look to you for assistance and instruction whenever I may need them, and hope you will never withhold from me any advice or caution you may see necessary.

For some years I have been perfectly my own mistress, subject to no *control* whatever—so far from it, that my sisters who are many years older than myself, and even my dear mother, used to consult me in every case of importance, and scarcely ever doubted the propriety of my opinions and actions. Perhaps you will be ready to accuse me of vanity in mentioning this, but you must consider that I do not *boast* of it, I have many times felt it a disadvantage; and although, I thank God, it never led me into error, yet, in circumstances of perplexity and doubt, I have deeply felt the want of a guide and instructor.

At such times I have seen and felt the necessity of supernatural aid, and by fervent applications to a throne of grace I have experienced that my heavenly Father is able and willing to supply the place of every earthly friend. I shall now no longer feel this want, this sense of helpless weakness, for I believe a kind Providence has intended that I shall find in you every earthly friend united; nor do I fear to trust myself under your protection, or shrink from your control. It is pleasant to be subject to those we love, especially when they never exert their authority but for the good of the subject. How few would write in this way ! But I do not fear that *you* will make a bad use of it. You tell me to write my thoughts, and thus as they occur I freely let my pen run away with them.

Sat. morn.—I do not know whether you dare show your face here again or not after the blunder you have committed. When we got to the house on Thursday evening, even before we were within the doors, we found that Mr. and Mrs. Bedford had been there, and that they had requested you to mention their intention of coming—a single hint of which you never gave ! Poor I too came in for a share in the hard words which were bestowed upon you, for they all agreed that I was the cause of it. Mr. Fennell said you were certainly *mazed*, and talked of sending you to York [asylum], etc. And even I begin to think that *this*, together with the *note*, bears some marks of *insanity* ! However, I shall suspend my judgement until I hear what excuse you can make for yourself. I suppose you will be quite ready to make one of some kind or another.

Yesterday I performed a difficult and yet a pleasing task in writing to my sisters. I thought I never should accomplish the end for which the letter was designed; but after a good deal of perambulation I gave them to understand the nature of my engagement with you, with the motives and inducements which led me to form such an engagement, and that in consequence of it I should not see them again so soon as I had intended. I concluded by expressing a hope that they would not be less pleased with the information than were my friends here. I think they will not suspect me to have made a wrong step, their partiality for me is so great. And their affection for me will lead them to rejoice in my welfare, even though it should diminish somewhat of their own. I shall think the time tedious till I hear from you, and must beg you will write as soon as possible. Pardon me, my dear friend, if I again caution you against giving way to a weakness of which I have heard you complain. When you find your heart oppressed and your thoughts too much engrossed by one subject let prayer be your refuge—this you no doubt know by experience to be a sure remedy, and a relief from every care and error. Oh, that we had more of the spirit of prayer! I feel that I need it much.

Breakfast-time is near, I must bid you farewell for the time, but rest assured you will always share in the prayers and heart of your own

Maria.

Mr. Fennell has crossed my letter to my sisters. With his usual goodness he has supplied my *deficiencies*, and spoken of me in terms of commendation of which I wish I were more worthy. Your character he has likewise displayed in the most favourable light; and I am sure they will not fail to love and esteem you though unknown.

All here unite in kind regards. Adieu.

To Rev. Patrick Bronte, A.B., Hartshead.

Wood House Grove, September 23rd, 1812.

My Dearest Friend, Accept of my warmest thanks for your kind affectionate letter, in which you have rated mine so highly that I really blush to read my own praises. Pray that God would enable me to deserve all the kindness you manifest towards me, and to act consistently with the good opinion you entertain of me—then I shall indeed be a helpmeet for you, and to be this shall at all times be the care and study of my future life. We have had to-day a large party of the Bradford folks—the Rands, Fawcetts, Dobsons, etc. My thoughts often strayed from the company, and I would have gladly left them to follow my present employment. To write to and receive letters from my friends were always among my chief enjoyments, but none ever gave me so much pleasure as those which I receive from and write to my newly

adopted friend. I am by no means sorry you have given up all thought
of the house you mentioned. With my cousin's help I have made known
your plans to my uncle and aunt. Mr. Fennell immediately coincided
with that which respects your present abode, and observed that it had
occurred to him before, but that he had not had an opportunity of
mentioning it to you. My aunt did not fall in with it so readily, but her
objections did not appear to me to be very weighty. For my own part, I
feel all the force of your arguments in favour of it, and the objections
are so trifling that they can scarcely be called objections. My cousin is
of the same opinion. Indeed, you have such a method of considering
and digesting a plan before you make it known to your friends, that
you run very little risk of incurring their disapprobations, or of having
your schemes frustrated. I greatly admire your talents this way—may
they never be perverted by being used in a bad cause! And whilst they
are exerted for good purposes, may they prove irresistible! If I may
judge from your letter, this middle scheme is what would please you
best, so that if there should arise no new objection to it, perhaps it will
prove the best you can adopt. However, there is yet sufficient time to
consider it further. I trust in this and every other circumstance you
will be guided by the wisdom that cometh from above—a portion of
which I doubt not has guided you hitherto. A belief of this, added to the
complete satisfaction with which I read your reasonings on the subject,
made me a ready convert to your opinions. I hope nothing will occur
to induce you to change your intention of spending the next week at
Bradford. Depend on it you shall have letter for letter ; but may we not
hope to see you here during that time, surely you will not think the way
more tedious than usual ? I have not heard any particulars respecting
the church since you were at Bradford. Mr. Rawson is now there, but
Mr. Hardy and his brother are absent, and I understand nothing
decisive can be accomplished without them. Jane expects to hear something more to-morrow. Perhaps ere this reaches you, you will have
received some intelligence respecting it from Mr. Morgan. If you have
no other apology to make for your blunders than that which you have
given me, you must not expect to be excused, for I have not mentioned
it to any one, so that however, it may clear your character in my
opinion it is not likely to influence any other person. Little, very little,
will induce me to cover your faults with a veil of charity. I already feel
a kind of participation in all that concerns you. All praises and censures
bestowed on you must equally affect me. Your joys and sorrows must be
mine. Thus shall the one be increased and the other diminished.
While this is the case we shall, I hope, always find "life's cares" to be
"comforts". And may we feel every trial and distress, for such must be

our lot at times, bind us nearer to God and to each other! My heart earnestly joins in your comprehensive prayers. I trust they will unitedly ascend to a throne of grace, and through the Redeemer's merits procure for us peace and happiness here and a life of eternal felicity hereafter. Oh, what sacred pleasure there is in the idea of spending an eternity together in perfect and uninterrupted bliss! This should encourage us to the utmost exertion and fortitude. But whilst I write, my own words condemn me—I am ashamed of my own indolence and backwardness to duty. May I be more careful, watchful, and active than I have ever yet been!

My uncle, aunt, and Jane request me to send their kind regards, and they will be happy to see you any time next week whenever you can conveniently come down from Bradford. Let me hear from you soon—I shall expect a letter on Monday. Farewell, my dearest friend. That you may be happy in yourself and very useful to all around you is the daily earnest prayer of yours truly,

Maria Branwell.

To Rev. Patrick Bronte, A.B., Hartshead.
Wood House Grove, October 3rd, 1812.

How could my dear friend so cruelly disappoint me? Had he known how much I had set my heart on having a letter this afternoon, and how greatly I felt the disappointment when the bag arrived and I found there was nothing for me, I am sure he would not have permitted a little matter to hinder him. But whatever was the reason of your not writing, I cannot believe it to have been neglect or unkindness, therefore I do not in the least blame you, I only beg that in future you will judge of my feelings by your own, and if possible never let me expect a letter without receiving one. You know in my last which I sent you at Bradford I said it would not be in my power to write the next day, but begged I might be favoured with hearing from you on Saturday, and you will not wonder that I hoped you would have complied with this request. It has just occurred to my mind that it is possible this note was not received; if so, you have felt disappointed likewise; but I think this is not very probable, as the old man is particularly careful, and I never heard of his losing anything committed to his care. The note which I allude to was written on Thursday morning, and you should have received it before you left Bradford. I forget what its contents were, but I know it was written in haste and concluded abruptly. Mr. Fennell talks of visiting Mr. Morgan to-morrow. I cannot lose the opportunity of sending this to the office by him as you will then have it a day sooner, and if you have been daily expecting to hear from me, twenty-four hours are of some importance. I really am concerned to find that this, what many would deem trifling incident, has so much disturbed my mind. I fear I should not have slept in peace to-night if I had been deprived of this opportunity of relieving my mind by scribbling to you, and now I lament that you cannot possibly receive this till Monday. May I hope that there is now some intelligence on the way to me ? or must my patience be tried till I see you on Wednesday ? But what nonsense am I writing ! Surely after this you can have no doubt that you possess all my heart. Two months ago I could not possibly have believed that you would ever engross so much of my thoughts and affections, and far less could I have thought that I should be so forward as to tell you so. I believe I must forbid you to come here again unless you can assure me that you will not steal any more of my regard. Enough of this ; I must bring my pen to order, for if I were to suffer myself to revise what I have written I should be tempted to throw it in the fire, but I have determined that you shall see my whole heart. I have not yet informed you that I received your serio-comic note on Thursday afternoon, for which accept my thanks.

My cousin desires me to say that she expects a long poem on her birthday, when she attains the important age of twenty-one. Mr. Fennell joins with us in requesting that you will not fail to be here on Wednesday, as it is decided that on Thursday we are to go to the Abbey if the weather, etc., permits.

Sunday morning. I am not sure if I do right in adding a few lines to-day, but knowing that it will give you pleasure I wish to finish, that you may have it to-morrow. I will just say that if my feeble prayers can aught avail, you will find your labours this day both pleasant and profitable, as they concern your own soul and the souls of those to whom you preach. I trust in your hours of retirement you will not forget to pray for me. I assure you I need every assistance to help me forward ; I feel that my heart is more ready to attach itself to earth than heaven. I sometimes think there never was a mind so dull and inactive as mine is with regard to spiritual things.

I must not forget to thank you for the pamphlets and tracts which you sent us from Bradford. I hope we shall make good use of them. I must now take my leave. I believe I need scarcely assure you that I am yours truly and very affectionately,

Maria Branwell.

But Jane Fennell did not obtain her "long poem" on her twenty-first birthday—Patrick's Muse was now working only for Maria. Hence a copy of *Cottage Poems* was presented: "To Miss Fennell—By the Author—as a token of his purest Friendship and Christian Love."

To Rev. Patrick Bronte, A.B., Hartshead.
                    Wood House Grove, October 21st, 1812.

With the sincerest pleasure do I retire from company to converse with him whom I love beyond all others. Could my beloved friend see my heart he would then be convinced that the affection I bear him is not at all inferior to that which he feels for me—indeed I sometimes think that in truth and constancy it excels. But do not think from this that I entertain any suspicions of your sincerity—no, I firmly believe you to be sincere and generous, and doubt not in the least that you feel all you express. In return, I entreat that you will do me the justice to believe that you have not only a *very large portion* of my *affection* and *esteem*, but *all* that I am capable of feeling, and from henceforth measure my feelings by your own. Unless my love for you were very great how could I so contentedly give up my home and all my friends— a home I loved so much that I have often thought nothing could bribe me to renounce it for any great length of time together, and friends with whom I have been so long accustomed to share all the vicissitudes of joy and sorrow? Yet these have lost their weight, and though I cannot always think of them without a sigh, yet the anticipation of sharing with you all the pleasures and pains, the cares and anxieties of life, of contributing to your comfort and becoming the companion of your pilgrimage, is more delightful to me than any other prospect which this world can possibly present. I expected to have heard from you on Saturday last, and can scarcely refrain from thinking you unkind to keep me in suspense two whole days longer than was necessary, but it is well that my patience should be sometimes tried, or I might entirely lose it, and this would be a loss indeed! Lately I have experienced a considerable increase of hopes and fears, which tend to destroy the calm uniformity of my life. These are not unwelcome, as they enable me to discover more of the evils and errors of my heart, and discovering them I hope through grace to be enabled to correct and amend them. I am sorry to say that my cousin has had a very serious cold, but to-day I think she is better; her cough seems less, and I hope we shall be able to come to Bradford on Saturday afternoon, where we intend to stop till Tuesday. You may be sure we shall not soon think of taking such another journey as the last. I look forward with pleasure to Monday, when I hope to meet with you, for as we are no *longer twain* separation is painful, and to meet must ever be attended with joy.

Thursday morning.—I intended to have finished this before breakfast, but unfortunately slept an hour too long. I am every moment in expectation of the old man's arrival. I hope my cousin is still better to-day; she requests me to say that she is much obliged to you for your kind enquiries and the concern you express for her recovery. I take all possible care of her, but yesterday she was naughty enough to venture into the yard without her bonnet!

As you do not say anything of going to Leeds I conclude you have not been. We shall most probably hear from the Dr. this afternoon. I am much pleased to hear of his success at Bierley! O that you may both be zealous and successful in your efforts for the salvation of souls, and may your own lives be holy, and your hearts greatly blessed while you are engaged in administering to the good of others! I should have been very glad to have had it in my power to lessen your fatigue and cheer your spirits by my exertions on Monday last. I will hope that this pleasure is still reserved for me. In general, I feel a calm confidence in the providential care and continued mercy of God, and when I consider His past deliverances and past favours I am led to wonder and adore. A sense of my small returns of love and gratitude to Him often abases me and makes me think I am little better than those who profess no religion. Pray for me, my dear friend, and rest assured that you possess a very, very large portion of the prayers, thoughts, and heart of yours truly,

M. Branwell.

Mr. Fennell requests Mr. Bedford to call on the man who has had orders to make blankets for the Grove and desire him to send them as soon as possible. Mr. Fennell will be greatly obliged to Mr. Bedford if he will take this trouble.

Poor Patrick could not forget the unfortunate affair of Mary Burder and its abrupt termination. Like all men who have the canker of unrequited love within their breasts he could not believe Maria returned his love in full measure. Always in his mind lurked the fear that someone would yet interfere to prevent his marriage taking place. But his doubts were eventually removed by Maria Branwell's love and patience; and her next letter shows that though all fears have not been quite cast out, there is a more happy spirit as the golden day approaches. We also learn that, in order to speed the happy event, Maria decided not to return to Penzance but ordered her belongings to be sent to Yorkshire. Thus she allowed to pass her last opportunity to see the old home she had loved so much.

To Rev. Patrick Bronte, A.B., Hartshead.

Wood House Grove, November 18th, 1812.

My Dear Saucy Pat, Now don't you think you deserve this epithet far more than I do that which you have given me ? I really know not what to make of the beginning of your last ; the winds, waves, and rocks almost stunned me. I thought you were giving me the account of some terrible dream, or that you had had a presentiment of the fate of my poor box, having no idea that your lively imagination could make so much of the slight reproof conveyed in my last. What will you say when you get a *real, downright scolding* ? Since you show such a readiness to atone for your offences after receiving a mild rebuke, I am inclined to hope you will seldom deserve a severe one. I accept with pleasure your atonement, and send you a free and full forgiveness. But I cannot allow that your affection is more deeply rooted than mine. However, we will dispute no more about this, but rather embrace every opportunity to prove its sincerity and strength by acting in every respect as friends and fellow-pilgrims travelling the same road, actuated by the same motives, and having in view the same end. I think if our lives are spared twenty years hence I shall then pray for you with the same, if not greater, fervour and delight that I do now. I am pleased that you are so fully convinced of my candour, for to know that you suspected me of a deficiency in this virtue would grieve and mortify me beyond expression. I do not derive any merit from the possession of it, for in me it is constitutional. Yet I think where it is possessed it will rarely exist alone, and where it is wanted there is reason to doubt the existence of almost every other virtue. As to the other qualities which your partiality attributes to me, although I rejoice to know that I stand so high in your good opinion, yet I blush to think in how small a degree I possess them. But it shall be the pleasing study of my future life to gain such an increase of grace and wisdom as shall enable me to act up to your highest expectations and prove to you a helpmeet. I firmly believe the Almighty has set us apart for each other ; may we, by earnest, frequent prayer, and every possible exertion, endeavour to fulfil His will in all things ! I do not, cannot, doubt your love, and here I freely declare I love you above all the world besides. I feel very, very grateful to the great Author of all our mercies for His unspeakable love and condescension towards us, and desire "to show forth my gratitude not only with my lips, but by my life and conversation". I indulge a hope that our mutual prayers will be answered, and that our intimacy will tend much to promote our temporal and eternal interest.

I suppose you never expected to be much the richer for me, but I

am sorry to inform you that I am still poorer than I thought myself.
I mentioned having sent for my books, clothes, etc. On Saturday
evening about the time you were writing the description of your
imaginery shipwreck, I was reading and feeling the effects of a real one,
having then received a letter from my sister giving me an account of
the vessel in which she had sent my box being stranded on the coast of
Devonshire, in consequence of which the box was dashed to pieces
with the violence of the sea, and all my little property, with the exception
of a very few articles, swallowed up in the mighty deep. If this should
not prove the prelude to something worse, I shall think little of it, as it
is the first disastrous circumstance which has occurred since I left my
home, and having been so highly favoured it would be highly ungrateful
in me were I to suffer this to dwell much on my mind.

Mr. Morgan was here yesterday, indeed he only left this morning.
He mentioned having written to invite you to Bierley on Sunday next,
and if you complied with his request it is likely that we shall see you
both here on Sunday evening. As we intend going to Leeds next week,
we should be happy if you would accompany us on Monday or Tuesday.
I mention this by desire of Miss Fennell, who begs to be remembered
affectionately to you. Notwithstanding Mr. Fennell's complaints and
threats, I doubt not but he will give you a cordial reception whenever
you think fit to make your appearance at the Grove. Which you may
likewise be assured of receiving from your ever truly affectionate

Maria.

Both the doctor and his lady very much wish to know what kind of
address we make use of in our letters to each other. I think they would
scarcely hit on *this* ! !

There is indeed a sad echo to the words "if our lives are spared
twenty years".

Happily for lovers of the Brontës, who rightly treasure every scrap
of their writings, Maria's little essay was not lost; and happily for
Patrick, who could retain it as another souvenir of his wife, one of her
books was not in the box but had been brought with her when she came
to Yorkshire. It was a small copy of the *Imitation* inscribed "M. Branwell, July 1807". The title page read:

"An extract of the Christian's Pattern : or, a treatise on the imitation
of Christ. Written in Latin by Thomas à Kempis. Abridged and
published in English by John Wesley, M.A., London. Printed at the
Conference office, North Green, Finsbury Square. G. Story, agent.
Sold by G. Whitfield, City Road. 1803. Price bound 1s."

Patrick passed this little book over to the safe keeping of Charlotte, as we learn from the fly leaf :

"C. Brontë's book. This book was given to me in July 1826. It is not certainly known who is the author, but it is generally supposed that Thomas à Kempis is. I saw a reward of £10,000 offered in the *Leeds Mercury* to any one who could find out for a certainty who is the author."

At last December arrived and Maria wrote her final letter to Patrick before their wedding :

To Rev. Patrick Bronte, A.B., Hartshead
                    Wood House Grove, December 5th, 1812.

My Dearest Friend, So you *thought* that *perhaps I might* expect to hear from you. As the case was so doubtful, and you were in such great haste, you might as well have deferred writing a few days longer, for you seem to suppose it is a matter of perfect indifference to me whether I hear from you or not. I believe I once requested you to judge of my feelings by your own—am I to think that *you* are thus indifferent ? I feel very unwilling to entertain such an opinion, and am grieved that you should suspect me of such a cold, heartless, attachment. But I am too serious on the subject ; I only meant to rally you a little on the beginning of your last, and to tell you that I fancied there was a coolness in it which none of your former letters had contained. If this fancy was groundless, forgive me for having indulged it, and let it serve to convince you of the sincerity and warmth of my affection. Real love is ever apt to suspect that it meets not with an equal return ; you must not wonder then that my fears are sometimes excited. My pride cannot bear the idea of a diminution of your attachment, or to think that it is stronger on my side than on yours. But I must not permit my pen so fully to disclose the feelings of my heart, nor will I tell you whether I am pleased or not at the thought of seeing you on the appointed day.

Miss Fennell desires her kind regards, and, with her father, is extremely obliged to you for the trouble you have taken about the carpet, and has no doubt but it will give full satisfaction. They think there will be no occasion for the green cloth.

We intend to set about making the cakes here next week, but as the fifteen or twenty persons whom you mention live probably somewhere in your neighbourhood, I think it will be most convenient for Mrs. B. [Bedford] to make a small one for the purpose of distributing there, which will save us the difficulty of sending so far.

You may depend on my learning my lessons as rapidly as they are given me. I am already tolerably perfect in the A B C, etc. I am much obliged to you for the pretty little hymn which I have already got by heart, but cannot promise to sing it scientifically, though I will endeavour to gain a little more assurance.

Since I began this Jane put into my hand Lord Lyttleton's "Advice to a Lady". When I read those lines, "Be never cool reserve with passion joined, with caution choose, but then be fondly kind, etc.," my heart smote me for having in some cases used too much reserve towards you. Do you think you have any cause to complain of me? If you do, let me know it. For were it in my power to prevent it, I would in no instance occasion you the least pain or uneasiness. I am certain no one ever loved you with an affection more pure, constant, tender, and ardent than that which I feel. Surely this is not saying too much; it is the truth, and I trust you are worthy to know it. I long to improve in ever religious and moral quality, that I may be a help, and if possible an ornament to you. Oh let us pray much for wisdom and grace to fill our appointed stations with propriety, that we may enjoy satisfaction in our own souls, edify others, and bring glory to the name of Him who has so wonderfully preserved, blessed, and brought us together.

If there is anything in the commencement of this which looks like pettishness, forgive it; my mind is now completely divested of every feeling of the kind, although I own I am sometimes too apt to be overcome by this disposition.

Let me have the pleasure of hearing from you again as soon as convenient. This writing is uncommonly bad, but I too am in haste.

Adieu, my dearest. I am your affectionate and sincere

Maria.

Soon after this letter was written all the doubts and anxieties under which both Patrick and Maria had laboured were to vanish, for on Tuesday, 29th December 1812, they were married at Guiseley Church.

CHAPTER 9

Marriage

THE church of St Oswald, Guiseley, stands on a knoll near the town cross and stocks, with an extensive churchyard sloping away from it on all sides. Dedicated to the second Christian king of Northumbria, A.D. 634-42, who was killed near Oswestry (Oswald's tree) while fighting Penda, the heathen king of Mercia, and who is buried in Durham Cathedral, a church has stood on this site since about 1150. The first evidences of Christian worship are fragments of Anglican cross carving and the shaft of an Early English cross dating from the ninth century. Guiseley with a large area of land centred in Otley was given by the king of Northumbria to the Archbishop of York in about the seventh century. Five hundred years later the parish of Guiseley was formed and included Esholt, Yeadon, Rawdon and Horsforth.

Since 1812 there have been many alterations and additions to the parish church but there remains much that Patrick and Maria would see as they came to its communion table to be married. There is the fourteenth-century tower, with its peculiar parapet overhanging on three sides, the Norman south doorway, the line of Norman quatrefoil pillars and semi-circular arches, the thirteenth-century chapel of St Mary now filled with pews and one box pew, carved in the style of the late seventeenth century, chairs of the seventeenth and eighteenth centuries, and St Oswald's chapel itself, originally built in the mid-thirteenth century and containing, on the north wall of the sanctuary, a rectangular opening, once fitted with a door, that had been used as an aumbry or cupboard for the church plate or, possibly, as an anchorite cell, reliquary, or outside confessional. Many other features survive, but for lovers of the Brontës the most important are the Jacobean wooden communion rails, dating from 1682, before which Patrick and Maria knelt on their wedding day.

In those days the organ and choir were at the back of the church by the tower, and oak Jacobean box-pews with their family table and chairs were to be seen in the body of the church. Finally, Patrick would have seen the Rectory Hall which stands at the bottom of the knoll on the south-east side of the church. Although restored in 1910, the building in its present form with its mullioned windows, wide-arched doorway and fireplaces, corbels and gargoyles, was reconstructed from an older hall in 1601 by the then rector whose name will interest lovers of *Shirley*, for it was Robert Moore. He placed the following inscription in Latin, over the doorway: "Anno domini 1601. The house of the faithful pastor, not of the blind leader; not of the robber; the house of Robert Moore, rector of the church, founder of the house."

To the "altar" then, came Patrick and his Maria; and it is to be hoped that a ray of winter sunshine broke in upon them as they knelt there, so full of love and hope. Their loyal old friend William Morgan married them. Then John Fennell gave his daughter Jane, a bridesmaid only a minute before, to William Morgan; and while Maria Bronté performed the role of bridesmaid to her cousin, Patrick joined William and Jane in holy wedlock, and down in Penzance Charlotte Branwell was united to her cousin Joseph. Thus two sisters and four cousins were married within that hour.

There followed an exodus to the vestry to sign the old registers, which dated in a complete form from 1584, although there were entries as far back as 1556. The excited and happy party crowded into the little room and the entries were made thus:

The Reverend Patrick Bronte of the Parish of Birstall and Maria Branwell of this Parish, Spinster, were married in this Church by License this 29th Day of December in the Year one thousand 800 & 12. By me W. Morgan officiating minister.
This marriage was solemnised
            between us   Patrick Brontě
                            Maria Branwell.
      in the Presence of   John Fennell
                            Elizabeth Parton
                            — Barber.

Then followed:

Wm. Morgan of the Parish of Bradford, Minister of Bierley and Jane Branwell Fennell of this Parish—
      Solemnised by me Patrick Brontě
            Between us   William Morgan
                            Jane Branwell Fennell.
      In the Presence of   Elizabeth Parton
                            Jane Parton
                            John Fennell.

After these two entries, that particular volume of the registers was not used again for the year was ending, and the rest of the book was left blank.

As the party came out of the church into the cold December air, there would be the usual knot of small boys standing down by the wall. No doubt they would run off in disgust—"it were only two parsons getting wed"—and they would miss the chance to say later that they had seen the parents of the Brontës on their marriage day.

In contrast to the narrative of Mrs Gaskell, who after describing their daughter Charlotte's honeymoon wrote, "Henceforward the sacred doors of home are closed upon her married life," our veil descends upon Patrick and Maria during that romantic period only. The probability is that there was no honeymoon; their secret will remain untold.

In the *Gentleman's Magazine* for 1813 appeared on page 179 : "Lately at Guiseley, near Bradford, by the Revd. W. Morgan, minister of Bierley, Revd. P. Brontë, B.A., minister of Hartshead-cum-Clifton, to Maria, third daughter of the late T. Branwell, Esq., of Penzance. At the same time, by the Revd. P. Brontë, Revd. W. Morgan, to the only daughter of Mr. John Fennell, Head-master of the Wesleyan Academy, near Bradford." (Again the printers gave Patrick's surname the diaeresis and anglicized his degree : Maria is described as the third daughter, not the fifth, as two of her sisters had died young, leaving her as the third surviving daughter.)

In the parish church of Guiseley, which the couple had just left, in the very St Oswald's Chapel where they had been united, there would one day be placed a plaque to commemorate that event. "At this rail on Monday [Tuesday] 29th December 1812, Patrick Brontë, minister of Hartshead was married to Maria Branwell. . . ." As they sped away to a new life together, Patrick and Maria could little have thought the event worth recording, but the reason would have surprised them even more. The plaque would continue, ". . . Among the most famous writers of our country are numbered their three daughters Charlotte, Emily and Ann[e]."

Maria must have liked her new home. Situated on high ground facing the top of Clough Lane, which dived down into a deep hollow and climbed up again to Hartshead Church, it was a strong three-storeyed stone building with a western aspect, and Patrick, returning from the church, would see his home facing him all the way as he descended into the "bottom" and mounted the other side.

Clough House contained three large living-rooms and a kitchen, five bedrooms and two attics. The main stairway, consisting of twelve stone steps, led up to a large staircase window which reached down to the level of the landing, and, being at the back of the house, gave a fine view over Cleckheaton. From the kitchen with its two stone mullioned windows, a small stairway led to a back bedroom. There was a short entrance hall, beautifully panelled throughout, as were the hall doors and the front door. The living-rooms were floored with oak boards, whilst the windows in the front of the house were very wide, and reached almost to floor-level. From these there was a splendid view towards the villages of Hartshead and Roberttown on the opposite rise. The main room on the left as you entered the house contained two massive oak beams.

The entrance to the house was a flat stone doorway, and there was a tiny plot of front garden railed off from the road. The back of the building gave directly on to fields. Built on to its right-hand wall and fronting on the road was a large two-storeyed barn.

This, then, was the home Patrick had rented for his bride, the house that would act as pro-parsonage in the absence of any official residence : a lovely house, happily still standing today.

Only three days before his marriage Patrick had obtained an invaluable "nest-egg" by selling two trees which stood in the field belonging to Clough House and near a house belonging to the purchaser.

Received from Mr. Thos. Milnes of Cliff Hill, Warley, £3-3-0, for two Ash-trees, consisting of twenty one feet of wood, and standing nearest to his house, which trees are to stand as long as they may be considered ornaments, by the said Mr. Milnes, and when they cease to be ornaments, to be cut down by him and carried away—Decr 26th 1812

P. Brontè, Minister of Hartshead-cum-Clifton.
N.B. The two ashes were valued at £3-3/ & the small plain [sic] tree adjoining was given in the value^n . . .

Patrick had engaged a local woman to act as servant at Clough House, but even so, it was very lonely for Maria whilst her husband was away on his duties in the parish. There still echoed the faint murmurings of Luddite discontent, and she would recall the threat that had been voiced against Mrs Cartwright. Patrick was often anxious as he walked across the heath to some outlying cottage ; there were but few houses in Hightown in those days and now that the military were somewhat dispersed, an attack on the two defenceless women in Clough House would have been easy enough. There was of course one loaded pistol that could be left at home with full instructions as to its use. The trouble died away, however, and no further violence occurred. There were certainly many growls of hatred during the first few days Maria spent in her new home—they were natural enough, for news of the executions had arrived from York. But all remained peaceful at Hartshead, although the hangings would never be forgotten.

When Patrick came home, it was very different: Maria was so happy, so contented, that she did not feel the lack of society. Even the distance that separated her from her relatives and friends, both in Cornwall and the other side of Bradford, was forgotten in that first flush of domestic bliss. Patrick would sit by the table working at his sermons—or were they new poems? Maria could not really tell, as she sat by the fire at her sewing. Most women of that time could ply their needle with skill, but Maria was especially talented in that direction, as her aunt had known well when she had suggested she should come to Yorkshire to aid her in running the domestic side of the school. On her eighth birthday she had finished the inevitable sampler, showing more than ordinary skill. Maria Branwell ended her sampler on 15th April 1791. It was embroidered with the following text: "Flee from sin as from a serpent, for if thou comest too near to it, it will bite thee. The teeth thereof are as the teeth of a lion to slay the souls of men." Now, however, it was the making of shirts with their frilled fronts and wrist-bands that occupied her time.

By and by Patrick would cease writing—he had to be more careful of his eyes now—and Maria would set aside her sewing. They would gather closer round the fire, and to each other, and talk of religion, politics, poetry and the like, often interspersed with many romantic nothings. After supper there would be more talk of the same nature, followed by a reading from the Bible, before going to bed. But it was by no means a life all as quiet as this: Patrick took his wife to Dewsbury to dine with the Buckworths on many occasions and return visits were often paid to Clough House. There were also calls on other of his old friends at Dewsbury—young Mr Halliley, and a Mr and Mrs Marmaduke Fox who lived at a house called Nab End at Hanging Heaton, outside Dewsbury. The Foxes had known Patrick when he had visited the district in the course of his clerical duties there, Hanging Heaton having no church of its own then, and were most pressing with their kind invitations. So there was gaiety and social intercourse and Patrick was proud of his Maria and she of him. But all who saw Maria noticed how very delicate she looked. Joseph Tolson, still faithfully following his former curate, continued to come over to hear Patrick preach at Hartshead Church and would often be invited home for a meal at Clough House. He would express the feelings of them all when he later reported that he often visited Patrick "and his fragile looking bride".

Occasionally Maria would accompany her husband on his walks across the moors, but generally found the high winds too trying and would wait his return at Lousey Thorn, where Mr and Mrs Bedford would make her welcome. On Sundays she would sit in the little church and listen to her Pat as he preached God's message to the congregation, afterwards leaning on his arm as they climbed Clough Lane to return home.

When Maria awoke on the morning of 15th April 1813, her thirtieth birthday, there was Patrick with a poem all ready for the occasion. To Mary Burder it had been "Verses—sent to a Lady on Her Birth-day", but this time it was "Lines, addressed to a Lady, on her Birth-day"; and Maria was favoured with a pleasanter poem than Mary had received. It would join "Kirkstall Abbey" in Patrick's third volume of verse.

> Sweet is this April morn, . . .
> Maria, let us walk, and breathe, the morning air,
> And hear the cuckoo sing,—
> And every tuneful bird, that woos the gentle spring.
> Throughout the budding grove,
> Softly coos the turtle-dove,
>   The primrose pale,
>   Perfumes the gale,
> The modest daisy, and the violet blue,
> Inviting, spread their charms for you.
> How much enhanced is all this bliss to me,
> Since it is shared, in mutual joy with thee ! . . .

Meanwhile John Fennell had left Woodhouse Grove to take Holy Orders in the Established Church; but not before complaints had been lodged against Mrs Fennell's management of the household and the poor, harassed matron was heartily pleased to lay down her office. Shortly afterwards the Rev. Jabez Bunting, who had done so much to lead the Methodists away from the Established Church, secured the appointment of headmaster at Woodhouse Grove Academy for his brother-in-law, the Rev. Thomas Fletcher, grandfather of "Deas Cromarty" (Mrs Robert Watson). Patrick was never asked to examine the scholars there again, for the Methodists in Yorkshire were completing their severance from the parent Church. But Woodhouse Grove had given him his bride and he was content; the journey to Apperley Bridge would now have seemed very long and tedious indeed. Yet Patrick would live to have the satisfaction of seeing his daughter Emily put this Jabez Bunting into the pillory and make his pompous antics in the pulpit look ridiculous. Her description of Jabes Branderham in *Wuthering Heights* and of the pandemonium in the overcrowded church, was a true account of the scene at the opening by Bunting in 1833 of the new school chapel at Woodhouse Grove. Thus one of Patrick's memories contributed a mite to that great classic !

Jabez Bunting, D.D., who died before Patrick, in June 1858, aged seventy-nine, had been superintendent of the Halifax Circuit during the recent Luddite Riots. He had attacked the Luddites severely from his pulpit and, inevitably, his life was threatened also. Of this he boasted : "The bullet is not yet cast that is to shoot me." Unlike Patrick, however, he refused to permit the burying of any rebel dead.

Yet both he and his brother-in-law, Thomas Fletcher, liked Patrick —as Bunting's son recalled. ". . . My Uncle always spoke of Mr Brontë in terms of the highest esteem, and did not recognise the picture of him which his daughter's friend [Mrs Gaskell] has drawn for the public amusement."

It was the personal arrogance of Jabez Bunting that disgusted Patrick and Morgan and finally alienated Fennell, godson of Fletcher of Madeley though he was. The energy of the man to free Methodism finally from liaison with the Establishment, from State control, was not in any way repugnant to them ; it would have retained the loyalty of Fennell and the sorrowful sympathy of Patrick and Morgan. The ecclesiastical history of England was largely shaped in their lifetime by three great men : Wesley, Simeon and Bunting ; but Patrick and his friends were too close personally to Bunting for them to see his purpose and his courage on a national scale.

Dr Bunting was a hard man who drew the cloak of unpopularity tightly about him—as great men often have to do if they wish to turn the tide of lesser thoughts into their wider stream of vision. He was a ruthless man who should be judged on his achievements, not on his personal character, on his sincerity, not on his lack of charm. Bunting's methods were harsh, often distasteful even to his supporters, yet it was his energy and independence that preserved and strengthened what many of his personal critics considered vital.

After a short while Fennell began his lengthy preparation for ordination, for which, in the words of his successor at Woodhouse Grove, "he was to undergo a purifying process of three years' abstinence from Methodism".

As for William Morgan, shortly after his marriage he obtained the transfer he had hoped for, leaving Bierley to live with his now almost blind vicar in Bradford, where he "resided some years under his roof, when he had the honour to act as his Curate, Secretary, and Accountant".

But he would not become the Vicar of Bradford, as he had hinted to Patrick. When the new Christ Church, Bradford, was consecrated in October 1815, he would be appointed its first incumbent, and Fennell, newly ordained, would succeed his son-in-law as curate to the elderly and ailing John Crosse at the parish church.

Meanwhile Patrick was a very happy man. True, 1813 was a quieter year than the preceding one, but it would yet bring events memorable in his life. He was now thirty-six, his hair not yet showing the flecks of white that would soon appear; the need for spectacles limited to those evening hours when he studied closely; his stock still of manageable proportions and not swathed round his chin as in later years when bronchitis became an annual visitor. In a word, he was still young, handsome, and with an unbroken chain of successes behind him.

Now that William Morgan was a curate in Bradford itself, he informed Patrick that he intended to issue a magazine entitled *The Pastoral Visitor*, and that he wished for contributions from his old friend. Patrick was only too willing, and later, when the project was launched, he was to be a frequent contributor. One article in this magazine, contributed by Patrick in 1815 and entitled "Conversion", aroused much interest in the district, showing as it did the manner in which an individual could be turned towards the Light of Eternal Truth. It also revealed that the influence of Methodism was still strong with Patrick at that time. The text is from St Matthew, chapter 18, verse 3 : " 'Except ye be converted, and become as little children, ye shall not enter into the Kingdom of Heaven.' Reader ! art *thou* converted ? Examine thyself without delay in this important subject. The following are the *Marks of the Unconverted*:—Open profaneness—formality (only) in religion—rejecting or making light of the gospel—want of sincerity in accepting salvation through Jesus Christ—Self-righteousness—Uncharitableness—indecision of character—Being satisfied with gifts without grace. Conversion is much more than taking upon us the Christian name in baptism, and a profession of the Christian religion. If this were all, Simon Magus and many others would have been safe. Nor is it enough to lead a decent life, free from scandalous and open sin. Nor again is that man truly converted who is satisfied with a partial reformation . . . in abstaining from sins to which he is not tempted. Conversion is a spiritual and universal change. It is effected by the agency of the Holy Ghost . . . it may be wrought suddenly or gradually. Its effects will be manifested in the heart and life. The understanding will be enlightened to discover the evil of sin, the need of a Saviour, the excellency of religion, the vanity of the world, and the importance of eternal things . . . Examine thyself . . . go then to some secret place, and there ask thyself seriously . . . Do I know myself to be a lost sinner ?—Do I feel the need of Christ as a Saviour ?—Do I forsake every sin ?—Do I seek my happiness in God only ?—Do I strive to please and serve God ?—Is Christ the foundation of my hope ? —Do I desire above all things the grace of God ?—Do I rejoice in God ? —Do I, like many, care for my soul ? Do I love God supremely, and do I love my neighbour as I love myself ?—Do I hate every sinful act, word, and thought ?—Do I grieve aright for sin ?—Do I follow after holiness of life in all its branches as God's word directs me to do ?— Am I sincere in this self-examination ?—Do I pray in the words of Psalm LI ?—Is this Psalm my form or model of my prayer to God ?— . . . Pause and think about it. Do not throw this paper aside, and forget the subject . . . think this paper as the message of a friend to your soul, sent for your everlasting good. O Reader ! 'the time is short !' Eternity is near ! Death levels his arrow at thy heart ! 'Escape for thy life !' 'Repent, and be converted, that thy sins may be blotted out.' "

In the meantime Patrick had plenty to occupy his mind : there were "two births" in the offing. He had barely realized that he had enough material ready to publish his next volume of poems, and was in the midst of discussing details with his printer, P. K. Holden of Halifax, when Maria announced the joyful news that she was with child.

In those happy autumn days, whilst preparation was made at Clough House to receive their first-born, Patrick hurriedly revised his poems and delivered them to Mr Holden. The book came to life first and was called *The Rural Minstrel*. It was the same size as his previous volume but with fewer pages, the poems running from pages 1-108. The title page ran :

The
Rural Minstrel :
a Miscellany
of
Descriptive Poems.
By the Rev. P. Brontë, A.B.
Minister
of
Hartshead-cum-Clifton,
Near Leeds, Yorkshire.

———

The smile of spring, the fragrant summer's breeze,
The fields of autumn, and the naked trees,

Hoarse, braying through stern winter's doubling storms;
E'en rural scenery, in all its forms,
When pure religion rules the feeling heart,
Compose the soul, and sweetest joys impart.

Halifax:
Printed and sold by P. K. Holden, for the author.
sold also by
B. and R. Crosby and Co., Stationer's-court, London.
And by all other Booksellers.

1813.

Following the usual short "Advertisement" were eleven poems:
(1) "The Sabbath Bell"—this, in calling us to prayer, gives a warning
that time is on the wing: the very tombstones in the graveyard as we
approach the church tell us there is little time to repent; (2) "Kirkstall
Abbey, a fragment of a Romantic Tale"—descriptive thoughts aroused
by his courtship of Maria amidst its ruins; (3) "Extemporary Verses,
written at a Reverend friend's house, during his absence"—a description of the "chaste simplicity" and quietude of the old vicarage at
Dewsbury; (4) "Lines, addressed to a Lady, on her Birth-day"—for
Maria, shortly after their marriage; (5) "An Elegy"—the poor labourer
has died after a life in which he worshipped God; Heaven will protect
his widow and young children: it concludes with "The Epitaph" of
the departed one; (6) "Reflections, by Moonlight"—the changing form
and uncertain light of the moon are fit emblems for the vain and
transient life on earth, "Though passing fair, thine's but a borrowed
light"; (7) "Winter"—in the fiercest storms let us remember the birds
as well as the poor and those at sea, and aid them all we can; (8) "Rural
Happiness"—the beauties of the world are in the countryside and
God made them all; but He must be in the heart for them to impart true
joy and peace of mind; (9) "The Distress and Relief"—Convictus,
leaning against an oak tree groans aloud to God that all this world is
sinful and leads to damnation; a golden volume appears which a voice
tells him to open; he reads that merciful God has pardoned all his sins:
he raises a gracious look to Heaven, "and all his soul had rest";
(10) "The Christian's Farewell"—the dying man tells his grieving
family that he sees the looks of Jesus; all is well, death has lost its
sting; (11) "The Harper of Erin"—an ancient harper, "high on a rock,
on sweet Killarney's shore", plays and sings to the glory of God.

It would be idle to pretend that Patrick had great talent as a poet, or even claim that what he wrote was really poetry. Nevertheless, a close study of his first three volumes of verse shows that *The Rural Minstrel* was a great advance on *Cottage Poems*; and furthermore that, anxious as he naturally was to transmit religious instruction through his poems, it was in his purely descriptive lines that he exhibited the greater skill. Here are four short extracts from *The Rural Minstrel*. The first is from "The Sabbath Bell":

> Erewhile, the morning o'er the blushing sky,
> In milder beauty, held the sovereign sway;
> The streaky east, with many a changing hue,
> Glowed on the confines of the ether blue,
> And gently ushered in the king of day.
> Now hangs the sun, his golden lamp on high,
>   Diffusing, brighter, warmer light;
> The sleepy charms dissolving, of the drowsy night,
> The spirits cheering, with a quicker flow,
> And fostering all the rosy flowers of health that blow.
>   How charming is the scene!
>   The fields in flowery green,
> Scent the soft breezes, with their fragrant smell:
>   The blackbird and the thrush,
>   Make vocal every bush;
> Perched on the milk-white thorn, the linnet sweetly sings;
> The labouring bee, shakes music, from his mellow wings:
>   Loud tolls the Sabbath Bell . . .

From "Winter":

> Ye feathered songsters of the grove,
> Sweet philomel and cooing dove,
>   Goldfinch, and linnet gray,
> And mellow thrush, and blackbird loud,
> And lark, shrill warbler of the cloud,
>   Where do ye pensive stray?
> The milk-white thorn, the leafy spray,
> The fragrant grove, and summer's day,
>   Are seen by you, no more;
> Ah! may you light on friendly sheds,
> To hide your drooping pensive heads,
>   From winter's chilling roar . . .

Next, from "Rural Happiness":

> As roves my mind, o'er nature's works abroad,
> It sees, reflected, their creative God,
> The insects, dancing in the sunny beam,—
> Whose filmy wings, like golden atoms gleam,
> The finny tribe, that glance across the lake,
> The timid hare, that rustles through the brake,
> The squirrel blithe, that frisks on yonder spray,
> The wily fox, that prowls about for prey,
> Have each a useful lesson for my heart . . .

Finally, the concluding lines from "The Harper of Erin":

> . . . But now the sun had kissed the western main,
> And hummed the beetle o'er the dusky plain,
> Killarney, matchless lake, could scarce be seen;
> A misty veil o'er spread the lovely scene.—
> The woods and mountains, could be viewed no more,
> And jutting rocks, that hem its flowing shore.—
> The sweet musician, homeward took his way,
> Resolved to tune his harp, another day.

But many of the clergy of those days wrote far worse verse, and after the publication of his third work, Patrick was known in the West Riding of Yorkshire as something of a scholar and poet.

As the year 1813 drew to its close Patrick's excitement grew at the prospect of his first-born. At long last the New Year arrived and, shortly afterwards, his first daughter : she was named after her mother— Maria. Of all the important dates in the history of the Brontés, the birthday of little Maria is the only one not recorded. But she is no less significant for that; if her life was brief it was also glorious.

Patrick, in his great happiness, informed all his friends of his news, and invited William Morgan to baptize his daughter at Hartshead Church. The good-natured Welshman readily assented; he would perform this service for his friend more than once and with no less pleasure because he and his wife Jane were childless.

It was, perhaps, only natural that Patrick should choose Saturday, 23rd April, as the date for the christening ceremony. It was Shakespeare's birthday and the anniversary of his degree day at Cambridge. Thus Maria was christened and the registers signed:

1814 April 23	Maria	daughter of	Revd. Patrick Brontë Minister of this church, and Maria, his wife	William Morgan officiating Minister.

William Morgan was the godfather, and in that capacity made his own responses during the baptismal service. Jane Morgan and Mrs Fennell were the godmothers.

It was a happy little party that left St Peter's Church, Hartshead, and drove back to Clough House.

The year 1814 was a contented one for Patrick and Maria, the latter showing no ill effects from having her first child. Patrick continued to serve the parish, making repeated visits to those who had been bereaved in the recent rioting and the punitive consequences. He still loved to walk across the moors, and was never loath to visit a cottage that stood at some distance across the hills from his church. Yet, as was only natural, he did not linger as of old. When darkness came on he was always anxious to return home to his wife and daughter; there was so much more to greet him than there had been at the old farm, for all the warm kindness of Mr and Mrs Bedford.

Occasionally, there would be a guest preacher at Hartshead Church, such as Hammond Roberson (for all his unpopularity), William Morgan, or Thomas Atkinson, A.M., the minister of Thornton. At such times Patrick would either preach at the church of his visitor or deliver a sermon as guest preacher to assist one of the neighbouring clergy. During that year he made several journeys into Bradford for that purpose and amongst the clergymen of that town he came to know really well was Thomas Atkinson.

This clergyman, who was born in Leeds on 10th June 1780, was thus thirty-four years of age at the time when Patrick became closely acquainted with him. He was educated at Magdalene College, Cambridge, where he obtained his A.B.; he gained his A.M. in 1814, whilst at Thornton. He was on very good terms with the Vicar of Bradford, John Crosse, friendly with Morgan and Fennell and, to complete the circle, was a nephew of Hammond Roberson.

Thomas Atkinson is not to be confused with *William* Atkinson of Bradford, who was minister of Thornton in 1799. The latter was, as already mentioned, a violent hater of Dissent and all Dissenters. So intense was his dislike, indeed, that he had a printing press installed in his house and issued pamphlets in which he expressed his views with great freedom. In a short serial entitled "The Looking Glass", he lashed out bitterly at all forms of Dissent. All his tracts, on ecclesiastical or political topics, were written under the name "The Old Enquirer". His output was considerable and continued over many years.

William Atkinson was extremely friendly with the Vicar of Bradford, John Crosse, who appointed him afternoon lecturer at the parish church there, a position he retained for a number of years.

Thomas Atkinson took Patrick to the Bradford Subscription Library and there they would meet Crosse and William Morgan, the latter by now well established as the Vicar of Bradford's assistant curate. John Crosse liked and respected Patrick more and more as their acquaintance grew, and this emboldened Atkinson to make a suggestion to Patrick that had been in his mind for some time.

One autumn day in 1814, he approached Patrick with the suggestion that they might find it beneficial to exchange livings. He was certain that both John Crosse and John Buckworth would agree to sanction such a move and that permission would be forthcoming if an application were made. Patrick agreed to discuss the matter with his wife, although he had no desire to leave Hartshead, where he had enjoyed so much both of excitement and domestic happiness. But he went home a puzzled man; it was strange that Atkinson should desire such a move, as Thornton, although of no greater importance than Hartshead as a church, was nevertheless near Bradford and closer to the centre of ecclesiastical matters. There was, however, no hesitation on the part of Maria; she was all in favour of a move to Thornton. Her cousin Jane was there and, now that he was about to be ordained, so were her Uncle Fennell and Aunt Jane. She would be sorry to leave her first home, such a fine one too, but nevertheless she would dearly like Patrick to accept; besides, it was in the nature of a slight promotion for him and he was on good terms with the Vicar of Bradford. It has been stated that Maria was anxious to leave Hartshead in favour of a quieter district owing to the unsettled conditions, but in view of the fact that matters were peaceful towards the end of 1814 and there existed no signs of a renewed social violence, this argument would have weighed little with her. There was only the natural desire to live near her Yorkshire relatives, as compensation for losing the society of her sisters in Cornwall.

Patrick met Thomas Atkinson again and agreed that, subject to permission's being obtained, they should exchange their duties. He then learned that the young clergyman's real desire to live at Hartshead was to be nearer a young lady of his acquaintance; or, as a Mr King of that district was to term it, "He had a bird to catch, near Hartshead." The "bird" was Miss Frances Walker, third daughter of Samuel and

Esther Walker, of Lascelles Hall, a lovely Georgian mansion, near Huddersfield.

Now Patrick understood the advantage to the already wealthy Atkinson—and to himself—for the living of Thornton was worth twice that of Hartshead. Thus, application for the exchange was sent to Mr Crosse and Mr Buckworth, who readily agreed to recommend the move. After a short while permission was granted, but before it was received, Maria told Patrick that they had better delay the move for a few months as they could expect a second child shortly after the New Year.

Patrick agreed, although he knew how much his wife was looking forward to being near her cousin again. To provide her with company in the meantime, he suggested she should invite her sister Elizabeth, now living alone in Penzance, to stay with them during the birth of their child: this proposal delighted Maria. Elizabeth Branwell readily agreed and prepared for her sojourn in the north.

Meanwhile Patrick, having agreed with Atkinson to defer the transfer of their livings until a more convenient time (no doubt to the latter's great exasperation), continued his daily duties at Hartshead. As he walked down Clough Lane towards the church, he thought much about the child so soon to arrive. There were many blessings he had to thank God for, so many favours had He shown him. Yet there remained one great longing in his heart, one further bounty that, should Heaven grant it, would complete his personal happiness in life: leaning his arms on a farm gate, he dropped his auburn head on to them and prayed fervently aloud that he might be given a son.

Miss Elizabeth Branwell duly arrived at Clough House and was reunited with her sister. She was of short stature, thin, and with a much sharper face than her younger sister's. She had soft brown hair, light brown eyes and a serious, even severe, expression. She had been born on 2nd December 1776, so that when Patrick first met her she was thirty-eight years of age. Her dress, at that time, was smart and in the fashion and she not infrequently took snuff. Like Maria, she had been left an annuity of £50. However, their father had stipulated that the capital sum should pass to his son on their deaths. (Benjamin Carne Branwell died in 1818, before these two sisters, but had issue: so Patrick and his children would not inherit Maria's annuity upon her death, only any capital she possessed.)

At first Elizabeth Branwell seemed rather a queer little woman, always telling Patrick of her home in Penzance and of her many *beaux* who would be anxious for her return. But he soon grew to like her although she seemed so very different from Maria. However, he found her strong Methodism rather a trial to bear, he did not know why. Also, he had a shrewd suspicion that, as her sister had gained a husband so soon after repairing to Yorkshire, Miss Branwell was hopeful of an equally speedy success.

Thus the New Year, like the previous one, was ushered in at Clough House in an atmosphere of excited expectancy : Miss Branwell and the servant bustled about busily, Patrick anxiously waited, only baby Maria looked completely calm as she gazed at her father with those grave eyes.

On Wednesday, 8th February 1815, a second daughter was born ; for a moment Patrick felt a keen pang of disappointment, but it quickly passed when he saw his new child for the first time. In view of the presence of the infant's aunt there could be no hesitation in naming the child after her—Elizabeth.

Little Maria gained her first glimpse of her sister and gazed at her with a solemn expression ; Patrick quietly left the room to thank God for his latest gift.

Mrs Brontë was soon about again and it was agreed that the move should take place in May. Patrick's incumbency at Hartshead-cum-Clifton drew to a close. He had been there, at St Peter's, for just over four years, and they had been momentous years for him. As he left the pulpit after his last sermon in the weather-beaten old church he remembered the excitements of the Luddite Riots and of the secret buryings by night. He recalled the happy days at Woodhouse Grove and the magic moments at Kirkstall Abbey. Then there was the contentment of these last two years, and the joy in his two young daughters.

On Monday, 15th May 1815, he officiated at a wedding in Hartshead Church and, with some sadness, signed its registers for the last time. Four days later he and his small family left Clough House for the parsonage at Thornton. His wife and two children (Elizabeth a mere babe-in-arms), his sister-in-law and the servant, were put into the waggon, and off they set on the journey.

The Rev. Thomas Atkinson moved to Hartshead, but did not occupy Clough House. Instead he took as the pro-parsonage Green House, a spacious and pleasant dwelling at Mirfield, not far from Roe Head. It had a beautiful garden in which, years later, Charlotte Brontë was to wander happily whilst a pupil at Roe Head School. Mrs Abraham Hirst was engaged as a servant. On 23rd December 1817 at Kirkheaton, Atkinson married Frances Walker, then aged twenty-four, of Lascelles Hall. Her mother had been a Firth of Kipping House, Thornton—a family Patrick was soon to know very well indeed. Thomas Atkinson remained minister of Hartshead for fifty-one years, until he retired through age and infirmity in 1866. He died at the Green House four years later, on 28th February 1870, in his ninetieth year. His wife died on 2nd May 1881 at the age of eighty-eight.

Whilst the final preparations for the exchange were taking place, Miss Elizabeth Firth at Thornton had made the following entries in her diary :

1815   March   5th.   The last time I heard Mr. Atkinson preach.
             16th.   We met Mr. Atkinson, he wished me goodbye.
             17th.   I came to Lascelles Hall.

And from Lascelles Hall she continued to keep in touch with the news from Thornton.

April 30th.   Mr. Atkinson preaches his farewell sermons at Thornton Chapel from these words—Romans, c.x.v. 1st ; 2 Corinthians, c.xiii, v.11th—"Finally, brethren, farewell." The congregation appeared much affected, and at the conclusion sung the hymn beginning :
"With all Thy power, O Lord, defend Him whom we now to Thee commend."

As Patrick's little party sped towards Thornton on 19th May 1815, Miss Firth's pen was poised ready for the report of his safe arrival.

May   19th.   Mr. Bronte came to reside at Thornton.

Miss Firth allowed the ink to dry and closed her diary for the day ; Maria took her first look at the new home in Market Street ; Patrick took a quick glance at the surrounding hills and followed her into the house.

At Thornton, Patrick Brontë was edging nearer to Haworth, some seven miles across those moorland hills : Haworth, that would prove to be, at one and the same time, the summit of his hopes and the well of his sorrows.

Thornton

IN 1815, Thornton was a small hamlet, a mere cluster of houses some three miles to the west of Bradford. Its main street was called Market Street and consisted of only twenty-three houses: at one end, by the Black Horse Inn, it curved round and dived into Pinchbeck Valley, at which point it was known as Lower Kipping Lane. This was the only road through from Bradford to Halifax. As in all these parts of Yorkshire, the houses were built of grey stone quarried from the immediate neighbourhood. Below Thornton, to the south, the fields sloped away into a deep valley. To the east the village looked down over Bradford; to the west and north it was ringed with hills—Thornton Heights and Moors, Denholme Moor and, behind them, Oxenhope Moor that led across to the Worth Valley and Haworth. In the centre of Market Street, facing south, stood the parsonage; in the fields below the village stood the Old Bell Chapel, Patrick's new charge; and a few yards down Lower Kipping Lane stood the home of the Firth family—Kipping House.

In Domesday Book, Thornton appears as *Torenton*—the town of thorns—so called because of the large number of thorn bushes that were found in the district. Apart from the local quarries, the main living of the people was hand-loom weaving and at the time Patrick arrived there the innovations had not yet reached the village and many of the inhabitants continued their weaving in the cottages.

The parsonage stood in a row of houses separated from the street by only a tiny patch of railed-off ground. Four steps led from the street to the front door. Unlike Clough House, the building was only two storeys high. On the ground floor were two rooms, each with a double window overlooking Market Street, neither of them as large as at Clough House; the hall was also somewhat shorter. The room on the left of the entrance was the dining-room, that on the right the parlour; the latter, however, would come into use as a spare bedroom or "state" room when children were born—a usual procedure in those days. Behind these rooms was the kitchen. Upstairs were five bedrooms; of the two larger rooms at the front, one was Patrick and Maria's bedroom, the other Patrick's study. Between these was a narrow dressing-room used by Miss Branwell. At the back of the house were the children's bedroom and the servant's chamber—the latter connected to the kitchen by a short back stairway, as at Clough House. It was a good deal smaller than the home at Hartshead, and soon there would be more children and more servants to pack into that stone house.

The house still stands, but the ground-floor parlour where the famous Brontës were born has had another room added to it, jutting into the street, and used as a butcher's shop. But those who serve the memory of the Brontës have eased their consciences with a plaque to commemorate the births.

This then was Patrick's new home. There was certainly not much space for a growing family, but Thornton was a small village and in those days the fields came almost to the back door, there being only a small stable intervening. This stood in a cobbled yard above the level of the kitchen and was reached by three steps. If Patrick could not guess that one day there would be a commemorative plaque on the wall, he would see the cornerstone over the doorway marked

J A S

1802

—the initials of John and Sarah Ashworth, former residents.

Down the fields at some little distance to the south-east, stood the Old Bell Chapel, dedicated to St James. Erected in 1612, although repaired many times before Patrick's arrival in Thornton, St James's Church was one of three chapels-of-ease attached to Bradford Parish Church, the others being St Michael's, Haworth, and Holy Trinity, Low Moor. (As recently as 1st July 1809, however, a fourth chapel-of-ease had been consecrated at Horton.) The purpose was to provide Christian services for the inhabitants of Thornton, Denholme, Allerton, Clayton and Wilsden, to save the communities of those scattered villages from the necessity of travelling into Bradford. Indeed, the Old Bell Chapel was for a long time the only place of worship connected with the Church of England between Bradford and Haworth, the Black Horse Inn providing the stone horse-mount and stabling for those worshippers who came by pillion. The chapel had been built at the time that Bradford had for its vicar a Puritan clergyman, the Rev. Caleb Kemp, and, indeed, the building gave every appearance of being a Dissenting House.

In 1815 the Chapel was in a very bad condition, far worse than Patrick had found at St Peter's, Hartshead; inside the building it was damp, dark and extremely dismal; the two galleries all but blocked out the light emitted by the small square windows; the aisles were paved with gravestones that were moist and slippery. In addition, the south wall was crumbling and the very roof was rotten and dangerous, with fragments likely to fall when voices were raised during a service. Only the vestry, with its cosy fireplace, was cheerful.

Inside the church were at least three old stones bearing inscriptions. One read, "This Chappell was builded by [Lillye] Freemason in the Yeare of our Lorde 1612." The others bore the dates 1587 and 1756— the latter signifying the year when extensive repairs had last been carried out. Many of the surrounding gravestones were of great antiquity. The old stone font, at which five of Patrick's children were to be baptized, dated from 1679.

Surrounded by its sloping churchyard the Old Bell Chapel stood in the midst of many fields, commanding a fine view over the surrounding countryside of soft grazing land, with the high moors overlooking the scene. Today the ancient chapel has all but disappeared, only a fragment of the east wall and the cupola remaining amidst the mouldering tomb-stones, with the vestry a crumbling tool-shed. Just above it runs the new main road leading out from Bradford; and on the other side of the road, on higher ground, towers the newer church of St James, built in 1870, and with its memorial stone dated 26th October of that year. In its porch is housed the Brontë font, together with another of even earlier date, whilst inside, the organ has affixed to it a small brass plate inscribed "The Brontë Memorial Organ—1897", the money having been raised largely by local working men, rather than by lovers of the Brontës who resided outside the parish. It cost £1,200 to install.

Patrick at once displayed great energy in restoring the Bell Chapel into a place fit and safe for worship. The cupola, to house the bell, was erected during his incumbency at Thornton. In addition, he ordered many alterations—the chapel to be completely re-roofed, and the south wall pulled down and rebuilt. In so doing, Patrick showed that drive and determination that would characterize his life's work in the church. A faculty was obtained for this work on 26th June 1818, and by the late autumn all was completed.

Thus the Old Bell Chapel was soon to be restored to something approaching a decent condition, despite its antiquity and the large amount of neglect it had suffered, Patrick making sure that all the ancient memorials, and an old oak kist or chest that had been in con-tinuous use since 1685, were safely preserved during the restoration work.

Near the chapel stood Thornton Hall, a lovely old mansion, and not far off was Leventhorp Hall.

Thornton was, however, a scattered parish, but one that suited

Patrick because of his love of walking over the hills. There were many isolated farmsteads to visit as well as the neighbouring villages, such as Denholme, over two miles away across the fields. Then there was the Pinchbeck Valley, full of snow through parts of the winter but a lovely spot to linger in on a summer's day. Patrick often took Maria there; it was a shelter for her from the moorland winds, a place of tranquillity.

Above Pinchbeck, near the top of Kipping Lane where it became Market Street, stood Kipping House, home of the Firth family. It was a Restoration building, giving directly on to the south side of the street. It was, however, the back of the house with its kitchen and pantry that faced Lower Kipping Lane. From the street entrance, or back door, a long corridor ran right through the house to the front door, which looked out on to a very large and beautiful garden, sloping down towards meadows and a hollow through which a small stream swiftly flowed. The front of Kipping House had a fine portico with flat Corinthian columns—a vast drawing-room overlooking the garden on the right hand side of the entrance, the dining-room on the other; in the former were two deep-set, high Georgian windows. The main hall, lobby and staircase were all stone-flagged. On the first floor were several large bedrooms, and above these, an attic floor with three fine rooms, all panelled in oak. The usual dormer windows admitted light to this floor. Built entirely of stone, as was the roof, the house was surmounted by chimneys that were unusually high and extremely crooked.

But lovely as was the house, Patrick in his numerous visits there would find the garden an added charm. Full of splendid old trees, it dropped steeply down to the narrow hollow, where at the stream's edge grew giant elms, ash and beech trees. In summer the fields behind Kipping were full of sorrel, meadow-sweet and buttercups, whilst on the other side of the hollow the ground rose sharply towards a high heath beyond. This private part of Pinchbeck Hollow was even more beautiful than that reached by the winding, tree-bordered Kipping Lane.

Immediately below Kipping House a gate in the thick stone wall of the lane opened into a small courtyard with out-houses and a large laburnum tree growing near the centre, its branches reaching to the roof of the house.

Above Kipping and adjoining it, stood the old barn, used in the seventeenth century for prayer meetings by the Independents, of whom Dr John Hall, the original owner of Kipping, was a fervent member. This was a long building with the roof running straight from the street wall; four old stone steps led up to the door in the street wall that was the main entrance to the barn, which bore the date 1669. It was first used as a meeting-house in 1672 when the Declaration of Indulgence made it possible for such prayer-gatherings to be held, a licence having been granted to Dr Hall for that purpose.

In that old building several famous men had preached. Oliver Heywood, that political paradox, who was both Royalist and Presbyterian and suffered under Cromwell and King Charles II because of his twin loyalties, was a frequent visitor to Thornton. Joseph and Accepted Lister preached at Kipping: Joseph as "a gifted brother" in the absence of the minister, his son, Accepted, as minister from 1702 to 1709. Both died in 1709, the father a fortnight after Accepted, and were buried together in the grounds of the Old Bell Chapel. In 1760 a brother of the celebrated Dr Priestley was minister. Dr Hall of Kipping is mentioned in both Oliver Heywood's diary and Joseph Lister's autobiography.

But long before Patrick's arrival at Thornton, the new Kipping Chapel had been built in Market Street and the old barn abandoned as a meeting-house. In addition, the Firths of Kipping House, although descended from Dr Hall and originally a Dissenting family themselves, had become firm adherents of the Established Church.

Happily Kipping House and its famous barn still stand: the former very little altered and beautifully cared for by its present owner, the latter in good condition and the home of swallows which nest in the eaves near the rounded arch.

Upon Dr Hall's death, his son John succeeded to the house; his daughter and heiress Mary married John Firth of Halifax, and thus the possession of Kipping passed into the latter family. Their son Joshua married Abigail Dixon, an heiress from Bradford, thus further enriching the Firths. Joshua died in 1769 and his only son, John, in 1782. The latter had three children of whom the eldest, John Scholefield Firth, was head of the family when Patrick arrived at Thornton: his brother Joshua, who lived for a time at Allerton Hall nearby, had died in London in 1814 at the age of sixty-two; his sister Esther had married Samuel Walker of Lascelles Hall and was the mother of the future Mrs Thomas Atkinson.

In 1815 Mr Firth was a widower, aged fifty-seven, and living with his only child Elizabeth. Miss Firth, who was born on 2nd January 1797, was eighteen years of age. She had been sent in the years 1811 to 1813 to the famous ladies' school, Crofton Hall, near Wakefield, which was under the direction of Miss Richmal Mangnall, author of *Mangnall's Questions*. She returned home in June 1813.

On 2nd July 1814, her mother (formerly Elizabeth Holt) was thrown violently out of a gig as the horse stumbled down Kipping Lane and was instantaneously killed before the door of Kipping House. She was fifty-six. Since the death of Mrs Firth, Elizabeth had kept house for her father.

As Thomas Atkinson was hoping to marry her cousin Frances Walker, it was only natural that young Elizabeth Firth should have been on friendly terms with the departing minister of Thornton; but she was the kind of young lady who was anxious to make friends with, and offer assistance to, any clergyman of the Church that came within her ken. So on Friday, 19th May 1815, she made the entry in her diary respecting the arrival of the new incumbent and looked forward with impatience to her return home, that she might meet him and his family.

But Patrick, had she been at Thornton, would have had little time for social intercourse in those first few days after the move, for he was a busy man on his arrival at Thornton. After seeing his family safely housed and a few of their belongings disposed in some order, he rushed down the fields to the Bell Chapel to officiate at a baptism, after which he signed the registers for the first time: "Patrick Brontë, Minister". He then remained there to meet his church-wardens—Timothy Riley, John Hill, William Downs, John Lockwood and the others. At once he saw the terrible condition of the church and made a note to report the need for urgent repairs to his vicar at Bradford, John Crosse.

As he stood alone in the dank, almost putrid-smelling church, Patrick determined that, with repairs, the old building could be saved to serve for many more years. As mentioned, his hopes for restoring the church would be fulfilled, and in 1818 the Old Bell Chapel was "Repaired and Beautified, the Rev. Patrick Bronte being then minister", as the plaque would read.

At the same time the parsonage was returned as "fit for residence", although Patrick later called it "very ill constructed" and spent "no small sum to keep it in repair".

The living of Thornton, augmented by a gift of £200 from Mr Firth in 1802, was valued at £140 per annum—a great improvement for Patrick.

As was customary with a chapel-of-ease, Patrick had to pay certain dues to the vicar of the parish: in one of the books at Bradford Parish Church (now Bradford Cathedral) he had entered the following under the date 13th March 1815

Whereas the Reverend John Crosse, the present Vicar of Bradford, hath nominated and appointed the Reverend Patrick Brontë to be perpetual Curate of the Chapel at Thornton. Now be it known unto all men that I, the said Patrick Brontë, do hereby solemnly promise and declare in the presence of Almighty God that I will at all times, so long as I shall continue Curate of the said Chapel, regularly pay, or cause to be paid, to the said John Crosse and his successors, the Vicars of Bradford ten pence for every Funeral, if an Infant, and for every Adult twenty pence, and sixpence for every Christening or Churching which shall be done or performed at the Chapel of Thornton aforesaid, as is the custom with the other Chapels of Ease in the said Parish. In confirmation of the above Agreement I have hereunto set my hand this thirteenth day of March, in the year of our Lord one thousand eight hundred and fifteen.

Patrick Brontë.

So ended Patrick's first day at Thornton and he went home across the fields with a contented mind; there was much work to be done but he felt he could be useful here and his young family happy.

As he settled in and grew to know Thornton and its people, he found that Nonconformity was in a flourishing condition; but Patrick was determined to live at peace with his Dissenting brethren. This was a broadminded and charitable view he would bring to his religious dealings all his life. There would be the occasional argument, fiercely written to the press or in pamphlet form, but however much he might differ from his fellow clergy who had other persuasions on questions of doctrine, he was ever on the friendliest of terms with most ministers of other denominations.

During four of the five years that Patrick remained at Thornton, the Rev. Robinson Pool was the minister of Kipping Chapel. He also was a man anxious to preserve the peace and became very friendly with the new incumbent of the Old Bell Chapel. At no time was the amicable intercourse between them disrupted.

The people of Thornton would remember Patrick Brontë as a pastor who was always at the bedside of the sick, one in whom the poor and destitute of the parish found a true friend who sought to be acquainted with all their griefs. As always he was prepared to walk miles at any time of the day or night if his presence or advice could bring comfort or relief. Never once was a call refused or postponed. At Thornton he continued to hold his cottage meetings. His sermons were considered by his congregation as simplcity itself: he spoke the language they could all understand, yət his deliveries were full of sound doctrine. It was early perceived at Thornton that his theological views were much more Arminian than Calvinistic. He remained on the very warmest terms with his vicar, John Crosse, both sharing the same views on most points of theology. ("Surely the people of this town are highly favoured, having both a Vicar and a Curate that preach the truth," wrote John Wesley in 1786, two years after Crosse came to Bradford.) Mr Crosse was now completely blind and relied on his curate, William Morgan, and the ministers in his parish to assist him as much as possible. At the old Bradford Subscription Library (founded 1774) many of the leading clergymen in the West Riding of Yorkshire would meet. Amongst the names in the books as subscribers were Crosse, Morgan, William Atkinson and Brontë. Here they would discuss various topics of the hour, together with problems of the parish. By 1815 Mr Crosse had ceased to attend: the books would have to be read to him and, in any case, he was now much enfeebled. It cannot be too sufficiently stressed that, in 1815, Patrick Brontë and his friend William Morgan were surrounded by some of the *élite* amongst the Evangelical Churchmen who had remained faithful to the Establishment. Crosse, Fennell, Buckworth, Roberson, Heald, Thomas Atkinson and Charnock at Haworth were all men with great power and influence in both Church and Yorkshire affairs. Patrick, as he went on his parish duties or strolled with Maria down in Pinchbeck, knew this only too well and considered his move to Thornton in the Bradford parish a wise one.

There is a story concerning Patrick in his early days at Thornton, reported later by an old resident of the village, Mrs Akeroyd: it is an example of the crushing and sarcastic answers Patrick frequently gave to meddlesome people who appeared to him to lack common sense.

One Sabbath morning he was observed by a Dissenting woman neighbour in Market Street, shaving in front of the window. Hearing of this, Mrs Akeroyd reproved him sternly at the first opportunity and received this reply. "I should like you to keep what I say in your family but I never shaved myself in all my life or was ever shaved by anyone else. I have so little beard that a little clipping every three months is all that is necessary."

But now that he had become accustomed to Thornton, there would be time for a considerable social life—this despite his manifold duties, his growing family and his plan to publish his fourth book that year.

Elizabeth Firth was at last free from her visit to Uncle and Aunt Walker at Lascelles Hall and could hurry home. Her next diary entry read:

"June 6th. Came home in the evening."

The next morning she was up betimes and along Market Street as fast as her young legs could carry her.

"June 7th. I called at Mr. Brontes."

From now on it would be a pleasant, happy time for Patrick—and

Maria also when there was time between her confinements. There were visits and counter visits, tea parties and walks, lectures and politics; and Miss Firth put them all down in her diary. If for no other reason every lover of the Brontës will be eternally grateful to her : every scrap of information, so it be authentic, is worth its weight in gold. If she did not record some of the more important events in Patrick's sojourn at Thornton, there are nevertheless many living details that help fill in the picture. William Morgan was already a regular visitor to Kipping House. Some of the items from 1812 to 1815 set the scene for Patrick's entry into her diaries.

"1812. January 1st. We were afraid we had offended Mr. Atkinson by a note we wrote to him. We had a party to dinner and a dance. 7th. Miss Outhwaite [later Anne Brontë's godmother] went home. February 12th. Miss Greame [later Miss Firth's stepmother] came here. We played at cards in the evening. 29th. Mr. Atkinson dined here. March 8th. Mr. Franks [later her father-in-law] called after tea. 30th. . . . My mama and I to Crofton. April 15th. Miss Outhwaite [her schoolfellow and closest friend] wrote home. 18th. I danced with Miss Outhwaite. June 21st. [Holidays] Mr. Atkinson breakfasted here. 24th. My Papa went to Casterton.

"Cash Account. ½ years Pocket Money 13/-.

"1813. June 12th. I left school. My Papa came for me. 27th Mr. Morgan preached. 28th. I wrote to Miss Mangnall. July 6th. We called at Mr. Morgans. 24th I bottled some wine. 31st I rode the first time on my pony Prince. August 1st Mr. Atkinson came and talked to me in the Chapel. 8th. It was Thornton-tide. 22 We went to Mr. Cookham's Chapel in the morning the new church in the afternoon, Methodists at night. 31. Drank tea at Mr. Atkinsons. September 30th I took Snap to walk with me. October 3rd. I received the sacrament the first time. November 11th. Took tea at Mr. Rands. 13th. Mr. and Mrs. Morgan drank tea here. December 3rd. Miss Greame came. 25th. We had the singers in the evening.

"1814. January 25th. Betty, Hannah Colly left Kipping. Sarah Smith came. [Later Patrick would also employ sisters as servants.] February 14th. I received a Valentine. 18th. I received another Valentine. April 11th. There was a sheep roast in Thornton in commemoration of Bonaparte giving up the throne of France and Louis 18th ascending it. 15th. My Papa was thrown out of the gig but not much hurt he had a providential escape. June 28th. Mr. Atkinson set off for Cambridge to take the degree of Master of Arts. Saturday July 2nd. My ever to be lamented Mother was thrown out of the gig and killed on the spot, by a blood vessel breaking in the head, aged 56 years, the accident happened in the lane opposite the kitchen windows. 4th An inquest was held over the body of my dear Mother. Miss Greame came yesterday and stopped with us. 6th. My dear mother was interred by Mr. Franks in the vault under our pew in Thornton Chapel. 7th. Mr. Atkinson called immediately on his arrival at home from Cambridge. 18th. Miss Greame went home in the evening. May I ever pay great respect to the memory of a most affectionate Mother . . . Mr. Atkinson preached my poor Mother's funeral sermon a very excellent one from the text Psalm 39 –4th Lord let me know mine end . . . August 29th. I weighed 7 stones in weight and measured 5.3½ in without shoes.

"1815. February 27th. Miss Greame and I had a tete a tete [about marrying Papa]."

Taken from over a thousand entries these give, nevertheless, a picture of the young woman who later could have become stepmother to the Brontés.

To continue the diary for June 1815: "9th. We met Mr. Bronte's family at Mr. Kay[e]'s. 11th. See St. Matthew, c.xiii, vs 3-9, The Parable of the Sower. The first time I heard Mr. Bronte preach. 12th. Mrs Bronte and Miss Branwell called. 14th. Drank tea at Mrs. Brontes. 15th. I called at Mr. Brontes. 20th. We had the Outhwaites, Brontes, and Miss M. Ibbotson to dinner. 26th. We walked with Mr. Brontes to the top of Allerton." It will be noticed Miss Firth used the term Brontes to cover Mr and Mrs Bronte or, sometimes, the Bronte family.

Elizabeth Firth frequently taught at the Sunday school, and there was an amusing incident when the parish clerk of Thornton Chapel, John Drake, announced this in church on one occasion. He was something of a curiosity, being almost illiterate and much of a comic besides. "Miss Firth will teach the graces," he solemnly informed the congregation. After the service, Patrick discovered that it was his rendering of "will teach gratis".

During that month of June 1815 Napoleon had been finally overthrown at Waterloo; and to the West Riding of Yorkshire, with its woollen mills, the Duke of Wellington was as much a hero as anywhere in the country. At long last the war was over, and the bells could ring in earnest.

Wellington became Charlotte Bronté's hero, as he was her father's. But for Patrick he was a link with other ideals: had he not entered the Army as Arthur Wesley, born into a Meath estate once offered to, but refused by, Charles Wesley?

"July 4th. I walked to Swill Hill with Mr. Brontes. 19th. I called at Mr. Bronte's. 23rd. See Psalm XLVI. A collection was made for the widows and orphans of those who fell at the battle of Waterloo. 24th.

Mrs Bronte and Miss Branwell called. August 1st. Mr. Bronte called. 3rd. I went to sit with Mrs. Bronte in the evening. 21st. Mrs Bronte, Miss Branwell, and I drank tea at Mr. Tom Ibbotson's." These extracts from the diary are those that mention the Brontés, but Miss Ann Greame of Bradford made several calls at Kipping House, for Mr Firth was shortly to marry again.

By this time Patrick was quite at home in the spacious drawing-room at Kipping, and knew every inch of the delightful garden and shallow beck. What more natural than that he should ask Miss Firth to become the second godmother to his daughter Elizabeth? Did she not bear the same name as the child, like the other godmother, Miss Branwell? So it was settled, with Mr Firth readily agreeing to be the godfather.

There had been no time for the christening to take place at Hartshead, but now that Elizabeth was over six months old it should be delayed no longer. As William Morgan had baptized little Maria, to please his wife Patrick asked John Fennell to perform this ceremony.

On Saturday, 26th August 1815, Elizabeth Bronté was baptized in the Old Bell Chapel at Thornton.

1815 August 26th	Elizabeth daughter of	Patrick and Maria	Bronté	Thornton	J. Fennell officiating minister.

Miss Firth scribbles on:

"26th, Sunday [Saturday] Mr. Bronte's second daughter was christened Elizabeth by Mr. Fennel [sic]. My papa was godfather Miss Branwell and I were godmothers. September 2nd. I called at Mr. Bronte's. 6th. My papa was married to Miss Greame at Bradford Church by Mr. Morgan. The bridal party dined at Exley and came here in the evening. 18th. Mr. Brontes called. 21st. Mr Brontes and Mrs Morgan drank tea here. 22nd. We called at Mr. Bronte's." And so on. The new Mrs Firth, who was fifty-four, was a most amiable person and she and her stepdaughter became, and remained, bosom friends.

As the year grew older Patrick was ready with his new manuscript and arranged to have it printed by the same Bradford firm that John Buckworth had dealt with. Again Patrick was having a volume published, his fourth, with the knowledge that another child was expected, his third. It was a short moral tale in prose this time, followed by some verses to illustrate points of the story. It was an even smaller book than his previous works, only $5\frac{1}{2}''$ by $3\frac{1}{2}''$. There were 68 pages.

The
Cottage
in the Wood,
or the
Art of becoming Rich and Happy.

By the Rev. P. Brontë, A.B.
Minister of Thornton, Bradford, Yorkshire.

Happy is the man that findeth wisdom, and the man
that getteth understanding. For the merchandise of it is
better than the merchandise of silver, and the gain
thereof than fine gold.—Prov.iii. 13, 14.

Bradford:
Printed and Sold by T. Inkersley;
Sold also by Sherwood & Co. London; Robinson
and Co. Leeds; Holden, Halifax; J. Hurst, Wakefield; and all other Booksellers.
1815.

There was a frontispiece showing "The good old Cottager" discovering "by the light of a candle a young man": it bore the names
James, del. Stather, sculp. *The Cottage in the Wood* was a simple tale of
the cottager who discovers a drunken young man of quality collapsed
outside his dwelling. He and his wife tend him and try to reform his
character; but William Bower was a hardened case and departed
unmoved, save for his interest in the cottager's daughter Mary. He
accosts her one day on the way to market " '. . . Mary, I have long
looked upon you with an eye of affection . . . now I shall make you a
proposal, which, if you accept, will place your father and mother and
yourself in comfortable circumstances . . . consent to come and live
with me, and you shall have one hundred a year, and another hundred
shall be given to those whom you shall leave behind in the Cottage.' "
Mary in her simplicity believes that he intends her to be his servant.
"To which, with an air of triumph, that bespoke his confidence of
success, he jocosely replied, 'I intend to advance you far above the rank
of a servant: you shall be my wife in every thing, the ceremony of
marriage only excepted. Come, Mary, let us be parson and clerk ourselves. Mutual consent is all that's required.' " Mary leaves him in
disgust and anger and returns home. After her parents' death she finds
a pious old lady prepared to be her benefactress, who leaves her four

thousand pounds. Whereat Mary commences good works. Bower continues his depraved life until one night he and two of his "wicked companions" narrowly escape death when lightning strikes a nearby oak tree during a storm. His companions continue "their idle songs and blasphemous conversation", but Bower lingers behind, sobered by his narrow escape. The others are shot dead by robbers and Bower, realizing anew the error of his ways, escapes. He reforms, convinces Mary that his reformation is complete and they marry to spend a holy life together. At the end of the tale, Patrick's first poem is "The Pious Cottager's Sabbath", followed by "The Nightly Revel; or the circumstances of William Bower's Conversion". The book ends with "Epitaphs" on Mary and William Bower. Patrick could indeed be pleased with the sales of this work, for it sold better than any of his volumes of verse. It had a second edition in 1818, and the prose section of it appeared in volume 6 of the *Cottage Magazine* in June 1817.

In his magazine *The Pastoral Visitor* for August 1816, William Morgan reviewed it for his friend.

"This is a very amusing and instructive tale, written in a pure and plain style. Parents will learn in this little book the advantages of Sunday Schools, while their children will have an example well worthy of the closest imitation. Young women may here especially obtain a knowledge that the path of virtue leads to happiness. We would therefore most cordially recommend this book to all sorts of readers."

Years later Mr Abraham Holroyd obtained Patrick's permission to reprint the prose portion, substituting "Incumbent of Haworth" for "Minister of Thornton" after the author's name. It appeared thus in 1859. Some of the unsold stock was issued with new printed covers in the following year and sold at twopence a copy, Holroyd speaking of the tale as founded on facts. Again in 1865 the prose story of *The Cottage in the Wood* was reprinted by J. Harrison & Son, Bingley, and quickly sold.

Shortly after Patrick's latest publication, before he could judge as to its possible success, it was confirmed in Bradford that William Morgan would be appointed as first incumbent of the new Christ Church shortly to be opened in that town. At the same time it was announced that the Rev. John Fennell would succeed him as curate at the parish church. This was in the nature of a promotion for Morgan, for all that he had hoped for the parish church. For Fennell, newly ordained, it was considered a useful training prior to granting such an experienced preacher a church of his own: not that St Peter's, as the parish church was called, was an unimportant curacy, particularly as the vicar was blind and ailing.

On 12th October 1815, Christ Church, Bradford, was consecrated and Morgan duly performed his proud part in the ceremony. John Crosse was too elderly and feeble to take part in the service, but donated £100 towards the cost of the building. Patrick's name is not mentioned in connection with the consecration, but on 7th July 1816 he preached in his friend's new church the sermon he had delivered at Wellington, from the text, "Judge not and ye shall not be judged." This was afterwards inserted in Morgan's magazine *The Pastoral Visitor* with the intimation that it had been delivered previously in the parish church of Wellington.

In addition to Patrick, Morgan could rely on his father-in-law to preach from the pulpit at Christ Church, and John Fennell obliged frequently. Unhappily, this church was demolished in 1879.

William Morgan, who remained at Christ Church, Bradford, until 1851, when he exchanged livings with the rector of Hulcott, Buckinghamshire, had almost white hair at this time and wore spectacles. His round cheeks were, however, as red as ever. He was a strenuous worker in the cause of religion and temperance. At times he was choleric and irascible and could appear as something of a buffoon to those who did not know him well: such an opinion was greatly to undervalue the man. He had a sound judgment and an unlimited capacity for hard work. Although sadly harassed by a heavy debt left on the church at its erection and by an insufficient salary, he still financed a charity child: "To Miss Arthur's half-year's account for Mr. Morgan's little boy— £8.12.9." It would be Morgan who would write an account of his old vicar, John Crosse—'The Parish Priest". Indeed, he became a prolific author, and his works included *Christian Instructions*; *The Welsh Weaver*—a tale; and *Selections of Psalms and Hymns*. Three days after the consecration of Christ Church, John Fennell signed the registers at the parish church for the first time as the new curate.

So ended the historic year 1815, with Patrick and his friends more firmly entrenched than ever. Patrick had another book to his credit, had made numerous friends in Thornton and was the father of a growing family; but there was little thought of ambition now, for he was happy and busy with his many parish duties, including the repairs to the old chapel. But the year's end brought news to Patrick, Morgan and Fennell that Mary Fletcher was now their sponsor in Heaven. She died at one o'clock in the morning on 9th December 1815.

A few more extracts from Elizabeth Firth's diary usher in the New Year.

"October 4th . . . Called at Mr. Rands and Mr. Redheads. 11th. Oratorio and concert. 12th Oratorio of the 'Messiah'. Christ's Church at Bradford was consecrated. 24th. Miss Branwell called. 25th. We drank tea at Mr. Bronte's. 30th. Mr. Brontes drank tea here. November 6th. Drank tea at Mr. Morgan's. 16th. Miss Branwell and I went to J. Jowett's. 27th. William Greame went back to Mr. Redheads. 30th. Miss Branwell came to tea. December 6th. I attended a chemical lecture by Mr Webster. 12th. Mr Bronte called. 21st. I attended Mr. Webster's second astronomical lecture. 25th. Mr Bronte took tea here.

"1816. January 6th. Mrs Firth and I called at Mr Bronte's. 13th. I called at Mr Bronte's. 18th. a day of public thanksgiving for the restoration of peace. 23rd. Mr Bronte drank tea here. 30th. Mrs Bronte and Miss Branwell called. February 3rd. Sunday. Mr Fennell [sic] Mr Morgan and Mr Bronte called. 5th. Mrs Bronte and Miss Branwell called. 7th. Mr. Bronte called. 8th. Elizabeth Bronte was a year old this day. 9th. Mrs Bronte and I called at Mrs J. Ibbotson's. 14th. I called at Mr Bronte's. 18th, Sunday. Mr Morgan preached. 21st. I called at Mr Bronte's. March 13th. Miss Branwell drank tea here. Mr. Bronte came in the evening."

On Sunday, 21st April 1816, Patrick's third daughter was born. She was named after the aunt who had been married in Penzance at the same hour as her parents—Charlotte.

In the front parlour of the parsonage in Market Street the fire in the old grate glowed brightly, illuminating the figures of two naked boys with flute and mandolin and the rabbits that decorated the ironwork of the fireplace. If Patrick, as he held the tiny baby in his arms, felt again that flicker of regret that he was still denied a son, he hid his feelings from Maria. Little could he know that this, his third child, would be to him what she herself would write in later years when describing the daughters of England, ". . . your tenderest nurses in sickness ; your most faithful prop in age."

Miss Firth excitedly entered in her little book, "April 21st, Sunday. C. Bronte was born." The child's godfather was Thomas Atkinson, whilst his fiancée, Frances Walker, was a godmother. Despite reports that Miss Firth was also a godparent, she did not record that fact and it is most likely that Charlotte Branwell of Penzance, after whom the child was named, filled that position.

Charlotte was baptised on Saturday, 29th June 1816, this day of the week being chosen as more convenient for William Morgan, who was required at Christ Church on the Sabbath. Patrick was most anxious that his old friend should officiate. The registers read:

1816 29th June	Charlotte daughter of	The Rev. Patrick and Maria	Bronté	Thornton	Minister of Thornton	By whom the ceremony was performed.
						Wm. Morgan Minister of Christ Church Bradford

With three children to care for, and Miss Branwell shortly to return home, Patrick decided that Maria would need more than one assistant in the house, and applied to Mrs Richardby at the School of Industry in Bradford for a nursemaid. A thirteen-year-old girl was sent to the parsonage, and Maria, liking her appearance, gave her a trial. She proved most satisfactory in washing, dressing and feeding the young children and thus Nancy Garrs was employed as nurse to the little Brontés. One of twelve children, she was born on 29th March 1803, the daughter of a shoemaker in Westgate, Bradford. He was of French extraction, his name being de Garrs, but the Napoleonic Wars necessitated the abbreviation.

But in this June, whilst Patrick was busy with these domestic activities, word came up from Bradford on the 17th that the old vicar, John Crosse, was dead. He was seventy-seven. On 23rd June 1816, the Rev. John Fennell, his curate, preached the funeral sermon in Bradford Parish Church. It was fitting he should do so, for in addition to his curacy there, the late vicar had been a close friend of Fennell's godfather, John Fletcher of Madeley. The curate gave a most moving address, which was afterwards printed. It was all of a piece that the late John Crosse had been first married to the daughter-in-law of Parson Grimshaw of Haworth, the widow of his unfortunate son John. The new Vicar of Bradford was appointed—the Rev. Henry Heap.

During this time, Mr Firth had been seriously ill to the great concern of his wife and daughter. Patrick went frequently to pray with and comfort him, in his room overlooking the beck. On the evening of Sunday, 28th July 1816, Elizabeth Branwell left Thornton to return to Cornwall. She took a sad farewell of everyone, being most sorry to return. If her hope had been to find a husband she had been unsuccessful. When the call to Yorkshire came again, it would be under far less happy auspices : then she would yearn to return to her native town, but would never leave the north again.

Miss Firth continues :

"May 23rd. My papa was worse again ; another blister. 24th. Papa had twelve leeches on. 25th. Mr. Bronte went to prayer with my papa. 27th. Mr. Bronte again. My papa was very ill. 29th. My papa's disorder came to a crisis and, thank God, took a favourable turn. June 4th. Mr Bronte called. 7th. Called at Mr Bronte's. 9th. I was most happy to see my dear papa once more downstairs. May I be truly thankful for this great mercy. 17th. Mrs Bronte called. 18th. Mr and Mrs Bronte and Miss Branwell came to tea. July 1st. Mr. Bronte drank tea here. 4th. Called at Mr. Bronte's. 17th. We drank tea at Mr Bronte's. 18th. The ladies assisted me in altering a gown. 25th. Mrs Bronte and Miss Branwell drank tea here the last time. 28th. I took leave of Miss Branwell. She kissed me and was much affected. She left Thornton that evening. 29th. We called at Mr. Bronte's. 31st. We called at Mr. Bronte's. August 1st. Mr Brontes to tea. 11th. Thorntontide ; a wet day ; did not go to Church. 12th. Called at Mr. Bronte's. Had a party of twenty-nine, chiefly from Bradford."

After this, Elizabeth Firth went away for her summer holiday, bringing back a frock for one of the young Brontes. In her cash account for September she entered : "Frock for one of the Brontes, 16s."

"September 23rd. Came home. Mr. Bronte called. 30th. I called at Mr. Bronte's. October 12th. Mr. Bronte drank tea here. 22nd. Mrs. Bronte called. 30th. Came with my aunt Smith to Casterton. [Miss Firth's connection with Casterton later played its part in the recommendation to Patrick of the Clergy Daughters' School, whose founder lived at Casterton Hall.] November 14th. Mr and Mrs Bronte to tea. 19th. Tea at Mr. Bronte's. We observed a beautiful eclipse of the sun ; the sky was very clear till it arrived at its greatest obscurity ;it was afterwards enveloped in clouds—a great gloom. 30th. We called at Mr Bronte's. December 11th. Mr. Bronte at tea. 13th. Mr and Mrs Bronte to tea. 16th. Mr and Mrs Bronte to dinner, 28th. I called at Mr. Bronte's."

So ended the year 1816. Soon after the New Year Maria knew that a fourth child would be born to them that summer and the parlour would again become her bedroom. Patrick continued his hard work in the parish, where that winter there was much sickness. His preaching at the Bell Chapel was extremely popular with the people of Thornton and even the devotees of Thomas Atkinson helped to fill the church.

Here is a brief description of the Morning Service as celebrated by Patrick Bronté at Thornton and, later, at Haworth. Patrick was quietly conducted by the verger to the reading-desk, which was the middle platform of the three-decker pulpit. He wore no surplice of any kind. (Where an organ existed it was often at the back of the church, and under its loft was the singing pew occupied by a mixed choir.) On the bottom deck of the wooden pulpit sat the clerk, who intoned the responses and was indeed a most important person in the conducting of the service. The *Venite* and psalms were read alternately by the minister and clerk, the choir singing *Gloria Patri* after each psalm. Metrical hymns (psalms in metre by Tate and Brady, Sternhold and Hopkins, Bickersteth) were used, as well as a selection of hymns sung to sober tunes. One of these was sung after morning prayer, followed by the Litany, which was a duet for parson and clerk. After a second hymn, there continued the ante-Communion part of the service up to the Creed. During the singing of the third hymn, the minister was conducted by the verger to the vestry, where he was robed in a black Geneva gown with white bands ; thus dressed he was ushered back, mounting to the top of the pulpit, where under the overhanging sounding-board, he would deliver his sermon. The entire service usually lasted some two hours, of which it was invariably Patrick's custom to preach for an hour.

The Old Bell Chapel having no organ, the singers and fiddlers performed from the east gallery. Fearing its structure unsound, however, Patrick had them brought down and placed immediately before the pulpit. This three-decker pulpit, with its white plaster dove surmounting the sounding-board, stood in the centre of the south side of the chapel, surrounded by box pews, the Firth pew being the second to the west of the pulpit.

Regularly once a year Patrick, remembering his early struggles, would announce that the collection was for "the Poor in Ireland".

Soon after his appointment, the new Vicar of Bradford confirmed John Fennell's appointment as minister of Cross Stone Chapel, a high moorland hamlet near Todmorden, in the parish of Halifax. This had been the earlier recommendation of John Crosse, who had once been incumbent there, as had Parson Grimshaw's brother, the Rev. John Grimshaw. John Fennell signed the registers at St Peters, the parish church, for the last time on 13th April 1817, and left Bradford to take up his first full ministry. It was sad for Maria to say farewell to her uncle and aunt, as it was for Jane Morgan also, and the happy circle was broken; although, fortunately, Cross Stone was not too many miles away. The Rev. Henry Heap, who was only twenty-seven, obtained a new curate to replace Fennell.

Life continued to be pleasant for Patrick at Thornton and Maria was happy. The children were very quiet and good and young Nancy was proving a most kind and capable nurse. Here are a few more entries from the diary at Kipping House, chosen from among the many calls and tea-drinkings.

"1817. January 30th. Mrs Bronte called. February 15th. Got two new shillings. A new silver coinage was exchanged for the old. March 18th. Miss Thomas came to Mr. Bronte's. [She stayed a few weeks to assist Maria during her latest confinement]. 19th. Mrs Kay[e]s and Mr. Bronte to tea. 27th. Went to Bradford. 28th. I came home with Mr. and Mrs. Bronte. Bought 'Mason' on 'self-knowledge'. April 22nd. Called at Spring Head with Mr. Bronte and Miss Thomas. 23rd. Walked with Mrs. Bronte and Miss Thomas. May 9th. Mr. Horsfall and Mr and Mrs Bronte's family dined here [a first visit by little Maria and Elizabeth]. 11th. Sunday-school commences. 13th. My papa and Mr. Bronte went to Wakefield to vote for Mr Scott. [Candidate for the post of Registrar of Deeds.] Stopped all night at Longlands. 14th. They came home. 18th. I began of attending Sunday-school. F. Greame and Miss Thomas with me. June 9th. Mrs Bronte called. 21st. Read "Old Mortality"; did not like it. 24th. Called at Mr. Bronte's."

On Thursday, 26th June 1817, Patrick received the gift he had prayed for back in Clough Lane, Hartshead: his son was born early that morning. How very changed would have been his feelings in that hour had he known that, whilst sorrow would come to him through all his children, only his son would bring him shame.

The child was named Patrick Branwell, after his parents; to those who knew him in the village of Haworth he would always be Patrick, but at home and, later, to the world, he became Branwell.

The christening was on Wednesday, 23rd July, with John Fennell coming over from Cross Stone to baptize Branwell. The godparents were Mr and Mrs Firth, with, possibly, Fennell as second godfather. After the signing of the registers the proud Patrick led the small party back to the parsonage, and was never more gay. Elizabeth Firth was not sure which name would have precedence and wrote straight away: "June 26th. Went to see Mrs. Bronte. Branwell Patrick was born early in the morning." The five most interesting of her remaining entries for 1817 were: "July 18th. We saw the confirmation and Visitation at Wakefield. September 23rd. Mr. Sterndale sketched Kipping. November 6th. I went to Bradford with Mr. Bronte. The Princess Charlotte of Wales died. 12th. Mr and Mrs Franks and Mrs Naylor came and Mr. Redhead and Mr. Brontes dined here. [The Rev. Samuel Redhead, then Minister of the New Horton Chapel, who later was offered Haworth by the Vicar of Bradford.] 18th. The ever to be lamented Princess Charlotte was interred. Service in all places of worship."

The year 1818 would see the publication of Patrick's fifth book, his best work. It would also bring the birth of his fifth child, the most brilliant of his family.

One day in March, Patrick was in charge of a party of sixty children

13

and youths to be taken to Bradford Parish Church for Confirmation. They set off at a brisk pace from Thornton, singing hymns as they marched along—Patrick keeping his eyes open for any lout that might care to interrupt their progress. However, they reached the town unmolested and were passing down Kirkgate towards the high mound at its foot where stood St Peter's, when a violent snowstorm came on. As the troop passed the Talbot Hotel on their right, Patrick suddenly deserted his army and rushed into this large and comfortable hostelry. There he immediately ordered hot dinners to be ready for the whole party at the time they were due out of Church.

After the Confirmation service the party trooped out with the visiting Bishop's blessing on their heads. But the snow continued to fall and it was everywhere freezing. Patrick re-formed the procession and headed them straight up Kirkgate and into the inn. The hot food was consumed and the party remained there three or four hours, greatly enjoying themselves. When the snow had ceased, Patrick led them home in high spirits.

Before his critics rush in, let it be cheerfully admitted that Patrick almost certainly regaled himself with some warming whisky—Irish whisky at that! But the young people would always look back and remember their Confirmation Day with happiness and pleasure. The Parish church was the less cold because of the warming meal in prospect ; and when the considerable account was rendered, Patrick would quietly pay it himself—there were no expenses for the Church to meet. May the whisky have warmed Patrick's heart as his generous and truly Christian act gladdened the hearts of his flock. This was 1818, when such charity was rare, such action unorthodox, to say the least. But Patrick loved young people—had he not children of his own ?—and when those sixty boys and girls reached maturity it would be Patrick's kindness and humanity that would keep them good, perhaps more than the Bishop's blessing.

Patrick's next work was a prose tale, *The Maid of Killarney*, and again he went to T. Inkersley of Bradford.

Thomas Inkersley was a well-known citizen of that town, being considered a sound churchman and firm Tory. He was treasurer of Morgan's Christ Church. He became very fond of Patrick and was only too pleased to print another of his works, particularly as *The Cottage in the Wood* had been so well received. *The Maid of Killarney* was published anonymously, but after its appearance in Buckworth's *Cottage Magazine* in April 1821, with an introduction by that cleric, and years later Patrick's own signed admission, there has long been no doubt that the author was Patrick Brontë. It is a not uninteresting tale, giving Patrick's views on many aspects of social life. In addition, there are

some fine descriptive scenes of an Irish Wake, and a forcible account of
an attack on a house by "Whiteboys". This work will be fully dealt with
later, for it certainly merits attention, not only in its own right but
because it affords a picture of Patrick's views on political and religious
aspects of the day as well as his opinions on dancing, card-playing,
music, the theatre and so forth. The British Constitution and the
British and Foreign Bible Society are not exempt from criticism. The
book was 7″ by 4″ and contained 168 pages, including a three-page
preface. The full title read, *The Maid of Killarney ; or, Albion and
Flora : a modern tale ; in which are interwoven some cursory remarks on
Religion and Politics*. It was published in London by Baldwin, Cradock,
and Joy, of Paternoster Row, and "sold by T. Inkersley, Bradford;
Robinson and Co. Leeds ; and all other Booksellers, 1818".

That summer, Patrick congratulated himself on having his new
work recorded as published in London, but its readers in Bradford soon
guessed he was the author, and the attacks made on some aspects of life
gained him respect, even where his views were not completely shared.

In July, Maria again moved downstairs to the front room. Nancy
Garrs kept the four children quiet upstairs—not that that was very
difficult. Patrick on his return home would inquire after his wife before
going in to see her.

Was there a violent storm on Thursday, 30th July 1818 ? Did the
lightning fork its way across the Yorkshire sky ? Did the thunder,
locked in the Pennine hills, roar a wild greeting from dawn to dusk ?
At night did the stars seem brighter and nearer to earth ? Perhaps not,
but who knows what happened out on the moors. On that day there
must have been a stirring in the hills that stretch from Thornton across
to Haworth and beyond. The heads of the budding heather and ling
nodded in expectancy and homage ; the curlews flew lower and called
in greeting ; the lapwings hovered lovingly over Thornton and flew
with the good news to their haunts on Haworth Moor. Rabbits were
less timid that day, less eager to seek their homes in the grey rocks.
The black-faced sheep ceased to graze and stood waiting for they knew
not what. That day all moorland life found a friend and a champion.
Across the moors the west wind came with a soft welcoming murmur
which, by nightfall, grew into a triumphant cry that swept the starlit
hills. Even in July there was, that night, the sweet scent of heather.

As usual Patrick went in to see his new-born child. He looked at
her fondly for some moments, kissed his wife and left the room. Emily
Jane Brontë was born. Patrick walked slowly upstairs to his study and
gazed out of the window across the hills. How could he guess that a few
minutes before he had been gazing into the eyes of genius ?

CHAPTER 11

Trustees

On Thursday, 20th August 1818, Emily Jane was baptized in the old stone font at the Bell Chapel of St James, Thornton, by William Morgan. Her godparents were Mr and Mrs Fennell and their daughter, Jane Morgan. She was given her second name after both her godmothers, although Patrick also had a sister called Jane. The name Emily, like the girl who bore it, was quite original in the family. The registers read:

1818 20th August	Emily Jane daughter of	The Rev. Patrick and Maria	Bronte A.B.	Thornton Parsonage	Minister of Thornton	Wm. Morgan Minister of Christ Church Bradford.

Now that there were already five children in that little parsonage, Patrick and Maria decided that further domestic help would be necessary, especially as the young woman from Hartshead was anxious to return soon to that village where lived her family and her young fellow.

On hearing this, Nancy Garrs bustled in to see Maria and respectfully suggested that her sister Sarah might suit. Sarah was a year younger than her sister and therefore, at this time, about fourteen years of age. If Mrs Brontë would enquire, Mrs Richardby at the School of Industry would give her the highest reference.

Maria, anxious that the two young sisters should be united, employed Sarah Garrs at once as nurse to the children, promoting Nancy, after two years of devoted service, to the position of cook and assistant housekeeper. Great was the joy in the parsonage kitchen when the two girls were together again; and the house seemed a happier, merrier place than ever.

Patrick continued his preaching from the old three-decker pulpit. This was the summer when the workmen would finish their repairs and depart, leaving the Old Bell Chapel a much finer place in which to worship. When it was complete Patrick would proudly show his friends the great improvements. The new Vicar of Bradford, the Rev. Henry Heap, in particular was delighted that so much neglect had at last been rectified. He blamed the former state of the Chapel on his predecessor, John Crosse, who he feared had allowed matters to slide in his chapels-of-ease. Indeed, in 1817, Heap had paid an Easter visit to Haworth and found many complaints from the people there that, besides paying their dues to Bradford, "they had to maintain their own edifice", scores of the people coming down from the hills to complain at a vestry meeting in Bradford.

With his domestic contentment greater than ever, his church "beautified" and plaudits from many on *The Maid of Killarney*, the year had been a most pleasant one for Patrick, foretelling nothing of the change so soon to come upon him and the sorrow that would rapidly overtake his fortunes. Of course the usual tea-parties and visits had continued unabated and Miss Firth had jotted them down. Ten quotations will suffice to cover the year and usher in 1819 :

"1818. February 12th. Expected Mr. Bronte to tea, but Mrs. B. was poorly. March 16th. Spent a happy day at Mr. Atkinson's. May 19th. Mr. Bronte, F.O. [Miss Fanny Outhwaite of Bradford] and I went to Ogden Kirk. 22nd. Read Remains of H. K. White. July 30th. Emily Jane Bronte was born. November 10th. Went to look at the Angel in Thornton Chapel [a part of the new interior decorations]. November 19th. Heard of the Queen's death. 22nd. Put on mourning for the Queen. December 9th. Repaired Chapel books. 1819. January 8th. M.E. and C. Bronte to tea."

During this New Year there was nothing of importance recorded in the diary—indeed Miss Firth was away during the summer months—and for the rest, she mentioned only the usual social round.

But in that period of May to September, during her absence, a very important matter was being debated and fought out between the various parties concerned, and for some time the issue would be poised in the balance. The outcome was anxiously awaited by the Brontë family. For them all it was important, but for the youngest, Emily Jane, then attempting her first faltering steps, it would be more than happiness that was at stake, it would be life itself.

On 25th May 1819 word came over the brown hills from Haworth that the Rev. James Charnock, A.M., was dead. He had been ill for some considerable time and had preached only occasionally in recent months. He was fifty-seven and had been the incumbent of that moorland village since 1791. Patrick heard the news with regret and wondered much who would be appointed to succeed Charnock in Grimshaw's old pulpit—and hoped a little too !

Down in Bradford the Rev. Henry Heap advised the Rev. Samuel Redhead to continue the curacy until a successor could be appointed.

Mr Redhead, who had often taken duty for James Charnock during his lengthy illness, readily obliged. The Vicar of Bradford then gave thought to the matter, and in June announced that Patrick Brontë was the new incumbent of Haworth, after which he sat back contentedly. He was to be most astonished at the storm clouds that gathered, came over those moorland hills, and burst about his ears.

As will be mentioned more fully in the next chapter, the trustees of Haworth Church, from a deed dating from the time of Queen Elizabeth the First (1559), retained the right to refuse the nominees of the vicars of Bradford for the incumbency of Haworth Church if they so desired. Indeed, under such circumstances they could refuse to pay him, and the emoluments of the living were in their hands. Thus, although the patronage of Haworth was in the gift of the Vicar of Bradford, it could be bestowed only with the full concurrence of the Haworth Church Land Trustees. Henry Heap, either from ignorance or design—almost certainly the former—did not consult the trustees prior to his appointment of Patrick. What an error to undervalue or ignore the people of Haworth ! Also in view of the importance that attached itself to Patrick's being accepted as minister of that moorland chapelry, what unwitting folly ! Yet, in fairness, the Rev. Henry Heap was not alone in wishing for Patrick's appointment to Haworth. Only a few days after Charnock's death, and before even the Vicar of Bradford had quite made up his mind, the trustees of Haworth Church had wind of the decision likely to be made. One of their leading members, Mr Greenwood, received the following letter from a clerical friend of their late incumbent.

To Mr. Greenwood. Moor House Haworth.

Dear Sir, May I beg leave to recommend the Revnd P. Brontè as a proper person to succeed my late Reverend Friend Mr. Charnock as perpetual curate of Haworth and I trust that you will feel no objection to him on account of his possessing the confidence of the Vicar of Bradford, as I am confident you will find in him every qualification necessary to the spiritual Pastor of your Parish.

I beg leave to subscribe myself, Yours very respectfully

M. Stocks.

Catherine House June 1st 1819.

Accordingly the trustees met and decided to await the Vicar of Bradford's suggestion, guessing that Patrick Brontë would be the man. A few days later his name was duly sent up to them from Bradford, not as a nominee for their approval, however, but as the new incumbent, appointed by the Vicar.

Back from those moorland hills came the retort, like a crack of mountain thunder : it was not for the Vicar of Bradford to appoint any man to Haworth Church without their complete assent ! As for this Patrick Bronté, they knew next to nothing about him.

In Thornton, Patrick had been overwhelmed with mixed feelings when Henry Heap told him of his decision. He was so happy at Thornton and had so many friends. Would Maria really care for another move, and one that would take her into a wild moorland village away from all friends, all sympathetic society ?

Yet Haworth *was* Haworth. It was the greatest of honours to be offered Grimshaw's old pulpit ; besides, this was wonderful moorland country, ridge after ridge sweeping up to the sky. Patrick had once or twice walked as far as Oxenhope Moor and gazed across to that promised land. The village clinging to the steep hillside had been almost hidden from view but he had seen the high heathery hills and knew that it was beautiful. It was just the scene Patrick loved most : there, above all places, he would feel nearer to God and amidst such surroundings could tend the needs of those sturdy people who sought shelter and livelihood in that little village.

Maria was very brave, as he had known she would be : it was indeed a great tribute to Pat that he should have been chosen for the appointment so speedily. Besides Haworth was not far away from Thornton : visits could easily be made to all their old friends.

Thus in early June the Bronté family was braced for an early move across the hills. Then Patrick was told of the trustees' attitude, was informed only in the vaguest manner of the terms of the Elizabethan Charter, and confusion ensued. As will be seen, that confusion continued for many months as the most vital tug-of-war ever connected with British literature commenced. Once again the fate of our greatest novel and some of the best writing in the English language hung in the balance. Could *Wuthering Heights* have been written without the intimate knowledge and understanding of the moors around Haworth ? Could the genius of those young girls have thrived on any other soil than that ?

Patrick decided that the best thing to do—indeed, the only course—was to go over to Haworth and see the trustees, or at least one of them, and learn the facts of the matter. Maria agreed at once, and the Vicar of Bradford, now much put out, saw no harm in such an idea. Nevertheless, he warned Patrick that they were a wild lot up there and he had best look to himself. This was just the stuff for Patrick and he was now more eager than ever to make the visit.

On a very hot summer's day in early July, Patrick walked from

Thornton to Denholme and thence across Oxenhope Moor to the village of that name. From there he struck up across the fields to Marsh (a small cluster of houses) until, continuing, he saw Haworth Church below him on the right. Uncertain of his bearings and not realizing that to continue straight ahead would bring him to the top of Haworth, he struck down a lane towards the church, passing, although he did not realize it at the time, the old parsonage of Sowdens—once occupied by William Grimshaw himself. Again he was uncertain as to his best route and, instead of turning left along a lane which would have led him into the churchyard to the south of the church, he continued downhill, past some quarry workings, until he came to Haworth Old Hall at the foot of the steep main street of the village.

As he strode up Kirkgate (now, alas, called Main Street) several of the villagers gave him a glance. Without looking at his face they knew he was a stranger : no inhabitant of Haworth was so foolish as to take that narrow cobbled street at such a gait. (They are not true cobbles but end-ways blocks of stone known in the north as setts.)

At the top, Patrick, without taking in his surroundings, made enquiries and soon found some of the trustees. Not a word of sense could he gain from any of them—it was always the same answer : he had best see Stephen Taylor of the Manor House at Stanbury. This hamlet stood a mile to the north-west of Haworth so off Patrick went. If he was now angry and inclined to the idea that Haworth and its people were perhaps best served if placed under the care of the Devil, the view that met his gaze as he left the village behind him was one to check any good-humoured blasphemy on his lips, and his stride besides. On his right he looked down into a deep valley, with old farmsteads dotted around the stream that glistened up at him in the blazing sunshine. On his other hand, the moor came down to the very lane, whilst in front was hill after rolling hill as far as the eye could see. Hardly a tree in sight and yet those moors, dotted with black-faced sheep, were not bleak in any way, but beautiful. Here was space—the very epitome of freedom. Patrick continued to stride it out, resisting any impulse to fall on his knees in the wayside heather and thank God for such a sight, for such a marvel.

Below him on his right he saw Stanbury, a mere cluster of houses grouped together on a knoll of its own. He passed a solitary cottage on his right (Hill Top Cottage) with a small fairy ring of trees opposite it across the little lane. Soon afterwards he turned down a shallow path and mounted the opposite slope to Stanbury. (The bottom of this path is now under the reservoir since opened in this stretch of the Sladen Valley.) Almost the first house he encountered was the Manor House.

He enquired after Mr Stephen Taylor and was told he was out in the fields, haymaking. Patrick, clutching his stick, went off on a further search and soon discovered a group of men engaged in that task.

The gentleman he sought was pointed out to him and Patrick approached. His opening words were a blunder and no mistake. "Mr Taylor, I am the new incumbent of Haworth. The Vicar of Bradford has appointed me as incumbent of Haworth." Stephen Taylor looked up slowly and gazed at Patrick for a minute. "Nay, the Vicar of Bradford cannot do that. Come with me up to my house." By now Patrick did not care if he ever saw Grimshaw's pulpit, let alone preach from it regularly.

They returned to the Manor House in silence. Patrick glanced at the house before entering. Facing the main road on the right at the beginning of Stanbury, the house had a most impressive front and over the doorway was a stone bearing the date 1753. There was a grass plot, a causeway up the centre, a passage-way, a room on each side of the door, and a kitchen at the back. Like all the houses in Haworth and Stanbury, it was built of the local stone, the dark grey millstone-grit.

The Taylors were one of the oldest families in Stanbury, if not the oldest, having deeds dating back to 1500. Stephen Taylor's three sons, George, Robert and John, were also trustees, but as they were busy in the fields, the two men were able to enjoy a quiet talk together—and enjoy it Patrick certainly did. For in a few minutes of conversation with Mr Taylor a light dawned on him : he began to have the first glimmerings of understanding of the people who lived on these heights, and he liked what he found. Patrick then came to the point : "What shall I do ?" Stephen Taylor was thoughtful for a moment. He already knew, from the brief outline he had gleaned of Patrick's story and beliefs that he liked him and that this was the man for Haworth. He looked at Patrick suddenly and smiled, "Go to the Vicar of Bradford and give in your resignation, and then apply to the trustees in about two months' time and I will see all the trustees in the meantime, and I can answer for most of the trustees." Patrick's heart sank at the word "resignation" but rose as Mr Taylor finished speaking. How strange that it now seemed so important to him to gain the position. He had good friends at Thornton, he was happy there : why wish to leave ? He did not wish it really, and yet those moors, those miles of heathery hills, seemed to draw him on irresistibly.

Stephen Taylor made a few mumbled remarks about seeing the Heatons down at Ponden House first, and then assured Patrick all would be well. He led his visitor to the gate and shook him warmly by the hand—follow his advice and matters would proceed slowly but surely towards the appointment of Patrick as perpetual curate at Haworth—official appointment, this time.

As Patrick walked down the path towards the Sladen Valley, and up again towards Hill Top Cottage, Stephen Taylor waved adieu and then stood looking after the retreating figure for some minutes. He thought the tall striding cleric now reaching the top of the opposite hill just the very man who was needed locally. In fact, he had decided this indeed would be the man they would have, and for that decision the world should hold ever blessed the name of Stephen Taylor!

Patrick walked back to Thornton at a much slower pace than that by which he had come, and by a more direct route. Avoiding the village of Haworth, he turned right across the moors towards Marsh and Oxenhope. He would dearly have loved to spend an hour in the church, but for once prudence ruled uppermost in his mind. His appearance there and natural interest would only be interpreted by the villagers as presumptuous nosiness on the part of an aspirant for the living.

As he walked along he could glance back across the hills. Soon it would be August, and with a warm summer like this, following such a wet spring, those moors would then be a vivid splash of purple. Above his head several peewits circled, guarding their young in a field to his left; in the distance the lonely cry of a curlew floated down from the heathery slopes. It was a scene to prompt reflection on the petty squabbles that went on unceasingly in the towns below—such a contrast to the peaceful beauty of these highlands—a scene to help him prepare next Sunday morning's sermon for the Old Bell Chapel.

Back at the parsonage in Market Street, Patrick could reflect on his day in Haworth and Stanbury, those few hours that had seemed so very much longer. He could not but agree with the trustees—it was their undoubted right to be consulted as to the appointment of their new incumbent, and consulted they had not been. In Patrick's opinion their further strongly worded, though not discourteous letter to the Vicar of Bradford had been justified to the hilt. In it (and a copy addressed to himself) they had stated that there was no personal objection to Patrick Brontë but, as they had not been brought into consultation with the Vicar about the matter, they must decline to accept him as their perpetual curate.

Someone with a personal interest in hearing Patrick's account of his day at Stanbury was the Mrs Kaye of Allerton Hall mentioned in Miss Firth's diary. Mercy Kaye was kinswoman to Stephen Taylor and his three sons, and into their ears a word in season had doubtless been whispered long since. That her opinions were favourable is certain, for there is evidence that after the Brontés had left Thornton, Charlotte once stayed at Allerton Hall.

Patrick knew well that the living of Haworth was a benefice or perpetual curacy. Should it become his, no one could ever remove him from that position (subject of course to the usual conditions that a sermon be preached on the Sabbath and the moral code pertaining be adhered to). But likewise, it would mean that once arrived at Haworth he was there for life. At Thornton there were friends and known happiness; at Haworth the beautiful moors and unknown wonders. There was also Grimshaw's pulpit. But Patrick did not allow ambition to play a part in his attitude during these vexed arguments. He would be honest and open in his dealings and leave it to God's will to decide where he, Patrick Brontė, might best serve Him.

He decided to take the advice of Stephen Taylor and retire from the field, leaving the vicar and the trustees to reach an agreement between themselves in accordance with the terms of the Elizabethan Charter.

He therefore informed Maria of his decision and wrote a number of letters intimating his withdrawal to the gentlemen most nearly concerned, the Rev. Henry Heap and Mr Taylor among them. But his clerical friends, together with the Vicar of Bradford, urged him to remain as the latter's nominee: the Archbishop of York had been advised of the position and would think poorly of him if he avoided his duty so readily. (Prior to 1836 Haworth had been in the diocese of York, but in that year was included in the new Ripon diocese.) Patrick decided he had best explain these matters to the trustees at once and on 8th July 1819 he wrote again, as follows, to Stephen Taylor:

". . . When the living of Haworth was offered to me by the Vicar of Bradford, I knew but little of the circumstances of the case, and consequently, I accepted the nomination. This I was induced to do for two reasons, which I am persuaded, no one can blame; first, because it seemed to hold forth some desirable advantages, and secondly, because as I never asked for it, it appeared to be a gift and a call of Providence. After I had seen you, however, and some of the other trustees I doubted if it was my duty to have anything more to do with Haworth, and I therefore wrote several letters to some gentlemen who were nearly concerned, signifying my intention to proceed no further.

"It seemed, however, to be the general opinion of my learned and pious friends, that I should not in honour, and with propriety recede, as I had gone so far: and that if I were to draw back, another might accept the place who would be less fit for it, and I should run the greatest hazard of seriously displeasing the Archbishop, who had received and approved my nomination.

"In consequence of this remonstrance, and, a kind proposal of his Grace, to permit me to hold both Thornton and Haworth, till affairs should be settled to my satisfaction, I now feel it to be my duty, with the help of God, to go on till I see the conclusion."

The letter then continues :

"I have been educated at Cambridge, and taken my degree at that first of Universities; I have resided for many years in the neighbourhood, where I am well known—I am a good deal conversant with the affairs of mankind—and I do humbly trust that it is my unvarying practice to preach Christ faithfully, as the only Way, the Truth, and the Life. From considerations such as these, I do think that Providence has called me to labour in His vineyard at Haworth, where so many great and good men have gone before me. I therefore request your kindness, and your prayers, and that when I come to preach amongst you, you will use your endeavours to prevent people from leaving the Church, and will exhort them to hear with candour and attention, in order that God's name may be glorified, and sinners saved. . . ."

What else could he say but this, now that his Grace of York requested him to take charge of both Thornton and Haworth ? It had certainly been an honour for him, but the position was more obscure and unsatisfactory than ever. He had thought Mr Taylor's idea a sound one and had meant to carry it through but could hardly fly in the face of the Archbishop. However, this visit was never paid and Patrick's request that the people be kept in order whilst in the church was not necessary : the people of Haworth are quite happy to fly in the face of an Archbishop, or Emperor for that matter. There came another crack of defiant thunder from those hills and Patrick, who sympathized with their attitude and realized its full justice, wrote again to Stephen Taylor giving him the letter he wanted, the letter that would strengthen his hand in his discussions with the other trustees. It was dated 14th July 1819.

". . . I have just written to the Archbisop and the Vicar of Bradford to acquaint them with my resignation of my nomination to the living of Haworth—I thought it best to give you the earliest notice of this. . . ."

Patrick despatched the three letters of resignation and sat back with a sigh. This could so easily end any hope he had of becoming the incumbent of Haworth, and he knew it. As far as he was concerned he would never go there; but he had now decided that he would ally himself to no side in the dispute, play no part in subterfuge or underhand dealing, for there was work in plenty at Thornton. Reaching for his staff he sallied forth to visit an elderly woman who was very sick out Denholme way.

Meanwhile up at Haworth, Patrick's letter of resignation, coupled with the sincere endeavours of Stephen Taylor, had worked the oracle— the trustees were won over to a man. Brontë was no doubt their man, but ought they not to hear him preach ? True, he had resigned all pretensions to the curacy, but nevertheless if they could see and hear him preach it would help decide the matter beyond all doubt. If he proved satisfactory, then the Vicar of Bradford could be told that the Haworth Church Trustees agreed with his nomination and felt they could concur in the appointment.

The Rev. Henry Heap was advised of this decision accordingly and passed the letter on to Patrick. But the men of Haworth had met their match at last. They were dealing with Patrick Brontë this time and in such a struggle neither side could win. Let them contend for ever, only the fusion of Haworth and Brontë could spell invincibility ! Patrick read their letter and exploded ! This time the thunderous roar came up from Thornton and rocked the trustees back on their heels.

Patrick has often been described as a social climber, who wanted desperately to go to Haworth to be minister of a church which had been made famous by the illustrious William Grimshaw, for the prestige and standing it would give him. His reply to this letter of the trustees is hardly that of a man so described. Any man can preach one good sermon and Patrick knew that well, but it can never be the yardstick of his true value. Had Patrick been so very anxious and so very ambitious he would never have replied in such a strain. It is perhaps the finest letter Patrick ever penned, and shows in full measure that independent and noble spirit that has rendered the name of Brontë for ever unique.

July 21st 1819

. . . My conscience does not altogether approve to a circumstance of exposing myself to the temptation of preaching in order to please, especially when I consider that the human heart is deceitful above all things and desperately wicked—through divine grace my aim has been, and I trust, always will be, to preach Christ and not myself, and I have been more desirous of being made the instrument of benefit rather than pleasure to my own congregation. Besides all this, I really am of the opinion that the best way by far is for the Trustees and some others of the people of Haworth, who are good judges of preaching, to come and hear both me and others in our own Churches at a time when we do not expect them, and then they will see us as we usually are, and such as they would find us after many years' trial. It is an easy matter to compose a fine sermon or two for a particular occasion but no easy thing always to give satisfaction. Now there are some who may be so far distant, as to render it difficult to act as I have just stated, yet as I am but five or six miles off it will be no very difficult thing for such of the Trustees, and people of Haworth, as may be inclined to hear me in my own Church to come over at a time when I do not expect them—and they may even learn my character both as a preacher and liver, from others—as I have been for four years and upwards within five or six miles of them. I shall, if it please God, preach at Thornton, every Sabbath for some time, excepting for the first Sabbath of next month, when I shall perform Divine Service for the Missionary Cause both morning and afternoon in Mr. Dury's Church at Keighley, and, believe me, the character and conduct of man out of the pulpit is as much to be considered as his character and conduct in, and we are most likely to know those best who live nearest to us—my wish is, that if it should please the All-Wise Dispenser of Events to call me to Haworth, rather to grow in the esteem and affection of my congregation, and neighbours, than greatly to please them at the first and then constantly to lose ground after the charms of novelty were over. . . ."

There is an answer for the Haworth trustees to put in their clay pipes and smoke! But, as anyone who knows Haworth folk will appreciate, it was just the response they would respect. Here was a man of mettle, no mealy-mouthed sniveller. With this reply Patrick had won their hearts and it was agreed amongst them that one day, and soon at that, "they would have him".

Meanwhile, however, the impasse must continue; no face could be lost on either side, and as Patrick Brontë would not deliver a "show" sermon the matter must be deferred again. There was no help for it, and the harassed Henry Heap gave instruction that the Rev. Samuel Redhead should continue to minister as often as possible, as he had done during Mr Charnock's lengthy illness; and a local cleric, the Rev. William Anderton, was asked to take the main share of the duties in Haworth. The registers show plainly that these two men carried out the full duties assigned to them there, with the latter taking the main burden of the work. There are also a few signatures of the Rev. W. Cann, who assisted occasionally during this long interregnum.

So matters remained as the glorious summer of 1819 passed away. On 29th September Elizabeth Firth returned to Kipping House. "Came home in safety, thank God"; and on the very next morning: "September 30th. Mr Bronte to breakfast". She heard the full story of the exciting happenings that had occurred during her absence, and applauded Patrick on the stand he had taken, together with his action in the matter throughout. But all this news took time to impart, so on the very same day, "He and Mrs Bronte to tea".

Maria also had some exciting information to give the Firths, if they had not already taken the hint from the letters she and Patrick had sent them—she could expect her sixth child in the New Year! There was a flutter of the tea-cups as Elizabeth Firth feigned her astonished delight. A few days later and it was the turn of the five Brontë children to come to Kipping House to prattle out their news: "October 4th. The little Brontes called." They loved the old house and its grounds and were ever happy there, although only the three eldest would recollect it— Charlotte but faintly—in after years.

Patrick tried hard to forget the unpleasant dispute that raged over his head and quietly continued his many duties at Thornton. He was still officially responsible for both that parish and Haworth, under the Archbishop of York's permission and desire, but with Redhead and Anderton looking after the latter there was no occasion to add fresh fuel to the fire by visiting that moorland village. He was free to minister at the Old Bell Chapel—or so he thought! But a few days after the visit to Kipping House by the children, Patrick received a command from the Archbishop to preach in Haworth Church, an order he could hardly refuse to obey. His Grace considered that such an action would break the deadlock and put an end to the strife. Patrick, however, was not so sanguine. True, he and the trustees were sympathetic to each other and understood one another's point of view, but Patrick felt that even if he was the man they wanted, even if Stephen Taylor had won the others over, his own refusal to preach a trial sermon could not have pleased them over much. Above all, he knew full well that until the Rev. Henry Heap conceded them their right to concur in the choice of the perpetual curate of Haworth, the trustees would be inclined to oppose anyone sent there to preach a sermon. (By now Patrick had learned that William Grimshaw's appointment nearly eighty years earlier had been at the insistence of the trustees and not the wish of the Church.) Not a little anxious, therefore, Patrick sat down and penned a few lines to the Trustees informing them of his impending visit.

"Oct: 9th 1819.

". . . His Grace the Archbishop of York sent me word yesterday that he wished me to take the duty at Haworth Church tomorrow. This, which was certainly very contrary to my inclination, I could not refuse— I therefore write to inform you of the circumstances, lest you should mistake my motive. My mind, and my inclination, are the same on the subject as when I last saw you. . . ." Namely, that he had offered his resignation, as advised by Mr Taylor, and would wish to come to Haworth only if it were the wish of all. Furthermore he would not consider that this one sermon preached there could tell the trustees or people of that village anything of his true worth either as a preacher or a man. He was most concerned lest his visit should inflame the situation further and concluded: ". . . I hope you will receive me in a friendly manner tomorrow, as I am obliged to go to you, in compliance with the wishes of the Archbishop. . . ."

Thus on the following day, Sunday, 10th October 1819, Patrick mounted the steps of William Grimshaw's famous pulpit for the first time, and preached to the people of Haworth in St Michael's Church.

There, under the overhanging sounding-board, bearing such an inscription as Grimshaw was likely to select, "I determined not to know anything among you save Jesus Christ and Him Crucified.—W.G."— there under the old sounding-board, Patrick preached quietly, sincerely and briefly. It was a sermon devoid of pomp, showmanship or fuss; and there were no disturbances of any kind. What the trustees thought of the address is not known; what the congregation felt, has been lost in the mists of the past. But Patrick made it clear that he understood fully the right of the trustees to be considered in the appointment of a new incumbent, and the trustees again informed the vicar of Bradford that they could not accept Mr Brontë as the nominee of the vicar but only as the minister approved by both sides. Again Mr Heap made no attempt to meet the trustees half-way, again he made a gross blunder: very well, if the people of Haworth would not accept Brontë as his nominee, perhaps they would be happier if he gave the living to another. So he appointed the Rev. Samuel Redhead as perpetual curate of Haworth.

Rumour of this reached Haworth but was at first discounted—the vicar surely knew better than to do that? But a few days later and it was official.

"Edward Ebor appoints the Rev. Samuel Redhead to the Perpetual Curacy of Haworth in the County of York. October 28th 1819. In the Archbishop's twelfth year at York." To that effect ran the document and there was the Archbishop's seal to prove its validity! The people of Haworth rubbed their eyes in amazement. Down in Market Street, Thornton, Patrick heard the news and was incredulous and, somehow, in his heart of hearts, not a little disappointed. This would mean trouble and no mistake—Patrick knew that the people of Haworth would not stomach this further slight.

They certainly did not! This time there was no single clap of thunder from those hills but a cracking storm that continued for three weeks and finally drove the unhappy Samuel Redhead down Kirkgate for his life.

During the long interregnum and earlier, when James Charnock had been so ill, Redhead had conducted the service at Haworth many times, and was extremely popular. But now he was the Vicar of Bradford's choice of minister for the villagers—there had been no consultation. They still held no personal grievance against him, but would not tolerate him under such circumstances. He must go!

On the first Sabbath he officiated, the church was crowded even in the aisles. During the reading of the second lesson, the entire congregation rose to its feet, as by one impulse, and marched out, making as much noise as possible to drown Mr Redhead's voice—no difficult feat as practically the entire assembly wore clogs. So they all clattered and banged their way out, until Samuel Redhead and his clerk were left alone in the church to continue the service as best they could. Many men from outlying farms and even from across the Lancashire border had walked in from the moors to take part in this demonstration.

Mr Redhead tried again the next Sunday—and the proceedings were far worse. The church was full, but this time the aisles were left quite clear. As the luckless minister was again attempting the second lesson, the reason for this became only too apparent. A man rode into the church upon an ass, face to tail, with as many old hats piled on his head as he could carry. He urged the beast round the aisles to the accompaniment of screams, hoots, yells and laughter from the congregation. Poor Mr Redhead gave up his endeavour to read from the Holy Book, and that ended another service. Redhead decided to make one more attempt—to the intense irritation of Haworth—and thus brought disaster on himself.

On the third Sunday, 14th November 1819, he rode up the village street accompanied by several gentlemen from Bradford. They reached the top and left their horses at the Black Bull, which stood in front of the church steps. They moved into the church followed by a determined and rather confident congregation, who had with them a chimney-sweep, covered in soot, whom they placed right in front of the reading-desk. Mrs Gaskell states that he had been plied with drink until he was in a state of solemn intoxication or "three-parts fresh" as the locals have it; but the truth is, the poor fellow, although sober enough, was half-witted.

As the Rev. Samuel Redhead commenced the service this fellow nodded his blackened face in stupid assent to all that was said. Redhead became disconcerted and there were titters from the pews. Then it happened. Suddenly springing to his feet, the sweep walked forward and clambering up the steps of the pulpit endeavoured to embrace the minister. Now the whole building was in uproar. The time had arrived— down the hill with him! The people pushed the chimney-sweep against

14

Mr Redhead as the latter tried to escape, then grasping them both they led them out of church and into the churchyard.

Here was a black pile, where the soot-bag had been emptied that morning, and into this mess the minister and his tormentor were hurled.

With his face covered with soot, the wretched Samuel Redhead was chased between the tombstones by the infuriated mob ; he barked his shins on several, fell flat on his face across a slab-tomb and slid on his back across another that was slimy and green with age. Somehow he regained his feet, and with the cat-calls of the crowd in his ears fell down the church steps, nearly broke his neck over the stocks that stood beside them, and dived head-first into the doorway of the Black Bull which was immediately locked behind him.

Outside the barred door the crowd gathered—the experience of being locked out of the Bull was very far from their taste—and they threatened to stone Redhead and his friends if they dared appear.

Inside the Bull the terrified clergyman found his only friend in Haworth, the landlord, Mr Sugden. The latter did not want any damage to his property, but he was a most kindly man withal and did not care for the odds against Mr Redhead. He decided at once to assist him in an escape, believing that, such was the temper of the Haworth people, the fugitive was in real danger of his life. Sugden led the unpopular inmates to a side door (through which, together with the various windows, many had escaped from Parson Grimshaw's whip in earlier times) and advised them to go behind the barn and make their way downhill behind the houses, until they reached the foot of Kirkgate where they would be met with horses. Without further query Redhead and his Bradford friends crept away over the rough ground where the fields sloped down almost to the very back walls of the houses, then round a narrow side street (later called Lodge Street) until they reached the bottom of the main hill. Meanwhile, Sugden and some of his stable boys emerged from the Black Bull and rode the visitors' horses backwards and forwards before the front door, amongst the fiercely expectant crowd. Seeing the figures emerge at the foot of the street they struck spurs and dashed down Kirkgate, where Samuel Redhead and the others quickly mounted. Turning left past the toll-bar or turnpike, the fugitives sped down Bridgehouse Lane, across the bridge, and away towards Keighley. By the time the crowd had realized their plan and run down to Bridgehouse, the prey had got clear away, and the pursuers found the turnpike gate closed against them.

But the people of Haworth were content. They had rid themselves of Samuel Redhead and had asserted what they considered to be their rights; and that night, in the old Black Bull, the landlord was as popular as ever.

Fortunately for the luckless cleric, the vicar of Bradford, fearing an abrupt termination to the appointment, had promised not to present to Horton for two months. Thus, after he had scrubbed away the soot, Samuel Redhead could return to his former ministry.

It is by this single incident that he is remembered outside the West Riding, as a figure of ridicule. Posterity was unkind to Samuel Redhead, for it dragged him into the Brontë legend because of those three weeks and ignored his years of inspired ministry. Some of the injustice Patrick suffered spilled on to his shoulders.

Samuel Redhead was born on 24th December 1778. He built up Horton Chapel, was for a time Second Master to Bradford Grammar School, and after the Haworth *débâcle*, in 1822 commenced a faithful, evangelical ministry as Vicar of Calverley, not far from Apperley Bridge, a ministry that called forth the comment, "We prayed for silver, but God has given us gold."

He became the annual examiner in classics at Woodhouse Grove, a further example of Evangelical-Wesleyan harmony in the north of England—rekindled once Jabez Bunting, having organized independent Methodism on a sure foundation, became anxious to work again with what he termed "the Wilberforce Evangelicals".

At Woodhouse Grove Redhead was remembered "as a fresh-looking, sprightly little gentleman, neat in his dress, and very kind and considerate in his manner". Indeed, it was Redhead who did much to soften Bunting and, before long, the pupils of the Grove were in Calverley Church where "the boys outsung everybody".

Although Patrick sometimes took duty at Calverley, it was many years before Redhead appeared in Haworth again. But Patrick invited him to preach on 21st July 1844, and he was given a hearty welcome, for the villagers bore him no grudge.

Nor did he bear any malice towards them, and in his two sermons to large and attentive congregations, he good-humouredly reminded them of the treatment meted out to him in 1819.

Through marriage Redhead was connected with many of the leading Bradford families—Rand, Mossman, McTurk—all of whom Patrick knew well. Patrick and Morgan remained close friends with Redhead, whom they had first met at Kipping House, until his death on 26th August 1845. He was succeeded at Calverley by his son-in-law, the Rev. Alfred Brown, M.A. A Memoir, with portrait, was published the year after his death.

Patrick Brontë played fair with Mr Redhead, and was not anxious to refer to those riotous scenes of long ago when questioned about them by Mrs Gaskell. She gained her story from the villagers and the grandson of Redhead's clerk. Patrick would merely say, "My predecessor took the living with the consent of the Vicar of Bradford, but in opposition to the Trustees—in consequence of which he was so opposed that, after three weeks' possession, he was compell'd to resign." Patrick restrained himself as he had no desire to make fun of the late gentleman, but for all his old age, he was longing to tell Mrs Gaskell the whole story as it had first reached his ears at the parsonage in Thornton.

Thus thwarted, the Rev. Henry Heap, after accepting Redhead's resignation, nominated two or three other clergymen—the Rev. William Anderton among them—but the trustees stood firm as mountain rocks and refused to consider the appointment of any of them. Matters were back where they had been, with Patrick responsible for both Thornton and Haworth and Mr Anderton still bravely filling the gap at the latter parish, although, happily, without any trouble. But it was a most unsatisfactory state of affairs as far as Patrick was concerned. He would be glad when all was well settled one way or another. He saw Mr Taylor again and explained his perplexities. He also wrote to the trustees again, saying that he was still prepared to accept Haworth if it was the unanimous wish of the Archbishop, the Vicar and the trustees. Otherwise, he thought to himself, I only wish to be left in peace at Thornton.

But for all this the year 1819 ended peacefully enough at Thornton, Miss Firth recording the everlasting visits and counter-visits for the purpose of drinking tea and gossiping. There are only two variants in her diary:

"November 3rd. My mother and I walked to Swirrel, Mr Bronte with us. [Swirrel was a farm at Thornton belonging to Mr Firth.] December 30th. Mr Bronte and I went to Bradford."

Only once or twice did Patrick have to walk the long way over those wintry hills to Haworth, but they were cold journeys with raw biting winds and snow threatening to fall from a leadened sky. One such journey was made on Wednesday, 17th November 1819, to officiate at a burial. Afterwards Patrick went into the vestry and, for the first time, signed the old Haworth registers: "P. Bronte". He raced home against a freezing wind, anxious to be by the fire with Maria and the little ones, and did not know the significance of the speck of ink he had washed across that page in the old vestry. For these journeys Patrick could draw expenses at Thornton amounting to 2s.

But with the New Year came a temporary banishment of his clerical cares. On Monday, 17th January 1820, his sixth and last child was born—Anne. She has always been called the quiet and gentle Anne, as indeed she was. But she was far more : she was the bravest of the Bronté children who grew to maturity. Charlotte, for all her courageous perseverance, would sometimes sink; Branwell lacked courage of any kind; Emily the fearless, the undaunted, the noblest of all women, remained so only when in her own moorland domain; but Anne never gave way, never lacked courage and endurance. She loved her home as much as Emily did, yet she alone laboured in a foreign field without complaint of any kind.

Anne Bronté, who was named after her maternal grandmother and her aunt, Anne Branwell, was born into a quiet house in Market Street. As Miss Firth entered in her diary : "January 17th. Anne Bronte born. The other children spent the day here." Of course, on the very next day, "18th. I called at Mr Bronte's."

At this time, with six children and no strong hope of Haworth, Patrick wrote to the Governors of Queen Anne's Bounty, asking for financial assistance and advised the Archbishop of his action. Had he but waited a few more days these letters would have been unnecessary.

Richard Burn, Esq. Secretary to the Governors
Bounty Office, Dean's Yard, Westminster.

Thornton, near Bradford, Yorkshire, 27 Jany 1820.
Sir,
The perpetual Curacy of Thornton, of which I am the Incumbent, has not, I believe, for many years, received any Augmentation from the Governors, under an idea I should suppose, of its having already arrived at the standard, which for the present, they are not inclined to exceed. I have, however, lately understood that they intend to raise all small Livings, especially when the population is considerable, to one hundred and fifty pounds a year exclusive of the Glebe House, or parsonage. Should my information in these respects be correct, then I hope to lay before the Governors, some particulars which may induce them to consider my case and afford me some assistance.

Thornton, has generally been returned for one hundred and forty pounds a year ; but in this have been included the dues, which average about five pounds, and a voluntary contribution, frequently made under exceedingly unpleasant circumstances—amounting for the most part to seven or eight pounds. Nothing arises from pews, or from any other service. The inhabitants, too, are so poor, in general, that presents which in some situations are very considerable, are here, not worth mentioning. So that all things duly weighed, and the proper deductions being made, the regular and certain salary of this Living, is not more than one hundred and twenty seven pounds yearly.

There is, it's true, besides this, a very ill constructed Parsonage House, which is, not only inconvenient, but requires, annually, no small sum to keep it in repair. There are, besides, these, some peculiarities in the situation, which, I should hope, the Governors will allow, give me a claim prior to many, whose salary is smaller. There are two full Services in the Church, every Sunday; the Chapelry is very extensive, being about 5 miles long and nearly 4 broad; the population is, at least, 9,000. The place swarms with disaffected people, who omit no opportunity that offers, to bring our excellent Establishment into contempt. Embarrassed as I have sometimes found myself, this has often half inclined me to give up the yearly contribution, and always induced me to exert myself to keep up a respectable appearance. I fear however, that in this, which as a Christian and a Churchman, I conceive to be my duty, I shall find myself sore beset, unless my salary receive some little augmentation. If I were a single man, I might find what I have sufficient, but as I have a wife, and six small children, with two maidservants [the Hartshead lass was shortly to return home], as well as myself to support, without I can obtain something more, in a just and honourable way, I greatly fear, that with the most rigorous economy, I shall be unable, any longer to uphold in appearance the due degrees of clerical respectability. By laying this before the Governors, you will greatly oblige, Sir,

Your most obedient, and humble servant P. Brontë

His Grace the Archbishop of York.

Thornton, near Bradford, Yorkshire, 4th Feby 1820.
My Lord,
I have just written a letter to be laid before the Governors of Queen Anne's Bounty, of which the following is a copy—would your Grace have the goodness to peruse it, and should it not meet with your disapprobation, by kindly condescending to use your influence in my behalf, you would greatly oblige,

My Lord, Your Grace's most obedient and humble servant,

P. Brontè.

But before Anne's christening could take place something rather important occurred. The Vicar of Bradford, Henry Heap, had a light of sweet reason flash into his head and decided to end the deadlock with a compromise. He conceded the choice of the perpetual curate for Haworth to the Church Land Trustees, but strongly recommended Patrick Brontë's name for their deliberations. Victory for Haworth!

They knew that Patrick had agreed with their stand for their rights; they had heard him preach; Mr Stephen Taylor was an enthusiastic supporter of that gentleman's claim, and they chose Patrick Brontë. On Friday, 25th February 1820, the Archbishop of York signed the order appointing Patrick Brontë perpetual curate of Haworth, and did so with a deep sigh of relief.

At Thornton Patrick heard the news also with relief, and then followed those inevitable mixed feelings of joy and sadness. Maria tried to appear pleased for herself as well as for Pat; the children were naturally excited, and certainly Emily had every reason to be. The young servant from Hartshead was vastly pleased and was prepared to pack her things straight away, to return home. Elizabeth Firth pulled a wry face and, with less enthusiasm than usual, brought her diary up to date: "February 25th. Mr Bronte was licensed to Haworth."

The protracted struggle over, the appointment of a new minister for Haworth was recorded down in Bradford Parish Church. Patrick's resignation-letter to Stephen Taylor was not considered official by Henry Heap until the latter had nominated Samuel Redhead, and Patrick's final appointment was, of course, dated some days before the Archbishop of York's confirmation.

Vicar Heap's clerk recorded Patrick's first acceptance as 2nd June 1819, his resignation as 21st October. Redhead's appointment was 25th October, followed by his hasty resignation on 19th November (five days after he had fled from Haworth).

In the final appointment of Patrick, Vicar Heap was forced to capitulate from the stubborn and senseless stand he had taken; although he made his clerk word the statement so as to include as much face-saving as possible:

"Whereas the Reverend Henry Heap, Vicar of Bradford, hath . . . consented to *permit* the Trustees of the Estates for the benefit of the Curate of Haworth, to join with him in a nomination, it is distinctly to be understood to all future generations and particularly when a vacancy shall happen in the Curacy of Haworth, that the rights of the Vicar of Bradford as Patron, and the Trustees of the Estate for the benefit of the Curate, shall remain untouched—Therefore be it known to all men that the Revd Patrick Bronte is duly nominated and appointed by the Revd Henry Heap, Vicar of Bradford, and the Trustees of the Curacy of Haworth."

The statement concludes with Patrick's promise to pay "half of all the Dues for *Marriages, Funerals, Baptisms and Churchings* —which shall be paid on Easter Monday in every year—and lastly, if required by the Vicar of Bradford, to preach a sermon in the Parish Church of Bradford every *Trinity Sunday*, in the afternoon as a mark of *Reverence* to the Mother Church—I have herewith set my hand and seal this 8th day of Feby in the Year of Our Lord 1820. Patrick Brontè."

On the same day, 8th February, Patrick's testimonial from Thornton was sent to the Archbishop, signed by Heap, Morgan and Redhead. It was enclosed with the nomination, which guaranteed to both parties that "their Rights shall remain in the same Condition and Force as they were in at the signing and sealing". Henry Heap's signature was followed, for the trustees, by those five stalwarts of Haworth independence—William Greenwood, John Beaver, James Greenwood, Stephen Taylor and Robert Heaton.

The next day Heap wrote to the Archbishop explaining his recent trials.

Vicarage, Bradford 1820 Feby 9th

My Lord,

I was honoured with your Grace's Letter for which I beg leave to return my best thanks. The difficulties stated therein of my holding Haworth with Bradford appeared so many and great that I thought it better to wait upon the Trustees at Haworth in order, if possible to settle the business — After many *altercations* they have at last agreed to take Mr. Brontè on my permitting them to *join with me* in a nomination similar to what was done by Mr. Kennett [*sic*—Kennet] late Vicar of Bradford, when Mr. Grimshaw was appointed to Haworth—I had offered to do this some time ago, but the Trustees *positively refused* then to have Mr. Brontè—Your Grace will see by the nomination, which will be sent by this day's Post that the question of Right between the Vicar of Bradford & the Trustees remains untouched. [Again the Vicar makes a virtue of necessity.] I feel truly thankful that the matter is now settled for it has been attended with very great trouble & expense to me—If your Grace could save Mr. Brontè a journey to York, by permitting him to take the Oaths before me for his Licence, it would be considered a great favour & *some expense* would be saved by this means, which to Mr. Brontè, with six small children, is certainly *an object*—

With my warmest acknowledgements to your Grace for the patience with which you have attended to my representations of the business through its various stages, & for the regard manifested for the *Interest* of the Establishment in my Parish—

I remain, my Lord, Your Grace's most faithful & obliged servant

H : Heap.

At the same time Patrick wrote to the Archbishop to ensure that his own postion and the trustees' rights were secured.

His Grace the Archbishop of York.

Thornton, near Bradford, 9th Feby 1820.

My Lord,
I have sent my Testimonials, and License to the Perpetual Curacy of Haworth for the inspection of your Grace, and should they be approved, I beg leave to request that your Grace will mention in my License, that I am Licensed in consequence of the conjoint nomination of the Vicar and Trustees; for if the Vicar's name only, were to be inserted, on my reading myself in, it would in all probability give rise to very serious tumults in the Church [certainly !], and might ultimately lead to the necessity of my resignation.
I remain, my Lord, Your Grace's most obedient and humble servant
P. Brontè

To this day the validity of the Elizabethan Charter remains, and a new licence read in Haworth Church maintains the trustees' rights.
For Patrick it now meant more frequent journeys over the moors to visit his new chapelry, where he would serve for the rest of his days; and as soon as Maria was strong enough for the journey, the move would take place.
On Saturday, 25th March 1820, Anne was christened, her godparents being Mr Firth, Elizabeth Firth, and the latter's great friend, Miss Fanny Outhwaite, from Bradford. Once again, William Morgan was called in to officiate.

1820 March 25th	Anne daughter of	The Rev. Patrick and Maria	Bronté	Minister of Haworth	Wm. Morgan Minister of Christ Church in Bradford

Note that the "Minister of Haworth" was entered under the heading "Abode", the column for "Profession" being left blank !
From Miss Firth—"March 25th. Anne Bronte was christened by Mr. Morgan; F. Outhwaite and I were godmothers." And in her cash account for January 1820 is found, "Gave at A. Bronte's christening, £1."
Shortly after this happy event, there was some unrest in Thornton and district, and Patrick, remembering the rebellion in Ireland and the

recent Luddite trouble alarmed Mr Firth so greatly by his prophecies of what might occur in England that that gentleman had all his windows in Kipping House barred up. The trouble, which in the event never materialized, seemed to have reached its most dangerous moment on Good Friday and Patrick was begged to be ready at hand. Thus the amusing entry in the diary: "March 31st. Good Friday; no service. We sat up expecting the Radicals."

So Patrick's life at Thornton drew to its close—he and his family were to move to Haworth in April. He had been so happy there: it had been a quiet, a social, a domestic life, in contrast to the storms of Dewsbury and Hartshead, but it had been bliss for Patrick—such complete joy as he would never know again. Elizabeth Firth was to be away from home on the day of departure and bade her sad farewells before leaving Kipping House: "April 5th. Took leave of Mr Bronte before leaving home." There is almost a tear-stain on the page.

Patrick performed his last baptism in the Old Bell Chapel of St James on 13th February 1820, christening the child of a coalminer from Denholme, and on Sunday, 16th April, he preached his last sermon from the pulpit as minister.

It was a sad moment for Patrick. He had served at Thornton for only a few weeks short of five years. He had been popular and made many friends, not only at Kipping House but amongst the people of the district. The poor in the parish owed him much and were distressed that he was leaving them. The future was a mystery, Patrick realzied that. He was going among strange people and was still uncertain as to what lay before him.

Patrick was not yet sure who his successor was to be, indeed it seemed another interregnum would occur. That indeed was the case for a short time—from 20th April until June. During that period payment was made every Sunday to the officiating clergymen, mostly from Bradford, who took the services. The faithful William Morgan agreed to come up from Christ Church to take any additional duties, such as burials and weddings, during the interregnum. In June, however, the Rev. William Bishop was appointed to succeed Patrick at Thornton. He remained there some years and is buried in the churchyard of the Old Bell Chapel. Bishop had been appointed curate at Bradford Parish Church on 22nd December 1819 and, not surprisingly, was "late of Madeley".

The final preparations for the journey were completed, the waggons ordered. Stephen Taylor kindly sent over two carts with horses—proof positive that Haworth wanted Patrick! Nancy and Sarah Garrs were to accompany the Bronté family to Haworth, as they were most willing to do. The young servant from Hartshead was at last released and returned there, where she promptly married her young fellow.

The children had their final glimpse of Kipping House and the magical garden with its flashing stream (although Maria and Elizabeth would return in a year's time); Mr and Mrs Firth said their adieus; Patrick paid his last visits to those who had grown to love his calling upon them; and all was ready.

When tragedy had burst fully upon him, Patrick would look back on his days at Thornton with an aching heart. True, he would walk from Haworth across the hills to visit Kipping House; true, he would often return to the Old Bell Chapel and preach the Anniversary Sermon to the Sunday school, but the magic would be gone. As some of his later letters will show, memory of happy times past made but a mockery of his old haunts. One such letter, written some years after the full tide of grief had swept over his head, shows he would never forget his carefree days at Thornton. It is written to his opposite number in that village, his friend the Rev. Robinson Pool, the Dissenting minister of Kipping Chapel, who by then was living in Driffield. It also contains an interesting reference to Mrs Gaskell's famous biography, published a year previously.

Haworth, Nr. Keighley. March 18th, 1858.
Revd. and Dear Sir,

I have read your kind letter, with a high degree of interest and melancholy pleasure, old times, and old circumstance, which have never escaped my memory, have been brought to view in more lively colours, and I can fancy, almost, that we are still at Thornton, good neighbours, and kind, and sincere friends, and happy with our wives and children.

But it has pleased the Lord, that a change should come over us, and that we should be reminded, that this is not our abiding place, that there is now, no paradise here below, and that pure and lasting happiness, is reserved only for those who are in heaven.

You have had your trials, both sharp, and severe, but God has given you grace, and strength sufficient unto your day—My trials you have heard of—I feard [sic] often, that I should sink under them; but the Lord remembered mercy in judgment, and I am still living, till I am in the eighty second year of my age.

You I think are considerably younger. I am still able to preach once on the Lord's day, but cannot do more. At present, however, I am troubled with an attack of chronic Bronchitis, and a severe cough, but am something better than I was a few days ago.

About eleven years since, I lost my sight, through cataract in my

eyes, but having undergone a surgical operation, I have through Divine
Mercy, been able since that time, to see to read and write, and find my
way without a guide. Mr Craven gave an account of your health and
circumstances and from what he said, and what you tell me, I have
derived especial pleasure.

The Memoir, which you refer to, though in general, well, and ably
written, contains some extravagant aneckdotes [sic] about me, which are
utterly untrue, and without the least foundation.

I remain, Revᵈ and Dear Sir

Yours, very respectfully, and truly, P. Brontë.
The Revᵈ R. Pool, Driffield.

(Before the final words of his letter, "least foundation", Patrick had
written the word "shadow", but crossed it through.)

Thus remembered the lonely old man who had lost everyone and
everything, except his faith!

On the morning of Thursday, 20th April 1820, a bright but blustery
day, a light, covered waggon, followed by seven carts, was driven quietly
out of Market Street in Thornton and made the steep ascent of Thornton
Heights. In the first sat Maria and her six children, the eldest only a
little over six years of age, the baby, Anne, who was in her mother's lap
but three months. Behind them all crouched Nancy and Sarah Garrs,
gazing a little anxiously at what they could see of the high moorland
countryside.

Patrick walked by the side of the waggon, giving the horse many a
pat and tasty titbit. From time to time he would lift one of the eldest
children out to give them exercise for a few yards. Behind rumbled the
carts, all loaded with furniture and personal possessions.

The moorland road, if road it could be called, was pitted and
cratered from the winter rains that had flowed over it from the hills, and
only Patrick who strode quietly on, was free from the danger of having
his head badly knocked about as the waggon jolted poor Maria and her
family from one side to the other.

Slowly the cavalcade proceeded. It was warmer now, as the noon
sun struck its heat through the coverings of the waggon. They went by
Denholme, Flappit Springs and Braemoor, the moorland road climbing
and diving alternately, until they reached Oxenhope Moor. Avoiding
the descent to that village they passed the old Fleece Inn on their right
and continued straight ahead. Suddenly they reached a crest and
Patrick halted the procession. For a moment he stood there on the Brow
side of Haworth and gazed across the narrow valley to where, on the
other side he saw, at the top of Kirkgate, the tower of his new church.
He pointed it out to Maria in silence. It was late in the afternoon and

the sun, although now watery, was setting on the moors behind the church. Against the bright yellow sky the tower was a strong black silhouette. Patrick had reached the highest rung in his ladder of destiny. From this time forward it would be passive endurance rather than assertive courage that he would require; and he would not be found wanting.

He gave the order to move forward and they climbed slowly down the Brow to the bottom of Bridgehouse Lane, crossed the little bridge over the Worth and mounted to the top of the lane, opposite the Old Hall. Here the turnpike-keeper enquired who they were. "Mr Bronté and family." There was to be no payment; the way was cleared. They passed through and the gate closed behind them.

As the waggon swung right and climbed slowly up Kirkgate the people came out of their houses to watch the arrival of their new incumbent—an unusual proceeding on their part. Usually, if "t'Parson" let them be they cared not who he was or what he looked like. But the recent challenge to their ancient rights and the exciting scenes during the ejection of Mr Redhead had aroused their interest in clerical matters. There they stood ranged along that steep, narrow cobbled street and clustered on the little plateau of space at its summit. Toothill the barber, Hartley the postmaster, Sugden of the Black Bull, the Taylors, Greenwoods, Heatons, Rushworths, and Mr Pighills, representing the trustees. Also represented in that crowd of onlookers were nearly all the well-known family names that have existed in Haworth since Saxon times: Appleyard, Aykroyd, Binns, Brown, Feather, Holmes, Horsfall, Hoyle, Murgatroyd, Pickles, Ratcliffe, Shuttleworth, Sutcliffe, Whittaker, Wood. There were, of course, several other names, but surprisingly few would complete the list.

As the waggon neared the summit of Kirkgate, one of the children moved forward under Maria's arm and gazed intently at the grey stone houses so close on either side. The walls of the village stared dumbly back. Emily Bronté and Haworth exchanged their first mutual glance; they alone, in all this world, were worthy of each other.

The waggon swung round to the left, passing the door of the King's Arms, and climbed up the short and narrow Parsonage Lane.

On the left was the north side of the church, and then the graveyard; on the other side was a small cottage and then an open space running up to a large stable at the top of the lane. (The Sunday school and sexton's house had not been built at that time.) The sexton, William Brown, and his sixteen-year-old son, John, stood at the entrance to the churchyard and touched their hats.

At the top of the lane, behind the churchyard, stood the parsonage, and as the procession reached the door in the side wall of the front garden, the waggon came to a halt. Behind it the carts stretched nearly the length of the lane.

Patrick assisted his cramped family to alight, then helped the Garrs sisters down. The Brontés walked along the path and up the steps. Patrick opened the door and they all crowded into the hall. A local woman, warned of their coming, had been busy and fires blazed cheerfully in both the living rooms.

Young Maria, with Emily at her heels, was soon halfway up the stairs. They had caught sight of the landing window ; there would be a splendid view of the moors from there. Maria picked up her sister and lifted her to the window ; and with wide eyes Emily Jane Bronté gained the first glimpse of her kingdom.

The rest of the family stood still in the hall for a moment and then Patrick shut the parsonage door behind them.

The Brontés had arrived in Haworth ! Save perhaps for the youngest, Anne, none of them would ever quite escape from it again ; nor, in their innermost hearts, would they ever really want to.

CHAPTER 12

Haworth

To GIVE a complete history of Haworth, to write a full account of the story of the parish church and its clergy, to mention completely the religious life of that village, even without adding a description of the wild and beautiful moors that sweep round it on every side and have given so much spiritual benefit to many—all this would take ten volumes. Add to this the story of the people of that moorland village— and the tales about them are legion—and there is no end.

They are Yorkshiremen. True. Of the West Riding. True. Typical moorland folk. Untrue. The fact is that the people of Haworth are unique, a race apart. Their nobility is without equal; their faults, bad beyond belief. They make the most loyal of friends, the most inveterate of foes. Nothing is negative in Haworth, nothing sweet and simpering. Everything resembles the local millstone grit—tough, sturdy, independent, defiant and yet beautiful. Haworth is beyond the realms of compromise, it is undeviating truth. It is a country where there is no place for faint hearts or sophisticated niceties or pretty men. It is a village of strength surrounded by primitive moors that are everlasting and lovely, with the freedom and beauty of the soul.

To describe Haworth, then, would take many books, but here it must be attempted in a few pages.

There is no mention of Haworth in Domesday Book. Although there is ample evidence of their reaching this district some years afterwards, even those intrepid warriors the Normans appear to have heard of the fierce reputation of Haworth folk and to have left it late to climb that hill in search of land.

That the Romans were there in the neighbourhood, although not interested in the ground on which the village stands, is obvious. The Pennine Way runs through the valley below Haworth, up past Stanbury, and then climbs over the crests of the high moors beyond, until it plunges down into Lancashire and finds its way to Colne (*Calunio*, the colony of the Romans). Hence it is not improbable that Stanbury (Stane or Stonyburgh) was a small fortification or station on the high Penine Way.

But beyond Stanbury, away above Ponden Hall, above Ponden Valley, above even that stone kirk or crag that overhangs the valley, on one of the highest parts of the moors there still loom out of the mists of antiquity something far older than the Romans : the Alcomden (or Oakenden) Stones. Composed of an outer circle with a high central rock, these stones are, in the opinion of most experts, the remains of a Druid "temple". Certainly the large, high, hollowed-out stone in the centre bears out that contention, being most unnaturally shaped like a sacrificial altar.

According to Lewis's *Topographical Dictionary* : "On Crow Hill, the loftiest eminence of the ancient chapelry of Haworth, and at a height of 1,500 feet above the level of the sea, is a cromlech, an evident Druidical remain, consisting of one flat stone, weighing about six tons, placed horizontally upon two huge upright blocks, now half embedded in the heather."

But around village and hamlet, farm and crag, around the very stones themselves, stretch the miles and miles of heather and bracken, ling and bilberry, grass and moss-crop—the moors themselves. They are the oldest of all, for they were here before there came the humans to build their houses of the local millstone grit, and they will remain long after man and stone have crumbled into dust.

Just how long there has existed some kind of chapelry on the present site of Haworth Church, it is not possible to tell. The assertion that a monastery was founded there by St Autest in A.D. 600 has been shown to arise from an erroneous translation of the Latin inscription over the door on the south side of the tower. But it is quite possible that a Christian community did exist in Haworth at that time. As early as A.D. 314 Britain was represented at the Council of Arles by three bishops, one of them from York.

The first direct notice of Haworth is from the record known as Kirkby's Inquest in 1296, the twenty-fourth year of Edward the First's reign. There it is mentioned that Godfrey de Haworth, Roger de Manyngham and Alicia de Bercroft had four oxgangs in Haworth, where twenty-four carucates made a knight's fee. These three acquired their property as heirs of John de Haworth. Similarly, at that time, most of the land at the neighbouring village of Oxenhope was held by the de Oxenhope family, the last lineal descendant of that name, Jane de Oxenhope, marrying Adam Copley de Batley.

The *Nomina Villarum*, 1316, gives Haworth and Oxenhope as in the possession of Nicholas de Audley, who held Bradford Manor.

In 1380, under Richard the Second, the poll tax mentions forty persons as inhabitants of Haworth, all save one paying the tax of four pence. Indeed there are several references to the chapelry of Haworth in the Archbishop's Registers at York in Plantagenet times,

PLATE 9   *All Saints, Dewsbury, and Vicarage*

PLATE 10   *St Peter's, Hartshead*

PLATE 11 (*Above*) *Hammond Roberson*

PLATE 12 (*Above right*) *Lousy Thorn Farm*

PLATE 13 (*Below right*) *The Wesleyan Academy, Woodhouse Grove, in 1812*

the first dated 1317. In that year a monition was issued commanding the Rector and Vicar of Bradford and the freeholders of Haworth to pay to the curate of Haworth Chapel the salary that was due to him in the proportions to which they had been liable from *ancient times*—thus proving that a chapel existed at Haworth long before 1300. The rector of Bradford was the owner of the "Great Tithes" and the vicar was his deputy and owned the "Small Tithes". Again, in 1320, a monition was issued from the Archbishop's Court, this time stating definitely the amounts due to the Haworth curate.

The rector of Bradford (not an ecclesiastic, but, as mentioned, owner of the tithes) was commanded to pay twenty shillings, the vicar of Bradford two marks and a half and the inhabitants of Haworth one mark.

In 1338 the curate's slender income was further augmented by the founding of a chantry in the chapel, which was added to the existing annual stipend. A chantry was a chapel or separate place of worship in a church, set aside for the celebration of masses for the souls of some departed this life.

The Haworth Chantry was endowed by Adam de Copley (or Adam Copley de Batley) for the repose of his soul and that of his wife, Jane de Oxenhope. Adam, who had died in 1337, left a messuage, seven acres of land and twenty shillings rent to support a chaplain at Haworth who should "celebrate Divine Service for the soul of the said Adam, and the souls of his ancestors, the souls of Thomas de Thornton and Ellen his wife, for all whose goods he had ill gotten, and all the faithful deceased in the Chapel of St. Michael at Haworth, every day".

After an inquisition had been held on the suit of Roger de Thornton and eleven others it was agreed that no damage would be done to King Edward the Third by the carrying out of Adam's bequest and the transaction was completed the year after his death.

This chantry appears to have provided the curate's main income until the final abolition of the chantries in 1547. In that year (the first in the reign of young Edward the Sixth) a statute was passed granting the crown the revenues of all chantries that had survived the grasp of Henry the Eighth, except in the cases of the colleges of Oxford, Cambridge, Eton and Winchester.

Haworth was certainly a remote place in those days, but it was not overlooked. The chantry endowment was confiscated, together with the original income which it had augmented. During the reigns of Edward the Sixth and Mary Tudor, the curate of Haworth was left without income from endowment. But the people of Haworth take nothing lying down and they ensured that their chaplain was provided for ; and shortly after Elizabeth the First ascended the throne they took steps to provide

15

a new endowment among themselves. They took matters into their own hands (happily not for the last time) and thus there came into being that famous Elizabethan Charter which was such a thorn in the side of poor Henry Heap.

A subscription was raised among the inhabitants of Haworth and a sum of £36 was provided: with this money they purchased land at Stanbury which was vested in trustees who have since, right up to present times, been responsible for paying the incumbent of Haworth. With this obligation the trustees (all local men) secured to themselves the right of choosing or rejecting their clergy, whose nomination depended on the Vicar of Bradford.

The famous deed was drawn up in 1559 and stated fully the conditions of the Trust which was formed. The original document, which is still preserved, reads as follows:

"This Indenture made the eighteenth day of December in the second year of the reign of our Sovereign Lady Elizabeth by the grace of God Queen of England, France and Ireland, between Henry Savile, Thomas Darley and William Adame of the Chappelrys of Hwaorth in the Parish of Bradford and County of York on the one parte and Andrew Heaton and Christopher Holmes of the same Chappelrys within the Same County on the other parte whereas the inhabitants within the Chappelrye of Haworth aforesaid have raised the sum of £36 which said moneye is agreed upon by the said inhabitants to be laid out in the purchase of lands and the security of such said lands and estate to be taken and kept on foot in the names of some of the principal menne who are inhabitants of the Said Chappelry and so to be transferred from time to time as occasion is requiring and for this and the above said Andrew Heaton and Christopher Holmes are chosen and appointed Trustees in Trust by the inhabitants of the Said Chappelrye to purchase lands and take and receive the rents dues and profits annually arising therefrom and the same apply and pay over to the minister for the time being who doeth the usual duties of Divine Service in the Said Chappel of Haworth being first lawfully licensed and admitted thereunto."

But that was not enough for the people of Haworth. They gained a greater point than that: the power to decide who was acceptable and who not as a minister in that moorland village. The deed goes on to explain that the aforementioned trustees and their successors shall from time to time "take and receive the actual rents dues and profits thereof and the same apply and pay over to the minister who preach and perform the usual duties of Divine Service in the Chappel of Haworth aforesaid, yet provided nevertheless upon these conditions, that if the said Andrew Heaton and Christopher Holmes and heirs and successors or a major part of them shall at any time hereafter be debarred in their choice or in the nomination of a minister to supply the place when any vacancy shall happen, or if a minister already licensed and admitted who is negligent in his duties in the Said Chappel or is of an infamous character or who is latigious [*sic*] with the inhabitants of the Said Chappelrye, that then and in any way of the cases aforesaid it shall and may be lawful to and for the said Andrew Heaton and Christopher Holmes and heirs and successors or a major part of them to make and receive the rents dues and profits annually growing and arising from the said arable land and unleased premises and the same convert apply and distribute to and amongst the poor of the said Chappelrye of Haworth or any other good and charitable use or uses for the benefit of all the inhabitants of the Said Chappelrye until such time that a minister of better merit and more worthy desert shall be chosen and approved of."

It will be noticed from this deed that land was placed in the possession of local trustees and they were directed to pay the rents to the minister, with the provision, however, that if they did not concur in the appointment of a curate they could withhold the income; similarly, if they considered the existing incumbent unworthy of his position. This is the provision which makes the Haworth Trust exceptional and the various disputes which have arisen between the vicars of Bradford and the trustees regarding the appointments of the incumbents of Haworth —notably in the case of Patrick Brontë—are accounted for by the terms of this document. The vicars of Bradford may be patrons of the living but no appointment has a chance of being satisfactory without the agreement and assent of the Haworth trustees. Thus the people of Haworth retained their independence in this, as in all matters, and did not hesitate to show their power if forced to. The driving out of Samuel Redhead was a prime example.

There had been trouble over the appointment of Patrick's predecessor, James Charnock—John Crosse disputing Haworth's right; whereupon the trustees entered a *caveat* in the Archbishop's Court on 9th June 1791, and obtained his appointment only nineteen days later, after their full consent had been sought.

But of the greatest importance was the stand taken by the trustees in March 1741. Haworth wanted Grimshaw, and the then Vicar of Bradford, Benjamin Kennet, refused to give him the nomination. Up in Haworth there was an immediate agreement between the trustees and principal inhabitants to pay money in entering a *caveat* in the Spiritual Court to prevent Kennet from choosing an alternate minister, backed by the threat that unless they got Grimshaw, they would let the church go empty. On 17th December 1741, the *caveat* was considered, and five months later Grimshaw was at Haworth!

Without this stubborn stand there would be no Brontë story. Grimshaw gave Haworth its fame and first glory, made it the stronghold of the Evangelical revival which swept like a moorland wind over Britain, and turned a small Pennine village church into a living of the first importance, a place of promotion for men who were considered worthy of preferment like Patrick Brontë. Had Grimshaw not gone to Haworth, Patrick would not have followed. He would have been sent elsewhere, most of the Brontë genius would have withered away without its peaty moorland soil, and no one would yet know of Haworth. But the world did not thrust greatness upon that village. It was not the gift of the Church. The people of Haworth gained it for themselves through their Church Land Trustees when they demanded William Grimshaw, and won him!

The registers at Haworth Parish Church date from 1645, although some of the earliest records are not in their original form but in an eighteenth-century copy. From them are learned news of tempests, landslides, hailstorms damaging the crops, drunken men drowning in the beck and, most furtively recorded by the Royalist minister, the execution of Charles the First. "Notable for this year 1649, As it was known Carolum Regem mag: Brit: et Hyber: decap: fuisse"—the sentence proceeds, after only a semi-colon, to mention the frosty weather and the spring. The Rev. John Collier, a local man, was ejected by the Parliament and succeeded by two Cromwellian ministers, Edmund Garforth and Robert Town. But after the Restoration this supporter of the Stuarts was reinstated and, no longer needing to hide his loyalties, boldly entered the following, relative to the coronation of King Charles the Second, the proclamation of which he had witnessed in the market place of Skipton on Saturday, 12th May 1660: ". . . which was proclaimed with such great and matchless Solemnity, Joy, Pomp and State as was never before heard or seen in England . . . so that the giddy Brethren (who desired all to be Rulers and would have no other) were forced to confess that, as we never had such a King, so we never had such a Coronation."

Although loyalties were divided in Haworth—it was a district that stood to benefit by Cromwell's trade policy—there was no doubt the village welcomed back John Collier with great enthusiasm. Royalists or no Royalists, they bitterly resented having two ministers foisted upon them without their consent, even if it had not been by the vicar of Bradford this time, but by Oliver Cromwell.

In 1638 a free grammar school for boys and girls was founded at

Haworth by the bequest of Christopher Scott, who gave a schoolhouse and an annuity of £18 towards the maintenance of the schoolmaster. This was situated across the fields to the south of Haworth Church at Marsh (Oxenhope).

Another seventeenth-century picture of Haworth is given by the famous Oliver Heywood; "... upon thursday June 13 72 upon a solemne invitation I went to Jonas Fosters house in Howarth parish, where I was never before in all my life, a very ignorant place, where there was never good preaching, multitudes of people flockt to hear me, some were affected." Again, "... on Lords day July 12, 1680, there was a rushbearing at Howarth and their Tyde (as they call it) on which multitudes of people meet, feast, drink, play, and commit many outrages in revellings, in rantings, riding, without any fear or restraint ... oh dreadful!" Oliver Heywood also gives another picture, that of the then Vicar of Bradford collecting his dues (£10) on Easter Monday, 1692, and who "sat all day in an Ale house, gathering his dues in Howarth parish, theres wont always to be a Sermon in the church that day, but Mr Pemberton hath laid it aside. . .". There is no mention as to the preference of Francis Pemberton, the Black Bull or King's Arms, the latter frequently used then as the court-house.

But with the turn of the century, a very different scene opens, for with the advent of the eighteenth century, Haworth became one of the most important strongholds of the Evangelical revival.

On 26th May 1742 there came up Kirkgate the new perpetual curate to Haworth, William Grimshaw. He came at a time when the Church was at the lowest ebb of its prestige, and he came amongst a wild and independent populace. But Grimshaw understood his flock and remained for twenty-one years. At his old parsonage, Sowdens (still standing), he held prayer meetings for the destitute whose foul clothing was their pretext for not attending church, and gave so liberally of his hospitality that with food and lodging given to many he was forced to sleep in his own stables. But he knew his parishioners and applied to them the "market language" they understood. He was a mixture of brutality and compassion, of coarseness and sensitivity. He would spare no pains to comfort the sick and dying, walking over thirty miles across the moors to Lancashire and back if he could bring comfort. He would preach as many as twenty sermons a week, including his cottage meetings. But he could be ruthless too. He would raid the inns, driving the unwilling hearers to the church at his whip's end, and many a game of hide-and-seek was played out on the Sabbath between the parson and the villagers. If he met anyone riding on the moors "he would rive them off their horses to make them pray".

By his fierce charity, his rough language, his devotion to the sick and poor, William Grimshaw effected radical changes in the lives of his parishioners. They were won over by a minister who, if the dying refused to see him, could pray loudly outside the window so that, in his own words, "At least he will die with the word of God in his lugs."

To Haworth came Charles and John Wesley over and over again at Grimshaw's invitation.

On 15th September 1751 Charles Wesley recorded, ". . . hastened to Haworth. I never saw a church better filled : but after I had prayed in the pulpit, the multitude in the churchyard cried out, they could not hear, and begged me to come forth. I did so, and preached on a tomb stone. Between three and four thousand heard me gladly. At two I called again, to above double the number, 'Behold the Lamb of God, which taketh away the sin of the world !' The church leads and steeple were filled with clusters of people, all still as night. If ever I preached Gospel, I preached it then. The Lord take all the glory !

"I took horse immediately, and followed our nimble guide, Johnny Grimshaw, to Ewood. His father came panting after us. . . ."

On Sunday, 12th July 1761, John Wesley "appointed to be at Haworth ; but the church would not near contain the people who came from all sides : however, Mr. Grimshaw had provided for this by fixing a scaffold on the outside of some one of the windows, through which I went after prayers, and the people likewise all went out into the church-yard. The afternoon congregation was larger still. What has God wrought in the midst of those rough mountains !

"Mon. 13. At five [a.m.] I preached on the manner of waiting for 'perfect love'; the rather to satisfy Mr. Grimshaw, whom many had laboured to puzzle and perplex about it. . . ." Had the young Patrick stopped the preacher as he rode through the Irish lanes, he could have learned much from him about the village that was to be his own place of destiny.

In addition to the Wesleys, all the leading Evangelicals preached at Haworth during Grimshaw's incumbency, including George White-field and John Newton. Selina, Countess of Huntingdon, recorded how, being in the congregation at Haworth Church in September 1749 as Whitefield was preaching, a man shrieked and fell dead. Grimshaw jumped to his feet and shouted: "Brother Whitefield, you stand amongst the dead and the dying—an immortal soul has been called into eternity—the destroying angel is passing over the congregation, cry aloud, and spare not." Whereupon the person next to Selina fell dead also.

William Grimshaw was born at Brindle, near Preston, on 3rd

September 1708, was admitted to Christ's College, Cambridge, in his eighteenth year and was ordained deacon in 1731. In his younger days he delighted in jovial company : his great loves were hunting, fishing, and playing cards. But after 1734 he awoke to a full sense of religious responsibility and became the leading preacher in the north of England. After only four years of married life, he lost his wife in 1739 ; he was her third husband and loved her deeply. (Grimshaw's daughter had died young, whilst his son, John, became a drunkard, declaring to his late father's horse, "Once thou didst carry a saint, but now thou carriest a devil.")

In the church registers at Haworth he recorded the following :

The Reverend William Grimshaw, A.B., of Christ's College, Cambridge, succeeded the Revd. Isaac Smith, A.M. last Incumbent deceased in the parochial Curacy of Haworth, having been Minister of ye parochial Curacy of Todmorden in ye County of Lancaster, ten years and nine months.

He was born in Brindle, in ye county aforesaid, and was educated at the Free School of Blackburn by George Smith, Headmaster thereof for some years, but was afterwards removed to the Free School of Heskin and put under the care of Mr. Thomas Jackson, Headmaster thereof, and from thence was sent to and admitted member of the University and College above mentioned.

Witness my hand,
                                    William Grimshaw, Minister de Haworth.

From the moment of his arrival in Haworth a great religious revival began and so great was the change in the spiritual attitude of the people locally, so large the crowds who wished to hear him preach that, in 1755, the church was not only repaired and some small alterations made but was extended two bays eastwards to accommodate the growing congregation. Yet even this enlargement proved quite insufficient and often not only the church, but even the churchyard, could not contain the people who came to worship—as the Journals of John and Charles Wesley testify.

Small wonder then, that at the beginning of 1763 Grimshaw was ranked third among the Methodists, John Wesley decreeing that should death come to him, his brother Charles should become trustee for the Methodist circuits, and if Charles died, William Grimshaw.

Small wonder also that it was said of Haworth before the Brontës enriched it further : "It is one of those obscure places, which, like the fishing towns of Galilee, favoured with our Lord's presence, owe all their celebrity to the Gospel. The name of Haworth would scarcely be known at a distance, were it not connected with the name of Grim-shaw."—(John Newton).

Many stories are yet told of William Grimshaw's ministry at Haworth, of his great spiritual power and physical courage. His friend the Rev. John Newton (also friend to Cowper, the poet) recorded hundreds of interesting anecdotes dealing with his hospitality to the destitute at the old parsonage of Sowdens and his racy manner with his moorland parishioners.

"It was his frequent and almost constant custom to leave the Church while the psalm before sermon was singing, to see if any were absent from worship, and idling their time in the church-yard, the street, or the alehouses; and many of those whom he so found he would drive into the church before him. A friend of mine passing a public house in Haworth, on a Lord's day morning, saw several persons making their escape out of it, some jumping out of the lower windows, and some over a low wall; he was at first alarmed, fearing the house was on fire; but, upon inquiring what was the cause of the commotion, he was told, that they saw the parson coming.

"He was equally zealous and bold in expostulating with the guilty, wherever he met them. Thus, when once a man, who had been often guilty of adultery, came into a shop where Mr. Grimshaw was, he charged him with his crime upon the spot, and said to those who were present, 'The Devil has been very busy in this neighbourhood; I can touch the man with my stick, who lay with another man's wife last night; the end of these things will be death, the ruin of body and soul for ever.'"

He was particularly hostile to hypocrisy and those who made great yet insincere pretences to religion, and was always ready to try out their sincerity in various ways.

"He then went to another house, to a woman who was almost blind; he touched her gently with his stick, and persisted to do so, till she, supposing it was from some children in the neighbourhood, began not only to threaten them, but to swear at them. Thus he was confirmed in his apprehensions; for he had no good opinion of the religion of those who were not, at least, gentle to the poor, or of those who did not bridle their tongues."

There are no end to the tales and memories of William Grimshaw at Haworth, of his transports and visions, his prodigious feats of walking and preaching and of the great Methodist wave that swept across England from his pulpit. One story tells how he climbed to the flat plateau of heather between two quarries just above Haworth where the annual races were held.

"There are at Haworth two feasts annually. It had been customary with the innkeepers, and some other inhabitants, to make a subscription for horse-races at the latter feast. These were of the lowest kind, attended by the lowest of the people. They exhibited a scene of the grossest and most vulgar riot, profligacy, and confusion. Mr Grimshaw had frequently attempted, but in vain, to put a stop to this mischievous custom. His remonstrances against it were little regarded ; and perhaps any other man would have been ill treated, if he had dared to oppose, with earnestness, an established practice, so agreeable to the depraved taste of the thoughtless multitude. But his character was so revered, that they heard his expostulations with some degree of patience, though they were determined to persist in their old course. Unable to prevail with men, he addressed himself to God, and for some time before the races began, he made it a subject of fervent prayer, that the Lord would be pleased to stop these evil proceedings in his own way. When the race time came, the people assembled as usual, but they were soon dispersed. Before the races could begin, dark clouds covered the sky, which poured forth such excessive rains, that the people could not remain upon the ground ; it continued to rain incessantly during the three days appointed for the races."

It was certainly a most effectual prayer ! There have been no further races in Haworth from that time to the present day.

Grimshaw fought through a mob to defend a Wesleyan preacher, roaring, "Out of the way, Tommy, with thy spindle shanks and let them kick me" ; at Communion the same preacher received with the cup of remembrance a tap on the ear, "And for thee, Tommy." Grimshaw resolved never to flag whilst he could "ride, walk, creep or crawl".

As in life, so also in death did William Grimshaw display his utter fearlessness. Early in 1763, a putrid fever raged through the village. Some few, who could afford to, fled, urging their minister to go with them. This he refused to do and continued his preaching and his visits to the homes of his people. Although a strong man, he caught the fever and died at Sowdens on 7th April 1763. ". . . I have nothing to do but to step out of my bed into Heaven, I have my foot on its threshold already." He was in his fifty-fifth year.

His influence had extended outside the Church of England. It was a feature of his ministry to be in concord with all other genuine sections of religious thought. "I love Christians, true Christians of all parties ; I do love them, I will love them and none shall make me do otherwise." He later came to deplore the gradual breaking away from the Anglican Church of some of its greatest elements in the religious revival, yet he remained in friendship with all denominations. During his ministry in

Haworth one of his own converts and former lay preachers, who had lived with him at Sowdens, James Hartley, became the first minister of West Lane Baptist Church, Haworth (erected in 1752).

In 1758 he helped to erect the first Methodist chapel in the village— also situated in West Lane; and now, in death, his will directed that a Methodist minister should preach the funeral sermon from his favourite text, "For me to live is Christ, to die is gain."

It was painted upon his plain elmwood coffin, which was carried by many mourners over the moors to his first wife's old home at Ewood; from there he was taken to Luddenden Church and buried at her side. His friend the Rev. Henry Venn (then Vicar of Huddersfield) preached the funeral sermon at Luddenden and on the following day, being Sunday, in Haworth Church.

So ended one of the most outstanding ministries the Church of England has ever known, and to this heritage came Patrick Brontë in 1820.

It was largely Grimshaw's church Patrick came to when he arrived at Haworth, although the galleries had been added in 1779. Dedicated to St Michael and All Angels the old church would appear to people today, for all its passionate interest, as crowded and obscure. There was only a small window on the west side; there were six large stone pillars down the centre of the nave, whilst heavy galleries were ranged round the east, north and west walls. The three-decker pulpit with its over-hanging sounding-board was placed near the centre of the south side. The high, enclosed square pews of old black oak mostly contained six seats, and bore the name of the family (or farm) on the doors. These pews filled the nave (and almost the two aisles) as well as parts of the galleries above. Even the pulpit was hemmed round with pews. There were six large windows along the north and south sides and two high windows at the east end of the church, with a smaller one between them. None of them was of stained glass. Each had a rounded fanlight and consisted of small panes of leaded lights that cast a dim green light on to the stone pillars and oaken pews within. The entrances to the church were from the south-west and north-west, opposite each other. Inside the north-west door and immediately to the right were the steps to the gallery and on the left was Grimshaw's stone font, bearing the inscription, "Wm. Grimshaw—A.B. Minister—A.D.1742." (This font is still to be found in the churchyard.) On the south-west corner of the building stood the old tower (where it still stands today, although the crenellations and pinnacles were lifted a fraction in 1870 to allow for the clock-face on all four sides: during Patrick Brontë's life at Haworth there was only one clock on the tower, on its eastern wall looking over Kirkgate).

There was no Sunday School, no organ and no bells when he arrived, all of which omissions he was soon to rectify. (The organ loft was eventually placed in the gallery in the north-west corner of the church.)

Already in 1820 there was a musty atmosphere which hardly improved as time passed. But it was a fine old building for all that and full of memories when Patrick first came there to preach. The sounding-board of the famous three-decker pulpit had to be destroyed recently, being found in an impossible condition for preservation, but the top deck of Grimshaw's pulpit, from which Patrick preached all his sermons at Haworth, has survived and is now the pulpit in the little church at Stanbury.

To the west of St Michael's, at the other side of the then treeless graveyard, on higher ground stood the parsonage. It was built in 1779 for the then incumbent of Haworth, the Rev. John Richardson, being known as "the Glebe House"—thus it replaced Sowdens as the official residence of the incumbents of that village. (Sowdens had been the parsonage since 1739, although Richardson resided for a short while at the Cook House before the new parsonage was ready.) If the aspect of crowded slab tombs, where at that time over 40,000 lay buried, was bleak, the further view over the Worth valley to the moors beyond was certainly not so. Nor yet the view of the old tower, or the sweeping vistas from the back windows, nor yet the house itself.

So famous has it become that many tens of thousands visit it each year. Built of the local millstone grit (as are all the houses of Haworth) which weather soon turns a dark grey, the parsonage is a typical late Georgian house with pedimented portico. Facing east, it is entered by a wooden side-door in the garden wall and a flagstone path leads up to seven steps. There is a wide hall with graceful arch leading to stone stairs that turn by a landing window. On the right as you enter is Patrick's study, on the left the dining-room. Behind the latter is a small peat-room and behind the study, the kitchen.

Upstairs on the right is the little servants' room and in front of that the large bedroom for Patrick and Maria. Facing the head of the stairs is the little narrow nursery over the front door; to the left of this at the front of the house Patrick's dressing-room (alas, soon to be his bedroom) and behind that at the back of the house another small bedroom.

The house had fine old cellars and a small yard at the back which led to the fields and then moorland. In the 1840s Patrick had a small scullery and wash-house built on to the back of the parsonage. There was also a small yard between the house and Parsonage Lane (where the new wing, added in 1872 by Patrick's successor, now stands). The water supply was from a pump in the kitchen.

That was Patrick's new home—the one he would never leave—and it was beautiful. When the sun shone after rain on the stone of the parsonage, his house was no longer grey but suddenly blue and green and the colour of heather.

Haworth too has been described many times, usually in one word: "bleak". There is nothing bleak about it or the surrounding country-side. It is strong, simple, unsophisticated, sturdy and very beautiful. It is natural, unpretentious and very, very old. Cobbled narrow streets with stone Tudor, Jacobean and Georgian houses, a few Victorian additions, and all blended into the appearance of medieval strength.

From the Keighley road, Bridgehouse Lane climbs to join the bottom of Kirkgate (now Main Street) and on the left, the end of Stubbing Lane (now Sun Street). Kirkgate, one of the steepest streets in Britain, reaches a small plateau or square at the top, with the Black Bull on the left and behind it the church and churchyard. Facing the top of the street was the old White Lion Hotel. Three narrow lanes led off from this square: Parsonage Lane (now Church Street) to the left, and West Lane and Changegate ahead on the left and right of the White Lion. They are connected later by Back Lane (now North Street), whilst West Lane continues out to the moors, joining the flagged-stone path that crosses the fields behind the parsonage. Thus it was when Patrick first saw it, and happily the village is little altered today.

From the end of West Lane the moors stretch for miles, with only little Stanbury below on the west to break the open view: rolling hills of heather slashed through with many becks, hidden valleys with cliffs of rock and thundering waterfalls. There are wonders beyond the counting, surprises beyond the telling; in winter snow or howling gale, in summer storm or warming sun, it is bliss to roam those moors. Nor yet is the climate as severe as has been made out by two-hour visitors. Those who have called Haworth bleak, indeed those who have omitted to call it beautiful, have surely sold their souls to sophistication and lost truth and beauty from their hearts.

Thus, at the age of forty-three, Patrick Brontë came to dwell in this moorland village, this veritable eagle's nest, and was happy and honoured to do so.

Now that he has arrived at Haworth he shall be called Patrick Brontë, except when quoting from letters or documents, for it was not until his daughters became famous that he adopted the diaeresis for himself. However, his children, taking their cue from the printed works of Papa, made no hesitation in adopting this spelling even in their childhood manuscripts.

Thus Patrick commenced his long labours as incumbent of Haworth, labours so totally ignored by the outside literary world. Yet his great work was carried out against the background of his children's lives, the sorrows and happiness, the tragedy and glory of which affected him so closely.

On the morning of Friday, 21st April 1820, Patrick was awake early and from the bedroom window watched the first flush of dawn as it spread round the tower in the eastern sky. There was work to be done, people to meet, and much to see. He had over 5,000 parishioners, and they were well scattered; for as well as Haworth, the chapelry included Stanbury and Far and Near Oxenhope, none of these other hamlets having churches of their own.

Patrick dressed himself and went downstairs. He opened the front door and walked along the path. Suddenly he looked up. There at the nursery window a face was pressed tight against the glass, gazing at the hills on the other side of Haworth. It seemed that Emily was glad to be here and that she also was too excited to sleep. He waved up at the window, but she did not notice him. Patrick let himself out of the gate and walked down the lane to the church door. Inside he stood for a moment; it was still too dark to see clearly about the church. Then he walked to the three-decker pulpit and gazed up at it for a moment. He moved down the aisle to the Communion table and flung himself down on his knees.

Patrick had been in good hands all the way, handed over from one safe keeping to another. From the Presbyterian Harshaw to the Methodist Tighe, and so along an unbroken Evangelical chain: from Tighe to Simeon, Martyn, Wilberforce, Jowett, Storry, Cox, Nunn, Mary Fletcher, Morgan, Gilpin, Buckworth, Fennell, Roberson, Crosse —until he had earned the rich inheritance of Grimshaw's pulpit of glory.

When he returned to the parsonage, Nancy and Sarah Garrs were in the kitchen preparing breakfast, Maria was in the dining-room and the children seemed to be in every room at once. It was such a happy start to life at Haworth.

CHAPTER 13

Grief

BREAKFAST was soon over and Patrick went back to the church. Within a few hours of his permanent arrival in Haworth he held his first vestry meeting. There he met those of the trustees with whom he was still unacquainted: there was a very crowded vestry that morning, as all the leading members of the Church were anxious to meet their new incumbent—Stephen Taylor and his sons, George, Robert and John, the two Heatons of Ponden House (now termed Ponden Hall), two Rush-worths who lived at Mouldgreave, Pighills from over the Brow side of the village and all the other gentlemen. There was Stephen Paslow, who had been parish clerk for two years (and would remain so until his death in February 1826, aged sixty); and Patrick also spoke to William Brown, who had been sexton since 13th March 1807. Brown, who was thirty-eight, would remain in that office until his death on 13th February 1835 (aged fifty-three), when his son, John, would succeed him.

But Patrick was anxious to commence business and, after a few words with each person, he opened the meeting. After so long an interregnum and the recent turbulence caused by it, the affairs of Haworth Church had sadly declined from the wonderful days of the illustrious William Grimshaw. Patrick resolved to put matters in order from the very start. It had been the practice for the churchwardens to be elected by the people (as represented by the trustees) during the absence of a permanent incumbent; and the right of the minister to have a say in the appointment of at least one or two wardens had been whittled away. If this practice were allowed to continue it would place the incumbent in a most unhappy position in the event of a dispute. Patrick determined that one churchwarden should be his own choice and that of his successors.

In the Minute Book dated 21st April 1820, there was recorded in Patrick's own hand: "At a Vestry Meeting, legally convened in the Vestry of Haworth Church on the 21st April 1820, the Revd. P. Brontë A B—Incumbent Minister, in the chair, it was passed as a Law, without one dissenting voice, that the Incumbent Minister of Haworth has a right to chose one Church or Chapel Warden, but not two, and it was voted also at the same meeting, that a memorandum of this circumstance, should be recorded in the Trust Book to stand as a president [*sic*] and a Law, in this place, forever. P. Brontë, Incumbent Minister." (Then follow fifteen other signatures.) The last line "and a Law in this place forever" sounded a warning bell to the people of Haworth, could they have but realized it. It was an early taste of the thorough and painstaking ministry that would be his and showed Patrick's fondness for the law and the readiness he would always display to bring the law into action if his desire for justice was thwarted. There would be many instances of this during his incumbency at Haworth.

Patrick had gained his point with goodwill on both sides and the meeting proceeded to elect the wardens for the year.

"At a Vestry Meeting held this 21st April 1820, for the purpose of appointing Churchwardens for the ensuing year, the following persons were duly elected, namely: Robert Heaton, John Thomas, George Greenwood, James Feather. In witness whereof, we have hereunto subscribed our hands. . . ."

It was a pleasant summer for Patrick and his family: the weather was warm and fine and long walks were taken over the moors. The children loved the great expanse of freedom and even the youngest stumbled out to the heather with Nancy and Sarah. Maria and Elizabeth often accompanied their papa on his visits to the sick in Stanbury and Oxenhope, but Patrick was forced to leave them behind when he walked across the moors to some of the farmsteads that dotted the slopes of the hills—farms such as Top Withens that, some four miles out on the moors, has been a landmark since Tudor times. Of an evening, when there was not too much wind, Patrick and Maria would stroll out to the waterfall in the Sladen Valley, and there in that delightful dell they would feel rekindled that tender first love of Kirkstall Abbey.

On 6th June Patrick went over to Thornton to see William Morgan and learn the news of Bradford. He visited Kipping House to have a word with his old friends, walking back across the moors in the cool of the evening and leaving Elizabeth Firth to record the event in her diary.

Nancy had been asked to clean his boots for this journey, but "I forgot, and when Mr. Bronte called for his boots they were not touched . . . he did not say a word, but just put on his hat and walked all the way to Thornton and back in his slippers!"

A return visit was intended but, as Elizabeth Firth wrote: "July 19. Intended going to Haworth rain prevents us."

Patrick learned to know and value his new parishioners, to appreciate the honest, hard-working hearts that beat beneath the blunt exteriors. Most of them were either farmers or workers in the mills that were hidden away beside the valley streams. Some few worked in the quarries, sending the millstone-grit to various parts of the north to help build the new towns and expand such cities as Manchester. Quite a number earned their livelihood at home in their cottages, weaving on the hand-looms by the wide windows that admitted enough light. But the hardest lot of all was that of the farmers, fighting to glean a living from the soil generations had cultivated, knowing that a moment's negligence or relaxation would allow the moor to creep back and reclaim its own; fighting also to save their flocks from the winter snows—for the black-faced sheep ranged far over the wild moorland— and every one was precious, as those grey dots on the moors meant wool, and wool was the life-blood of Haworth.

Patrick soon knew the moors well. Again his love of walking in the hills could be incorporated in his duties to those of his chapelry who lived far from the village, and that peace of heart and mind that always came to him when alone with nature was upon him stronger than ever before. Yet, even now, Patrick always carried with him one of the pistols from his Hartshead days. Haworth folk appeared to have taken him and accepted him. If so he had the loyalest parishioners a clergyman could wish for, but it was too early to be certain, and should any action of his displease them, then of a surety the pistol would be useful. He had grown quite fond of this particular pistol. It lay on his dressing-table at night next to his watch—loaded. Every morning he opened the bedroom window and discharged it across the garden and graveyard, sometimes hitting the old tower (the marks are still there as witness). He would then reload it and place it in his pocket, again next to his watch. It was a practice he continued nearly all his life, and even when on his death-bed, he sent for the local watchmaker (Mr Feather) to regulate the trigger.

One morning, shortly after Patrick's arrival at Haworth, one of the churchwardens was walking up Paronage Lane when an upper window of the parsonage was flung up and the new minister, without hesitating, pointed a pistol at the tower and discharged a shot at it. The warden was horrified; he knew well the reputation Patrick had earned at Dewsbury, but this really was too much. This was sacrilege of a high order. With some trepidation he called up to enquire why Mr Brontë had fired at the church and why point his pistol over the graveyard?

"Because by emptying my pistol in that direction, should I hit any person, the chances are that they will be already dead. Better that than shoot the living!" And the window went down with a slam.

But most of Patrick's time was taken up in the village attending to the many parochial matters that needed attention. Vestry meetings

PLATE 14 *William Morgan*

PLATE 15 *Kirkstall Abbey*

PLATE 16 *Maria Branwell*

were continual, as will be seen in a later chapter dealing exclusively
with his great work as the incumbent of Haworth. (In addition, shortly
after his arrival in Haworth, he took duty in Keighley for the Rector,
Mr Dury, whose first wife, Caroline, had died at Hastings.) He soon
knew every corner of St Michael's as well as many of the tombs in the
churchyard. He had early been shown various treasures including the
two large pewter flagons from Grimshaw's day inscribed A.D. 1750,
and the new twelve-light chandelier for the candles.

As for the parsonage, it was a great improvement on the cramped
quarters of Thornton and, once Maria had overcome the sadness of
separation from her kinsfolk and friends, Patrick was certain she would
be happy at Haworth. His financial position had improved as a result
of his transfer to Haworth, the trustees providing a more generous
living that was to be found in most chapels-of-ease. His salary was now
some £180 per annum for life, together with the house, rent free. This
was certainly not poverty, and had it not been for the great cost of his
wife's illness there would have been no money worries in those early
days at Haworth Parsonage. He also received various other emoluments
in kind. An interesting one, taken from the registers, reads: "To
grazing in the churchyard—15 lbs. wax candles, there being three to
the pound. This to be paid annually."

From the very start Patrick's sermons were a great success with his
congregation, and even the oldest amongst them who could still
recall Parson Grimshaw's addresses were no less enthusiastic. From
Ellen Nussey, Charlotte's great friend, we have a wonderful description
of a service in Haworth Church in Patrick Brontë's time. "The services
in church in these days were such as can only be seen (if ever seen again)
in localities like Haworth. The people assembled, but it was apparently
to *listen*. Any part beyond that was quite out of their reckoning. All
through the prayers, a stolid look of apathy was fixed on the generality
of their faces. There they sat, or leaned, in their pews; some few,
perhaps were resting, after a long walk over the moors. The children,
many of them in clogs (or sabots), pattered in from the school after
service had commenced [this was after Patrick had opened the Sunday
school], and pattered out again before the sermon. The sexton, with a
long staff, continually walked round in the aisles, 'knobbing' sleepers
when he dare, shaking his head at and threatening unruly children;
but when the sermon began there was a change. Attitudes took the
listening forms, eyes were turned on the preacher. It was curious, now,
to note the expression. A rustic, untaught intelligence, gleamed in their
faces; in some, a daring, doubting, questioning look, as if they would
like to offer some defiant objection. Mr Brontë always addressed his

16

hearers in extempore style. Very often he selected a parable from one of the Gospels, which he explained in the simplest manner—sometimes going over his own words and explaining them also, so as to be perfectly intelligible to the lowest comprehension."

A villager would also recall Patrick's sermons : "Before commencing he placed his watch on the cushion of the desk, and almost without exception he concluded with the words, 'Through our adorable Lord and Saviour, Jesus Christ.' "

So passed 1820, a happy year in which all the Brontës settled down to their new moorland surroundings and Patrick was able to restore the ravages an unsettled interregnum had caused. Soon Patrick would keep the promise he had made to himself down in the lanes of Wethersfield : to have a dog for a companion. But there is no evidence of any pets at the parsonage in that year. However, it would not be long before there were several.

But 1820 ended on a sad note. Mr Firth was taken very ill in early December, and Patrick, on hearing this, went over to Kipping House on the 13th. A few days later he heard that his old friend was in a most depressed state of mind and, knowing recovery was out of the question, returned there on the 21st and prayed and talked with the dying man. That his visit was able to heal the mind and prepare his old friend's heart and soul for death is evident from Elizabeth Firth's diary.

"1820. December 3rd. My papa complained of shivering. 5th. My papa was very ill. 9th. My papa worse. 10th. My papa was carried into the drawing-room. 13th. Mr Bronte dined here. 17th. Alarmed with my father. 18th. My papa very ill. 20th. My dear papa suffered great depression of mind. 21st. By God's blessing and Mr Bronte's conversation became more happy. 22nd. In holy ecstasies all day, blessed be God. 23rd. Pretty composed. 24th. My poor father's ideas still wandering, but very cheerful. 26th. My dear father's last words at half-past eleven—All's well, all's happy. 27th. At half-past two a.m. he breathed his last without a struggle. 1821. January 2nd. My dear Father was interred—Mr Bronte officiated. 4th. Mr Greame and Mr Bronte left. Fanny Outhwaite came."

But if 1820 ended on a sad note at Haworth Parsonage, the New Year would bring far greater sorrow to Patrick before it was very old.

In later life Charlotte would have only one memory of her mother, playing in the twilight with her only son, Branwell. Patrick would carry in his heart memories of his Maria until his dying day, and in the smile of his youngest child there would be a reminder of her until that smile too was taken from him. On returning home on Monday, 29th January 1821, he found his wife had collapsed with a rending pain in her stomach : she was dangerously ill. The doctor was summoned and he asked for further advice. From Leeds came a medical specialist of great experience and he went up to see Maria.

Patrick was in the hall as he came downstairs, and was told Maria must die. There was no hope : she had an internal cancer. For the very first time Patrick retired into his parlour and shut himself in. This was a refuge, this room, from a mortal blow. In the years to come he would retreat here as sickening blow after sickening blow fell upon his head until very experience had given him strength ; but now it was a new shock, and he was so unprepared. He sank into his chair and placing his head on his sleeve wept aloud with grief. He saw her as she first appeared to him at Woodhouse Grove. He remembered her letters and her words, "I think if our lives are spared twenty years hence I shall then pray for you with the same, if not greater, fervour and delight than I do now." Twenty years ! It had been only eight and now she was dying !

When he emerged from the parlour the pale blue eyes were dry, the smile ready for Maria and the little ones. Prayer had soothed him out of the first gush of sorrow and prepared him for the iron-hard duty ahead. He comforted her as cheerfully as he could, but it was apparent Maria had divined the truth. As he came downstairs he noticed how still and quiet was the house : in the kitchen not a sound from Nancy or Sarah. He opened the dining-room door and there were his children ; five of them, even the baby, ranged round the fire in a circle whilst in the centre sat little Maria reading softly to them from a book. The grave, quiet Maria also had divined the truth and had already assumed her mantle of the little mother.

There was much for Patrick to do. He hired a day nurse to assist in the sickroom (she it was who was Mrs Gaskell's main witness as to domestic life in the parsonage at Haworth) ; he wrote to several medical men asking them to see his wife ; and he advised Miss Elizabeth Branwell of the sad news.

As for the nurse, she was rather unsatisfactory. The Garrs sisters found her difficult to tolerate and her eventual dismissal, when her services were, alas, of no further use, seems to have rankled in her mind, for to Mrs Gaskell, as an old lady, she poured forth a stream of abuse against Patrick and the two young servants. Doctors came and went, and Patrick spared no expense to try to save his beloved Maria, but all in vain. There was no cure ; her intense pain could not be alleviated. Miss Branwell would come to Haworth as soon as she could. Meanwhile Patrick did all he could to lessen the agony of Maria. He stayed up at nights to comfort her until, through sheer fatigue, he fell asleep at her side. Elizabeth Firth forgot her own sorrows and did what she could.

"February 9th. I went to see Mrs Bronte who was very poorly. 21st. I dined at Mr Bronte's. April 17th. Wrote to Mr Bronte. May 26th. F.O. and S brought Maria and E. Bronte to Kipping. June 22nd. Mr Walker went home also M and E. Bronte."

So the weeks passed, with Maria biting her lips to suppress the cry of pain and Patrick dividing the time between his duties as parson and his wife's bedside. The house remained quiet, the Garrs sisters stealing about on tiptoe and the children, with young Maria as an example, as good as gold. Yet Maria knew that Patrick was never far away and it was a comfort to her ; it gave her a sense of normality that every morning at the same moment there would come the crack of a pistol as a bullet whistled over the churchyard.

Maria lay there fighting the pain that never ceased, thinking of the happy days of Woodhouse Grove and Thornton and dreaming a little of Mount's Bay. Patrick prayed for her and with her, until, overcome by exhaustion, he could pray no longer.

The children were brought in one by one to see their mother : to have them all in her room at one time would have been too much for Maria. Sarah had been teaching the girls needlework, and Charlotte, although only five, could show Mamma with great pride a chemise she had made. Maria was much pleased with the neat work and gave her tiny daughter a loving kiss. Yet Branwell was her favourite and paid the most visits to the sickroom.

As for Nancy and Sarah Garrs, their loyalty and humanity were beyond praise. During Maria's long and painful illness Nancy became engaged to a local man, Patrick Wainwright. Hearing of this, Patrick went into the kitchen one evening, before commencing his nightly vigil. "Nancy, is it true, what I have heard, that you are going to marry a Pat ?" "It is," replied the girl, "and if he prove but a tenth part as kind a husband to me as you have been to Mrs Brontë, I shall think myself very happy in having made a Pat my choice." But it was to be no rushed desertion on Nancy's part ; she was little more than seventeen and would never contemplate leaving the household at such a sad time. In the event, Nancy remained some three years after Maria's death. Save for the temporary day nurse, all the servants employed by Patrick would love him and his family, and be worthy of the deep affection the Brontës returned them.

Month followed month and the vigil continued ; more doctors were called in to see Maria. Patrick spent all his savings in a despairing attempt to save his wife, but the answer always came, "There is no hope."

One day in particular came in gloomier than ever. Maria seemed to be sinking rapidly and three of the children went down with scarlet fever. The next day the remaining three were ill of the same complaint.

At such a moment only Patrick's great and unwavering faith in God's wisdom prevented him from pointing the morning pistol in the other direction and lodging the bullet in his brain. But Maria rallied somewhat, the children survived the worst of their dangerous illness, and, at the beginning of May, Elizabeth Branwell arrived from Penzance. She would never see Cornwall again. During the hours of the nurse's attendance, there were thus twelve people living in the parsonage, seven of them ill in bed, one of them never to quit it again.

Maria was happy to see her sister again, but her improvement was not long maintained; by August she began to sink and her spirits became most depressed. Patrick wrestled for hours in her room fighting to help her maintain her faith in God and cling to her life's beliefs. By his strenuous efforts he helped her to face the end calmly. As Patrick knelt by Maria's bedside there died in Ireland the man who had helped give him that faith, now so sorely tested. Thomas Tighe died on 25th August 1821, in his seventy-eighth year.

No longer able to carry out his parish duties Patrick called in the Rev. William Anderton, who had helped so often at Haworth during the preceding interregnum, and this clergyman officiated for some days at St Michael's. On 14th September he conducted the funeral of a five-week-old baby girl from Oxenhope. On the next day, Saturday, 15th September 1821, Maria Brontë died with her Patrick kneeling by the bedside, her last words ringing in his ears, "Oh my poor children, my poor children."

On the following Saturday, 22nd September, the little gate of the dead, that small wicket opening at the centre of the stone wall dividing the parsonage garden from the graveyard, was opened, and along the path that ran through the middle of that garden they carried Maria Brontë. She was the vanguard of that glorious family. From henceforward the gate would appear to the people of Haworth to spring open and shut with sickening regularity. Who was to bury her? There could be only one answer, and up the hill came the loyal William Morgan who had married her at Guiseley Church less than nine short years ago. She was thirty-eight years and five months old. William Morgan made his entry in the registers thus:

Name	Abode	When Buried	Age	By whom the ceremony was performed.
Maria, the wife of Patrick Bronte A B. Minister of this Church	Haworth	22nd Septr	38 years	W. Morgan. Minister of Christ Church, Bradford.

Only two of the children—the eldest, Maria and Elizabeth—were present in the church as they laid Maria Brontë to rest under the flags of St Michael's. Miss Firth, who had last seen Patrick on 17th August when he dined at Kipping, entered in her diary: "September 15th. Mrs. Bronte died after an illness of 8 months."

Patrick returned slowly to the sanctuary that was his parlour and shut himself in with his memories and Maria's love letters. The first shock of sorrow had come months ago when he knew she would die; now, after watching these weeks of suffering he felt almost emptied of grief. In the days that followed Patrick resumed his parish duties and found the balming consolation of the moors—"those rough mountains", as John Wesley termed them in his journal. On the vast expanse of rolling hills, Patrick soon found that, if his beloved companion was gone, God had not deserted him, and His strength and wisdom bore him up in the midst of his tribulation. It was on these sad walks that Patrick saw the last of the eagles swooping down from the rocky heights; soon they too would be gone, becoming extinct in those parts a year or so later and never seen since. But the curlew is now the monarch of the moors and those who love him regret not the passing of the Pennine eagle.

So Patrick braced himself and made that recovery of mind and spirits that life has always demanded of survivors. Then came another blow. Never in all his long life would Patrick be permitted to digest his sorrows with *one* bitter pill at a time. Only a very few months after Maria's death, news reached him from Ireland that his mother had died. Ambition left him of a sudden; there remained his belief in God's mercy and his anxiety for the children, so poignantly expressed by his wife on her death-bed. And with these two major interests remaining to him, he wrapped himself up in the soothing escapism that Haworth can give and resigned his strong physical activity to the service of that chapelry where he would live for the remainder of his days.

The nurse was dismissed with no regret on the part of the household, although all were forced to admit her skill in the sickroom, and Aunt Branwell agreed to remain for a time until matters were more settled.

Now that Anne no longer required the Brontës' cradle, Patrick sent it to Mrs Garrs, then expecting her twelfth child.

On 27th November 1821 Patrick answered a kind letter of condolence from his old vicar, John Buckworth at Dewsbury. From his reply, which was afterwards published by Buckworth in his *Cottage Magazine*, or Plain Christians' Library (Volume XI, 1822) and bearing only the initial letters of people and places mentioned, it will be seen how straitened financially Patrick became as the result of the extensive medical advice he paid for during his wife's illness. In addition, his notebook showed that he owed £50 to at least one business man in Bradford, a debt he was able to clear through the kindness and generosity of his many friends.

Haworth, near Keighley, Yorkshire. Nov: 27th 1821
My Dear Sir,
    I have just received yours of the 23rd instant, and it is like good news from a far country, or the meeting of old friends after a long separation. Your kind letter breathes that good sense, that Christian spirit and brotherly tenderness, which I have ever considered as prominent features in your character, and which are well-suited to soothe and benefit a mind like mine, which, at present, stands much in need of comfort and instruction. As I well know, that you, as well as a much-esteemed friend of mine, who is near you, will take an affectionate interest in my affairs, whether they be prosperous or adverse, I will proceed to give you a brief narrative of facts, as they have succeeded one another, in my little sphere for the last twelve months.
    When I first came to this place, though the angry winds which had been previously excited, were hushed, the troubled sea was still agitated, and the vessel required a cautious and steady hand at the helm. I have generally succeeded pretty well in seasons of difficulty; but all the prudence and skill I could exercise, would have availed me nothing, had it not been for help *from above*. I looked to the *Lord*, and He controuled [*sic*] the storm, and levelled the waves, and brought my vessel safe into the harbour.
    But no sooner was I there, than another storm arose, more terrible than the former—one that shook every part of the mortal frame, and often threatened it with dissolution. My dear wife was taken dangerously ill on the 29th of January last; and, in a little more than seven months afterwards, she died. During every week, and almost every day, of this long, tedious interval, I expected her final removal. For the first three months, I was left nearly quite alone, unless you suppose my six little children, and the nurse and servants, to have been company. Had I been at Dewsbury, I should not have wanted kind friends; had I been at Hartshead, I should have seen them, and others, occasionally; or had I been at Thornton, a family there, who were ever truly kind, would have soothed my sorrows; but I was at Haworth, a stranger in a strange land. It was under these circumstances, after every earthly prop was removed, that I was called on to bear the weight of the greatest load of sorrows, that ever pressed upon me. One day, I remember it well, it was a gloomy day, a day of clouds and darkness—three of my little children were taken ill of a scarlet fever; and the day after,

the remaining three were in the same condition. Just at that time, death seemed to have laid his hand on my dear wife, in a manner which threatened her speedy dissolution. She was cold and silent, and seemed hardly to notice what was passing around her. This awful season, however, was not of long duration. My little children had a favourable turn, and at length got well ; and the force of my wife's disease somewhat abated. A few weeks afterwards, her sister, Miss Branwell arrived, and afforded great comfort to my mind, which has been the case ever since by sharing my labours and sorrows, and behaving as an affectionate mother to my children.

At the earliest opportunity, I called in different medical gentlemen, to visit the beloved sufferer ; but all their skill was in vain. Death pursued her unrelentingly. Her constitution was enfeebled, and her frame wasted daily ; and after above seven months of more agonising pain than I ever saw anyone endure, she fell asleep in Jesus, and her soul took its flight to the mansions of glory. During many years, she had walked with God ; but the great enemy, envying her life of holiness, often disturbed her mind in the last conflict. Still, in general, she had peace and joy in believing ; and died, if not triumphantly, at least calmly, and with a holy, yet humble confidence, that Christ was her Saviour, and heaven her eternal home.

Do you ask how I felt under all these circumstances ? I would answer to this, that tender sorrow was my daily portion ; that oppressive grief sometimes lay heavy upon me ; and that there were seasons, when an affectionate, agonizing *something*, sickened my whole frame, and which is, I think, of such a nature, as cannot be described, and must be felt, in order to be understood. And when my dear wife was dead, and buried, and gone, and when I missed her at every corner, and when her memory was hourly revived by the innocent, yet distressing prattle, of my children, I do assure you, my dear Sir, from what I felt, I was happy at the recollection, that to sorrow, not as those without hope, was no sin ; that our Lord Himself had wept over His departed friend ; and that He had promised us grace and strength sufficient for such a day. Indeed, throughout all my troubles, He stood by me and strengthened me, and kindly remembered mercy in judgement ; and when the scene of death was over, and I had incurred considerable debts, from causes which I could neither foresee, nor prevent, He raised me up friends to whom I had never mentioned my straitened circumstances, who dispensed their bounty to me in a way truly wonderful, and evidently in answer to prayer. I received on one day, quite unexpectedly, from a few wealthy friends in Bradford, not less than *one hundred and fifty pounds* ! I received also several pounds from my old and very kind friend at Bradford [William Morgan, bless his heart], *fifty pounds* as a donation from the Society in London; and what is, perhaps, not less wonderful than all, a few days ago, I got a letter, containing a bank post bill, of the value of *fifty pounds*, which was sent to me by a benevolent individual, a wealthy lady, in the West Riding of Yorkshire. [Miss Currer? Miss Firth had joined with her stepmother, Dr and Miss Outhwaite and Charlotte Brontë's godmother, Mrs Atkinson of the Green House, Mirfield, in £150. In addition she entered in her cash account for 1821 : "March 1st. Expenses to Haworth 3/4. September. Subscription for Mr Bronte 2-2-0."]

How true, how memorable, the saying, "Seek ye first the Kingdom of God and His righteousness, and all these things shall be added unto you".

Should you still enquire how I now feel? I would also answer to this, the edge of sorrow, which is still *very keen*, is somewhat blunted. The tide of grief, which once threatened to overwhelm me, has, I trust, been at its height; and the slowly receding waves, often give me a breathing time; though there are periods when they swell high, and rush momentarily over me; yet I trust, through the mercy of the Lord, that time will produce its effects, and that I shall be enabled to pursue my ministerial labours with the necessary degree of alacrity and vigour.

I wish you had mentioned more particularly to me the state of your health, as well as that of my dear friend, Mrs Buckworth, for whom I have been lately much concerned. Perhaps if you can not do it, she may find a leisure moment, to tell me more particularly how you both are.

I remain

Yours most sincerely P. Brontë.

This letter was published under the heading, "A Letter from a Clergyman—In answer to a letter of Sympathy on the loss of his wife".

Patrick kept a small home-made notebook bound in brown leather : inside the front cover he wrote, "Always keep every page of this book for the sake of reference". The first entry was the settlement of his debt incurred during Maria's long illness. "I paid Wm. Tetley Esq— Bradford, Yorkshire, the £50-0-0 which I owned [sic] him in 1821, in the presence of Mrs Tetley and his son and burnt the note." There is then added, "Mr Tetley made me a present of half a dozen of port in Aug: 1830."

For the next two and a half years, Patrick instructed the eldest of the children himself, whilst Elizabeth Branwell had the complete charge of Emily and her favourites, Branwell and Anne. Patrick taught them English, Geography, and History, and then, Maria showing such signs of genius, he added to her lessons, Latin and politics. She could converse with him on any topic of the day. The newspapers were eagerly devoured by her upon their arrival, and she rapidly became a fully intellectual companion to her father—although only nine! Her grasp of parliamentary procedure and the debates held at Westminster was phenomenal, her knowledge of the political figures of the day and their various tenets, complete. But it was her emerging faith that was his greatest joy and pride. Truly, she lived "in calm, looking to the end".

It was during this time that Patrick made the famous discovery of his six children's extraordinary talents—of the seed of genius that flowered in them all. He was to relate the incident to Mrs Gaskell in a letter dated 30th July 1855.

". . . When my children were very young, when as far as I can remember the oldest was about ten years of age, and the youngest about four—thinking that they knew more than I had yet discover'd, in order to make them speak with less timidity, I deem'd that if they were put under a sort of cover, I might gain my end—and happening to have a mask in the house, I told them all to stand and speak boldly from under cover of the mask. I began with the youngest [Anne]. I asked what a child like her most wanted. She answered, age and experience. I asked the next [Emily] what I had best do with her brother Branwell, who was sometimes a naughty boy. She answered, reason with him, and when he won't listen to reason, whip him. I asked Branwell what was the best way of knowing the difference between the intellects of men and women. He answer'd, by considering the difference between them as to their bodies. I then asked Charlotte what was the best book in the world. She answer'd, the Bible. And what was the next best? She answer'd, the Book of Nature. I then asked the next [Elizabeth] what was the best mode of education for a woman. She answer'd, that which would make her rule her house well. Lastly, I asked the oldest, what was the best mode of spending time. She answer'd, by laying it out in preparation for a happy eternity. I may not have given you precisely their words, but I have nearly done so, as they made a deep and lasting impression on my memory. The substance, however, was what I have stated. . . ."

Even allowing for pardonable parental pride and an aged memory, what truly wonderful answers are these! And each terse reply contains in a nutshell the various characters of the six children. They would all have answered their respective questions thus, had they been ninety years of age.

So the lessons at the parsonage continued, Patrick telling the children tales to illustrate a Scripture, Geography or History lesson and for them to write about next day. Thus they pondered it out in bed, a habit Charlotte would continue all her life when writing.

In 1823, Maria and Elizabeth were sent to school for a short time, to Crofton Hall School at Wakefield, on the recommendation of Miss Firth, who, as already mentioned, had been there from 1811 to 1813. But this famous establishment for young ladies was beyond Patrick's present means and they remained there only a few months. Had matters been different, had Patrick been able to afford to keep them at this splendid school, how different would be the story: their lives might have been spared for many years. But there came another suggestion for Patrick. It sounded reasonable and sensible, but was in reality the worst piece of advice he was ever given.

There was to open on 30th January 1824, at Cowan Bridge near Kirkby Lonsdale, Westmorland, a Clergy Daughters' School, to provide a reasonably inexpensive education for the girls of the poorer clergy. Wilberforce and Simeon were subscribers; the Rev. Theodore Dury, Rector of Keighley, was one of the first trustees; Miss Currer, patron of Morgan's former living, possessed great influence at Cowan Bridge and Tunstall—where could be the harm? Yet harm there was. The founder, the Rev. William Carus Wilson, Vicar of Tunstall, was a Calvinist and one who lacked the humanity of Lady Huntingdon and George Whitefield. True, Simeon had shown him much kindness as a young man but later became alarmed at his extreme views.

On 12th November 1815 Simeon wrote: ". . . Five pious young men are running into Huntingdon's and Dr. Hawker's principles . . . there have also been two most excellent young men refused Orders for inclining towards Calvinism, (Mr. Wilson's eldest son, of Casterton Hall, and Mr. Blackburn) . . . it has made a great noise. . . ." On 30th October 1815, Simeon warned Carus Wilson: ". . . You lean more to one side than I do. View me on the Calvinistic side, and I am as strong as you could wish : so that my statements are not from fear, or partiality, but from conviction, and from a determination to follow Scripture *fully* . . . turn this in your mind, and see if it be not right . . . my views are truly scriptural, and at the same time more calculated to unite men of real piety, than the partial statements of either party [Arminian and Calvinist]." Yet the idea of the school seemed wholly worthy, the situation beautiful; if Charles Simeon was still prepared to support its inception, how could Patrick divine the harsh extremity of Wilson's beliefs? It would be 1847 before Simeon's warning letter to Wilson was published.

Maria and her sister returned home from Wakefield towards the end of 1823, promised as pupils for the opening of the new school. But illness prevented them from attending as arranged. At the year's end, Maria and Elizabeth were very ill, with measles, followed by whooping cough. The younger ones caught the infection, but happily, in a milder form.

At this stage Nancy Garrs, soon to leave the parsonage, became disgusted with Elizabeth Branwell. No sooner were the two girls over the worst of their illness and back on their feet again, than their aunt set them to work in her stuffy bed-sitting-room (where the windows were never opened, for all the roasting fire) making underclothing for them to wear at their new school. Nancy was indignant; "Keeping them at needlework instead of allowing them to walk on the moors and regain their health, as the four younger children did." Well might Nancy wax angry. The harm done to those girls by Aunt's folly in denying them both fresh air, by shutting them in an overheated room for hours on end, so weakened their resistance against the consumption that raged within them that it would need but little of the neglect and unnecessary hardships imposed upon them at Cowan Bridge by the Rev. William Carus Wilson and his minions to end their young lives. By her action Aunt Branwell lost the affection of the two servants, who would later describe her as "a bit of a tyke". Patrick, overwhelmed at this time by family responsibilities and church duties had, however, made two determined attempts to end her *régime*.

CHAPTER 14

Rejection

AT THE end of 1821 Patrick had proposed marriage to Elizabeth Firth, and was rejected. She was not yet affianced to the Rev. James Clarke Franks, later Vicar of Huddersfield, son of an old family friend, the Rev. James Franks, incumbent of Sowerby Bridge, Halifax (she left Kipping House on 27th April 1824, and married him on 21st September of that year); but she would not look twice at Patrick's proposal. In December 1821 Patrick stayed two days at Kipping House. Miss Firth recorded his arrival on the 8th, his departure on the 10th and the receipt of a letter from him on the 12th. "14th. I wrote my last letter to Mr. Bronte. Mr Franks to dinner."

It was not to prove the end of the friendship; but the need to secure a suitable stepmother for his children remained.

Nor was that all Patrick's troubles, not by any means. A youngish clerical widower with or without a family is always the object of prey or, at least, gossip, in any age. Several young ladies' names were linked with Patrick's, to his intense rage and despair. In a village rumour always sets the fashion, but in the town of Keighley, gossip spreads a hundred times faster and farther than in Haworth. There, fair names were bandied about, particularly if they had a clerical connection or background.

Miss Isabella Dury, the Rector of Keighley's sister, is discovered writing to a friend, Miss Marriner:

To

Greengate, Keighley, Yorkshire

. . . I heard before I left Keighley that my brother and I had quarelled about poor Mr Bronte, I beg if you ever hear such a report that you will contradict it as I can assure you it is perfectly unfounded. I think I never should be so very silly as to have the most distant idea of marrying anybody who had not some future, and six children into the bargain it is too ridiculous to imagine any truth in it. . . .

"Too ridiculous," indeed, to imagine the author of those flippery lines sustaining the future that did await "poor Mr Bronte" and the "six children".

But so it continued, and there was no course open to Patrick, but to turn the wheel full circle and return to his first love, Mary Burder. Here was someone who, he knew, would make a wonderful mother to the children. Here was someone he had once loved very dearly. If she be still free of heart, there could be no other choice so satisfactory for his needs—and for his heart. He had written first to Mary's mother.

To Mrs Burder, The Broad, Wethersfield, Essex.

Haworth, April 21st, 1823.

Dear Madam,

Fourteen years have now gone by since I have either seen you, or heard from you, or from any other of my acquaintance in that part of the country where I spent the first years of my Ministry. During that interval of time many events have taken place which once were little thought of, and who can tell what may occur during the lapse of fourteen years to come ? You may remember to have heard me often say that I should like to live in Yorkshire. In consequence of this, after I left your neighbourhood, I spent only a year at Wellington, in the county of Salop, and then came into this County, where I have resided ever since, and where I am likely to reside as long as life lasts. The first situation I had in Yorkshire was a Curacy at Dewsbury near Leeds. From that place I wrote twice to my old Friend, Miss Davy, from whom I received no answer. In about a year and a half after I was promoted to the Living of Hartshead near Huddersfield, and still I received no answer to my letters to the South, from whence I concluded that all my Friends there were either dead or had forgotten me. Shortly after this, I married a very amiable and respectable Lady, who has been dead for nearly two years, so that I am now left a widower. I have at length removed to a Living in this place, where I have been for upwards of three years, and where, in all human probability, I shall continue during the remainder of my life. This Living is what is here called a Benefice, or Perpetual Curacy. It is mine for life, no one can take it from me. The only difference between it and a Vicarage is that in a Vicarage the salary arises from tithes, and in the Living I have it arises from the rent of Freehold Estates, which I like much better. My salary is not large, it is only about two hundred a year. But in addition to this two hundred a year, I have a good House, which is mine for life also, and is rent free. No one has anything to do with the Church but myself, and I have a large congregation.

Should you, or any of your relations, or of my old friends come down into this part at any time and favour me with a call, I shall be very glad to see them, and shall make them as comfortable as I can.

You will much oblige me if you will write ere long, and let me know whatever you may think will prove interesting. I should like to know whether Miss Davy be still alive, how you are yourself, how all your children are, whether they be married or single, and whether they be doing well, both as it respects this life, and that which is to come. It is sometimes good to lay up treasure on earth, but it is always far better to lay up treasure in Heaven, where moths do not corrupt, and where thieves do not break through nor steal. An interest in Christ Jesus is the best interest we can have, both here and hereafter. I would be much obliged to you to tell me also who is now the Curate of Wethersfield. If all be well I shall probably go up into the South this summer, and may pass through your neighbourhood. I long to revisit the scene of my first ministerial labours, and to see some of my old friends.

As this letter is written entirely of my own affairs, and I know not into whose hands it may fall, I have taken the liberty of post-paying it, which I hope will be excused. Into whatever hands, however, this letter may fall I shall be greatly obliged by an answer. Be so kind as to write an answer as soon as you can and to direct "The Rev. Patrick Brontë, Haworth, near Keighley, Yorkshire".

I remain, Dear Madam,

Your Sincere Friend and Humble Servant, P. Brontë.

After some lapse of time, there returned a brief and guarded answer and, a visit to Essex being quite out of the question that year, Patrick had no alternative but to write direct to Mary.

To Miss Burder, Finchingfield Park, near Braintree, Essex.

Haworth near Keighley, Yorkshire. July 28th, 1823.

Dear Madam,

The circumstance of Mrs Burder not answering my letter for so long a time, gave me considerable uneasiness; however, I am much obliged to her for answering it at last. Owing to a letter which I received from Miss Sarah, and to my not receiving any answer to two letters which I wrote subsequently to that, I have thought for *years* past that it was highly probable you were married, or, that at all events, you wished to hear nothing of me, or from me, and determined that I should learn nothing of you. This not unfrequently gave me pain, but there was no remedy, and I endeavoured to resign to what appeared to me to be the will of God.

I experienced a very agreeable sensation in my heart, at this moment, on reflecting that you are *still* single, and am so selfish as to wish you to remain so, even if you would never allow me to see you. *You* were the *first* whose hand I solicited, and, no doubt, I was the *first* to whom *you promised to give that hand*.

However much you may dislike me now, I am sure you once loved me with an unaffected innocent love, and I feel confident that after all which you have seen and heard, you cannot doubt respecting my love for you. It is now almost fifteen years since I last saw you. This is a long interval of time and may have effected many changes. It has made me look something older. But, I trust I have gained more than I have lost, I hope I may venture to say I am *wiser* and better. I have found this world to be but vanity, and I trust I may aver that my heart's desire is to be found in the ways of divine Wisdom, and in her paths which are pleasantness and peace. My Dear Madam, I earnestly desire to know how it is in these respects with you. I wish, I ardently wish, your *best* interests in *both* the worlds. Perhaps you have not had much trouble since I saw you, nor such experience as would unfold to your view in well-defined shapes the unsatisfactory nature of all earthly considerations. However, I trust you possess in your soul a sweet peace and serenity arising from communion with the Holy Spirit, and a well-grounded hope of eternal felicity. Though I have had much bitter sorrow in consequence of the sickness and death of my dear Wife, yet I have ample cause to praise God for his numberless mercies.

I have a *small* but *sweet* little family that often soothe my heart, and afford me pleasure by their endearing little ways, and I have what I consider a competency of the good things of this life. I am *now settled* in a part of the country *for life* where I have many friends, and it has pleased God in many respects to give me favour in the eyes of the people, and to prosper me in my ministerial labours. I want but *one* addition to my comforts, and then I think I should wish for no more on this side eternity. I want to see a dearly Beloved Friend, kind as I *once* saw her, and as *much* disposed to promote my happiness. If I have ever given her any pain, I only wish for an opportunity to make her ample amends, by *every* attention and kindness. Should that very dear Friend doubt respecting the veracity of any of my statements, I would beg leave to give her the most satisfactory reference, I would beg leave to refer her to the Rev. John Buckworth, Vicar of Dewsbury, near Leeds, who is an excellent and respectable man, well known both as an *Author* and an able Minister of the Gospel to the religious world.

My dear Madam, all that I have to request at present, is that you will be so good as to answer this letter as soon as convenient, and tell me candidly whether you and Mrs Burder would have any objection to seeing me at Finchingfield Park, as an *Old Friend*. If you would allow me to call there in a friendly manner, as soon as I could get a supply for my church, and could leave home, I would set off for the South. Should you object to my stopping at Finchingfield Park, over night, I would stop at one of the Inns in Braintree—as most likely my old friends in that town are either dead or gone. Should you and Mrs Burder kindly consent to see me as an old friend it might be necessary for me before I left home, to write *another* letter in order that I might know when you would be at home. I cannot tell how *you* may feel on reading this, but I must say *my* ancient love is rekindled, and I have a *longing* desire to see you. Be so kind as to give my best respects to Mrs Burder, to Miss Sarah, your brothers, and the *Little Baby*. And *whatever* you resolve upon, believe me to be yours,

Most Sincerely P. Brontë.

In many ways this letter was deserving of a rebuff, and Patrick certainly received one. Mary had not forgotten, or forgiven, his ambitious nature and the ease with which he had given up the fight and quit the field. Here is her stinging reply:

To the Rev. Patrick Brontë, Haworth, near Keighley, Yorkshire.

Finchingfield Park, August 8th 1823.

Reverend Sir,

As you must reasonably suppose a letter from you presented to me on the 4th inst. naturally produced sensations of surprise and agitation. You have thought proper after a lapse of fifteen years and after various changes in circumstances again to address me, with what motives I cannot well define. The subject you have introduced so long ago buried in silence and until now almost forgotten cannot I should think produce in your mind anything like satisfactory reflection. From a recent perusal of many letters of yours bearing date eighteen hundred and eight, nine and ten addressed to myself and my dear departed Aunt, many circumstances are brought with peculiar force afresh to my recollection. With my present feelings I cannot forbear in justice to myself making some observations which may possibly appear severe, of their justice I am convinced. This review Sir excites in my bosom increased gratitude and thankfulness to that wise, that indulgent providence which then watched over me for good and withheld me from forming in very early life an indissoluble engagement with one whom I cannot think was altogether clear of duplicity. A union with you under then existing circumstances must have embittered my future days and would I have no doubt been productive of reflections upon me as unkind and distressing as events have proved they would have been unfounded and unjust. Happily for me I have not been the ascribed cause of hindering your promotion, of

17

preventing any brilliant alliance, nor have those great and affluent friends that you used to write and speak of, withheld their patronage on my account young, inexperienced, unsuspecting, and ignorant, as I then was of what I had a right to look forward to. Many communications were received from you in humble silence which ought rather to have met with contempt and indignation ever considering the sacredness of a promise. Your confidence I have never betrayed strange as was the disclosure you once made unto me, whether those ardent professions of devoted lasting attachment were sincere is now to me a matter of but little consequence. "What I have seen and heard" certainly leads me to conclude very differently. With these my present views of past occurrences is it possible think you that I or my dear Parent could give you a cordial welcome to the Park as an *old friend*? Indeed I must give a *decided* negative to the desired visit. I know of no ties of friendship *ever* existing between us which the last eleven or twelve years have not severed or at least placed an insuperable bar to any revival. My present condition upon which you are pleased to remark has hitherto been the state of my choice and to me a state of much happiness and comfort tho' I have not been exempted from some severe trials. Blessed with the kindest and most indulgent of friends in a beloved Parent, Sister, and Brother, with a handsome competency which affords me the capability of gratifying the best feelings of my heart. Teased with no domestic cares and anxieties and without any one to control or oppose me I have felt no willingness to risk in a change so many enjoyments in possession. Truly I may say, "my Cup overfloweth", yet it is ever my desire to bear in mind that mutability is inscribed on all earthly possessions. "This is not my rest," and I humbly trust that I have been led to place all my hopes of present and future happiness upon a surer foundation, upon that tried foundation stone which God has laid in Zion. Within these last twelve months I have suffered a severe and protracted affliction from typhus fever. For twenty-eight weeks I was unable to leave my bedroom and in that time was brought to the confines of an eternal world. I have indeed been brought low but the Lord has helped me. He has been better to me than my fears, has delivered my soul from death, my eyes from tears, and my feet from falling, and I trust the grateful language of my heart is, "What shall I render unto the Lord for all his benefits?" The life so manifestly redeemed from the grave I desire to devote more unreservedly than I have ever yet done to his service.

With the tear of unavailing sorrow still ready to start at the recollection of the loss of that beloved relative whom we have been call'd to mourn since you and I last saw each other [a brother], I can truly

sympathise with you and the poor little innocents in your bereavement.
The Lord can supply all your and their need. It gives me pleasure
always to hear the work of the Lord prospering. May he enable you to
be as faithful, as zealous, and as successful a labourer in his vineyard as
was one of your predecessors the good old Mr. Grimshaw who occupied
the pulpit at Haworth more than half-a-century ago, then will your
consolations be neither few nor small.

Cherishing no feelings of resentment or animosity, I remain,
Revd Sir,
       sincerely your Well Wisher, Mary D. Burder.

Patrick really should have let it go at that; there was nothing but
futility in continuing the correspondence. But he wrote one more letter
to Mary, a rather pathetic letter that could not possibly save the day.
But it points out some truths about their relationship at Wethersfield
and helped Patrick to ease his mind before ending the affair for ever.

To Miss Burder, Finchingfield Park, near Braintree, Essex.

      Haworth near Keighley. January 1st, 1824.
Dear Madam,

In the first place, I wish you the compliments of the season. My
earnest wish and ardent prayer is that you may soon recover from the
effects of your late severe illness and that every New Year's day may
add to your blessings, as well as privileges and comforts in this life, and
open to your view brighter and more cheering prospects in reference to
another world. This world with all its pains, pleasures, fears, and hopes
will soon have an end; but an eternity of utterable happiness or misery
is the grand characteristic of the next world. When we take this just
view of the subject through the medium of faith all the concerns of this
life are at once immerged and lost in the vast and sublime concerns of
the life to come. From some expressions in your last letter to me I am
led to suppose that you have directed your face heavenward, and are
taking the Blessed Saviour for the pillar of fire and cloud to guide you
on your way through this wilderness. Yet, my dear Madam, I must
candidly tell you that many things in that letter surprised and grieved
me. I only made a civil request, which I think, and do verily believe,
no one in all England but yourself would have refused to grant me, and
not only did you do this but you added many keen sarcasms, which I
think might well have been spared, especially as you knew the pale
countenance of death was still before my eyes and that I stood far more
in need of consolation than reproach. I do solemnly assure you that no
consideration whatsoever could have induced me to treat you in the

same manner—no, nor I trust, anyone living. When I had the pleasure of knowing you, you seemed to me (and I shall still believe it) to be considerate, kind, and forgiving. But when I look at your letter and see it, in many parts, breathe such a spirit of disdain, hatred, and revenge— after the lapse of so long an interval of time—I appear to myself to be in an unpleasant dream; I can scarcely think it a reality. I confessed to you that I had done some things which I was sorry for, which originated chiefly in very difficult circumstances that surrounded me, and which were produced chiefly by yourself. This, I think, might have satisfied you; at least, it might have disarmed you of everything like a spirit of hatred, scorn, and revenge. However, you may hate me *now*—I am sure you *once* loved me—and perhaps, as you may yet find, better than you will ever love another. But did I ever in any one instance take advantage of this or of your youth or inexperience? *You know* I did *not*. I, in all things, as far as it was then in my power, behaved most honourably and uprightly. The letters, which were written in your absence and which I entreat you never more to read, but to burn, were written when my mind was greatly distressed, and the only object of which was to hasten your return. These letters, I say, greatly distressed me soon after, and have greatly distressed me many a time since. For this, and every other word and action towards you and yours in which I have been wrong, I ask your pardon. I do not remember the things you allude to, but as far as I can collect from your letter I must have said something or other highly unbecoming and improper. Whatever it was, as a Christian Minister and a gentleman, I feel myself called upon to acknowledge my great sorrow for it. Such an apology becomes me, and is I deem, required of me. And such an apology I now make. Your Aunt and Mother were always kind to me, and if there were any others that wished me ill or spake ill of me I freely forgive them. And should it ever be in my power, instead of doing them harm, I would do them good. You wonder what my reason was for wishing to call on you. I will honestly tell you. I said, and resolved, that if my circumstances changed for the better I should, if I was spared, return on a visit to your neighbourhood. They have changed for the better, and I wished to keep my word. You also distinctly promised (they were nearly the last words I heard you utter), when I last saw you in Wethersfield, that if I called again *you would see me, as a friend*. I, moreover, loved you, and notwithstanding your harsh and in some respects cruel treatment of me, I must confess I love you still. The reason of this, I suppose, is I retain in my mind the *lats* impressions. I see you still as you once were—affectionate, kind, and forgiving, agreeable in person, and still more agreeable in mind. I cannot forget our walks from Wethersfield to the Broad, and some of our interviews there. But I will say no more on this subject ; it may be disagreeable to you, and it greatly disturbs my own mind. You may think and write as you please, but I *have not* the *least doubt* that if you had *been mine* you would have been happier than you *now* are or *can* be as one in *single* life. You would have had other and kindlier views and feelings. You would have had a *second self*—one nearer to you than Father or Mother, sisters or brothers ; one who would have been continually kind, and whose great aim would have been to have promoted your happiness in *both* the worlds.

Our rank in life would have been in every way genteel, and we should together have had *quite enough* of the things of this life. We should have had even *more* than the prophet, Agar, prayed for in his most judicious prayer. Once more let me ask you whether Mrs Burder and you would object to my calling on you at the Park some time during next spring or in the summer ? If you cannot see me as a *friend*, surely you can see me without feelings of revenge or hatred and speak to me civilly. I give you my word, on honour, that I will say *nothing* in reference to what is passed, unless it should be as agreeable to you as to me, and that I will not stop a moment longer than you wish me. Surely you cannot object to this. It can do *no one living* any harm, and might, I conceive, be productive of some good. Remember me very respectfully to Mrs. Burder and all her family, and believe me yours very respectfully and sincerely, P. Brontē.

Patrick had certainly scored some hits in his response, but there are lines in the letter that must make his defenders tear their hair in despair. So Mary Burder, who had had many suitors since Patrick had known her, refused to see him. The letter remained unanswered and Patrick sat back with a sigh and resigned himself to hearing the eternal click of pattens and swish of the silk dress as Elizabeth Branwell moved about the house.

In the same year, 1824, at the age of thirty-five, Mary Burder married the Rev. Peter Sibree, then Dissenting Minister of the Wethersfield meeting-house, and took up her abode with him in the vine-covered manse that faced the village green. The marriage had been in the offing at the time of her correspondence with Patrick and this fact, allied to the religious views of her intended husband, gave the sharp tone to her refusal to entertain Patrick at her home. Four children were born to her and grew to love their mother dearly. Some twenty-five years after the birth of her youngest child, she received one day a photograph of the old father of the famous Brontës, sent her with Patrick's kindest regards. She outlived her first suitor and died in 1866, in her seventy-seventh year.

If her rejection of Patrick had sadly disappointed him, it was equally a blow to Miss Branwell. She longed for her beloved native county, detesting the moorland village of Haworth. But, hard as one has to be with her sometimes, she was a loyal and devoted woman. She did not hesitate an instant: it was her duty to stay and help Patrick run his home, her duty to look after her late sister's children. She would live at Haworth Parsonage as housekeeper. She had an income of £50 a year, but insisted from the very start that she would prefer to pay all her own expenses and not become a burden to the household. She rarely left the house—the moors were a desert for her—yet the villagers did sometimes catch a glimpse of the large yet dainty cap, the inevitable purple or mauve shoulder shawl, her favourite black silk dress and if not the daintiest of shoes, then the rough pattens with their iron rings clashing against the cobbled streets. She took many of her meals in her bedroom. As for the young children, they puzzled her. Maria was untidy; Elizabeth gentle and quiet, yet stubborn; Charlotte excitable and hot-tempered; Emily had the eyes of a half-tamed creature, cared for nobody's opinion and seemed happy only with pets. Really, only baby Anne and the handsome auburn-haired Branwell were manageable! But in his heart, Patrick was truly grateful to Elizabeth Branwell. She was sometimes a trial, but she had proved a true friend in the past and, now she was so sorely needed, had made a great sacrifice in order to help him. He remembered that whilst at Thornton he had given her a copy of his *Cottage Poems* (as well as "The Rural Minstrel") some three weeks before Charlotte was born. He had really meant what he had written inside: "Gift of the author to his beloved sister Miss Branwell as a small token of affection and esteem. Thornton nr. Bradford. March 29th 1816."

In October 1823 Patrick had met Elizabeth Firth for the last time. She had recently become engaged to Mr Franks and he went over to Kipping to confirm this (before writing his last letter to Mary) and to give her his good wishes. "October 4th. Mr. Bronte called renewed acquaintance. 6th. Mr. Bronte went home. Mr. Franks came." There would still be letters between them, but as Patrick left Kipping House, giving way to Franks, he made his final exit from Miss Firth's diary.

As for sending the children away to school, there was now no alternative. With no mother to care for them, no possibility of a step-mother, it was the only way they could obtain that education and knowledge denied him in his youth. His many parish duties precluded him from giving them anything but a smattering of knowledge and he knew their hungry and remarkable minds demanded much more.

It has often been stated that had either Mary Burder or Elizabeth

Firth married Patrick Brontë, the children's lives would have been saved, that they would have been happier. Yet Mary Burder would have been too late to prevent the heated, stuffy room provided by Aunt Branwell and too late to save the two eldest girls from Cowan Bridge; as for Elizabeth Firth, the Clergy Daughters' School was partly her suggestion, and neither she nor Mary could have eradicated the consumption that Maria Branwell's family bequeathed to the children. In addition, the Brontë girls had to be free from supervision and control for their great talents to reach maturity, and in this connection they had the greatest good fortune in the father who gave them life.

CHAPTER 15

"Helen"

IT WAS arranged that Maria and Elizabeth should go to Cowan Bridge School for the start of the quarter beginning in July 1824, and on the 21st of that month Patrick took them by coach from Keighley and gave them in charge to the superintendent. On hearing of the recent attacks of measles and whooping-cough, the latter hesitated to accept them; it would hardly do to permit them to mix with other girls, ought they not to have a longer holiday? Patrick thought the change of air would be beneficial. Indeed, after Miss Branwell's room any air would do them good. So they were accepted. Patrick slept at the school that night and took his meals there. Every institution is a showplace at its inception, and he left his two children, quite happy and contented in his mind that they would be in good and kind hands. Indeed, on 10th August of that year he sent Charlotte to join her eldest sisters at the Clergy Daughters' School. (Thomas Plummer, the Keighley curate whom Patrick later employed as a "drawing-master" at the parsonage, had sent his fourteen-year-old daughter, Margaret, to Cowan Bridge on 21st February. She survived the ordeal and left on 4th July 1826.)

Some six weeks after Charlotte's arrival at the school she was to pillory so memorably in *Jane Eyre*, Elizabeth Firth, now Mrs Franks, called there with her husband whilst on her honeymoon. She saw Maria, Elizabeth and Charlotte, giving them each some pocket money. In her account book for that time she wrote, "3 Miss Brontes, 2/6 each". Despite her rejection of Patrick's suit, she remained on the friendliest of terms with him and, as will be seen later, they continued to correspond.

Meanwhile in Haworth, the three youngest children were soon involved in an exciting adventure that certainly one of them, Emily Jane, would never forget. On Thursday, 2nd September 1824, at 6 o'clock in the evening, the bogs on the moor at Crow Hill, near the site of the druidical Alcomden Stones, erupted with tremendous fury, sending a flood of water, mud and slime cascading down the moors and over the steep cliffs into the Ponden Valley. Boulders and stones were hurried by the torrent and hurled over the abyss into the valley beneath, some of the largest embedding themselves over a mile from their former position. The destructive torrent was kept in bounds for a time as it passed down the narrow Ponden Glen, but just above Ponden House it ran over some cornfields to a depth of several feet, destroying the crops. It filled the millpond, choked the watercourse, flooded the mill and carried away a stone bridge. An old gentleman, Mr J. Craven, had time only to cross the bridge with a youth under his care, when the muddy waters reached it; as he turned round he saw the bridge collapse. Much devastation was caused, several bridges were damaged or destroyed, but there was no loss of life. The torrent was seen seven feet high pouring down the hillside by a person who gave the alarm and was able to save several children playing in Ponden Valley. Robert Heaton was out shooting with some friends on the moor a short time before the eruption, but as the sky grew a dark fierce red, they started for home, fearing a storm. They reached Ponden House just ahead of the slimy waters. On the following morning at 8 o'clock there was another discharge from this peaty part of the moors and a black deposit was cast over banks and fields. The rivulets polluted the Worth, killing the fish, and down at Stockbridge near Keighley the poisonous water joined the Aire, keeping the water of this river in such a turbid state that for some time afterwards it remained unusable at Leeds, either for household or manufacturing purposes. Near Crow Hill, the scene of the outburst, over 1,000 feet above Keighley, there was left across an area of 1,200 yards a great crater some four to six yards deep, surrounded by many smaller pits.

Under the care of Nancy and Sarah Garrs, Emily, Branwell and Anne were out on the moors that afternoon, although happily at some distance from the Ponden Valley. But Emily saw the threatening sky, felt the gathering strength of her beloved moorlands and heard with exultation the defiant boom as the heath hurled its wrath on the heads of the valleys below. Only the danger to the sheep could mar that moment for her.

Ten days after this long-remembered eruption, on Sunday, 12th September 1824, Patrick preached a sermon in St Michael's Church, taking as his text, the 97th Psalm, verses 4 and 5: "His lightnings enlightened the world; the earth saw, and trembled. The hills melted like wax at the presence of the Lord, at the presence of the Lord of the whole earth." In his sermon Patrick revealed to the congregation that he had watched the skies from the back chamber of the parsonage and of his anxiety for his three children. ". . . As the day was exceedingly fine, I had sent my little children, who were indisposed, accompanied by the servants, to take an airing on the common, and as they stayed rather longer than I expected, I went to an upper chamber to look out for their return. The heavens over the moors were blackening fast. I heard mutterings of distant thunder, and saw the frequent flashing of the lightning. Though, ten minutes before, there was scarcely a breath of air stirring; the gale freshened rapidly, and carried along with it clouds of dust and stubble; and, by this time, some large drops of rain, clearly announced an approaching heavy shower. My little family had escaped to a place of shelter, but I did not know it. I consequently watched every movement of the coming tempest with a painful degree of interest. The house was perfectly still.

"Under these circumstances, I heard a deep, distant explosion, something resembling, yet something differing from thunder, and I perceived a gentle tremour in the chamber in which I was standing, and in the glass of the window just before me, which at the time, made an extraordinary impression on my mind; and which, I have no manner of doubt now, was the effect of an Earthquake at the place of eruption. This was a solemn visitation of Providence, which, by the help of God, I shall endeavour to improve. . . ."

This sermon was shortly afterwards printed in Bradford by Patrick's old friend T. Inkersley of Bridge Street, and sold at sixpence. "A sermon preached in the Church of Haworth, on Sunday, the 12th day of September, 1824, in reference to an Earthquake, And extraordinary Eruption of Mud and Water, that had taken place ten days before, in the Moors of that Chapelry. By the Rev. Patrick Brontë, A.B., Incumbent of Haworth, near Keighley."

Then followed the lines of Cowper commencing,

> When were the winds
> Let slip with such a warrant to destroy. . . .

Patrick's advertisement to the reader ran as follows: "I wish the Reader to understand, that in preparing this Sermon for publication, I have condensed and shortened it, as much as the nature of circumstances would admit, in order, that as it was principally intended for the poorer classes of the people in Haworth, and the adjoining parishes, it should, both in the perusal and purchase, require as little as might be of their time and money. I am also desirous that the Reader should know, that it appeared to me to be a duty incumbent on some one, to afford them an opportunity of procuring, at an easy rate, a plain and practical statement of an extraordinary occurence, of a monitory nature, which ought to be remembered and improved."

Patrick considered two main points: "How and for what reason Earthquakes are produced"; "And then by making some particular observations in reference to that Earthquake which forms the immediate object of our attention."

He proceeded to explain in the simplest terms the various natural causes that produce eruptions and the like, using Etna and Vesuvius as examples. Then he expounded the belief that God "sometimes produces earthquakes as manifestations of his power and majesty. In this sense He employed them at the delivery of the Ten Commandments to Moses; when 'Mount Sinai was altogether on a smoke, because the Lord descended upon it in fire; and the smoke thereof ascended as the smoke of a furnace; and the whole mount quaked greatly'."

Patrick pointed out that "sometimes, God produces earthquakes as awful monitors to turn sinners from the error of their ways", and then gave examples of the attitude of some of the groups of people whom he had seen when surveying the scene at Crow Hill a few days after the bog-burst. "As I proceeded up the channel, along which the overwhelming and ruinous flood had lately passed, I heard some, whilst surveying the ruins of overthrown bridges and walls, lament in pathetic terms the great expense that must be incurred by the different townships"; others "whose sorrows were confined within the narrow limits of their own fields of corn, so lately their hope, but now laid prostrate and ruined". But the greater part "rushed on, impelled by mere idle curiosity". Here and there "I was able to discern one in deep contemplative mood, who saw by faith through nature to nature's God". Some, being mere scientific men, "could neither penetrate so far, nor rise so high as this; who only looked at second causes, and grovelled here below". Again, "Several graceless persons wrangled and disputed with each other, even in the very bottom of the cavities, and on their edges; utterly regardless of the warning voice of Providence, that so lately spoke to them in thunder. . . ." ". . . Many, I perceived, on their return home, who in all the giddy frivolity of thoughtless youth, talked and acted as if they dreamed not either of heaven or hell, death or judgment."

Soon the terror of a moment, the serious impression created, was lost: it is the same with a family bereavement or other calamity—the greater part continue to indulge their bad passions and practices, disregarding every warning. "We have just seen something of the mighty power of God: he has unsheathed his sword, and brandished it over our heads, but still the blow is suspended in mercy—it has not yet fallen upon us. As well might He have shaken and sunk all Haworth, as those parts of the uninhabited moors on which the bolts of his vengeance have fallen." He ended with a plea that they all take warning to heart and "Be thankful that you are spared". (Patrick had read

John Fletcher of Madeley's "A Dreadful Phenomenon described and improved. Being a particular Account of the sudden Stoppage of the River Severn, and of the terrible Desolation that happened in consequence thereof, May 27th 1773. And the Substance of a Sermon, preached the next day on the Ruins, to a vast concourse of spectators.")

At the same time Inkersley published, at twopence a copy, "The Phenomenon, or, an account in verse of the Extraordinary Disruption of a Bog" which Patrick wrote for the children—"Intended as a Reward Book for the Higher Classes in Sunday Schools". "To my Young Readers", Patrick gives in the simplest and easiest terms the message of his sermon, warning them however that ". . . This talent of reading which you possess, will prove a blessing or a curse, just according to the use you make of it. If you read the scriptures and other good books only, your souls will be edified and comforted; but if you read every tract that is put into your hands by cunning and designing people, or eagerly search out for, and peruse such tracts and books as you know before to be bad, then you are sure to be corrupted and misled, and your talent of reading will become a source of sin and misery to yourself and others."

As Patrick Brontë's writings are all out of print, here are a few lines from "The Phenomenon":

> . . . On whirring wings the startled moorcocks fly;
> The fleeing gunners pass unheeding by;
> The labouring peasants haste, with sturdy stride,
> To 'scape the danger of the coming tide;
> The bleating sheep, or heedless, or too slow;
> The cattle with a loud, last dismal low; . . .

Both pamphlets were printed in 1824. The sermon appeared also in *The Cottage Magazine* for January 1825. In addition, Patrick sent a letter to the *Leeds Mercury* three days after the occurrence, giving his explanation of the physical causes of the outbreak. This letter landed Patrick in a bother; its reference to "an earthquake" caused the newspaper to send a representative up to Crow Hill to investigate. He could not agree with Patrick's conclusions and the *Leeds Mercury* told its readers as much. Patrick then wrote the newspaper a stiff letter: "the phenomenon in question was what justly deserves the appellation of an earthquake", although he admitted that he had "written at an Inn [Stanbury], in great haste, and without the requisite premeditation".

On 16th September the *Leeds Intelligencer* also published a letter from Patrick on the eruption.

Three months after bringing her young charges safely home from the moors Nancy Garrs left the parsonage, to marry her Patrick and live in Bradford; a few weeks later Sarah too left the service of the Brontës.

Years later, when Nancy was ill with fever in Bradford, Charlotte visited her, and regardless of infection, rushed to the sick-bed and kissed her old nurse, bursting into tears at finding her so very ill. But Nancy recovered, and lived to be a mourner at Patrick's funeral. She long outlived all the family she had served so well, but, alas, died in the Bradford workhouse, on 26th March 1886, three days before her eighty-third birthday. She was buried in the Undercliffe cemetery. She was twice widowed, her second husband being John Malone.

Sarah Garrs became Mrs Newsome and emigrated to the United States of America, where she lived for the rest of her days. She always delighted to tell of her time with the Brontës and, late in her life, developed a fetish for reminding people that her correct name had been de Garrs. After the publication of Mrs Gaskell's *Life of Charlotte Brontë* Patrick and his former servants were forced to rush to one another's defence. On the authority of Mrs Brontë's day nurse (who was then living in Burnley) and whose spite against the parsonage household is incomprehensible, Mrs Gaskell wrote: "There was plenty, and even waste in the house, with young servants, and no mistress to see after them." Both the sisters, thus branded as being wasteful, appealed to Patrick to save them from the imputation. Nancy called on him in Haworth. "Wasteful!" Patrick told her, "had you and your sister been wasteful, I should have found it out; but I can truly say that no master was ever blessed with two more careful and honest servants." So Patrick wrote out a reference for Nancy and gave it her.

Haworth, August 17th, 1857.

I beg leave to state to all whom it may concern, that Nancy, and Sarah Garrs, during the time they were in my Service, were kind to my children, and honest, and not wasteful but sufficiently careful in regard to food, and all other articles committed to their charge.

P. Bronte, A.B. Incumbent of Haworth, Yorkshire

For Nancy, it was a great shock to hear of the violences which Mrs Gaskell had attributed to Patrick. She was hotly indignant. "There never was a more affectionate father, never a kinder master. He was not of a violent temper at all; quite the reverse." From America Sarah wrote later: "The Brontës were well brought up . . . lively and cheerful in their own home. Mr Brontë was a kind and loving husband and father, kind to all about him." Even Martha Garrs, the eldest sister, who had met Patrick only once or twice, rose in his defence. But Mrs Gaskell had done the harm, and Patrick's reputation is unfairly tarnished to this day. It is to be deplored that she did not make a protracted stay in Haworth instead of employing a local gentleman to gather all the village information on her behalf. It is a thousand pities the day nurse was allowed to pour forth her poison, whilst Nancy Garrs remained unquestioned : a completely false picture of those early days of the Brontës at Haworth was created.   It was said that Patrick would fire off his pistol in anger, disturbing Maria in her sick-bed, whereas he fired off his pistol every morning whether angry or no ; that he stuffed the hearth-rug up the chimney and stayed in the smoky room to watch it burn : he was far too afraid of fire to commit such folly ; that he sawed off the backs of the chairs in a rage : too ludicrous to merit a retort ; that he burned in the kitchen grate the red boots William Morgan had given the children, because they were too gay and would foster an undue love of dress : Nancy was never absent from the kitchen for more than five minutes at a time and remembered no odour of burning boots, nor the children ever missing any ; and that he did not allow his children to have flesh meat to eat, they had only potatoes for dinner : Nancy remembered meat and plenty of it, only butter being restricted. "The children had meat every day of their lives, cooked on that very meat-jack," she recalled, pointing to the roasting-jack bequeathed her by Patrick "upon his death-bed".

Emily would mention in her 1834 diary paper that "we are going to have for dinner Boiled Beef, Turnips, Potatoes and apple pudding". It was reported too that Patrick entered his wife's bedroom in her absence and cut into shreds her favourite silk dress because of its lack of propriety. Here is Nancy's report of what really happened : "One morning Mr Brontë perceived that his Mrs. had put on a print gown, which was made in the fashion of that day, with a long waist and what he considered absurd-looking sleeves. In a pleasant humour he bantered her about the dress, and she went upstairs and laid it aside. Some time after, Mr. Brontë entered her room, and cut off the sleeves. In the course of the day, Mrs Brontë found the sleeveless gown, and showed it me in the kitchen, laughing heartily. Next day, however, he went to Keighley, and bought the material for a silk gown, which was made to suit Mr Brontës taste." A piece of folly certainly, but one for which Patrick would pay dearly when Mrs Gaskell's twisted version had become current. Yet fear of injury by fire would have dictated his action. The gown had *not* been of silk (as was its replacement) and Nancy also described it as "buff" with "balloon sleeves".

So by the end of 1824 the Garrs sisters had left the parsonage, and when Sarah was leaving, Patrick gave them £10 each in gratitude for their loyalty and devotion to his family. In November he had advised his banker, Marriner of Greengate, Keighley (head of a worsted-spinning firm founded in 1784, and brother to Isabella Dury's friend) that he was going to send Emily to Cowan Bridge, and would replace the Garrs sisters by an elderly woman.

Mr. Marriner, Worsted Manufacturer Keighley.

Haworth, near Keighley Novbr 10th 1824.

Dear Sir,

I take this opportunity to give you notice that in the course of a fortnight it is my intention to draw about twenty pounds out of your savings bank. I am going to send another of my little girls to school, which at the first will cost me some little—but in the end I shall not loose [sic]—as I now keep two servants but am only to keep one elderly woman now, who, when my other little girl is at school—will be able to wait I think on my remaining children and myself.

Remember me very respectfully to Mrs. Spence and Mrs. Marriner, not forgetting another important personage, though young and little.

Yours very respectfully P. Bronte.

Emily joined her three sisters on the 25th of that month and was more than loath to leave the moors; she was heart-broken. At the beginning of 1825 the "elderly woman" arrived at the parsonage—Tabitha Aykroyd.

Dear old "Tabby" was fifty-four years of age and, save for an interval of under three years, would stay with the Brontës until within a few weeks of her death, thirty years later. Tabby's maiden name had been Wood. She had been early widowed but had several relatives in the village. She had lived away from Haworth for a few years and immediately before returning to her native village worked on a farm. As Patrick well knew, she was a Methodist ; indeed, for a time she was a Class-leader among the Wesleyans in Haworth under the Rev. Jonathan Crowther. She spoke with the broad local dialect, had a quaint face full of character and remembered the days when the pack-horses went through the village once a week with their tinkling bells and gay worsteds, carrying the wool from Keighley over the Pennine Way to Colne.

She had also known the bottoms (valleys) in the days when "the fairies frequented the margin of the beck on moonlight nights and had known folk who had seen them". But that was when there were no mills—"it wur the factories as had driven 'em away". Did Branwell never paint Tabby ? If so, the portrait has been lost to the world. To those who have loved her, her kind face remains a shadow. She was abrupt in her manner, sharp with strangers, but had as large and warm a heart as can be met with. She was a typical example of the Haworth peasant woman of olden times, and no finer race existed. In the years that followed her arrival, when Maria the child-mother was gone, it was Tabby who became the foster-mother to the surviving children, and they could not have had a finer one. Bereft of social graces, devoid of education, she was yet wise in the ways of humanity and nature. Emily especially would find her kitchen tales of old moorland life irresistible and invaluable. Yes, Tabby was the servant of the Brontës, but it is as their close and loving friend for thirty years that she will be ever remembered.

Meanwhile at Cowan Bridge, the four Brontë girls endured the burnt and unwholesome food and harsh conditions. For each of them Patrick paid £7 on entrance and £4 for books and clothing. In 1825 he paid £7 for three of them, £3 for French and drawing for Maria, £1 14s 8d for extra clothing, as well as 18s 7½d for "clothes for Miss Charlotte" and an extra 13s for Emily. The entry reports for the girls read as follows :

"Maria Bronté aged 10 . . . Reads tolerably, writes pretty well. Ciphers a little. Works very badly—knows a little of Grammar. Very little of Geography or History. Has made some progress in reading French, but knows nothing of the language grammatically. . . ." "Elizabeth Bronté, aged 9. (Vaccinated. Chicken Pox, Scarlet fever, Whooping cough.) Reads little. Writes pretty well. Ciphers none. Works [Needlework] very badly. Knows nothing of Grammar, Geography, History, or Accomplishments." "Charlotte Bronté [8] . . . Reads tolerably. Writes indifferently. Ciphers a little, and works neatly. Knows nothing of Grammar, Geography, History, or Accomplishments —Altogether clever of her age, but knows nothing systematically. . . ." "Emily Bronté . . . [aged 6¼]. Reads very prettily and works a little. . . ." In addition to their dates of entering and leaving the establishment, the report gives the dates of Maria and Elizabeth's death and the subsequent career of Charlotte and Emily as "Governess". In view of their lives and writings, how farcical that word "Governess" appears ! Yet the entire report is little short of a farce, were it not the prelude to stark tragedy.

On 13th February 1825, Patrick received a sudden notification that Maria was very ill and should be sent for at once. He went the next day by the coach from Keighley to fetch her home. One glance at her pale, shadowed face and wasted limbs was sufficient to tell him that his eldest daughter, his dear companion of many a happy hour, was doomed to die.

The other girls appearing to be well, though naturally subdued, Patrick left at once with Maria to return to Haworth. They placed her in Aunt's bedroom, where her mother had died less than four years previously.

Again the doctors pronounced no hope. She had consumption and was in a rapid decline. Aunt nursed her niece, helped by the grief-stricken Tabby, who had hoped to meet her eldest charge under happier circumstances. Branwell and Anne were allowed in to talk to her and were not afraid, for Maria had a saint-like aspect and unswerving faith in God's mercy. She spoke only of the happiness that would so soon be hers and told them not to grieve when they heard that she was dead. She was going to her last great home where they were all sure to meet one day if they were good. She counted the hours until she was restored to Him who was her Father in heaven. Patrick was greatly moved at this example of faith and goodness. There was no need to pray for her, as she rarely ceased to supplicate for her own salvation. There were no hours of dark uncertainty and despair to assist her through, as had been the case with her mother. All was serene and holy in the sickroom. This helped to blunt the agony of sorrow that Patrick felt, yet even so, he would leave her and quietly break his heart in the sanctuary of his parlour. As he later said of his little Maria, "She exhibited during her illness many symptoms of a heart under Divine influence." Maria felt no pain during her long weeks of waiting, but was very wasted at the end. On Friday 6th May 1825, her golden moment arrived and she was safely home.

It was then Aunt Elizabeth held Branwell up so that he might look long upon his dead sister's face as she lay in her coffin, an act certainly not unusual in those days, but one which helped to unhinge a delicately balanced mind. Anne was too young to remember, but all his days Branwell would be haunted by the memory of Maria's features reposed in death. He would never quite escape the horror and sudden agony of that moment as several of his poems attest. Drunk or sober, he would have that scene always before his eyes.

Once again William Morgan came up Kirkgate, this time to bury the child he had christened at the little old church at Hartshead. The funeral was on Thursday, 12th May. Maria had been in her twelfth year.

Maria, Daughter of the Revd Patrick Bronte B.A. Incumbent of Haworth	Haworth	May 12th	12	W. Morgan Officiating Minister

18

There was hardly time for grief. Before Patrick and his family had gone into mourning, before he could become accustomed to the idea that his darling Maria was gone, there came another message from Cowan Bridge. He must suffer a double blow. This time it was Elizabeth who was ill: they were sending her home in care of a Mrs Hardacre. This news reached Patrick at the end of May, only three weeks after Maria's death, and it stunned him.

Elizabeth left the Clergy Daughters' School on 31st May, the school account book showing these items debited to Patrick:

Elizabeth's fare home, guard and coachman	13 – 0
Mrs Hardacre to take Elizabeth home	18 – 0
Horse, gig, pikes and man	2 – 6
Mrs Hardacre's bed at Keighley	1 – 0
Mrs Hardacre's letter at Keighley	8

Patrick met his daughter at the parsonage gate and once again looked into the eyes of death. He rapped out questions to Mrs Hardacre and her answers pulled him out of the pit of despair and galvanized him into action. There had been typhus fever in the school, it was there yet, and many of the girls were ill. He knew at once that he must save his other children. Leaving Miss Branwell to look after Elizabeth and after sending the distracted Tabby for the doctor, he set off at once for Cowan Bridge, his whole frame racked with anxiety and anguish. On arrival he was told that Charlotte and Emily were not there, but on the day that Elizabeth was sent home they had been taken to The Cove, Mr W. Carus Wilson's seaside home at Silverdale, on the shores of Morecambe Bay.

Patrick rushed off to find a conveyance to Silverdale. There he found the girls pale but well and hurried them home at once. Their bedroom had been at the back of the house; thus Charlotte lost her first opportunity to look at the sea she loved so much in her imagination. It is a thousand pities that, later, in a letter to Mrs Gaskell, Patrick, in endeavouring to remember early happenings that would be useful for her biography, made a bad error of memory. "I left Emily and Charlotte at the school, where they remained a year and then came home." His tired and grief-stricken old brain had dug a pit for him and Mrs Gaskell pushed him in. She made no effort to see the school registers (showing that the girls had left on "June 1st 1825", and never returned), but took Patrick at his word and wrote to the effect that he sent them back to Cowan Bridge for a further period. Patrick has been much blamed for his callous behaviour, whereas the truth is that upon seeing Elizabeth's condition he did not hesitate but removed the others on the following day from "the jaws of death".

In the event, before the year was over, twenty-eight of the seventy-seven pupils had left the school, many because of ill-health, at least three of them dying that year, whilst another died at the school. The probable casualties were, no doubt, higher, as the registers simply state "left" against twenty of the names. On 23rd September, Patrick's account with the school—totalling £82 16s 4d—was declared closed and he was refunded nearly £7 for his two eldest girls and £5 2s 4d for clothing.

When they reached home, the news was exactly what they had expected—consumption. Elizabeth Brontë died as she had lived, quietly, gently, without expressing any fervent fears or hopes. Tabby kept the four children occupied with tales in the kitchen. Aunt Branwell tried to take Patrick's mind off the impending loss by reading him *Blackwood's Magazine*. When they stayed with Elizabeth for a spell, she seemed quietly grateful. There was a happy smile on her thin, drawn face. Patrick knew that she sought only the company of her beloved sister Maria.

Miss Evans, a teacher at Cowan Bridge (the sweet Miss Temple of *Jane Eyre*), would remember Elizabeth by one single incident. She wrote to Mrs Gaskell: "The second, Elizabeth, is the only one of the family of whom I have a vivid recollection, from her meeting with a somewhat alarming accident, in consequence of which I had her for some days and nights in my bedroom, not only for the sake of greater quiet, but that I might watch over her myself. Her head was severely cut, but she bore all the consequent suffering with exemplary patience, and by it won much upon my esteem. Of the two younger ones (if two there were) I have very slight recollections, save that one, a darling child, under five years of age, was quite the pet nursling of the school [Emily]."

It has been said earlier that Anne was the bravest of the Brontës who grew to maturity, yet she could teach Elizabeth nothing of courage. The house was silent, the sickroom still. Elizabeth waited for death and the coming of Maria to fetch her, with a smile of contented resignation. The sullen pout had left those lips for ever. She died on Wednesday, 15th June 1825, less than six weeks after her sister. Maria and she were not long separated. Less is remembered of Elizabeth Brontë than any of her family, but she was by no means the least of them.

On the following Saturday, 18th June, the little gate of the dead was opened yet again, for the third time in under four years. Patrick, and Elizabeth Branwell, the godmother, followed the little coffin down the garden path and through the graveyard to the church. Charlotte and Emily followed, then Branwell and Tabby. The lad had again been shown the dead sister, but it was still Maria's face he saw. Anne stayed at home, in charge of a village girl. At the church entrance waited William Morgan. They laid Elizabeth to rest under the church flags beside her devoted Maria and her mother.

Again Morgan completed his sad duty:

Elizabeth, Daughter of the Revd Patrick Bronte B A Incumbent of Haworth	Haworth	18 June	10 yrs	W. Morgan Officiating Minister

As they left the church, Charlotte remembered Maria's goodness and grace; she recalled the dying Elizabeth, whose death-bed had been the first she had attended. As her sisters' ashes merged in the vault of the church, so their memory merged in Charlotte's mind and became "Helen Burns".

When they reached the house, Patrick asked Miss Branwell to take the children into the kitchen so that Tabby might give them something to eat. He went into his parlour followed by William and Jane Morgan. It was a warm day but there was a chill at his heart. His two beloved daughters had been taken from him so suddenly, so soon after their mother. Then he remembered the four surviving children in the kitchen and a shudder of fear suddenly convulsed his frame.

From that moment onward, Patrick would live in daily dread of a sudden death in his family. Every cough would strike a note of terror until, as the last survivor, there was no longer need for him to fear.

CHAPTER 16

Papa

THERE they were on parade in their little box : twelve wooden soldiers, with feet placed firmly in their respective stands, all dressed in the smartest uniform, yet not one of them facially resembling another ; the slightest touch of paint giving each a characteristic all his own. Patrick stared in at them through the shop window, regarding them intently with an almost professional eye. This was just the "platoon" he was seeking, a fine body of men indeed. Branwell had asked for reinforcements to assist his battle-scarred survivors ; he would surely be proud to command this splendid troop. With the inward hope that the remainder of his shopping would prove as easy, Patrick entered the Leeds toyshop and demanded of the assistant the surrender of the wooden fusiliers in their cardboard fortress. There being no resistance, providing that the ransom marked on the price-ticket was duly forthcoming, Patrick obtained the soldiers, and then cast his eyes over dolls, models and toys of all description. There was a large choice and it did not take him very long to complete his purchases : a set of ninepins for Charlotte ; a toy village, that with a little imagination might be Haworth, for Emily ; and finally a sweet dancing doll for Anne.

He left the shop clutching his parcels and feeling rather pleased with himself. He had earlier bought a small gift for Miss Branwell and a little something for Tabitha ; now he felt he could escape from the hot city and return home. The long clerical conference and the shopping expedition had been quite tiring in the heat of summer ; he would welcome the cool evening breeze as he walked up to Haworth from Keighley. Certainly, as he trudged away with his armful of toys, he had every reason to be pleased, particularly with regard to the box of soldiers. There had to be some spark that would set alight the bursting talents of the little Brontës—gifts maturing so rapidly under the shelter of those inspiring moors, and Patrick all unwittingly carried home with him that spark, that key which would set the little minds free of hesitation : the dozen soldier-men that marched up the hill from Keighley with him in the evening light.

It was quite late that night, Monday, 5th June 1826, when Patrick reached the parsonage. He handed Elizabeth Branwell her present and those for the girls, then went into the kitchen to give Tabby her little souvenir. Next he went quietly upstairs to the little back bedroom behind his own, the soldiers in his hand. Branwell was asleep, and he placed the box quietly beside the bed. It wanted three weeks yet to the boy's ninth birthday, but Patrick had neither the heart nor the patience to delay the pleasure until then.

It can be supposed that he stood there for a moment gazing down at the faint outline of his son's face, so reposed, so very tranquil in sleep. There were the same features he had seen so often in his mirror—the aquiline nose, the same hollow under the cheekbones, the same auburn hair. This was his young Patrick, his Branwell, his only son, the hope and pride of his heart, the being he had prayed for in the lanes of Hartshead and in his nightly bedroom-prayer. All Patrick's plans for the future (as far as he dare nurse any) centred on this handsome youth sleeping so peacefully in his bed. Here was his son and heir, the boy who, when grown to man's estate would protect and cherish his sisters (if God should spare them) and bring honour to the white hairs of his old father. So Patrick fondly thought that night, as he looked down on the slumbering Branwell. Is there a father in the land who has not at some time made his only son the very core of his existence? Patrick loved his boy more than any living being, and later, when forced to realize that Branwell was the least worthy of the family, the only one lacking in courage and determination, he never abandoned hope and would wrestle with him to the end. Patrick quietly closed the door and came downstairs, his heart full of happiness. However, there would be many other nights when he would be forced to watch his son as he lay in his bed; but they would not be nights of tranquillity and repose. Instead there would be the ravings of the drunkard, the restless fits of the drug addict, and the eyes would not close in sleep but stare wildly round with the light of madness. But Patrick had given Branwell the soldiers he had asked for, and though his son would, in later years, fall out from the parade, the three remaining girls would march on with them to ultimate victory!

Both Charlotte and Branwell have recorded the arrival of the soldiers and the former has given a picture of the excitements of the following morning, when Branwell burst into his sisters' room calling on them to see the new troops. Charlotte chose one to be her hero the Duke of Wellington, Emily chose a serious-looking fellow, called "Gravey" by the others, and later Anne chose "Waiting-Boy", whilst Branwell picked on "Buonaparte".

Around these wooden effigies, which replaced earlier ones bought by Patrick in Bradford in the summer of 1824 (twelve for 1s 6d) and others bought by Branwell in Keighley, the four children built many characters, battles and campaigns. Then the "Young Men", as they called the soldiers, were given divers occupations and credited with various exciting exploits. Soon the various adventures were set down on any minute pieces of paper available. These were stitched together with grey worsted and strengthened by coarse sugar paper for covers. Thus came into being the countless tiny books of the Brontë juvenilia. The wooden soldiers inspired a dream world that would lead Charlotte and Branwell to their "Angria" and Emily and Anne to "Gondal". When Branwell had abandoned everything, Charlotte would have to wrench herself out of her exotic dreams of Angria to relate life as it was in *The Professor*. Anne would make a gentle transition to describing her own experiences in *Agnes Grey* but for Emily there would be little change. The northern wastes of Gondal and the moors of Haworth were one and the same, her *Wuthering Heights* only the culmination of all she had felt and written since childhood. No doubt the model village served to set the scene for some of Emily's Gondal sagas, yet had she not, around her home, a live village of her own? Perhaps, also, the doll and the skittles were not completely ignored.

Since the tragedy of Cowan Bridge, Patrick had decided to keep his surviving children safe at home, where he would instruct them himself, and keep an eye on their health. The three eldest seemed to him well enough, but little Anne was somewhat delicate. He never could quite forget the time when she was yet a baby and Charlotte had rushed into his study exclaiming that there stood an angel by Anne's cradle. He had gone straight up, of course, and found nothing, but there was enough of the Celt in him for such conviction on Charlotte's part to make him uneasy. He would look well to Anne and watch over her closely.

Patrick often kept fond mementoes of his children, such as a woven strand of Anne's hair tied in a blue thread, taken when she was thirteen. Such things would be trivial to a biography if one had not read through the mass of ignorant accusations against Patrick over the last hundred years—in which lack of love for his family sets the theme. Indeed, *his* reputation is the chief sufferer from the destruction of all but a few of the Brontë inter-family letters.

At this time the regular weekday routine was family prayers, breakfast (in the dining-room with Papa), lessons in Patrick's room, early dinner (Patrick dining alone in the parlour), afternoon walk on the moors with Tabby, tea in the kitchen, followed by sewing in Aunt's room for Charlotte and Emily, when Aunt would often read to them from the newspapers. Occasionally Patrick went upstairs to take over the reading. Patrick, although a staunch Tory all his life, determined to read both views and took each week the *Leeds Intelligencer*, which accorded with his principles, and the Whig *Leeds Mercury*. In addition, as Charlotte wrote, "We see the *John Bull*; it is a high Tory, very violent. Dr. Driver lends us it, as likewise *Blackwood's Magazine*, the most able periodical there is."

During the morning lesson, Patrick instructed his four children in Scripture, history, reading, writing, arithmetic, geography and (for he never could forget his little Maria) politics. For the geography lesson, Patrick used the old book he had possessed for so long. Again young Charlotte records, "Once Papa lent my sister Maria a book. It was an old geography book; she wrote on its blank leaf, 'Papa lent me this book'. This book is a hundred and twenty years old." Anne had her own Bible in red morocco, inscribed: "To Anne Brontë, with the love and best wishes of her godmother Eliz:Firth, Oct 1823." Patrick added: "To read it and keep it for the sake of the donor." Soon Emily possessed a similarly bound Bible, inscribed: "To Emily Jane Brontè, by her affectionate Father, Febr 13th 1827." Although Patrick had always enjoyed teaching, it was strange acting as tutor to his own children: many parents did, but in his case he found it difficult. They were so eager for knowledge that he sometimes felt quite overwhelmed, yet very proud.

In some of their exercise books he wrote in the traditional manner: "Everything that is written in this book must be clear and legible." Many of those "exercises" were devoted to legends and tales that never reached Patrick's eye for correction. When he was too busy to take the morning class owing to his parish duties, Elizabeth Branwell stood in as deputy teacher, to the regret of the children. But from their earliest days of reading the little Brontës were allowed to select any and every book from their father's small but select library. Never once was a volume hidden from them or its perusal prohibited. Indeed they were encouraged to foster self-selection and no pressure was ever put upon them as to the subject-matter of their reading. When they were a little older they were further encouraged to use the library at the Mechanics' Institute, Keighley, and bring home whatever they cared to select. In addition, there was the lending library of Mr Hudson, bookseller and druggist, in High Street, Keighley, frequently visited by Charlotte.

Patrick never forgot his early days when he hungered for books and he determined that his children should be fed, without the imposition of any course of diet. This most enlightened attitude on the part of Patrick Brontë (so different from most clerical fathers of his day) was invaluable to his children and was his great contribution to their ultimate achievements.

Whenever a moment could be spared, however, the children were at their writing. They always carried a pencil in their pocket, and Tabby watched with open-mouthed concern as they frequently darted into the corner of a room to scribble down their thoughts on odd pieces of cardboard or any stray bit of paper. By seven o'clock they all had to be in bed; but for many an hour the two older girls would whisper together in the narrow nursery they shared before sleep overcame them both. Anne, alas, was still condemned to sleep with Aunt. Patrick knew they were "making out", as he had done as a child. He envied them their enthusiasm and guessed the happiness it was giving them. It could do no harm!

There are many happy pictures of Patrick and his children at this time, perhaps the most touching being the one of Prince Charles hiding in his oak tree. On one occasion, Oak-apple Day, 29th May, these young loyal devotees of the Stuarts determined to enact the escape of Charles into the tree. As the parsonage garden contained no oak tree, the cherry tree outside Patrick's study was nominated as the royal hiding-place. Emily, being the tallest and having the longest legs, was dressed up to represent the Prince. She climbed out of her father's bedroom window and secreted herself in the branches of the tree. Alas, Emily trod on one of the slender branches and off it snapped. True, there were none of Cromwell's men waiting to pounce on the royal prize, but there would be Papa coming home soon—it was his favourite tree!

Tabby rushed out and saw what had happened. She ran back into the house again and returned with a paper bag full of soot. She proceeded to blacken the broken end in the hope that the fresh break would escape her master's notice. But Patrick's eagle eye soon detected that his cherry tree had been unceremoniously pruned. He never pursued the matter with any ardour and the culprit remained undiscovered; but he was very fond of that cherry tree and wished "the Prince" had been more careful.

One of Mr Thomas Inkersley's printers at Bradford would often, as an old man, recall Patrick Brontë calling at the office in Bridge Street to correct the proofs of one of his printed sermons. He thought it had been the sermon on the bog-burst at Crow Hill and the year 1824, but as he maintained Charlotte came also, his memory must have been at fault as she was at Cowan Bridge at the time. But whatever the date or sermon concerned, he clearly remembered Patrick discussing politics with the equally fervent Tory, Thomas Inkersley, whilst Charlotte calmly corrected the entire proofs unaided—and she not more than nine years of age.

The story is still told in Haworth of how one of the church trustees invited the four parsonage children to a birthday party. To the intense astonishment of the village children they found that the Brontës knew absolutely nothing of any childish games such as "hunt the slipper" or "here we go round the gooseberry bush". In addition, their extreme shyness was most painful to behold. They remained awkward and silent during the party and seemed intensely relieved when the time came to return home. How they would have astonished the other children could they have acted one of their own original plays, which certainly needed more brain-power than was required of them at the party. At home they often performed their own plays, dragging in the assistance of the unwilling Tabby.

All this time Patrick was busy with his parish work and, as will be seen in a subsequent chapter, there was plenty to do. It is of little more than local interest, but on 25th July 1825, Patrick baptized a young child, Timothy Feather. "Owd Timmy" of Stanbury is now a legend in the West Riding of Yorkshire; he lived until 30th November 1910 and was the last of the hand-loom weavers in the Haworth district.

After the death of Elizabeth, Patrick was in great financial difficulties, the trustees presenting several bills for repairs to be deducted from his salary. Patrick again appealed to the Governors of Queen Anne's Bounty.

Post Paid
To Richard Burn, Esqr. Secretary to the Governors,
Bounty Office, Dean's Yard. Westminster.

Haworth, near Keighley August 25th 1825

Sir,

This case which I am about to lay before the Governors, will, I doubt not, when duly considered, urge as strong a claim on their attention and support, as any case that has come before them, for several years. This, will scarcely appear at first sight, as I shall begin with stating that the perpetual Curacy of Haworth, according to the present rental, is nominally worth, about one hundred and eighty pounds a year; besides the Surplice Fees, amounting annually, to about fourteen pounds. In addition to which, there is a house in which the Incumbents have been permitted to live rent free—This House, the adjoining garden, and the Lands from which the one hundred and eighty pounds, yearly, arise, are vested in Trustees, whose power, according to the respective Deeds, is almost unlimited. The Deed of the House and garden, says nothing at all, in reference to the Incumbent. It only mentions the House, and garden, & that they may be sold or let, or converted to any purpose, the Trustees may judge most proper—

They have, however, been occupied by the several Incumbents free of
rent, for upwards of forty five years. The following abstract from the
Deed of the Lands, will clearly illustrate a studied attempt, to keep the
Incumbent in perfect thraldom. . . .

The Governors, will readily perceive from this abstract, that the
Minister can claim nothing with certainty, but the fourteen pounds a
year, arising from the Surplice Dues, inasmuch, as under one plea, or
another, however circumspectly he may walk, he may be deprived of
his salary—or at least involved in a tedious, and expensive case of
litigation ; from which course, however, even to recover his rights, the
Deed, is contrived, so, as if possible, to debar him. The Governors, will,
however, perceive, that under the plea, of not being satisfied with the
Vicar of Bradford's nomination, the Trustees may object, to every
Minister, that he might nominate—and thus throw the whole salary
into the poor rates, a measure, calculated, ultimately to benefit themselves—Hence, it will appear evident, that this perpetual Curacy has
no certain endowment, at all, and is in a much worse situation, than
those churches, where the whole of a competent salary arises from the
rent of the pews—I have lately felt this to be the case, in various
instances, when bills, for repairs, and other things, have been brought
in to me, by the Trustees—to a very large amount, rendering the salary
inadequate to support my family, even with the most rigorous economy
—But another feature, and, perhaps the worst in the whole concern, is
the circumstance, that a part of the Trustees, who are much the
Wealthiest, and who have a preponderating influence, are Dissenters,
and have to support the Interest of a Baptist Chapel of their own, lately
erected within about one hundred yards of the Church—Though, I
have had no quarrel with the Trustees, and am on good terms with the
Inhabitants, I would now appeal to the Governors with a humble
confidence, that they will decide in my favour, and agree with me, that
this is a situation, in which no Church, or Minister of our Excellent
Establishment ought to be placed. Nor is this Church of small importance. The nearest Churches to it are at the distance of about four miles
—It is capable of accomodating above a thousand hearers, and is very
well attended—and there are in the Chapelry, nearly five thousand
Inhabitants. Surely then, it would be most desirable, that it should
stand upon a more respectable, and a more solid foundation. By laying
this letter before the Governors, and informing me, in due time,
respecting their decision, you will greatly oblige, Sir,

Your Obedient, Humble Servant, Patrick Bronte, Perpetual
Curate of Haworth, near Keighley—In the Diocese of his
Grace, The Lord Archbishop of York.

The reply, dated 6th September, was negative: the benefice of Haworth could not be augmented as the Archbishop of York had not certified that the living was worth less than £150 per annum, and therefore it was not on the Governors' list of augmentable livings. The Elizabethan Charter was inviolate. Patrick tried again and Vicar Heap forwarded this letter with one from himself dated 10th December.

Richard Burn, Esqr. Secretary, to the Governors—
Bounty Office, Dean's Yard, Westminster.

Haworth, near Keighley, Dec. 1st 1825. Yorkshire

Sir,

I some time ago, through the medium of you, stated to the Governors, the very unfavourable situation, in which I am placed here, as a Minister of the Establishment. I informed you, that, except, about fourteen, or sixteen pounds, annually, of surplice dues, all my salary, was in the hands of Trustees, of Different Denominations, and by virtue of a Deed held in their possession, vested with extraordinary powers—so as to enable them on certain occasions of ordinary occurrence, to keep back from the Incumbent, all the salary, except the fourteen or sixteen pounds, annually, alluded to above. I also, observed, that, notwithstanding, these gentlemen, were generally civil, in their deportment, I was nevertheless, greatly straitened in my circumstances, and that, my salary which was about one hundred and eighty pounds a year, nominally, was virtually, but very small—I further stated that I was under circumstances, so dependent, as to be altogether foreign, and detrimental to the rules, and Wellbeing of our Church. In answer to my letter, you informed me, that as my salary was not returned by My Diocesan, as being under one hundred and fifty pounds a year, the Governors, could not at present, Augment my Living—From this, I cannot help thinking, that the Governors misunderstood me; for, otherwise, they surely, never would have judged it expedient, to leave this Church, almost entirely dependent, and without any certain Endowment at all, with the single exception of about fourteen, or sixteen pounds a year of surplice fees, as before stated—I was encouraged to make application to the Governors, by many of the neighbouring Clergymen, who knew, the peculiarly unpleasant circumstances of my case—and particularly, by the Vicar of Bradford, the Patron—who would, I doubt not corroborate, what I have here stated, and readily come forward, as he always has done, to promote the interest of the Church—in any part of his extensive parish—as I have now stated my case, more fully to the Governors—I trust they will give it a favourable reception, and after the strictest investigation find, that no Act of Parliament, militates against an Augmentation. Begging, that the Governors and you, will excuse that importunity, which naturally results from the peculiarity, and urgency of my circumstances,

I remain, Sir, Your Obedient, Humble Servant, Patrick Brontē.

The Governors informed Heap that Patrick's only course was to apply to the Archbishop for a certificate. Such an application was doomed to failure (the stipend was unchanged over fifty years later), but happily, however, Patrick and the trustees continued to work well together for the good of Haworth, and many of the bills were met by the latter.

In September 1827 there came news to grieve Patrick. For years it had been his dear old friend William Morgan who had served him as minister in all his family needs. He had married Patrick, christened four of his children and, recently, buried his wife and two little girls. Now it was Patrick's turn to console Morgan—on the loss of his young wife Jane. She died on 24th September 1827, aged thirty-six. There being no burial ground at Christ Church the funeral was at her father's chapel, on the 27th, conducted by the Rev. Joseph Cowell, minister of Todmorden. Jane Morgan was buried in the east churchyard of Cross Stone Chapel, with its powerful view high over the Calder Valley to the moors beyond. Morgan gave Patrick his wife's Greek prayer book inscribed: "J.B. Morgan 1813. A Memorial of Mrs. Morgan presented to Rev. P. Bronte, B.A. Haworth, Sepr 29th 1827: presented by the Rev. William Morgan B.D. Octr 2nd 1827."

Poor Mrs Fennell never fully recovered from her daughter's death and died less than two years afterwards, on 26th May 1829, in her seventy-sixth year. Although Patrick would continue to meet Morgan and Fennell and remain in contact with them until their deaths, the bare facts of their remaining lives may best be given here. In 1836, Morgan married again—Miss Mary Alice Gibson of Bradford. The wedding was at Calverley Church solemnized by Samuel Redhead. A son was born of this marriage and Morgan paid tribute to his friend by choosing as one of the Christian names—Brontë. He left Christ Church in 1851, exchanging livings with the Rector of Hulcott in Buckinghamshire. In the following year, 1852, the second Mrs Morgan died and her husband's last work was entitled, "Simplicity and Godly Sincerity exemplified in the Life and Death of Mrs Morgan of Hulcott, Buckinghamshire, and late of Bradford, Yorkshire." Shortly afterwards, in old age, he married a third time. William Morgan died at 10, South Parade, Bath, on 25th March 1858, aged seventy-six.

John Fennell was married again shortly after his wife's death, at Halifax in 1830. His bride was Elizabeth, daughter of John Lister, a

Leeds merchant. They had five children, three daughters and two sons. The eldest, Mary Elizabeth, married the Rev. W. G. Mayne of Ingrow, between Haworth and Keighley. A son, Charles John, became a doctor in the Royal Navy. John Fennell remained the incumbent of Cross Stone Chapel, Todmorden, until his death on 13th October 1841, at the age of seventy-nine.

As a further example of how Patrick outlived nearly all his friends of earlier days it must be mentioned again that John Buckworth died on 2nd April 1835, aged fifty-six. A few months before his death, in November 1834, Charlotte wrote to her friend Ellen Nussey about the failure, "or rather the suspension of payment", of "Halliley, Son, and Brooke". ". . . Do you know whether the fortunes of Mrs. Brooke, Mrs. Buckworth, Mrs. Carter and Mrs. Jackson were in their brother's hands [Young Halliley] ? . . . I am thus particular in my enquiries because Papa is anxious to hear the details of a matter so seriously affecting his old friends at Dewsbury, and because I cannot myself help feeling interested in a misfortune, which must fall heavily on some of my late schoolfellows. Poor Leah and Maria Brooke ! . . ." Leah and Maria were at Roe Head with Charlotte; their father, John Brooke, had been taken into partnership with Halliley. Again in May 1835 she writes to Ellen, ". . . Poor Mr Buckworth, who was only ill when you wrote, is now, dead and buried. He had a troubled sojourn in Dewsbury; but undoubtedly he has now found rest in heaven. . . ." Neither was Patrick without losses in Haworth. On 26th December 1831 he buried Stephen Taylor, who had befriended him from the moment of his first visit to Haworth and who had been so largely responsible for his obtaining the living. He was fifty-nine. His son, George Taylor, succeeded him at the Manor House, Stanbury, and as a leading member of the church trustees.

On 13th February 1835, William Brown died, aged fifty-three. He had been sexton for twenty-seven years. As will be seen, his son John succeeded him in that capacity.

In the summer of 1830 Patrick was himself in some danger. He was ill for several weeks with severe inflammation of the lungs. (From this day onward the stock would be wound higher round his throat until it covered his chin, as a guard against bronchitis.) On Tuesday, 22nd June, at 6 o'clock in the evening, with Patrick confined to bed and very weak, there came a loud knock on the door of the parsonage. Charlotte and Tabby were alone in the kitchen. Tabby opened the door and an old man appeared before her. Charlotte has related the conversation thus :

Old Man—"Does the parson live here ?"
Tabby —"Yes."

Old Man—"I wish to see him."

Tabby　—"He is poorly in bed."

Old Man—"I have a message for him."

Tabby　—"Who from ?"

Old Man—"From the Lord."

Tabby　—"*Who ?*"

Old Man—"The Lord. He desires me to say that the bridegroom is coming, and that we must prepare to meet him ; that the cords are about to be loosed, and the golden bowl broken ; the pitcher broken at the fountain."

The stranger then left abruptly and Charlotte ends her narrative : ". . . I could not forbear weeping at his words, spoken so unexpectedly at that particular period." Happily it was no ill omen (for all that George IV died four days later) and Patrick recovered. It cannot be too sufficiently stressed that if Patrick had to worry continually about the health of his children, they in turn would be anxious all their lives about their father. Apart from their warm affection for him, his death would have been an irreparable blow. They would have lost the parsonage as a home, and would have been forced to seek their employment for life almost certainly away from Haworth.

Let Charlotte and Branwell prate all they may about the confinement of a little moorland village where there was no intellectual stimulus, but the loss of Haworth and the moors would have been spiritual disaster for them all. For Emily it would have meant an even speedier death. For the Brontës were happy in Haworth. They loved it, were wretched when away, and all who love them and their writings must count it a blessing that their father lived to provide them, all their lives, with the very home it was essential they should have. From the Branwells they inherited their sad physical weakness, for the Brontës from Ireland were a long-living and hardy race. From neither parent but only from Haworth and the moors did the girls obtain their inspiration. It has never been sufficiently recognized that if the Brontës made Haworth famous, it was that village, its people and its surrounding hills that gave the Brontës their immortal fame. Only the fusion of the two in 1820 made possible the flood of genius that was to follow.

How many scores of pictures could be given of the Brontës as happy and gay in their home, especially Emily and Anne, to refute the rubbish that has been written of their gloomy and sombre existence. They were brief in their lives but glorious. If they occasionally plumbed the depths of greatest anguish they also soared to heights of dazzling beauty and joyous understanding denied to all their fellows.

For many years Tabby was the only servant at the parsonage, but several local girls were called in to do the washing, the regular assistant in this task being Sally Mosley. But in December 1836, Tabby, whilst walking down the steep Kirkgate, slipped on the frosty cobbles (setts) and broke her leg. Patrick and Miss Branwell decided (with regret on the part of the former and relief by the latter) to send her to live with her relatives in the village. The children at once went on hunger strike until the order was rescinded. Tabby made a partial recovery, but the leg never set perfectly and she remained lame for the rest of her life. By the end of 1839 her lameness became worse and was further exacerbated by a large ulcer in her leg. There was then no help for it but to send her to live with her sister down in Stubbing Lane. For a time there was no regular servant at the parsonage, but John Brown, the sexton, sent his elder daughters there, to serve as errand girls and do the shopping. One of them was eleven-year-old Martha.

About a year after Tabby had left, this other loyal and devoted friend of the family, Martha Brown, was established as housemaid at the parsonage. Save for one short break, she was to remain until there were no longer any Brontës left to live in that old stone house at the top of the lane.

Towards the end of 1842, Tabby returned to the parsonage. From now on her usefulness was somewhat limited, but Patrick kept her in his employ until her last illness, and was happy to do so. At times of strain such as Aunt's illness and the visit of a clerical party, Hannah and Tabitha Brown would help with the work until the time came when their sister Martha had, as she grew older, obtained that degree of efficiency that served the Brontës so well.

Martha Brown was born on 22nd April 1828 and, as may be expected, had been baptized by Patrick.

"1828—June 8th. Martha, daughter of John and Mary Brown, Haworth, Stonemason. P. Brontè."

It has been hinted that Tabby and Miss Branwell found it difficult to rub along together. But on one point they were largely in agreement : a dislike of the domestic pets, and a horror of wild ones. True, Tabby would grow to like some of them, but Aunt Branwell—never !

For years the parsonage was the refuge and home of many stray cats from the village and injured birds from the moors ; and behind Miss Branwell's back, Patrick encouraged his children in these acts of mercy and affection. The first animal friend of whom there is record is Patrick's dog, Grasper, an Irish terrier, if Emily's drawing of him is to be the guide. When Grasper came to the parsonage or when he died is not known, but it is Grasper who in 1831 cost Patrick 8s tax under

Schedule G, for keeping a house dog. Emily drew him from life in January 1834 and he probably lived until 1837 or the beginning of 1838 when his successor is first mentioned.

Then there are, in November 1834, Rainbow and Diamond (no specification given), Snowflake (a cat), and a pheasant called Jasper. Later there were to be two more cats, black Tom, who died in June 1841, and Tiger, who died in March 1844. There were several geese, including Victoria and Adelaide, Little Dick the canary (acquired in 1841) and Hero the hawk. The last was brought down from the moors by Emily who, finding it injured, carried it home to nurse, ignoring the bites the wild bird gave her fingers, bites that caused the blood to flow over her hand. She nursed it to health and it became a favourite pet. But whilst Emily and Charlotte were in Brussels and Anne at Thorp Green, Elizabeth Branwell gave away Victoria, Adelaide and, cruellest act of all, Hero. As Emily wrote in her 1845 diary paper : ". . . lost the hawk Hero which with the geese was given away, and is doubtless dead, for when I came back from Brussels I inquired on all hands and could hear nothing of him. . . ." It is not possible to forgive Aunt Branwell for that !

But of all the pets the two famous ones are Keeper and Flossy. Keeper, like his predecessor, Grasper, belonged to Patrick, as the house-holder. His massive brass collar was engraved with Patrick's name ; but Emily made both these dogs her own and it is with her name that Keeper will be ever linked. Keeper, a mastiff, came to the parsonage as a puppy at the beginning of 1838 and on 24th April of that year Emily painted her magnificent water-colour sketch, "Keeper from Life".

Flossy, a King Charles spaniel, belonged to Anne. She had been given to her in 1843 by her employers at Thorp Green when she pleaded for the puppy's life, to save her from being drowned. Charlotte gave the world two brilliant studies of Flossy, one in repose, the other showing her at full stretch after grouse. But the most delightful sketch of all is the group of Keeper, Tiger and Flossy.

Having given these details of all the domestic companions Patrick found himself living with, some of the incidents of his life during the years 1826-1842 (both large and small) must now be given, it being beyond the province of this book to follow his children to schools, to the various houses where they were governess or tutor, or to drift with Branwell on his futile visit to London and in his besotted career as a railway clerk.

Patrick joined the Mechanics' Institute, Keighley, shortly after its foundation in 1825, his membership number being 213. Founded with the purpose of bringing the Arts and Sciences within the reach of the most humble, one of the guiding spirits of the Institute was the Rev. Theodore Dury, M.A., Rector of St Andrew's, the parish church of Keighley from 1814 to 1840. (He was presented to the living by the patron, the Duke of Devonshire, with whom he was at Harrow, contemporary with Lord Byron.) One of the four foundation members was John Bradley, a house-painter. As a hobby he painted in oils and his portrait of Patrick was most striking, showing the subject's handsome and determined features. Regularly every week Patrick or his children would walk the eight miles to Keighley and back, returning with their arms full of books from the Institute's Lending Library. These were a great assistance to Patrick in educating his children, although they needed no encouragement to read, but avidly devoured as many books as they could lay their hands on. Patrick had decided to keep Branwell at home also. There is a report that he did, for a time, attend the free grammar school at Oxenhope and was soon removed as the local boys were too rough and uncouth. However, there is no evidence for this, and it seems Patrick felt that Branwell's education could be effected more satisfactorily at home. Certainly there was no money to spare to send his son away to college as he would have wished. It was a matter of deep anguish to Patrick that, despite his own labours as a youth, it was now impossible for him to provide Branwell with the classical education that he himself had so nearly missed. But he endeavoured to instruct the boy as well as he could, believing rightly that his years at Cambridge had well qualified him to do so. It has been argued that Patrick was responsible for Branwell's ultimate collapse by keeping the boy at home and robbing him of the chance to mix with men and learn of life the hard way. Yet Branwell was sent to London to become an artist, he worked away from home in the capacity of clerk, and later tutor, and as soon as he was away from Haworth would collapse and completely lose all sense of direction. The critics remain blind to the magnetic powers of Haworth and the moors—powerful to all who have once lived there, and for the Brontës irresistibly potent. There is a kind of genius that will flourish only in the wild, lonely places of this earth, that is hardy amidst nature, yet so fragile amidst sophistication as to be soon choked to death.

In a small brown leather concordance to the Holy Scriptures, Patrick noted some of his later lessons with his son, tuition given preparatory to Branwell's becoming a tutor in the Postlethwaite family of Broughton-in-Furness.

"In June 1839—I agreed with Branwell, that under Providence, we should thoroughly read together, the following classics, in the following order only—

"1st the first 6 Books of the *Aeneid*—and the four gospels in Greek and 2ndly the first 3 or 6 books of Homer's *Iliad*—and some of the first odes of Horace, and the *Art of Poetry*—besides translating some English into Latin. The progress of the reading, is to be regularly set down in this, and the *following pages*. B.

"In Virgil, read to the the [*sic*] line of the 1st *Aeneid*—
To the 105=211−497=to the end.
2 *Aen'd*−200=505=
3 *Aen'd*=320.

"Read to the end of the verse of the first ch. of Matthew—the 11 ch—12 ver—verse the last. 3rd ch—end. 4th — "

They got no further, and it takes little imagination to realize whose fault that would be. But does this quotation show a father who shut himself away in his study and never interested himself in his children?

It had long been Patrick's dream that Branwell would become a very great artist—a painter of the front rank. He had earlier paid for a drawing-master (Thomas Plummer of Keighley) to come to the parsonage and give lessons to his children in painting and drawing. All four excelled, particularly Charlotte and Branwell, and their father and aunt were at once captivated by their sketches. The Brontës would go down to Mr Wood, the village carpenter, who lived in Kirkgate, and ask for frames for their sketches. Too proud to accept them as gifts they would give him in exchange some of their drawings. Patrick soon decided that the two elder children should receive more efficient training and he engaged William Robinson, the Leeds artist, to come to Haworth and give lessons to Charlotte and Branwell, at two guineas a visit.

William Robinson, the successful portrait painter, was trained by Sir Thomas Lawrence and numbered amongst his illustrious sitters the Duke of Wellington.

Charlotte's eyesight alone prevented her from becoming a successful artist (although her draughtsmanship was superb and she has left scores of wonderful sketches), and so, instead, she painted her vivid, immortal scenes with words. Branwell, through idleness and conceit, failed to reach any great heights as an artist; yet his portraits of John Brown and other local people are invaluable to the Brontë lover, whilst the portraits of his sisters that survive, although made famous only by the everlasting renown of the three subjects, have given him an honourable place in the National Portrait Gallery. Those who knew the girls said that Branwell "had painted them to the life" and that, surely, is worth more than all the subsequent portraits, however cleverly executed.

In September 1835 Branwell went to the Leeds studio of William

Robinson, in order to finish his course of lessons, and shortly afterwards, in early October 1835 went down to London on his abortive attempt to complete his studies at the Royal Academy. There, he soon frittered away the generous allowance his father had given him—at great sacrifice to the rest of the family—as well as money provided by Mrs Firth. He was not accepted at the Academy. Indeed, it is not certain that he made any great endeavour to gain admittance, and he spent his time with "sporting gentry" of the pugilistic type, drinking hard until the small hours. Soon his allowance was gone and he asked for more money, giving as his main excuse that he had been robbed by a fellow-traveller. Patrick, with a sigh, ordered him home at once. During the following years it was the Black Bull for Branwell. He would entertain the travelling guests with his brilliant conversation until, his mind befuddled with intoxication, he would stagger home up the lane. Sometimes Patrick would go down to the Bull himself and enquire if his son was there, or send Emily to fetch him home. On more than one occasion Emily would flit through the churchyard to tap a warning on the window of the room where her brother always caroused. But at all such times Branwell would escape either through that window or the one in the kitchen, or by the back door. This enabled the innkeeper, Sugden, to reply truthfully to his parson that Branwell was not on the premises. When, years later, Sugden was taxed with having sent for Branwell in order to entertain the guests, he responded, "I never sent for him at all; he came himself, hard enough."

In the solitude of his study Patrick broke his heart almost daily over the hopeless failure of his son. He searched his soul to find out if he was responsible for Branwell's dismal moral fibre. Patrick liked a drink of whisky (Irish preferably) or wine, but had never in his life been intoxicated. He had always endeavoured to face the trials of life bravely and, with God's help, had acquitted himself well. He remembered with pride and relief the courage of his two departed little ones and the three daughters who had been spared. Why then this insidious corruption in Branwell's being? He resolved to make yet one more attempt to assist his son to become the artist his family believed he could be. So it was that in 1838-1839, Branwell rented a studio in Fountain Street, Bradford. With a great deal of determination he painted William Morgan (who also lived in Fountain Street at that time) and one or two other portraits, and then his determination was washed away in the various inns of that town—the George, the Talbot, and so on. He made many friends: J. H. Thompson, the artist; John James, the historian of Bradford; Wilson Anderson, landscape-painter; Geller, the mezzo-tint engraver; Richard Waller, portrait painter; and J. B. Leyland, the sculptor; but he soon ceased to paint. Again he was costing his father a great deal of money and the studio was given up. So it would be all his life: begging, borrowing and wheedling money from his family. Towards the end of his life he even threatened his father with suicide if money was not forthcoming. At such a time Patrick's faith was sorely tested.

Happily there were generous and kind friends who assisted in paying for the girls' education. Charlotte's godmother, Mrs Atkinson, had again come to the assistance of Patrick in 1831 and offered to pay her godchild's education at Margaret Wooler's School, Roe Head. The cost of Emily's brief sojourn there (she soon pined away for lack of the moors of home) and the board of Anne who replaced her, had also been offered, but was largely met by Charlotte's later acceptance of Miss Wooler's offer to her to return as a teacher in exchange for free schooling for one of her sisters. During the summer of 1837 Miss Wooler's school would move to Heald's House, Dewsbury Moor, and in December of that year, Anne became seriously ill with influenza. Charlotte, ever mindful of consumption, badgered Margaret Wooler; the latter wrote to Patrick, and remembering Cowan Bridge he ordered both daughters home the next day.

But now it was only too apparent that Branwell would never earn a penny, or rather, would drink away his money faster than he could earn it. It had early been obvious that the girls would have to earn a living for themselves as governesses. Now the failure of Branwell, to whom they had all looked for some support, made some occupation for the sisters even more necessary. So Charlotte and Anne went away to their various positions as governesses in different families and even Emily made her attempt at supreme sacrifice by becoming a teacher for a time at Law Hill School, Southowram, near Halifax. They all suffered because they were separated from home, from each other, and because there was no time for them to give more than a partial release to the creative force that welled up in their breasts. Later, they would plan for a school to be opened in the parsonage, and Charlotte and Emily would go to Brussels to polish their accomplishments (Aunt Branwell was the generous one this time) to fit them as teachers. But the plan would come to nothing and, having done their duty to the utmost, they remained at home—to write.

Branwell earned a little as a railway clerk at Sowerby Bridge and Luddenden Foot, and drank himself into debt. Anne helped him to a post at Thorp Green where she was governess and disaster overtook Branwell again—although this time not all of his own making. By the end of his life, his greatest companion, Charlotte, had turned from him

in disgust, Anne in sad despair, and Emily attended him only because
of the endless flow of loyalty that was hers; he had long since killed her
love for him. Only his father, whom he had so cruelly shamed, struggled
to remember the golden-haired lad playing with his soldiers, and at the
end fought as parent and parson to save his soul.

But in the period with which this chapter deals, there are happier
pictures of Branwell Brontë: busily sketching from nature with his
sisters in September 1829, when Aunt Branwell had taken them over to
the Parsonage House, Cross Stone, to stay with their bereaved Uncle
Fennell; or proudly walking down Kirkgate with Patrick to visit
Mr Toothill the barber at the top of Butt Lane. Here, in the wooden
shop half-way down the main village street, they would all sing carols
whilst having their hair cut. Patrick would talk of the political problems
of the day and Branwell would join in with his brilliant comments on
leading figures in Parliament. It was said in Haworth that Branwell
used to persuade Toothill to crest his hair up as high as possible to add
an inch or two to his short stature.

Another picture of Branwell, an amusing one, derives from Patrick's
first curate at Haworth, the Rev. William Hodgson. Patrick's eyes were
no longer strong when, in 1835, he applied for an assistant. William
Hodgson arrived just before Christmas—indeed his first signature in
the registers is on 25th December 1835—and was given lodgings in a
house at the beginning of West Lane.

Hodgson's son-in-law has related the great respect he felt for
Patrick. ". . . he spoke of him as a man of a very nervous temperament
. . . often when he had promised to preach he would send to Mr Hodgson
at the last moment and tell him that he was unable to do so. This was
the case on the first or second Sunday on which Mr Hodgson officiated
at Haworth." It seems that Patrick asked his assistant to take the
morning service whilst he would preach in the afternoon. But during
the afternoon Sunday school Patrick sent for him and said he felt
unequal to the task of taking the service. Hodgson urged that he had no
sermon ready. " 'Oh,' said Mr Brontë, 'you must preach extempore;
the people like it better.' " It was said afterwards that the curate never
gave a better sermon. But that was the least of his troubles, for his
lodging was haunted!

Hodgson lived in the house of three women—mother, daughter and
granddaughter. The youngest, when three years old, had seen "a lady
standing in the middle of the room with something tied round her
throat". At once the bedroom had been searched but nothing found.
Upon his arrival, the curate was told the tale but took no notice of it.
One evening, however, when returning from a visit "he saw a light

moving about from one chamber to another in the upper regions of the house". He thought the family were retiring for the night, but found them sitting round the kitchen fire. None of them had been upstairs. Once he went to his room to fetch a book, "when close to his ear he heard what sounded to him like the shaking of a silk gown". Again, "more than once as he was sitting reading or preparing his sermon he would hear the crack of a whip in the room above him. He would rush upstairs and the whip would resound in the attic. He would follow it there, and there it was again in the room below." Nor did the ghost leave him unmolested at night. He slept in a four-poster with an understructure of sacking. "When he had got comfortably settled the bed would begin to heave as though someone underneath were uplifting it." He would light the candle, and find nothing. Hodgson informed Branwell of these disturbing visitations and, not surprisingly, received a sceptical reply. The curate, in exasperation, invited Branwell to come and share his bed for a night and then see whether he was inclined to scoff. Branwell at once accepted the challenge, and after examining the room thoroughly and locking the door and windows, climbed into bed alongside the persecuted cleric. They had barely lain down before the bed began to heave and jump with great gusto, threatening to throw Branwell on to the floor. This continued for some considerable time, but there was no sign of the cause of the disturbance. "One night's experience was quite enough for Branwell, and he would not renew it." Shortly afterwards William Hodgson was somewhat mollified—and became assured that the ghost intended him no harm. ". . . One night, at Haworth, I had fallen asleep while reading in bed, my candle burning on the chair beside me, when an unconscious movement of mine would probably have pushed the bed curtain into the flame of the candle. Judge my surprise and thankfulness when in the morning I found the candle burnt down into the socket and removed to a safe place at the bed's foot."

Had Hodgson's name been Redhead, or had he been unpopular with, and unwanted by, the people of Haworth, the explanation would be simple enough—they were trying to get rid of him—but as the following document shows, he was extremely popular there.

A requisition to the Revd. William Hodgson, Assistant Minister of Haworth, Yorkshire, April 30th 1837.

Revd. Sir,—We the undersigned inhabitants of Haworth, aforesaid, being fully satisfied with your faithful and diligent services, both in the desk, pulpit, Sunday School, and Parish, earnestly desire (if you can see it to be the path of duty pointed out by Providence) that you would continue in your present situation for another year, at least, or as long as you conveniently can. And at the same time we wish to state it is our hope and belief that, notwithstanding trade is depressed, your subscription will be conducted in a spirit, similar to that which gave rise to it, last year. [Then follow the signatures of 236 people, headed by Patrick Bronté and Branwell. It concludes as follows :]

All the preceding names or signatures, which are two hundred and thirty-six, were procurred [sic] in a few hours, and had the requisition been sent round the parish I am persuaded from what I have heard and seen that it would have been signed by all the churchpeople in Haworth and its vicinity.

P. Bronté, Incumbent.

Besides the subscription mentioned, the Pastoral Aid Society granted Hodgson an annuity of £50. Had the curate needed any additional salary at any time, the extra money would have had to be found by Patrick, as the minister.

William Hodgson remained for some months after this petition by the Haworth people and then obtained the living of Christ Church, Colne. On 22nd July 1838 he came over the moors from Lancashire to preach for Patrick at the six o'clock service (following William Morgan who came up from Bradford to take the service at two). At the beginning of August 1839, he visited Haworth Parsonage, accompanied by his own curate, David Bryce. The latter, who had come expressly to find a wife from amongst the three daughters of the incumbent, proposed to Charlotte and was immediately refused. It was as well for her that Charlotte gave the young Irishman the answer she did, in more than one respect, for a few months later he died of tuberculosis at Colne, on 17th January 1840, aged twenty-nine.

To complete the picture of Patrick as a father to his growing family are some extracts from Ellen Nussey's account of her first visit to Haworth Parsonage in 1833, some details of Patrick's tax returns for 1831 and those of his letters applicable to this chapter.

During the summer of 1833, for the end of July and most of August, Ellen Nussey came to the parsonage for her first visit. She had met Charlotte when she first arrived at Margaret Wooler's school at Roe Head on 25th January 1831. They would remain the closest of friends (save in the literary sense) until Charlotte's death. That other companion of Roe Head days, Mary Taylor, never became so close to either of them, largely because of her later emigration to New Zealand.

In old age Ellen Nussey's mind became confused, but this devoted friend of Charlotte's remembered with clarity her first visit and related it whilst the details were still fresh in her mind. She travelled by gig from her home, The Rydings, in Birstall and described the "terrific hill" that led her to her destination. Charlotte met her at the garden gate. Miss Branwell took possession of the guest and treated her with care and solicitude. "Mr Brontë, also was stirred out of his usual retirement by his own kind consideration, for not only the guest but the man-servant and the horse were to be made comfortable. He made inquiries about the man, of his length of service, etc. with the kind purpose of making a few moments of conversation agreeable to him. Even at this time [he was then fifty-six], Mr Brontë struck me as looking very venerable, with his snow-white hair, and powdered coat-collar. His manner and mode of speech always had the tone of high-bred courtesy. He was considered somewhat of an invalid, and always lived in the most abstemious and simple manner. His white cravat was not then so remarkable as it grew to be afterwards. He was in the habit of covering this cravat himself. We never saw the operation, but we always had to wind for him the white sewing-silk which he used. Charlotte said it was her father's one extravagance . . . his liability to bronchial attacks, no doubt, attached him to this increasing growth of cravat. Miss Branwell was a very small, antiquated little lady. She wore caps large enough for half a dozen of the present fashion, and a front of light auburn curls over her forehead. She always dressed in silk. She had a horror of the climate so far North . . . she talked a great deal of her younger days; the gayeties [sic] of her dear native town, Penzance, in Cornwall. . . the social life of her younger days she used to recall with regret; she gave one the idea that she had been a belle among her own home acquaintances. She took snuff out of a very pretty gold snuff-box, which she sometimes presented to you with a little laugh, as if she enjoyed the slight shock and astonishment visible in your countenance. In summer she spent part of the afternoon in reading aloud to Mr Brontë. In the winter evenings she must have enjoyed this; for she and Mr Brontë had often to finish their discussions on what she had read when we all met for tea. She would be very lively and intelligent, and tilt arguments against Mr Brontë without fear.

" 'Tabby', the faithful, trustworthy old servant, was very quaint in appearance . . . we were all 'childer' and 'bairns' in her estimation. She still kept to her duty of walking out with the 'childer', if they went any distance from home, unless Branwell were sent by his father as a protector. . . . Emily Brontë had by this time acquired a lithesome, graceful figure. She was the tallest person in the house, except her father. Her hair, which was naturally as beautiful as Charlotte's, was in the same unbecoming tight curl and frizz, and there was the same want of complexion. She had very beautiful eyes—kind, kindling, liquid eyes; but she did not often look at you: she was too reserved. Their colour might be said to be dark gray, at other times dark blue, they varied so. She talked very little. She and Anne were like twins— inseparable companions, and in the very closest sympathy, which never had any interruption.

"Anne—dear, gentle Anne—was quite different in appearance from the others. She was her aunt's favourite. Her hair was a very pretty, light brown, and fell on her neck in graceful curls. She had lovely violet-blue eyes, fine pencilled eyebrows, and clear, almost transparent complexion. . . . Branwell studied regularly with his father . . . all the household entertained the idea of his becoming an artist, and hoped he would be a distinguished one. . . .

"The interior of the now far-famed parsonage lacked drapery of all kinds. Mr Brontë's horror of fire forbade curtains to the windows; they never had these accessories to comfort and appearance till long after Charlotte was the only inmate of the family sitting-room,—she then ventured on the innovation . . . it did not please her father, but it was not forbidden. [Patrick never forgot "A Brand plucked out of the Burning".]

"There was not much carpet anywhere except in the sitting-room and on the study floor. The hall floor and stairs were done with sand-stone, always beautifully clean, as everything was about the house; the walls were not papered, but stained in a pretty dove-coloured tint; hair-seated chairs and mahogany tables, book shelves in the study, but not many of these elsewhere. Scant and bare indeed, many will say, yet it was not a scantness that made itself felt. Mind and thought, I had almost said elegance, but certainly refinement, diffused themselves over all, and made nothing really wanting.

"A little later on, there was the addition of a piano [in Patrick's study]. Emily, after some application, played with precision and brilliancy. Anne played also, but she preferred soft harmonies and vocal music. She sang a little; her voice was weak, but very sweet in tone. [Branwell also played the piano—and the organ.]

"Mr Brontë's health caused him to retire early. He assembled his household for family worship at eight o'clock; at nine he locked and barred the front door, always giving as he passed the sitting-room door a kindly admonition to the 'children' not to be late; half-way up the stairs he stayed his steps to wind up the clock, the clock that in after days seemed to click like a dirge in the refrain of Longfellow's poem, 'The Old Clock on the Stairs': 'Forever-never! Never-forever!' Every morning was heard the firing of a pistol from Mr Brontë's room window.

... Mr Brontë's tastes led him to delight in the perusal of battle-scenes, and in following the artifice of war; had he entered on military service instead of ecclesiastical he would probably have had a very distinguished career. The self-denials and privations of camp-life would have agreed entirely with his nature, for he was remarkably independent of the luxuries and comforts of life. The dread he had was of *fire*, and this dread was so intense it caused him to prohibit all but silk or woollen dresses for his daughters ... [As will be seen later, Patrick had a good practical reason for this dread that he had inherited from his father. At Haworth alone, he buried nearly a hundred children who had been burned to death as the result of their clothing catching fire, *all* wearing cotton or linen, *none* silk or wool.] Mr Brontë at times would relate strange stories, which had been told to him by some of the oldest inhabitants of the parish, of the extraordinary lives and doings of people who had resided in far-off, out-of-the-way places, but in contiguity with Haworth [moorland farms]—stories which made one shiver and shrink from hearing; but they were full of grim humour and interest to Mr Brontë and his children. . . . During Miss Branwell's reign at the parsonage, the love of animals had to be kept in due subjection. There was then but one dog [Grasper] . . . Emily and Anne always gave him a portion of their breakfast, which was, by their own choice, the old north country diet of oatmeal porridge. Later on, there were three household pets—the tawny, strong-limbed 'Keeper', Emily's favourite: he was so completely under her control, she could quite easily make him spring and roar like a lion ... without any coercion. 'Flossy'— long, silky-haired, black and white 'Flossy'—was Anne's favourite, and black 'Tom', the tabby, was everybody's favourite. . . . The Brontë's love of dumb creatures made them very sensitive of the treatment bestowed upon them. For any one to offend in this respect was, with them, an infallible bad sign, and a blot on the disposition. . . . The villagers would have liked Tabby to talk to them about the family in the parsonage; but Tabby was invincible and impenetrable. . . . What the Brontës cared for and *lived* in most were the surroundings of nature, the free expanse of hill and mountain, the purple heather, the dells, and glens, and brooks, the broad sky view, the whistling winds, the snowy expanse, the starry heavens, and the charm of that solitude and seclusion which sees things from a distance without the disturbing atmosphere which lesser minds are apt to create. For it was not the seclusion of a *solitary* person, such as Charlotte endured in after days . . . it was solitude and seclusion shared and enjoyed with intelligent companionship, and intense family affection."

In addition to the foregoing, Ellen has also given a delightful description of walks across the moors with the Brontës. Also from Ellen Nussey we have the picture of the dinner-table in the parsonage : at one end Miss Branwell, at the other Charlotte, with Emily and Anne on either side (Branwell was then absent and Patrick always dined alone in his room); on the table a joint and vegetables, followed by a milk pudding. She gives us Emily as, "Her extreme reserve seemed impenetrable, yet she was intensely lovable. She invited confidence in her moral power. Few people have the gift of looking and smiling, as she could look and smile—one of her rare expressive looks was something to remember through life, there was such a *depth* of soul and feeling, and yet shyness of revealing herself, a strength of self-containment seen in no other—She was in the strictest sense a law unto herself, and a heroine in keeping to her law. . . ." And the most moving scene Ellen has drawn is of the three girls putting away their writings late in the evening and walking round and round the dining table—Charlotte with Ellen, then Emily and Anne. Years later when Mrs Gaskell was staying at the parsonage she would hear the solitary survivor continuing the walk she and her sisters had rarely missed.

The tailor who made clothes for Branwell rarely had Patrick as a customer. His son recalled that "while Mr. Brontë got almost everything he required from Haworth tradesmen, he always had his coats made in Cambridge, at an establishment that he had patronised during his collegiate days. But after a garment had been worn twelve months it was sent to the Haworth tailor to be 'turned', and the material was of so good a quality that the coat then looked like a new one. The coat always bore, in the parson's own rough sewing, two pockets designed to accomodate the two pistols which he invariably carried with him."

An examination of the tax returns of Haworth in the years 1829 and 1831 gives a good indication of Patrick Brontë's position in the village. He was the only clergyman whose return was recorded by the collectors. (Haworth was then in the East Morley district, and the returns were made to the commissioners in Bradford.) In Haworth there were 104 persons who paid tax, only two of them paying more than Patrick. The total amount collected was £117 19s 3d, of which Patrick was taxed £4 19s 9d, including £1 3s 6d under Schedule I, Hair Powder Duty. He was the only person in Haworth so charged. "You are to assess every Person who shall have used or worn any Hair Powder. . . ."

Patrick's assessment for the year ending 5th April 1831 shows that he was taxed £2 13s 3d under Schedule A, because he lived in a house with thirteen windows. Under Schedule B, inhabited house duty was paid on houses of £10 annual value or more : here Patrick was assessed at the lowest scale of 1s 6d in the £, namely, 15s for £10 rent. There were no charges against him for "male servants, carriages, horse for riding, other horses and mules". As already mentioned, he paid tax on a house dog. John and James Greenwood of Bridgehouse, gentlemen, were assessed together, paying £19 3s 9d for a house with twenty windows—a rent of £15, a clerk, for whom they paid £2 4s, one wheeled carriage, two horses exceeding thirteen hands, three other horses and two house dogs. The other resident paying higher taxes than Patrick was Abraham Wilkinson, innkeeper: thirteen windows costing £2 13s 3d, rent £12, which cost him 18s in tax; one horse and one house dog, total £5 8s.

Certainly the parson stood financially high among his parishioners. James Ogden, schoolmaster, paid only 8s tax. The farmers appeared to be more prosperous than the manufacturers. It is interesting to note from these returns that Patrick claimed the right to pay his taxes in two instalments; and every reader will have the deepest compassion for "Stansfield, John, transported".

One of the most charming letters Patrick ever penned was written in 1835 to William Robinson, the artist he had engaged to teach Charlotte and Branwell. His love of children is clearly shown in this letter:

To William Robinson, Artist, of Leeds.

Haworth, near Bradford, Yorkshire. Sept: 7th 1835.

Dear Sir,

I am greatly obliged to you, for your very acceptable present, both on account of the good principles, and great talents of the man whom it represents, and the fidelity and skill of the execution. I thank you, also, for your great kindness, towards my son. Your picture which he has brought home, has so much in it of truth and life, and that something which cannot be expressed and which genius alone can give, that when it is not in use I frequently have it in my own room—for the pleasure of looking at it—for, though I have comparatively, but little skill in the fine arts—I greatly admire them—and in their excellence, they afford me peculiar pleasure. The child has a fine, expressive countenance—I trust that under providence, as she grows up, her mind will harmonize with her features. I wonder how you could get her to sit. If I were in Leeds, I would buy her a pretty little Book or something else that would amuse, and profit her.

But as I am not likely, soon to be there, I have taken the liberty of enclosing under a seal, in this letter—half a sovereign, which I beg you to present her with, in my name, and to lay out for her, as my proxy, in the manner, in which you may think, will correspond best with her infantile fancy; telling her, at the same time, that I am greatly obliged to her for the trouble she has had, on my account.

If all be well, Branwell hopes to be with you on Friday next, in order to finish his course of lessons.

I remain, dear Sir, Yours very respectfully and truly P. Brontê

As mentioned, Charlotte had become a pupil at Roe Head in January 1831. Whilst there, she received many kindnesses from Elizabeth Firth (now Mrs Franks) whose husband was vicar of nearby Huddersfield. Patrick soon wrote to his old friend expressing his gratitude.

Mrs Franks, Vicarage, Huddersfield. [Postal charge 6d.]

Haworth, near Bradford, Yorkshire, April 28th, 1831.
Dear Madam,

Having heard of your kind attention to Charlotte, I have taken the liberty of writing to thank both Mr. Franks and you for this, and to assure you that we have not forgotten, in our little family, your other various acts of kindness. Charlotte would be highly gratified. She still remembered having seen you at Kipping, and has often heard us speak of you, whilst we took a retrospective view of Good Old Times. I have just received a letter from our mutual friend, Miss Outhwaite, which has given me some uneasiness. It appears that some whose opinions I highly value greatly misunderstand my motives, in being an advocate for temperate reform, both in church and state. I am in all respects *now*, what I *was* when I lived in Thornton—in regard to all political considerations. A warmer or truer friend to church and state does not breathe the vital air. But, after many years' mature deliberation, I am fully convinced that, unless the *real* friends of our excellent institutions come forward and advocate the cause of temperate reform, the inveterate enemies will avail themselves of the opportunity which this circumstance would give them, and will work on the popular feeling—already but too much excited—so as to cause, in all probability, general insurrectionary movements, and bring about a revolution. We see what has been lately done in France. We know that the Duke of Wellington's declaration against reform was the principal cause of the removal of him and the other ministers from power. And there is now another instance before our eyes of the impolicy of this perverseness. The anti-reformers have imprudently thrown the ministers into a minority, and consequently Parliament is dissolved by the King in person, and in all probability another Parliament will soon be returned, which may be less

particular than the other, and perhaps go too far in the way of reformation.

Both, then, because I think moderate, or temperate reform, is
wanted—and that this would satisfy all wise and reasonable people, and
weaken the hands of our real enemies, and preserve the church and
state from ruin—I am an advocate for the Bill, which has been just
thrown out of Parliament [Lord Grey's Reform Bill]. It is with me
merely an affair of conscience and judgment, and sooner than violate the
dictates of either of these, I would run the hazard of poverty, imprisonment, and death. My friends—or some of them, at least—may differ
from me as to the *line of conduct* which ought to be followed, but our
motives and our *good wishes* towards church and state are the same.

But to come nearer home. I have for nearly a year past been in but
a very delicate state of health. I had an inflammation in my lungs last
summer, and was in immediate and great danger for several weeks. For
the six months last past I have been weak in body, and my spirits have
often been low. I was for about a month unable to take the church duty.
I now perform it, though with considerable difficulty. I am, certainly, a
little better; yet I fear I shall never fully recover. I sometimes think
that I shall fall into a decline. But I am in the Lord's hands, and hope
that he will at the last give me a happy issue out of all my troubles, and
take me for ever into His heavenly kingdom. We have been much
concerned to hear from time to time that you have not been quite so
strong as usual. It is our earnest wish and prayer that the Lord may
support and comfort you, and spare you long and in mercy to your
husband and your children. I have only once been at Kipping since I
last saw you and Mrs Firth there. The family were kind to me, but I
missed my old friends, and I could not feel comfortable, and I soon
departed, intending never to call again. Miss Branwell still continues
with me, and kindly superintends my little family, and they all join
with me in the kindest and most respectful regards. When you write to,
or see, Mrs Firth, be so kind as to remember us all to her in the most
respectful and affectionate manner. Be so good also to thank Mr Franks
in our name for his kind attention to Charlotte, and believe me to be,
dear Madam,

very respectfully and truly yours, P. Brontê

Elizabeth Franks had six children, of whom four survived: a
stillborn daughter, John, James (died a month old), Henry, Elizabeth
(born on the day of Patrick's letter) and, in January 1833, William
Walker.

In July 1835 it was decided that Charlotte should return to Roe

Head as a teacher, accompanied by Emily as a pupil, and Branwell was to go to London to the Royal Academy Schools. Again Patrick wrote to his old friend from Kipping House.

Mrs. Franks, Vicarage, Huddersfield.

Haworth, near Bradford, Yorkshire. July 6th 1835.

My Dear Madam,

As two of my dear children are soon to be placed near you, I take the liberty of writing to you a few lines in order to request both you and Mr Franks to be so kind as to interpose with your advice and counsel to them in any case of necessity, and, if expedient, to write to Miss Branwell or me if our interference should be requisite. I will charge them strictly to attend to what you may advise, though it is not my intention to speak to them of this letter. They both have good abilities, and as far as I can judge their principles are good also, but they are very young, and unacquainted with the ways of this delusive and insnaring [sic] world [Charlotte was nineteen, Emily seventeen]; and though they will be placed under the superintendence of Miss Wooler, who will I doubt not do what she can for their good, yet I am well aware that neither they nor any other can ever, in this land of probation, lie beyond the reach of temptation. [All very true, no doubt, but he also wanted an outside opinion on their food, etc. Cowan Bridge had not been forgotten.] It is my design to send my son, for whom, as you may remember, my kind and true friends, Mr Firth and Mrs Firth, were sponsors, to the Royal Academy for Artists in London; and my dear little Anne I intend to keep at home for another year under her aunt's tuition and my own. For these dispositions I feel I am indebted, under God, to you, and Miss Outhwaite, and Mrs Firth and other kind friends; and for every act of kindness I feel truly grateful. [Mrs Franks had first suggested Margaret Wooler's school to Patrick—a happier choice than her previous one.] It has given us all unfeigned pleasure to learn that your health is nearly restored, and that Mr Franks and your dear little children are all well. Several years ago I saw in Bradford a fine little child of yours, whom I took into my arms and would have nursed, but it took the alarm and would not stay with me; and so I was obliged to return it to Miss Outhwaite, in whom it placed greater confidence. My own health is generally but *very* delicate, yet through a gracious Providence, and with great care, I am for the most part able to perform my various ministerial duties; indeed I have never been very well since I left Thornton. My happiest days were spent there. In this place I have received civilities, and have, I trust, been civil to all, but

I have not tried to make any friends, nor have I met with any whose mind was congenial with my own. I have not been at Thornton or Kipping for many years. The last time I was there I travel'd over some of my ancient paths and thought of my dear wife and children whom death had removed, and when I was in the church and reflected that my beloved friend, with whom I was wont to take sweet counsel, was beneath my feet [Mr Firth], sadness came over my heart; and afterwards, as I walked round your garden, I called to mind *all* my dear friends who were removed from thence—by the vicissitudes of life—and I soon found the *whole* aspect of affairs to be *entirely* changed; and so I returned home, fully intending to visit Thornton and Kipping no more, unless I should be in a great measure forced by reason of circumstances. I have heard, however, that some alterations and perhaps a few improvements have been made there. But of those you must know more than I do, as probably you often revisit the place of your nativity and the scenes of your early youth.

Amidst all the chances, changes, and trials of this mortal life, we have still the glorious conviction on our minds that we may have our hope immovably anchored in heaven, by the throne of God, in whom there is no variableness, neither shadow of turning. And I trust this blessed consideration will be a never-failing source of comfort to you during the remainder of your journey through life, and especially at that last hour when you will step out of time into eternity. We are now, as members of the Church of England, placed under peculiar trials outwardly from the numerous and inveterate enemies of both the church and state, and we may have enemies within. Yet still, if we look to the Lord in humility, patience, and faith, and use the appropriate scriptural means, we shall at last come off more than conquerors over death and hell, and obtain houses, not made with hands, eternal in the heavens.

Be so good as to give my very kind and respectful regards to Mr Franks, and to my old and kind friends, Mrs Firth and Miss Outhwaite, when you see them; and also excuse the trouble which I have here given you, and believe me, my dear Madam,

Ever yours, very sincerely and truly, P. Brontè.

There is certainly something moving about the picture of Patrick strolling alone in the garden of Kipping House and, no doubt, down the Pinchbeck Valley. In the following year he wrote again to Mrs Franks, probably for the last time. Anne had replaced Emily at Roe Head. Here it is difficult not to censure Patrick for his action in delaying the return home of his two children. His happy days had been at Thornton: could he not know how deeply they found their happiness at Haworth?

20

Mrs Franks, Vicarage, Huddersfield, Yorkshire.

Haworth, near Bradford, Yorkshire. June 13th, 1836.

My Dear Madam,—My dear little Charlotte has informed me that you and Mr Franks have been so kind as to invite her and Anne to pay you a visit for a week, but that through impatience, as is very natural, they have curtail'd that invitation to a few days. I have written to them to countermand this intention. I esteem it as a high privilege that they should be under your roof for a time, where, I am sure, they will see and hear nothing but what, under Providence, must necessarily tend to their best interest in both the worlds. You I have long known, Mr Franks' character I am well acquainted with through the medium of authentic report; and hence I came to this conclusion. I have written to Charlotte and Anne to this effect, but as my letter may not reach them (owing to a bye-post) in due time, I will thank you to communicate to them this intelligence. I will send the horse and gig for them to your house, and if necessary, they may return from thence by Roe Head. In these sentiments, Miss Branwell perfectly agrees with me and at the same time joins with me and my family in the most respectful and kind compliments and regards to you and Mr Franks, and to Mr and Mrs Atkinson when you see them. [Charlotte also endured visits to her godmother at The Green House, but the lovely garden was a compensation.] For many years I have visited no friends in Bradford, but, having heard that our old friend, Miss Outhwaite, had broken her arm, I went over a few days ago to that town, when I saw those who awakened in me many lively recollections of *Auld Lang Syne*.

On some, perhaps on all, time had made a difference; but there was only *one* whom I did not at first recognise. They complimented me, in general, on *renewing* my age; but perhaps this was owing to their kind partiality.

Sincerely and ardently wishing and praying for your health and happiness, both here and hereafter,

I remain, my dear Madam,

Your old friend and obliged servant, P. Brontè.

"Your old friend"—Patrick, as he sat back after finishing the letter, remembered again with a sigh the days of Kipping, when Maria and all his children had been with him. Then, in the dark days, he had asked Elizabeth Firth to become his wife. Now she had children of her own, yet was still kind to his girls. He did not forget to pray for her health that night: since the severe attack of influenza the previous year, she had not been really strong.

Fifteen months after writing that letter, Patrick learned that she was dead. Elizabeth Franks died on Monday, 11th September 1837, whilst on a visit to her friend, Miss Fanny Outhwaite, in Bradford. She was forty years of age. Patrick Brontë had lost yet another companion of the days when he was young, happy, and when sorrow had yet to pay the first of many calls.

CHAPTER 17

Weightman

As THE year 1839 arrived, Patrick decided that he must have a new curate—Hodgson had been gone for well over a year now—and his sight was slowly getting worse: at times there was a mist over his eyes that completely obscured his vision. Happily these were still rare inflictions, but they served him as a warning for the years ahead. Patrick wrote to Morgan, Fennell, and several other friends requesting their assistance; then to the Apostolic Bishop of the diocese (Ripon); and finally to Mr Franks.

Rev. J. C. Franks, Vicarage, Huddersfield.

Haworth, near Bradford, Yorkshire, Jany. 10th 1839.

Revd and Dear Sir,

I have lately written to several Clergymen requesting that they would exert themselves to find for me a suitable Clerical Assistant. I have got a grant from the Pastoral Aid Society, in case I can procure a man congenial with their sentiments, and who would be active, as well as zealous. Their conditions, though not unreasonable, are somewhat strict—a good deal more so, I believe, than those generally imposed by the Clergy Aid Society. Will you be so good as to give me your advice and assistance on this occasion? The Bishop, to whom I have applied, has been very kind and attentive to my case, and offers, if no better may be, to ordain on my Nomination. I know not what your religious opinions may be on some particular points, but it is expedient that on this occasion I should candidly tell you some of mine, lest inconvenience might arise from a collision with my future Assistant in our preaching and exhortation. As far as I know myself, I think I may venture to say that I am no Bigot. Yet I could not feel comfortable with a coadjutor who would deem it his duty to preach the appalling doctrines of personal Election and Reprobation. As I should consider these decidedly derogatory to the Attributes of God, so also I should be fearful of evil consequences to the hearers from the enforcement of final perseverance as an essential article of belief. [Patrick had not forgotten Carus Wilson.] I am well aware that many Clergymen, far wiser and better than I am, do not accord with me here ; but as I freely leave them to the possession of their views, so I hope that they will kindly permit me to enjoy mine. I want for this region a plain rather than an able preacher ; a zealous, but at the same time a judicious man—one not fond of innovation, but desirous of proceeding *on the good old plan*—which alas ! has often been *mar'd*, but never *improved*. I earnestly wish that some of the clergy in our excellent Establishment were as solicitous for improvement as they are for change, and that they would give less way to the hazardous fitful air of popularity. The signs of the times in which we live are of ominous portent. Without our Citadel we have numerous vigilant, inveterate, and active enemies ; and within, many who are utterly unsafe either through shallow ignorance or evil design. Yet, blessed be God, there has lately been an increase of men of great learning, genuine piety, and vast resources of the most valuable kind, and who are as willing as they are able to stand forward at all hazards, in order to do their duty, as Ministers of the Gospel, and good members of society. God and His Holy Word, too, are on our side, and thus, after all, it may prove, ere long, that the gloomy season we have may only be the immediate forerunner of an early dawn and a bright and cheering day.

I have written a longer letter than I intended—but I felt I was addressing the late partner of one of the best and most esteem'd friends that my family and I have ever had, and whose memory is still held in lively remembrance by us, though she is herself removed to another, and a better, world.

All my little flock join with me in the kindest and most respectful regards to you and yours—

I remain, Revᵈ and dear Sir, yours very truly, Patrick Brontè.

The Rev. J. C. Franks, Vicar of Huddersfield.

This letter, which gives some details of Patrick's religious convictions, was almost the last communication between him and the Franks family. In 1840, the Rev. James Clarke Franks left Huddersfield for Cambridge and neither he nor his children saw the Brontës again.

The "grant from the Pastoral Aid Society" mentioned by Patrick was £80 per annum. The "conditions" of the Society, founded in 1836, were to promote true religion, and give support for Evangelicals consistent with "distinctly Protestant and Evangelical doctrine and principles".

It was the Bishop who eventually found Patrick the curate he was looking for : the Rev. William Weightman, M.A. It would be August of that year (1839) before he arrived at Haworth, yet he would bring the delights of spring into the village, the parsonage, and yes—into the very hearts of the three girls. Patrick could work well with him, Aunt Branwell could tolerate him, Branwell found the companion he so badly needed, Charlotte was fonder of him than she has admitted, Emily was amused by him and, when he was dead, Anne realized she had loved him. For only three years would he live in Haworth, and then become another echo for one member of the parsonage to listen for on windy nights.

Willy Weightman was a native of Appleby in Westmorland and after his schooling went to Durham University, where he graduated as a Bachelor and Master of Arts. He had been at the University when Patrick first enquired for an assistant, and came straight down from his ordination to Haworth at the age of twenty-five. He was a fine young classical scholar and very handsome—Charlotte mentions the "blue eyes, auburn hair, and rosy cheeks". The Brontë girls soon dubbed him "Celia Amelia". But this "bonny-faced" youth was neither foolish nor effeminate. He was a cleric of the highest attainments and sincerity, and he flirted with all the young ladies in a more than robust manner. Patrick was most pleased to obtain assistance at last. Save for some help from his old curate William Hodgson, who had come over from Colne to help him in January 1839, he had received no aid in his pastoral duties; and from the very commencement of his appointment Patrick was satisfied with Weightman's religious tenets, his capabilities and his youthful enthusiasm. On the four young people at the parsonage the new curate acted as a summer rainstorm upon parched earth. Their shyness was soon washed away in a flood of laughter, pranks and good-humoured fun. He was the most amusing person they had met, the gayest they would ever know.

Willy Weightman commenced his work at Haworth in the middle of August 1839, his first signatures in the registers being on the 19th of that month, when he officiated as "Assistant Curate" at a baptism and a funeral. For the next three years he was invaluable to Patrick by his hard work in the parish, his cheerfulness and his warm-hearted friendship. Three times he left Haworth: in July 1840 to pass his final examinations at Ripon, followed by a protracted stay in his home district; in January 1841 to be ordained as priest, and spend two weeks at home; and in the spring of that year when he again took a holiday in Westmorland.

Many are the references to "Celia Amelia" in Charlotte's letters, many the happy scenes drawn of this lively young man, but they must be briefly touched on, for if Aunt became quite young and giddy sometimes with his banter, she knew but half of what was going on under her nose, and Patrick knew even less.

He flirted with all and sundry; with Charlotte and Anne; with Ellen Nussey when she visited the parsonage; and he teased even that formidable and serious-minded young woman, Mary Taylor, when she came, their games of chess ending "in a species of mock hostility". He made his most unremitting advances to a girl from home, Agnes Walton, but found time to break the heart of a lass in Swansea, and heaven knows how many local belles. Charlotte writes, "Keighley has yielded him a fruitful field of conquest. Sarah Sugden is quite smitten, so is Caroline Dury." Alas, the latter romance was soon nipped in the bud, for early in 1840, Caroline's father, the Rev. Theodore Dury, Rector of Keighley, was appointed to Westmill in Hertfordshire; but Weightman kept hope alive by sending many letters and some "most passionate copy of verses". Caroline (aged twenty) and Agnes appear to have been the leading contenders for his fickle heart, for there is no further mention of Sarah Sugden (a magistrate's daughter), and the Welsh girl had all her letters returned in a bundle.

Charlotte related all these events in detail, claiming a detached heart, but she "protests" too much for that to have been the case. Anne said nothing, but had some painful thoughts. Like her father, she preferred to judge him as a very true and Christian minister working hard for the common good of the parish. Emily is reported as having danced with joy when they were all walking together on the moors— Weightman and the Brontës. But did not Emily always dance for joy when alone on her beloved heath? It needed not the presence of the dashing curate for those heather hills to impart spring to her heels. She too liked him much, saw the worth in him, yet she alone could regard him with a dispassionate eye. Once, when Weightman offered to escort Ellen Nussey on an evening stroll, Emily insisted on being the chaperone, for she knew her man too well. Thus she earned the soubriquet, "The Major". Branwell much admired the curate and desired his friendship above all things. It is not certain whether Weightman kept him from the Black Bull or if Branwell managed to entice him in. When Weightman was away they corresponded regularly.

Charlotte sketched a portrait of him, robed in his gown, and painted for him a picture of Agnes Walton. He returned the compliment by drawing a horse's head with great pomp, "the eye is a little too elevated", said Charlotte, and a representation of the flying figure of Fame inscribing his own name across the clouds. When Weightman learned in 1840 that no such thing as a valentine had ever entered Haworth Parsonage, he promptly sent the three girls one each, and repeated these tributes in 1841. He wrote the verses himself and walked ten miles to Bradford to post them, to disguise the source from Patrick.

Ellen Nussey told the story of Weightman wishing to have the Brontë girls hear his lecture on the Classics in the Mechanics' Institute, Keighley. He gained Patrick's permission, after obtaining the consent of a local married clergyman to invite them to tea and then escort them to the hall. He gave a splendid address, which was long remembered in Keighley, and then came the four-mile walk home. "The Parsonage was not reached till 12 p.m. The two clergymen rushed in with their charges, deeply disturbing Miss Branwell, who had prepared hot coffee for the home party, which of course fell short when two more were to be supplied. Poor Miss Branwell lost her temper, Charlotte was troubled, and Mr Weightman, who enjoyed teasing the old lady, was very thirsty. The great spirits of the walking party had a trying suppression, but twinkling fun sustained some of the party."

Nor was this young philanderer without a generous side to his nature: indeed it was ever uppermost. In August 1840, whilst still away in Westmorland, he sent Ellen Nussey a present of ducks; and in September, just prior to his return, there arrived at the parsonage "a brace of wild ducks, a brace of black grouse, a brace of partridges, ditto of snipes [sic], ditto of curlews, and a large salmon". Was not this gay, irrepressible whirlwind something for the Brontë sisters to look forward to, when they came home on holiday from their duties as governess!

But Patrick saw the other side of Willy Weightman's character, and liked what he saw. He knew little or nothing of the young curate's lightness of love with the fair sex, only his unswerving attachment to God and the Established Church. Patrick grew to understand much of Weightman's mind and heart, not only when engaged on parish duties, but on those long sporting tramps over the moors when, in late August, there were plenty of grouse to shoot. The young man was a keen shot but more than found his match in the marksmanship of his senior. Patrick, for all that his eyes were weak, had drilled well at Cambridge, and rarely missed his bird. Yet there was a difficulty. Such forays had to be made when Emily was out of reach, or there would be a blazing scene that, Patrick knew well, would equal, if not surpass, any violent rage that had ever encompassed him; for she was, more than any of them, the child of her father. Her views were only too well known; use fixed targets for such sport, or, if you must have living prey, shoot at each other, but leave harmless dumb creatures alone!

In his parish duties Patrick could not fault Weightman, but the latter's sermons caused the older man some anxiety. The trouble was that the curate was *too* much of a classical scholar, and would preach above the heads of his simple-minded congregation. Again and again

Patrick told him to "speak plain", but never quite succeeded in altering his style of address.

Patrick's affection for his curate grew very warm. When he made his application for the £80 grant from the Church Pastoral Aid Society for the second year, he requested "that in consideration of the valuable services of his Curate, the grant may be augmented on renewal to £100". It was immediately recommended. "P. Brontë £100 for Curate to Revᵈ P. Brontë of Haworth in Bradford."

In the beginning of August 1840, whilst Willy Weightman was still away, Patrick received a visit from his wife's and Miss Branwell's cousin, John Branwell Williams, with his wife, and daughter Eliza. They had previously been staying with "Uncle Fennell". (Mr Williams was the son of Maria Brontë's Aunt Alice.) It was hard going at the parsonage. Eliza, a good-looking, bouncing girl, talked only of the Low-Church evangelical clergy, the Millennium, Baptist Wriothesley Noel (one of the most popular preachers of his day who left the Church of England for the Baptists in 1848), botany and her own conversion. It was all well enough for Aunt Branwell, but Patrick wished that his ardent young "High-Church" curate had been there to lash them with his tongue. As host it would not do, so Patrick bit his lips and said nothing. After all, they were dear Maria's relatives; nevertheless, their high and mighty ways were irritating.

He recalled how Weightman's cheerfulness had helped the young people through a three-day visit by his old friend William Morgan earlier, in March. Really he had never known Morgan quite so talkative. Of this visit Charlotte wrote, "Mr Morgan came, stayed three days and went—by Miss Weightman's aid we got on pretty well—it was amazing to see with what patience and good temper the innocent creature endured that fat Welshman's prosing—though she confessed afterwards that she was almost done up by his long stories." (Charlotte often wrote of the curate in the feminine gender.) Poor Weightman found Morgan quite a trial but remained most good-natured; and Patrick was glad, for he was very fond of his oldest remaining friend.

There are four other pictures of Willy Weightman that Charlotte has given us: his lashing of the Dissenters from Grimshaw's pulpit, his other lecture at Keighley, when he persuaded Patrick to give an address, his kindness to a village girl who was dying and, most moving of all to the Brontë lover, his glances at Anne during service in Haworth Church. In April 1840 there was a meeting in the Sunday school at Haworth, about the thorny question of Church rates. Patrick took the chair, supported by Weightman and a local clergyman, Mr Collins. The latter was later assistant curate to the Rev. James Chesterton

Bradley, incumbent of Oakworth, a high village between Haworth and Keighley.

'Little Haworth has been all in a bustle about Church rates since you 'were here—we had a most stormy meeting in the school-room. Papa took the chair, and Mr Collins and Mr Weightman acted as his supporters, one on each side. There was violent opposition, which set Mr Collins's Irish blood in a ferment, and if papa had not kept him quiet, partly by persuasion and partly by compulsion, he would have given the Dissenters their 'Kale through the reek'. . . . He and Mr Weightman both bottled up their wrath for that time, but it was only to explode with redoubled force at a future period. We had two sermons on dissent, and its consequences, preached last Sunday—one in the afternoon by Mr Weightman, and one in the evening by Mr Collins. All the Dissenters were invited to come and hear, and they actually shut up their chapels and came in a body; of course, the church was crowded. Miss Celia Amelia delivered a noble, eloquent, High-Church, Apostolical-Succession discourse, in which he banged the Dissenters most fearlessly and unflinchingly. I thought they had got enough for one while, but it was nothing to the dose that was thrust down their throats in the evening. A keener, cleverer, bolder, and more heart-stirring harangue than that which Mr Collins delivered from Haworth pulpit, last Sunday evening, I never heard. He did not rant; he did not cant; he did not whine; he did not sniggle; he just got up and spoke with the boldness of a man who was impressed with the truth of what he was saying, who has no fears of his enemies and no dread of consequences. His sermon lasted an hour, yet I was sorry when it was done. I do not say that I agree either with him or Mr. Weightman, either in all or half their opinions. I consider them bigoted, intolerant, and wholly unjustifiable on the ground of common-sense. My conscience will not let me be either a Puseyite or a Hookist [followers of doctrines preached by Walter Farquhar Hook, then Vicar of Leeds, and afterwards Dean of Chichester]; 'mais', if I were a Dissenter, I would have taken the first opportunity of kicking or of horsewhipping both the gentlemen for their stern, bitter attack on my religion and its teachers. But in spite of all this, I admired the noble integrity which could dictate so fearless an opposition against so strong an antagonist."

In November 1840, Mrs Collins came to Patrick with a tale of her husband's "drunken, extravagant, profligate habits". There was nothing but ruin facing them. There were many debts that could not possibly be met. Her husband's dismissal from his curacy was expected immediately, his vices were incurable. He treated her and the child in a most savage manner: what should she do? Patrick's answer is a further proof that, however much his language was tied to the times in which he lived, his ideas were often greatly in advance of them. "Papa advised her to leave him for ever, and go home, if she had a home to go to." Few early Victorian clerics would have given such an enlightened answer. Years later, on the evening of 3rd April 1847, Mrs Collins was shown into Charlotte's room by Martha Brown. She had not had the courage to take Patrick's advice, and it had been her husband who had deserted: "after running an infamous career of vice, both in England and France, abandoning his wife to disease and total destitution in Manchester, with two children and without a farthing, in a strange lodging-house." Mrs Collins had, happily, recovered from her illness and, after a great struggle, procured a living for herself and the children, by keeping a lodging-house.

About the time of Weightman's attack on the Dissenters in Haworth Church, he gave another lecture at the Keighley Mechanics' Institute and persuaded Patrick to give an address. Charlotte writes, "Both are spoken of very highly in the newspaper, and it is mentioned as a matter of wonder that such displays of intellect should emanate from the village of Haworth, situated amongst the bogs and mountains, and, until very lately, supposed to be in a state of semi-barbarism. Such are the words of the newspaper." Such remains the opinion of many ill-informed people today!

One Saturday night, late in September 1840, shortly after his return from Westmorland, Willy Weightman spent an hour with Patrick in the parsonage parlour. But he was in dull sorts and, as he rose to leave, Patrick asked him, "What is the matter with you? You seem in very low spirits to-night." "Oh, don't I know," answered the curate, "I've been to see a poor young girl, who, I'm afraid, is dying," "Indeed, what is her name?" "Susan Bland, the daughter of John Bland, the Superintendent." But Weightman had the door open by now, and in the dining-room across the passage, Charlotte had heard all. Susan was her oldest and best scholar in the Sunday school and the news sent a chill to her heart. She must visit the girl as soon as possible. "I did go on Monday afternoon, and found her very ill and weak . . . After sitting with her some time, I happened to ask her mother if she thought a little port wine would do her good. She replied that the doctor had recommended it, and that when Mr Weightman was last there he had sent them a bottle of wine and a jar of preserves. She added that he was always good to poor folks, and seemed to have a deal of feeling and kind-heartedness about him." Little Susan Bland recovered!

But the glimpse of Willy Weightman that is most indelible is the one given by Charlotte in January 1842, just prior to her departure for

Brussels with Emily. "He sits opposite to Anne at Church, sighing softly and looking out of the corners of his eyes to win her attention—and Anne is so quiet, her look so downcast—they are a picture." There is sweet sadness in that scene of the "delicate and pale" young curate Charlotte would never see again, and of the youngest sister whose love for him was hidden in her heart.

All was bustle and rush at Haworth Parsonage, as Charlotte and Emily prepared to leave for Belgium; Papa was to escort them to Brussels. Aunt Branwell, recently returned from a visit to the dying John Fennell, was financing the project of sending the two girls to complete their education so that they could, with Anne, open a school of their own. On 29th September 1841, from Upperwood House, Rawdon, where she was completing her duties as governess to John White's children, Charlotte wrote to Miss Branwell regarding the £100 which the latter had offered as a "loan". ". . . You always like to use your money to the best advantage ; you are not fond of making shabby purchases ; when you do confer a favour, it is often done in style ; and depend upon it £50, or £100, thus laid out, would be well employed. . . . I feel an absolute conviction that if this advantage were allowed us, it would be the making of us for life. Papa will perhaps think it a wild and ambitious scheme ; but who ever rose in the world without ambition ? When he left Ireland to go to Cambridge University, he was as ambitious as I am now. I want us *all* to go on. I know we have talents, and I want them to be turned to account. I look to you, Aunt, to help us. . . ."

There were several changes of plan. Charlotte clung for a while to her dreams of the Château de Koekelberg ; then, the French schools in Brussels being reported as unsatisfactory, an institution in Lille was recommended by Baptist Noel and others, and the girls were to be escorted there by a French lady, Madame Marzials. At this point, Elizabeth Branwell consented to pay an extra sum so that her two nieces might enjoy a separate room, for which act she can be forgiven much.

Shortly after this decision had been taken, the Rev. Evan Jenkins, M.A., Chaplain to H.M. King Leopold and minister to the English congregation of the Chapel Royal (brother to Patrick's immediate predecessor as curate of Dewsbury), wrote to Patrick recommending most strongly the Pensionnat Heger in the rue d'Isabelle. Plans were changed accordingly and all was at last ready. Anne had returned after Christmas to her employers, the Rev. Edmund Robinson and his wife, Lydia, as governess to their children at Thorp Green, near York ; and Branwell had gone back to his post as a clerk to the railways, from which position he was soon to be dismissed.

On Tuesday, 8th February 1842, Patrick escorted an eager Charlotte and a desperately reluctant Emily down the garden path to the waiting gig. At the gate the girls turned and waved farewell to Aunt Branwell who had made it all possible. Perhaps as Charlotte looked back at the little lady in her absurd bonnet as she stood on the top step waving her handkerchief, she forgave her all her failings, and forgot all her previous dislike of this queer Cornish aunt who had been present at her birth and had watched over her since childhood. Emily could hardly thank Aunt for being the means of sending her away from that home that was life to her; but perhaps Charlotte, as she waved farewell, had warm gratitude in her heart. Let it be hoped so, for neither of the girls would ever see Aunt Branwell again.

So it was that, with mixed feelings in his heart, Patrick took his two daughters down to London, to the very Chapter Coffee House by St Paul's where he had stayed after coming down from Cambridge. William Weightman was left in charge of Haworth Church. The idea of furthering their education on the Continent had been entirely Charlotte's, but Patrick had helped to arrange matters and now that the time had come there was a gnawing terror in his mind: Cowan Bridge still seemed only yesterday. Then there was the additional worry because his girls would be living amongst Roman Catholics, even instructed by them. Yet Charlotte was now nearly twenty-six years old and Emily approaching twenty-four: he was confident they could fend for themselves and avoid the cunning papist snares. The Brontës had been joined by Mary Taylor and her brother Joe. The former, who had spent a holiday in Brussels the previous summer, was to join her younger sister Martha as a pupil at the Château de Koekelberg, the latter was travelling on business.

The party remained at the Chapter Coffee House for four nights, but in the days between much sightseeing was accomplished. Patrick, although now sixty-five years of age, had not been to London since his Wethersfield days, but was anxious to show his girls those places of interest he remembered. Charlotte made a great effort to see as many pictures and statues as time and her father's preferences would allow. Mary Taylor reported that "Emily was like her in these habits of mind, but certainly never took her opinion, but always had one to offer." It is fitting that the Brontës would always stay at this Coffee House, that famous rendezvous of writers, not the less so because women did not frequent it and all the servants save one were men. Dr Johnson, Oliver Goldsmith and many other illustrious men dined and talked in that famous house, yet surely its greatest honour was to give hospitality to Charlotte, Emily and, later, Anne Brontë.

On Saturday, the 12th, they made the fourteen-hour voyage from London to Ostend. They left Ostend on Monday morning and the diligence rolled on its way to Brussels. It was seven o'clock in the evening when they reached the Porte de Flandres, where Charlotte caught her first glimpse of the lights of Brussels, "through streaming and starless darkness".

As Mr Jenkins lived outside the gates of Brussels, beyond the Porte de Namur, in the Chaussée d'Ixelles, the party made for the Hôtel d'Hollande, 61 rue de la Putterie, a street close to the rue d'Isabelle. The next morning Patrick's arrival was recorded by the police under the date 14th February 1842.

"No. 457. Patrick Bronté—63 [sic]—'Gerant d'Affaires' [as with Joe Taylor they entered : business man]—born : England—usual place of residence : England—place of issue of Passport : Ostende 13th February 1842 [endorsed only ; Patrick obtained his in London] date of arrival : 15th February—name of Hotel : Hollande."

This hotel was advertised in the *Indicateur Belge* for 1840 as "the Hotel which is distinguished by the number of persons in high-society who frequent it".

After breakfast Jenkins arrived at the hotel. Having taken leave of the Taylors, Patrick, Jenkins, Charlotte and Emily proceeded to the pensionnat in the rue d'Isabelle. Madame Heger had a few words with them, and Patrick must have been lighter in heart : Madame Heger seemed a capable, motherly woman. After staying a night or two with Mr and Mrs Jenkins, Patrick was able to call for his daughters and walk with them in the Brussels streets and parks. Then came the farewell : it was difficult to make conversation at such a time, in such strange surroundings. Charlotte managed somehow to maintain her eager, inquisitive look, Emily to retain her expression of defiant determination to endure and not fail as she had done at Roe Head. Patrick put an arm round each daughter, hoping they would not notice the tears in his tired old eyes. Then he took them back to Madame Heger and entrusted them to her and God's keeping. He turned quickly and strode rapidly away down the rue d'Isabelle—at no time had he met Monsieur Heger.

It was long assumed that Patrick returned straight home, but a little home-made notebook which he kept, shows plainly that he used this unique opportunity to treat himself to a little holiday. Bound in black leather there are thirty-six pages stitched together. On the first page : "The following conversational terms, suited to a traveller in France, or any part of the Continent of Europe—are taken from Turenne's New French Manual for 1840—and with those in my pocket book will be sufficient for me—and must be fully mastered—and ready—semper—

All these must be kept—semper. There are first the French—2—the right pronunciation—and lastly the English. Revᵈ P.B. A.B. Haworth, near Bradford, Yorkshire."

There follow pages of simple French expressions, ranging from "Où est la chambre" to "S'il vous plait montrez moi le privy". The various phrases are divided under headings embracing all the everyday needs: "Of the mind—of food—Spices & etc—Dessert and Drink—Numerals—Days and Months—French coin," and so on, the first of these being subdivided into "Virtues of the Mind" and "Vices of the Mind."

He adds, "English sovereigns pass everywhere and so in general do English Bank Notes—but not the copper or silver."

Then on page 21 he writes: "I went to Brussels, Lille, Dunkirk and Calais in Feby 1842—and found the expenses of travelling, under all circumstances, generally to be neither below, nor above one fifth less there than in England. 1842. B."

He continues: "I was only between 2 and 3 weeks away—and the whole expenses of my journey amounted to about £23-10-0, not more—My passport, procured at the Belgian Consul's Office, in London, cost 5s though at the French Consuls, it would have amounted to ten—At the ports, on landing, as numbers of porters bellow out, in recommending their respective houses, it is best, directly, to name your Inn—when they will cease and the porter will take you to it without delay. A traveller may and must, always have a good bedroom to himself alone. I have thus made extracts once over all Turenne's excellent French Manual. May—1842—B."

Yet Patrick failed to record in this notebook a pilgrimage near to his heart. However, he mentioned it in the first sermon after his return to Haworth. A member of the congregation long recollected Patrick "describing in vivid and vigorous language the field of Waterloo, which he had visited from Brussels".

Now that he was alone in the parsonage, Patrick had time to swallow a disappointment received by letter only five days before leaving home for Belgium. It arose from a letter he had sent to General Sir George Murray in November 1841, after much experimenting with his pistols and other firearms on the moors.

For the Honourable General, Sir George Murray,
Master General of the Ordnance, London.

Novʳ 19th 1841

Honourable Sir,
　　Having lately read Mr. Greener's able and just remarks on the bad qualities and construction of the musket at present in use, I take

the liberty of making a few observations of my own, in the hope that if they are judicious, they may reach and influence those in high quarters. In doing this, I shall be as brief as possible, speaking at the same time, as intelligibly as I can. I should propose, that the new muskets be constructed as follows. That they should be at least three inches longer, than those hitherto used, and that they should be little more than two thirds, as wide in the bore. But what I wish to bring more prominently forward is, the position of the lock, and in some respects its formation. The lock, I conceive, should be placed on the top, as is the case, generally, with pocket pistols, and of course the pipe, or tube on which the percussion cap is to be fixed, on the upper part of the barrel. There should be an aperture, or hole through the cock which when it was raised to the full, ready for firing, should form the sight at the breech, and tend in a proper direction to the sight at the muzzle. This aperture should be wide above, and drawn to a point at the bottom, being only just large enough for the soldier to take a ready aim. The Line of Aim should pass directly over the percussion cap, to the sight at the muzzle—which sight should have a sufficiently conspicuous knob, raised high enough, to correspond with the elevation of the aperture at the breech, so as to give the proper direction to the bore, at the time of the discharge.

As this plan may be entirely new, it is but right, that I should give my reasons for it, so as to enable the reader to form his judgment with a fair chance of coming to a just conclusion. With the tube on which the percussion cap is placed, at the upper part of the barrel, in case of destruction the touchhole can be readily and effectually pricked—which appears to me to be a matter of vast moment—this facility of pricking can never be so great, when, as in the side lock the line of communication, is either angular or curved. Moreover in a lock of my construction, an obstruction, could scarcely ever take place, as must be obvious to every one who duly considers the subject. The sight through the cock is the necessary consequence of having the apparatus on the upper part of the barrel—But, independently of this, the sight thus placed has, I feel confident, its peculiar advantages. It comes at once, to the soldier's eye, and the cock, sights, and object are all rectilinear, a circumstance of itself calculated to produce, both a scientific and mechanical habit of straight shooting. There are here no lateral objects on the piece to distract the attention, or confuse the vision. All, which, at point-blank distance, is necessary to be done, is to see the *under part* of the *aperture* in the Cock, the *Knob* of the Sight at the muzzle, and the *object* in a right line, and this any man, with ordinary powers of vision, and a steady hand might learn to do, in ten minutes, if he had

never before, applied a gun to his shoulder. An achievement, frequently
not to be accomplished, according to the present construction of
muskets, in as many years. Another argument, might be adduced
in favour of my proposed construction. It would altogether give the
musket a more agreeable, and lighter appearance : the Instrument would
seem of itself, to indicate its projectile avocation, and to invite the
spectator to a trial of its merit and powers.

Should the bayonet, be also made three inches longer than at
present, it would be a great improvement. I am fully convinced, that all
this might be effected, leaving sufficient strength,—at two pounds less
of weight than we now have, admitting due regard was paid, in the
construction, to due proportion, as well as the qualities of all the
materials. Judging from various experiments which I have seen, I
should not hesitate to say, that a scientific gunmaker could turn out a
musket of my construction, that would be sufficiently effective, if
properly elevated, at the distance of eight or ten hundred yards, and
very sure, at two or three hundred, rendering in many instances
artillery less necessary—and in most cases the bayonet altogether useless.
The plan, if duly carried into effect, would tend powerfully to save our
brave men, and give full scope to their unequalled courage and energy—
It would also do away with the most torturous and mangling modes of
death in the field of battle, and thus be a kind of mercy in disguise.
On these grounds, chiefly, I have been induced to entertain this somewhat appaling [sic] subject.

I remain Sir, Your most obedient servant, P. Bronte, A.B.—
Perpetual Curate of Haworth, near Bradford, Yorkshire.

This letter was endorsed: "24 Nov' 1841. Referred by the Master
General's desire to the Select Committee". Patrick received a polite
acknowledgment and elaborated his ideas in a further letter :

To the Honourable General, Sir George Murray,
Master General of the Ordnance, London

Haworth, Near Bradford, Yorkshire Novr 29th 1841.
Honourable Sir,
I have just received a kind and attentive answer to my letter to you,
on the subject of muskets. For this answer I would beg leave to thank
you, and G.S. Belson Major Rl.Artillery, and Secy.
I have no recompense in view, my motives are merely love of
Queen and Country, and the greatest admiration of the Gentlemen of
the Army and Navy. I wish them to be provided with Instruments of
War, equal in excellence to their courage, and then, I am sure, they

will not meet with their match in the world. I am not a Military man, and never was, but I have had much experience in fire arms, and have long been an enthusiastic admirer of them, when rightly constructed— I have also made many scientific experiments with them, in all their possible positions, and I might nearly say, in all their possible forms,— though on a small scale. You, and the Gentlemen who constitute the Select Committee, are too wise, and considerate, therefore, not duly to examine my plan.

Archimedes, an Old Mathematician, and no Soldier, was the grand Instrument, through his instructions of protecting Syracuse for several years against all the Military skill and power of Rome—But, I wish to be as brief as possible, and consequently, I shall proceed directly, to explain my plan—which I beg you will lay before the Honourable, Committee, as owing to the sacredness of my Office, and other considerations, I cannot, with propriety attend, since, though humanity, and justice are at the bottom of my proceedings, I cannot openly appear as an advocate in the Arts and Science of War—I am no draughtsman, and must not call in the aid of another—And so I must try in a rude way, to give you something like a representation of my musket, and then, the proper explanation and my reasons— [There follows a passable sketch of his musket, followed by many more verbal details]. . . .

With every apology for thus troubling you, I remain, Honourable Sir,

Your most obedient servant, Patrick Bronte, A.B.
Incumbent of Haworth, near Bradford, Yorkshire.

This was endorsed : "Referred to the Select Committee—2 Decr 1841".

The Committee's answer was sent to Sir George who informed Patrick of their decision.

Woolwich, 2nd February 1842.
Sir,

I have the honour to report that agreeably to your Order, the Select Committee have been assembled for the purpose of considering and assessing upon some Papers relative to alterations in the Muskuet [sic] at present in use in the Service as proposed by the Revd P. Bronte. Mr. Bronte declined attending, but his Letters having been read, and the Sketches therein of his proposed Muskuet examined by the Committee, it did not appear desirable to them, that his alteration should be adopted into the Service. . . .

Patrick's naïvety had surely deserved some explanation for the refusal; but he was rarely granted much personal pleasure and it seems a pity that the rejection of his ideas came only a few days before he fulfilled his wish to stand on the field of Waterloo.

The early summer of 1842 was a quiet time for Patrick, yet not without grief: Branwell had been dismissed the railway—accused of negligence—and was now at home. At first he seemed quite broken in spirits and drank heavily, but by the end of June he made an attempt at recovery and busily engaged himself in obtaining orders for John Brown in the latter's capacity as monumental mason. Yet he could write to his friend, the railway pioneer, Francis H. Grundy, ". . . I can now speak cheerfully and enjoy the company of another without the stimulus of six glasses of whisky . . . I feel my recovery from *almost insanity* to be retarded by having nothing to listen to except the wind moaning among old chimneys and older ash trees. . . ." And again, "As for the Church—I have not one mental qualification, save, perhaps, hypocrisy, which would make me cut a figure in its pulpits." As if Patrick had not made more than one effort to launch his son out into the world! Yet always the Brontës were drawn back to Haworth. Even Branwell found it easier to hide there amongst the hills he pretended to loathe. There is a rare germ of talent that can blossom into genius or, by the single negligence or slip of a lifetime, can germinate instead into insanity, the division between genius and insanity being a thin border-line of control. Branwell lacked all such restraint.

But the comparative lull of early summer did not last; it was but the peaceful prelude to another sudden storm of suffering. On 14th August 1842, Willy Weightman baptized a child in Haworth Church, signing the registers as "Curate". A few days later he was struck down with cholera. Patrick visited his assistant twice each day, to comfort and pray with him, for he had seen at once that Weightman was dying. Patrick, as he walked from the curate's lodging in West Lane one evening in early September, feared that Weightman's impending death might presage another. Weightman had been like a son to him; his passing would strike very near home; would there be another double bereavement to endure? As he walked up the garden path of the parsonage, Martha Brown ran down the steps to inform him that Miss Branwell was unwell.

Branwell was almost distraught. He spent hours by Weightman's bedside and then rushed home to comfort his aunt. Although he always remembered that it was she who had held him up to see little Maria, only the picture of his dead sister remained to him as a source of pain, and he, alone of all the children, loved Miss Branwell.

William Weightman died on Tuesday, 6th September 1842. He was twenty-eight. The news was sent to Charlotte and Emily in Brussels, plunging them into gloom. Then Anne was sent a letter informing her of his death: a letter she could take with her, when permitted, along the lanes to grieve over in the small, empty Holy Trinity Church at Little Ouseburn.

The funeral was on the Saturday, 10th September, Patrick taking the service. Aunt Branwell, though somewhat better, was not able to attend and, in the Brontë pew, Branwell sat alone. As they laid his young friend to rest under the flags of the north aisle, his loud sobs echoed throughout the church.

The Revᵈ William Weightman M.A.	Haworth	10th Septʳ	26 years [28]	P. Brontè

On Sunday, 2nd October, Patrick preached a funeral sermon for his late curate: it was afterwards printed by J. U. Walker of Halifax, and priced 6d, "the profits, if any, to go in aid of the Sunday School". The text was the fifteenth chapter of the first epistle of Paul to the Corinthians, and the fifty-sixth, fifty-seventh, and fifty-eighth verses, commencing, "The sting of death is sin, and the strength of sin is the law. But thanks be to God, which giveth us the victory, through our Lord Jesus Christ." Before expounding this truth, Patrick started by telling the congregation that "for more than twenty years, during which time I have ministered amongst you, this will be the first sermon I shall have read to this congregation, and it may be the last. This is owing to a conviction on my mind that in general, for the ordinary run of hearers, extempore preaching, though accompanied with some peculiar disadvantages, is more likely to be of a colloquial nature, and better adapted, on the whole, to the majority." He then explained that, on that solemn occasion, it had been requested that his sermon be published. He had therefore written it out in advance so that "there should be no discrepancy between the pulpit and the press". After stressing that a funeral sermon should not tend to flatter but have a due regard to the truth, Patrick expatiated on the importance of truth as a guiding principle. We must all, in the end, "seek out the strait gate and narrow way, which is Christ, the truth and life. . . . This may puzzle or perplex, and disgust the fallen proud man; the infidel may sneer, the scorner may laugh, the philosopher may despise, the lukewarm may disregard, and the sophist cavil; and Satan, and the evil deceitful heart may join the unholy alliance; yet the cause of God must stand." He continued, ". . . our

frail bodies must soon perish . . . but by the Power of Him who has
said, 'Let it be', and the universe was created, they shall be raised in
their own proper identity, in a manner far surpassing the comprehension of man, and probably of the highest Archangels, when this mortal
shall put on immortality, and shine with unfading splendour for ever
and ever. These were the scriptural doctrines preached, practised, and
maintained by him whose loss we deplore."

Here follow some of Patrick's remarks about Willy Weightman.
"In his preaching, and practising, he was, as every clergyman ought to
be, neither distant nor austere, timid nor obtrusive, nor bigoted,
exclusive, nor dogmatical. He was affable, but not familiar; open, but
not too confiding. He thought it better, and more scriptural, to make
the love of God, rather than the fear of hell, the ruling motive for
obedience. He did not see why true believers, having the promise of the
life that now is, as well as that which is to come, should create unto
themselves artificial sorrows, and disfigure the garment of gospel peace
with the garb of sighing and sadness. . . . The Rev. William Weightman
was a native of Westmorland, and born of respectable parents, who
spared no expense within the range of their power in the education of
their children; wisely judging this to be the best, the most intrinsic, and
abiding fortune they could give them. From school he went to the
University of Durham. . . ." He then mentioned how the apostolical
Bishop had made an admirable choice of Curate for Haworth—"which
more than answered my expectations, and probably yours. The Church
Pastoral Aid Society, in their pious liberality, lent their pecuniary aid,
without which all efforts must have failed. [Sweet breath of honesty!]
. . . His character wore well; the surest proof of real worth. . . .
Agreeable in person and manners, and constitutionally cheerful, his
first introduction was prepossessing. But what he gained at first, he did
not lose afterwards. . . . He had classical attainments of the first order
. . . this was manifest in his sermons . . . which, though sometimes above
the reach of ordinary capacities, always exhibited clearness, truth, and
argument, well calculated to edify the generality of attentive hearers.
When I stated to him that it would be desirable he should descend to
the level of the lowest and most illiterate of his audiences, without
departing from the pure and dignified simplicity of the scriptures, he
would good-naturedly promise to do so—and in this respect, there
evidently was a gradual, but sure improvement. As it ought to be with
every Incumbent, and his clerical coadjutor, we were always like father
and son—according to our respective situations—giving and taking
mutual advice, from the best motives, and in the most friendly spirit;
looking on each other, not as rivals, but as fellow labourers in the same

glorious cause, and under the superintendence of our common Lord and Master. [Father and son indeed—how understandable are those words.] In visiting, and cottage lectures, a most important part of a minister's duty, he . . . was as active and sedulous as health and circumstances would permit; and in the Sunday School, especially, he was useful in more than an ordinary degree. He had the rare art of communicating information with diligence and strictness, without austerity, so as to render instruction, even to the youngest and most giddy, a pleasure and not a task. . . . I do not, however, mean to represent the subject [of these remarks] as faultless; I have no such anti-scriptural views of human nature. . . . But wherever there might have been a deficiency, it would, through the grace of God, necessarily have been supplied in due time, by sage experience afforded through the rough but salutary discipline of this unsparing and unceremonious world. As he was himself a friend to many, and an enemy to none, so by a kind of reaction, he had, I think I might say, no enemies and many friends. He was a conscientious Churchman, and true Protestant—but tolerant to all his differing brethren; where he could not cordially unite, he determined that separation should be no ground of hostility. . . . Thus, our reverend friend lived—but, it may be asked, how did he die? During his illness, I generally visited him twice a day, joined with him in prayer, heard his request for the prayers of this congregation . . . heard of his pious admonitions to his attendants, and saw him in tranquility close his eyes on this bustling, vain, selfish world; so that I may truly say, his end was peace, and his hope glory. . . . But our privilege as Christians is to look forward to a joyous resurrection, in the hope of being for ever re-united above, with those who have been taken from us by death, and whom we have loved here below. . . . Our late lamented friend ran a bright, but short career. He died in the twenty-sixth year of his age [twenty-ninth] . . . let us walk by faith and not by sight . . . longing for a glorious resurrection, and eternal salvation, through Jesus Christ, our Lord and Saviour; to whom, with the Almighty Father, and Holy Spirit, we would ascribe all glory, praise, power and dominion, both now and for ever. Amen!"

There, perhaps, is the finest portrait of all of the dashing young Willy Weightman, and much is learned, also, of Patrick Brontë. Anne could not have felt anything but pride when she read her father's tribute to the man she loved. Patrick slowly climbed down from the top deck of the pulpit and only then remembered that he still had a son left. Yet his eyes were still moist with tears when he came out into the autumn sunshine.

Branwell was now able to devote himself to nursing his aunt, whose recovery seemed his only care in life, now Weightman was dead and buried. The true facts behind his recent dismissal were now known to Patrick, and the explanation was an ugly one. Yet this seemed hardly the time to upbraid him. His recent grief and the touching sincerity of his anxiety for the sick Miss Branwell precluded anger for a time. It seemed that money had been missing from the station at Luddenden Foot and, for a while, Branwell, whose responsibility it was, had been suspect. The porter had now been discovered and punished, Branwell's guilt consisting only of negligence in the proper supervision of the office; but Patrick knew his son well enough by now to appreciate that his heavy drinking would soon have placed him in the way of an equal temptation to theft—and God knows where the end would have been.

About two weeks after the funeral sermon for William Weightman, Elizabeth Branwell suddenly had a relapse and became gravely ill. She had an internal obstruction and the doctor held out little hope for her recovery. Branwell wrote to Grundy again: ". . . I have had a long attendance at the death-bed of the Rev. Mr. Weightman, one of my dearest friends, and now I am attending at the death-bed of my aunt, who has been for twenty years as my mother. I expect her to die in a few hours. . . ." This was written on 25th October. Two days afterwards Elizabeth Branwell became agonized with pain, and when Patrick saw the tender way Branwell tried to ease her suffering through long day and weary night, he forgave his son all his past failings.

Elizabeth Branwell died on Saturday, 29th October 1842, aged sixty-six. Again Branwell writes to Grundy: ". . . I have been waking two nights witnessing such agonising suffering as I would not wish my worst enemy to endure; and I have now lost the guide and director of all the happy days connected with my childhood. . . ."

Anne had been advised of her aunt's grave illness, but was quite unable at first to obtain leave of absence from the Robinson family. Charlotte and Emily received a letter in Brussels on 2nd November informing them of Miss Branwell's condition, and decided to return home at once. Then the girls were told that she had died: Anne arrived home (too late to see her aunt and possibly too late for the funeral), the other two received the second letter on 3rd November, the day of the funeral, and sailed from Antwerp on 6th November, reaching home two days later. They had only recently left the graveside of young Martha Taylor who had died in Brussels in October, like Weightman, of cholera. Charlotte, upon her return wrote to Ellen Nussey, ". . . I have seen Martha's grave—the place, where her ashes lie in a foreign country. Aunt, Martha Taylor, and Mr Weightman are now all gone; how dreary and void everything seems. . . ."

Miss Branwell was buried on Thursday, 3rd November, by the Rev. James C. Bradley, incumbent of Oakworth.

Elizabeth Branwell	Haworth	Nov : 3rd	66 years	James C. Bradley Officiating Minister.

At her request she was laid to rest in the vault under the church, where her sister and two little nieces slept. "Should I die at Haworth, I request that my remains may be deposited in the Church in that place as near as convenient to the remains of my dear sister." Her will, dated 30th April 1833, shows that, "My Indian workbox I leave to my niece, Charlotte Brontë; my workbox with a china top I leave to my niece, Emily Jane Brontë, together with my ivory fan; my Japan dressing-box I leave to my nephew, Patrick Branwell Brontë; to my niece Anne Brontë, I leave my watch with all that belongs to it; as also my eye-glass and its chain, my rings, silver spoons, books, clothes, etc. etc., I leave to be divided between my above-named three nieces, Charlotte Brontë, Emily Jane Brontë, and Anne Brontë, according as their father shall think proper. . . ." All the money that remained was to be divided equally between the three Brontë girls and her niece Elizabeth Jane Kingston, after being placed in "some safe bank or lent on good landed security". The will concluded, ". . . I appoint my brother-in-law, the Rev. P. Brontë, A.B., now Incumbent of Haworth, Yorkshire; the Rev. John Fennell, now Incumbent of Cross Stone, near Halifax; the Rev. Theodore Dury, Rector of Keighley, Yorkshire; and Mr. George Taylor of Stanbury, in the Chapelry of Haworth aforesaid, my executors." (Accordingly Elizabeth Jane, daughter of John Kingston, a Wesleyan minister, would pay the Brontë sisters their share accruing from Miss Branwell's rents in Penzance. On 8th May 1846 Charlotte writes to her cousin at 17 St Clare Street, Penzance: "Papa wishes me to acknowledge for him the receipt of the Post-office order for the rent.")

The witnesses to Miss Branwell's signature were the then sexton, William Brown, John Toothill, and William Brown, junior. The will was proved on 28th December 1842, in the prerogative court of York by the oaths of Patrick, and George Taylor. (John Fennell was dead and Theodore Dury had renounced when he left Keighley.)

It was a quiet Christmas in Haworth Parsonage, after the storm. Patrick had cast a quick glance over his girls and saw no immediate danger: they all seemed as well in health as circumstances allowed. Anne had had to return to Thorp Green for a while, and Charlotte had spent a week with Ellen Nussey at her home in Birstall (Ellen had left

the Rydings and now lived at Brookroyd); but now it was Christmas
and they were all at home, and in early January Ellen was to come for a
short visit.

Patrick had finished writing his short tribute to William Weightman
for the memorial tablet to be placed in the church. He later gave it to
Branwell's friend, J. B. Leyland the Halifax sculptor, to execute.
Patrick had entertained Leyland the previous May when the latter
visited Haworth in connection with the memorial to Dr Thomas
Andrew.

"This Monument was erected by the Inhabitants in Memory of the
Late William Weightman—who died September 6th, 1842, aged 26 yrs.
[28]. And was buried in this Church—on the tenth of the same month.
He was three years Curate of Haworth—and by the congregation and
parishioners in general was greatly respected—for his orthodox principles, active zeal, moral habits, learning, mildness and affability : his
useful labours will long be gratefully remembered by the members of the
congregation ; and Sunday school teachers, and scholars."

This monument remains in the new church today. Anne too, in
later years, would write those many verses that would be her heart's
monument to Willy Weightman.

> Life seems more sweet that thou didst live,
> And men more true that thou wert one ;
> Nothing is lost that thou didst give,
> Nothing destroyed that thou hast done.

But in January 1843, the Brontës broke up again, Anne to return to
her duties at Thorp Green accompanied by Branwell who, through her
efforts, had been given the post of tutor in the Robinson household.
Charlotte was to return to Brussels, as an English teacher at the
Pensionnat Heger : for this she would receive a nominal salary and the
continuation of her lessons. Patrick was very much against her
returning to Brussels alone : he would need someone at home now that
Aunt was gone. But there was Emily ; she had no desire to leave
Haworth again. He re-read Monsieur Constantin Heger's letter to him,
the one that Charlotte had brought home with her. ". . . We know, Sir,
that you will weigh with better judgment, and more wisely than we, the
consequences which a complete interruption of your daughters' studies
would have on the future. . . ." He read again : "Miss Emily was
learning the piano, receiving lessons from the best professor in Belgium,
and she herself already had little pupils. She was losing whatever
remained of ignorance, and also of what was worse—timidity. Miss

Charlotte was beginning to give lessons in French and to acquire that assurance, that aplomb, so necessary to a teacher. . . ." Patrick recalled again his own early thirst for knowledge, looked at Charlotte's eager face, and gave way. Charlotte could return; Emily would remain to look after the home! It was a decision that sent a thrill of happiness into the hearts of both his daughters. Patrick once more took up the letter and gazed at the words Charlotte had translated to him twice already. "I have not the honour of knowing you personally, still I hold you in sincere veneration; for in judging of a father of a family by his children one cannot be greatly deceived; and, in view of this, the education and sentiments we have found in your daughters can only give us a very high opinion of your merit and your character. You will no doubt learn with pleasure that your daughters have made very remarkable progress in all branches of teaching, and that this progress is entirely owing to their love of work and their perseverance. With such pupils we have had but little to do; their advancement is your work more than ours. We have not had to teach them the value of time and instruction; they had learnt all that in their paternal home, and we, on our part, have had only the feeble merit of directing their efforts and providing suitable aliment for the praiseworthy activity for which your daughters are indebted to your example and teaching. . . ." Patrick smiled quite happily to himself—well, it appeared Monsieur Heger had some discernment! But, as he put the letter away, Patrick was a very proud father indeed.

By the end of January, Anne and Branwell were at Thorp Green, where the latter would meet with the disaster that would finally wreck his life; Charlotte had arrived in Brussels (she left home on the 27th), where she would suffer torments because of her growing love for Constantin Heger; and Patrick was left with the uncomplicated and singleminded Emily to look after him.

CHAPTER 18

"'T' Parson"

BEFORE glimpsing Patrick Brontë sharing the tranquil peace of Haworth Parsonage with his beloved Emily, a quick survey should be made of his very great work for over forty-one years as the incumbent of Haworth, followed by a glance at his literary attempts. If in the latter capacity he was a failure, it is hoped the following pages will prove that as t'parson (as he was always called by the villagers) he was a very considerable success. He proved indeed a more than worthy successor to the great Grimshaw. There is a vast amount of material available recording his work in that moorland chapelry. The church registers and minute books will be quoted from extensively, together with many unpublished diaries and letters.

Patrick Brontë, until prevented through blindness or old age, was an insatiable walker in the cause of his people. No farmstead was too far across the moors for him to visit, no night too wild and stormy to preclude his holding a cottage meeting, if one had been requested. He preached simple, homely sermons that his congregation could understand, and endeavoured to preach at least one sermon a week until his last illness. Many addresses were given when he was completely blind; many when the family pew in front of him was missing a well-beloved face; many again when that pew was empty save for Martha Brown; and when the sermon was over, he would climb down and walk towards the Communion-table, crossing the stone flags that covered all his loved ones, save Anne.

During his incumbency the church was given its first organ and its first peal of bells, the Sunday school was built in Parsonage Lane, and Stanbury and Oxenhope were given little churches all their own. Vice and crime were checked and effectively dealt with, and a new prison was made available. Reforms were carried out to help the poor: cottages were purchased so that the destitute could be more comfortable there than in even the most improved of workhouses; road repairs, so long neglected, were put under way; frequent attempts were made to obtain freedom for the chapelry of Haworth from the parish of Bradford (to save the high rates that had to be paid to Bradford); the dwellings of the poor were whitewashed and cleaned to prevent the spread of cholera; all the houses in the village were ordered to be numbered; and so on. In all these matters Patrick was the driving force, his energy never flagging during his long hours of duty. Nor must mention be omitted that, during his administration, Haworth Church was always full on the Sabbath day—without the aid of a whip !

All this and a score of authentic cameos of Patrick Brontë amongst his parishioners, tell the tale of a conscientious clergyman doing more than his duty, of a man determined to cling to what was best in late Georgian and early Victorian England and equally eager to eradicate forever what was unjust ; a true-blue Tory who led the van for social reform ; a cleric who fought cruelty, ignorance and oppression no matter from what quarter it came, rich or poor, Whig or Tory, High Church or Low ; a man with unlimited funds of physical and mental courage, who, when bereft of all his earthly loves, died confidently, holding out a firm hand to God. A snob, perhaps, in those matters that are eternal, but the undeviating enemy of all earth-bound cant and hypocrisy, a loyal servant of his Church, and the head of a family whose like we shall never see again. Now let his labours amidst the hills of the Pennines, amongst the unique race that is the people of Haworth, speak for Christianity and himself.

"Copy of a Notice read in Haworth Church. Upon order received from the Chief Constable on the 3rd inst : There is wanted one man to serve in the old Militia for this Township. Therefore Notice is hereby given that a Meeting will be held in the Vestry of this Church on Friday the 9th Inst. at 2 o'clock in the afternoon to take into consideration how and in what manner such man is to be raised—likewise to consult respecting the removal of a Family from Thornton to this Township. Haworth, 3rd June 1820. [The Brontë family.]"

"At a Vestry meeting Legally convened in the Church or Chapel of Haworth on the 6th of October 1820, the Rev. P. Brontë Chairman, to take into consideration whether a Law suit should be entered into and maintained against James Greenwood of Bridge House in Haworth, in his attempt to obtain Damages according to Act of Parliament for his Plantation which was burnt by some Incendiary or Incendiaries on the 26th April last past. It was carried by a large majority—7 votes—that no such opposition should be made and consequently that the Damage, which was estimated at Twelve Pounds sterling should be laid on as a Rate and paid by the Church or Chapel Wardens or overseer or overseers of the said Parish, Township or Chappelry [sic]. P. Brontë. Witness our hands this 6th Oct : 1820. . . . Please to take Notice that a meeting of the Township will be held in the vestry of this Church on Friday the 13th Inst. at half past two o'clock in the afternoon, to determine whether, or not, the new intended burial ground, adjoining

the churchyard on the west side, shall be purchased by the Inhabitants
of the said Township for their general use, and also should this purchase
be approved by a Majority, to resolve upon and adopt the best mode of
laying on a Rate for that purpose. Those who have advanced sums
towards purchasing the aforesaid ground, are particularly requested to
attend. Haworth April 8th 1821."

"At a Vestry Meeting . . . on the 13th April 1821, it was agreed
without one dissenting voice, that the new intended burial ground . . .
should be properly conveyed and consecrated for burial ground . . . the
necessary expenses attending the same, as well as for paying those
gentlemen who had previously advanced sums of money for purchasing
the said ground . . . to be collected by the churchwardens. P. Brontè.
Chairman. [Churchwardens, at that time, were elected at a meeting held
on Easter Monday.]"

"At the last mentioned meeting . . . it was also agreed that the
Church wardens in future shall refrain from dining as usual four
Sundays in the year, at the Town's expense, but dine on Easter Monday
only out of that fund. . . . this 23rd day of April 1821. P. Brontè.
Chairman."

". . . A meeting will be held in the Vestry . . . for the purpose of
considering the Propriety of Purchasing a set of Music Books . . . which
may be had at about six pounds owing to their being second-handed.
By order of P. Brontè Minister, Haworth April 28th 1821."

". . . We the undersigned do consent for the Purchase of the aforesaid
Music Books . . . the Purchase money to be paid out of the Church Rate
and that Thomas Parker is hereby authorised to Purchase the same with
reasonable expenses for his trouble."

"There will be a meeting of the Inhabitants held in the Vestry of
the Church for the purpose of choosing a certain number of gentlemen
as Trustees to whom the intended Burial ground lately purchased, is to
be conveyed for the use of the Parish . . . Haworth, Septr :2nd 1821.
[This ground was purchased from Mr Thomas Brooksbank Charnock—
son of the late incumbent.—later the Rev. Charnock, M.A., of Cullingworth who was buried by Patrick at Haworth on 29th October 1847
aged forty-seven.]"

"Whereas a number of ill-behaved and disorderly persons have for
a long period colleagued together, not only to destroy the property but
to endanger the lives of the peaceable inhabitants of this township, in
consequence of which, Notice is hereby given that a meeting will be
held in the Vestry of this Church on Tuesday the 1st of January 1822 at
2 o'clock in the afternoon in order to adopt such measures as may be
conducive to Peace and tranquility. Haworth, 22nd Dec : 1821."

". . . 1st January 1822, the following resolutions adopted by the Majority of those present. 1st . . . An Association be formed in Haworth to be denominated 'The Association for the Suppression of Vice', and that its operations shall extend to all who shall be guilty of Murder, or of assaulting unoffending Individuals or of robbing and stealing, or committing any depredation etc. . . ."

"23rd day of January 1822 . . . that subscriptions are to be opened at Stephen Taylor's, Stanbury, Wm. Thomas, Haworth, Joseph Hartley, near Oxenhope, John Greenwood, far Oxenhope, at the sum of four shillings each man in order to clear those persons liable to be balloted for eight men now wanting to serve in the old militia for this township."

"1st Day of January 1823. It is unanimously agreed that all persons not belonging to this Township shall pay 10s for each burying place in the New Ground and that each Burying Place contain seven feet in length and three feet six inches in Breadth. . . . the same money shall be converted for the use of the Town. Jan: 17th 1823 . . . no support to the Singers shall be allowed out of any of the Parish Rates. . . . Paid £65 for the overseer with allowance for journies on his going ten miles from home as usual. The grave-maker for a Common grave to have two shillings for one three feet deep for all residing in the Parish . . . 22nd March 1823. . . . 17th May 1823, that part of West Lane from *White Lion Inn* in Haworth to the *Sun Inn*, shall be sett [sic] or paved, to be completed in Four Years, the first year to be sett [sic] or paved at Well Lane Head."

". . . Three singing Books were delivered by David Feather in this Vestry on the 17th Oct: 1823. Viz: Boy's Anthems 2nd Volume, one book Ratcliff's Anthems, one ditto Ebdon's Services . . . July 14th 1826 . . . for the purpose of raising more money to meet the demand of the present distress."

"Dec: 29th 1826, That in compliance with a requisition of, and from, the principal inhabitants and householders of the township of Haworth, requesting a Public meeting to be called and held for the purpose of . . . adopting proper and efficient measures for the suppression of the notorious practices of selling illicit Beer, the which practices are productive of every imaginable Evil. We do hereby accordingly appoint a Public Meeting to be held in the Parish Church on Friday next at 2 o'clock in the afternoon for the aforesaid purposes and all persons who have an interest for the security of property and the well-being of society will do well to attend. At a Vestry Meeting legally convened in Haworth on 5th January 1827.—the Rev. Mr Brontë in the Chair. *1st Resolution.* That Whist Shops, as they are usually called, which abound in the Parish of Haworth, and the surrounding neighbourhood, have a constant and direct tendency to lower and vitiate the minds both of those who keep them and those who frequent them, and from their unseasonable hours—to sow the seeds of various diseases and greatly to injure the body as well as the soul. Moved by the Revd. C. Ratcliff and seconded by John Greenwood. *2nd Resolution.* That in consequence of the inward pollution they naturally produce, and the facility they afford, when money is expended, for the disposal of articles of every kind and however got, Whist shops offer a great variety of strong temptations to licentious conduct—to outrage—and to theft and robbery of every description. Moved by Mr. Greenwood of Bridgehouse —seconded by John Pickles. *3rd Resolution.* That the officers of Excise, Constables, Churchwardens and all others whom it may concern be requested to exert themselves to the uppermost to detect and bring to condign and legal punishment—as speedily as possible—all, who keep Whist Shops, and likewise those who frequent them whenever they shall be found cognisable to the Law, and when the Law is not capable of reaching their offence to report them to their Masters and to request that they will turn them out of their employ unless they give satisfactory proof of their repentence and amendment, by immediately desisting from their illegal practices. Moved by Mr. Greenwood of Springhead and seconded by Simeon Townend. *4th Resolution.* And that those who are the owners of dwelling houses be also requested to enquire into the characters of their tenants—and if they continue their illegal practices in reference to selling Whist, to give them notice to quit ; and deliver up possession, and should they not deliver up, means to be taken by the township in regard to expenses consequent on any legal proceedings. Moved by Mr. William Garnett. Seconded by Mr. Isaac Sharpe. *Fifth Resolution.* That all expenses necessarily incurred in legal proceedings to put down Whist Shops be paid by the whole township in connection with the constables. Moved by Mr. James Hartley, Seconded by Mr. James Wright. *Sixth Resolution.* That the late Prison be fitted up and one pound one shilling a year rent be paid to Mr. William Garnett for the occupation of it. Moved by Mr. William Brown. Seconded by Mr. William Thomas. P. Brontè, Chairman. Resolved that the thanks of this meeting be given to the Revd. P. Brontè for his able conduct in the chair."

"To the Gentlemen, in vestry assembled &c

"Please to take notice, that I choose Mr Stephen Taylor of Stanbury, to be my churchwarden, for the ensuing year—

Haworth, April 16th 1827—

P. Brontè, Minister, of Haworth, aforesaid."

"Wednesday November 12th 1828 [at Lower Town or Far

Oxenhope] . . . the repairing of the Highways of that part of the Township of Haworth called Far Oxenhope. Also at the same time to let a certain Stone Quarry on the waste ground for the benefit of the aforesaid Highways. . . . repairing a certain piece of road from the west end of Mill Lane to Moorhouse Bridge formerly repaired by Stephen Sutcliffe. . . . that James Feather be allowed to get stones in the above mentioned Quarry and pay the sum of one pound one shilling per year . . . 1829. John Ogden [he was the constable in 1821] be appointed assistant overseer . . . salary of £55 a year, to collect Rates Bastardy and Pay Poor. . . . [the former was the payment levied by the church against fathers of illegitimate children—for the maintenance of the child]. The Select Vestry . . . to have two shillings each person for attending and any person . . . not attending shall have no allowance . . . to take into consideration the propriety of erecting a workhouse on the Common waste ground belonging to Haworth Hamlet . . . June 11th 1829. [Here Patrick intervened with a kinder and more homely idea]— . . . not to erect a Workhouse but . . . to take two or three cottage houses in as good a situation as can be met with, for the use of such poor as belongs to this Township, and fit the said houses up with such necessaries as will be required. June 17th 1829.

"... August 28th 1829, the Rev. P. Brontè in the chair . . . in May 1830 . . . all the slates and lathes should be taken off the church—that the woodwork should be repaired wherever it was necessary—that it should be all well lathed and slated, and ciseld or underdrawn . . . but that no alteration be made in the form of the Church. P. Brontè. Chairman. July 1830 . . . all constables . . . shall be duly protected in their duty as far as consistent and legal for the preservation of peace. [Can devotees of Mrs Gaskell still wonder why Patrick did not throw away his pistols ?]"

Then follow two or three meetings to discuss in detail further extensive road repairs.

"10th Dec. 1831 . . . and adopt such measures of precaution as may be deemed essential for the prevention of *Cholera Morbus* and to urge the necessity of white washing, cleaning, and removing all nuisances of dirt in or near the dwellings of the poor. . . . December 14th 1831 . . . Present, Rev. P. Bronte in the Chair . . . Rev. Moses Saunders, Mr. Thomas Andrew, Surgeon . . . to procure the immediate removal of all offensive Objects and Nuisances in the Roads, Lanes, Alleys, and Entries, belonging to the Township . . . to supply such of the Poor with Bedding and Clothing as are in a destitute condition in that respect. . . . [In this drive against cholera Patrick worked harmoniously with the strict Baptist Minister, Moses Saunders, although, as will be seen in the

next chapter, they often clashed good-humouredly in print.] March 1832
. . . that the houses throughout the Township be numbered with black
ground and white figures and that each Hamlet be numbered separately.
Sep : 28th 1833 . . . John Feather (Constable) to call a meeting for the
purpose of erecting a *lock up* for the custody of Felons and Disorderly
persons . . . that there be a *lock up* or *prison* immediately erected in this
town for the purpose stated above."

"19th day of January 1834 . . . The Rev. P. Brontè, Incumbent, in
the Chair, . . . that it be attempted to procure a final separation of the
Chapelry of Haworth from the Parish of Bradford . . . that a proper
statement be laid before one of His Majesty's Ministers, respecting our
situation and connection with Bradford, and the vast disproportion of
Rates we have to pay to Bradford, to our great disadvantage . . .
[there had been an earlier petition to Parliament in September 1831].
March 1st 1834, It having been agreed . . . that a Prison should be
erected in Haworth . . . whether it will be advisable to build the Prison
separate or erect a Dwelling House above it, for the use of the township.

"Feby : 13th 1835 . . . the Revd. P. Brontè in the Chair, and adjourn-
ed to the School Room [built in 1832] . . . that John Brown of Haworth
be appointed Sexton. [This meeting was held on the day John Brown's
father died.] April 11th 1835 . . . to take into consideration the propriety
of adopting means to obtain certain rights and monies belonging to this
township arising from a farm at Withins and Upper Horking Stone.
That Council's opinion be got on the distribution and clothing the
10 Poor children from the Farm situate at Withins. . . . [David Midgley
of Withens Farm—Emily's setting for *Wuthering Heights*—by his will
dated 5th March 1723, directed that out of the rents from that land
the Trustees should annually pay on Martinmas Day, for ten poor
children under seven years old to be clad with good blue clothes and
other necessary wearing apparel.] November 7th 1835 . . . to consider
the propriety of sending Thomas Arnold of Haworth to the Pauper
lunatic asylum . . . Resolved that another place be obtained if possible
. . . where he can be comfortably kept. . . ."

And so it continues throughout the years. It can readily be seen that
the clergy of those days, particularly in districts like the moorland
heights of the West Riding, more than earned their keep. A salute is
surely due to Patrick Brontë and his loyal little band of churchmen when
it is remembered that they did the work now attempted by a town
council, a mayor, a sanitary inspector, a health officer, a borough surveyor, local officials of the Ministry of Works, the constituent Member
of Parliament, the social workers, the moral welfare workers, the

22

lawyers and the police, as well as that host of indefinable public bodies that have sprung up like mushrooms. When one considers the foregoing activities together with such items as, "Feby 6th 1841 . . . the most equitable plan of putting out orphans and other children as Town apprentices"—one is inspired by their energy and not a little dismayed at the thought of their expenses. Small wonder that in 1842 it was "carried by a large majority—that a collection be made every month, in order to answer for church expenses. P. Brontë. A.B. Incumbent-Chairman".

A close look at some of the domestic expenses is not without interest : "August 1833—keeping the clock in repair—10/-. September 1834—4 sacrament wine bottles—16/-. Cleaning candlestick—7/6. Candles 8/-. Postage—5/-. Keeping the clock in repair—12/6. Oct : 17th 1834 . . . to take into consideration the propriety of erecting a stove in the said Church. 1841 Prayer Book—£6-0-0. Coal—£5-10-0. White-washing Church—£24-0-0. Repairing North-side of Church [estimate]—£123-8-4." From these accounts it is learned that there was "gass" to light the church with in 1841 ; and that a survey was ordered of the stone-quarries and coal-pits (there were one or two small coal-mines on the moors, long since disused and overgrown). When crime was at its height four special constables were appointed, and two guineas were offered to any villager who gave information respecting a crime. But the most heartbreaking burden of all was the Bradford church rate, levied on the chapelry of Haworth towards the maintenance of the Bradford parish. In 1834 Haworth paid £23 8s ; by 1841 it was £76 12s 10d. When the meeting was held to approve this last sum, John Brown moved the motion but Patrick himself led the opposition to such a payment and the motion was defeated. "Oct : 23rd 1841. Resolved that this meeting disapproving of the demand of the Bradford Church Wardens from the Township, resolved not to pay that demand, but to defend the Church Wardens against any Proceedings that may be commenced against them." Thus, having promised support to those of his wardens who were responsible to Bradford for collection of the rate, Patrick and Haworth, acting together this time, defied Bradford and refused to pay. By thus openly opposing the payment of the dues claimed by the mother-parish of Bradford, Patrick was only continuing that agitation that he had begun in January 1834 to free Haworth from its dependency on Bradford. He would continue the fight until his death, and it is ironical that only three years afterwards, on 30th August 1864, Haworth would be freed, no longer a chapel-of-ease in the parish of Bradford but a new and independent parish. It would have gladdened a heart sorely in need of solace had

Patrick lived to see that day, the accomplishment of a cause for which he had worked unceasingly and with no little personal courage.

One of the most serious problems Patrick had to face was that of the church rate. All over England men were murmuring against it, and matters eventually came to a head in Haworth in 1836. The trouble was that the rate was used for the sustentation of the church fabric. This was, no doubt, well enough for those who belonged to the church and thus received the benefit, but hardly just to those who professed some other faith. As a result, many Nonconformists had for some time resisted payment, advancing the unfairness of this all-embracing rate. (In Haworth it was 7½d in the £ in 1827, 10d in 1831, 1s 5d in 1841.) The following extracts from two letters written by Patrick on this subject, show his sound common sense when faced with a very delicate situation and also his genuine courtesy towards those whose opinions differed from his own.

"October 1st 1836. After having consulted both the Leeds newspapers of to-day, I sit down to write a few things to you respecting Church Rates—I see that in many of the neighbouring towns the churchwardens, and their friends, have laid on a Church Rate, in direct opposition to the majority of votes, at their vestry meeting, and that on the other side, associations have been formed to counteract this by legal measures. I do not think that these proceedings will tend either to lessen expense or to promote the best interest of our excellent Establishment, and I am of opinion, that in Haworth especially, all attempts at force would involve the churchwardens in great expense, and do much harm, and no good. I have lately sounded the inhabitants in general, and find that they are, for the most part, of my opinion, and that with me they think (all things considered) it would be the best way for the churchwardens to make an estimate of the rate, and to go round both to churchmen and dissenters and receive what they would be disposed voluntarily to give, and if what might be raised in this way should fall short, a collection should be made in the Church. They have acted thus in Keighley, and have no reason to rue it."

Patrick's fair and sensible idea was soon adopted, for shortly afterwards he writes, "I have drawn out the document as follows: 'Wishing and believing that the Church Rate question will be finally and satisfactorily settled during the next session of Parliament, we take the liberty of proposing that the sums following should be raised by voluntary subscription, pledging ourselves, at the same time, that if this desirable end should be accomplished we shall make no further claims for the past and present year.' " Patrick ends by expressing his desire that the Dissenters should be free to attend at the Meeting—

"that the meeting referred to shall not be called on any day on which the Dissenters may have a sermon, for any public, or pecuniary purpose, and I think our best plan, as our course is good, is to act openly, fairly, and Scripturally. Miss Branwell, my children, and myself, join in very kind regards to you."

At the beginning of 1844 Patrick received a long letter from Dr William Scoresby, the famous Whitby Arctic whaler, who had become Vicar of Bradford on the death of Henry Heap. Patrick had often cause to cross swords with this worthy particularly over the question of church rates, of which Scoresby was a fanatical supporter.

To the Revᵈ P. Brontë A B—Incumbent of Haworth.

Field House. Jan 4th 1844.

My Dear Sir,

I have long purposed writing to you on a subject of much importance to the children of the poor and the working-classes under your spiritual care—I refer to the present condition of the free Grammar-School of Near Oxenhope. This school by its constitution and trust should be I believe conducted by a graduate of Oxford or Cambridge, the will of the Testator of the endowment fund specifies I understand this express condition. Yet the school I am told is at present under the direction of a Wesleyan local preacher—at all events of a person not answering the description of the Headmaster declared by the will of the Testator. Conceiving it to be of great importance to my parishioners that any benefits of this kind should be fully carried out for their children ; and that it is a great privilege to the working classes and poor to have superior masters for carrying on the instruction in the Schools ; I feel it my duty to write to you on the subject, with the view of getting the Oxenhope Grammar School put under a proper master.

Will you therefore be so good as to call a meeting of the Trustees, and lay this letter before them, as I would rather trust to their good feeling and to their desire to fulfil the sacred objects of their trust faithfully, than seek by any other means to accomplish the object desired.

Should the Trustees be disposed to follow the course which is plainly their duty to pursue—their first object will be to give notice to the master for a specified time—to give up the charge of the School. On this being done, I shall be very ready to assist yourself and them as far as I am able, in taking measures for the appointment of a proper master.

I should be obliged if you will report to me the result of your meeting—which I would suggest should be regularly summoned, specifying the object of the meeting and minutes made of all the proceedings and the minutes signed by the Chairman is in the event of an application to the Lord Chancellor being necessary, the proceedings, with a copy of your circular summoning the Trustees and the names and quality of the Trustees will be required.

I remain, my dear Sir, yours faithfully W. Scoresby.

Patrick at once passed a copy of this letter to "Mr Robert Heaton. Ponden, Haworth". The meeting was convened, but as may be guessed, action was somewhat slowed. Scoresby was correct in his reading of the endowment fund, but as there was little or no demand in Haworth for a classical education, the then master, William Ramsbottom, competent to teach Latin, was considered adequate, although he was a graduate of neither of the Universities. Had he not been a Dissenter no squeak of protest would have emanated from the Vicar, who lacked Patrick's broad tolerance. Scoresby was so detested by the Dissenters in Bradford, particularly over the Church Rate Levy, that he resigned in June 1847, retiring to Torquay, yet not before receiving a letter threatening, "if he but dared to collect the obnoxious rate, he might get a bullet where he expected to receive a shilling".

Besides being anxious to obtain more land for the graveyard and to purchase small stretches of waste ground for prisons, etc. (at 1½d a yard), Patrick was always eager to introduce improvements into the church itself, and in his desire for an organ he received the enthusiastic support of his son. But before the question of installing an organ was fully under way, there was some difficulty with the singers in the church. Patrick writes to George Taylor at the Manor House, Stanbury:

June 6th 1832.

Dear Sir,

Since I had the pleasure of seeing you, I have written and spoken on the subject of the oratorio, and I got the gentlemen concerned to engage that there shall be nothing in the affair respecting Sunday Schools, and that all will be conducted in a decent manner as formerly on such occasions—I have also consulted the proper law authorities and have found that when the licensed minister gives leave, no other can hinder any performance of the kind in the Church, and it will not do for me to be dictated to by the singers. I can see no better way, therefore, than to let the matter go on as usual—I am much obliged to you for your open and friendly conduct, and remain,

Yours respectfully and truly P. Brontë.

P.S. Miss Branwell joins me in kind regards.

In 1833, Patrick, anxious to improve the musical side of the worship in Haworth Church, writes, "Since I last saw you I have spoken to several people concerning the organ. All seem desirous of having one if the money can be procured. Miss Branwell says she will subscribe five pounds, and some others have promised to give liberally. Mr. Sunderland, the Keighley organist, says he will give his services *gratis*, on the day of opening of the organ, and in general, the real friends of the Church are desirous of having one. A player, also, can be readily procured." Abraham Stansfield Sunderland, the Keighley organist, gave music lessons at Haworth Parsonage. Indeed, at this time, Patrick was paying liberally for both a drawing master and a music teacher for his children. Where, then, the accusation of the total neglect of their education and talents so often hurled at his head ?

In 1834 a list of names of the members of the organ committee was drawn up by Patrick and amongst them was that of Branwell. The secretary was Thomas Andrew, surgeon, the Brontë's family doctor at that time. The organ was installed and first played in the following May. Charlotte wrote that Sunderland and John Greenwood (of Leeds) were the organists and that there rang through the old church, "I know that my redeemer liveth". This choice was certainly dictated by Branwell : Handel was his favourite composer. In 1845, St Michael's Church had but the one bell (Great Tim, survivor of three) to summon the villagers to worship, but in that year there was a desire for a peal of bells and Patrick writes to one of the Trustees :

Mr Joseph Rushworth Mouldgreave.

Haworth April 21st [1845]
Sir,—In conformity with what appears to be the wish of the Inhabitants —respecting a Peal of six bells, in order to consider the propriety or impropriety of such a measure—it is requested that you will be so kind as to attend in the Vestry of the Church of Haworth on the 29th Instant, at six o'clock in the evening.—

P. Brontè—Incumbent.

A gilded inscription in the belfry chamber of Haworth Church shows that : "This peal of bells was hung by William Wood ; Joseph Redman being Architect, and were opened and prizes given—March 10th, AD 1846." On the tenor bell, weighing nearly twelve hundredweight, is inscribed, "C & G Mears, London. These bells were raised by subscription. Rev. Patrick Bronte A.B. Incumbent. Mr. George Feather, Mr. James Lambert, Churchwardens." The bells have the date 1845. It is pleasant, on a Sabbath morn or eve, to hear those bells pealing out from the old tower across the grey, uneven roofs of Haworth until their music is lost in the moorland wind. Whether we answer the summons or no, Patrick's bells are calling us to come to God.

Haworth Church has long been noted for the work of its Sunday schools, and the credit for the beginning of this work belongs to Patrick. In 1832, he had built, in Parsonage Lane, the first school (next to which John Brown the sexton erected his new house) and, at sixteen, Charlotte was appointed the first Superintendent. Helped by her two sisters Charlotte endeavoured to set aside a day each week to help the local milliner with her work, the latter being a widow with a young family to maintain. For a time, Branwell also taught at the Sunday school.

The school that Patrick built still stands. Of recent years it was a hostel welcoming from all over the world young people who found in the parish church the message of eternal things; in the moors, the beauty and wonder of Nature; and in the writings of the Brontës all that is noblest and best in English literature. Now, however, the church Sunday school has returned to the old building, which again rings with the sound of children's voices, thus fulfilling the text that Patrick caused to be carved over the doorway. Taken from the Book of Proverbs, it reads: "Train up a child in the way he should go; and when he is old, he will not depart from it."

Although as a young man Patrick was never loath to walk over the moors to the far-scattered parts of his parish—he was often seen walking briskly with his young children—as blindness threatened and old age grew ever nearer, he thought of the future and decided that both Oxenhope and Stanbury ought to have churches of their own. In 1843 he writes: "I have lately had communication with the Bishop, who has been very, and unusually kind, respecting getting a curate for Oxenhope. His Lordship has been graciously pleased, in the most handsome manner, to grant my desire. Consequently, at the expense of great fatigue, I went over on Thursday last, in the heat of the day, and took over a room—nine yards long and six wide." The letter ends, "I am in the way of getting a daily teacher for the National Church Sunday School. The salaries in both cases will be paid by the London Institutes —so that if the Lord should spare my life a few years longer, our Church affairs will be put into a better condition than they were ever before." This letter is edged in black because of Miss Branwell's death.

By the beginning of 1845, Patrick had appointed his then curate, the Rev. Joseph Brett Grant, B.A., to be in charge of Oxenhope. The district, for ecclesiastical purposes, was formed that year under Sir Robert Peel's Act, and included Far and Near Oxenhope. Until then the services there had been held in cottages, and later in a wool-combing shop. Grant, recently down from Emmanuel College, Cambridge, raised funds for a day and Sunday school and was greatly helped by Mrs Ferrand of Bingley, who gave a school for that purpose. With Patrick's continued support, Grant now agitated for a church. It is said he wore out fourteen pairs of shoes whilst walking the district for subscriptions. On 14th February 1849, the foundation stone was laid and on 11th October of that year the church was consecrated by the Bishop of Ripon. It was dedicated to St Mary the Virgin. Perhaps its most striking feature was that it was a perfect copy of Anglo-Norman architecture in its severest form. Another rarity was the fact that the estimated cost of £1,308 was not reached—£930 plus site and walling £218. The living was worth £150, with residence (built shortly after the church) and was a vicarage in the gift of the Crown and Bishop, alternately. Grant, who was the Master of Haworth Grammar School at Marsh (replacing Vicar Scoresby's "unqualified" Wesleyan), remained as Vicar of Oxenhope until his death, thirty-five years later.

About a year previously to the consecration of St Mary's at Oxenhope, the little village church of Stanbury was erected. In 1848, Patrick had raised a subscription for this purpose, aided by the Charity Commissioners. Stanbury had no churchyard then, and the small church stood in pleasantly wooded grounds. As already stated, the top deck of Grimshaw's pulpit today serves in this Stanbury Church, which remains in the parish of Haworth. Towards the end of his life, Patrick obtained an order closing the old burial ground at Haworth. Only the new part was used for burial. Today there is a burial field out of the village on high ground by the moor's edge, with tender flowers within and the heather of home embracing the outer wall.

Yet these were only the major material improvements Patrick instigated at Haworth. True, in forty-one years much was bound to be improved, yet judged by any standards, Patrick's incumbency was energetic in the extreme. There were a host of smaller improvements too numerous to record, such as, in 1824, the erection of gates and pillars at the entrance to the yard of the church. In 1859 the Yorkshire Penny Bank was founded, Patrick becoming president of the Haworth branch. He persuaded many parishioners to invest their savings in the bank. But the greatest work Patrick accomplished can have no visible monument; it is hidden away in the souls of men. Much evil was corrected, much doubt was given certainty, the disbelievers were given a glimpse of the true God, many who suffered in body or mind were comforted and healed. When he died Patrick left behind him a better place. No one can alter the characters of the people of Haworth, no one should seek to. Yet they knew the goodness he had done, the kind example he had shown, and when he died they mourned, not the father of his children, but "t'parson on the hill".

It will have been noticed that Patrick had no lack of interest in the law, and would never hesitate to bring the law into action if he thought the best interests of the village (or his own) were being thwarted.

"March 17th 1842... As I have lately been at great expense, you will oblige me, by getting for me, and sending, the £7-12-6, of rent due. If it is not paid this week, or the next at the latest, I shall be under the necessity of taking proceedings." In 1850, when Arthur Bell Nicholls was his curate, we find him writing thus: "April 27th 1850 . . . As you are the acting Trustee, I should like you to come, and by the help of some joiner, or carpenter, to examine the house in which I reside. The roof, I fear, stands in need of renewal, or repair, and some plan should be laid for the accomplishment of the work—I have been made rather uneasy by information from Mr. Nicholls, respecting a path leading through the Church Lands to the Mill. With regard to all paths and ways, as stated in Mr. Griffith's Book of Law, a right is procured in one of two ways. An express agreement gives a right—and there is a right by prescription, that is, when a path, or way has been used time immemorial, or time out of mind. There may be a protest made against the use of it, or there may be fines for trespass, or there may be a sort of rent or charge for the privilege of use. But much would have to depend on the persons who paid, whether the mill-owner, or those who went to the mill, and also whether some did not go over, who never paid at all. But, however these things might be, the expense of a law suit might amount to hundreds of pounds—I have known hundreds of pounds to be spent under such circumstances, when the object contended for was not worth 10s.

"There may be many ways tried before you go to law. You can deprive the mill-owner of some water, which may, perhaps, bring him to reasonable terms, you may fine for trespass, or you may protest and threaten, and if after all, the Trustees felt bound in duty to go to law, the best way would be, I conceive, in the first instance, to have Counsel's advice, and then defray the expenses of the law suit, either by using the money, or a portion of it lent on mortgage, or to borrow a certain sum, the interest of which should be paid by me and my successors, since all who follow me, would as much as myself, be interested in the concern."

It seems that Patrick's long interest in the law had given him an intimate knowledge of the members of that profession, as the following amusing extract shows:

"December 19th 1854 . . . You will remember that a considerable time ago, I had the pleasure of seeing you in my house, when I avail'd myself of the opportunity to tell you that, though it was not absolutely necessary to renew the Church Deeds of Appointment, at that time, yet the Trustees would have it renewed, should the expense be small. Therefore I asked you what the expense would be, and your answer was, that as the Deed would not require to be enrolled and registered, the expense would not exceed £6 and that, if it did, you yourself would pay the difference.

"You cannot wonder then, that I am rather surprised to find from your bill, that the expense is nearly three times the sum which you mentioned. Now I certainly do not expect, that you will pay the differences, 'for what Gentleman of the Law, would do such a thing?' But, I hope, that without detriment to yourself, on a revision of the case, you will be able to make a considerable reduction, and that you will be so kind, as to give me notice of this, at your earliest opportunity, in order that I may lay your final statement before the Trustees."

From law to politics, and in those days it was quite impossible for a clergyman to remain aloof from such worldly strife. As today, there were certain fundamental issues that could not be shirked. The fate of a district could hang on the wool tax, the peace of a village on the question of new machinery. Patrick had always keenly interested himself in political affairs, and that interest, so marked during the Luddite risings, continued with him at Haworth. He often addressed the local Conservative Club at its meetings in a large upper room of the White Lion Hotel in the very centre of the village. Patrick was too much a man of sincerity to balance himself hypocritically on the fence of neutrality. Yet his rigid bias towards the Tory camp was not always a help to those he was attempting to assist on the platform. He would attack the Whigs with great fervour and freedom of speech, but if anything was said in the Tory cause that he felt to be wrong he was as likely as not to commit a *volte face* and lash out at his allies. There would rage within him that conflict between his convictions and his sense of fair play. Indeed, his appearances on political platforms were few, for once there, he was in great danger of losing both temper and dignity and saying things he would afterwards regret. On the occasion of a meeting in Haworth in 1832, during the Reform Bill agitation, he maintained that the working classes had no right whatever to the franchise it was then proposed to extend to them. There was an aristocracy in the country far better qualified to be the governing power than a multitude of uneducated people. The government of the land should be left in their hands. All this was well and good for Viscount Morpeth, then seeking election as the member for the West Riding: he was a Whig and could slash this argument to ribbons. But he made an error : he began discussing Church matters. It was the duty of the State to provide more churches in large towns—"the large churches of the rural districts are but so many dark lanterns, as most of them are but thinly attended". This was the moment for Patrick : he was on his feet with flashing eyes and the veins swelling in his forehead. He resented the assertion in "strong and excited" language, and concluded by asking "how that could be called dark which was filled with spiritual light ?" Lord Morpeth was elected and remained the member for several years. In 1851, when Charlotte was in London attending one of Thackeray's lectures, Lord Morpeth, then the seventh Earl of Carlisle, came over to speak to her and, as Charlotte told her father, "He asked after you, recalled the platform electioneering scene at Haworth, and begged to be remembered to you."

But in 1837 Patrick made a great speech, a slashing indictment of the New Poor Law Act, which deservedly gained for him great prominence in *The Times*. In the issue for Monday, 27th February 1837, his speech was chosen from among the many then being made up and down the country, and in particular, Yorkshire.

"In pursuance of a requisition signed by several of the most respectable inhabitants, a public meeting was appointed to be held on Wednesday in the Church Sunday-School Room, Haworth, for the purpose of petitioning Parliament to repeal the New Poor Law Act ; and although the liberal manufacturers of the place had sent round, commanding their workpeople to abstain from defiling themselves by attendance on the meeting, which they stigmatized as a Tory trick, so large a number of persons had assembled at the hour that it became necessary to adjourn the proceedings into the open street, where the Rev. P. Bronte, incumbent, having taken the chair, first rose to address them.

"He declared that upon that occasion neither speakers nor hearers had met to promote the interests of party, but to plead the cause of the poor, and, in so doing, to oppose the continuance of a law which had been introduced for the apparent purpose of amending all former legislation with regard to them ; but he cautioned every one against being misled by terms, for what would men think of a surgeon who should propose to amend the human system by lopping off a nose here and a finger there, without regard to either the soundness or utility of the members ? Now the old bill, though not a perfect one, was sufficient for our wants, and like John Bull himself it was generous as well as testy, shaking a cudgel over our heads at times, but closing the punishment with shaking of hands over a quart of ale ; while the new bill was a nose-hewing, finger-lopping quack, a legal deformity, hunchbacked, and one-handed, though that one hand grasped the trenchant dagger.

"He had found from that day's papers, that Whigs, Tories, and Radicals had joined in congratulating the Government upon the introduction into Ireland of a bill like this, therefore what were the people to do amid such treachery among their representatives ? They must stand up as Englishmen and demand their natural rights. The working men and labourers trampled on by this bill were the material of the country ; remove them, and what were King, Lords, and Commons worth ? All these ranks must fall with them ; nor was rank wholly exempt from the chance of feeling the effects of this bill, for riches often made unto themselves wings to fly away. He had heard, too, of plurality of sovereigns in a country ; he had heard of two Kings of Lacedaemon, of the Saxon Heptarchy, of the two Kings of Brentford [in the Restoration comedy *The Rehearsal*, 1672], but not before of the hundred Monarch Guardians, and the three Royal Commissioners, incontrollable by Parliament, unanswerable to Crown ! This poor law was termed a remedy for the poor, but in that sense a man might take a strong dose of opium for a remedy while in the cholic, and then, as now, the remedy would prove worse than the disease. Then again, 'guardian of the poor' seemed a pretty name, and the guardians of Haworth were all honest men,—but there's many a pretty name for an ugly thing, and three honest men would possess no power but to do mischief.

"Guardians were in the situation of the fox guarding the goose. Supposing the fox gives his ward a loving pinch by the neck, the poor goose might complain, but the fox assures it that all is for its good, though the pinch might end in worrying. However, he hoped that in the case before him, the geese would soon turn to eagles triumphing, with talons clinched in their prostrate enemy, and he could assure them that Yorkshire and Lancashire united, would prove more than a match for all opposition to their welfare. He entreated them to rouse themselves, for their laws, and bodies, and souls, were equally concerned in that matter—and country too, for if dear times and general distress should come on, starvation, deprived of relief, would break into open rebellion ; but the time for healthy action was now or never, and if Englishmen only exerted themselves they would in the end come off more than conquerors."

Abraham Wildman spoke next against the bill, to cries of, "That's reight, owd lad." His was a fighting speech—"Where was the working man who could wish to be classed in gangs ? . . . if they [the authors of the bill] love gangs and grinding so much . . . he could wish that 'gang' to grind for one month in the House of Correction !" "The Rev. P. Bronte seconded the motion, which, on being put, was carried without a dissentient voice . . . The Rev. W. Hodgson then came forward, expressing his belief that the resolution he held would meet with the support that those before had done. He had heard it said in Haworth, that 'there seldom comes a better' " and the curate applied that maxim to the bill. The petition to Parliament was drawn up and read by Patrick, "who moved that it be adopted and presented to the two Houses of Parliament, to the Commons by Mr Hardy, and to the Lords by the Archbishop of Canterbury". Wildman seconded the motion which was carried unanimously, after which three cheers were given to the Chairman and to the speakers. ". . . and the multitude dispersed with feelings which neither the tyranny of Commissioners nor the professions of mock Reformers will ever confound or wipe away."

In March, Patrick and his friends continued the attack with a statement, "to the Rate Payers of Haworth".

There is much of politics in the next two letters of Patrick's to be quoted: the first is to John White, a Bradford merchant, in whose family Charlotte had been governess in 1841, prior to her departure for Brussels.

For John White, Esq. Upper Wood House Rawdon, Nr. Leeds.

Haworth, near Bradford, Yorkshire. Sept: 22nd 1842.

My Dear Sir,

I thank you for your kind letter, and as a proof of this, I answer it immediately—and least [sic] I should forget it, in the important affairs I now mean to speak of, I beg leave to say that Miss Branwell, and all at home join with me, in the most respectful and kind regards to you, Mrs White, Mrs Fennell [the widowed second Mrs Fennell] and all your amiable family. With regard to your children, and your governess, it gives me great pleasure to learn, that all is going on, well—May God grant that it may continue so, since much of your peace of mind, must necessarily depend on the probable results, in regard to these, and similar matters.

My daughter, has always spoken well of you, and Mrs White, and your Family [not quite always, in her letters], but she has been very much engaged, and has had scarcely time to write, even to me—Both my Daughters, who are on the Continent, as well as the one, who is near York, as a governess, are exceedingly well received—For which, and all his other mercies, I desire to thank God, the great, and glorious Giver of all good—When you see Mr. Readhead [sic—our old friend, Redhead], his Lady, and Family, be so good as to remember me very kindly to them—In regard to politics, it must now appear to all rational and unprejudiced men, that had the poor, unprincipled, temporizing Whigs, remain'd much longer in power, we should have been utterly ruined, as a nation, in respect to both the worlds—May the Most High, enable the Conservatives to do their duty, and protect them from all the evil designs of their enemies !—I remain, My Dear Sir,

Yours, most respectfully, and truly, P. Brontè.

That is plain enough. In the Whig defeat of 1841, Morpeth had been ousted and the member for the West Riding was now the Brontës' favourite—John Stuart-Wortley, the second Baron Wharncliffe. The next letter is to his brother Hugh. In addition to the dull red Queen Victoria penny stamp, the envelope bears four postmarks : Haworth (no date) Bradford-Yorks (Nov. 20th) a diamond-shaped mark (Nov. 21st) and the green stamp of Rathfriland (Nov. 22nd). As the letter was written on the 20th, it thus took only two days to reach Hugh Brontè in Ireland.

To Mr Hugh Brontè Ballinasceaugh Near Rathfriland, Ireland.

Haworth, near Bradford, Yorkshire. Nov: 20th 1843.
Dear Brother,

I wish to know, how you are all doing, in these turbulent times, as I learn from the Newspaper, Ireland is at present, in a very precarious situation, and circumstances there, must, I should think—lead to civil war—which, in its consequences, is the worst of all wars—I hope, that the protestants, of *all* denominations, are, by arming themselves, and laying down, proper plans, or orginazation [*sic*], duly, on their guard— otherwise, they may be taken by surprise, and murdered by their insidious, and malignant enemies—as the Army cannot be every where all the protestants in Ireland, ought to remember, what a few determined men, did at the seige of Derry—But, whatever, in these cases, be done, should be in strict accordance with the Laws—If all the protestants in Ireland, were rightly armed and organized, they need not—owing to their good cause, and their superior intellects, and wealth, fear their opponents—should the Romanists gain their ends, they will destroy, and utterly exterminate, *both Churchmen, and dissenters*—and, I hope, that both dissenters, and Churchmen, see this, and will act, accordingly. I like not war, but Christ has said, in reference to a case of necessity, like this "let him who has no sword, sell his garments and buy one."—Yet, whilst I say these things, I would admonish you, and all my Brothers, and friends, not to be rash, and neither to break the Laws of God, or Man—and I would say, let prudence, and justice, be joined to courage—and due precaution—

With all our kindest regards, to you, my Brothers, and Sisters, and all old friends, who may now be living—I remain, dear Brother,

Yours, truly, P. Brontè.

P.S. Write soon, and let me know how you all are—and tell me, where my Brother William lives—so that I may know how to direct a letter to him.

William Brontè, known as Billy Brontè, was always a wild one, a United Irishman who fought at Ballinahinch. Patrick was anxious to caution prudence before civil war should begin.

There are several other letters and documents of Patrick's, extant, that have a bearing on his work as the incumbent of Haworth Church. They are best given here.

"Believing that it will be for the comfort, and convenience of all parties, we the undersigned, agree, that for building, repairing, and all other things, on the Church Lands in Haworth, and Stanbury—ten pounds of English currency—but not more—during the time Mr. Brontè, is the Licensed Minister of Haworth, shall be deducted from his rents, yearly—and that the remainder shall be duly paid by him, as Incumbent of the aforesaid Living—as long as he shall be in possession of it, in conformity with the conditions of his Licence. As witness our hands this 28th of July, 1834." Then follow the trustees' signatures, and "P. Brontè, Licensed Minister. Mr. Bronté has the duplicate of this—"

Next, a testimonial given late in his life—only the signature is Patrick's—the writing being that of Mr Nicholls:

Haworth, Bradford. Yorks.

We, who subscribe our signatures to the present testimonial, feel pleasure in stating from our personal knowledge of the bearer—Joseph Holmes—that he has always borne an excellent character for industry, and sobriety, and appears to us to be well qualified to fulfill [sic] all the duties in such an employment as that of Porter or Policeman on a Railway, where good character, health and activity are held as recommendations to an applicant. P. Bronte A.B. Incumbent of Haworth.

Mr. Simeon Townend, Ebor House Haworth.

Haworth, Feby: 27th 1827.

Dear Sir,

I have just received the papers, which you sent—and your resignation—and will take care to execute your orders, in reference to our committee—Without flattery, I can say to you, that in my own opinion, and in the opinion of many, with whom I have conversed—you have executed your office, *fearlessly*, *faithfully*, and *impartially*, and I assure you, that both you, and your Fair Partner in life, will have my sincere good wishes, for your welfare, wherever, in this changeable world, you may go, or under whatever circumstances, you may be placed—and I, earnestly pray, that, however we may be parted here, we may all reassemble around the throne of Grace in heaven, to spend together, a Blessed Eternity. I remain, in haste, yours truly,

P. Brontè—

In 1831, Patrick tried to help the brother of the Keighley school-master to enter into Orders, but received a rebuff from the Archbishop of York.

Mr. Metcalfe, Schoolmaster—Keighley.

Haworth, June 30th 1831.

Dear Sir,

You will find from the enclosed, that both your brother Mr Anthony Metcalfe, and myself, have met with a disappointment. I have written to you on the subject, as I understand that he would be from home, about this time. Have the goodness to inform him of this matter, at a convenient opportunity=We must, you see, meet with trials, here below—but it is our part to resign to the will of God—and where we cannot comprehend—to worship and adore.

I remain, yours truly P. Brontè.

The "enclosed" was a letter from the Archbishop, posted in Oxford.

The Reverend P. Bronté, Haworth, Bradford. Yorkshire.

Nuneham June 27th 1831.

Rev: Sir—

As you do not mention the circumstances which have occasioned your *disappointment* in the two cases to which you allude in your letter of the 24th, I can only regret the fact *of your disappointment*—my rule of not admitting Literates as candidates for orders, whose age exceeds 30 and who have not complied with the prescribed regulations as to the conduct of their studies, for the 2 *years* immediately previous to their offering themselves for ordination must of course prevent my acceding to your wishes in favor [*sic*] of Mr. Metcalf. I am Revd Sir,

Yrs. faithfully E. Ebor.

In 1834, Patrick, faced with an extended list of Trustees, decided to prevent confusion by allocating duties.

PLATE 17 *St Oswald's, Guiseley*

PLATE 18 *Clough House, Hightown*

PLATE 19 *The Old Bell Chapel,
Thornton*

PLATE 20 *The Parsonage, Market Street,
Thornton*

PLATE 21 *The Manor House, Stanbury*

Written by P. Bronte Haworth.

Haworth Feb 1st 1834.

To the Trustees for the Church Lands of Haworth.

Gentlemen, it is the opinion of many of the Trustees, that a division of labour in collecting the rents, would be the best and most effectual plan, and that consequently there should be four acting Trustees, and not more for each year in rotation. Whilst it is to be understood, that on all occasions of importance the whole of the Trustees, should be convened, and that Mr Joseph Greenwood of Spring Head, would then and on all other occasions, be so good as to attend, since his consent and signature might be wanted for the sale and exchange of lands waterfalls & etc—Should this method be generally agreeable the Trustees are requested to write their names at the bottom of this document, a copy of which will be sent to each Gentleman in order that he may know his years of acting as they occur,

I remain, Gentlemen, Yours & etc, P. Brontè, Minr—

Then follow the names of twelve trustees.

Patrick often wrote to the Heatons of Ponden House, near Stanbury —at that time leading trustees. Ponden House was immortalized by Emily Brontë as "Thrushcross Grange"!

Mr Heaton, Ponden.

Haworth, Jany 20th 1835.

Dear Sir,

There is to be a meeting of the Trustees for the Church Lands— at Stanbury, on Monday the second of February next, at one o'clock, and you are requested to attend—

I remain, Dear Sir, Yours, truly P. Brontè.

Mr Heaton, Ponden, Near Stanbury, Yorkshire.

Haworth, May 11th 1837.

Dear Sir,

There is to be a meeting of the Trustees for the Church Lands—in the vestry on Monday next, at two o'clock in the afternoon, in order to choose new Trustees, and transact other business of importance. I hope you will attend.

Remember me, kindly to Mrs Heaton, and your family, and believe me

Yours truly, P. Brontè

Mrs. Can[n]an, Clitheroe, Lancashire.

Haworth. Octr: 10th 1842.

Dear Madam,

Happening to be at Mr Greenwood's of Spring Head, and one of his hands, being rather weak, he has desired me to write to you on a solemn occasion. Mr Cannan, surgeon, in this place has been rather unwell, for some weeks past, but, for three or four days lately, he became very ill—and this morning at two o'clock he died—His funeral, and its consequent expenses, are now to be thought of—and therefore, as you stood in such close connexion [sic] with him, it was judged proper to acquaint you with the circumstance as soon as possible. I saw him a little before his death, and had some spiritual conversation with him, and after that went to prayer—in which he joined with great earnestness —I trust, that you will be supported, and comforted by the Lord—so that you may have peace here and glory and bliss, forever hereafter— you will, no doubt see the propriety of an early answer to Mr Greenwood—or rather of coming over—to his house, in order to give directions, in regard to the requisite proceedings. Mr Greenwood, and his sons, send their kindest condolence and regards.

I remain, Dear Madam, your obedient servant—P. Bronte

P.S. Excuse great haste and its usual consequences.

William Cannan, aged forty-six, was buried by Patrick on 21st October 1842. He had been the successor to Thomas Andrew, surgeon, who died that year aged fifty and was buried by Patrick on 3rd May.

The next letter is to Mr Rand—formerly of Haworth, then at Staley Bridge, as Master of the National School.

Mr. Rand.

Haworth—June 5th 1845.

Dear Sir,

We must now make up our minds for an occasional wound from the briars and thorns, which everywhere beset our path—and this, whilst it is calculated to wean us off this world, is equally well fitted to point us to the only paradise which is above. I trust that you have not too much to do. You can, I know, do a good deal, and you would be disposed to do more than might be suited to your constitution. But Scripture, and reason, lay upon us no heavier burden than we may conveniently bear— but next to true religion, health is above all things the most desirable— beyond that, we require nothing but convenient food and raiment, the objects of the prophet Agar's prayer. I hope your son and heir [recently born] is doing well. He will now be very interesting. Our school is getting on tolerably well—and we have raised £230—for a peal of new bells!!!... Patrick Brontè.

Through suffering, Patrick had learned to share in the sorrows of others, as the following two letters show. The first is addressed to a parishioner whose family requested anonymity. Here, and in a later letter, their wish is still respected.

Haworth, Augt 1st 1843

Dear Sir,

I have often thought of your case, but never so much as since I last saw you, and consequently I now venture to say to you a few things which I hope you will either receive or excuse. I perceive that your troubles are making some inroads on your spirits and constitution, whilst I know that your life is of great value to your family and neighbours. I am well aware that, as Solomon says, "The heart knoweth its own bitterness, and a stranger doth not intermeddle with its joy; but at the same time, those who stand aloof are often better fitted for judging of our own affairs than we are, owing to their judgment being more free to come to just and impartial conclusions. Hence I would say to you, as an old neighbour and friend, settle if you can your affairs with a certain personage, as soon as you possibly may do, without law. It would be far better to do this at the loss of two or three hundred pounds, than to spend as many thousands with the lawyers and be nothing better.

Remember Dr. Swift's saying respecting two that were about to go to law and had some money, when the letter of one of the opposing attorneys was opened—

> There are two woodcocks in the west,
> They are well feather'd in their nest,
> Take this advice, my brother,
> Pluck you the one and I will pluck the other.

Send for this weak man, who has got into the snares of those who are cunning and designing. Speak to him Scripturally and kindly. Make him sensible of his danger and folly, and endeavour to persuade him to come to Scriptural and just terms.

Had you taken my advice at first, things would not have gone so far. But what is passed cannot be recalled, and we can now only "redeem the time". Remember that, however it may be, you ought, according to the Word of God, to possess your soul in patience and not to grieve as those "without hope"—and to receive by faith the gracious promise that "all things work together for good to those who love God"—

I remain, dear Sir, Yours very respectfully and truly, P. Bronte.

The next letter, written in 1844 refers to Enoch Thomas, one of Patrick's churchwardens, who was suffering from melancholia. In the 1846 voting register for Haworth, his address is given as the Black Bull Hotel, and his property included freehold houses in West Lane.

George Taylor, Esq. Stanbury.   Haworth, Feby, 29th 1844.

My Dear Sir,
     I doubt not, you have heard of Mr. Enoch Thomas's, *very severe* and great affliction, one of the greatest that can fall to our human nature—In consequence of this, I requested him to come up here, this morning, and when he came, I gave him the most consolatory advice, within my power—But what can console a man, under his circumstances?—I am aware, that you have kindly sent for him, and given him good advice, but I wish you, to have a tea party, soon, and to invite him among, the number of the guests; His mind, which is, in a very disordered state should be diverted, as much as possible, from his present way of thinking—He is a good, well-meaning, and honest man; and, in many respects, unfit, for his present arduous, situation—yet still, his friends, ought to do for him, all that lies, within their power—I have understood, that your son, and heir has met with an accident—for this, I am very sorry, and as soon as the snow goes away, I shall, do myself the pleasure, of seeing how you all, are—as my eyes, are very weak, I cannot, very well, go out whilst the snow, is on the ground—With my kind respects, to you, Miss Parrot, and your Family, I remain, my dear Sir,
         Yours, most respectfully and truly, P. Brontè.

To the Revd W. Cartman, Schoolhouse—Skipton.
       Haworth, Nr. Keighley Jany: 27th 1854.
My Dear Sir,
     I have safely received the Ice apparatus, which fits me admirably, and for which, I sincerely thank you—and which I value, as much for the sake of the doner, as its own intrinsic worth—It will serve as another prop to old age—Charlotte joins me in very kind regards,
         Yours, very sincerely and truly, P. Brontè.

This gift of "ice-prods"—square pieces of metal with spikes, to be strapped to the heels of his boots in frosty weather—was frequently used by Patrick.

The Revd James Cooper, Bradford, Yorkshire.
       "Haworth" Nr. Keighley. Feby: 21st 1854.
Revd, and Dear Sir,
     We are much obliged by your kind invitation to meet the Deputation from that Excellent Institution, the Church Pastoral Aid Society—but

advanced age, and its usual consequences, have laid me under the necessity of declining for several years to go far from home, so that I shall not have the pleasure of going to Bradford, on the interesting occasion you mention.

I remain, Rev^d and dear Sir, yours, very respectfully, P. Brontë.

At last the fame of his children has swept across the land, and Patrick now follows their practice of using the diaeresis.

Next a letter to the five Heaton brothers of Ponden, postmarked Haworth and Keighley, at the time of the Crimean War.

Messrs. Heaton, Ponden, Stanbury, Keighley.

Gentlemen. Decr 13—1854

You are requested to attend a meeting to be held in the Haworth National School on *Saturday next* at 3.0 p.m. to take into consideration the best means of raising a general subscription in this Township in aid of the Patriotic Fund—

yrs. truly P. Brontë.

Next a letter to Sir Joseph Paxton, showing that at the age of eighty-one the fire is not extinguished in Patrick Brontë, and giving an answer to the false accusation that Patrick attempted to profit from Charlotte's fame.

Sir Joseph Paxton, Bart. Hardwick Hall, Chesterfield.

Sir, Haworth, Nr Keighley. January 16th, 1858.

Your letter, which I have received this morning, gives both to Mr Nicholls and me, great uneasiness. It would seem that application has been made to the Duke of Devonshire, for money to aid the subscription in reference to the expense of apparatus for heating our church and schools. This has been done without our knowledge, and most assuredly, had we known it, would have met with our strongest opposition. We have no claim on the Duke. His Grace honour'd us with a visit, in token of his respect for the memory of the dead [the famous Brontë sisters], and his liberality and munificence are well and widely known ; and the mercenary, taking an unfair advantage of these circumstances, have taken a step which both Mr Nicholls and I utterly regret and condemn. In answer to your query, I may say, that the whole expense for both the schools and church, is about one hundred pounds, and that, after what has been and may be subscribed, there may fifty pounds remain as a debt, but this may, and ought to be raised by the inhabitants in the next year after the depression in trade shall, it is hoped, have passed away. I have written to His Grace on the subject.

I remain, Sir, your obedient servant, P. Brontë

Dr. W. Law, Binridden [Ben Rhydding], Ilkley.

Haworth Nr. Keighley July 27th 1858.

Dear Sir,

Greenwood Wood, of this parish, who has formerly been under your care, and been greatly benefited by it, is earnestly desirous of your advice and aid, and wishes to know, whether you have a vacancy for him—He is labouring under the sad effects of indigestion and is very reduced, and feeble—His employment, as a Tailor, being ill suited, to his condition. An early answer, will much oblige,

Yours very respectfully P. Brontë Incumbent of Haworth.

The next letter is addressed to a member of the big mill-owning family of Haworth.

Mr. Merrall, Springhead.

Haworth, March 21st 1859

Dear Sir,

You will greatly oblige me if you will continue to be my Church-warden for the ensuing year.

Mr. Nicholls joins me in kind regards to you, and Mrs Merrall—

I remain yours, truly P. Bronte.

The Revd Welbury Mitton, Bradford, Yorkshire.

Haworth, Nr. Keighley, July 8th 1859.

Revd and Dear Sir,

I have heard, that you are so obliging, as sometimes, to preach for Charitable Institutions—I therefore, venture to request that you will be so kind, as to preach for us, on Sunday the twenty fourth Inst, a sermon in the afternoon, and another in the Evening—in behalf of our Sunday School—the Service in the afternoon will begin at a quarter past two o'clock and in the evening at six. An early answer will oblige,

Yours very faithfully, P. Brontë.

Next, a testimonial for the eldest son of John Greenwood, the Haworth stationer.

Haworth, July 13th 1859.

Richard Greenwood, the bearer hereof, is a young man, the son of respectable parents, and is a native of my Chaperly [sic]; He is moral, and steady, and well qualified, for performing his duty, in the line of life which he has chosen [dentist]—

P. Brontë, A.B. Incumbent.

To complete the present group of letters is another testimonial—

Haworth Oct: 20th 1860.

To whom it may concern. We the undersigned do hereby certify that [Mr] Squire Thornton the bearer hereof, is of honest, steady, sober and industrious habits, sufficiently respectable in his station in life, and in our humble opinion is a fit and proper person for a situation as Railway Porter—

P. Brontë A.B. Incumbent of Haworth.
A. B. Nicholls A.B. Curate.

It can be seen from these documents and letters, that if Mrs Gaskell was correct in seeing Patrick as a man chained to his chair in the parsonage parlour, he could only just have sat down, in his old age, after years of unceasing and unflagging activity in his parish.

As was customary, Patrick, as the minister, was frequently called upon to contribute a page of "wisdom" to the albums of young women in Haworth. One such request resulted in:

To Miss Thomas, Haworth, near Bradford, Yorkshire. July 28th 1837.

> Dear Madam trust not to thy youth,
> For many years to come,
> To Him alone, the God of truth,
> Is known their final sum.
> With time-redeeming skill improve
> The moment, as it flies—
> And let it be in faith and love,
> And *still be timely wise*.
> As wise physicians well can state,
> An antidote is better,
> Than remedies applied too late ;
> They're oft a mere dead letter.
> Trust not to worldly smiles, though bland,
> They often lead to ruin,
> And those, who here will take their stand,
> Shall work their own undoing.
> But all who look upon this Globe,
> As full of sin and death,
> And clothe themselves in Christ's pure robe,
> When they resign their breath,

Shall rise on Angel wings above
The lucid starry sky,
To reign with Him the God of love,
Where joys shall never die.

These few lines I have composed hastily, and off hand—but they may serve as a kind memento.

P. Brontè, A.B.
Incumbent of Haworth, near Bradford, Yorkshire.

On the opposite page are written some lines by Charlotte.

After the death of Weightman, Patrick had a quick succession of curates: the Rev. James William Smith (graduated at Trinity College, Dublin) from the end of 1842 until September 1844; Joseph Brett Grant from September 1844 until his appointment at Oxenhope in 1845; and, in May 1845, there came the Rev. Arthur Bell Nicholls. In addition, in 1847, whilst Nicholls was visiting his native Ireland, the Rev. James Stuart Cranmer, D.D.—then Master of the grammar school—assisted Patrick as temporary curate. Of Grant, something has already been written; of Nicholls, and another curate named De Renzy, there will be mention later; a quick glance, however, at James Smith. The story that he and Patrick caroused together has long been refuted. Charlotte, in her misery over Monsieur Heger, had, alas, given the rumour its birth by once expressing her concern for her father as a reason for the hurried exit from Brussels. Indeed Patrick disliked Smith intensely and was glad when he was appointed curate at Keighley. Charlotte writes to Ellen Nussey in July 1844: ". . . Papa has two or three times expressed a fear that Mr Smith paid you too much attention . . . he keeps saying that I am to write to you and dissuade you from thinking of him. I never saw papa make himself so uneasy about a thing of the kind before; he is usually very sarcastic on such subjects. . . ." Friend Smith had been enquiring if Ellen had money!

Add to all this a few authentic pictures of "t'parson on the hill" and Patrick's record as incumbent of Haworth stands—can it be doubted how it will be judged? He was president of Haworth Temperance Society of which, ironically, his son Branwell was secretary in 1834 and 1835.

On 2nd September 1833, the "Three Graces" Lodge of Freemasons having rented a room (at £4 per annum) in Lodge Street, Haworth, decided to hold a public procession to mark the occasion. At the church, Patrick preached a sermon at midday for the Masons, preparatory to their dinner. His fee was 10s. John Brown, the sexton, was the Worshipful Master and on 1st February 1836, Branwell was proposed as a candidate in the Lodge, aged only nineteen. By 25th April of that year, he had become a full member.

The first Masonic meeting at the new room in Lodge Street was held on 23rd September 1833, nearly three years before Branwell joined the Lodge. Thus, although the dinner at the Annual Festival of St John (on or near 27th December) continued for a time to take place at the Black Bull, it is not true, as often stated, that Branwell attended Masonic meetings there. Branwell's last attendance at the Lodge was on 26th December 1842.

Charlotte has given the picture, in one of her letters, of the parish clerk sitting in the parsonage kitchen making up his accounts; and John Greenwood, the Haworth stationer (and most kindly of friends to the Brontës), has left many pictures of them in his diary. His daughter, Mrs Jane Ellen Widdop, long recalled Patrick Brontë calling each Friday, when she was a little girl, and commissioning her to take some tripe up to the parsonage. There, she was always rewarded with a slice of bread and butter, generously spread with jam—then considered a great luxury.

Another tale, so typical of Patrick's tolerance and broad-mindedness in religious matters of the chapelry, was told by Mr J. F. Greenwood of Haworth. His uncle (a Baptist) was invited by Patrick to become a churchwarden, and replied that that was not possible as he was a Nonconformist. Patrick's answer was, "that did not matter—he wanted him, as a personal friend, to help in some useful parish works, one of which was the restoration of the tower of the church". William Greenwood accepted the position with gratitude. In 1848—when Anne was dying—influenza swept Haworth, causing untold distress. In forceful language Patrick represented the insanitary state of Haworth to the local authorities and obtained a recommendation that means be set on foot for obtaining a water-supply to each house, instead of every bucketful having to be carried up Kirkgate or over from Sowdens. As shown in a later chapter he fought hard for the implementation of this decision, but was for a long time "baffled by the ratepayers". In the *Leeds Intelligencer* for 6th May 1830, Patrick made an enlightened, passionate plea for the revision of the too "bloody" English criminal code. In Haworth he organized a petition wherein the "Dissenting and Methodist" ministers (Patrick's distinction) supported him with "cheerful alacrity"—not one of the 4,000 inhabitants objecting. Patrick praises the Quakers, whose humanity should be imitated. He claimed that the savage laws encouraged rather than reduced crime, "for not a few prefer to let malefactors go free rather than exact the dire penalties provided for their crimes". Two comments of Patrick's, so typical of his honest outspokenness, are worth recalling. Charlotte tells Ellen Nussey in April 1852 of his reaction to the unusually severe diet Mr and Mrs Joe Taylor are giving their sick infant. ". . . he said if that child died, its parents ought to be tried for infanticide! . . ." Mrs Edith Farrar of Salisbury recalled, "My father, Edwin Feather, although a younger man than the Rev. Patrick Brontë, was a close friend of his, and the latter was a frequent visitor to our home, and he would often (after taking his customary tot of whisky) quote the following: "It is not what goeth in but what cometh out that defileth man."

Another villager recalled Patrick's attending concerts in the village —"taking with him the members of his family. It was his invariable practice—no matter what the occasion—to leave for home at nine o'clock. . . . Old Brontë was passionately fond of Oratorio, and at least one of Handel's sublime works was given at the church . . . he lent newspapers to Mr. Winterbotham—the Baptist Minister." Another memory of his was of calling as a lad at the parsonage parlour to do some repairs: "There old Brontë, in accordance with his wont, was sitting in a plain, uncushioned chair, upright as a soldier." Noticing the youth's interest in the pictures on the wall, Patrick took him round, explaining the various subjects: "engravings of Martin's once-celebrated allegorical paintings, 'The Plains of Heaven', 'The Last Judgment', etc."

It has been recorded, not by Dissenters, but by members of his own congregation, how in old age, when Nicholls was his permanent curate, Patrick on a Sunday evening would go along West Lane to the Wesleyan Chapel to worship. Perhaps as he knelt there, under the memorial tablet to William Grimshaw, Patrick remembered Thomas Tighe with his library, so lacking in martial exploits; Henry Martyn's brief life of sacrifice; Vicar Crosse emptying his pockets to beggars in the Bradford streets; and above all, that old preacher who came to the Irish lanes all those long years ago. In the new Puseyite age, such unorthodoxy could not be considered as treachery by the true Evangelical.

There is no finer picture of Patrick Brontë with which to end this summary of his life as the incumbent of Haworth than the one given by Ellen Nussey to William Scruton, when she recalled an occasion long remembered in Haworth. There was held a missionary meeting of the Wesleyans, to which ministers of all denominations were invited. "Mr Brontë, then old and blind, accepted the invitation, and he entered the large Wesleyan Chapel leaning on Charlotte's arm." Patrick was led on to the platform, "where, with outstretched arms, he repeated in tremulous accents and amid breathless silence, the short but beautiful Psalm beginning, 'Behold, how good and how pleasant it is for brethren to dwell together in unity'! Having done this, and without adding a word of his own, he was taken back to his daughter, who led him gently home."

The assembly watched the tall erect figure of the Rev. Patrick Brontë as he was guided down the chapel, this elderly man, for the second time temporarily deprived of his sight, now helped by his only surviving child. There were tears in many eyes. Then the great doors of the chapel clanged behind them and he was gone.

CHAPTER 19

"Sydney"

To DEVOTE a chapter, however short, to a critique of Patrick's work as an author may seem unjustifiable. His writing was not in any way distinguished, for all the joy he gained in wielding the pen. There is nothing whatever of literary value. Yet to know a man one must study what he does, what he says *and* what he commits to paper. Therefore a quick glance should be taken at those of his works not yet touched upon. As mentioned, in December 1810, Patrick set out fully in the *Leeds Mercury* the detailed story of William Nowell, in whose defence he had been actively engaged. At this time he used the pseudonym "Sydney", and we shall complete our survey of the writings of Patrick Brontë under this title. Before dealing with his best work, *The Maid of Killarney*, mention must be made of his political treatise of 1835, his poem on Halley's Comet, of the same year, a treatise on baptism, written in 1836, and a short hymn composed for the children of Haworth in 1849.

"The Signs of the Times; or A Familiar Treatise on some Political Indications in the year 1835—By P. Bronte, A.B., Incumbent of Haworth, near Bradford, Yorkshire", was a twenty-four page pamphlet, with a blue paper cover, and cost 6d. It was printed in Keighley by R. Aked, Bookseller, of Low Street, and sold at 19, Chancery Lane, London, by W. Crofts, "and all Booksellers". The treatise is prefaced with the text, "Can ye not discern the signs of the times? Matthew, xvi 3", and is addressed to the "Courteous Reader". Patrick commences by describing the growing danger to the established religions; the fashion is to denounce them all as "anti-scriptural, and to talk much about the all-sufficiency of the voluntary principle". He goes on to deplore this new trend.

"What would any reasonable man think of a king or government that would contrive with much study and labour, a code of laws, and enforce their execution at the public expense, and after all, say to the nation,—We leave all the concerns of immortal souls and the great cause and honour of God to the voluntary principle. We will make no certain religious provision for those who either cannot, or will not, provide in this way for themselves. They may go to any place of worship, or no place of worship, as they please. A good father lays down a system of religious instruction for his children, and so does a good master for his servants; but we, the guardians of the state, and the commonwealth, devise no plan, and execute no plan of spiritual edification for you; we cannot devise a system that will please you all, and therefore, we will not call upon you all to support any system of religion. Think, plan, and execute for yourselves, or, if it please you better, neglect all these concerns entirely and for ever. However shallow and inconclusive this mode of argumentation may seem, yet all the arguments used against an established religion, when divested of rhetorical attire, come to the same conclusion. [Patrick concludes that the best plan is for every government to establish] that religion which they deem to be the most agreeable to Scripture, and the best adapted to the wants of the community; taking, at the same time, due care that all religions are tolerated, and that there is full liberty of conscience. Had that mighty hierarchy which domineered for ages over the bodies, as well as the minds, of men, only maintained its establishment, whilst it allowed liberty of conscience, as long as the various governments of Europe coincided, their subjects would have had no just grounds of complaint. But where racks and wheels and fire were employed to extort from the lips of the sufferer, assent to doctrines which his judgment rejected, and his heart abhored, then his complaints were the voice of reason and conscience, uttered against acts of injustice, cruelty, and oppression. I am not charging the Church of Rome, alone, with the foul and loathsome crime of persecution, I know, alas! and the world knows full well to its cost, that, for not performing an impossibility, for not believing what their reason, as well as their conscience, necessarily contradicted, and could not by any possibility receive, thousands and hundreds of thousands of men and women were doomed by the gloomy superstitions and unrelenting cruelty of that church, to languish in dungeons, and perish under horrid devices, whilst nature, in her last agony, was denied every earthly source of consolation, and overwhelmed with every species of mockery and insult. But to the utter disgrace of our common nature, I must in candour confess, that the impartial history of the last five centuries presents to our view, Churchmen, Presbyterians, and Independents, all persecuting in their turn. . . ."

Patrick then notes a great improvement, save for three or four melancholy exceptions where Roman Catholic nations have failed to relax "in their intolerant deeds of blood. . .". He then turns to the thorny question of finance within the Church.

"They tell you, that as the property of the Protestant Establishment was wrested from the Church of Rome, it is but fair to lay violent hands on that property ; they declare, that what an Act of Parliament has given, an Act of Parliament may take away ; they maintain, that where churches are not well attended by a superstitious population, those churches should be desecrated, their altars torn down, and their property confiscated. These are, indeed, bold pretensions, so many sure proofs that intellect has marched so fast, and so far beyond true religion, that it has fairly distanced it, and lost sight of it altogether. I never attempted to justify the spoliation of the Church of Rome ; this act was unscriptural, and worthy of Catholic Henry the Eighth, who mainly performed it. But his crimes, and the crimes of some who resembled him, cannot be laid to the charge of William of glorious memory, and his protestant successors on the throne of Britain. . . . I have never been able to discover, that because an orthodox church was but ill attended by a superstitious people, averse to its doctrines, that could be urged as a sufficient reason why it should be pulled down, especially in places where the inhabitants are numerous. The greater their mental darkness, the greater is their need of gospel light, and the more urgent we should be to enlighten that gloom. No one thinks of removing a missionary station, because the natives around are backward in their attendance for a season, and given up to the destructive pursuits of idolatry. . . .

"I am far from saying, that our excellent Establishment is perfect. Time may have wasted or worn some of its parts . . . the variations in the value of property may have occasioned disproportionate inequality of recompense. Hence reform, but not destruction, is wanted, and the sooner this reform is effected, by wise and good heads, the better. But let not an unholy, selfish, motley coalition of enemies do this great work. Their professions would be insincere, their policy hollow and tortuous, and their end bad. But what shall we say of the voluntary principle ? Man, in a state of graceless nature, has a perverse will ; but if he should be left to the operation of that will, for the most part he would, as he has ever done, think about any thing rather than building churches or chapels. He would build and frequent houses of lucre or licentiousness ; and they would be the places of his dearest and most frequent resort. Houses for religious worship would generally be found in the last pages of the books of his reckoning. . . . There is another sign of the times. I refer to the manifest indications of a growing conviction that, in our generation, we are wiser than our forefathers. Hence we hear of the march of intellect, the wisdom of the nineteenth century, and are often reminded, that the schoolmaster is abroad . . . some discoveries, of modern date, have certainly led to the acquisition of knowledge; such are the properties of the magnetic needle and the telescope,—the circulation of the blood,—the composition and force of gun-powder,—the nature of electricity,—and the power and application of steam. Not so long as the names of Wellington, Bonaparte, Marlborough, Nelson, Newton, Milton, Burke, Pitt, Fox, and many others, shall be remembered, shall it ever be denied that modern times have not had a large share of illustrious heroes, philosophers, poets, and orators. But let us not suffer our eyes to be dazzled and blinded by the closer view of these luminaries. Let us look back nearly two or three thousand years into time, and we shall discover stars of the first magnitude, which, though remote, still shine with matchless splendour. If we turn to the Sacred Volume, where shall we find a legislator or an historian, who, for brevity and perspicuity, pathos and elegant sublimity, can bear a comparison with Moses? Many of the Psalms are the most sublimely simple of all pastorals. The books of Job and of Isaiah are sublime in the extreme, and the Epistles of Paul, for colloquial elegance and force of argument, have no equal. And if we come to uninspired men, we shall find that no poets ever equalled Homer and Virgil : no orators, Demosthenes and Cicero ; no generals, Alexander, Caesar, and Hannibal ; no painters, Apelles ; no philosophers, Aristotle and Socrates ; and no physicians, Galen and Hippocrates. And that the sculptors of the ancients left all the modern sculptors far behind, the historical accounts of their works, and the fragments which still remain, put beyond a doubt. The art of painting elegantly and durably on glass, and superlative skill in architecture, are in the wane, as may be fully demonstrated from history, and the astonishing ruins yet to be seen in Greece and Rome, and various other parts of the world. These architectural relics of antiquity, even in their mutilated state, produce a simple, grand, and overwhelming effect, and totally eclipse the puerile efforts of modern times. And when we consider the vigour, sublimity, comprehensiveness, and applicability of the Greek and Roman languages, we shall have no difficulty in discovering that those who invented and needed them, in their daily intercourse with each other, excelled most of the moderns, as far in their mode of thinking, as they did in their manner of speaking and writing. What real grounds have we then for our self-complacency ? . . ."

He continues to enlarge his theme, giving printing as the great modern boon, ". . . but in ancient times, whilst the rivers of knowledge ran in narrower channels, they, also, frequently were deeper, and more rapid and powerful. Greater numbers of the present, than of the former, generation know a little, but fewer know much . . . where but little learning, and much pride, and no religion, enter into the human heart, the necessary consequence will be, daring speculation, impatience of control, a restless spirit of innovation, and a desire of change. 'Before honour there is humility ; and after pride cometh a fall'. . . ." If the moors gave the Brontës their love of beauty and freedom and Haworth their love of independence, can it be doubted, after reading the foregoing lines, that their craving thirst for knowledge came uniquely from their father ? Patrick ends his treatise with an appeal for reason and calmness at election time: ". . . should the end of all our efforts be confined to party, and limited by time and the grave, we may gratify our pride, or foster our vanity, and sell our eternal interest for the sake of perishable gain ; but if breaking through the partialities of our nature, by faith, we advocate for conscience' sake alone, the cause which we deem best . . . God, in his infinite mercy, will, for his Son's sake, . . . cause our darkness to disperse, and our light to shine brighter and brighter till the perfect day. . . ."

Patrick was not always so lenient with Roman Catholics, as we have seen. Years later he rejoiced to his friend the Rev. James Cheadle, Vicar of Bingley, at the evidence of decline in the popish influence, "that ghastly Incubus of the human mind" which formerly held "but slippery footing in this our highly favoured Island".

However, in three letters to the *Leeds Intelligencer* (15th and 29th January, and 5th February 1829) on the question of Catholic emancipation he adopts a moderate view, although he had "observed Roman Catholic domination in his native country for twenty years".

Amongst Patrick's many "fugitive pieces" is his poem "On Halley's Comet in 1835", which was signed and dated: "P. Bronte—Haworth, Oct 20th, 1835." It was later published by Abraham Holroyd in *The Bradfordian*, 1861. This short poem is addressed to the Comet, and tells of the wickedness that abounds on earth, of the sins that have been committed since its last visitation, and how, before it next returns, most of the existing wickedness of the world will have perished. It is a stainless planet: "The Mighty God himself alone—Can reign thy speed, and guide thee on." Here are a few lines from the poem :

> Full seventy years have pass'd away
> Since last we saw you, fresh and gay . . .
> Vast changes in this world have been,
> Since by this world you last were seen :
> The child, who clapped his hands with joy,
> And hailed thee as a shining toy,
> Has pass'd, long since, that dusky bourne,
> From whence no travellers return ;

PLATE 22 *Samuel Redhead*

PLATE 23   *William Grimshaw*   PLATE 24   *Mary Burder in later life*

PLATE 25   *Interior of Old Haworth Church, showing the pulpit used by the*
Wesleys, Whitefield, Newton, Grimshaw and Patrick Brontë

Or sinking now in feeble age,
Surveys thee, as a hoary sage . . .
Or if the sun, as Newton says
Still issues forth substantial rays,
Emitting from his body bright,
Exhausting sparks of rapid light—
To give him back each spark and ray,
Well gather'd, on thy airy way;
Lest he should sink in wrinkled years,
And leave in night the rolling spheres,
Say, dost thou, then, all things that burn,
Give to the Sun in thy return ?
And thus maintain his shining face
In all the pride of youthful grace ?
If so, thou art less selfish far,
Than many another shining star—
Less selfish, far, than those below,
Who gaze upon thy brilliant glow. . . .

In 1836, Patrick had printed by R. Aked of Keighley "A Brief Treatise on the Best Time and Mode of Baptism—Chiefly in Answer to a tract of Peter Pontifex, alias the Rev. M. S—, Baptist Minister. By P. Bronte, A.B. Incumbent of Haworth, Yorkshire." There were twenty-four pages and the cost was 3d. He sent a copy to William Morgan inscribed over the title, "To the Revd Wm. Morgan, with the Author's kindest regards". Peter Pontifex, whom he wished to answer on the question of baptism, was the Rev. Moses Saunders, the first minister of the Hall Green Strict Baptist Church, Haworth, which had been opened at the top of Bridgehouse Lane in 1824. It was known amongst the Baptists as "the Second Baptist Church", the older Church being along West Lane where, in 1836, the minister was the Rev. W. Winterbotham.

"My friend, Peter Pontifex, I am glad to see you once more. But ere I proceed much farther, I must correct a mistake, of which I was guilty in my first publication, entitled 'Paul Telltruth'." Patrick expresses regret that he had imagined that "Peter Pontifex" was both Saunders and Winterbotham and he tenders his apology to the latter: ". . . And now that I know the *real Peter Pontifex*, I shall lay the burthen on the shoulders which ought to bear it. You talk, my friend Peter, of *windows* of glass, but, were I like you, to be regardless of harsh expressions and allusions, I should have need only to go back from the present time, to the era of L[or]d M[orpe]th's appearance at Haworth,

24

to give *you* a *house* of glass. But this I wish to avoid. You were the first to throw stones. . . ."

There is a good deal of banter over the use of organs and musical instruments in churches and chapels, and then he comes a trifle nearer to the core of the matter : the mode of baptism.

". . . You appear, my dear Peter, to be very angry at my criticism ; and then have recourse to Holy Writ, in order to prove that it is right and lawful to say, that a child has issued from the press ! Can it be wondered at, after this, that you should, by scriptural quotations, demonstrate that infant baptism is wrong ; and that *total immersion* is the only legitimate mode. I see you are very sore about Horace, and that you labour as hard as his mountains did, when they were pregnant only with a mouse. Why not confess the truth at once, and have done with it. I have not, to my knowledge, quoted your Latin unfairly. A typographical error was made in mine. There is an *i* where there should have been an *e*. Oh ! had you but seen this, what a noble opportunity it would have afforded you of displaying your critical acumen; since we hear you just afterwards, in one of your transformations, crow loudly, because the printer happened to leave out a letter in the word Japheth ! Ah ! my friend Peter, this is *small* criticism indeed ! No one that knew anything about the feet and measure of Latin versification, would have floundered and blundered as you did, in quoting even from *memory*. An examination in Homer and Horace, previously to the ordination of clergymen, seems to fill you with horror. I can tell you, that before ordination, the candidate is not only examined in the learned languages, but also in Scripture and church history, and on such various points of doctrine, as the bishop and chaplain may deem expedient.

"Such strictures as yours, have often enabled me to see into some of the reasons why you wished the two Universities to be opened. One week in any one of them would teach you more humility and self-abasement than you are likely to learn, in twenty years, under your present circumstances. You truly say, that 'a *little* learning is, indeed, a dangerous thing'. My friend Peter observes, that the propriety of infant baptism is not to be found in the Word of God ! Should my friend Peter intend to say, that it is no-where said in Scripture, 'Thou shalt baptize infants', I perfectly agree with him. But should he mean to assert that infant baptism is anti-scriptural, that it is any where *expressly forbidden*, and no-where *understood*, I totally disagree with him. Our friends, the Baptists, very properly admit females to the communion table, as Pedobaptists do. But I ask Peter whether he can produce in all the Scriptures one direct command for this ? I am fully confident that he cannot . . . I *sincerely* believe, that females are entitled to sit down at the Lord's table, and he, I know, does the same; but at the same time, after due reading, on both sides of the subject, I *aver*, that he has *no better* scriptural authority for this *his* practice, than we have for *infant baptism*. Let him prove the contrary if he can. . . . Peter, in a learned note, refers to the mode of servants in washing clothes, in order to prove his point; but I can tell him, that a servant of mine [Tabby] is in such *high dudgeon*, at her name appearing *in print*, that I do believe if she should unfortunately meet him with a pail of water in her hand, he might be satisfied, by personal knowledge and experience, that a man *might be thoroughly washed* by sprinkling or *pouring*. I should be very sorry to see my friend Peter baptised a second time in this manner; therefore, in all neighbourly and fraternal kindness, I give him *timely warning*. The maid servants, in general, are, I understand, greatly exasperated against him; as they stoutly maintain, that in washing their cups and pots, they but seldom or never *dip* them; but on the contrary, *dip* the *towel*, and then rub them with it after, after it has been thoroughly wetted. My friend Peter, suffer me just to remind thee, that if thou dost quarrel with thy fellow men, thy case may be hazardous; but if a contest arises between thee and the ladies, thou wilt be placed beyond the utmost confines of hope; so that all thy priestly dignity will not save thee from *utter ruin.* . . ."

There is much more of this good-natured and humorous bantering before a serious tone is adopted and the question of infant baptism examined in detail. ". . . I am still of opinion that it is scriptural and right to baptize infants, or if you like it better, to sprinkle, but that if, through the criminal neglect of the parents, or the unsoundness of their doctrinal views, children should die, without the rite of baptism, by sprinkling or otherwise, the infinitely merciful Saviour, who loved them, and kissed and blessed them, will not shut them out of his heavenly kingdom. . . ."

There follows a long argument that the Greek word *baptizo* means to wash by sprinkling and that it is better to baptize a person whilst yet a child, as an insurance against their dying unchristened. Then Patrick attacks the Baptist method of complete immersion. ". . . I will give you the opinion of your favourite, the Rev. Daniel Isaac . . . you will find that he writes in much stronger terms than I did, and has not at all *minced the matter*. He observes, 'There is neither command nor example for immersing people with their clothes on. If immersion be the mode, the only legal mode of administration, it cannot be an immaterial circumstance whether the candidate be clothed or naked: it is a question of the utmost importance to morals . . . all the religious immersions of the Jews were performed in a state of nudity . . . now, we think it indecent, though the thoughts of the parties may be quite pure, for a man to grasp a woman, especially when both are young, raise her off her feet, bend her body backward, and set her on her feet again, whether it be done in the water, or out of it ; and if the man does not do all this, he does not baptize her . . . one thing is quite certain, that there is no authority whatever, in the Bible, for performing religious immersions, with the body clothed'. Now, Peter Pontifex, what do you think of this passage ; it is not mine, but another's. Has the Rev. Daniel Isaac a polluted mind ? If he has, I can assure you, that in this United Kingdom of Great Britain and Ireland, there are more than ten millions of minds polluted. . . ."

Then follow some most amusing references to the Irish, with Patrick assuming a "mock pride" for his race. ". . . You break some of your jokes on Irishmen. Do you not know, that an Irishman is your lord and master ? Are you not under the King's ministry ? And are they not under Mr. O'Connell, an Irishman ? And do not you or your friends pay to him a yearly tribute under the title of *rent* ? And is not the Duke of Wellington, the most famous, and the greatest of living heroes, an Irishman ? And dare you, or your adherents, take one political step of importance without trembling, lest it should not meet the approbation of your allies in Ireland ? Then as an Irishman might say to you, refrain from your *balderdash* at once, and candidly own your inferiority. . . . I have been able to number some of my best friends amongst Dissenters ; yea, even amongst *Baptists*. One I had in Bradford, who is now gone to a better world [not Robinson Pool] : two, I had in Haworth, who are in heaven ; and one is still living, and is still connected with me in my secular concerns, and who faithfully does his duty ; and there are also others, to whom I need not refer. For do I imagine that *any* liberal minded Dissenter will think the worse of me, for defending myself, when I am rudely attacked. . . ." Having explained that Peter Pontifex had thrown the first stone and that "before I ever wrote *one* sentence in reference to my dissenting brethren, they had held their public meetings in Manchester, Leeds, Bradford, and other towns, and openly harangued, and wrote against that church, of which I am an unworthy but conscientious member. . .". Patrick asserts ". . . that I wish to live in peace, and to be on good terms with all my ministerial brethren, of *every* denomination, and to co-operate with them in every good work of charity. . .".

This answering blast to the Rev. Moses Saunders is followed by "a solemn address to the Inhabitants of Haworth", a simple précis of the treatise. It is addressed to "My Dear Friends" and concludes, "With real kindness, I remain, yours truly, P. Bronte." The booklet ends with "a few concluding remarks", signed "P. B."

As shown in the previous chapter Patrick and Moses Saunders worked closely together for the village good on the committee named the Haworth Board of Health.

Patrick had also greatly admired the Rev. Miles Oddy, Baptist minister along West Lane from 1785 to 1831. On the latter's death in March 1841, Patrick composed the lines on his slab tombstone in the Baptist chapel yard, after a plea by John Brown (in his capacity as stone mason) to make it lengthy, as he would have it to cut!

> Firm in the Faith, he heavenward held his way,
> Unchecked by fell relapse, or dull delay.
> In trials keen, he shrank not from the rod,
> He owned the Father in the chastening God;
> And when a ray of joy divinely shone,
> He gave the praise to God, and God alone.
> In friendship firm and true, to none a foe,
> He had that calm, which bad men never know.
> The Cross of Christ, was aye, his glowing theme,
> Illumin'd by the spirit's heavenly beam;
> And as he preached he liv'd and shew'd the road,
> That leads to peace on earth, and joy with God.
> Then, reader, think, believe, repent, and pray;
> That, so, through Grace Divine, on the Last Day,
> You may triumphant, wear a Crown of Gold,
> When Christ shall all the Deity unfold;
> Whilst countless saints and angels loudly raise
> Their heavenly notes of wonder, love, and praise.

Yet "Peter Pontifex" had some sly digs at Patrick also. In his "Baptism Without Controversy", also printed by Aked in 1836, he mentions the forming of the counter-attack against his beliefs by the churchmen. ". . . Some naughty people have said that the embryo was formed at Haworth, on Easter-Monday last, 1836. It may not be generally known, but it is nevertheless a fact, that the worthy Vicar of Bradford [Henry Heap] visits his Haworth parishioners every Easter-Monday, on some business connected with *Easter-Dues*, *& etc*, and preaches a sermon in the church. On that occasion it is said that the Vicar and another clergyman of pugnacious celebrity [Patrick] 'dined together', in company with a few others of somewhat dubious fame. After dinner, under a certain kind of inspiration, while the *bottle* went round, a consultation was held among the chiefs of the party respecting what was to be done to prevent the increase of the Baptists in Haworth, for they were making great advances.

"One said he would *drive* them out ; another observed it would require *spirit* to set about it ; a third vowed he would thrash them till his *green* stick became dry before they should go on as they had lately done ; a fourth said he was afraid it would require a *stronger antidote* than they could *prescribe* to put a stop to the prevailing epidemic. All however concurred in the opinion that some old thing, or some new thing, should be sent to the press without delay. Some say that a certain *Clericus*, of newspaper renown, who has lately been studying too closely "the Signs of the Times", bravely offered, in true Hibernian style, to draw his sword and vanquish the foe. It was at once agreed that he should lead the van. . . . A subscription was forthwith made to defray the cost of publication. In a short time a manuscript was produced, but it was thought it *would not do*. Besides, the Rev. Mr — [Brontë] said there was a large stock of Mr. Wesley's Tract on Baptism, which had been lying on the shelves of the Methodist Book Room, in London, for many years (for it was there judged most politic *not* to circulate them, as bad consequences had sometimes followed from it), and they would just answer the purpose.

"Accordingly, in a short time some hundreds of them arrived, and the Rev. Mr — announced from the pulpit of Haworth Church the several places at which this famous tract was to be sold. . . ."

Such enthusiastic partisanship from all sides, however restricting, is refreshing in this age of indifference.

In December 1849, Patrick had printed a short, simple hymn for the children of the Sunday school, and gave each a copy personally.

> Our Church, it is pure and unstain'd,
> And founded on Christ as a Rock ;
> His truth it has ever maintain'd,
> And cherish'd and shielded his flock.
> Though winds of iniquity blow,
> And enemies come like a flood ;
> This building they cannot o'erthrow,
> For it is the building of God.
> Then haste at the sound of its bell,
> The sabbath bell calls you away,
> With God for a season to dwell,
> In His temple to praise and to pray.

To those who meet there in His name,
His presence and blessings are sure
And these will be ever the same,
When time shall no longer endure.
God prosper the Church in our land,
Of Truth may she long be the stay,
A light at Jehovah's command,
To guide, and to cheer, on our way.

Haworth, December 18th 1849.   P. B.

Patrick was in need of God "to guide, and to cheer" him on his way for, in the preceding year or so, he had received three crushing blows of which only the first could appear as a blessing in disguise.

By far the longest and best work Patrick ever wrote was *The Maid of Killarney* which, as already mentioned, was published in 1818 whilst he was at Thornton. It contained 168 pages (with eleven chapters) and there is a Preface rendered brief, as Patrick explains, because "a long Preface to a book, like a long introduction to a sermon, generally meets with no better reception from the reader or hearer, than a surly and tedious sentinel does from a veteran soldier, who is impatient to see the interior of an ancient and famous castle". Unlike his daughters after him, Patrick hid under a cloak of complete anonymity in this case, scorning even a pseudonym, and to his great delight his tale was received very well. Many inhabitants of Haworth who read *The Maid of Killarney* at the time have testified that it was Patrick's own work. But the final proof of Patrick's authorship came towards the close of his life, as the result of a visit from his friend the Rev. Dr Cartman of Skipton, and two clerical colleagues. In a copy of *The Maid of Killarney* Patrick wrote on the title page, "P. Brontë, A B. Incumbent of Haworth", whilst overleaf one of his visitors added, "The autograph of the Revd P Brontë on the title page thereby acknowledging the authorship of this volume was kindly written by him on Saturday April 7 1860 at the request of the Revd J. H. Mitchell who visited the Parsonage at Haworth for the purpose on that day in the company of The Revd W. Cartman D.D. and The Revd S. Parkinson B.D."

Briefly, it tells of Albion, a young Englishman, and his divers adventures whilst wandering in Ireland; and ends happily with his betrothal to Flora, daughter of Captain Loughlean. In Chapter 2, there is a glimpse of an Irish Wake—or funeral. "By this time they had reached the cabin. What was Albion's surprise on beholding the strange motley scene that presented itself! The good old woman, whom he had visited the day before, lay dead, stretched out, and covered with a white sheet, on a bed of straw, in the middle of the floor. Around the corpse, in a circle, were placed about twelve elderly women; some with handkerchiefs tied on their heads, and others, with striped petticoats and aprons. They all held cheerful conversation with each other, except two or three, who sat at the head, and were weeping bitterly. In one corner of the cabin, were a group of young men and women, at various kinds of plays; and in another, a number of old people smoking and drinking! 'Now,' said Albion's fellow-traveller [Captain Loughlean], 'attend!' In an instant all the old women that surrounded the corpse, began to sing out, or chaunt [sic], in a most melancholy strain, all the while clapping their hands, as if in the bitterness of grief! After they had repeated this several times, Albion's guide, lightly touching him, whispered, 'This is what, in your country, you denominate the Irish howl, and what we term the Irish Cry. It is used only at the funerals of Roman Catholics, and is altogether a very unmeaning ceremony'. . . . [Albion asks for an explanation of the enactment before him.] . . . 'these three who sit weeping at the head of the corpse, are near relations, and the only real mourners, all the rest are but feigned; they are either neighbours who offer their service gratis, or a few practitioners who are hired for the purpose'. . . ."

Captain Loughlean invites Albion to his home, Loughlean Hall, and during the dinner-party and over the subsequent tea-table many topics are discussed; as is only too obvious, Patrick uses his little tale of Irish life, as he remembered it from his youth, as a peg on which to hang his own views of various topical and social questions. There are assembled on this occasion, Loughlean, Albion, a Doctor Laurence O'Leary (Flora's uncle) and, of course, Flora herself. ". . . 'What think you,' said Albion to Doctor O'Leary, who sat opposite, 'what think you of Roman Catholic Emancipation? Would it benefit Ireland?' 'No, Sir,' answered the Doctor, 'it certainly cannot benefit the Protestants, and I think it will add but little to the comforts of the Roman Catholics themselves. They already possess full liberty of conscience, are under the protection of the laws, and may all get as high in the scale of power and influence, as their giddy heads, and still giddier principles, will carry them.' 'But supposing, Doctor O'Leary, that they should be emancipated, do you think they would then be satisfied?' 'Satisfied, do you say, Sir, satisfied? Observe their ruling motive. They have already a great deal of power, but they want much more. If they now say, 'Why should our tenets preclude us from the British Senate?' But give them admittance, and they will then exclaim, 'Why might not a Roman Catholic sit on the British Throne?' . . ." O'Leary then expresses the conviction that

". . . should ever Protestants and Roman Catholics sit together in Parliament, they will constitute a mixture of powder and sparks, that will blow the fabric of the State to atoms!" Albion asks why it is that statesmen do not more strenuously oppose the emancipation, to which O'Leary answers that some are bad Christians who care not what religion is uppermost, whilst others wield the Catholic question for purely private ends. Loughlean then puts in a word for the Romanists. ". . . 'Many of them are good friends and neighbours, and none make better soldiers. Many of them, under myself and others, fought valiantly in the Field of Waterloo. At home, we have numberless political skirmishes, and dangerous party commotions; but when abroad, and opposed to the common enemy, Scotch and English, Welsh and Irish, Whig and Tory, melting and mixing, form but one mass, and that is borne against the foe, with irresistible destruction!' "

Naturally, these remarks lead to praise of the Duke of Wellington and a discourse on martial tactics from the Captain:

". . . 'Hannibal was wily and persevering; Alexander was bold and rapid; Caesar was wise to combine, and swift to execute; but Wellington, as a general, is wily, persevering, bold, and rapid; his powers of combination are immense, and his execution like thought! In all forward movements, his great antagonist, Napoleon, shewed himself an able Commander, and worthy of that martial renown his achievments [sic] acquired; but, in his retrograde movements, his fortune and abilities forsook him, and left him but little whereby to distinguish him from the crowd of Generals, that are carried, every age, into the gulph of oblivion. Of our great Duke and of him alone, perhaps, it can justly be said, there is a General who never conquered by chance, whose every victory is the natural and obvious result of powerful combination, and noble execution'. . . ."

Patrick then has a few words to say about the tea-table: ". . . all Doctors, whether of divinity or physic, unequivocally assert, and satisfactorily, prove, that there is more scandal over a tea-table, than can be found at the tables of drunkards, gamesters, or any other table whatsoever. It is a great pity there should be any ground for this heavy accusation. Tea, which is the most social, ought at least to be a harmless repast. . . ."

Doctor O'Leary then gives some of his views on political problems of the day.

". . . 'I always lay it down as a maxim, that it is intended the laws should be universally obeyed. In order to do this, they ought, most certainly, to be universally understood. But how impracticable is this! Consider the phraseology of our law-books. Here is a snatch of Latin;

there, a scrap of French, and every where, tautology and perplexity without end. Even the most common instruments, a lease, or indenture, have so much repetition, obscurity, and nonsense in them, that he must have a good memory, and no ordinary share of leisure and patience, who can read them through, and understand them when he has done. And what quirks, and quibbles, and fine spun subtilties ! Should your case be ever so straight and just the most learned Doctor of the Law cannot tell what may be the issue. In attention to unmeaning punctilios, or the absence of even a word or letter, may cause you to lose all ! How useless and burdensome are most of the law's ceremonies ! How detrimental its delays ! And as a necessary consequence, how great its expense ! The losing man may indeed be painted naked, and the winning man in rags . . . consider, moreover, the inadequacy of punishment. A man will be hanged for stealing a fat sheep, though he be hungry ;—he will incur no greater punishment for murdering twenty men ! In the name of common sense, what is the necessary tendency of this ? Most undoubtedly, the man who robs, will find it his interest to murder also, for by so doing, he will be more likely to prevent discovery, and will, at all events, incur no greater punishment. It has always been a sorrowful reflection to me, when I have heard of robbers being hanged on the evidence of the person robbed, that in all probability they came to their melancholy end, through that little remains of conscience, and tenderness of heart, which they still possessed, and which prevented them, even at their own peril, from imbruing their hands in their fellow creature's blood'. . . ."

Then follow remarks on card-playing, dancing, and the theatre. Loughlean asks Albion if he sometimes plays a "Rubber at Whist".

" 'Yes, Sir, I occasionally do, but I am no slave to the amusement.' 'I am glad, Sir, that you are not ; for we never give a night's lodging to a pack of cards . . . all things are liable to abuse, but cards have a natural and constant tendency that way. At best, they are but murderers of time. And this is not all. Those who are fond of cards, will play for money ; this gives a taste for gaming, and gaming produces covetousness, dissimulation, malice, and sometimes even worse effects . . . I object to dancing on the very same ground that I object to cards . . . they may call it if they please a healthy exercise, the art of acquiring graceful attitudes and airs, and the school of politeness : but I call it the destroyer of constitutions, the underminer of morals, the consumer of time. Consider the dress, the heat and bustle, the nightly air, and the trifling and giddy manners of a ball-room : justly weigh these, and many other necessary appendages, and when you have done, tell me, whether in your cooler moments of reflection, you would choose for your wife the heroine of such a scene ?' 'I suppose, Captain Loughlean, that to be consistent with yourself, you would condemn the Theatre also ?' 'Most certainly, Sir, to be consistent with the *Christian character*, I would. This evil you have mentioned, though last, is not the least. Take the *double meanings, the buffoonery, the meretricious ornament* of the stage, blend them well together, and tell me whether history records any composition so poisonous and destructive ! . . .' "

Flora then plays her harp and enchants Albion with a song, "The Tempest", after which many of the latest songs come under attack : their Italian words often convey "ideas—very unfit for female ears". O'Leary expresses the view that he always likes "to see more of nature than art in music. Many prefer execution ; but I cannot bear to have the eye entertained at the expence [*sic*] of the finest feelings of the heart." Finally, the general run of novels are severely criticized as containing much pollution beneath the surface. In the subsequent chapters Albion visits the death-bed of a defiant sinner, whose last moment of horrified repentance silences the sarcasm of his two most hardened followers, and meets Ellen Green, a poor crazed girl whom Loughlean had befriended when he found her wandering through the countryside. She had a small house built for her in one of his fields and his fiercest dog, Lion, is her chosen companion and guardian.

Chapter 8 describes a night attack by Whiteboys on Loughlean Hall. The Whiteboys were an insurrectionary group who gave much trouble to the authorities in Ireland during the latter part of the eighteenth century and early part of the nineteenth. They derived their name from their habit of wearing a linen garment over their shoulders. Several of the ringleaders were executed. Albion is awakened by a crashing at his door and the voice of John O'Flacharty, the footman, shouting "Arrah ! dear Master, rise as fast as you can—they are here !" The Captain believes there are nine or ten armed men in the garden and asks the footman to ascertain this.

"John . . . taking up the Captain's bolster, and rolling it round his head, he thrust it out at the window with considerable difficulty. . . . 'Who's there ?' . . . The only answer he had, was first one shot, and then another, and another. John, drawing in his head rather hastily, let fall his bolster on the outside of the house, and a voice was instantly heard, savagely bawling out—'Huzza, we have hit him—he is down !' But John's precaution, ludicrous as it was, saved his life. Several shots struck his headpiece, but he remained unhurt ; and immediately vociferated, in a triumphant tone, 'You scoundrels, you shall soon know to your cost, that I am not down.' Then running for his musket, he returned them a very unceremonious compliment. . . . The Captain, like a good soldier, began immediately to muster his forces, and to order them, in the best manner he could, for attack and defence. He sent John to the garret, to fire from above. He gave a blunderbuss to the Doctor, and assigned him his station. To Albion, he handed a double-barrelled gun saying . . . 'stand and fire out at that window—I will guard this entrance.' So saying, he took with him two large horse pistols, and his broad sword, and placed himself in the post of honour. This was the most vulnerable part. It was a back passage, where both the door and windows were but weak and ill secured . . . Now the firing was carried on briskly, though irregularly, both from within and without."

Old Mary, the housekeeper, runs about in great trepidation but, as may be supposed, Flora remains coolness itself. She visits each station in turn, and whilst with Albion ". . . a ball at this instant entering in at the window, struck the opposite wall, breaking the looking-glass that hung upon it, but doing no other mischief. Flora now bethought herself of a stratagem . . . there was a watchman's rattle, which had lain neglected in an upper chamber for some years. Up she ran, and putting her hand out at the window, she sprung her rattle five or six times, with such good effect, that it might have been heard half a mile round [what, then, of the shots ?]. Shortly after, the firing on the outside of the house began to abate, and in a little time, entirely died away. . . ."

It is dawn and all the defenders are unhurt. Bloodstains are found in three parts of the grounds and it is later reported that six men from the next village are missing and that three men were seen, at break of day, making good their escape, " 'one had his arm in a sling, the other had his head bound up, and the third had a handkerchief tied round his hand' ". There are refreshments for the victors and the Captain requests that his faithful footman (who had served him at Waterloo) should sit down with them. ". . . 'He has fought bravely. Like gallant fellow-soldiers, let us for this time drink out of the same cup, and sit at the same table'. . . ." Here again is that striking Brontë trait—kindness for, and respect of, their servants.

After divers adventures, visits to the sick and poor, and so on, Albion wins the consent of Captain Loughlean for the fair Flora's hand, and there is a peaceful close. The final quotation from *The Maid of Killarney* is taken from Chapter 6, and is a passing glimpse of the famous Lake.

". . . the weather was mild, the sky a cloudless blue, the wind was still, and the glassy Lake reflected in its bosom the heavens, and all the surrounding scenery. The woods and groves seemed to grow downwards ; the lofty mountains to point their rocky tops towards the nether skies ; and a mock sun, as if he would rival the real one, blazed beneath in all his glory ! . . ."

When Patrick came to read his daughters' books, he would sense, to the full, how feeble were his best efforts. Yet he had had something to say, something to tell the people, and had seen his works printed. Never for one single instant did he regret the endeavours he had made.

In addition to his main published works, all of which have been dealt with in this book, Patrick wrote scores of articles for magazines and very many letters to the newspapers. (Indeed, he became so well known, nationally, as to receive personal letters from the Duke of Wellington (Prime Minister) and Peel (Home Secretary) dated 21st November 1828.) One such contribution was twenty-six light-hearted lines of verse called "Church Reform", concerning the ejection of the village housewives from the graveyard which they had used for drying their garments on wash days. One of the letters, written to the *Leeds Mercury* and appearing on 16th March 1844, strikingly bears out his statements that he always advised his family to wear only silk or wool, and was written long before Mrs Gaskell's biography had given world-wide publicity to this insistence. This letter, which gives a more than valid reason for his preference in the matter of clothes, concludes the survey of the writings of "Sydney".

Cremation. To the Editors of the *Leeds Mercury*.

Gentlemen, You have given a solemn warning to all your numerous correspondents not to trouble you with long or needless articles during the session of parliament, and therefore I will be as brief as possible; nevertheless, I hope that you will permit me to say that your readers in general, and I amongst the rest, fear nothing more than a long parliamentary speech. Half a column we can do with, but when it comes to two or three columns we put the whole aside in despair, and have recourse to the leader, as a wise and good abridgement of that which in general means anything or nothing. You may not, perhaps, be aware of the distressing nature of the circumstance under which you have laid your various and numerous correspondents. Who, except the writers, can tell with what anxiety and heart-palpitating eagerness every man looks for the next number of the paper, in which he expects and hopes that his lucubrations will be read, and perhaps admired by thousands? You have very properly and ably written against the burning of Hindoo widows, and have applauded the law which put a stop to such an abomination, but though I have been a subscriber to your paper for more than thirty years, I can remember only one article in it respecting the misconduct of parents in regard to the death of children, in consequence of their clothes catching fire. How, with your critical acumen, this important case could have been overlooked by you, I can hardly conjecture. I know that you have admonished mothers to stay at home with their children; but when a little village gossip is afloat, you might as well tell mankind to chain the sunbeams, in a cloudless summer day. You know, and those less knowing than you are must be conscious that all garments of linen, or cotton, are particularly inflammable, and that clothes of woollen, or silk, are much less so, and cannot be ignited at all without the most careless and wanton neglect. Hence it is evident that if women and children were, in general or always, to have their garments of silk or wool, there would be little or no danger of their losing their lives by accidental ignition. You may, and perhaps some of your readers may, think me to be trivial. Well, I cannot help it; nor do I wish to write or state my sentiment otherwise. I like to talk plainly and openly, and I may say faithfully; and then I leave the consequences to the Supreme Disposer of events, and the Controller of all hearts. I have been at Haworth for more than twenty years, and during that long interval of time, as far as I can remember, I have performed the funeral service over ninety or a hundred children, who were burnt to death in consequence of their clothes having taken fire, and on inquiry in every case I have found that the poor sufferers had been clothed in either cotton or linen. Believing this to be an important lesson, and by giving it to the world, in all its simplicity, I shall be amply gratified should I be the means of saving only one life in this our state of probation.

I remain, Gentlemen, your most obedient servant, Patrick Brontè.

For a hundred years, Patrick's great fear of fire has been used as one of the jeers against him. His refusal to have curtains and his strictures as to the material his family could wear have been levelled against him as acts of tyranny. But there were the hundred children! Patrick did not limit his love of children to saving them only from the flames of Hell. There was the more real danger: the fires of home.

CHAPTER 20

Emily

IT WAS May 1843 and the sun shone on Haworth Parsonage; it was always shining these days and a hot summer seemed promised. There were four human inhabitants of the old grey building. Emily divided her time between the kitchen, the moors and the solitary nursery. Towards evening, the clouds would make a moorland in the sky but the western winds came with the darkness and breathed them away; and Emily would sit half the night, stared at by her moon and smiled at by her stars. Tabby was back again, trying all she knew to hide the limp that could never leave her again. She tried hard to find fault with young Martha, but it was not easy and, as the days passed, it became almost impossible. Martha Brown was clean; she was honest; she was hard-working; she was thorough; and she was the most faithful young child on earth. Tabby recognized all this at a glance, particularly the last-named attribute, for there was nothing Tabby could be taught of loyalty or fidelity. Patrick had recently returned from a brief visit to Anne and Branwell at Thorp Green. Anne looked well and Branwell seemed full of enthusiasm for his new employment; both were in very good odour with their employers.

As Patrick came away from the lush and pleasant Vale of York he had no reason to be worried. If his weakening eyesight had failed to detect the character of Lydia Robinson he cannot be blamed for negligence. Was she not the daughter of the Rev. Thomas Gisborne, closest of friends to the late William Wilberforce, and whose home, Yoxall Lodge, had been the latter's favourite retreat for study?

My dear Gisborne,
    I turn from my wearisome track . . . to answer the call from Yoxall Lodge, whence every voice is always heard with pleasure . . . with kind remembrances to all under your roof. . . .

So wrote Wilberforce in 1810, as Patrick had later read, and little Lydia Gisborne, aged ten, was under that pious roof. Why should Patrick distrust her now?

From Brussels came Charlotte's letters. All seemed well, yet a certain tautness in them puzzled him : the other teachers seemed a most disagreeable set of women.

There were, of course, other inhabitants of the parsonage, several of them, and none found the heat of day more trying than Keeper. Tiger, however, was contented and basked and smiled by the hour in the back yard. But soon Tabby and Martha became more used to each other in the kitchen, Patrick forgot his worries about the three absentees, telling himself that he was, naturally, over-anxious on their account; whilst Emily tolerated the heat of the house, found hidden breezes on the moor tops, and waited eagerly for the night wind and the moon and the stars. There was a fine harvest of hay in the fields that summer, the heather was never so thick on the moors, the bilberry seemed a more vivid splash of yellow than ever, and during those warm moorland days there took immortal root the first fibres of *Wuthering Heights*. There was an easy relationship between the white-haired father and his tall daughter. His golden-haired son in his childhood days had been his hope; in old age necessity would make Charlotte his only support; but nature had made Emily Jane his most beloved, his favourite. Charlotte was invaluable to him in the Sunday school and, although there is no proof of this, the deeply religious Anne may have assisted there, but she was so seldom at home during her brief days of womanhood. Emily never taught there, nor did Patrick ever insist that she should. It was a measure of his great understanding of, and sympathy with, his nature-adoring daughter, that she could spend a Sunday on the highest plateau of the moors where the long grasses wave and the cotton-ball moss crop nods even on the stillest day. Patrick would smile in quiet understanding when he read his daughter's lines :

> What have those lonely mountains worth revealing ?
> More glory and more grief than I can tell :
> The earth that wakes *one* human heart to feeling
> Can centre both the worlds of Heaven and Hell.

Indeed, outside the family circle, Emily was only once heard to comment on the subject of religion, and her remark was as laconic as it was typical. Mary Taylor has related how she once told Charlotte, ". . . that some one had asked me what religion I was of (with a view of getting me for a partisan) and that I had said that that was between God and me. Emily (who was lying on the hearthrug) exclaimed, 'That's right.' This was all I ever heard Emily say on religious subjects. . . ." When Emily was present in the Brontë box-pew, she would sit with her back to the pulpit. Whereas "Charlotte almost tried to hide herself from observation", Emily made a lasting impression. One who saw her many times told of "the stolid stoical manner of Emily as she sat bolt upright in the corner of the pew, as motionless as a statue. Her compressed mouth and drooping eyelids, and indeed her whole demeanour, appeared to indicate strong innate power. A large protruding tooth added to her peculiar aspect."

Emily had indeed become, for Patrick, the son he had so longed for. When a mad dog had bitten her there had been no fuss : she had walked quietly into the kitchen and cauterized the wound herself. Again, when Keeper and a powerful village dog were fighting in Parsonage Lane, Emily had rushed out with the pepper pot and dredged their noses with pepper, before pulling Keeper off. There were several men standing by gaping at the scene ; she did not deign to give them even a glance. These incidents gave Patrick much food for thought, particularly the former. As a boy Branwell had been bitten by a dog, and the bite had not been cauterized : Patrick pondered much over this fact and wondered how far the omission could be responsible for his son's lack of control. Yet Emily loved and understood all animals, their natures were half her own. That wild streak of fierce pain when she beat Keeper with her fists as a punishment for lying on the bed-covers—before bathing his eyes so tenderly—would not Patrick understand that outburst ? There had been, no doubt, that fierce light in the eyes, that swelling temple, that grief and shame at having dealt harsh justice to a best friend. Patrick would be struck with horror on hearing of Keeper's thrashing, a strong reprimand ready on his lips ; then he recalled his own youthful outbursts, and said nothing. He understood that Keeper must be cured of his fault instantly. Punishment from another's hands would not be tolerated by either the dog or Emily.

Happy were those early summer days for Patrick and Emily. In the Parsonage garden they found great enjoyment in shooting at a mark, Emily having expressly forbidden her father to shoot grouse on the moors and advising him firmly that he might look to August in vain. Yet there was no need for this stricture. Patrick's eyes were but very dim. The diary of the then Haworth stationer, John Greenwood, gives the following picture of them together in the garden. "Mr. Brontë formerly took very great pleasure in shooting—not in the way generally understood by the term, but shooting at a mark, merely for recreation. He had such unbounded confidence in his daughter Emily, knowing, as he did her unparalleled intrepidity and firmness, that he resolved to learn her to shoot too. They used to practice with pistols. Let her be ever so busy in her domestic duties, whether in the kitchen baking bread, at which she had such [a] dainty hand, or at her ironing, or at her

25

studies, wrapt in a world of her own creating—it mattered not; if he
called upon her to take a lesson, she would put all down. His tender and
affectionate 'Now, my dear girl, let me see how well you can shoot today,'
was irresistible to her filial nature, and her most winning and musical
voice would be heard to ring through the house in response 'Yes, papa!'
and away she would run with such a hearty goodwill, taking the board
from him and tripping like a fairy down to the bottom of the garden,
putting it in its proper position, then returning to her dear, revered
parent, take the pistol, which he had previously primed and loaded for
her. 'Now, my girl,' he would say, 'take time, be steady.' 'Yes, papa,' she
would say, taking the weapon with as firm a hand and as steady an eye as
any veteran of the camp and fire. Then she would run to fetch the board
for him to see how she had succeeded. And she did get so proficient, that
she was rarely far from the mark. His 'how cleverly you have done, my
dear girl!' was all she cared for. She knew she had gratified him and she
would return to him the pistol, saying, 'Load again, papa!' and away she
would go to the kitchen, roll another shelf-full of teacakes, then, wiping
her hands, she would return again to the garden and call out, 'I'm
ready again, papa,' and so they would go on until he thought she had
had enough practice for that day. 'Oh!' he would exclaim, 'she is a
brave and noble girl. She is my right hand, nay, the very apple of my
eye!'"

A brave and noble girl. Patrick's simple words echo in that small
garden. There have been many less satisfactory summaries of Emily
Jane Brontë than that. But then her father *understood* her. She remains
a sphinx *only* to those who cannot or will not comprehend the message
of the moors.

Anne and Branwell were welcomed home for their June holidays,
bringing with them a new inmate for the parsonage, Flossy. Then they
were gone and Patrick and Emily were alone again until the year's end.

This, then, was the period in which *Wuthering Heights*, so long
rooted in the heath, burst into moorland bloom; this the time when
Patrick and Emily knew and loved each other best. Freed from the
companionable walk with her sisters round the dining-room table,
Emily could stride straight across the hall into Papa's parlour. She
would play to him on the rosewood piano—such hours of delight for
Patrick that when she was gone the instrument, which served to support
his books, became a sore reminder of his daughter.

During these quiet months, even for those away from home, the
stuff of the Brontë novels was being shaped, for Charlotte and Anne
painfully, for Emily serenely. At Haworth Parsonage Patrick learned
with undivided attention the real worth of Emily. He first sensed that

of all his talented friends of early days, of all the genius in his own house, Emily Jane was the greatest of them all and her faith in eternity the most sure.

She could know much of her independent-minded, unorthodox father : Evangelical Anglican who never really ceased to be a Wesleyan Methodist ; rigid Tory who stormed at his party for needed reforms ; leading opponent of the Luddites who alone showed them ruth : worker amongst men, finding inspiration and solace from wild nature ; a man of God whose Irish humour, reinforced by Yorkshire gusto, made him a man of violent action.

During these peaceful months—was the parsonage ever so serene ? —Emily came home in the evenings, her feet dusty with heather knots, those storm-blue eyes worlds of satisfaction and elation, and put down in solitude Heathcliff's indestructible love for Cathy, and her own enduring faith in the immortality which those moors imparted. But even Heathcliff shared Emily with her father and, with Keeper padding in by her side, she often spent the evening with Papa. Local tradition, which in Haworth is both reluctant and reliable, tells how after such evenings Patrick would be very late to bed and would quite forget to stop to wind the clock.

There was much to discuss as they sat there, the west wind up and rushing over the house with a sobbing cry, blowing the smoke of the summer-evening fire into the parlour as it always did on that side of the Parsonage. Patrick perceived that for his daughter his own words of promise were inadequate, that Emily had found everlasting life for herself up there amid the curlews and the heather. Once on the moors she seemed to stride through life's boundaries, to pass beyond all Christian benefits, to enter an existence of beauty and splendour that he had never quite known. Perhaps God had chosen that moorland paths should be her way to heaven.

Patrick sensed that to Emily his influence seemed tied and limited ; the very walls of that grey church a confining influence, where half-truths were pent up. Yet for him it was different. Patrick knew that the villagers came there to be comforted ; if all that Emily embraced alone on those heights were available to everyone—even those completely devoid of imagination—none would go there to seek it. At the church he could give to all who repented of their sins solace and shining hope, and the truth in God's message to all who came. For Emily the valleys were crowded with fickle vanities, the valleys where shadows creep and make things appear what they were not ; on the high moors there was no shadow, all was light and truth and eternity.

Patrick also gained an insight into Emily's belief that everyone had his own God, to worship in his own fashion. Each was different. God, nature, truth, beauty, inspiration, eternity, call it what you will, was for her not only nearer on the moors—it was there! Emily's God resembled the good earth that gives life to all things and then takes them back to her breast until they shall be born anew.

Thus, surrounded only by the kind servants and the faithful dogs, Patrick and Emily drew ever closer in their understanding of each other. These two, the only tall members of the family, had, strangely enough, more in common than the others. They were not the Christian and the pagan, the platitudinous, hide-bound cleric and the young feminist rebel, the practical man and the visionary girl. They were both enthusiasts. They alone of the family who survived had no doubts or qualms about their faith. Their path was undeviating and with no pitfalls. It was a differing track they travelled over so confidently, but it led to the same destination in the hills: through death to immortality.

CHAPTER 21

Manchester

IF PATRICK was deeply interested in politics, the law and military matters, there was yet one other subject in which he became immersed, namely, medicine. His interest in the causes and cures of every known disease or sickness, and the various scientific innovations in that field during his latter years, was undeviating. As will be seen later in this chapter, he spent many hours noting the various improvements in medical knowledge, and his own physical reactions to the numerous medicines he had tried, in a copy of Graham's *Domestic Medicine*. Indeed, next to the work of composing his sermons and attending to parochial matters, the question, "What did Patrick Brontë do with himself, shut away alone in that parlour ?" could be answered quite truthfully, "By spending hours learning how the sick could be cured, first in soul, then in body."

In reading through the various ailments marked down for attention by Patrick, and his own notes on them, one cannot but wonder how often he turned to his favourite medical book for help, as one by one his family were brought down by sickness and death : certainly many times in connection with his four grown-up children, for the book was published in 1826.

But before giving some extracts from Patrick's most extensive notes there are three letters of his which deal with medical matters : the first is to young John Milligan, the surgeon, whom he was anxious to help establish in Keighley, out of friendship for his father, whom he had known during his Thornton days.

Mr Milligan, Surgeon. Keighley, Yorkshire.

Haworth, Near Bradford, Yorkshire. Oct. 9th 1838.
Dear Sir,

On the last occasion in which I had the pleasure of being in your company—after, I had given you a true, and circumstantial account of my ordinary complaint which is dyspepsia—you were so kind as to prescribe to me according to the object, which I had in view—I have taken your prescription, and after due time, and after having fairly weighed the effects, I can from my own experience (which I judge to be the best authority) honestly assert, that nothing received from the hands of any medical gentleman, has ever done me, more good. Your advice, accorded in many points, with that given to me, by the late Mr. Sharp of Bradford, who, as many yet remember, was an able surgeon, and skilful medical adviser—as, with professional benignity you charged me nothing—for your prescription—I wish in the same spirit, to make to you such a return as I can, by bearing testimony to your skill, as well as your liberality. I ought, perhaps here to observe, that I have not gone, *beyond* or *on this side* of your prescription—as I I [*sic*] considered this line, to be the only one, which could do both you, and myself, justice.

I have frequently thought, that you might have wondered, why I was so *particular* in requiring your signature—the truth is—I wished to have *medical authority*, for what I might do—in order that I might be able to counteract—(under providence) the groundless, yet pernicious censures, of the weak—wicked—and wily—who are often on the alert—to injure those, who are wiser and better, than themselves. I profess, to have no great skill in medicine, though I have studied it, both at the University and since I left it—yet I feel confident, that I can soon discriminate between, scientific medical men, and mere pretenders. My humble opinion is, that if you go on, to cultivate and improve your natural and acquired talents you will, by the blessing of God, rise to eminence, in your high, and honourable profession—Remember me, very kindly to your Dearer Half—and when you see your Father, and Uncle in Bradford, give my best respects to them—and tell them *from me* that I hope they will see the necessity of walking in politics with *all* a *Scotch mans*, wonted precaution—in these critical, wayward and dangerous times—I have, of course—post paid this—which I beg you to excuse, in yours, very truly

Patrick Brontè. Incumbent of Haworth—Yorkshire

(John Milligan, M.R.C.S., L.S.A., did indeed rise in his profession. In 1849 he won the Fothergillian Gold Medal for his essay on "The Influence of Civilization upon Health and Disease".)

The "weak—wicked—and wily" mentioned by Patrick were a handful of villagers who spread the tale that, like his son, the parson was a tippler and that he spent his time in that little parlour not studying anything in particular, but imbibing heavily. The next letter, addressed to Mr Greenwood, the church trustee, refers to this local gossip against Patrick.

To Mr. Greenwood.

Haworth, October 4th, 1843.

Dear Sir,—When you see John Crabtree, you will oblige me by desiring him to pay the debt which he owes. Since you and Mrs Greenwood called on me on a particular occasion, I have been particularly and more than ever guarded. Yet notwithstanding all I have done, even to the injury of my health, they keep propagating false reports. I mean to single out one or two of these slanderers, and to prosecute them, as the Law directs. I have lately been using a lotion for my eyes, which are very weak, and they have ascribed the smell of that to a smell of a more objectionable character. These things are hard to bear but perhaps under Providence I may live to overcome them all.

With all our kindest regards to you and your family,

I remain, dear Sir, Yours very truly, P. Brontè.

This mention of "a smell of a more objectionable character" is another reference to Patrick's reputed liking for the liquid refreshment of his native land; and the herbalists' prescription books contemporary with this time generally give the formula of an eye lotion as "Sulphate of zinc and one pint of water". There is certainly nothing there that savours of Irish Whiskey! Add to this the date of the last letter, October 1843, and the case against Patrick grows blacker. Friend Smith is still the Curate. In less than three months' time Charlotte will be home from Brussels and will express her anxiety over her father as the reason for her precipitate return. Add again the fact that Patrick shares the parsonage with the wild, untamed and beautiful Emily; that Tabby is lame and retires to bed early; that Martha often slips down the lane to sleep at her parents' home; and the critics are convinced they have a case to support the gossips. Branwell must have inherited his drunkenness from his father: the parson was a confirmed toper.

As always the gossips are half right. Patrick was a drinker of whisky, but never to excess. To those who might wish it so, a lotion of sulphate of zinc with which to bathe the eyes could appear to emanate from the mouth, as do the fetid fumes of whisky, gin, port, ale, or what you will. As for Smith the curate, he had many faults, as his later curacy at Keighley confirmed. He was a place-seeker, desirous of finding for himself a rich wife, but there is no record that he was a heavy drinker. Charlotte's unexpected return from Brussels was dictated by fear for no one but herself: she was concerned only with the powerful yet wholly innocent growth of love and veneration for Constantin Heger that had sprung to life in her heart. Emily was certainly wild and unorthodox, yet she quenched her parched and craving thirst only from the cool crystal springs of the moors. Again, Tabby was lame but rarely retired early to bed, earlier, that is to say, than her master. The kitchen was her fortress until the fire there had flickered into sleep. True, Martha often used to sleep at the sexton's house down Parsonage Lane, but was active until late in the evening at the parsonage and never left old Tabby until all the household work was completed. Never once did Martha (or any of her sisters who assisted at the parsonage) find the little parlour rancid with the stale fumes of spirits, when they came there to clean up early in the morning.

Branwell was a drunkard because his talents were great and his frame incapable of turning them to worthy account. There was no hereditary explanation whatsoever. Patrick loved a drop of port, better still a noggin of whisky, as most men did in those days, and still do today. But he was at no time in his life a drinker to excess. In his sermons, his published works and in his various notes there is a constant reiteration of the evils of debauchery: he had a prime example of its ruinous effects in his own household. Whatever else may be levelled against him, Patrick Brontë was no hypocrite.

The third letter concerning his interest in medicine is again addressed to Dr Milligan.

Mr Milligan—Surgeon, Keighley.

Dear Sir,
Haworth, Nr. Keighley. Jany 25th, 1859.

I thank you for the able scientific work which you have sent me, and which I hope, will make a useful addition to many important discoveries, and improvements, since the days of Galen. Yet I apprehend, that the Healing Art, is but in its infancy, and that the time may not be far distant, when the vital principles, will be better understood, and antidotes, and remedies, and specifics more numerous than at present. The Author of every Good and perfect Gift, will I trust throw light upon a subject so import, [sic] and necessary for the comfort and happiness of his creatures—I should have written sooner, had it not been that I have been confined to bed by an attack of bronchitis. However I thank God I am better. Give my kind regards to Mrs Milligan, and believe me, yours, respectfully and truly

P. Brontë.

As this letter shows, Keighley had become a separate postal district (in November 1847) and Haworth was no longer "near Bradford". Also, as already stated, after the fame of his girls had burst upon the world, Patrick adopted their usage of the diaeresis.

There are 562 pages to Patrick's prized copy of *Modern Domestic Medicine* by Thomas John Graham, M.D.—and on almost every page he has scribbled a dozen or so notes. In both pencil and ink are long remarks, terse comments, underlinings, question marks : in all over a thousand comments of one kind or another. Many reflect his great anxieties over his family's health and his own; others illustrate his enquiring mind wrestling with medical problems of the day. It is purposed here to quote as many as possible of the former kind and a few of his general comments. The book, 8½ inches by 5¼, is a mottled brown with dark green leather binding. On the second blank page Patrick writes, "price 15s in boards and binding 2s", followed, in pencil, by "*Vide*, page 207=For wash Leather". This refers to a cure for asthma, from which Anne Brontë was a frequent sufferer, and Graham writes as follows : "A waistcoat of wash leather or of flannel, worn constantly next the skin, from October to May inclusive, is highly to be recommended." On the fourth blank page Patrick writes, "Vide the 111th page, for nervous, and toothache tinctures—and the 1st page for the explanation of weights, and measures. For the recs for Indigestion, vide pages 353, and 359." As is known, Patrick suffered acutely from indigestion, and as in most households of those days, everyone had toothache from time to time, especially Charlotte and Martha.

"Typhus Fever. Something worth knowing—nitrous acid gas possesses the property of destroying contagion of Typhus Fever. To produce gas—place a little powdered saltpetre in a saucer and pour over it as much oil of vitriol as will cover it. A copious discharge of nitrous acid gas will instantly take place. . . ."

Opposite the title page Patrick remarks, "I have read many works, of Dr Elliotson, and the ablest medical writers, and found this Book, as far as it goes, perfectly to accord with them, both in its description of the symptoms of diseases, and their causes and remedies. P.B. 1848."

Then follows a marginal note on "Mesmerism". "In 1850, I read a Treatise on Mesmerism—from which I learned that in order to mesmerise a subject he must be placed in a sitting position and the mesmeriser must stand before him, moving his hand, with the fingers pointed towards him, from the back of the cranium, and about an inch distance, slowly for half an hour. When the mesmeric sleep takes place, in order to de-mesmerise the person, the backs of the hands must be brought into contact before him, and quickly separated in a horizontal line, for half an hour. To effect the sleep, steady looks are required, and both the operator and the patient must have their minds absolutely on the undertaking. There is no danger. P.B."

On the title page itself Patrick continues—"Dr K—S work, and as I read, and proved it was greatly inferior to this and tended only to puzzle and etc. I therefore parted with it—and will retain only this work of Dr Gr—m and B—ch—n [Buchanan], which must gen-lly rem-n.—1831. B."

Thus Patrick possessed this volume long before the deaths of Weightman, Miss Branwell or his four remaining children. The habit of omitting letters is frequently practised by Patrick in these notes, but, having given an example, we shall take the liberty of completing the words in future. At the foot of the title page is written, "This work was published after Buchanan's pieces—and etc—and was perfered [sic] to them, and highly recommended in the 'Literary Chronicle'— 'Wessleyan [sic] Magazine'—'Oriental Herald' and etc—and cost 15s—in boards."

The author's preface follows and is dated, "Croydon, Surrey, July 1826." Next comes a cutting from the Leeds Mercury of 1851 concerning successful experiments with chloroform. Patrick comments: "Dr. Simpson truly stated that if persons, under the full influence of Ether or chloroform were to have liquids poured into their mouths, they would be suffocated. . . . Chloroform would blister the skin." Alongside the contents page he adds, "The celebrated Dr. Forbes told Charlotte, in 1853, that Chloroform was regularly used in all the London Hospitals with continual and uniform success. B." Again on the same page— "Drs Jackson and Norton in America . . . care must be taken not to bring the flame of a candle near the operator, otherwise there might be a destructive explosion. P.B." And again, "As was discovered in 1849 —sulphuric ether inhaled through a suitable apparatus destroys, for some minutes, all consciousness—so that all surgical operations, may now be effected without any sense of pain. Limbs have been amputated, teeth extracted, and persons have been operated on for hernia and the stone, without their having any knowledge whatever of what had been done. The *liquid* must not be swallowed." We now turn the pages giving the appropriate headings, followed by Patrick's own comment. Where the ailment concerned the Brontë household, mention will be made of this fact. The book gives a clear picture of medical knowledge and beliefs in the early Victorian age.

Aloes—"too frequent a use of aloes, often produces piles." *Carbonate of Ammonia*—"I tried and found Carbonate of Ammonia greatly to irritate and injure my nerves and stomach." *Chamomile of Flowers*—"This is the safest and best of all. . . ." *Chloride of Lime*—"As I have read in able medical works, chloride of lime, which costs only 2/6 a quart, is the best of all things for purifying the air—a teaspoonful may be sprinkled in a room, once a day.—B." *Common Salt*—"Two table spoonful of salt, melted in water—would produce vomiting." *Compound Rhubarb Pill*—"This was ordered by Mr Ingham, surgeon [of Haworth] and is the *best* I ever used. B. 1854." This refers to another of Patrick's troubles. *Croton oil*—"According to medical advice I rubbed on some of this oil, to raise pimples, which it did—but it produced inflammation in my eyes and other parts—as I have heard is the case of others—so that I will never use it anymore. B." *Epsom Salts*—"Oxalic acid—a deadly powder, has sometimes been mistaken for Epsom Salts." Diet—onions—"Onions- *ob me, sunt valde mala.*"

Now follow two quotations to be seized upon by those who accuse Patrick of tippling. *Ether*—"I tried Ether, and found it to be rather too heating, and irritating, like fiery spirits.—B." "A teaspoonful of Ether in a little Brandy and water is good for flatulency—Mr. Snow, surgeon makes *dixit*, that Ether, produces no subsequent injury, like Laudanum or opium." (Branwell took to both these towards the end of his life.) *Glauber's Salt*—"Some have been killed by mistaking Nitre for Glauber's Salts." *Honey*—"Much honey, if eaten, will produce griping pains in the bowels." His note beside *Senna Leaves*—"seidlitz powders, according to the direction on the box, have generally been found excellent for indigestion, constipation & etc. B. 1842." *Squill*—"This dose may be taken three times a day—The form of syrup is the best." *Sulphate of Zinc. or white vitriol*—"This salt dissolved in rose-water, in the proportion of ten grains to half a pint of rose-water forms an excellent collyrium—or ointment for the eyes." Here Patrick has drawn a hand with the index finger pointing to his own words. "Dr Outhwaite recommended this to me in Oct. 1843. The eyes are to be closed, and the collyrium to be placed over the eye lids, only. B." Mention need hardly be made of Patrick's poor eyes. *Sulphuric Acid*— "This is excellent for heartburn, acidity . . ." "N.B. Tinctures . . . contain ardent spirits—and consequently would soon injure the constitution—syrups, contain no ardent spirits" *Turpentine*—"This is often one of the component parts of gin—instead of juniper berries, which were used, formerly." Now comes an important note of Patrick's— "Vinegar is mentioned as one of the best means of counteracting the fatal effects of over doses of *opium*, hemlock, and other narcotic poisons —such as tobacco & etc." How often must poor Patrick have reached for the vinegar bottle as he struggled with his doped son! *Wine*—"As a wine merchant told me, dealers often mix brandy, and other articles of a pernicious kind, with the ordinary sorts of port, sherry, and other similar wines—and the most salutary wines, are genuine sherry, not

less than three, or four years old—which costs from 38s to 48s a dozen—
the inferior kinds cost only 30s—and Madeira, sent to the Indies, to be
rendered mellow, by the voyage : this costs 60s a dozen, but—Madeira
made from grapes which grow on vines transplanted from Persia, is the
best of all and costs 80s a dozen=champagne and port are not salutary
—Burgundy Hermitage . . . are the dearest of all wines and are sold at
from 80s to 90s a dozen. B." *Compound Decoction of Sarsaparilla*—"I
found it best to boil it, over a slow fire for about half an hour. B."
Purging Mixture—". . . the Epsom Salt and the tincture of Senna—only,
will form the best mixture." *Purgative Pills*—"only six grs. of calomel
would be sufficient and best." *Sir H. Halford's Pile ointment*—"Neither
blue pill or calomel—much Rhubarb or Ipeacauanha & etc will do for
me—as they irritate my stomach by far, too much—and nothing will
answer, but the compound calacynth & oil of carroway . . ." *Mild
Aperient Pills*—"Not for me." *Plaster for cough*—"Burgundy pitch
plaster, is excellent for a cough and etc. B." *Tincture for toothache*—
"As a chemist told me, and as I proved, the following is the same as
Mr Sutens and better than the above—if applied to the teeth=Half an
ounce of spirits of Ether—as much of the tincture—and thirty drops of
oil of cloves mixed. The above mixture costs only five pence but is
better—and etc. B."

Now follows a note which would have interested those who accused
Patrick of never allowing meat to be eaten at home. *Diet*—generally
speaking, the flesh of tame animals is more wholesome than that of wild
animals, the flesh of quadrupeds than birds, and that of birds than fishes
—"Yet I have read in an able medical work that in various cases, wild
birds—as having more exercise than tame ones—and living on food less
gross are for the most part more wholesome—B." "Milk should always
be mixed with only a desert spoonful of magnesia to the pint—to correct
acidity and prevent costiveness"—*Butter-milk blancmange* : "Not
pruderi, ob me valde malam est—". *Oats*—". . . proved that gruel,
except about a pint or two in the week as medecine—is rather heating,
and difficult to digest—and porrige [*sic*] can be digested only by people
who are very strong." *Chocolate/Cocoa*—"Chocolate is the cacao nut,
mixed with some oily substance which renders it unfit for very weak
stomachs." *Well fermented malt liquors*—"British Brandy, (as I have
heard and proved) is very heating and bad, and so are rum, whisky,
Hollands and Gin, which are mixed with a large proportion of spirits of
Turpentine—*aqua fortis*—and all wines and malt, or fermented liquors,
whether bottled, or not, are for the most part detrimental—and above
a wine glass, or two in the week, even of French Cogniack [*sic*], Brandy
or any quantity of this or any other spirit daily or twice a day or on every

other day—or without four times its quantity of water, would, as I have read and heard, injure the stomach and nerves, though the old French Cogniack Brandy is occasionally only medicinal—1835—B." "Many drunkards often use daily eight, or ten wine glasses of ardent spirits—B." Not "as I have proved" in this case but "as I have read and heard" ! *Intoxication*—"Cold water may answer best—B." Graham tells of an inebriate being calmed by twelve drops of water of ammonia in a glass of sugar and water ; Patrick comments—"only some little effect . . . cost only 8d per ounce. B. 1837." No doubt he had already had several occasions on which to test its efficacy on Branwell ! *Animal Poisons— Vipers, Rattle-Snake etc*—"If soft paper and spirits of wine & etc be kindled in a glass and it be speedily pressed on the skin, there will be firm adhesion and consequent suction on account of the expansion and expulsion of the air—and the fire will go out." *Apoplexy*—"Though nervous people, from polar attraction, sleep best with their heads towards the North—this might not suit apoplectic persons, owing to the properties of iron, in the blood—B."

We return to Anne again with *Asthma*—"Were the nostrils to be stopped or pressed close by the fingers—during the proceeding—as is customary, the inhalation of the vapour, would, in three or four minutes, produce insensibility. B." *Burns and Scalds*—"N.B. I have heard and seen that the best application for a burn, or scald is dry, raw, fine cotton, or rather wheat flour—diachylum plaster—would be too hard and inflammatory." Now his comment on the scourge that had killed his wife. *Cancer*—"As I have read, excision, by a caustic, or the knife, is the surest method of removing cancer in its first stage, but after cancer has been fully form'd, and absorbed by the system, neither excision, nor any other remedy will perform a cure—B . . . As Mr. Wilson, Surgeon, said, and I have read & seen, frequently, but not always—when cancer is radically cut out in one part, it breaks out in another. B." "Drinking a table spoonful of brandy, and water and salt, four times a day, and bathing with this mixture, the parts affected, is said to be good for a cancer—This remains to be proved. B." *Catarrh*—"The fumes of tobacco must be carefully avoided. B."

Then follow some comments on *cholera morbus* (from which Willy Weightman died)—including praise of "mustard poultice placed on the pit of the stomach for ten minutes—will produce blisters and often do good" and of pure naphtha [*sic*], lately discovered and a powerful remedy. Next, Patrick's greatest curse in life, consumption, which certainly concerned his six children. *Pulmonary Consumption*—"playing on wind instruments is bad for the Lungs. B." *Consumption*—"Mr Teale, Surgeon, Leeds, said that change of place and climate, could

prove beneficial only in the early stages of consumption—that afterwards, the excitement caused by change of scenes, and beds, and strange
company, did harm. B." Thus Dr Teale had reported, after examining
Anne. There, then, is yet another answer to those ill-informed critics
of Patrick Brontë. Now the answer is given as to why Patrick hesitated
in allowing Charlotte to take the dying Anne to Scarborough.

More than Charlotte, Patrick was under no delusions about his
youngest child's condition. He had seen it all too often not to doubt that
Anne was far gone in decline. Branwell had died, Emily had followed;
now one glance sufficed to inform Patrick that the change of air might
kill instantly, that it could never cure. But Charlotte dared not face this ;
and Anne so wished to see the sea once more that Patrick gave way at
last and, in waving farewell to his little Anne on the parsonage steps, he
knew it was goodbye, that but a few hours of life might be left. Patrick,
on Teale's advice, kept Anne from Scarborough to keep her alive, and
when there was *no* hope left, he let her go, to die in that place she had
chosen. *Costiveness*—". . . generally should make water once in 3 or 4
hours and not more, nor less—*semper*. B." "Brown bread is very
irritating, heating and injurious to delicate sensitive stomachs." In
1848, when Anne was racked with coughing, he writes—"For a cough,
the following recipe got by Mrs Amos from Dr Mossman, is excellent.
Three ounces of syrup of squill, one ounce of syrup of poppys [*sic*], one
drachm of elixir of vitriol, one drachm of spirits of sweet nitre, one
drachm of Laudanum, and three ounces of water—mixed, and only two
teaspoonful to be taken thrice in the day. P.B. 1848.—price 6d or 1s—"
In June the red-haired Miss Mossman visited the Parsonage. Dr George
Mossman of Bradford published works on the use of digitalis for consumption and scrofula. ". . . pitch plaster is excellent for a cough. This
plaster may be removed from one part to another . . . for cough—*vide*
consumption. . . . Balsaam is recommended—but it costs 10s or 15s a
bottle. . . . Dr Laycock's pulmenil wafers are very good." "A roasted
onion, with a little water and sugar mixed and eaten with bread, is an
excellent remedy for a hard dry cough—*probatim est*." And again he
scribbles with despair—"Roper's Royal Bath plaster to be had at the
druggists, and put on the chest is excellent for coughs and diseases of
the lungs." *Cow-pox*—"Experience has proved that vaccination, does
not prove a sure antidote, unless it be repeated every six or seven years.
—B. . . . if 300 children be vaccinated, only one will be susceptible of
small-pox afterwards, but not otherwise than in a mild and safe form—
whereas, if 300 be inoculated one will surely die." Patrick then recommends common shoemakers' wax, made only of resin and oil, for cuts,
and diachylum plaster spread on linen or leather. *Nervous deafness*—

"In this case, the best plan is with a silk handkerchief to rub ears, repeatedly—taking care at the same time, that the bowels be regular. This generally effects a cure . . ." *Ear-ache*—"Should a flea, or other insect get into the ear—it will produce dreadful uneasiness—but oil poured in will kill the insect and effect a cure." *Gravel and stone*—". . . a quart in the day of water drunk, in which potatoes with the skins on have been *duly* boiled. P.B." "It has been said, that a decoction of heath, frequently drunk, will dissolve the stones and gravel . . . I have seen many who have been afflicted with red gravel—notwithstanding they were in the habit of using only soft water . . . Beer, and all kinds of spirits, even gin, often produce gravel." *Heartburn*—"The Carbonnate [*sic*] of Soda, is of great utility in various cases of heartburn." *Hypochondriasis*—". . . for four or five days at a time . . . only 5 or 6 times a year . . . accompanied generally by diarrhea. . . ."

More comments on various purgatives tried follow, leading to the statement—"a correct regimen is of the utmost consequence . . . all sedentary occupations must be forsaken as much as possible, and if they can be entirely given up, the prospect of complete relief will be far greater . . . by quitting the confined atmosphere and late hours of the crowded city, for the pure, dry, bracing air of the country—and active exercises." The next entry is surprising : "I never remember having once taken the smallest quantity of P. Wine with impunity . . . W.W." Did Willy Weightman indulge too freely on one occasion and have to pay penance by writing this confession in Patrick's medical book ? Certainly the writing is in his hand. *Mild home-brewed beer* : "this is dangerous practice. . . ." *Inflammation of the lungs or bronchitis*—"which, according to Keller and others frequently, but not always proves fatal." "Nitre is very bad for an inflammation in the lungs . . . two or three nuts of nitre, will prevent or cure a quinsy B." *Insanity*—"There is also 'delirium tremens' brought on sometimes by intoxication—the patient thinks himself haunted by demons, sees luminous substance in his imagination, has frequent tremors of the limbs . . . if intoxication be left off, this madness will in general gradually diminish."

It is interesting to note from this quotation that, in his search for an explanation of Branwell's diseased mind, Patrick has underlined the sub-heading to insanity, "*hereditary disposition*". Next follows a survival from his worries as the father of a young family : *Mumps*—"According to Dr Buchanan, . . . there should be no bleeding nor purging—and great care should be taken, against cold—since when the swelling is struck in, it often proves fatal." *Night-mare*—"Dr McNish . . . has justly described the sensations of night-mare . . . as being amongst the most horrible that oppress human nature—an inability to move, during the paroxysm—dreadful visions of ghosts & etc—and he recommends due attention to diet—and the circumstance of *lying* with the *head neither more* nor *less* than on a level with the body, or nearly so . . . it was worst towards the morning 1838—B. . . . people, when oppressed with the night-mare, groan in their sleep, and should be waked [*sic*]."

Now we turn to *Rupture*—which affected both Patrick and William Morgan. "1852. In my case, as Mr Kirk, the surgeon told me, it will [be] best to remove the truss, when in bed—since the tumor then subsides and the pressed muscles get rest. B. . . . a double truss is best—*Both* sexes, are subject to rupture. . . . when the truss fits very well, it will be the most convenient plan, to wear it next the skin. The pads should be three or four inches wide, not more and a little raised in the middle. Some wear the truss over the shirt, but this is very often inconvenient. The Dr. placed it next my skin, which mode generally answers best . . . Mr Morgan, who tried it, informed that bandages, do not answer, and that nothing but a well-constructed elastick [*sic*] steel truss, will do, and two trusses, should [*be*] kept. 1852—B." *St Anthony's Fire*—"Some have died of this complaint when it attacked the head—B." *Scrophula, or King's Evil*—"It is generally hereditary."

Again a frequent unwelcome visitant to the parsonage—*Spitting of Blood*—". . . thirty drops of nitralick or sulphurick [*sic*] acid, taken in a glass of water, twice or thrice a day is good. . . ." Now a complaint of which Charlotte and Martha Brown were frequent victims—*Tic Douloureux*—"These are french words, signifying a painful convulsive fit, and pronounced tick tooleorau. B." *Toothache*—"The following mixture, applied by a camel's hair brush or fine lint or cotton is . . . very good for the toothache—one ounce of the Tincture of Myrrh—half an ounce of the rectified spirits of turpentine—or as much ether—and eighty drops of the oil of cloves—B. . . . the nitrous spirits of Ether and the powdered Alum, must be well shaken, ere used. I tried this and found it not to answer very well. B. . . . when the toothache arises from acidity in the stomach, a desert spoonful of magnesia and three grs. of ginger, taken in a table spoonful or two of milk and water—and drinking warm tea—and lying in bed—and rinsing the mouth with brandy or rum frequently—and spitting out—will generally give relief. B—1834. . . . It was a practice at one time to extract the sound tooth—and to put in its stead, a tooth just warm from a sound subject . . . this unnatural mixture produced dangerous diseases and was not persisted in—B. . . . gin will not do—since aqua fortis, and other articles in it would greatly augment the pain—and the inflammation . . . Mr Morgan of Bradford . . . found great relief from pain in his teeth, by rubbing his gums and teeth daily with a mixture of the tincture of bark, and myrrh, in equal parts—B . . . a hard brush is very pernicious . . . rubbing and pressing the gums, and jaws inside, and outside, tends to mitigate the pain of the toothache. . . . In my case the best remedy is cold water, held in the mouth and sprinkled over the head and face—and a night cap put on without drying—which may be safely done—*vide*, under 'Headache'—B."

In all this catalogue of the crude ways in which the early Victorians struggled to find out measures that would ease pain, the example just given is at once the most ludicrous and the most tragic. Again there is *Typhus Fever*—"Sometimes, as I have seen, in the last stage of debility *after* the fever was gone, the patient was rescued from death, by drinking small quantities of the best brandy—if taken whilst the fever continued it would be fatal—B." *Warts*—"Oil of vitriol will soon burn away warts, but great care must be taken not to let it touch the skin—the point of a pen is best for putting on the oil. . . . Lunar caustic, wetted and rubbed on warts is the best thing for removing them—B." *Houseleek*—"Not above ten drops, or twenty, of these, should be kept in the house at one time—as they are poisnous [*sic*]."

Apart from the reference to his eyes and the operation he underwent for the removal of a cataract, our last quotation from Patrick's medical notes concerns *hydrophobia*, and it will be remembered that whilst Emily's bite was cauterized, Branwell's was not. "Dr Elliotson says, all things have been tried to cure this disease, and all have failed—Chloroform has failed—and he adds, that generally, not above one third of those bitten by a mad dog—go mad—and that some recover of themselves—but that the greater part die—and that the disease begins within two months after the bite. B . . . When a dog bites through clothes, as the poison is wiped off, the person bitten will probably not go mad. . . ."

There is no doubt that this long recital of notes makes Patrick appear, to modern eyes, an absurd figure; yet it is a detailed picture of his times, and has been presented as such in this book. Was he not the incumbent, one of the few educated men in the village of Haworth? True, there was a doctor there, yet should that preclude Patrick from endeavouring to learn something of sick bodies as well as sick souls? Of course not: it was his bounden duty to God and man to learn all he could for the benefit of his parish. Can anyone, having glanced through this medical book, still accuse Patrick Brontë of carelessness over his children's health? Surely this evidence proves that, within the narrow limits of medical knowledge then pertaining, their health was his daily concern.

As Patrick once wrote, regarding scientific knowledge, ". . . In this age of innovation and scepticism, it is the incumbent duty of every man of an enlarged and pious mind to promote, to the utmost

26

extent of his abilities, every movement in the variegated, complex system of human affairs, which may have either a direct, indirect, or collateral tendency to purify and expand the naturally polluted and circumscribed mind of fallen nature, and to raise it to that elevation which the Scriptures require, as well as the best interests of humanity."

Patrick's eyes grew steadily worse. There was now a cataract formed in his left eye and his sight was fading fast. It was the summer of 1846 and the July sun was warm and bright. Patrick, though he felt its heat, lived in a world of sullen skies. As will be seen from the next chapter, the family were all at home again, Charlotte from Brussels, Anne and Branwell from Thorp Green. For some time the girls had urged their father to undergo an operation for the removal of the growth but Patrick had hesitated. Not that he was afraid for himself—there was no physical fear in his make-up—but there were the children to think of. He knew well the risk such an operation would bring : after all, he was now nearly seventy. (He would recall, too, how the venerable John Crosse, his old Vicar of Bradford, had actually set off to undergo couching, but had returned blind, rather than undergo the necessary confinement.) But his sight was so very precious to him : never to see the heather bloom in August; never to read a book again but always be read to—it was unthinkable. By July 1846, he agreed to try whether couching his eyes would restore sight. At the beginning of August Charlotte and Emily went to Manchester to find medical advice. Charlotte writes to Ellen Nussey on August 9th, ". . . In a fortnight I hope to go with papa to Manchester to have his eyes couched. Emily and I made a pilgrimage there a week ago to search out an operator, and we found one in the person of a Mr Wilson. He could not tell from the description whether the eyes were ready for an operation. Papa must therefore necessarily take a journey to Manchester to consult him. If he judges the cataract ripe, we shall remain,—if, on the contrary, he thinks it not yet sufficiently hardened, we shall have to return—and papa must remain in darkness a while longer. . . ."

Leaving the drunken, half-crazed Branwell in the charge of Emily and Anne, with strong injunctions on Mr Nicholls, the curate, and John Brown to keep a watch on matters, Patrick was led to Manchester by Charlotte on Wednesday, 19th August 1846. They went straight to Dr Wilson. William James Wilson, M.R.C.S., was born in Leeds and was honorary surgeon to the Manchester Infirmary 1826-1855. He was largely instrumental in founding the Manchester Institution for curing eye diseases. He died at Tickwood, near Wellington, on 19th July 1855. Charlotte's next letter to Ellen details their arrival.

83 Mount Pleasant, Boundary Street. Oxford Road, Manchester.

August 21st '46.

. . . Papa and I came here on Wednesday; we saw Mr. Wilson, the oculist, the same day; he pronounced papa's eyes quite ready for an operation, and has fixed next Monday for the performance of it. Think of us on that day dear Nell. We got into our lodgings yesterday—I think we shall be comfortable; at least, our rooms are very good, but there is no mistress of the house (she is very ill, and gone out into the country), and I am somewhat puzzled in managing about provisions; we board ourselves . . . papa's diet is so very simple; but there will be a nurse coming in a day or two. . . . Papa requires nothing, you know, but plain beef and mutton, tea and bread and butter; but a nurse will probably expect to live much better. . . . Mr Wilson says we shall have to stay here for a month at least. It will be dreary. I wonder how poor Emily and Anne will get on at home with Branwell? They too will have their troubles . . . one cheerful feature in the business is that Mr Wilson thinks most favourably of the case. . . ." In the event, the operation did not take place on the Monday, but a day after that—Tuesday, 25th August. Before it began, Dr Wilson informed Patrick that, not believing in couching, he would perform the more serious operation of extracting the cataract. (There was, of course, no anaesthetic.) For a moment, just for a moment, Patrick despaired of life. At seventy he doubted if he should survive the ordeal. He turned to Charlotte with the cry, "I shall never feel Keeper's paws on my knees again!" Then the spasm was past and that iron control was restored; he was quite ready. It was so typical of the man, that in that fleeting second of panic, his thoughts were on his beloved dog. Their passionate love for animals was another trait the Brontë sisters inherited from their father. Before we quote Patrick's own notes on the operation, let Charlotte tell the tale in her letters to Ellen Nussey.

"Manchester, August 26th 1846. Dear Ellen,—The operation is over; it took place yesterday. Mr Wilson performed it; two other surgeons assisted. Mr Wilson says he considers it quite successful; but papa cannot yet see anything—The affair lasted precisely a quarter of an hour; it was not the simple operation of couching Mr Carr described, but the more complicated one of extracting the cataract. Mr Wilson entirely disapproves of couching. Papa displayed extraordinary patience and firmness; the surgeons seemed surprised. I was in the room all the time, as it was his wish that I should be there; of course, I neither spoke nor moved till the thing was done, and then I felt that the less I said, either to papa or the surgeons, the better. Papa is now confined to his bed in a dark room, and is not to be stirred for four days; he is to speak and be spoken to as little as possible. . . .

"Manchester, August 31st 1846 . . . Papa is still lying in bed, in a dark room, with his eyes bandaged. No inflammation ensued, but still it appears the greatest care, perfect quiet, and utter privation of light are necessary to ensure a good result from the operation. He is very patient, but of course depressed and weary. He was allowed to try his sight for the first time yesterday. He could see dimly. Mr Wilson seemed perfectly satisfied and said all was right. I have had bad nights from the toothache since I came to Manchester. . . .

"Manchester, September 13th 1846 . . . Papa thinks his own progress rather slow, but the doctor affirms he is getting on extremely well. He complains of extreme weakness and soreness in the eye, but I suppose that is to be expected for some time to come. He is still kept in the dark, but he now sits up the greater part of the day, and is allowed a little fire in the room from the light of which he is carefully screened. . . .

"Manchester, September 22nd 1846 . . . I have nothing new to tell you except that papa continues to do well, though the process of recovery appears to me very tedious. I dare say it will yet be many weeks before his sight is completely restored, yet every time Mr Wilson comes, he expresses his satisfaction at the perfect success of the operation, and assures me papa will ere long be able both to read and write. He is still a prisoner in his darkened room, into which, however, a little more light is admitted than formerly. The nurse goes to-day; her departure will certainly be a relief. . . .

"Haworth, September 28th, 1846 . . . When I wrote to you last, our return to Haworth was uncertain indeed, but Mr Wilson was called away to Scotland; his absence set us at liberty. I hastened our departure, and now we are at home. Papa is daily gaining strength; he cannot yet exercise his sight much—but it improves, and I have no doubt will continue to do so. I feel truly thankful for the good ensured, and the evil exempted during our absence. . . .

"Haworth, November 17th 1846 . . . Papa continues to do very well. He read prayers twice in the Church last Sunday. Next Sunday he will have to take the whole duty of the three services himself, as Mr Nicholls is in Ireland. . . ." To Miss Wooler, Charlotte writes towards the end of the year, ". . . his spirits are improved since his restoration to sight . . . those were indeed mournful days—when papa's vision was wholly obscured, when he could do nothing for himself, and sat all day long in darkness and inertion. *Now* to see him walk about independently, read, write, etc., is indeed a joyful change . . . he continues to see spots before the very eye which has been operated on, and from which the lens is removed ; he mentioned the circumstance to Mr Wilson, who put it off as a matter of no consequence. . . . I should much like to know Mr Wm. Wooler's opinion on the point. Will you ask him some day when you have an opportunity ? . . ."

William Wooler, a doctor, was Miss Wooler's eldest brother.

Thus, having been chained down in the dark, Patrick recovered his sight : and when one considers how much he shared Emily's love of the free moors, one can more readily appreciate his torment of mind. In his beloved medical book he recorded the following : "*Cataract*. In Augt. 1846—Mr Wilson, Surgeon,—72, Mosley St. Manchester, operated for cataract in one of my eyes—the left one. He informed me, and others, also, that, generally, they do not operate on both eyes—for fear of inflammation, which would destroy the sight. Belladonna, a virulent poison, prepared from the deadly nightshade, was first applied, twice, in order to expand the pupil—this occasioned very acute pain, for only about five seconds—The feeling, under the operation—which lasted fifteen minutes was of a burning nature—but not intolerable—as I have read is generally the case in surgical operations. *My lens* was extracted so that cataract can never return in that eye—I was confined on my back a month in a *dark room*, with bandages over my eyes for the greater part of the time and had a careful nurse, to attend me both night and day— I was bled with 8 leeches, at one time, and 6, on another, (these caused but little pain) in order to prevent inflammation— Through Divine Mercy, and the skill of the Surgeon, as well as my dear Charlotte's attention, and the assiduity of the nurse—after a year of (nearly total blindness) [these last three words are crossed through] blindness—I was so far restored in sight, as to be able to read, and write, and find my way, without a guide—The operation is critical, and ought not to be ventured on, without due precaution. P.B. [There is a touching note of pride in that last sentence.] Leeches must be put on the *temples*, and not on the *eyelids*—B. Darkly coloured glasses should be worn in a strong light—B. Mr Wilson charged me only £10—I believe he often charges £20 or £30. The whole expenses, however, amounted to nearly £50—as I had to take three rooms at £1-5-0, per week and to board myself besides . . . the nurse was paid 15s per week and boarded besides at Mr Balls. Mr Redscar, Surgeon, was the assistant, on whose proper management of the eye, during the operation, much depends.

"Before the operation, for about a year, I could neither see to read, or write, or walk without a guide—Jany 1847 P.B. After an operation for cataract, Mr Cooper—Surgeon, says convex glasses must be used— but not whilst the sight continues to improve—without them. B.

Mr. Wilson said that in couching, cataract often returned, and the operation had to be repeated. B. The frequent application of rose-water tends to strengthen the eyes . . . The extraction of the lens will not be proper when the eye is very flat—since in that case it would become concave, and the power of vision lost. The best wash for strengthening the eyes, is a decoction of half an ounce of gunpowder tea boiled down in a pint of water to a quarter of a pint—to be bottled, and the eyes bathed daily with it. The spectacles which suit me best for reading—are those of a 2½ inch focus—and for walking 4 or 5 inches . . . as teas are all of the same nature, a decoction of ordinary tea may do nearly as well—I will use this daily—*semper* B. . . . My right eye recovered *half* its tone—after acute inflammation in Augt. 1852. B. My right eye was injured by effluvia from paint varnish on my spectacles. B. In August 1852, I had acute inflammation, in my right eye for three weeks with severe pain, fever, and nausea. B. For inflammation of the eyes, do not bleed in the arm, but apply immediately 8 or 10 leeches to the temples : Take an half a wine glass of sherry, a table spoonful or two of castor oil, every other day ; darken the room, avoid animal foods—and bathe the eyes with lukewarm milk and water till the disease is subdued. All intoxicating liquors must be avoided."

There is something more than noble in that scene in those dreary rooms in Manchester : Patrick surprising even the hardened medical men by his patience and courage under pain—in his heart the fear of blindness, and the fear also that his brave Emily and Anne would find his raving son more than they could manage, back in the old parsonage. If he died, what would become of his dear girls ? Bereft of their father, they would be turned from their home, with a drunken lunatic as their charge ! What of his beloved Haworth ? Was Nicholls capable of discharging his full duties ? And in the outer room sat Charlotte, racked with anxiety for her father, and those beloved sisters at home wrestling with the hopeless Branwell. Before her on the table lay the manuscript of *The Professor*, returned to her yet again from unwilling publishers. Toothache tore at her mouth until it was agony to sit still. At that moment she reached for a sheet of paper and wrote upon it : "There was no possibility of taking a walk that day. We had been wandering, indeed, in the leafless shrubbery an hour in the morning ; but since dinner (Mrs Reed, when there was no company, dined early) the cold winter wind had brought with it clouds so sombre, and a rain so penetrating, that further outdoor exercise was now out of the question." At such a moment of low ebb, of complete misery and heartbreak, *Jane Eyre* was born. The enduring courage of the Brontës had triumphed once again.

CHAPTER 22

"Bell"

ON New Year's Day 1844, Charlotte left Brussels for home, where she arrived on 3rd January. She came home to a sublimely happy Emily, and an almost blind father. Mr Smith was still the curate. Yet as he welcomed his daughter back, Patrick did not need his sight to sense that she had brought with her from Brussels a heart pent up with emotion. Emily too saw the matter in a moment, and knew its cause. There was an extra curl to her lips : she was sorry for Charlotte, but really ! such a little monkey as Monsieur Heger—who had a wife older than himself. She turned in scorn and went back to Cathy and Heathcliff. The scenes of home brought forcibly to Charlotte the first true measure of her feelings for her master, and her heart was opened to release that flood of anguish that would spill into *The Professor*. Patrick divined the reason, if not the object of her attachment, knew that his daughter could never act in any but the most honourable fashion, sensed a sacrifice on her part, and tried to interest her in the project for opening a school at the parsonage. Charlotte pushed ahead with the scheme, circulars were printed and issued, Ellen Nussey and Margaret Wooler did what they could to help, but no parent cared to send his girls up to Haworth. Besides there were established schools in plenty. It would mean some alterations to the house if a school were launched there : at this point Patrick looked at Emily and Emily at her father with a sudden glance of dismay—peace and quiet would be at a premium. Then the idea of opening a school in the East Riding, where there might be a better opportunity, was suggested by the energetic Charlotte. But nothing came to fruition, happily for the world of letters.

Anne and Branwell came home for holidays as usual. Charlotte informs Ellen, "June 23rd 1844 . . . Anne and Branwell are now at home. . . . Jany 13th 1845 . . . Branwell and Anne leave us on Saturday. Branwell has been quieter and less irritable on the whole this time than he was in summer—Anne is as usual always good, mild and patient—I think she too is a little stronger than she was. . . ."

There were visits by Charlotte to Ellen Nussey and the latter came to stay at the parsonage. And, in 1844, James William Smith was appointed curate of Keighley. "July 29th . . . Papa wishes he could hear

of a curate, that Mr. Smith may be at liberty to go . . . August 15th . . .
Mr Smith leaves in the course of a fortnight . . . Sept : 16th . . . Mr
Smith has gone hence. He is in Ireland at present, and will stay there
six weeks . . . nobody regrets him . . . Mr Grant fills his shoes at present
decently enough. . . ." Nevertheless, they were not quite rid of friend
Smith, for the registers show that upon his return from holiday he
officiated at a baptism and a burial on 13th October 1844, although
omitting the word "Curate" after his signature. Even after he had
commenced his duties at Keighley there would be occasional returns
to Haworth. In June 1845 he came to tea at the parsonage with the
three local curates—Nicholls of Haworth, Grant of Oxenhope, Bradley
of Oakworth. Charlotte records that ". . . they began glorifying themselves and abusing dissenters in such a manner—that my temper lost its
balance and I pronounced a few sentences sharply and rapidly which
struck them all dumb—Papa was greatly horrified also. . .". Again in
July 1845 he officiated at a mass baptism in Haworth Church. Finally,
on 26th February 1848, Charlotte told Ellen : ". . . about a fortnight
since Papa received a letter from a brother of Mr. Smith. It expressed
shame and indignation at what the writer termed 'the shameful termination of his ministry in England . . .' :" it seems that Smith disappeared
owing a lot of debts including "£5 of Miss Sugden for some charitable
purpose" which he went off with. Smith, an Irishman, after suffering
from the Irish famine of 1847, emigrated to Canada with his young
family and was last heard of in Minnesota as a lumberjack. However,
after Smith had departed in October 1844 he was succeeded by Joseph
Brett Grant, who remained until May 1845, when he became the
incumbent of Oxenhope. Patrick was delighted at the former's departure ; he found Grant a more sincere man to work with. Indeed Patrick
was a frequent visitor at Oxenhope when Grant was there. Mrs Grant
liking "the Reverend Pat", as she called him, but complaining that "he
talks so much he gives me an headache". But if 1844 was largely
uneventful, the following year was not : it drew together all the actors
in one of the world's most moving, most noble tragedies.

The year 1845 was the beginning of that golden period in the life of
the Brontës, a year which saw the first glimmer of that vivid sun that
would blaze and scorch for a brief span and then turn into an unforget-
table sunset, leaving Patrick alone in a dark, cold world. In May there
came up the steep Kirkgate a tall, dark, bearded young man of twenty-
seven, the new curate, Arthur Bell Nicholls. Patrick met him at the
parsonage door, and inwardly cursed his failing eyesight. He saw the
man and yet he did not ; he trusted him and yet he could not ; he was
satisfied with his new curate's appearance and yet he was not. As he

returned to his parlour after directing him to his lodgings at the home of John Brown the sexton in Parsonage Lane, he reflected that only time would tell of the true value of Mr Nicholls. But he was wrong as far as world opinion is concerned, for Arthur Bell Nicholls remains the enigma of the Brontë story. He was the intruder from the outside world who penetrated the Brontë fastness, yet he loved a woman and not a legend. How many worshippers of that famous family are able to divorce these two aspects ? He saw Charlotte's courage, not her genius, her loyalty, not her fame, he brought her happiness, not praise. It was a perfect match, because it was brief. Had the fates protracted the union, it could have ended in disaster.

Patrick, having seen his new curate handed over to the safe keeping of Mrs Mary Brown, turned his thoughts to the new Sunday school master, Mr Purnell, whose satisfactory service was certain. It was an unhappy fact for Patrick that even with help from the Evangelical Pastoral Aid Society, he rarely received an Evangelical assistant : this man Nicholls was a positive Puseyite.

Arthur Bell Nicholls, T.C.D., B.A., was born of Scottish descent at Killead, County Antrim, Ireland, on Tuesday, 6th January 1818. From the age of seven he was brought up by his maternal uncle, Dr Alan Bell, headmaster of the Royal High School, Banagher. His father's name is said to have been originally Nicoll and he appears himself as "Arthur Nichols" in the catalogue of Dublin graduates. Nicholls entered Trinity College, Dublin, in 1840, where he obtained a second class in Divinity and graduated in the Trinity term of 1844. He was ordained deacon on Letters Dimissory granted by the Bishop of Ripon to the Bishop of Lichfield for Trinity 1845 and was licensed to the curacy of Haworth on 9th June 1845. He was ordained priest by the Bishop of Ripon, 20th September 1846. He first performed duty in Haworth Church on Sunday, 25th May 1845, and on the following day Charlotte informs Mrs Rand ". . . Papa has got a new Curate lately, a Mr Nicholls from Ireland . . . he appears a respectable young man [almost two years younger than Charlotte], reads well, and I hope will give satisfaction. . . ." Mr Nicholls first signed the registers on 28th May 1845, when he conducted a wedding—"A.B. Nicholls" ; and on the following day he took a funeral, adding this time the word "Curate". His salary was £100 per annum.

But before Patrick or Charlotte or the disinterested Emily could get to know and understand the new curate with his brusque ways, there came in mid-June, two more people up that steep, narrow main street : Anne and Branwell. Anne, looking pale and drawn, announced at once that she had decided not to return to Thorp Green, that she had left the

Robinsons' household for ever. Charlotte was pleased at this news; besides, it gave her greater freedom of movement, she could visit Ellen Nussey. Emily and Anne had planned a short holiday together at Scarborough, but cancelled it in favour of an excursion to York so that Papa should not be left alone; and because they had heard from Branwell that the Robinson family would be there. Anne had no desire for a chance encounter with them. After a week at home, Branwell, flushed and agitated, returned to Thorp Green, intimating that he was not to accompany the Robinsons to the East Coast and would soon be home again—which he was! Charlotte stayed with Ellen from 26th June until 19th July at the vicarage, Hathersage, Derbyshire, where they made preparations for the return of Ellen's brother, the Rev. Henry Nussey, and his bride from their honeymoon. It was a trying return journey for Charlotte: there was a Frenchman in her carriage, and that accent always brought back memories of Constantin Heger. She was tired and dispirited when she reached home at ten o'clock in the evening. As soon as she put her nose inside the hall she scented trouble, and one swift look at Anne's ashen face confirmed that something was amiss.

It had all started a day or two after she had departed for Derbyshire. Patrick was not a little anxious about Anne. He knew she had almost as great a love for her home as had Emily, that there had been long periods of unhappiness for her at Thorp Green and that she had for some time been anxious to leave her position as governess there. Yet, now that she was home, she seemed wretched and unable to enjoy her new freedom. In his heart Patrick divined the source of her worry. He guessed, Charlotte guessed and Emily, being Anne's confidante, no doubt was certain that it could only be Branwell. He had boasted much lately of his expected rise in the world, of how Lydia would see that his talents had the requisite financial backing and so forth. Patrick well knew his son and his little Anne: there was a dryness in his mouth when he realised the possibilities. Small wonder that Anne had left her employment of her own accord. One look at Branwell's face when he returned home helped to confirm his worst fears, his deepest suspicions. Branwell was more flushed and agitated than ever, was in a highly nervous state. Had there been a quarrel with his Lydia? On Thursday, 17th July, the matter was put beyond all doubt, and Anne was free to unburden her mind to all and sundry. Patrick was in his parlour when the post came. Tabby, as always, shuffled rapidly to the door, beating Martha by a few yards: it really was surprising how quickly she could move to the postman's knock, her lameness seemed quite to leave her! Patrick went on reading Graham's *Domestic Medicine* as peace once more settled over the house. Suddenly there came from upstairs a cry like that of a wounded animal, then a roar, then a moan, then a veritable shriek. He heard the kitchen door burst open and Emily's footsteps pounding up the stairs. He heard her overhead, thundering away in that deep voice of hers, and the moans and sobs ceased. Then the dining-room door slowly opened and a gentle tread crossed the hall. Anne put her head in at the door and Patrick saw she was trembling. "It was a letter from them, Papa; Branwell had a letter from the Robinsons." Her voice shook, yet there was a strong note of relief in it.

Patrick went upstairs and found his son whimpering, whilst Emily stood before him, her arms folded and a look of scorn on her face. It had been a note from the Rev. Edmund Robinson, not Lydia, and it had sternly dismissed Branwell from his employ. It went on to state that Branwell's proceedings, which were bad beyond expression, had been discovered; that unless he broke off instantly, and for ever, all communication with the entire family, Edmund Robinson would expose Branwell's conduct to the world. Patrick looked at his son for a full explanation of the meaning of this letter but could get nothing coherent from him save that he loved Lydia, that Lydia loved him, that Mr Robinson was an invalid and would soon be dead, the sooner the better; and Branwell continued to alternate between gusts of grief and anger. Patrick was only anxious to learn the extent of his son's guilt; was he an adulterer with another man's wife? But there was no answer to be had from Branwell and it was left to Anne to explain to Patrick that it was her conviction that Branwell, for all his faults, had not been guilty of such a wicked act. Patrick let out a breath of relief; that, at least, they had been spared. Yet there would be disgrace enough before all was done.

Anne gave it as her opinion that Lydia Robinson was weak and deceitful; that, her husband being an invalid, she had certainly encouraged Branwell and had toyed with his affections; but Branwell could not see that what was to him a desperately serious matter was to her a mere pastime. He was besotted with love for her, and she was utterly worthless. She did not care a jot for her young tutor. Patrick listened to Anne gravely and knew it was the truth, but how that would help them all manage Branwell was another matter altogether.

That evening Branwell went to the Black Bull, and it was the early hours before he returned, quite drunk. All the next day it was the same: he drowned his distress in spirits. So it was when Charlotte arrived home on the Saturday, and heard the full story from Anne. So it would be, with scarcely a respite, until he had killed himself off. Charlotte wrote to Ellen, ". . . no one in the house could have rest. At last we have been obliged to send him from home for a week, with some one to look after him . . . but so long as he remains at home I scarce dare hope for

peace in the house. We must all, I fear, prepare for a season of distress
and disquietude . . . I cannot now ask Miss Wooler or any one else. . . ."
There was to be only one good aspect of Branwell's unhappy troubles ;
he had finally squashed all hopes of setting up a school at the parsonage.
Now at last all three girls were free to write at home, that home that
alone could maintain their inspiration. Emily had progressed with
Wuthering Heights, Charlotte had *The Professor*, which needed only a
polish, and Anne had not come back from Thorp Green empty-handed.
She had brought back with her the first two volumes of *Passages in the
Life of an Individual* and noted in her diary paper of 31st July 1845
that "I have begun the third volume. . .". This would reach the world
as *Agnes Grey*. But as yet there was no thought of being published
(save, perhaps, in Charlotte's active brain) and the Brontës wrote simply
because they had to : the impulse was too great to resist.

Branwell returned on 3rd August from a week's holiday in Liverpool
and North Wales. Patrick had sent John Brown, his sexton, to act as
guardian over his drunken son. It has often been suggested that the
sexton's bad example was a contributing factor to Branwell's dissipation.
More will be said about this matter in the next chapter ; yet it is unlikely
that Patrick would confide his son at such a time to a man whom he
could not trust implicitly. The fact was that Patrick, having worked
with his sexton for many years and having employed his daughters in
his own home, had a very high opinion of the man. John Brown has been
much maligned.

Upon his return, Branwell drank more heavily than ever, until
forced to abstain through lack of funds. Then, driven to desperation,
he commenced borrowing and running up that series of debts that
would drain Patrick and his daughters until the day of Branwell's death.
He was out of the house a good deal, and when at home would usually
be upstairs too drunk to know what passed. Thus he knew next to
nothing of what his three sisters were about. For their part, when they
were being published, they would keep all the news from him : the
sense of his own failure would have been intensified and have pushed
him downhill the faster.

One day, in the autumn of 1845, Patrick was again sitting in his
parlour poring over various medical remedies recommended by Graham,
when there came an interruption to his studies. Branwell was out, so he
had counted on some peaceful hours. Suddenly from the dining-room
opposite he heard Emily's voice raised in a white-hot fury. There was
an unceasing torrent of angry words which grew louder and louder.
Then they ceased and he could make out Charlotte's "Oh, Emily, I
didn't mean to . . ." Then Emily was at it again, louder than before, and

more violent. Patrick shut his book and wondered what had overtaken
the girls. For a moment he was inclined to go in and inquire but
prudence whispered to him that he had best remain where he was. In
such a mood Emily's temper was not to be faced with impunity. Again
Emily stopped her tirade and he heard the dining-room door slam to
behind her as she rushed into the kitchen. Then came another crash
and he knew she was away, across the fields and on to the moors.
Shortly afterwards the door opposite opened again and there was a quiet
tread up the stairs. That was Anne. After a minute she returned, and
Patrick heard Charlotte and Anne talking quietly together. Well, the
storm was over for the time being, but Patrick was greatly perturbed.
It was so unlike the dear girls, what could possibly have upset Emily?
Was it something to do with Keeper again? Had Patrick understood his
Emily the less, had he blundered across the hall, he would have known
the truth. Charlotte had inadvertently come across Emily's open desk,
and her eyes had seen those sheets of verse. At the top was a poem but
newly completed; it bore the date 9th October 1845. Charlotte had at
once seen these lines:

> He comes with western winds, with evening's wandering airs,
> With that clear dusk of heaven that brings the thickest stars;
> Winds take a pensive tone, and stars a tender fire,
> And visions rise and change which kill me with desire. . . .

For fully a minute Charlotte stood transfixed, then she read on. Here
was genius. There is no moment in the Brontë story more vital than
this. Charlotte had seen Emily's soul. She could not fully comprehend
it, but she knew it was immortal.

Now the world can read those poems and be equally puzzled; yet,
for those who understand, there is everlasting bliss. But Emily had
come in and accused her sister of snooping. She did not write for the
world's vulgar gaze, but for herself. Anne had sensed the importance
of the occasion and, when Emily had stormed out of the house, had
brought down some of her own verses for Charlotte to look at. The
latter read them carefully and knew their greatness. Her own verse was
vastly inferior to that of her sisters yet they must publish a volume of
poems jointly, each contributing what were considered best. The rest is
known. What will never be discovered for certain is whether Emily and
Anne were planning to publish a little book of poems on their own.
Certainly they would have succeeded better without Charlotte's poor
verse; yet it does not appear possible that such was their intention.

Emily's rage was not at *Charlotte's* discovery of her innermost heart but that *anyone* should have gazed therein. Even the soul-mate Anne had not been allowed to read every poem. In that moment of blind fury, Emily must have been perilously close to pitching her poems into the fire; she would have been fully justified in so doing; yet she forbore. The world is thus fortunately enriched and because of that fortune should tread gently into Emily Brontë's soul; and if failing to understand what is there, should retire and enter never more.

In his parlour, Patrick re-opened his medical book and resumed his reading. How much did he know of his daughters' literary ambitions? What were his views of their poems and novels? There is some evidence.

It has been suggested that Patrick Brontë knew nothing of his daughters' hunger to write, that he saw them scribbling away but did not take their great industry seriously. Yet as early as March 1837 when Charlotte had received an answer to her letter to Robert Southey, she would write to the poet referring to his answer thus: ". . . That letter is consecrated; no one shall ever see it but papa and my brother and sisters. . . ." Patrick must then have long known that the scribbling had an ambitious bent, that it also brought the girls' hearts great release. He remembered *The Maid of Killarney* and his other hopes, and wished his children well. When on 28th January 1846, Charlotte first wrote to Messrs Aylott and Jones of Paternoster Row, asking if they would consider publishing the joint collection of poems, she gave direction that the answer should be addressed, "C. Brontë; Rev. P. Brontë, Haworth, Bradford, Yorkshire." This was continued in all subsequent correspondence until 28th March when she wrote, ". . . As the proofs have hitherto always come safe to hand under the direction of C. Brontë *Esq*—I have not thought it necessary to request you to change it, but a little mistake having occurred yesterday—I think it will be better to send them to me in future under my *real* address which is Miss Brontë, Revd. P. Brontë and etc." There certainly appears to be no great attempt to hide the approaching publication of the poems from Papa. One can imagine what the "little mistake" was: Martha had for once beaten Tabby in the race and handed the letter to Patrick. There is little doubt the latter knew all about the forthcoming book, and the pseudonyms Acton, Currer and Ellis Bell. As is known only two copies were sold (one purchaser, whose name is thus deservedly immortalized was F. Enoch, Corn Market, Warwick: he wrote to the Bells and requested their autographs). Thus Charlotte after this failure would be anxious to keep all news of their pending novels from her father, lest another failure should ensue. In such a case, he might well attempt to dissuade them from further literary attempts.

Both Patrick and the servants, however, had a suspicion that something was brewing, as indeed they admitted later. The real difficulty for the girls was to keep Branwell out of the dining-room. Yet even he must have felt it in his bones, and the landlord of the Black Bull would later relate how Branwell was anxious to collect local traditions in order to pass them on to his sisters for their books. But when Charlotte commenced her correspondence regarding the three novels, and sent the famous manuscripts to publisher after publisher under the name "Currer Bell", old James Feather, the then carrier for the post office, could bear the mystery of these continuous streams of thick, coarse paper parcels no longer. He accosted Patrick in the street one day; "You have a gentleman staying at the Parsonage, called Mr Currer Bell ?" Patrick answered at once, "You are mistaken, there is nobody in the whole of my parish of that name." James Feather had to be content with that reply. Patrick had expressed no surprise, had asked no questions regarding the name, although it was obvious from the nature of the query that letters had been delivered to the parsonage for a Mr Currer Bell. Certain it is that Patrick knew fully what was in the wind and, although not sanguine as to the chances of success, was quite happy to let his girls have their head. Meanwhile he wrestled with Branwell through many a night of torment and helped clear the way for his daughters to write. For Emily it was the easiest task. As Martha and her sisters have recalled, Emily's favourite retreats for writing were in the little front garden, sitting on a stool in the shade of the currant bushes or, better still, out on the moors where the only inquisitive intruders were the sheep. There "Ellis Bell" need fear no human inter-ference !

When *Wuthering Heights* was attributed in part to Branwell, Patrick was greatly annoyed. He stated that his son was quite incapable of writing a line of such a book. In 1879 Martha Brown told William Scruton that Patrick was indignant that people should say Branwell had helped Emily write the novel. "He maintained that Branwell had no share or part whatever in the book." Martha added that Emily was her favourite : she would never lend herself to any form of subterfuge, being "the very embodiment of truth and honour".

The circumstance of Patrick's first real knowledge of *Jane Eyre* has been told to Mrs Gaskell by Charlotte. There are two versions : one in a letter Mrs Gaskell wrote in August 1850, the other appearing in her Life of Charlotte. We take the latter, as it was written after the bio-grapher had met Patrick Brontë. ". . . Her sisters urged Charlotte to tell their father of its publication. She accordingly went into his study one afternoon after his early dinner, carrying with her a copy of the book, and one or two reviews, taking care to include a notice adverse to it. . . . 'Papa, I've been writing a book.' 'Have you, my dear ?' 'Yes, and I want you to read it.' 'I am afraid it will try my eyes too much.' 'But it is not in manuscript : it is printed.' 'My dear ! You've never thought of the expense it will be ! It will be almost sure to be a loss, for how can you get a book sold ? No one knows you or your name.' 'But, papa, I don't think it will be a loss ; no more will you, if you will just let me read you a review or two, and tell you more about it.'

"So she sat down and read some of the reviews to her father ; and then, giving him the copy of *Jane Eyre* that she intended for him, she left him to read it. When he came in to tea, he said, 'Girls, do you know Charlotte has been writing a book, and it is much better than likely ? . . .' "

There is another reference to Patrick and *Jane Eyre* in a letter Charlotte wrote in August 1849, at a time of crushing bereavement. ". . . I should grieve to see my father's peace of mind perturbed on my account ; for which reason I keep my author's existence as much as possible out of his way. I have always given him a carefully diluted and modified account of the success of *Jane Eyre*—just what would please without startling him. The book is not mentioned between us once a month. The *Quarterly* I kept to myself—it would have worried papa. . . ." Patrick was dreaming of *Wuthering Heights* and *Agnes Grey*, and of the authors who were no longer there.

What Patrick thought of Anne's two novels is, alas, not known, yet one cannot doubt his complete approbation.

It is known that when Charlotte had finished *Shirley*—originally to be named *Hollow's Mill*—Patrick was desirous that she should write another novel, that he was anxious *Villette* should have a happy ending and that he was delighted with the reviews of that book. As will be seen in a later chapter, he corresponded a number of times with Charlotte's publisher. There is no doubt that Patrick became a great enthusiast for his daughter's writing and had not his beloved Emily and Anne been taken from him just when their fame was on the wing and their novels being sold, he would have taken an active interest even sooner.

In 1853 he sent his brother Hugh a copy of the fourth edition of *Jane Eyre*, writing above the "Note to the Third Edition" the following words :

To Mr. Hugh Brontè. Ballynaskeagh, near Rathfriland, Ireland—This is the first work published by my daughter, under the fictitious name of "Currer Bell", which is the usual way at first by authors, but her real name is everywhere known. She sold the copyright of this and her other two works for fifteen hundred pounds ; so that she has to pay for the books she gets, the same as others. Her other two books are in six volumes, and would cost nearly four pounds. This was formerly in three volumes. In two years hence, when all shall be published in a cheaper form, if all be well, I may send them. You can let my brothers and sisters read this.

P. Brontë A.B.

Incumbent of Haworth, near Keighley. Jany. 20th 1853.

This was written eight days before *Villette* was published; it had been held back a week or two so as not to clash with Elizabeth Gaskell's *Ruth*. Patrick is, of course, incorrect regarding the question of author's free copies. Charlotte had received six copies of *Jane Eyre* from her publishers, Messrs Smith, Elder & Co.

Yet if Patrick showed enthusiasm for Charlotte's writings only after he had recovered somewhat from his crushing bereavements, it is certain that he early became aware as to what was afoot. It is to Mrs Gaskell that Patrick summed up his attitude to his daughters' hours of writing. In a letter dated 20th June 1855 he writes:

". . . When my daughters were at home they read their manuscripts to each other and gave their candid opinions of what was written. I never interfer'd with them at these times—I judged it best to throw them upon their own responsibility. Besides, a clergyman, bordering upon the age of eighty years [he was seventy when *Jane Eyre* and *Wuthering Heights* appeared in 1847], was likely to be too cold and severe a critic of the efforts of buoyant and youthful genius. Hence it came to pass that I never saw their works till they appear'd in print. . . ."

"I never interfered"—how many Victorian fathers, and clerical ones at that, could truly say as much?

Patrick never pried. He allowed his daughters to write books and have them published without once acting as a censor. He trusted his girls implicitly and gave them complete freedom. The "Bells" were grateful for this—and so should be posterity!

CHAPTER 23

Absalom

BRANWELL grew steadily worse. He drowned his sorrows in spirits, then laudanum, and finally opium itself. The autumn and winter of 1845, the two following years and the first half of 1848 slipped by almost unnoticed. He wrote letters to Francis Henry Grundy and Joseph Bentley Leyland during his more lucid moments, but knew little of his sisters' great literary efforts and nothing of their ultimate success. The rejection of *The Professor*, the appearance of *Poems by Currer, Ellis, and Acton Bell*, the immediate triumph of *Jane Eyre*, the spreading appreciation of *Wuthering Heights*, the publication of Anne's *Agnes Grey* and *The Tenant of Wildfell Hall*, all this happened under his very nose, yet he knew it not. Whilst Emily and Anne struggled with the rascally publisher Newby, whilst Charlotte poured forth letter after letter to Smith, Elder & Co., when Charlotte and Anne went down to London in July 1848 to see Mr George Smith and reveal to him their true identity, when Newby was publicly pilloried and even Emily's closely wrapped cloak of anonymity was finally removed, whilst all this occurred Branwell was in an almost continuous drunken or doped stupor. He had been finally moved into Patrick's bedroom, so that a watch could be kept upon his feverish nights, but not before he had almost caused the realization of his father's great horror—fire. From John Greenwood's diary we learn the following : "Poor Branwell, in the latter end of his life, had a habit of reading in bed ; and on one occasion had retired rather early to his room, more, I suspect, to indulge in the gin bottle than to read. At all events, he fell asleep with the loose [unbound] periodical in his hands, and which [he] had evidently let slip from [his] fingers. In falling to the floor, [it] had come in contact with the blaze of the candle, placed at his bedside, and consequently ignited, and set the bed on fire. Miss Anne, who had not retired, and having occasion to pass his room door, was the first to discover what had occurred, and in her own meek, quiet way, tried to rouse her brother by calling out— 'Branwell ! Branwell ! Your bed is on fire !' 'O, it's all right' was his unconscious reply, still asleep. 'Branwell ! Branwell !' she again exclaimed, 'do get up, your bed is on fire.' 'Well, well, we'll make it all right by and by,' still asleep. Seeing she could not awaken him, she went,

wringing her hands, to her sister Emily's bedroom door, crying,
'Emily! Branwell has set his bed on fire and I cannot wake him!' The
words were no sooner spoken than out came Emily, without uttering a
word, rushing at once into the room, seizing her brother and lifting him
apparently without an effort from the bed and threw him into one
corner of the room, where he cowered, stunned and bewildered. Then
she tore the bedding off—now all in flames, and threw that into the
middle of the room—the safest place—then flew downstairs into the
kitchen, seized a large can, which happened to be full of water at the
time, then upstairs she went and threw the whole of its contents on the
blazing pile and quenched it at once. The first words she uttered were
'Don't alarm papa!'"

That there was a can of water ready to hand is not surprising, for it
was always Patrick's ruling that full pails of water should stand in the
hall at night, against just such an emergency (also the blue and white
china ewer in Patrick's bedroom, when Branwell slept there).

As Branwell continued to disintegrate, both morally and physically,
Charlotte turned from him in disgust. Her comrade of Angrian days was
forgotten and she removed the last slender prop he could cling to—not
that ten thousand loving Charlottes could have saved him. Charlotte
had herself suffered the keenest pangs of frustrated love in honourable
silence (save to Monsieur Heger himself). She could only hold in
contempt her weak brother who thus bared his soul to the world.
Indeed, at this time of glorious creation there were three bruised hearts
in the parsonage: Charlotte's bled for her master, Branwell's for his
Lydia, and Anne's mourned secretly for Willy Weightman. Only the
shrinking heart of an old man and that other which had long since
been dedicated to the goddess Nature remained whole.

For Patrick, his son's abysmal homecoming had ruined what
promised to be a pleasant interlude in his life: he had so looked forward
to having all his family together again at home. Save for his one journey
to Thorp Green and a visit once to Charlotte at Heald's House, Dewsbury Moor, whither Miss Wooler's school had removed, he had seen
nothing of his children when they were from home.

Before we give a glimpse of Branwell's final decay in his own words
and those of Charlotte, a further glance must be taken at John Brown,
the sexton. That John Brown drank both ale and spirits is not denied;
that he often visited the Black Bull and other Haworth taverns is also
true; there is, in addition, evidence that he supplied Branwell with gin
shortly before the latter's death; yet that cannot amount to responsibility
for Branwell's long years of dissipation. True, he was fascinated by the
talents and conversational powers of the parson's son. Like most of the

villagers he was fond of Branwell, and enjoyed his witty and courteous company. The sexton was a well-read man and possessed a small library of books, unlike most of his Haworth contemporaries. Even after Branwell's final debauchery had commenced, Patrick made no move to separate his son from the sexton's company. Indeed, he sent Branwell away in the charge of John Brown.

It should be remembered that a sexton was appointed and dismissed by the incumbent. No one could possibly suggest Patrick was lacking in courage, and it is certain that if he had felt Brown's influence was bad for Branwell, he would very quickly have terminated his appointment. In such a personal matter as that, it was unlikely the trustees would have opposed his wishes. Yet John Brown remained as sexton and was honoured by all. Certainly his wages were far from princely, as the following extracts from the Vestry Book at the time of his appointment clearly show:

> To kindling fires — £1-10-0
> For clothes — £3- 0-0
> For tools — 10-0
> [These sums are for a full year's service.]
> Common Graves. For every one 3 feet deep, 2/-

The remuneration increases with the depth of the grave until he receives 10s for one 8 feet deep. Walled graves range from 12s for a six foot depth to £1 2s for nine feet. For reopening walled graves and walling again the fee was 5s 6d for three feet and 15s 6d for eight feet. "For removing any grave stone 6d. For replacing the same with walling 1/6. Without walling 6d. The attending on the funeral, filling up the grave, cleaning away the earth and removing the stones, is of course, included." The notice of John Brown's appointment ends: "that the foregoing statement of wages be by him strictly adhered to".

It is as well that Brown, who was the father of a large family, did not rely on his payment as sexton for a living: that indeed would not have allowed him to drink to excess in the Black Bull. Fortunately he had great skill as a monumental mason—his yard was beside the parsonage—and evidence of his skill still abounds in Haworth Churchyard and other churchyards in the district.

After his return from Wales Branwell writes to J. B. Leyland, ". . . I found during my absence that wherever I went a certain woman robed in black, and calling herself 'Misery' walked by my side, and leant on my arm as affectionately as if she were my legal wife. Like some other husbands I could have spared her presence. . . ." In the same

month Charlotte writes, ". . . My hopes ebb low indeed about Branwell
—I sometimes fear he will never be fit for much—his bad habits seem
more deeply rooted than I thought—the late blow to his prospects and
feelings has quite made him reckless. It is only absolute want of means
that acts as any check to him. . . ." And again, ". . . his health and
consequently his temper have been somewhat better this last day or
two, because he is now *forced* to abstain. . . ." In September she writes,
". . . Branwell makes no effort to seek a situation, and while he is at
home I will invite no one to come and share our discomfort. . . ."

To Francis Grundy in October 1845 Branwell gives an account of
the circumstances attending his dismissal from Thorp Green Hall.
". . . This lady [Mrs Robinson] (though her husband detested me)
showed me a degree of kindness which, when I was deeply grieved one
day at her husband's conduct, ripened into declarations of more than
ordinary feeling. My admiration of her mental and personal attractions,
my knowledge of her unselfish sincerity, her sweet temper, and un-
wearied care for others, with but unrequited return where most should
have been given. . . . Although she is seventeen years my senior, all
combined to an attachment on my part, and led to reciprocations which
I had little looked for. During nearly three years I had daily 'troubled
pleasure soon chastised by fear'. Three months since, I received a
furious letter from my employer, threatening to shoot me if I returned
from my vacation, which I was passing at home; and letters from her
lady's-maid and physician informed me of the outbreak, only checked
by her firm courage and resolution that whatever harm came to her,
none should come to me. . . . I have lain during nine long weeks utterly
shattered in body and broken down in mind. The probability of her
becoming free to give me herself and estate, never rose to drive away
the prospect of her decline under her present grief. I dreaded, too, the
wreck of my mind and body, which, God knows during a short life
have been severely tried. Eleven continuous nights of sleepless horror
reduced me to almost blindness. . . ."

Of course Branwell believed all that the lady's-maid (Ann Marshall)
and physician (Dr Crosby) had told him; all that Branwell did with his
brief life was weak and wicked enough, but here he was no liar. These
two were simply carrying out the orders of Lydia Robinson and her
brother-in-law, William Evans, Member of Parliament for North
Derbyshire. Lydia had not the slightest wish to see Branwell again.
Indeed she had long since repented of her flirtation with him—it could
lead to trouble for her, and she had a far greater prize in view, far
greater, that is, in her estimation. In November Branwell again sends a
letter to Leyland, ". . . I send through yourself the enclosed scrap for

the *Halifax Guardian*—and I ought to tell you why I wish anything of so personal a nature to appear in print. I have no other way, not pregnant with danger, of communicating with one whom I cannot help loving. Printed lines with my usual signature 'Northangerland' would excite no suspicion—as my late employer shrunk from the bare idea of my being able to write anything, and had a day's sickness after hearing that Macaulay had sent me a complimentary letter, so *He* won't know the name. I sent through a private channel one letter of comfort in her great and agonising present afflictions, but I recalled it through dread of the consequences of a discovery. . . . I hope I shall hear of you on John Brown's return from Halifax. . . .''

The scrap mentioned in this letter was a poem, "Penmaenmawr", and it contained the following lines:

> I knew a flower, whose leaves were meant to bloom
> Till Death should snatch it to adorn a tomb,
> Now, blanching 'neath the blight of hopeless grief,
> With never blooming, and yet living leaf;
> A flower on which my mind would wish to shine,
> If but one beam could break from mind like mine.
> I had an ear which could on accents dwell
> That might as well say "perish!" as "farewell!"
> An eye which saw, far off, a tender form,
> Beaten, unsheltered, by affliction's storm;
> An arm— a lip— that trembled to embrace
> My angel's gentle breast and sorrowing face;
> A mind that clung to Ouse's fertile side
> While tossing— objectless— on Menai's tide!

When one reads these lines, these reflections on his journey into Wales; when one reads his letters, so trusting and believing of his lady love, when one sees the illustrations that accompanied those epistles, so redolent of a mind unhinged, criticism of Branwell Brontë all but melts into pity. As with his sisters, idealism was the dominant force, yet he alone of all the Brontës lacked the courage to bend that ideal vision into reality. Branwell was abject, wholly unworthy of his parents or his sisters, yet, poor, hopeless, drifting creature that he was, he was fundamentally honest and good. Lydia Robinson it is whose name merits eternal execration.

In his introduction to *The Cottage in the Wood* Patrick had used wise words which applied forcibly to Branwell's condition. " . . . beings of depraved appetites and sickly imaginations, who having learnt the art of *self-tormenting*, are diligently and zealously employed in creating an imaginary world, which they can never inhabit, only to make the real world, with which they must necessarily be conversant, gloomy and insupportable . . . being utterly incapable of tracing good and evil to their proper sources. The truth is, that happiness and misery have their origin within, depending comparatively little on outward circumstances. The mind is its own place. . . ."

In December 1845 Charlotte writes again to Ellen Nussey: ". . . You say well in speaking of Branwell that no sufferings are so awful as those brought on by dissipation—alas! I see the truth of this observation daily proved. . . ." Again in the following month, ". . . no changes take place here—Branwell offers no prospect of hope—he professes to be too ill to think of seeking for employment—he makes comfort scant at home. . . ." On 30th January 1846, Charlotte writes to Margaret Wooler, ". . . You ask about Branwell; he never thinks of seeking employment and I begin to fear he has rendered himself incapable of filling any respectable station in life, besides, if money were at his disposal he would use it only to his own injury—the faculty of self-government is, I fear almost destroyed in him . . . they [men] are not half sufficiently guarded from temptation—girls are protected as if they were something very frail and silly indeed while boys are turned loose on the world as if they—of all beings in existence, were the wisest and the least liable to be led astray. . . ." It can hardly be said of Patrick Brontë that he turned Branwell "loose on the world".

Unable to invite any of her friends to stay at Haworth, Charlotte visited Ellen Nussey in February 1846.

To Ellen Nussey. Haworth, Feb. 25th 1846.

Dear Miss Nussey;—I fancy this note will be too late to decide one way or other with respect to Charlotte's stay. Yours only came this morning (Wednesday), and unless mine travels faster you will not receive it till Friday. Papa, of course, misses Charlotte, and will be glad to have her back. Anne and I ditto; but as she goes from home so seldom, you may keep her a day or two longer, if your eloquence is equal to the task of persuading her—that is, if she still be with you when you get this permission. Love from Anne.

Yours truly, Emily J. Brontë.

Emily's letter was in good time, for Charlotte did not return home until 2nd March, when ". . . I went into the room where Branwell was, to speak to him about an hour after I got home—it was very forced work to address him—I might have spared myself the trouble as he took no notice and made no reply—he was stupefied—my fears were not vain. Emily tells me that he got a sovereign from Papa while I have been away under the pretence of paying a pressing debt—he went immediately and changed it at a public-house—and has employed it as was to be expected—she concluded her account with saying he was a hopeless being—it is too true—In his present state it is scarcely possible to stay in the room where he is—what the future has in store I do not know. . . ." On 31st March 1846 she reveals to Ellen some other troubles at the Parsonage ; ". . . our poor old servant Tabby had a sort of fit a fortnight since but is nearly recovered now—Martha is ill with a swelling in her knee and obliged to go home . . . I am thankful papa continues pretty well—though often made very miserable in mind by Branwell's wretched conduct—*there*—there is no change but for the worse—" In the absence of any direct record of Patrick's feelings at this dreary season, we continue to quote from the letters of Charlotte and Branwell as they give an authentic and good description of the father's sufferings as his son became steadily more depraved.

Charlotte writes to Ellen on 14th April 1846 : ". . . how can we be more comfortable so long as Branwell stays at home and degenerates instead of improving ? It has been lately intimated to him that he would be received again on the same Rail-road where he was formerly stationed if he would behave more steadily but he refuses to make an effort, he will not work— and at home he is a drain on every resource— an impediment to all happiness. . . ."

Branwell's next letter to Leyland, written at the end of April, reveals that he had been over to Halifax for three days, doubtless drinking heavily at his favourite taverns in that place.

On 26th May 1846 the Rev. Edmund Robinson died, and from this moment Lydia Robinson's infamy knew no bounds. She sent her coachman George Gooch, to Branwell, with a string of lies upon his lips : Mrs Robinson was left powerless ; if she were to marry Branwell she must forfeit the property and all monies ; Mr Robinson's cruel will made it impossible for them to continue any relationship, and so on. In actual fact Lydia had been left everything in the way of property and money she could desire and wished only to be well rid of the former tutor. Her plans were to marry Sir Edward Scott, whose wife was dying. It was the final crushing blow for Branwell, who was quite incapable of perceiving the falsehood of the entire Robinson household. In June he writes to Leyland, ". . . Mr Robinson of Thorp Green is dead, and he has left his widow in a dreadful state of health. She sent the coachman over to me yesterday, and the account which he gave of her sufferings was enough to burst my heart. Through the will she is left quite powerless, and her eldest daughter who married imprudently is cut off without a shilling. [This last was the only truth in the coachman's story.] The Executing Trustees detest me, and one declares that if he sees me he will shoot me. These things I do not care about, but I do care for the life of the one who suffers even more than I do. Her coachman said that it was a pity to see her, for she was only able to kneel in her bedroom in bitter tears and prayers. She has worn herself out in attendance on him, and his conduct during the few days before his death was exceedingly mild and repentant, but that only distressed her doubly. Her conscience has helped to agonize her, and that misery I am saved from . . . for four nights I have not slept—for three days I have not tasted food—and when I think of the state of her I love best on earth, I could wish that my head was as cold and stupid as the medallion which lies in your studio. . . . What I shall *do* I know not—I am too hard to die, and too wretched to live. . . ."

Charlotte's version of this event is in her letter to Ellen dated 17th June: ". . . The death of Mr Robinson, which took place about three weeks or a month ago, served Branwell for a pretext to throw all about him into hubbub and confusion with his emotions, etc, etc. Shortly after, came news from all hands that Mr Robinson had altered his will before he died and effectually prevented all chance of a marriage between his widow and Branwell, by stipulating that she should not have a shilling if she ever ventured to reopen any communication with him. Of course, he then became intolerable. To papa he allows rest neither day nor night, and he is continually screwing money out of him, sometimes threatening that he will kill himself if it is withheld from him. He says Mrs Robinson is now insane; that her mind is a complete wreck owing to remorse for her conduct towards Mr Robinson (whose end it appears was hastened by distress of mind) and grief for having lost him. I do not know how much to believe of what he says, but I fear she is very ill. Branwell declares that he neither can nor will do anything for himself; good situations have been offered him more than once . . . but he will do nothing, except drink and make us all wretched. . . ."

Branwell repeats his tale of woe to Grundy, then writes again to Leyland: ". . . I have got my finishing stroke at last—and I feel stunned into marble by the blow. I have this morning received a long, kind and faithful letter from the medical gentleman who attended Mr R. in his last illness and who has since had an interview with one whom I can never forget. He knows me *well*, and he pities my case most sincerely [poor foolish, deluded Branwell]. . . . When he mentioned my name— she stared at him and fainted. When she recovered she in turns dwelt on her inextinguishable love for me—her horror at having been the first to delude me into wretchedness, and her agony at having been the cause of the death of her husband, who, in his last hours, bitterly repented of his treatment of her. Her sensitive mind was totally wrecked. She wandered into talking of entering a nunnery; and the Doctor fairly debars me from hope in the future. . . . I never cared one bit about the property. I cared about herself—and always shall do. May God bless her but I wish I had never known her! My appetite is lost; my nights are dreadful . . . when a young man like myself has fixed his soul on a being *worthy* of all love—and who for years, has *given* him all love, pardon him for boring a friend with a misery that has only one black end. I fully expected a change of the will, and difficulties placed in my way by powerful and wealthy men, but I *hardly* expected the hopeless ruin of the mind that I loved even more than its body. . . ."

Lydia Robinson, whilst eagerly waiting for Lady Scott to die, kept up the tale to Branwell of her collapsed mind. George Gooch, the coachman, was sent over again in July 1846 with an account of declining health.

It was at this stage of the proceedings that Charlotte took the now blind Patrick to Manchester for the operation on his eye. How much suffering the sightless old man had undergone as he wrestled night after night with his raving son may easily be conceived, also his anxiety in Manchester at having to leave his two youngest daughters to manage Branwell. Happily Emily was always a tower of physical strength. By December of 1846, Branwell was costing his family a small fortune. His debts were mounting everywhere, and at the beginning of the month Patrick suffered what would remain as the greatest humiliation of his life. Charlotte describes the sudden arrival of a "Sheriff's Officer on a visit to Branwell—inviting him either to pay his debts or to take a trip to York—of course his debts had to be paid—it is not agreeable to lose money time after time in this way, but it is ten times worse to witness the shabbiness of his behaviour on such occasions. . . ."

The next letter of Branwell's, written to Leyland at the beginning of 1847, reveals the main source of his money: Lydia Robinson herself. It is obvious that Patrick and his daughters could not clear all his debts and meet his craving for spirits and opium—Branwell had a further banker for his wants. Either Lydia paid him a regular sum of money to keep him quiet or Branwell blackmailed her on the threat of a public scandal; probably a combination of the two, for both parties had sunk so low morally that fresh sins could do no further harm. ". . . I wish Mr Thos: Nicholson of the *Old Cock* [Halifax] would send me my bill of what I owe to him, and, the moment that I receive my outlaid cash, or any sum which may fall into my hands through the

hands of one whom I may never see again, I shall settle it. That settlement, I have some reason to hope, will be *shortly*. But, can a few pounds
make a fellow's soul like a calm bowl of creamed milk ? . . ." Again, to
Leyland, on 24th January : ". . . an honest and kindly friend has
warned me that concealed hopes about one lady should be given up . . .
he is the Family Medical Attendant, and was commanded by Mr Evans,
M.P. for North Derbyshire to return me, unopened, a letter which I
addressed to Thorp Green and which the Lady was not permitted to
see. She too, surrounded by powerful persons who hate me like Hell,
has sunk into religious melancholy . . . I had reason to hope that ere
very long I should be the husband of a Lady whom I loved best in the
world, and with whom, in more than competence, I might live at
leisure to try to make myself a name in the world of posterity, without
being pestered by the small but countless botherments, which like
mosquitoes sting us in the world of work-day toil. That hope, and
herself are *gone*—*she* to wither into patiently pining decline—*it* to make
room for drudgery falling on one now ill fitted to bear it. . . ." In these
last few lines Branwell reveals his true self. He could not be bothered
with troubles of any kind ; he hoped to live at leisure to make a name for
himself. When one recalls that at this time Patrick endured his operation, that the three girls, two of whom had their own secret heartbreak,
were writing the finest novels in the English language, then Branwell's
words stick in the throat. Even if the guilt was Mrs Robinson's, Branwell's spineless behaviour made him unfit to be an inmate of that
parsonage or a member of that family. He goes on, ". . . my father
cannot have long to live, and that when he dies, my evening, which is
already twilight, will become night . . . for four years (including one
year of absence) a lady intensely loved me as I did her, and each
sacrificed to that love all we had to sacrifice, and held out to each other
Hope for our guide to the future. She was all I could wish for in a
woman, and vastly above me in rank, and she loved me even better than
I did her—now what is the result of these four years ? *Utter wreck.* . . .
I have received to-day, since I began my scrawl, a note from her maid
Miss Ann Marshall, and I *know* from it that she has been terrified by
vows which she was forced to swear to, on her husband's deathbed . . .
when that husband was scarce cold in his grave her relations, who
controlled the whole property overwhelmed her with their tongues, and
I am *quite conscious* that she has succumbed in terror to what they
said. . . ."

Charlotte writes again in March 1847 : ". . . Branwell has been conducting himself very badly lately—I expect from the extravagance of
his behaviour and from mysterious hints he drops—(for he never will

speak out plainly) that we shall be hearing news of fresh debts contracted by him soon—The Misses Robinson—who had entirely ceased
their correspondence with Anne for half a year after their father's death
have lately recommenced it . . . they speak with great affection too of
their Mother . . . we take special care that Branwell does not know of
their writing to Anne. . . . [12th May 1847:] . . . Branwell is quieter
now . . . he has got to the end of a considerable sum of money of which
he became possessed in the spring . . . you must expect to find him
weaker in mind, and the complete rake in appearance. . . ."

In one of his next letters, Branwell mentions the death of the old
landlord of the Black Bull: "Poor Dan Sugden has gone to the New
Jerusalem. Alas what is life?"

Ellen Nussey tried to relieve the gloom by sending presents to the
parsonage household. ". . . Papa says I am to remember him most
kindly to you. The screen will be very useful, and he thanks you for
it. . . ."

Towards the end of 1847, Branwell was taking drugs in a considerable quantity and his mind was completely unbalanced. He would
stagger about the village streets unwashed, unshaven, his clothes torn
and tattered. There was no pretence of hiding his hideous condition
from the villagers, many of whom saw Patrick find his son collapsed in
some corner, and although over seventy, pick up and carry the emaciated
Branwell home, slung over his shoulders. Charlotte writes in October of
that year, ". . . he leads Papa a wretched life. . . ". Never again does
Branwell refer to his Lydia who, so shortly after his death, became
Lady Scott. We have Patrick's view of Mrs Robinson, expressed just
once, when years later in a letter to Mrs Gaskell he wrote describing
her as his "brilliant and unhappy" son's "diabolical seducer".

In January 1848, Branwell paid another visit to Halifax; he writes to
Leyland, ". . . I was *really* far enough from well when I saw you last
week at Halifax, and if you should happen shortly to see Mrs Sugden of
the *Talbot* you would greatly oblige me by telling her that I consider her
conduct towards me as most kind and motherly, and that if I did
anything, during temporary illness, to offend her, I deeply regret it,
and beg her to take my regret as my apology till I see her again, which,
I trust will be ere long. I was not intoxicated when I saw you last . . . I
was so much broken down and embittered in heart that it did not need
much extra stimulus to make me experience the fainting fit I had, after
you left, at the *Talbot*, and another, more severe at Mr. Crowther's—
the *Commercial Inn* near the Northgate. . . ."

Charlotte writes, in the same month: " . . Branwell has contrived
by some means to get more money from the old quarter . . . Papa is

harassed day and night—we have little peace—he is always sick, has two or three times fallen down in fits. . . ." And again : ". . . Poor girls ! [the Robinsons] they still complain of their mother's proceedings ; that woman is a hopeless being ; calculated to bring a curse wherever she goes, by the mixture of weakness, perversion, and deceit in her nature. Sir Edward Scott's wife is said to be dying ; if she goes I suppose they will marry. . . ." This letter shows only too plainly that even Branwell knew the truth at last ; his last vestige of sanity now deserted him completely.

At this time of impending disaster, Ellen Nussey again tried to help. She offered Patrick a copy of *The Memoirs of the Life of Charles Simeon.* ". . . I dare say papa would like to see the work very much, as he knew Mr Simeon. . . ."

Three more letters from the wretched Branwell now follow in quick succession and then we hear him no more. He writes to Leyland in June 1848 : ". . . For mercies sake come and see me, for I have sought for you till I dare not risk my knee and my eyesight any more this evening. . . ." This was sent to the Old Cock, Halifax. Again he writes to Leyland on 22nd July. ". . . Mr Nicholson has sent to my Father a demand for the settlement of my bill owed to him, immediately, under penalty of a Court Summons. I have written to inform him that I shall soon be able to pay him the balance left in full—for that I will write to Dr Crosby, and request an advance through his hands, which I am sure to obtain, when I will remit my amount owed, at once, to the *Old Cock.*

"I have also given John Brown this morning Ten shillings, which John will certainly place in Mr N.'s hands on Wednesday next. If he refuses my offer and presses me with law, I am *ruined.* I have had five months of such utter sleeplessness, violent cough and frightful agony of mind that jail would destroy me for ever.

"I earnestly beg you to see Nicholson and tell him that my receipt of money on asking, through Dr. Crosby, is morally certain. If you conveniently can, see Mrs Sugden of the *Talbot,* and tell her that on receipt of the money I expect so shortly, I will transmit her the whole or part of the account I owe her. . . ."

Finally he writes to John Brown.

Sunday, noon.

Dear John,

I shall feel very much obliged to you if [you] can contrive to get me Five pence worth of Gin in a proper measure. Should it be speedily got I could perhaps take it from you or Billy [the sexton's younger brother] at the lane top or, what would be quite as well, sent out for, to you. I anxiously ask the favour because I know the good it will do me.

Punctually at Half-past Nine in the morning you will be paid the 5d out of a shilling given me then. Yours, P.B.B.

By now the seeds of consumption in Branwell were killing him quickly : his whole constitution was irreparably weakened by drink and drugs. How he dragged on as long as he did is the wonder, and the pity !

There was little respite for the household, save when Branwell was in one of his deep stupors. Patrick attempted some relief in another letter to the Ordnance, dated 4th July 1848. This time it was about a projectile, explained at length with a diagram. ". . . let it be supposed, that this globe is projected either from a mortar, or a cannon, so as to pass through only one side of a ship and rest in and explode in the interior—or if it did not explode, issue forth, a stream of intense fire . . . Might it not in this way, produce both the effect of a ball, and shell— and being capable of *horizontal* firing, be extremely destructive to the enemy ?—As I know but little of Howitzer practice, or the mode of projecting shells, these notions of mine may, I am aware, be not only crude, but incorrect—However this may be, I cannot submit them to a better Judge than your Lordship—

"I remain, My Lord Marquis,

"Your Lordship's most obedient & humble servant,

"Patrick Brontë, A.B.

"Incumbent of Haworth, near Keighley, Yorkshire."

"To The Right Honourable the Marquis of Anglesey,
"Master General of the Ordnance, London—"

On 2nd August the committee answered ". . . that the object which he proposes, has long since been fully accomplished by means of the present Wood Fuse of the Service applied to Shells, both for Vertical and Horizontal firing from Guns, Howitzers and Mortars in the Naval and Artillery Services ; the mode suggested by Mr. Bronte being a crude illustration of the early practice of Shell-firing". But the answer meant nothing to Patrick, for Branwell was now rapidly deteriorating.

Charlotte, at the end of July 1848, says : ". . . his constitution seems shattered. Papa, and sometimes all of us, have sad nights with him, he sleeps most of the day, and consequently will lie awake at night. . . ." In August she writes : ". . . Papa has been very much interested in reading the book [*Life of Simeon*]. There is frequent mention made in it of persons and places formerly well known to him ; he thanks you for lending it . . . The unhappy Lady Scott is dead . . . Mrs Robinson is anxious to get her daughters husbands of any kind, that they may be off her hands, and that she may be free to marry Sir Edward Scott. . . ."

It was well that Patrick could relive his days at Cambridge to take his mind temporarily off Branwell's condition. Yet the book was not a tactful choice of Ellen's, the author being the Rev. William Carus, cousin to the Rev. Carus Wilson, that sure reminder of death to the inhabitants of Haworth Parsonage. Now Patrick could read Simeon's strictures of the latter's Calvinism; yet he said nothing to his daughters of this tearing open of old wounds.

Just before Branwell's death, Francis Grundy went to visit him in Haworth. He went to the Black Bull and sent word of his arrival to the parsonage. ". . . Whilst I waited his appearance, his father was shown in. Much of the Rector's [sic] old stiffness of manner was gone. He spoke of Branwell with more affection than I had ever heretofore heard him express, but he also spoke almost hopelessly. He said that when my message came, Branwell was in bed . . . he had insisted upon coming, and would be there immediately. . . ." Branwell arrived carrying a carving knife secreted in his coat, in case he met the devil, and Grundy describes ". . . the sunken eyes, once small, now glaring with the light of madness. . . ". Two days before his death Branwell visited John Brown's house in Parsonage Lane. Tabitha Brown, Martha's sister (later Mrs Ratcliffe), recalled "teasing him because his clothes hung on him so loosely"; he was asked if he had his father's coat on. He looked a mere skeleton.

On the morning of Sunday, 24th September 1848, Branwell Brontë died. He was thirty-one. His last caller was his old friend, John Brown, the sexton. Shortly after Brown had left, Branwell became very ill suddenly, and the last paroxysm came on. Branwell did not attempt to get to his feet, as so often stated, but raised himself a little in sudden fear. Patrick later told John Brown that Branwell was very penitent and asked forgiveness from his family.

His old father, who had wrestled with him body and soul for many a long and bitter night, prayed as he had never prayed before. All his early Methodist faith, all his Evangelical Church training taught him that one last effort must be made to save this soul. Branwell, who had so insolently referred to his father's unceasing nocturnal vigils as "the poor old man and I have had a terrible night of it", turned to Patrick suddenly as there was a pause in the flood of prayer. "Amen!" It was the last word Branwell would ever utter and there was a smile on his face, a smile of peace that became instantaneously fixed in death. In that last second of life he had become again for Patrick that little golden-haired lad who had wanted a box of soldiers. In that last word, there had been a chance, surely, of salvation! At the moment of death, Patrick cared only for the soul; Anne breathed a sad sigh of relief;

Charlotte felt suddenly sick and faint now that the long trial was over. Emily walked slowly downstairs : never again would she need to light the little lamp and place it in the peat-room window, as a guiding star for the drunken brother as he left the Bull.

Only when he reached the solitude of the parlour did the worldly measure of his loss overcome Patrick. Only then did he think of the body as well as the soul ; grief engulfed him and he wept aloud for his only son. Charlotte wrote on 2nd October, ". . . My poor father naturally thought more of his *only* son than of his daughters, and, much and long as he had suffered on his account, he cried out for his loss like David for that of Absalom—my son ! my son !—and refused at first to be comforted. . . ."

CHAPTER 24

Anne

"WE HAVE buried our dead out of our sight." So wrote Charlotte on 2nd October 1848 to her friend W. S. Williams, the reader of Smith, Elder and Co. ". . . Branwell was his father's and his sisters' pride and hope in boyhood, but since manhood the case has been otherwise . . . my brother was a year my junior. I had aspirations and ambitions for him once, long ago—they have perished mournfully . . . My unhappy brother never knew what his sisters had done in literature—he was not aware that they had ever published a line. . . ." And again to Williams on 6th October, ". . . In the value, or even the reality of these two things [religion and principle] he would never believe till within a few days of his end, and then all at once he seemed to open his heart to a conviction of their existence and worth. The remembrance of this strange change now comforts my poor Father greatly. I myself, with painful, mournful joy, heard him praying softly in his dying moments, and to the last prayer which my father offered up at his bedside, he added 'Amen'. How unusual that word appeared from his lips. . . ." Finally, to Ellen Nussey on 9th October, ". . . Branwell's constitution had been failing fast all the summer, but still neither the doctor nor himself thought him so near his end as he was. He was entirely confined to his bed but for one single day, and was in the village two days before his death. The end came after twenty minutes' struggle on Sunday morning, 24th September. He was perfectly conscious till the last agony came on. His mind had undergone the peculiar change which frequently precedes death. Two days previously the calm of better feelings filled it. A return of natural affection marked his last moments. . . . Papa was acutely distressed at first, but on the whole has borne the event well. Emily and Anne are pretty well, though Anne is always delicate, and Emily has a cold and cough at present. . . ."

They had buried their dead out of their sight on Thursday, 28th September 1848, and, for the last time, William Morgan did service for his old friend. Patrick had no hesitation in calling upon Morgan yet again, especially since Branwell's godparent, John Fennell, who had baptized him, was dead.

For the first time since Miss Branwell's death, the little gate of the

dead at the bottom of the garden was opened to the churchyard, and
they carried the luckless Branwell into the church, to lay him in the
vault next his mother, his two sisters and his beloved aunt. The tiny
face of Maria would haunt him no more. Patrick walked behind the
coffin of his dearest hopes, as erect as if he were still on parade with
Palmerston at Cambridge. Behind him came Emily and Anne, both
deathly pale. Then followed John Brown and Martha, and behind
them again, other members of the Brown family. On her admission,
Charlotte, after bearing up for a day or two following her brother's
death, collapsed with a bilious fever and was confined to bed for a
week, so it seems unlikely that she attended the funeral. And if she
were not actually waiting for the funeral procession within the church,
it can readily be imagined that old Tabby was there to bid adieu to
another of her "bairns". When the service was over, William Morgan
went into the vestry to make his entry : Morgan has a sad claim as the
true memorialist of many of the vital moments of the Brontës' lives.

| Patrick Branwell Bronte | Haworth | Sept : 28th | 30 [31] yrs. | W. Morgan Off'. Minister. |

As William Morgan goes down Kirkgate after burying Branwell
Brontë, we take leave of this old friend of Patrick's ; apart from a great
kindness a year later, he played little further active part in Patrick's life.
As his carriage whirls him away from Haworth until he is lost to sight,
it is a suitable time to recall what an important part he played in
shaping the Brontë story : he had introduced Patrick to Mary Fletcher ;
and he had found him his bride. As he disappears down the road to
Keighley, it seems a shame that William Morgan is largely remembered
as an irascible Welshman who once sent his cook to jail for making thin
sauce !

On the following Sunday, 1st October, the funeral service was held.
The Brontë family sat in their pew. Mr Nicholls performed the service,
assisted by Mr Grant from Oxenhope. As they came out of the church,
a blast of cold moorland air swept down from the hills and crossed the
bare graveyard. There was already a chill in it that told of an early
winter season. Tabitha Brown watched from the lane as Patrick and
Charlotte walked slowly down the garden path and the father helped
his daughter, fresh from her sickbed, to climb the parsonage steps.
Martha and Tabby were up the lane and in at the kitchen door, as
Anne and Emily walked very slowly between the tombs. They entered
the garden and Anne went indoors. Emily slowly closed the little gate
and for a moment stood looking at it thoughtfully. Then she looked up

at the hills that circled the village on all sides. As she gazed at the moors there was a happy smile on her lips, yet two large tears rolled down her cheeks. She stood a moment longer, as still as a statue; then she slowly turned and went up the steps and into the parsonage. Emily Brontë had not only parted with her brother, but had bade farewell to those moors of fading heather that were her own paradise. She would never leave the old grey parsonage again until that little gate she had just closed was opened once more to let her pass through to glory.

Patrick sat in his parlour and worried about little Anne. Again he trembled at her delicate looks, her thin, pinched face. Had not bereavement always come to him as a double blow? Now that poor Branwell was gone, his fears for Anne became acute. But this time Death would pay Patrick the cruellest of visits, not twice in a short space of time but thrice! And it was not Anne who would die, not quite yet!

Emily's cold and cough grew rapidly worse. By the middle of October her shortness of breath was apparent to all the household. By the beginning of November she was very ill. Of the next seven weeks, the world well knows. Charlotte has given to posterity her very finest lines as she poured out her soul in anguish as she watched Emily die. Now, at last, she realized what her sister meant to her. ". . . I think Emily seems the nearest thing to my heart in this world. . . ." and ". . . she is dear to me as life. . . ." Anne had always loved Emily more than any, even her love for Weightman was less surely rooted; and in his lonely parlour Patrick knew full well the extent of his next approaching loss. Was she not "a brave and noble girl", his right hand, the very apple of his eye?

All the Brontë deaths were tragic for the survivors; death is always so. Yet Emily's death was the most anguishing of all. All three who watched her daily struggle loved her more than any other being on earth—a higher proportion than at any other time of heartache. In the kitchen Martha and Tabby kept silent with grief: Emily was their favourite too! In the village also there were stricken hearts. John Greenwood, whose admiration for Emily was unbounded, later wrote of his last meeting with her. "The last time I ever spoke to Miss Emily was one morning when I met her, returning from one of her rambles on the moor. I shall never forget the sweetness of manner—the rapture, with which she returned my morning salutation. Her countenance was lit up with a divine light. Had she been holding converse with Angels, it could not have shone brighter. It appeared to me, holy—heavenly! Oh! how precious are those Moors! . . . But now, and henceforth, they will be sacred ground."

All through November and early December, Emily continued to

carry out her share of the housework. She fed the dogs, did her sewing, and refused point-blank to see a doctor. Charlotte wrote letters describing her condition and received medical advice by post, as she wrote of Emily, ". . . she declares 'no poisoning doctor' shall come near her. . .".

Patrick looked keenly at Emily and agreed that no doctor should be sent for. One glance told him it was too late, that it would have been so even before Branwell's death, when she had taken a chill. Why disturb her last days by an insistence that could do no good ? Emily would only drag herself away up into the hills to die alone like a hunted wild animal. Charlotte writes again : ". . . My father is very despondent about her. Anne and I cherish hope as well as we can, but her appearance and her symptoms tend to crush that feeling . . . my father shakes his head and speaks of others of our family once similarly afflicted, for whom he likewise persisted in hoping against hope, and who are now removed where hope and fear fluctuate no more. . . ." Patrick was quite resigned to the fact that his Emily would die. She had her own mysterious beliefs in Nature that would give her courage. But he looked, as always, to God Almighty for the strength to bear this new blow.

By the second week in December Emily was greatly reduced and had a severe pain in her chest. The last lines she would ever pen were written. In her writing desk were reviews of *Wuthering Heights*, at least one of which was favourable enough to promise that, one day, the novel would achieve something of the fame and popularity it deserved.

Patrick tried to take his mind off the inevitable by reading one of the books from the box of volumes that George Smith, Charlotte's publisher, had sent her. He chose George Borrow's *The Bible in Spain*. In sending her thanks to Smith, Charlotte ends, ". . . Under present circumstances whatever agreeably occupies his mind must be truly beneficial. . . ."

There was no comforting to be done. Patrick dare show no added affection. Like his other two daughters, he must stand aside and say nothing. To make a fuss would only add to Emily's torment. On 9th December Charlotte describes Emily's condition as follows : ". . . Her appetite failed ; she evinced a continual thirst, with a craving for acids . . . In appearance she grew rapidly emaciated ; her pulse—the only time she allowed it to be felt—was found to be 115 per minute . . . her resolution to contend against illness being very fixed, she has never consented to lie in bed for a single day—she sits up from 7 in the morning till 10 at night. All medical aid she has rejected, insisting that Nature should be left to take her own course. . . ."

As Christmas drew daily nearer, Emily became weaker and weaker. She was now terribly emaciated. On the evening of Monday, 18th

December, she staggered into the stone-flagged passage on her way to the kitchen to feed Keeper and Flossy: at the kitchen door she fell against the wall. Charlotte and Anne rushed after her saying they would feed the dogs. Emily smiled faintly, but refused all aid. She went out into the yard and gave Keeper and Flossy their supper, the last they would ever receive from those loving hands. Later, Charlotte read to Emily as she lay on the horsehair sofa; ". . . the very evening before her last morning dawned I read to her one of Emerson's essays—I read on till I found she was not listening—I thought to recommence next day—Next day, the first glance at her face told me what would happen before night-fall."

Ellen had sent some crab-cheese for the patient; it was never tasted. Like Emerson's essay it was too late now.

Tuesday, 19th December 1848, dawned cold and clear. There had been little sleep for any of the inmates of that old Haworth Parsonage. Emily had, perhaps, slept more than anyone, yet even in her sleep the pain had wrung moans from her. She was now in the large front bedroom which had been Aunt's room, and her mother's before that. There could be a fire in this room, none in the narrow nursery. Tabby and Martha, next door, heard the moans and could not sleep. Charlotte, in the nursery would not have slept had all been silence. Anne in the small back room prayed half the night, and during the other half recalled happy moorland days spent with Emily. Patrick sat up in bed and with wearied eyes watched the dawn coming. In turns they had all crept to Emily's door, and perhaps one at least of them sat at her bedside for some time.

Charlotte was up and out of the house first. On to the moors she raced to look for a sprig of heather that might yet bear some faint trace of bloom. She brought home one dried withered branch and took it up to her sister. Listless eyes gazed at the precious growth, but recognized it not.

With exceeding difficulty, with many a pause to gasp for breath, Emily dressed herself unaided and tottered downstairs to the dining-room. Anne was dusting, Charlotte writing a note to Ellen: ". . . I should have written to you before, if I had but one word of hope to say; but I had not. She grows daily weaker . . . He [the London physician] sent some medicine which she would not take. Moments so dark as these I have never known. I pray for God's support to us all. Hitherto He has granted it. . . ."

Emily took up some sewing and attempted to work at it, but it soon slipped from her feeble fingers. As noon approached she became suddenly worse. She lay back on the sofa and whispered, "If you will send for a doctor, I will see him now !" Emily was safe now : no doctor could meddle with or poison her, prevent or retard her release from the chains of life.

Her own words blazed in her mind as she lay back on the cushion :

> Mute music soothes my breast—unuttered harmony
> That I could never dream till earth was lost to me.
> Then dawns the Invisible, the Unseen its truth reveals ;
> My outward sense is gone, my inward essence feels—
> Its wings are almost free, its home, its harbour found ;
> Measuring the gulf it stoops and dares the final bound !
> Oh, dreadful is the check—intense the agony
> When the ear begins to hear and the eye begins to see ;
> When the pulse begins to throb, the brain to think again,
> The soul to feel the flesh and the flesh to feel the chain !
> Yet I would lose no sting, would wish no torture less ;
> The more that anguish racks the earlier it will bless ;
> And robed in fires of Hell, or bright with heavenly shine,
> If it but herald Death, the vision is divine. . . .

Patrick was summoned by a white-faced Anne, and the three of them looked down on her whom they all held as dearer than life itself. Emily refused to be taken upstairs to bed : "No, no," she cried. These are the last recorded words of as great a poet or novelist as ever lived— fittingly defiant to the last.

Just before two o'clock she tried to raise herself up, and fell back dead into Charlotte's arms. Anne and Patrick knelt by the side of the black sofa. Perhaps that dried sprig of heather was on the couch by her side ; perhaps it had been left upstairs, it matters little, for the heady scent of moorland ling would ever remind Patrick of Emily. He returned to his parlour to grieve afresh. In the village they soon knew that "t'parson's Emily" was dead : Keeper's pitiable howl had been un- mistakable.

"She died in a time of promise" : so wrote Charlotte of her beloved sister. Yet for Emily it was a time of fulfilment. It is true, as Charlotte says, that the sisters' writings had burst upon the world like a rocket and would soon spread their shiny stars over the night sky of world literature, but for Emily it was all over. Read her poems in their entirety, every line of every verse ; read *Wuthering Heights*, the greatest novel the world has ever known ; what then remains to be said ? It was there, it had all been conceived and written down ; nothing was left now but fame and notoriety. The sullying of pure thought and feeling, the adulation, the flattery, the rank hypocrisy, the theorists and the cranks : there was nothing left that could interest Emily, only distortion and unhealthy speculation. Men and women whose feet had never trod the moors, whose ears had never heard the curlew, whose very hearts quailed at the crash of thunder and the blaze of lightning, who knew not ling from heather or bracken from fern, would sit sipping tea in their dainty salons and explain to a nicety the enigma that was Emily. But the moorland folk who knew the answer to that riddle could not read or write and kept their silence. The giant was dead ; now the pygmies could strut and grimace and explain at length what was a complete mystery to them—and the moor kept Emily's immortal vision locked in its quiet peaty heart.

The funeral was on Friday, 22nd December. Again the little gate was opened by John Brown. The coffin was carried down the garden path and through into the churchyard. Then followed Patrick, still erect and dignified, but holding firmly to his stick. This time he did not walk alone ; the other chief mourner was by his side. It was Patrick's express wish that Keeper be allowed to attend the funeral service, and the old dog padded along beside his master. It was what Emily would have wished ; it was what Patrick himself desired. Had they never written a word, the entire Brontë family would deserve eternal fame for the uniquely courteous way in which they always treated their servants and pets as complete equals.

Behind Patrick and Keeper walked Charlotte and Anne, then Martha and Tabby, the last insisting on taking part in the small procession. Arthur Nicholls met them at the south door of the church. Perhaps he took a quick glance at Charlotte's face, rendered almost hideous by the excess of grief, and knew for the first time that he loved her.

Nicholls committed Emily's body to the family vault and the coffin was slowly lowered into the dark depths. But in the Brontë pew not one pair of eyes followed it. Patrick, Charlotte, Anne, Martha, Tabby, even Keeper, looked up at the high church windows. Yet they did not see the square panes of coloured glass, only high waving heather and moss crop, long grass and clumps of bilberry. They heard not Nicholls's deep tones but only the lapwing and curlew. Emily was there at last, high on those moors from which she need never return again.

| Emily Jane Brontè | Haworth | Dec. 22nd | 29 [30] yrs. | A. Nicholls. Curate. |

But Emily is timeless, ageless.

When they were back in the parsonage, Keeper threw off all

restraint. During the entire service he had been perfectly quiet, but now he ran upstairs to the door of Emily's room and howled pitifully for many days to come. Martha's grief was very deep. She would speak for Tabby and her own sisters when she declared: "Emily we always thought to be the best-looking, the cleverest, and bravest-spirited of the three sisters."

If Charlotte had been the one to collapse at the time of Branwell's death, she was now to be the member of that dwindling family who would rally strongly. Anne was crushed with grief at the loss of Emily and was far from well. Patrick was quite stunned by his recent bereavements: he had once supposed Emily to be the strongest physically of them all. Although seventy-two years of age, it was only now that he suddenly felt an old man, whose great strength had ebbed from a powerful body. The late tragedies had only served to heighten his anxiety about little Anne: she seemed to be very weak. What would be the end of it all? He saw Charlotte busying herself about the house and suddenly felt that she alone was now the family's hope and strength. As she has recorded, on Christmas Day 1848, ". . . My father says to me almost hourly, 'Charlotte, you must bear up—I shall sink if you fail me'. . . ." She continues, ". . . The sight too of my sister Anne's very still but deep sorrow wakens in me such fear for her that I dare not falter. . . ."

The year 1849 came in cold and stormy; both Patrick and Anne were in bed with influenza. It must be stressed that Anne's case was very different from Emily's. True, both had "consumption" but, unlike her late sister, Anne was willing and eager to receive all the medical advice and attention that could be procured, and neither Patrick nor Charlotte hesitated in consulting the best available brains. It was only too much of a relief to their pent-up feelings to be able to render assistance to Anne, after having to watch helplessly as Emily refused all aid whatsoever. ". . . Anne is very patient in her illness—as patient as Emily was unflinching. I recall one sister and look at the other with a sort of reverence as well as affection—under the test of suffering neither have faltered. . . ."

Ellen Nussey came to stay at the parsonage at this time of trial and grief, as a comfort for Charlotte: that the latter was in dire need of encouragement is only too obvious. On 2nd January Charlotte writes to Mr Williams: ". . . hope has proved a strange traitor; when I shall again be able to put confidence in her suggestions, I know not; she kept whispering that Emily would not, *could* not die, and where is she now? Out of my reach, out of my world—torn from me. . . ." Medical advice was sought for Anne, and on 7th January Mr Thomas Pridgin Teale,

surgeon to the Leeds General Infirmary, came over to examine her.
Ellen has recorded the following note on his visit: "I made my visit to
Haworth and found the family wonderfully calm and sustained, but
anxious respecting Anne. Mr Brontë enquired for the best doctor in
Leeds. Mr Teale was recommended ; and came to Haworth. Anne was
looking sweetly pretty and flushed, and in capital spirits for an invalid.
While consultations were going on in Mr Brontë's study, Anne was very
lively in conversation, walking round the room supported by me.
Mr Brontë joined us after Mr Teale's departure, and, seating himself
on the couch, he drew Anne towards him and said, 'My *dear* little Anne.'
That was all—but it was understood. Charlotte afterwards told me that
Mr. Teale said—The disease of consumption had progressed too far
for cure ; and he thought so seriously of the case, he took the trouble to
acquaint my friends and urge them to call me home from my visit."
So Ellen left the parsonage, and Patrick and Charlotte could only pray
that Anne might be spared to them for a little while yet.

Anne quietly picked up her pencil and commenced the last poem
she would ever write, her now famous "Last Lines". By the 28th of
that month she would add the last two verses :

> If Thou shouldst bring me back to life,
> More humbled I should be ;
> More wise, more strengthened for the strife,
> More apt to lean on Thee.
> Should Death be standing at the gate,
> Thus should I keep my vow ;
> But hard whate'er my future fate,
> So let me serve Thee now.

By the 10th of January, Dr Wheelhouse, the local doctor, had
visited Anne and ordered that a blister be put on again : ". . . she bore it
without sickness—I have just dressed it—and she is risen and come
downstairs—she looks somewhat pale and sickly—She has had one dose
of the Cod-liver oil—it smells and tastes like train-oil . . . Papa continues much the same—he was very faint when he came down to
breakfast. . . ." By the middle of January, Patrick was recovered, but
Anne was no better ; ". . . Anne cannot study now, she can scarcely
read ; she occupies Emily's chair—she does not get well. A week ago we
sent for a Medical Man of skill and experience from Leeds to see her ;
he examined her with the stethoscope ; his report I forbear to dwell on
for the present . . . she must not travel—she is not to stir from the house
this winter—the temperature of her room is to be kept constantly

equal. Had leave been given to try change of air and scene, I should
hardly have known how to act—I could not possibly leave papa—and
when I mentioned his accompanying us the bare thought distressed
him too much to be dwelt upon. Papa is now upwards of seventy years
of age, his habits for nearly thirty years have been those of absolute
retirement—any change in them is most repugnant to him and probably
could not at this time especially—when the hand of God is so heavy upon
his old age, be ventured upon without danger. . . ." George Smith,
through Mr Williams, then suggested that his friend, Dr John Forbes,
would perhaps be willing to travel up to Haworth to see the sick Anne.
Forbes, who was sixty-two, was physician to the Queen's household ;
at the time Maria Branwell left Penzance for Woodhouse Grove, he had
just settled as a young medical practitioner in that Cornish town.
Charlotte answers Smith on 22nd January ". . . The proposal was one
which I felt it advisable to mention to my Father, and it is his reply
which I would now beg to convey to you. I am enjoined, in the first
place, to express my Father's sense of the friendly and generous feeling
which prompted the suggestion, and in the second place to assure you
that did he think any really useful end could be answered by a visit
from Dr. Forbes he would, notwithstanding his habitual reluctance to
place himself under obligations, unhesitatingly accept an offer so
delicately made. He is, however, convinced that whatever aid human
skill and the resources of science can yield my sister is already furnished
her in the person of her present medical attendant, in whom my Father
has reason to repose perfect confidence, and he conceives that to bring
down a Physician from London would be to impose trouble in quarters
where we have no claim, without securing any adequate result. . . ."
Nevertheless, Charlotte sent a version of Teale's report and treatment,
and asked for Dr Forbes's advice. Back came the answer and Charlotte
mentioned it to Ellen : ". . . Dr. Forbes said he knows Mr Teale well,
and thinks highly of his skill. The remedies were precisely those he
would have recommended himself. He warned us against entertaining
sanguine hopes of recovery . . . He, too, disapproved of the change of
residence for the present. There is some feeble consolation in thinking
we are doing the very best that can be done. The agony of forced,
total neglect, is not now felt, as during Emily's illness. Never
may we be doomed to feel such agony again. It was terrible. . . ." On
31st January came another parcel of books from Mr Williams. ". . .
Papa is at this moment reading Macaulay's *History*, which he had
wished to see. . . ."

All through February, March and April, Anne fluctuated in health
her complaint so often flattering to deceive. Meanwhile Patrick had

received several letters of condolence for his recent losses. His reply to Mr Rand has survived:

To Mr. Rand, St. Mark's School, Ducking Field, Nr. Manchester.

Haworth, near Keighley, Feby. 26th 1849.

Dear Sir,

I have indeed had my ample share of trouble—But it has been the Lord's will—and it is my duty, to resign—My only son has died, and soon after him, a beloved daughter, died also—For these things we may weep, since Christ himself wept over his dead friend—and also over the living inhabitants of Jerusalem—Yet, whilst we grieve, it should not be without hope. I am sorry to learn that Mrs Rand is in a delicate state of health, and that Mrs Bacon is not well—but pleased to know that your son is in good health. All my Family that remain, join me in kind regards to you all. I remain, dear Sir, yours truly,

P. Brontè.

Charlotte had been engaged in writing *Shirley* when Emily became ill. Her publishers were delighted with the start of the work, but for some time now it was put aside, neglected and almost forgotten. In March Charlotte writes, ". . . my Father, I am thankful to say, has been wonderfully sustained. . . ."

By the beginning of April, Anne was desperately anxious to get to Scarborough, where she had so often gone with the Robinsons, and which she loved second only to the hills of home. She hoped Ellen would accompany her, but the latter's friends were unwilling she should undertake such a responsibility. However, at the end of the month it was agreed that Charlotte, Anne and Ellen were all to go to Scarborough. Patrick said he would be quite all right left on his own. Anne was more than able to afford the journey as her godmother, Fanny Outhwaite, had died in Bradford on 14th February and left her £200. Rooms were booked, for 30s a week, at "No. 2 The Cliff", where Anne had stayed three or four times with the Robinsons, thus obviating the need to accept Margaret Wooler's kind offer of her house there, an offer which came shortly after the apartments had been booked. It was agreed that Wednesday, 23rd May, should be the day of travel. Ellen was to meet them at Leeds.

On the 16th Charlotte writes to Ellen: ". . . We shall leave Keighley about ½ 1 o'clock and expect to reach Leeds soon after two—Wednesday 23rd that is next week . . . I feel you will be shocked when you see Anne —but be on your guard—dear Ellen—not to express your feelings . . . I wish my judgment sanctioned this step of going to Scarboro' more fully than it does. You ask have I arranged about leaving papa—I could make no special arrangement—he wishes me to go with Anne—and would not hear of Mr. Nicholls coming—or anything of that kind. . . ."

But when 23rd May dawned, Anne was far too ill to contemplate the long journey. Ellen waited for several hours on the platform at Leeds railway station and became more and more depressed. Two coffins were carried past her from different trains as she waited; but there was no sign of Anne. It was a bad omen indeed! The next morning, Thursday, 24th May, she drove over to Haworth and arrived just in time to see the dying Anne being helped into the conveyance by Charlotte and Martha. Martha Brown said, years later, that death was written clearly on Anne's face. The sexton's family were very much against the journey. They stoutly maintained that when the girls gave up their moorland walks and scribbled away in the parsonage until midnight, they wrecked their health.

Anne was settled comfortably in the conveyance. There was a kiss for Patrick and a hug for her Flossy. Then, after explanations of the change of plan on the previous day, Charlotte and Ellen climbed into the vehicle. As it slowly went down Parsonage Lane, Patrick, Martha and Tabby stood at the gate and waved au revoir to Charlotte and Ellen and, in their hearts, good-bye to Anne. Keeper stood stock-still; Flossy made to run after Anne but Nicholls caught hold of her outside the sexton's house and held fast. John Brown stood there and slowly removed his hat: there was the touch of saintliness about Miss Annie, as the villagers always referred to her, that commanded respect. The conveyance turned out of sight by the King's Arms and Anne was never more seen in the Haworth she loved so dearly. The group standing by the parsonage gate returned to the house. Martha and Tabby went to the kitchen, Keeper and Flossy crept up to the nursery to be wretched together, Patrick retired to his lonely parlour, where he put back Graham's *Domestic Medicine* on his bookshelf; he prayed that God would render it unnecessary for him to take it down again for many years and that, when the time came, he would not be alive to do so.

Many will know of Anne's brief stay at Scarborough and of her heroic death. It is not our purpose to follow the conveyance from Haworth or to tell again of that magical last sunset for her on the east coast of Yorkshire. We must remain in the old grey parsonage with Patrick Brontë. Patrick heard that the girls had arrived safely. Then he waited alone in the parlour for the next letter and for the news it must bring. That letter, in Charlotte's well-known hand, soon came, on Wednesday, 30th May. It had been penned the previous day. He opened the letter and read it through, then he folded it up and replaced it in his pocket. He went into the kitchen and told them that Miss Anne was dead. Then he stroked Flossy's neck and asked Martha to see to it that the dog had an extra large supper that night.

Anne Brontë died on Monday, 28th May 1849, aged twenty-nine. Like her beloved Emily she died at two o'clock in the afternoon. Charlotte and Ellen Nussey were with her. Her last words were, "Take courage, Charlotte; take courage."

Charlotte was determined to spare her father a third funeral in so short a space of time, and on the very day Patrick received her letter, Anne was buried in St Mary's churchyard, Scarborough.

| Anne Bronte | Scarborough, from near York | May 30th | 28 [29] | J. W. Whiteside Vicar |

Patrick wrote to his daughter urging her to remain at the sea a while longer, now that all the strain was over. So Charlotte and Ellen went to Filey and thence to Bridlington and were a month away. To Williams Charlotte wrote on 4th June: ". . . Her quiet, Christian death did not rend my heart as Emily's stern, simple, undemonstrative end did. I let Anne go to God, and felt He had a right to her. I could hardly let Emily go. I wanted to hold her back then, and I want her back now . . . they are both gone, and so is poor Branwell, and Papa has now me only— the weakest, puniest, least promising of his six children. Consumption has taken the whole five. For the present Anne's ashes rest apart from the others. I have buried her here at Scarbro', to save Papa the anguish of the return and a third funeral. I am ordered to remain at the sea-side awhile . . . I have heard from Papa. He and the servants knew when they parted from Anne they would see her no more. All tried to be resigned. I knew it likewise, and I wanted her to die where she would be happiest. She loved Scarboro'. A peaceful sun gilded her evening. . . ." The inscription on Anne's tombstone reads, "Here lie the Remains of Anne Brontë, Daughter of the Revd P. Brontë, Incumbent of Haworth, Yorkshire. She died, aged 28 [29], May 28th 1849." Appropriately the headstone is embossed with carvings of two books, and the grave, under the shadow of the castle ruins, looks down over the south bay.

Charlotte wrote again to Patrick, then to Martha. From Filey she sent another letter to Williams on 13th June: ". . . Papa is resigned and his health is not shaken . . . my sister died happily; . . . the doctor —a stranger . . . wondered at her fixed tranquillity of spirit and settled longing to be gone. He said in all his experience he had seen no such death-bed . . . it but half consoles to remember this calm . . . I hardly know whether it is sadder to think of that than of Emily turning her dying eyes reluctantly from the pleasant sun . . . these two have left in

their memories a noble legacy. Were I quite solitary in the world—
bereft even of Papa—there is something in the past I can love intensely
and honour deeply—and it is something which cannot change—which
cannot decay—which immortality guarantees from corruption . . . It is
over. Branwell—Emily—Anne are gone like dreams—gone as Maria
and Elizabeth went twenty years ago. One by one I have watched them
fall asleep on my arm—and closed their glazed eyes. . . .''

Charlotte came home on Thursday, 21st June: ''. . . I got home a
little before eight o'clock. All was clean and bright waiting for me—
Papa and the servants were well—and all received me with an affection
which should have consoled. The dogs seemed in strange ecstasy. I am
certain they regarded me as the harbinger of others—the dumb
creatures thought that as I was returned—those who had been so long
absent were not far behind. . . .'' And again she writes: ''. . . I call it
home still . . . Haworth parsonage is still a home for me, and not quite
a ruined or desolate home either. Papa is there—and two most
affectionate and faithful servants—and two old dogs, in their way as
faithful and affectionate . . . but here my sisters will come no more.
Keeper may visit Emily's little bed-room as he still does day by day—
and Flossy may look wistfully round for Anne—they will never see
them again—nor shall I—at least the human part of me . . . it is only
the thought of my dear Father in the next room, or of the kind servants
in the kitchen—or some caress of the poor dogs which restores me to
softer sentiments and more rational views. . . .''

There was indeed an affectionate welcome for Charlotte when she
came home, alone. Yet Tabby and Martha, once back in the kitchen,
shook their heads sternly. As long as they lived they would never quite
forgive Charlotte for leaving Miss Anne all alone ''in a foreign grave''.

Patrick would never see the grave of his youngest child, but Charlotte
revisited it in June 1852 to see that some ordered alterations had been
carried out. For the rest of her days Charlotte worried about Anne's
lonely mound at Scarborough. Her hasty decision to leave her there
had been honourable enough but, as Ellen Nussey related, she came to
the conclusion that Anne would have preferred to rest in Haworth, next
to Emily. Even after her marriage she made a plan to have the remains
brought home, but Nicholls firmly objected.

For a few minutes Patrick and Charlotte talked together in his
parlour, the only survivors of a family of eight. Perhaps Patrick offered
up a prayer for all their dear departed. Certainly he gazed at his
daughter with anxious eyes, scanning her face for signs of the final
blow that could befall him. But she looked better than he had dared to
hope; the sea air had restored her to some degree of good health.

". . . I left Papa soon and went into the dining-room—I shut the door . . . I felt that the house was all silent—the rooms were all empty . . . The great trial is when evening closes and night approaches—at that hour we used to assemble in the dining-room—we used to talk—Now I sit by myself . . . Papa thought me a little stronger—he said my eyes were not so sunken. . . ." So Charlotte sat alone—surrounded by those ghosts that would always come over the moors to her at nightfall; and across the passage, solitary in his study, sat Patrick, who had lost three precious children in eight months. Yet even now he did not become that inactive old man, with the clay pipe and spittoon, loath to leave his little room, whom Mrs Gaskell met and painted as representing a true perspective, a life portrait, of Patrick Brontë.

CHAPTER 25

"Next to Godliness"

IN THAT spring and summer of 1849 it was not only Anne Brontë who died. There were many deaths among the Haworth cottagers, and the reason became more and more apparent: bad sanitation and lack of fresh water-supplies.

Patrick had striven for years to obtain improvements. Now he determined to put all his remaining strength into one great effort to secure better conditions. He organized a petition to be sent to the General Board of Health in London, and thus began a protracted struggle for water that was barely won before his death.

The petition, dated 28th August 1849, was signed: "P. Brontë A.B. Incumbent. A.B. Nicholls AB. Curate. E.S. Hall, Surgeon, John B. Wheelhouse, Surgeon", and by many of the people of Haworth. Patrick mentioned two good springs, and the necessity for only a few pipes to make water available to the poor, not only to the wealthy few who owned the land containing the springs. There was water always pouring down from the hills; all they wished was "to procure the salutary beverage in question".

Back came the answer that the Board had no power to interfere unless one tenth of the ratepayers signed. This was soon remedied, and a further petition was sent to Whitehall on 9th October. The additional signatures included those of Abraham Berry, the Baptist minister, and John Brown. "Early" consideration was promised, followed by mention of sending an investigator.

On 14th November George Spencer (solicitor) wrote from Keighley to advise the Board's inspector ". . . the place of meeting may be at the Vestry of Haworth Church" and that "the *Leeds Mercury* and the *Halifax Guardian* are the newspapers mostly taken in the hamlet, and notices are usually affixed at the Church Door, and outer Gate; the two Baptists Chapels and the Methodist Chapel and Primitive Methodist Chapel in Haworth. . . ".

But no inspector arrived. On 23rd January 1850 John Hudson, Chairman of the Haworth Health Committee, wrote to ask: "why he has not come." No answer. So Patrick took up his pen.

To Henry Austin, Esq Secretary to the General Board of Health,
Gwydyr House, Whitehall—London.

Sir,   Haworth, Near Keighley Feby, 5th 1850

Having long since petitioned for an authorized Agent, to come and
look into our situation, with regard to a sufficient supply of pure water,
we are much disappointed, at not having seen any such Agent, nor
having got any satisfactory answer to our petition : we would, therefore
request, that you would be so kind as to inform us, what we are to
expect, or do ; and we are the more anxious on this head, as spring and
summer are drawing nigh, when the want of pure water, would be
extremely detrimental, and the and the [*sic*] privilege of it, a great
blessing—
We consequently beg an answer, at your earliest opportunity,

P. Brontè, A.B. Incumbent.

There came the maddening answer that the "necessary preliminary
arrangements" were being completed.

However, on 4th April 1850, Benjamin Herschel Babbage started
enquiries in Haworth, all the local newspapers being informed. What
the inspector saw and reported was bad enough : no sewers, refuse
thrown into Kirkgate where it poured down an open channel; offal
from the slaughter-house piled up in the inn yard at the end of Parsonage
Lane ; middens overflowing and none with so much as a door : often
the farmers found the ash in them harmful in muck-spreading the
land, and left them unemptied. That and much more the inspector
wrote into his report, yet nearly a year later nothing more had been
done from Whitehall.

Again Patrick wrote.

To The Secretary, The General Board of Health,
Gwydyr House, Whitehall, London.

Sir,   Haworth, Nr. Keighley Feby 12th 1851.

Having made application, long since, to the General Board of
Health, respecting their assisting us, in making improvements here, by
procuring a supply of pure water, which is much wanted.—
We are greatly surprized [*sic*] and grieved that nothing has yet
been done towards the furtherance of this desirable end—We hope,
however, that the Board will take our case into their early consideration,
and promote our object as soon as practicable. Mr. Babbage, who has
visited this place, can give them, the requisite information.

I remain, Sir,   Your obedient Servant, P. Brontë, Incumbent.

29

More letters were exchanged, those from Haworth in the beautiful handwriting of Joseph Redman the parish clerk and also clerk to the Haworth Health Committee. Matters indeed seemed at last to be moving and then came treachery from some of Patrick's prominent church members : not the trustees so much as those wealthy church-goers who already had water and were now regretting the petition. The first rumblings of refusal are heard in Patrick's next letter.

To Henry Austin, Esq, Secretary, General Board of Health,
Gwydyr House, Whitehall, London.

Haworth, Near Keighley, April 1st 1851.

Dear Sir,

Deeming it best to call a Public Meeting of the Inhabitants, I have done so—and that opinion, which was unanimous, will be found, both expressed and defined in the accompanying resolution, and map, or plan, where some little alteration, is petitioned for—We petition for this alteration, on the grounds that the original plan, included some outlying farms, which do not require, our proposed improvements, and consequently could not be reasonably demanded to pay for what would go only to the benefit of others.

As far as the churchyard is concerned, it appeared to the Meeting, and still appears to me, that to shut it up, before new burial ground shall have been procured, would be the cause of great confusion, and seriously evil consequences.

New ground is, most undoubtedly wanted, and will be procured as soon as practicable—but even after that shall have been done, some newly made vaults would remain in the old ground, which might still be used with safety for many years to come—

It is hoped that this alteration, which we petition for, will not render it necessary, for the Board, to make another Survey—and that they will proceed, as soon as practicable in the execution of the laudable end in view, as Summer is approaching, and all that we petition for, and have petitioned for, will be most urgently needed—I know not that all this, is in the Ordinary form, but I send it, in the spirit of a petition—You will be so kind as to lay it before the General Board of Health—and should there be any deficiency, Mr. Babbage who has taken great pains, to understand our case, will I doubt not, be able to give the requisite information—

I remain, dear Sir, Your most obedient Servant

P. Brontë, A.B. Incumbent & Chairman.

This slight change of plan just when action was about to be taken from Whitehall, was the beginning of a desertion of Patrick by some leading members of his congregation. Several of them wrote to London behind his back to secure exemption from paying a small water-rate, as they already possessed wells and springs.

Haworth—Keighley. April 14th 1851.
Sir,
We hereby give notice that we object to the Sanitary Measures proposed for the Hamlet of Haworth being applied to Ebor, as shown in the map accompanying the Superintending Inspectors Report—the property is already well supplied with good water, for which according to the terms of purchase it is chargeable with an annual rent for Ebor— the Sanitary condition is also in other respects satisfactory—
We are Sir,
Yr Obt Servts Merrall (Brothers)

On the 17th William Thomas objected to his property "Buildings situate at Hollings Cottages at Rough Nook do. at Gaugers Croft do. in the main or principal Street Land and Cottages at Lower Brow Land and do. at Hawkcliffe" being included in any improvement scheme "as all the Property is well supplied with water".

Then there came so many objections that it must have seemed to Whitehall that there were plenty of water-supplies all the time. Richard Robert Thomas objected to the inclusion of the "*White Lion Inn* and the 8 Cottages adjoining etc" as supplied already with water. Tobias Lambert objected to the inclusion of his property at Hall Green which was supplied by Hough Spring, and Joseph Hartley at Church Gates wanted the exemption of his house Sowdens.

Confusion naturally followed in Whitehall, and Babbage planned a second visit. But Patrick was now aware of the proceedings of these few wealthy churchmen, foresaw further delays in London, and having delivered a strong sermon to his congregation on brotherly love, he wrote a stiff letter to Whitehall.

The Secretary, General Board of Health,
Gwydyr House, Whitehall, London.

Haworth, Nr. Keighley, July 10th 1851.
Dear Sir,
Our sanitary Committee held a meeting last night, and requested me to write to the General Board of Health, in order to petition them to proceed with our case as soon as practicable—

There has already been long, and tedious delay—there has been a deal of sickness amongst us, and there is now a great want of pure water, which ills might have been prevented, or palliated, had the remedial measures we hope for, been duly applied. A few interested individuals, might try to throw difficulties in the way, but by the large majority, consisting chiefly of the working people, there is an anxious desire that the work should on the earliest opportunity be done—

I remain, Dear Sir, Your most obedient Servant,

P. Brontë Incumbent

PS. Please to send me an early answer.

Despite powerful opposition in Haworth, Patrick and his local Health Committee battled on, backed by the Methodists and Baptists. Again Patrick wrote, a biting letter this time.

To the Secretary, General Board of Health,
Gwydyr House. White-Hall. London—

Haworth, Nr. Keighley Septr 8th 1851

Sir,

The Committee, here, have applied to me, in reference to some amelioration, with regard to local cleanliness—towards which the General Board of Health, have taken some steps, enough I should think, to enable them, should they be so desposed [sic], to go on, legally, as far as our case may require.

Yet, after, tedious delay, they, have, as far as we know done almost nothing—We might have thought, that this arose from a press of more urgent business, had it not been, that we have learned from good authority, that their salutary rules have been adopted, and enforced, in various other places, where there was less necessity for them, and from whence application was made, at a date long after ours—What we have to request, therefore, is, that you will be so kind as to inform us, as soon, as you conveniently can—whether, our case has been entirely given up—and if not, at what time we may expect a decisive, and final arrangement—

I remain, Sir, Your most obedient servant,

Patrick Brontë Incumbent.

The answer was that an "order in Council for the purpose is now in progress". Then came another note to say that the boundary alterations were likely to delay matters.

By now there was open hostility between the ratepayers and Patrick and his supporters. Richard Butterfield of Woodlands arranged a

petition of ratepayers dated 10th December 1851 and sent it to Whitehall signed by himself, the Merralls, Mrs Ferrand (the Lady of the
Manor of Haworth), W. B. Ferrand, Joseph Greenwood, J.P., John
and Richard Murgatroyd, etc. They claimed that property-owners were
not elected to the local Board of Health, only cottagers, and therefore
the elections to it were illegal.

London replied with a promise to send William Ranger to enquire
into these matters. Butterfield wrote to inform Whitehall that there
would be another election "next month"; would the Board tell Ranger
to come and see him? His visit was arranged for 17th March 1852.
Patrick countered this by getting Joseph Redman to complain to
London that property-owners and owners of springs were holding
matters up: had they the right to do so? London replied that "there is
no power of compulsory purchase": the owners were inviolate. Ranger
held a meeting in Haworth on 30th July 1852 and sent in his report in
September.

And so it dragged on. London called for a new enquiry to fix fresh
boundaries. Edward Baines, editor of the *Leeds Mercury*, explained to
Whitehall why he had failed to put their notice in his paper (it was
Christmas); the Haworth surveyor, Brierley, plotted the new plan to the
wrong scale; and the years dragged by. Certainly the local ratepayers
had a genuine grievance over the new water-rate, but their behaviour
soon lost them Patrick's sympathy on that score. Conditions were too
serious for such considerations.

The Haworth spring, Headwell Spring, ran only at one quart per
minute. All West Lane, Back Lane, and Changegate protested to
London, including William Summerscale, John Brown's brother
William, and Thomas Parker, a prominent Baptist temperance advocate,
who had an additional reason for wishing water made available to all
houses. But still the owners of wells refused to permit fresh springs or
reservoirs on their land.

Ranger recommended that the rate qualification for election to the
local Committee of Health be raised from £5 to £10, whereupon Patrick
protested that there were only ten houses so highly rated, five of them
inns! So 1853 came and went, and nearly five years had passed since
Patrick's first attempt to help the people.

Redman admitted that there were forty-three houses rated at £10
or upwards; but Whitehall switched its attention to drains, only to be
met with such a demand for compensation by the mill-owners and
others that their scheme was wrecked.

Patrick proposed two new springs for Haworth that would give
sixteen gallons of water a minute. Bradford was interested in obtaining

its water-supply from Haworth, then it abandoned the project and by 1854 still nothing had been achieved. In June of that year the Haworth Board "constructed a main sewer in the lower part of the main street 172 yards in length" and charged the owners of nearby property with the whole expense, at 12s 6d in the pound; whereupon these house-holders complained to London and at night tore up the drains. From then on it became an anarchy, such as could only happen in Haworth. Redman explained that the pipes had been put in to prevent buckets of filth being tossed down the street, and he forced the owners to pay for the sewer.

In September 1854 Whitehall thought of sending yet another inspector. Joseph Hartley refused to pay for fresh water-pipes, having plenty of water already. He also refused a bill for £1 16s 2d for a cottage "situate at Ducking Stool in Stubbing Lane", and took the local Board to court at Wakefield Quarter Sessions in January 1857. But Ranger acted as peacemaker and Hartley won his case out of court. Then, in true Haworth fashion, having proved himself legally right, he paid up!

But Patrick was winning. By 21st May 1856 a small reservoir was being built in Haworth (the Haworth Health Committee borrowed £800 and levied a water-rate). Stand-taps were put in the streets (another £300 being borrowed) and, after much resistance, all rates were paid. In 1858 the little reservoir was completed and walled and an attempt was made to obtain fresh water for every cottage. This was largely achieved by the year's end, with more borrowed money. Finally, in 1857, the Haworth Gas Company was established and by 1865 the lanes were lit by gas.

Thus, near the end of his life, after nearly ten years' continuous struggle, Patrick achieved his objective, having endured typical White-hall delays and, what was far harder to bear, selfish obstruction from his wealthier church members. It was a further measure of his independent courage that he fought the hands that fed him.

It had all been great fun, of course, with sewers and water-pipes torn up; only all the time the cottagers, most of them Dissenters, remained without water or sanitation, and continued to die. If the issue had been less grave and the interference had originated from outside, then such a typical Haworth attitude would have been justified and Patrick would have backed the ratepayers; but the lives of their fellow-villagers were at stake and what otherwise might have been another jolly Haworth riot turned into a real tragedy.

But if it had been a struggle for fresh water, it had also developed for Patrick into an inner conflict of faiths. His loyalty to the Established Church was not broken, but his sympathy, and love of justice for the

Wesleyans, never very dormant, was rekindled into all the old affection. Those few Haworth churchmen had behaved in a worldly manner unworthy of their Evangelical tradition. Patrick knew also that in several instances they were members of the same families who had fled the fever in 1763, vainly urging Parson Grimshaw to desert and go with them. These were two black periods in Haworth's noble history, and Patrick turned from the thought of them in disgust.

This then was the time when Patrick inclined back towards the pure Methodism of his youth. It was shortly after this battle was won that he was seen going to the evening service at the West Lane Wesleyan Chapel.

Nicholls's share in these events, for he was in Haworth during most of them, was not prominent. But Patrick's part was clear-cut. He fought for the poor and for those who were not of his flock. He served his God and not Cæsar, his people and not his financial backers. Those who have suggested that Patrick Brontë was negligent over the health of his family and of Haworth should shift the blame on to guilty heads.

CHAPTER 26

Charlotte

PATRICK lived for twelve more years after the death of his youngest child, six of them with his daughter Charlotte, and then when she also was dead, six quite alone save for his son-in-law, Arthur Nicholls.

The first of these two periods of his life is, perhaps, better known than any because of the light that has fallen on Charlotte; the latter's several journeys to London, the Lake District, Scotland, her meeting with many famous men and women of letters and her voluminous correspondence, all are well known and it is not the purpose in hand to repeat them here. A mention of the few visitors who came to the parsonage, a glimpse or two of Patrick's domestic life at this time, his letters written during this period and Arthur Nicholls's declaration of love for his daughter must be the main concern of this chapter.

In August 1849, Patrick again had a severe attack of bronchitis: ". . . Papa has not been well at all lately . . . I felt very uneasy about him for some days, more wretched than I can tell you . . . when anything ails papa, I feel too keenly that he is the *last*, the *only* near and dear relation I have in the world. . . ." William Morgan it was who went to York for Patrick on 5th September 1849, commissioned to take out the administration papers on Anne's estate, having visited Haworth two days earlier to obtain the signatures of Patrick, Nicholls and William Summerscale. On the 6th he sent Patrick a bill for administration and his personal expenses.

Bradford, Sepr 6th 1849.

Dear Bronte,

Herewith I send you the Administration, Bill of Charges etc. You will have to pay to me for the Court & myself £6–3–7. Our best love to you and Miss B.

I am, Dear Bronte, Yours very truly W. Morgan.

The letter containing the acknowledgment of the receipt of £15 I forwarded to you by Post yesterday.

Revd P. Bronte
  To W. Morgan

	s d
Septr 3rd Day Ticket by Railway from	
Bradford to Keighley and back	2– 6
Gig from Keighley to Haworth & back	5– 0
Horses & Boy at *Black Bull*	2– 2
Boy	2– 0
Bars	–11
	12– 7
Administration	20–11– 0
Paid Duty	15– 0– 0
Bal^{ce}	6– 3– 7

The first visitor from the outside world was James Taylor of Smith, Elder & Co.—who came on Saturday, 8th September, to collect the manuscript of the now finished *Shirley*. Shortly after his departure, both Tabby and Martha became ill. Tabitha Brown, the latter's sister, and Mrs Brown herself came up to the Parsonage daily to help: ". . . Martha's illness has been most serious; she was seized with inflammation ten days ago. Tabby's lame leg has broken out; she cannot stand or walk . . . there was one day last week when I fairly broke down for ten minutes, and sat down and cried like a fool. Martha's illness was at its height, a cry from Tabby had called me into the kitchen and I had found her laid on the floor, her head under the kitchen grate; she had fallen from her chair in attempting to rise. Papa had just been declaring that Martha was in imminent danger. I was myself depressed with headaches and sickness. . . ." Happily, ". . . Martha is now almost well and Tabby much better. . . ." For the last week of October 1849, Charlotte visited Ellen Nussey at Brookroyd, and during that time, on the 26th, *Shirley* was published.

By November all the inmates of Haworth Parsonage were well again and as Charlotte wrote on the 6th of that month, ". . . Papa's health has, I am thankful to say, been very satisfactory of late. The other day he walked to Keighley and back, and was very little fatigued. . . ." Nearly eight miles, with the return journey steeply uphill all the way,—and Kirkgate to climb at the end of it: no mean feat for a man approaching seventy-three! It saved five shillings.

On Thursday, 29th November, Charlotte went to London and wrote to her father on 5th December. Patrick could not help but feel anxious when she was away, although he was proud that London was making much of his girl. She came home on Saturday, 15th December. On the 21st Joe Taylor, Mary Taylor's brother, arrived. He came to dinner and Patrick found it next to impossible to be civil with such a stupid, bumptious young man. After Christmas Ellen came again. Hearing of this, Canon W. M. Heald, who was depicted in *Shirley*, wrote to Ellen, who was a leading member of his Birstall congregation, ". . . Fame says you are on a visit with the renowned Currer Bell . . . Pray give my best respects to Mr Brontë, also, who may have some slight remembrance of me as a child. I just remember him when at Hartshead."

By 1850, of course, the identity of "Currer Bell" was universally known. On 28th January Charlotte tells Ellen, ". . . Mr Nicholls has finished reading *Shirley*, he is delighted with it. John Brown's wife seriously thought he had gone wrong in the head as she heard him giving vent to roars of laughter as he sat alone, clapping his hands and stamping on the floor. He would read all the scenes about the curates aloud to papa, he triumphed in his own character [Mr Macarthey]. What Mr. Grant will say is another thing. . . ." In February: ". . . Mr Morgan has finished reading *Jane Eyre*, and writes not in blame, but in the highest strains of eulogy! He says it thoroughly fascinated and enchained him . . . Martha came in yesterday, puffing and blowing, and much excited. 'I've heard sich news,' she began. 'What about?' 'Please ma'am, you've been and written two books, the grandest books that ever was seen. My father has heard it in Halifax, and Mr George Taylor and Mr Greenwood, and Mr Merrall at Bradford; and they are going to have a meeting at the Mechanics' Institute, and to settle about ordering them!' . . ."

During this month of February, Charlotte was given her first glimpse of those sweet love-letters her mother had written so many years ago from the sheltered Woodhouse Grove. ". . . A few days since, a little incident happened which curiously touched me. Papa put into my hands a little packet of letters and papers, telling me that they were mamma's, and that I might read them. I did read them, in a frame of mind I cannot describe. The papers were yellow with time . . . it was strange now to peruse, for the first time, the records of a mind whence my own sprang; and most strange, and at once sad and sweet, to find that mind of a truly fine, pure, and elevated order. They were written to papa before they were married . . . I wish she had lived, and that I had known her. . . ." The same letter also gives an amusing description of the next visitor: "Yesterday, just after dinner, I heard a loud bustling voice in the kitchen demanding to see Mr Brontë, somebody was shown into the parlour; shortly after wine was rung for. 'Who is it, Martha?' I asked. 'Some mak of a tradesman,' said she, 'He's not a gentleman, I'm sure.' The personage stayed about an hour, talking in a loud vulgar key all the time. At tea-time I asked papa who it was. 'Why,' said he, 'no other than the Rev —— [John Barber], Vicar of Bierley!' Papa had invited him to take some refreshment, but the creature had ordered his dinner at the Black Bull, and was quite urgent with papa to go down there and join him, offering by way of inducement a bottle, or if papa liked, 'two or three bottles of the best wine Haworth could afford!' He said he was . . . in raptures with the wild scenery! He warmly pressed papa to come and see him . . . and to bring his daughter with him!!!Does he know anything about the books, do you think? he made no allusion to them . . . Martha said he looked no more like a parson than she did. Papa described him as rather shabby-looking, but said he was wondrous cordial and friendly. Papa, in his usual fashion, put him through a regular catechism of questions; what his living was worth, etc. etc. . . . Papa asked him if he were married. He said no, he had no thoughts of being married, he did not like the trouble of a wife; he described himself as 'living in style, and keeping a very hospitable house' . . ." On 22nd February; ". . . one or two curiosity-hunters have made their way to Haworth Parsonage—but our rude hills and rugged neighbourhood will I doubt not form a sufficient barrier to the frequent repetition of such visits. . . ." On 5th March: ". . . Various folks are beginning to come boring to Haworth, on the wise errand of seeing the scenery described in *Jane Eyre* and *Shirley*. . . ." What Charlotte would say to the 50,000 or more who now pour up the narrow Main Street and trample through her home annually can only be imagined, but fairly accurately so nevertheless. In March came Sir James Kay-Shuttleworth and his lady from Gawthorpe Hall, near Burnley. ". . . When here they again urged me to visit them. Papa took their side at once, would not hear of my refusing; I must go,—this left me without plea or defence. I consented to go for three days. . . ." Here, that indefensible strain of snobbery that was to cause Charlotte so much suffering, first reared its ugly head. Patrick was flattered at such attentions to his daughter, his courteous manners forbade refusal; yet in that moment he did *not* think of his only remaining child.

After her return from Gawthorpe, there were some quiet weeks, during which Mr Grant plainly showed his "forgiveness" for his portrait in *Shirley* by coming to tea very often and behaving in a most affable fashion. Towards the end of April, there was another visit to Ellen, followed by one from the insufferable Joe Taylor; happily Patrick was in bed with a cold and missed that treat. On Thursday, 30th May 1850, Charlotte again went to London, leaving Martha Redman, the daughter of the parish clerk, to assist the two servants. In her absence, necessary repairs were made to the roof of the parsonage ; "I cannot go home for the house at Haworth is just now unroofed. . . ."

During Charlotte's absence Patrick wrote to the Society for the Propagation of the Gospel concerning a friend from Bradford days.

Haworth, Near Keighley. June 22nd 1850

Revd Sir,

In reply to your letter of enquiry, respecting the Revd W.R. Thomas's qualifications, for the situation of an emigrant teacher, I would briefly but faithfully remark that I have known him for many years, and that from what I know of him, and what you want, I do not think that you could easily get another, who would suit your purpose better or so well —He is steady, judicious, pious, and consequently moral, and would I am sure, be most *ardently* devoted to his avocation ; he is active, and persevering, and a warm climate would, far better suit him, than a cold one. He, has, as far as I know, been hitherto, under independent circumstances, and cannot I imagine, be under any pecuniary embarrassment, nor do I think, that he is a character, that would, ever be likely to be so.

I remain, Revd Sir, Yours, most faithfully

Patrick Brontë A.B. Incumbent of Haworth, Bradford, Yorkshire.

To the Rev. Ernest Hawkins, M.A. Secretary to the Society for the Propagation of the Gospel, 79, Pall Mall, London.

Less than three years later Patrick would again have to write to the Society, on a matter closely concerning both Charlotte and himself.

From London Charlotte went to Birstall to stay with Ellen, then to Edinburgh (to join George Smith and party), back to Birstall and finally came home in the middle of July. ". . . Just at the foot of Bridgehouse hill I met John Greenwood—staff in hand, he fortunately saw me in the cab—stopped and informed me he was setting off to Brookroyd by Mr Brontë's orders to see how I was—for that he had been quite miserable ever since he got Miss Nussey's letter—I found on my arrival that papa had worked himself up to a sad pitch of nervous excitement and alarm—in which Martha and Tabby were but too obviously joining him . . . I have recently found that Papa's great discomposure had its origin in two sources—the vague fear of my being somehow about to be married to somebody—having 'received some overtures' as he expressed himself—as well as in apprehension of illness. . . ." "Miss Nussey's letter", mentioned here, had been answered as follows :

To Miss Nussey, Brookroyd, Birstall, Nr Leeds.

Haworth, near Keighley. July 12th, 1850

My Dear Miss Nussey,

Notwithstanding your kind letter is cautiously worded, it gives me considerable uneasiness. One thing comforts me, that in you she will have the kindest and best nurse. It may be that she is labouring under one of her usual bilious attacks, and if so, she will I trust, through a merciful providence, speedily recover. Should you see any feverish symptoms, call in the ablest medical adviser, for the expenses of which I will be answerable. But lose no time. And write to me, soon, as soon as you can. Charlotte well knows that I am rather prone to look at the dark side of things and cunningly to search out for it, and find it, if it has any existence. Tell her that I am well—that is, in better health than when she last saw me. And that after a host of labour amidst decayed laths and rafters and broken lime plaster, and busy carpenters, masons, and repairers of various descriptions, we have at length got our house put into order. And that, moreover, amidst all the bustle, both workmen and servants, as well as the more important trustees, have acted in good will, fidelity, and harmony. I have often thought when it has been otherwise, it has been as much owing to the employers as the employed. In general, people can be more easily led than driven, and respect has a far more prevailing influence than fear. Tell Charlotte to keep up her spirits. When, once more, she breathes the free exhilarating air of Haworth, it will blow the dust and smoke and impure malaria of London out of her *head and heart*. Remember me very kindly to Mrs Nussey, your mother, to Mr Taylor, and to Mr Carr, and other old friends. And tell Charlotte that, with all due affection, I hope soon to see her. I remain, my dear Miss Nussey,

Yours, very gratefully and truly, P. Brontë.
(Excuse haste and its usual consequences).

One of the labourers working in the parsonage at this time, an Irishman, told Patrick that he was a Roman Catholic. "Oh, very well," Patrick replied, "practise the religion you are taught, and you will be all right at last."

It was during this visit to London, that Charlotte sat for her portrait to Richmond: it was sent to Patrick as a gift from George Smith. At the same time he gave Charlotte a portrait of her hero, the Duke of Wellington, whom she had seen for the first time whilst in London. She writes to Ellen on 1st August: ". . . my portrait is come from London—and the Duke of Wellington's . . . Papa thinks the portrait looks older than I do—he says the features are far from flattered, but acknowledges that the expression is wonderfully good and life-like. . . ." On the same day she sends a letter to Smith: ". . . Papa seems much pleased with the portrait, as do the few other persons who have seen it, with one notable exception, viz, our old servant, who tenaciously maintains that it is not like—that it is too old-looking—but, as she, with equal tenacity, asserts that the Duke of Wellington's picture is a portrait of 'the Master' (meaning papa), I am afraid not much weight is to be ascribed to her opinion. . . ."

On the next day Patrick writes his own thanks for his daughter's portrait:

To George Smith, 76, Gloucester Terrace,
Hyde Park Gardens, London.

My Dear Sir,   Haworth, Near Keighley, Yorks. August 2nd 1850.

The two portraits have, at length, safely arrived, and have been as safely hung up, in the best light and most favourable position. Without flattery the artist, in the portrait of my daughter, has fully proved that the fame which he has acquired has been fairly earned. Without ostentatious display, with admirable tact and delicacy, he has produced a correct likeness, and succeeded in a graphic representation of mind as well as matter, and with only black and white, has given prominence and seeming life, and speech, and motion. I may be partial, and perhaps somewhat enthusiastic, in this case, but in looking on the picture, which improves upon acquaintance, as all real works of art do, I fancy I see strong indications of the genius of the author of Shirley and Jane Eyre.

The portrait of the Duke of Wellington, of all which I have seen, comes the nearest to my preconceived idea of that great man, to whom Europe, and the other portions of the civilised world, in the most dangerous crisis of their affairs, entrusted their cause, and in whom, under Providence, they did not trust in vain. It now remains for me only to thank you, which I do most sincerely. For the sake of the giver, as well as the gifts, I will lay the portraits up for life amongst my most highly valued treasures, and have only to regret that some are missing who, with better taste and skill than I have, would have fully partaken of my joy.

I beg leave to remain, with much respect, My dear Sir,

Yours faithfully, P. Brontë.

Please to give my kindest and most respectful regards to Mr Williams, whom I have often heard of, but never seen, and to Mr Taylor, whom I had the pleasure of seeing when he ventured into this wild region.

Later in August, Charlotte stayed with Sir J. Kay-Shuttleworth at The Briery, Windermere and met, for the first time, her future biographer, Mrs Gaskell. After her return, she tells Ellen of some visitors to the parsonage who had arrived just before she went to Windermere: ". . . Mrs Ferrand and sundry other ladies and two gentlemen . . . Lord John Manners, the other . . . was Mr Smythe, the son of Lord Strangford . . . Lord John Manners brought in his hand two brace of grouse for papa, which was a well-timed present; a day or two before, papa had been wishing for some. . . ."

In September Patrick was again struck down by bronchitis; ". . . Papa continues in an invalid state—still subject to bronchitis and often complaining of weakness—I have wished him to consult Mr Teale or to try change of air—but his objection to both these alternatives is insuperable. . . ." A touch, surely, of Emily in this attitude!

The next visitors were some friends of Mrs Gaskell's. They were ushered into the dining-room by Patrick, "an old gentleman very like Miss Brontë", who looked in again later to see that Charlotte was there entertaining the guests. Keeper was very much in attendance, and they noticed Richmond's portrait was in that room, "looking strangely out of place on the bare walls". Patrick issued forth to say good-bye as they took their leave.

On 31st October Charlotte tells George Smith: ". . . I showed Papa the 'Paper Lantern', he was greatly amused with it and would like to see the whole when it is completed to show the curates, whose case it will fit with much nicety. . . ." (A paper lantern for Puseyites by "Will O' the Wisp".)

In mid-December, Charlotte stayed at The Knoll, Ambleside, the home of Harriet Martineau, followed by a few days with Ellen. She was home again the day after Christmas. By February 1851 Charlotte found Patrick anxious she should write another book, but "I think I can pacify such impatience as my dear Father naturally feels. . . ."

It was about this time that John Stores Smith paid his visit to see Charlotte. He wrote his reminiscences in the *Free Lance* of 7th March 1868. They are written in a light-hearted vein and are in rather doubtful taste: poor old Keeper is ridiculed greatly. Patrick is described as being stone blind, which of course he was not. ". . . Mr Brontë was the ruin of what had been a striking and singularly handsome man. He was tall, strongly built, and even then perfectly erect. His hair was nearly white, but his eyebrows were still black . . . he was dressed very carelessly, in almost worn-out clothes, had no proper necktie, and was in slippers. . . the blind old dog curled himself on the hearth at his blind old master's feet [neither was blind] ' . . . he commenced conversation almost immediately upon his daughter . . . then he talked about Emily and the other sister, and told me how he had considered Emily the genius of the family. . . ."

In May 1851 Charlotte refers to marriage in a letter to Ellen: ". . . I believe he [Patrick] thinks a prospective union, deferred for 5 years, with . . . a decorous reliable personage would be a very proper and advisable affair—However I ask no questions and he asks me none . . . I enclose a letter of Mr Morgan's to Papa—written just after he had read *Shirley*. It is curious to see the latent feeling roused in the old gentleman—I was especially struck by his remark about the chap: entitled 'The Valley of the Shadow, &c'. he must have had a true sense of what he read or he could not have made it." In May, Flossy junior, a puppy, given to Ellen, died: ". . . I have not yet screwed up nerve to tell Papa about her fate. . . . I went to Hunt and Hall's [Leeds] for the bonnet . . . I saw some beautiful silks of pale sweet colours, but had not the spirit or the means to launch out at the rate of five shillings per yard, and went and bought a black silk at three shillings after all. I rather regret this, because Papa says he would have lent me a sovereign if he had known. . . " Towards the end of that month Charlotte plans another visit to London. Again there was concern in the parsonage: ". . . Papa seriously told me yesterday that if I married and left him—he should give up housekeeping and go into lodgings ! ! !" Naturally, Charlotte could be flippant : she had no thought of marriage (only hopes) but one can imagine the old man's worry lest his last child should leave him. At such moments of agèd distress even confidence in a loved one can be shaken.

Charlotte went to London on 28th May and left there on 27th June. Three days were then spent in Manchester with Mrs Gaskell before returning to Haworth.

"Dear Papa,

"I was very glad to hear that you continued in pretty good health, and that Mr Cartman came to help you on Sunday. I fear you will not have had a very comfortable week in the dining-room; but by this time I suppose the parlour reformation will be nearly completed, and you will soon be able to return to your old quarters. . . ." Poor Patrick always seemed to be left alone to face the decorators but no doubt it suited best when Charlotte was away. ". . . Hoping you are well, dear papa, and with kind regards to Mr. Nicholls, Tabby, and Martha, also poor old Keeper and Flossie . . . I am glad the parlour is done and that you have got safely settled, but am quite shocked to hear of the piano being dragged up into the bedroom—there it must necessarily be absurd, and in the parlour it looked so well, besides being convenient for your books

I wonder why you don't like it." Was Charlotte really so dense! Could she not remember that Emily had played to her father of an evening when they shared the house together ? Did she not realize that, like herself, Patrick was eating his heart out for Emily ? The presence of the piano in his room was too sad a reminder of happy hours that would never come again. Indeed, after Charlotte's death, he lent it to Mr Grant at Oxenhope ; whilst, as Charlotte had agreed, the family music sheets were given to William Summerscale, the Haworth National Schoolmaster and organist, and his wife.

During the summer of 1851, Ellen came again, then "Mr Morgan was here last Monday, fat—well and hearty—he came to breakfast by nine o'clock—he brought me a lot of tracts as a present. . . ". Then came a cousin from Cornwall, Thomas Brontë Branwell (son of Charlotte and Joseph Branwell who had been married on the same day as Patrick and Maria) ; and then came Margaret Wooler in October. Dear Miss Wooler : she was ever a true and loyal friend to the Brontës, and is the most undervalued person in the Brontë story. With Patrick and the two servants she was always the favourite guest. ". . . Papa and she get on extremely well ; I have just heard papa walk into the dining-room and pay her a round compliment on her good sense. . . ." And again : ". . . she is younger than when at Roe Head . . . she has been pretty comfortable and likes Haworth. . . ." When the visit was over : ". . . Papa enjoins me to give you his best respects and to say he hopes ere long to see you at Haworth again. He would not say this unless he meant it. Tabby and Martha have each with simple sincerity expressed the same wish. . . ." Margaret Wooler had made a hit, as she deserved to do ! At the end of October, Patrick, Martha and Tabby were all ill again, Martha with her second attack of quinsy : ". . . Martha at present looks feeble, I wish she had a better constitution ; as it is, one is always afraid of giving her too much to do, and yet there are many things I cannot undertake myself, and we do not like to change when we have had her so long. . . ."

On 1st December 1851 Patrick went again to his study to unburden his grief alone. Keeper, Emily's beloved companion, was dead. Charlotte writes : ". . . Poor old Keeper died last Monday morning ; after being ill all night, he went gently to sleep. We laid his old faithful head in the garden. Flossy is dull and misses him. There was something very sad in losing the old dog ; yet I am glad he met a natural fate ; people kept hinting he ought to be put away, which neither papa nor I liked to think of. . . ." ". . . We have got curtains for the dining-room . . . dyed crimson. . . ."

At the end of that year, Charlotte was ill—feverish and low-spirited.

30

Ellen came again for a visit to help cheer her and Mr Ruddock, then the local doctor, attended her. ". . . Poor Papa has been in grievous anxiety—on the point of sending for Mr. Teale, I had hard work to restrain him. . . ." Charlotte soon recovered, however, and the end of January 1852 saw her safely staying with Ellen. She came home on 11th February carrying a small gift for Patrick from Ellen. ". . . I found Papa well—he thanks you for the potted tongue and says 'old fellows get more kindness from the ladies than young ones'. . . ."

On 24th February: ". . . as to papa, his health has been really wonderful this winter; good sleep, good spirits, an excellent steady appetite—all seem to mark vigour; may it but continue! . . ." In April, Charlotte writes to an old Brussels schoolfriend: ". . . Tell your papa my father was seventy at the time he underwent an operation . . . nearly six years have now elapsed since the cataract was extracted . . . He has never once, during that time, regretted the step, and a day seldom passes that he does not express gratitude and pleasure at the restoration of that inestimable privilege of vision whose loss he once knew. . . ."

Then followed the summer visit to Filey, and to Anne's grave. Charlotte wrote to Patrick that she hoped soon to bathe, had seen a dog swimming like a seal—"I wonder what Flossy would say to that"— and had attended a church where singers turned their backs on congregation and congregation on the parson and pulpit—"had Mr Nicholls been there he certainly would have laughed out. . . ." Patrick read her long letter through, but did not notice that these days Mr Nicholls was mentioned more often with each succeeding letter.

Shortly after returning from Filey and whilst engaged in writing *Villette*, Charlotte was seriously interrupted. Patrick had a seizure: ". . . He was suddenly attacked with acute inflammation of the eye Mr Ruddock was sent for . . . and said papa's pulse was bounding at 150 per minute, that there was a strong pressure of blood upon the brain, that in short, the symptoms were decidedly apoplectic. Active measures were immediately taken, by the next day the pulse was reduced to 90. Thank God he is now better, though not well. The eye is a good deal inflamed. He does not know his state, to tell him he had been in danger of apoplexy would almost be to kill him at once, it would increase the rush to the brain and perhaps bring about rupture; he is kept very quiet. . . ." On 3rd August: ". . . papa is now considered out of danger . . . there was partial paralysis for two days, but the mind remained clear . . . one eye still remains inflamed . . . one cannot be too thankful that papa's sight is yet spared, it was the fear of losing that which chiefly distressed him. . . ." Ten days later Charlotte says,

". . . Mr Ruddock seems quite satisfied that there is now no present danger whatever—he says Papa has an excellent constitution and may live many years yet. . . . there is every prospect of his still being spared to me for many years. . . ."

For the rest of 1852 there were further visitors to see the famous "Currer Bell"; a visit from Ellen, which was returned towards the end of November; the finishing of *Villette* and its despatch to London on 20th November; and the fierce clash between Patrick and Arthur Nicholls.

It was on Monday, 13th December 1852, on a chill winter's night, that Nicholls asked Charlotte to be his wife. For some time Patrick had noticed his curate's low spirits, his threats to return home to Ireland and his indifferent health. He had almost certainly divined the cause if not the object of his attachment and, according to Charlotte, noticed these symptoms with "little sympathy and much indirect sarcasm". On the evening in question, Charlotte, Patrick and Nicholls had tea together in the parlour, after which, as usual, Charlotte returned to the dining-room. Until half-past eight Patrick sat talking with Nicholls, no easy matter as his curate was deathly pale and seemed to be under feverish restraint. At last Nicholls rose to go and Patrick saw the parlour door close behind his tall figure. He waited for the crash of the front door but it did not come. For some minutes there was silence, next, voices in the hall—the front-door closing hurriedly—and then Charlotte entered the room. She told him at once that Mr Nicholls had a wish to marry her; that he had not dared tell Patrick, that he had watched her for many years now with sympathy, then admiration, and finally love. Patrick's first reaction was a noble one and a true one : Charlotte marry ! Why, it would kill her ! She was as delicate as the others, in many ways more fragile; marriage, children to follow, oh God ! not his only remaining child. Why, she could never survive the birth of her first infant. Then there followed another thought : Nicholls ! a Puseyite ! a mere curate, not a good one at that, earning only £100 a year. Charlotte was worth more than he could ever offer. She would be throwing her talents, her very self, into the arms of an upstart. He hurled back his chair and poured forth a string of invectives that made Charlotte wince. ". . . The veins on his temples started up like whipcord, and his eyes became suddenly bloodshot. I made haste to promise that Mr Nicholls should, on the morrow, have a distinct refusal. . . ." Yet as Charlotte hurriedly gave that assurance and slowly closed the parlour door behind her, do not imagine for one moment that she was heartbroken, her dearest hope blighted, her most precious dream destroyed on wakening. At that time she had never entertained the slightest affection for Nicholls, indeed, her eventual fondness for him grew solely out of pity, and love would not blossom until after they were married. ". . . If I had *loved* Mr Nicholls and had heard such epithets applied to him as were used, it would have transported me past my patience; as it was, my blood boiled with a sense of injustice, but papa worked himself into a state not to be trifled with. . . ." Note the "if I had *loved* Mr Nicholls" and "a sense of injustice"—not the true passion of a Charlotte Brontë! She continues ". . . attachment to Mr Nicholls you are aware I never entertained, but the poignant pity inspired by his state on Monday evening, by the hurried revelation of his sufferings for many months, is something galling and irksome. . . ." It was indeed a shattering moment for poor Charlotte (it was well that *Villette* was finished) but no catastrophe, no heartbreak. For the moment it would be the village gossip that was hardest to bear. ". . . Papa's vehement antipathy to the bare thought of any one thinking of me as a wife, and Mr Nicholls's distress, both give me pain. . . ." Patrick knew only too well the precarious state of his daughter's health, and from this moment forward would suffer greatly lest his consent to the wedding should set the seal upon her early death. He had lost so much, had so little left to lose! Even when he knew beyond all doubt that, after her marriage, Charlotte would continue to live with him, he was not quite contented in his mind. His last-minute refusal to attend the wedding was certainly the churlish action of a selfish old man, but it was dictated by motives of a sudden recurring fear for Charlotte's precious life and the baby that could soon end it.

Martha Brown would later tell how, after the specialist had said there could be no hope of recovery for Charlotte, Patrick walked into the kitchen and said softly: "I told you, Martha, that there was no sense in Charlotte marrying at all, for she was not strong enough for marriage." Even when he had largely swallowed his pride over Nicholls (who was, of course, of a most excellent family) and all his unworthy motives were calmed, there remained his valid objection on the ground of health: an objection, alas! that proved only too reasonable in the sad event that was to follow.

CHAPTER 27

Nicholls

THERE was a feeling of latent hatred in the parsonage, and it was rapidly spreading through the village : some took Nicholls's part, others took Patrick's. Yet at the start of the affair, few sided with the curate ; many supported their venerable parson. Charlotte's feelings were almost forgotten, for there was an exciting struggle in prospect.

On 18th December she writes again to Ellen : ". . . You ask how papa demeans himself to Mr Nicholls. I only wish you were here to see papa in his present mood ; you would know something of him. He just treats him with a hardness not to be bent, and a contempt not to be propitiated. The two have had no interview as yet : all has been done by letter. Papa wrote, I must say, a most cruel note to Mr Nicholls on Wednesday . . . the poor man is horrifying his landlady, Martha's Mother, by entirely rejecting his meals. . . . You must understand that a good share of papa's anger arises from the idea, not altogether groundless, that Mr. Nicholls has behaved with disingenuousness in so long concealing his aim, forging that Irish fiction, etc. [Patrick and Charlotte did not, at this time, believe in the story that the Nicholls family had considerable property in Ireland.] I am afraid also that papa thinks a little too much about his want of money ; he says that the match would be a degradation, that I should be throwing myself away, that he expects me, if I marry at all, to do very differently . . . his manner of viewing the subject is, on the whole, far from being one in which I can sympathise. My own objections arise from a sense of incongruity and uncongeniality in feelings, tastes, principles. . . . Yours, wishing devoutly that papa would resume his tranquillity, and Mr. N. his beef and pudding . . . I am glad to say that the incipient inflammation in papa's eye is disappearing. . . ."

On Wednesday, 5th January 1853, Charlotte again went to London for the publication of *Villette*. ". . . Papa wants me to go too—to be out of the way—I suppose—but I am sorry for one other person whom nobody pities but me. Martha is bitter against him. John Brown says *he should like to shoot him.* . . . he carefully performs the occasional duty—but does not come near the church, procuring a substitute every Sunday. A few days since he wrote to Papa requesting permission to withdraw his resignation. Papa answered that he should only do so on condition of giving his written promise never again to broach the obnoxious subject either to him or to me. This he has evaded doing, so the matter remains unsettled. . . . Without loving him—I don't like to think of him, suffering in solitude, and wish him anywhere so that he were happier. He and Papa have never met or spoken yet. . . ."

From London, Charlotte tells Ellen on 19th January : ". . . Papa— I am glad to say—continues well—I enclose portions of two notes of his which will show you—better than anything I can say—how he treats a certain subject—one of the notes purports to be written by Flossy ! . . . You may burn Papa's notes when read."

But Ellen did not burn the notes. The one written as Flossy (a reminder of the days of the poem of Robin Tweed to his mistress) survives, and the accompanying letter in part. Charlotte had split the latter in two and sent one part to Mrs Gaskell ; it is her portion that survives. Here is the letter from "Flossy" :

To Miss Bronte. 112, Gloucester Terrace,
Hyde Park Gardens, London.

Flossy to his much respected and beloved mistress, Miss Brontë. My kind mistress, as, having only paws, I cannot write, but I can dictate and my good master, has undertaken to set down what I have to say— he will understand the dog's language, which is not very copious, but is nevertheless significant and quite sufficient for our purposes, and wants. Which are not many—I fear that my Master will not do my simple language justice, but will write too much in his own style, which I consider quite out of character, and wrong—you have condescendingly sent your respects to me, for which I am very grateful, and in token of my gratitude, I struck the ground three times with my tail—but let me tell to you my affairs, just as they stand at present, in my little world—little in your opinion, but great in mine. Being old now, my youthful amusements have lost their former relish—I no longer enjoy, as formerly, following sheep, and cats, and birds, and I cannot gnaw bones, as I once did—yet, I am still merry and in good health and spirits—so many things are done before me, which would not be done, if I could speak (well for us dogs that we cannot speak) so, I see a good deal of human nature that is hid from those who have the gift of language. I observe those manouevres [*sic*] and am permitted to observe many of them, which, if I could speak, would never be done before me— I see people cheating one another, and yet appearing to be friends— many are the disagreeable discoveries which I make, which you could hardly believe if I were to tell them—one thing I have lately seen, which I wish to mention—no one takes me out to walk now, the weather is too cold, or too wet for my master to walk in, and my former travelling companion [Nicholls], has lost all his apparent kindness, scolds me, and looks black upon me—I tell my master all this, by looking grave, and puzzled, holding up one side of my head, and one lip, showing my teeth then, looking full in his face and whining.—Ah! my dear Mistress, trust dogs rather than men—they are very selfish, and when they have the power, (which no wise person will readily give them) very tyrannical—that you should act wisely in regard to men, women, and dogs is the sincere wish of yours most sincerely—Old Flossy.

The remaining portion of the accompanying letter from Patrick, addressed the same, is as follows: ". . . a sin quite as great, and is derogatory to the attributes of the author of every good and perfect gift—You may wish to know how we have all been getting on here, especially in respect to *master* and *man*; on yesterday I preached twice, but my man, was every way very quiet—He shun'd me as if I had been a Cobra de Capello—turning his head from the quarter where I was, and hustling away amongst the crowd to avoid contact—it required no Levater to see that his countenance was strongly indicative of mortified pride and malevolent resentment—people have begun to notice these things, and various conjectures are afloat—You thought me too severe— but I was not candid enough—this conduct might have been excus'd by the world in a confirmed rake—or unprincipled Army officer, but in a *clergyman*, it is justly chargeable with base design and inconsistency— I earnestly wish that he had another and better situation—as I can never trust him any more in things of importance—I wish him no ill— but rather good, and wish that every woman may avoid him forever, unless she should be determined on her own misery—all the produce of the Australian *diggins* [*sic*] would not make him and any wife he might have, happy—Mr Grant has been here twice—and asked *kindly* after you, and about 'Vilette' [*sic*]—so that you see 'Mr *Donne*', has at least good policy—as he will not *don* the cap—showing thus to the world that it does not fit him—This, as far as he is concerned is wise and well— Tabby, is in her usual way—I give her your respects—Martha, is lively and brisk, looking at the best side of things, and, and [*sic*] busy on the household affairs, and in spare time, in making frocks, petticoats, and pinafores—They both desire to be kindly, and respectfully remembered to you, and are very anxious to see 'Vilette'—Ever your affectionate Father, P. Brontè."

Villette was published on 28th January 1853, and was immediately an overwhelming triumph. It was during this visit to London that

Charlotte met Dr Forbes, who had been consulted regarding Anne. On Wednesday, 2nd February, Charlotte arrived home, bringing with her Ellen Nussey. ". . . I hope to come home next Wednesday . . . I hope you and Tabby have agreed pretty well. . . ." So she wrote to Martha Brown to announce her return.

But before Charlotte returned, indeed on the day *Villette* was published, Nicholls, as if he had read Patrick's sarcasm of "the Australian diggins" applied officially to go as a missionary to that Colony. The reality of his loved one's third novel and his jealousy of all and sundry, especially George Smith—for now Patrick's uneasy hints could be used against the curate—proved too much to bear. He wrote to the Secretary of the Society for the Propagation of the Gospel:

Haworth. Keighley. Jany 28th 1853.

Revᵈ Sir

I beg to offer myself as a Candidate for Employment as a Missionary in the Australian Colonies. I return the "paper of Questions" with answers.

My present Engagement will be concluded by the end of May next.
I am Revᵈ Sir, Your obᵗ Servt. A.B. Nicholls

The enclosed application form showed his preference for "Sydney, Melbourne or Adelaide" and his declaration that he had no private property or income. His health was "very good, except that I have been affected with Rheumatism this winter, but never so severely as to be incapable of duty. I am now almost quite well." His reason for applying ? "I have for some time felt a strong inclination to assist in Ministering to the thousands of of [sic] our fellow Countrymen, who by Emigration have been in a great measure deprived of the means of Grace." He gave, as those clergy who knew him best, the names of Patrick, Dr Burnet, Vicar of Bradford, his friend Sutcliffe Sowden of Hebden Bridge, Grant, Mayne of Ingrow and William Cartman of the Grammar School, Skipton.

Of course the Society applied to Patrick and, as he wrote his answer, he must have been very relieved that Charlotte was still in London.

To the Revᵈ W. Thos. Bullock. M.A.
Assistant Secretary, To the Society for the Propagation of the Gospel, 79, Pall Mall, London.

Haworth, NR. Keighley, Jany 31st 1853—

Revᵈ Sir,

I shall briefly, plainly, and faithfully answer your questions, respecting the Revᵈ Arthur Bell Nicholls, A.B. He has been my curate for seven years, and during that time has behaved himself, wisely, soberly, and piously—

He has greatly promoted the interest of the National, and Sunday Schools; he is a man of good abilities, and strong constitution—He is very discreet, is under no pecuniary embarrassment, that I am aware of, nor is he, I think, likely to be so since, in all pecuniary and other matters as far as I have been able to discover, he is wary, and prudent—In principles, he is sound and orthodox—and would I think, under providence, make an excellent Missionary—

I am, Revd Sir, Your faithful servant, Patrick Brontë, A.B.

Incumbent.

The local clerics rushed to aid the application with a will. Sutcliffe Sowden wrote of Nicholls ". . . having frequently most of the responsibility of the Parish, thru [sic] the age of his Incumbent . . ." Grant, remembering Patrick's teasing over his portrayal in *Shirley* mixed malice with recommendation. ". . . I have had the pleasure of knowing Mr. Nicholls for the last eight years. When he first came to Haworth the Church was in a very sad condition . . . the National School which at *that period* did not number above 60 scholars now numbers between two & three hundred, while the service in the Church especially of an Evening has increased six-fold. In the neighbouring hamlet of Stanbury he has also been the means of building a Schoolroom: of a weekday & Sunday School & service there on Sundays . . . he had much to contend against both in the want of rich men to aid as well as in the strenuous opposition of Dissenters. But in all things he acted so discreetly, and wisely that I am sure he will be much regretted both by Churchmen & Dissenters. . . ."

William Cartman wrote: ". . . I had intended walking up to visit Mr. Brontè his incumbent the other day, but was delayed at the Parsonage of St. John's Keighley when I dined with Mr. Mayne, a mutual friend of ours, who hinted to me that he believed that Nicholls would leave Haworth soon. . . . Mr. Brontè has often detailed to me his invaluable services, and has frequently said, that sh^d he leave him, he should not know how to supply his place. . . ."

Finally the Vicar of Bradford added his recommendation and, like his predecessors, showed no love for Haworth. ". . . The Revd A.B. Nicholls has been curate at Haworth, a very wild & rough part of this extensive Parish for several years . . . amongst a rude, and dissenting population . . . by his exertions the Church has gain'd ground. . . ."

Thus matters stood when Charlotte came home.

Five days later Patrick wrote again to George Smith regarding his daughter's new book:

Haworth, near Keighley. February 7th 1853.

My Dear Sir,

I know not whether you are in the habit of canvassing for your publication the suffrages of the provincial press. There is, however, one provincial editor to whom it might be advisable to send a copy of my daughter's work, *Villette*, viz. Mr Baines, editor of the *Leeds Mercury*— his paper enjoys a wide circulation, and considerable influence in the north of England, and as I am an old subscriber, and occasional contributor, to the *Mercury*, a fair notice, I think, of *Villette* might be counted upon. Offer my kind regards to Mrs Smith, and also my acknowledgments for her late friendly hospitality to my daughter.

I am Yours faithfully, P. Brontë.

At the same time Patrick wrote to Baines:

To Edward Baines, Esqʳ Editor of the *Mercury*,
Mercury Office, Leeds.

Rev. P. Brontë, Haworth, Nr. Kighley. [*sic*] Feby: 7th 1853.
Dear Sir,

I having [*sic*] this day, written to the Publisher of *Villette*, My Daughter's last work, requesting him to send you a copy, in order, that if you thought proper it might be noticed in the *Mercury*—Already, several able, and just reviews, have appeared in the London papers— but from what I know of your Critical taste and talents, I have a strong desire to learn your opinion.

Yours, very respectfully, and truly, P. Brontë.

Late in the evening of 25th February, Thackeray's portrait arrived at Haworth Parsonage: another gift from Charlotte's publisher: ". . . My father stood for a quarter of an hour this morning, examining the great man's picture. The conclusion of his survey was, that he thought it a puzzling head; if he had known nothing previously of the original's character, he could not have read it in his features. . . ." There now followed important visitors to the parsonage, and some trouble with Nicholls: ". . . The Bishop has been, and is gone. [Dr. Charles Thomas Longley, first Bishop of Ripon, later to become Archbishop of York in 1860 and of Canterbury in 1862.] He is certainly a most charming little Bishop . . . his visit passed capitally well . . . he expressed himself thoroughly gratified with all he had seen. The Inspector also has been in the course of the past week . . . Martha waited very nicely, and I had a person to help her in the kitchen. Papa kept up, too, fully as well as I expected, though I doubt whether he could have borne another day of it. . . . We had the parsons to supper as well as to tea. Mr. Nicholls demeaned himself not quite pleasantly. I thought he made no effort to struggle with his dejection, but gave way to it in a manner to draw notice; the Bishop was obviously puzzled by it. Mr Nicholls also showed temper once or twice in speaking to papa. Martha was beginning to tell me of certain 'flaysome' looks also, but I desired not to hear of them. The fact is, I shall be most thankful when he is well away; I pity him, but I don't like that dark gloom of his. He dogged me up the lane after the evening service in no pleasant manner, he stopped also in the passage after the Bishop and the other Clergy were gone into the room, and it was because I drew away and went upstairs, that he gave that look which filled Martha's soul with horror. She, it seems, meantime, was making it her business to watch him from the kitchen door . . . he managed to get up a most pertinacious and needless dispute with the Inspector, in listening to which all my old unfavourable impressions revived so strongly, I fear my countenance could not but show them. . . ."

Nicholls was indeed in a state of agitation, for between Charlotte's return and the Bishop's visit in early March, (and despite his "strong inclination" to minister to emigrants "deprived of the means of Grace") he had already abandoned the project as easily as, later, he gave up the Church altogether. Patrick could note again the difference between the Puseyite and the Evangelical: this was not the stuff of Henry Martyn.

Nicholls had written twice more to the Society.

Haworth—Keighley. Feby 23rd 1853.

Revd Sir,

I some time ago addressed an application to the Society for an appointment in the Australian Colonies. As I have had no reply I shall feel obliged by your kindly informing me, whether my letter has been received, and if so, when it is probable that I shall have a definite answer.—

I am Revd Sir, Yr obt. Servt A.B. Nicholls.

This letter was at once endorsed "come to town". But Nicholls, still detested by Patrick and with no encouragement from Charlotte, drew back hurriedly.

Haworth—Keighley Feby 26th 1853

Dear Sir,

I beg to acknowledge the receipt of your note of 24th inst, inviting me to an interview in London with your Committee—Since the date of my application, owing to the Solicitation of friends some doubts have occurred to me as to the desirableness of leaving the Country at present—

When I have fully made up my mind upon the point I will again communicate with you—

faithfully yours A.B. Nicholls

Shortly afterwards Nicholls ended the matter with rheumatism as his feeble excuse.

Haworth—Keighley April 1st 1853

Revd Sir,

As, owing to the severity of the weather, the Rheumatic affliction, with which I have been troubled during the winter has not abated as rapidly as I expected, I have been induced by my friends to relinquish for the present my intention of going abroad—Will you therefore convey to your Committee my sincere thanks for their kindness in entertaining my application : & also my hope, that I shall meet with a like consideration, if in the course of a few months I should wish to renew the subject ?

I am, Revd Sir, Yrs faithfully A.B. Nicholls

The Committee marked this letter simply—"withdrawing".

Meanwhile, after a spate of praising reviews, the *Guardian* printed an attack on certain aspects of *Villette* and, with a touch of revengeful malice, it was Mr Grant who rushed into Patrick's parlour with the criticism in his hand.

On 6th April Charlotte mentions Nicholls again to Ellen : ". . . I hear he has got a curacy, but do not yet know where. I trust the news is true. He and papa never speak . . . He sits drearily in his rooms . . . He still lets Flossy go to his rooms and takes him [her] to walk. . . . He is now grown so gloomy and reserved, that nobody seems to like him, his fellow-curates shun trouble in that shape, the lower orders dislike it. Papa has a perfect antipathy to him, and he, I fear, to papa. Martha hates him. . . ."

William Morgan, now at Hulcott, Buckinghamshire, had promised to come up and see Patrick : ". . . Mr Morgan did *not* come, and if he had, the subject you mention would not have been touched on. Papa alludes to it to nobody ; he calls it 'degrading' and would not have it hinted at or known. . . ."

Towards the end of April 1853 Charlotte stayed with Mrs Gaskell at her home in Manchester, then on to Ellen's. Back home again, Charlotte was to obtain a fresh glimpse of the character of Arthur

Nicholls. It was in church on Whit Sunday, 15th May, and Charlotte had stopped behind for the sacrament. Nicholls was taking the communion service.

"... He struggled, faltered, then lost command over himself, stood before my eyes and in the sight of all the communicants, white, shaking, voiceless. Papa was not there, thank God! Joseph Redman [parish clerk] spoke some words to him—he made a great effort, but could only with difficulty whisper and falter through the service. I suppose he thought this would be the last time; he goes either this week or the next . . . what had happened was reported to papa either by Joseph Redman or John Brown; it excited only anger, and such expressions as 'unmanly driveller'. Compassion or relenting is no more to be looked for from Papa than sap from firewood. . . ."

There remain two more pictures of Nicholls before he left Haworth. Charlotte writes to Ellen on 19th May: ". . . I cannot help feeling a certain satisfaction in finding that the people here are getting up a subscription to offer a testimonial of respect to Mr. Nicholls on his leaving the place. [A gold watch, engraved with this inscription: 'Presented to the Revd A. B. Nicholls, B.A., by the teachers, scholars, and congregation of St. Michael's, Haworth, Yorkshire, May 25th, 1853.'] Many are expressing both their commiseration and esteem for him. The Churchwardens recently put the question to him plainly. Why was he going? Was it Mr Brontë's fault or his own? 'His own,' he answered. Did he blame Mr Brontë? 'No! he did not: if anybody was wrong it was himself.' Was he willing to go? 'No! it gave him great pain.' . . . Papa addressed him at the school tea-drinking, with *constrained* civility, but still with *civility*. He did not reply civilly; he cut short further words. This sort of treatment offered in public is what papa never will forget or forgive; it inspires him with a silent bitterness not to be expressed. . . ."

However, now that he was actually leaving, opinion in Haworth had largely swung round in sympathy with Nicholls. Finally, on 27th May, Charlotte again wrote to Ellen: ". . . You will want to know about the leave-taking . . . the testimonial was presented in a public meeting . . . Papa was not very well and I advised him to stay away, which he did. As to the last Sunday, it was a cruel struggle. Mr. Nicholls ought not to have had to take any duty. He left Haworth this morning at 6 o'clock. Yesterday evening he called to render into Papa's hands the deeds of the National School, and to say good-bye. They were busy cleaning, washing the paint, etc. in the dining-room, so he did not find me there. I would not go into the parlour to speak to him in Papa's presence. . . ." She then relates how she found the curate "leaning against the garden

door in a paroxysm of anguish, sobbing as women never sob". She
went to him and gave what comfort she could—"I trust he must know
now that I am not cruelly blind and indifferent to his constancy and
grief . . . for a few weeks he goes to the South of England—afterwards
he takes a curacy somewhere in Yorkshire, but I don't know where.
Papa has been far from strong lately. I dare not mention Mr Nicholls's
name to him. He speaks of him quietly and without opprobrium to
others, but to me he is implacable on the matter . . . I see no chance of
hearing a word about him in future unless some stray shred of intelligence comes through Mr Sowden [the Rev. Sutcliffe Sowden of
Hebden Bridge] . . . they all think, in Haworth, that I have disdainfully
refused him, etc. If pity would do Mr Nicholls any good, he ought to
have and I believe has it. . . ."

Arthur Bell Nicholls became curate at Kirk Smeaton, a few miles
south-east of Pontefract, whilst Patrick obtained a new assistant, who
arrived at the time Nicholls left.

When news of Patrick's refusal to allow Charlotte to marry Nicholls
reached the ears of Mary Taylor out in New Zealand, that arch-enemy
of all parental control was furious. Even after Charlotte's eventual
marriage and death she never forgave him and wrote to Ellen on 19th
April 1856: ". . . I can never think without gloomy anger of Charlotte's
sacrifices to the selfish old man. . . ."

In June 1853 Charlotte invited Mrs Gaskell to come to Haworth for
a few days, but on the eve of her visit Charlotte became ill and Patrick
wrote to postpone it. This was the first of the many letters he would pen
to Mrs Gaskell.

To Mrs Gaskell, 47 Wimpole Street London.

Haworth, near Keighley. June [7] 1853.
My Dear Madam,

I am obliged to act as amanuensis for my daughter, who is at present
confined for the most part to her bed with influenza, and frequent sharp
attacks of [tic-]douloureux in the head, which have rendered her utterly
unable to entertain you as she could wish—and, besides this, she is
afraid of communicating the complaints by contagion, which would be
cause for sad reflection, should you have to suffer from your intended
kind visit. I can assure you, that your not visiting us as we wished and
expected, will be a great disappointment both to my daughter and me
—From what I have heard my daughter say, respecting you, and from
the perusal of your literary works, I shall give you a most hearty welcome
whenever you may come. As soon as my daughter shall have got well—
which I trust in God will be ere long—she will let you know, and we

hope then to see you at your earliest convenient opportunity. With our united kindest regards, I remain, My dear Madam,

Very respectfully and truly yours, P. Brontë.

By the 16th Charlotte had recovered but she was now a little anxious about her father : ". . . the eyes, and etc. betrayed those symptoms that fill me with alarm. . . ." And to George Smith on 3rd July : ". . . there is no change for the worse in his sight since I wrote last . . . He says the sort of veil between him and the light appears thinner . . . he must become stronger than he appears to be just now, less liable to sudden sickness and swimming in the head. . . ." This was in response to an offer of attention should Patrick seek medical aid in London : ". . . I know, however, that my father's first and last thought would be to give trouble nowhere . . . he would, of course, take private lodgings. . . ."

Patrick had hoped for a brief visit to London that summer but now he was back in his parlour fighting off blindness again : ". . . My father's half-formed project of visiting London this summer for a few days has been rather painfully frustrated. In June he had a sudden seizure, which . . . brought on for a time total blindness. He could not discern between day and night. I feared the optic nerve was paralysed, and that he would never see more. Vision has, however, been partially restored, but it is now very imperfect. He sometimes utters a wish that he could see the camp at Cobham . . . I think him very patient with the apprehension of what, to him, would be the greatest of privations, hanging over his head. I can but earnestly hope that what remains of sight may be spared him to the end. . . ."

To the editor of *The Christian Remembrancer* Charlotte wrote on 18th July : ". . . My father is now in his seventy-seventh year ; his mind is clear as it ever was, and he is not infirm, but he suffers from partial privation and threatened loss of sight. . . ." Patrick's eyesight, although weaker, did not get worse, for which mercy he was the more grateful as his new curate, a pale, thin young man named George De Renzy, was by no means to his liking or that of the village. Yet his sight was not clear enough to notice that there came the occasional letter from Nicholls to his daughter.

In August 1853 Patrick received a handsome present of game from William Busfeild Ferrand, the squire of nearby Bingley. Ferrand, of Harden Grange, was a J.P., Deputy Lieutenant of Yorkshire and, as Member of Parliament, actively sponsored the Ten Hours' Factory Act, exposed the truck system and the harsh conditions of Poor Law administration. He is finely portrayed in Halliwell Sutcliffe's *A Man of the Moors*. At this time he was forty-four years of age.

To W. B. Ferrand Esq. Bingley

Haworth, Nr. Keighley. August 23rd, 1853.

Dear Sir,

I thank you for your kind remembrance of me, through your presents of game—they remind me of my youthful days, when I often traversed the moors and fields myself, and in a quick and steady aim, might have been not an unworthy competitor, even with you, though from what I learn, that would have been no easy matter; since I hear, you scarcely ever miss—well—you have strong nerves, quick sight, and a steady hand, good, and necessary qualifications for hitting the mark. I had the curiosity to weigh one of the birds—it weighed nearly twenty-six ounces—which was the greatest weight, I ever knew. But, to pass from moorcocks to statesmen, from powder to politics. What think ye of the materials of our present Government, and their proceedings—was there ever so heterogeneous a Mass, under the sun?—Whig, and Tory—Conservative and Radical, Romanist, and Puritan—all jumbled together! Are these the men, to make a long pull, a strong pull, and a pull, all together, for the public good? Where there must be so much sacrifice, of principle and consistency, it is not difficult to foresee, the inglorious and disastrous issue. Hoping that you, your Lady and family are well —I remain, Dear Sir, Yours respectfully and truly,

P. Brontë.

Patrick is, of course, referring to the coalition ministry of Peelites and Whigs, under Lord Aberdeen. His presagement soon came true. The Government drifted into the Crimean War, the conduct of which was disastrous, and after two years the ministry fell, unloved by all.

At this time, namely August, Charlotte was away for a few days in Scotland with Mr and Mrs Joe Taylor. It was a farcical trip. The Taylors' baby was supposed ill by its parents and they quit Scotland for Ilkley. Charlotte lost her box and after three days then came home, where "I found Papa far from well".

Mrs Gaskell was now free to make her belated journey to Haworth, and she intimated that she would arrive on Monday, 19th September. But when her letter arrived, Charlotte was back in Ilkley staying with Margaret Wooler, and again it was Patrick who answered:

To Mrs Gaskell, Plymouth Grove, Manchester.

Haworth, Near Keighley, Yorkshire. September 15th 1853.

My Dear Madam,

My daughter having gone from home, for only two or three days— when your letter arrived—I deem'd it best to open it, lest it should have

PLATE 26   *Elizabeth Firth*

PLATE 27 (*Above*) *The Sunday School, Haworth, and John Brown's house*

PLATE 28 (*Right*) *Haworth Parsonage and Church Tower in winter*

required an immediate answer. She will return on Saturday next—therefore she will be here to receive you on the Monday after. As I have given her the requisite information by post—you may probably have a letter from herself on the day on which you will receive this. As far as I am able to discover from what my daughter has told me, and from my perusal of your able, moral, and interesting literary works, I think that you and she are congenial spirits and that a little intercourse between you, might, under the strange vicissitudes and frequent trials of this mortal life—under providence—be productive of pleasure and profit to you both—We are gregarious beings and cannot always be comfortable if alone—and a faithful and intellectual friend—when such an one can be found—is often productive of pleasure and profit—and needed by us, next to that Greatest and Best of All Friends—who sticketh closer than a brother—We can promise you nothing here but a hearty welcome, and peaceful seclusion—nevertheless, this may not be without its use—for a season.

With my kind and respectful regards, I remain, My dear Madam,
Yours very sincerely, P. Brontë.

Patrick's note to his daughter brought her home post haste and she wrote telling Mrs Gaskell to come as promised on the Monday, Elizabeth Gaskell came to Haworth and went; and the world now knows well what she saw there, but not what she entirely missed. Whilst she was there, Francis Bennock called to see Charlotte, claiming "that he was a patron of Authors and literature". Naturally, Charlotte and her guest were contemptuous but Patrick was impressed and captivated by the man. He called them both "proud minxes" for their reluctance to see Bennock.

Whether Mrs Gaskell is quoting Patrick correctly is not known, for her entire description of everything that is not Charlotte is one long sneer from beginning to end, from "breakfast at 9, in Mr Brontë's room" to "he [Papa] begged Miss Brontë to go and see Prince Albert's armoury at Windsor; and when he is unusually out of spirits she tells him over and over again of the different weapons, & etc there".

True, she admitted that Patrick was "very polite and agreeable to me; paying rather elaborate old-fashioned compliments". Yet when Mrs Gaskell went down Kirkgate to return to her sophisticated friends she carried the poisoned image of Patrick Brontë and Haworth in her heart.

Political and religious bias was to be a difficult barrier for her to surmount: the sight of strong people living in primitive naturalness would prove insurmountable. There is a sadly ironic touch in the

31

letter that followed her down the hill: ". . . Papa, I am sure, derived real benefit from your visit; he has been better ever since. . . ."

The remainder of 1853 is soon told. After the departure of Mrs Gaskell, Charlotte left Patrick alone in the parsonage again, whilst she visited in turn Ellen at Brookroyd and Margaret Wooler at Hornsea. She arrived home on 5th October and found that all was well there. She also discovered that Arthur Nicholls, as hinted in his letters to her, had been in the district once or twice, staying with Mr Grant at Marshlands, near Oxenhope.

Charlotte had begun answering his correspondence; and on at least one occasion she glided along the lane that leads from the churchyard, past Sowdens where Grimshaw had lived, and so past Oxenhope Mill to Marshlands. The fidelity of the curate had warmed Charlotte's heart if not to love, then certainly to warm affection. Patrick too was wavering: De Renzy was by no means bone idle but Charlotte often heard her father complain that, with his feeble eyesight, he needed an active and assiduous curate such as Nicholls had been. Charlotte said nothing at this stage, though she hated hiding her association with Nicholls from him. But he was weakening and she felt sure that the New Year would see the matter put to rights.

In November Charlotte was on the eve of departure for London, her rooms taken, her portmanteau packed. But the visit was cancelled: this was certainly no time to leave Haworth, with Nicholls at Oxenhope and her father rating De Renzy more roundly than ever. It was now agreed between Nicholls and Charlotte that, should Patrick's consent be gained, they would be married. Charlotte wrote to Williams advising him not to trouble to send any more parcels of books. Her London friends were overthrown—"Currer Bell" was dead!

Some few weeks after the New Year, following an even worse lapse than usual on the part of the luckless De Renzy, Charlotte told her father all that had occurred between Nicholls and herself and left the matter in his hands. For a long time Patrick sat alone, staring through the window of his parlour across the churchyard, and through the very walls of the church, to see the vault where all his loved ones save Charlotte and Anne were sleeping. His old hatred of Nicholls had evaporated. Charlotte had stipulated only for the right to become even better acquainted before any irrevocable decision be taken. Certainly he could do with Nicholls back in the parish. It was so tedious and humiliating to have continually to ask local clerics like Cartman and Fawcett to assist him. And his eyes were no stronger; at his age he could scarcely hope they ever would be again. Yet marriage for Charlotte might easily mean her death: child-bearing in her feeble constitution was fraught with peril. It was almost dark in the little room before Patrick reached his decision with a long drawn-out sigh. A day or so later Charlotte was told she might continue to write to Nicholls and also see him.

On 8th March 1854 Charlotte wrote to an old Brussels schoolfriend : ". . . My dear Father has borne the severe winter very well . . . I can hardly tell you how thankful I was, dear Laetitia, when, after that dreary and almost despairing interval of utter darkness, some gleam of daylight became visible to him once more . . . a sort of mist remained for a long time, and indeed his vision is not yet perfectly clear, but he can read, write, and walk about, and he preaches *twice* every Sunday, the curate only reading the prayers. *You* can well understand how earnestly I pray that sight may be spared him to the end ; he so dreads the privation of blindness. His mind is just as strong and active as ever, and politics interest him as they do *your* papa. The Czar, the war, the alliance between France and England—into all these things he throws himself heart and soul. They seem to carry him back to his comparatively young days. . . . Of course, my Father's sympathies (and mine too) are all with Justice and Europe against Tyranny and Russia. . . ." On 28th March Charlotte makes some showing of a woman in love : she mixes her envelopes and sends to Ellen by mistake a letter intended for Nicholls. ". . . I wish you could come about Easter— Mr Nicholls, if not prevented, proposes coming over then. I suppose he will stay at Mr Grant's . . . he will be frequently coming here, which would enliven your visit a little. Perhaps, too, he might take a walk with us occasionally. . . . He was here in January and was then received, but not pleasantly. I trust it will be a little different now. Papa has breakfasted in bed to-day, and has not yet risen ; his bronchitis is still troublesome. . . ."

But Nicholls came earlier than Easter, on Monday, 3rd April, so Ellen was not present. On the 11th Charlotte informs her of her engagement : ". . . Mr Nicholls came on Monday, and was here all last week. . . ." Then follows a recital of the slow developments of the past months, and of the overcoming of Patrick's resentment and hostility. ". . . The result of this, his last visit, is, that Papa's consent is gained—that his respect, I believe, is won, for Mr Nicholls has in all things proved himself disinterested and forbearing. . . . In fact, dear Ellen, I am engaged. Mr. Nicholls, in the course of a few months, will return to the curacy of Haworth. I stipulated that I would not leave Papa, and to Papa himself I proposed a plan of residence which should maintain his seclusion and convenience uninvaded and in a pecuniary sense bring him gain instead of loss. What seemed at one time impossible is now arranged, and papa begins really to take a pleasure in the prospect. . . . It is possible that our marriage may take place in the course of the Summer—Mr Nicholls wishes it to be in July. . . ." Then Charlotte wrote to Miss Wooler : ". . . it gives me unspeakable content to see that—now my Father has once admitted this new view of the case—he dwells on it complacently . . . Mr Nicholls seems deeply to feel the wish to comfort and sustain his declining years. I think—from Mr N's character—I may depend on this . . . he is to resume the curacy of Haworth, as soon as Papa's present assistant is provided with a situation . ;. Papa has just got a letter from the good and dear Bishop—which has touched and pleased me much. It expresses so cordial an approbation of Mr N's return to Haworth (respecting which he was consulted) and such kind gratification at the domestic arrangements which are to ensue. It seems his penetration discovered the state of things when he was here in Jany. 1853. . . ." Again to Ellen on 15th April : ". . . Papa's mind seems wholly changed about the matter, and he has said both to me and when I was not there, how much happier he feels since he allowed all to be settled. . . . He is rather anxious things should get forward now, and takes quite an interest in the arrangement of pre-liminaries. His health improves daily . . . the feeling which had been disappointed in Papa was *ambition*, paternal pride . . . Mr Nicholls only in his last letter refers touchingly to his earnest desire to prove his gratitude to Papa, by offering support and consolation to his declining age. . . ." Finally to Mrs Gaskell on 18th April : ". . . The Rubicon once passed, papa seems cheerful and satisfied ; he says he has been far too stern ; he even admits that he was unjust . . . I could almost cry some-times that in this important action in my life I cannot better satisfy papa's perhaps natural pride. My destiny will not be brilliant, certainly, but Mr Nicholls is conscientious, affectionate, pure in heart and life . . . I am very grateful to him. I mean to try and make him happy, and papa too. . . ."

It is too obvious from this and all Charlotte's letters that there was still very little of love for Arthur Nicholls : that would ripen later. Meanwhile Tabby and Martha remained in their kitchen, busily digesting this volte-face. In fairness to Nicholls it must be mentioned that, in order to return to the curacy of Haworth, he rejected several offers of promotion in the Church.

Towards the end of April we learn that "Papa, thank God ! con-tinues to improve much. He preached twice on Sunday and again on Wednesday and was not tired."

In May, Charlotte stayed with Mrs Gaskell at Manchester, then went to Hunsworth, home of Joe Taylor, then to Ellen's. Nicholls had been invited to all three places but was obliged to remain on duty at Kirk Smeaton as his rector, Mr Cator, was in London.

Upon her return to Haworth, Charlotte found that De Renzy had complained bitterly to Nicholls about the termination of his curacy. She tells Ellen on 14th May : ". . . I found Papa well . . . He has already given Mr de Renzy the legal notice : that gentleman is still perfectly smooth and fairspoken to Papa ; he never told him a word of what he has written to Mr Nicholls—nor does he make any objection before Papa—but has the deplorable weakness to go and pour out acrimonious complaints to John Brown, the National Schoolmaster and other subordinates. This only exposes himself to disrespectful comment from those exalted personages. . . ." On 7th June : ". . . I was very miserable about Papa again some days ago—he was suddenly attacked with deafness and complained of other symptoms which shewed the old tendency to the head. His spirits too became excessively depressed —it was all I could do to keep him up . . . however he took some medicine which did him good. The change to cooler weather too has suited him . . . That unlucky Mr de Renzy continues his efforts to give what trouble he can—and I am obliged to conceal and keep things from Papa's knowledge as well as I can, to spare him that anxiety which hurts him so much. Mr de R's whole aim is to throw Papa into the dilemma of being without a curate for some weeks. Papa has every legal right to frustrate this at once by telling him he must stay till his quarter is up— but this is just the harsh, decided sort of measure which it goes against Papa's nature to adopt and which I *can* not and *will* not urge upon him while he is in delicate health. I feel compelled to throw the burden of the contest upon Mr. Nicholls, who is younger—more pugnacious and can bear it better. The worst of it is Mr. N. has not Papa's rights to speak and act—or he would do it to purpose. . . ."

On 11th June : ". . . Papa preached twice to-day, as well and as strongly as ever. . . ." Meanwhile the wedding day approached and all was bustle and preparation. The little peat room behind the dining-room was turned into a study for Mr Nicholls : "the green and white curtains are up ; they exactly suit the paper. . .".

Charlotte wrote again to Ellen on June 16th : ". . . Can you come next Wednesday or Thursday ? . . . I sadly wished to defer it [the wedding] till the 2nd week in July, but I feel it must be sooner, the 1st week in July, possibly the last week in June, for Mr de Renzy has succeeded in obtaining his holiday, and whereas his quarter will not be up till the 20th of August, he leaves on the 25th of June. This gives rise to much trouble and many difficulties as you may imagine, and Papa's whole anxiety now is to get the business over. Mr Nicholls with his usual trustworthiness takes all the trouble of providing substitutes on his own shoulders. . . . He and Mr Sowden [who was to marry them] will come to Mr Grant's the evening before. . . . Precisely at 8 in the morning they will be in the Church, and there we are to meet them. Mr and Mrs Grant are asked to the breakfast, not the ceremony. . . ." On the same day she wrote to Margaret Wooler: ". . . come as soon as you possibly can . . . Papa also seems much to wish your presence . . . Yourself, E. Nussey and Mr Sowden will be the only persons present at the ceremony. . . ."

Certainly there is no mention in this letter of Patrick's being expected at the ceremony and it is likely that his refusal to give his daughter away, a refusal made on the eve of the wedding, was far from being a surprise to Charlotte.

Wedding cards were sent out to friends, both local and otherwise, Charlotte's list appropriately beginning with "The Rev. W. Morgan, Rectory, Hulcott, Aylesbury, Bucks."

On the afternoon of Wednesday, 28th June, Ellen and Miss Wooler arrived by coach, and all was ready. Then after prayers at nine o'clock Patrick, instead of going to bed, went into his study. Charlotte crept in to say goodnight and found him in great distress. He would be at the wedding breakfast in the morning, but to the church he could not, he would not, go. As is known, the sex of the person who may give the bride away is not specified, so Margaret Wooler filled the breach for her old pupil.

Thursday, 29th June 1854, was "a dim, quiet June morning" as Charlotte Brontë, walking down the lane between Ellen and Margaret Wooler, went to her wedding. The previous day's arrivals had been noticed by the villagers and, for all the attempts at secrecy, a small knot of loyal friends from the village stood by the church door, with not one dry eye among them. Charlotte looked "like a snowdrop" in her white embroidered muslin.

From his bedroom window Patrick looked out at the scene and watched his last child enter the church of which he was the incumbent; then a wet mist covered his fading eyes and he was again blind, with tears. They were all in that church now, save his little Anne. Yet his was the tomb: that great grey parsonage which was a prison of loneliness echoing with voices that had long been hushed. The front door knocker crashed three times rapidly and startled him out of his reverie. He brushed his hand over his eyes to see again. The Grants had arrived.

There were eight people present at the wedding breakfast, nine really, for Martha Brown, in a simple black and white cotton gown—

a present from Charlotte—waited at the table, and her recollection was of a very happy time. Mr Nicholls, Mr Grant and Mr Sowden kept the conversation going. "Old Mr. Brontë behaved very well in his grandiloquent manner" (only Charlotte knew what it was costing him). Ellen and Miss Wooler chatted away to Mrs Grant.

Then the carriage came to the garden door. There were kisses for Ellen and Margaret; thanks for Mr Sowden and Mr Grant; a warm embrace for Papa, with exhortations to take care of his health; and Charlotte was almost ready, but not quite. She shook Martha by the hand, bent down to fondle Flossy and then went into the kitchen. It was only when she came out, having kissed and hugged Tabby almost to death, that there were tears in her eyes. That good old woman reminded her so much of other days—with Anne and Emily!

There was a last shout from the people of Haworth, and Mrs Nicholls was lost to view. Mr Sutcliffe Sowden and the Grants had remained in the hall and Charlotte did not notice Martha peering through the dining-room window, or the battered old head of Tabby, who had hobbled to the front door. She did not see Flossy held firm in the grip of her old schoolmistress Margaret Wooler, nor dear Ellen waving a very wet handkerchief. Her last picture was of her father, standing erect and alone by the garden door. There was a sad look on his face for all that he was smiling, and as the carriage turned out of sight Charlotte suddenly thought how very much like Emily he looked.

When all was quiet, and the visitors were departed, Patrick could slip down to his vestry and read:

1854 June 29th	Arthur Bell Nicholls Charlotte Brontë	full age full age	Bachelor Spinster	Clerk —	Kirk Smeaton Haworth	William Nicholls Patrick Brontë	Farmer Clerk

Married in Haworth, by license, by me, Sutcliffe Sowden.

This Marriage was solemnized between us—
      Arthur Bell Nicholls.   Charlotte Brontë.
In the presence of us—Ellen Nussey. Margaret Wooler.

Whilst the newly-married couple were honeymooning in Ireland, Patrick was left with Tabby and Martha and a host of memories. He wrote to Ellen Nussey in early July.

To Miss Nussey, Brookroyd, Birstall. Nr. Leeds.

Haworth, nr. Keighley. July 7th 1854.

My Dear Madam,

I thank you for your kind and considerate letter. You are perfectly right in what you say respecting the usual effects of changes in regard to those far advanced in years. They are often reminded of Solomon's description of the old man with whom "fears shall be in the way and the grasshopper shall be a burden". I was very glad that you and Miss Wooler, my daughter's old and faithful friends, were present on the important occasion, and it gave to my daughter, also, great pleasure. There are times, and this time was one of them, when the presence and conversation of friends answer a good end in more respects than one. I hope that, under Providence, the change that has occurr'd in my case will be for the good of all parties concern'd, in reference both to time and eternity. That a gracious providence may direct and bless you, in all your ways, is the sincere wish and ardent prayer of, my dear Madam,

Your sincere and faithful friend, P. Brontë

Towards the end of her honeymoon Charlotte tells Ellen: ". . . Papa has not been well, and I have been longing, *longing intensely* sometimes, to be at home. . . ." Mr and Mrs Nicholls arrived back at Haworth on Tuesday, 1st August, and the former re-commenced his duties as curate there, although he would not be officially licensed again to Haworth until 21st September 1854.

Brief was Charlotte's married life, only nine months, and brief must be our description of it. The first visitors were Mr Sowden and a friend, then the Grants. To Miss Wooler, Charlotte writes on 22nd August: ". . . My dear father was not well when we returned from Ireland—I am, however, most thankful to say that he is better now— May God preserve him to us yet for some years! The wish for his continued life—together with a certain solicitude for his happiness and health seems—I scarcely know why—stronger in me now than before I was married. So far the understanding between Papa and Mr. Nicholls seems excellent—if it only continues thus I shall be truly grateful. Papa has taken no duty since we returned—and each time I see Mr. Nicholls put on gown or surplice—I feel comforted to think that this marriage has secured Papa good aid in his old age. . . ." And to Ellen on 29th August: ". . . Papa, I am thankful to say is much better; he preached last Sunday. . . ."

The next visitor was Dr Burnet, Vicar of Bradford: ". . . Dr Burnet was here on Sunday—preaching a sermon for the Jews . . . he thought

Papa not at all altered since he saw him last—nearly a year ago. . . ."
Then came Ellen, and then Mr and Mrs Joe Taylor—to the horror of
Nicholls.

Charlotte found that her husband was still fond of his moorland
walks, and the aged Patrick and elderly Flossy would watch them with
great envy as they set off across the hills. It was during this month,
November, that Nicholls tried to persuade Ellen to burn all Charlotte's
letters, his horror of publicity being so intense. Mercifully Ellen dis-
regarded his threats. In November the Rev. Sutcliffe Sowden and his
brother, the Rev. George Sowden, came on a visit, followed by Sir
James Kay-Shuttleworth, who offered Nicholls the living of Padiham
near his home, Gawthorpe Hall. ". . . Arthur of course is tied to Haworth
so long as Papa lives. . . ." Nicholls recommended his friend Mr Sowden,
but it was of no avail.

On 28th November Nicholls took his wife on that fateful walk to the
waterfalls on Haworth Moor. It began to pour with rain as they watched
the winter's torrent, and Charlotte arrived home drenched to the skin
She changed her clothes at once, flimsy shoes included, but the damage
was considerable : she caught a chill which would play its deadly part
in the tragedy soon to follow.

Early in December Patrick lost another of those few remaining links
with his past, Flossy. Anne's beloved silky, lazy Flossy died. On the
7th, Charlotte tells Ellen : ". . . I did not achieve the walk to the waterfall
with impunity . . . I felt a chill afterwards, and the same night had sore
throat and cold . . . did I tell you that our poor little Flossy is dead ?
He drooped for a single day, and died quietly in the night without pain.
The loss, even of a dog was very saddening, yet perhaps no dog ever
had a happier life or an easier death. Papa continues pretty well, I am
happy to say, and my dear boy flourishes. . . ."

Then came the year 1855, and another double blow to remove from
life two more inmates of Haworth Parsonage. In January Charlotte
and her husband spent three days with the Kay-Shuttleworths at
Gawthorpe, and returned in time to receive Nicholls's cousin, the
Rev. James Adamson Bell. Then followed stark tragedy such as Patrick
could never have believed possible again after his terrible losses of six
years earlier.

A day or two following her return from Gawthorpe, where at least
one walk had been taken on damp grass, provided only with thin house
shoes, Charlotte's cold became aggravated, and she suffered from acute
nausea. Dr Amos Ingham of Haworth was sent for and examined
Charlotte. She was going to have a child ! The very words struck a
chill of horror in Patrick's heart. ". . . Don't conjecture—dear Nell—for

it is too soon yet though I certainly never before felt as I have done lately. But keep the matter wholly to yourself. . . ."

At this very moment, the middle of January, Tabby's health utterly gave way and she was carried to her bed, gravely ill.

To Dr Ingham.   Haworth, Tuesday Afternoon.
Dear Sir,

I regret to have to disturb you at a time when you are suffering from illness, but I merely wish to ask if you can send any medicine for our old servant Tabby.

Yours faithfully—C. B. Nicholls

Dr Ingham continued ill and the young local accoucheur, Crawshaw Dugdale, frequently attended Charlotte.

Again Charlotte writes to a friend: ". . . It is an hourly happiness . . . to see how well Arthur and my Father get on together now—there has never been a misunderstanding or wrong word. . . ."

By 23rd January Charlotte was very ill and confined to bed also. Nicholls informs Ellen that a visit from Charlotte cannot now be looked for, and in subsequent letters he describes her worsening condition. Patrick and Nicholls sent for Dr MacTurk, the most able physician in Bradford, and he came on Tuesday, 30th January. He announced that Charlotte was very ill, that she was likely to remain so for some time, but that there was no immediate danger.

There came a letter for Charlotte from Sir James Kay-Shuttleworth which Patrick was obliged to answer.

February 3rd, 1855.
. . . Owing to my dear daughter's indisposition, she has desired me to answer your kind letter by return of post. For several days past she has been confined to her bed, where she still lies, oppressed with nausea, sickness, irritation, and a slow feverish feeling; and a consequent want of appetite and digestion. Our village surgeon visits her daily, and we have had a visit from Dr Mackintosh [MacTurk] of Bradford, who both think her sickness is symptomatic, and that, after a few days, they hope her health will again return—nevertheless the trying circumstance gives much uneasiness in our little family circle—where till lately, considering our respective ages, we have all been in good health and spirits.

I have read with much interest, and a thorough sense of gratitude to you and the celebrated medical gentleman you consulted, the scientific opinion respecting the state of my eyes. . . . We rejoice that your health is improving, and that the horrid neuralgia is less frequent in its visits, and has lost some of that virulence which often extends its direful influence to body and mind.

Mr and Mrs Nicholls join me in the most respectful regards—and as soon as my dear daughter gets better she will no doubt give you a statement of circumstances in a manner more satisfactory than I am able to do. . . .

Martha, although helped by her sister Tabitha, could no longer nurse both the invalids and attend to her household duties, so Patrick came, reluctantly, to a heart-rending decision. It was his wish as well as Charlotte's that the faithful old woman, Tabby, should end her days at the parsonage, but it could not be so.

Her nephew, William Wood, came and took his aunt to his small cottage in Stubbing Lane, at the foot of Kirkgate. Poor old Tabby's loyal and devoted service to the Brontës was over. She would hobble painfully no more, but march proudly from life, and the last of her beloved "bairns" would not be far behind her. Tabitha Aykroyd died on Saturday, 17th February 1855. The sad though not unexpected news came up the hill and reached the parsonage. It came at a time when Charlotte was very much weaker and when Patrick was recovering from bronchitis. He told his daughter the sad tidings: there could be no keeping the news from her. To Ellen on 21st February: ". . . Papa, thank God! is better. Our poor old Tabby is *dead* and buried. . . ."

That was written on the day of the funeral, a Wednesday. Patrick stayed with his daughter and it was Nicholls who buried Tabby. Martha Brown attended the service. "Tabitha Aykroyd—Haworth—Feb: 21st —84 years—A. B. Nicholls, Curate."

They laid her to rest near the parsonage garden wall, to the right of the little gate of the dead as you face the house, and where her relatives were buried. It is fitting that she found a resting-place so near the scene of her long labours. "Also of Tabitha Aykroyd, of Haworth, who died Feby: 17th, 1855, in the eighty-fifth year of her age."

By the end of February, Charlotte was reduced to a shadow: ". . . Let me speak the plain truth—my sufferings are very great—my nights indescribable—sickness with scarce a reprieve—I strain until what I vomit is mixed with blood . . . As to my husband—my heart is knit to him—he is so tender, so good, helpful, patient. . . ." Tabitha Brown would later tell how "she was so worn and thin that the light showed through her hand when it was held up".

Martha was an untiring nurse, a devoted attendant. When she tried to cheer Charlotte with thoughts of the baby to come, the reply was: "I dare say I shall be glad some day, but oh, I am so ill and tired."

Whenever Patrick visited his daughter, she would make a supreme effort to sit up, exhausting herself in the process. "See, Papa! I am a little better; don't you think I look better?" Patrick would try to agree to comfort her, but he always left the room with an expression of sorrowful resignation on his face.

Nicholls kept Ellen informed of his wife's state and he it was who had to tell Charlotte of the death of her friend's brother-in-law, Mr Clapham. But nothing could affect Charlotte at this stage. Towards the end of March she became delirious and craved for food, "opening her mouth just like a little throstle" according to Tabitha Brown. Nicholls was quite beside himself with grief, and it was Patrick who had to steel himself yet again and make the supreme effort. He wrote to Ellen Nussey:

To Miss Nussey. Brookroyd, Birstall, Nr. Leeds.

Haworth, Nr. Keighley, March 30th 1855.
My Dear Madam,

We are all in great trouble, and Mr Nicholls so much so, that he is not so sufficiently strong and composed as to be able to write. I therefore devote a few moments to tell you that my dear Daughter is very ill, and apparently on the verge of the grave. If she could speak, she would no doubt dictate to us while answering your kind letter, but we are left to ourselves to give what answer we can. The Doctors have no hope of her case, and fondly as we, a long time, cherished hope, that hope is now gone, and we have only to look forward to the solemn event, with prayer to God that He will give us grace and strength sufficient unto our day.

Will you be so kind as to write to Miss Wooler, and Mrs Joe Taylor, and inform them that we requested you to do so, telling them of our present condition?

Ever truly and respectfully yours, P. Brontë

That same evening Charlotte sank rapidly. Patrick and Nicholls knelt and prayed by her bedside. Awakening from her stupor Charlotte heard the hope expressed that God would spare her. "Oh, I am not going to die, am I? He will not separate us, we have been so happy." They were the last words the world would hear from Charlotte Brontë. In the early hours of Saturday, 31st March 1855, she died, and the villagers heard of her death through the solemn tolling of the church bell. The certified cause of death was: "Phthisis—duration two months."

Yet can it be doubted that the unborn child she took to the grave with her had hastened her end? Certainly Patrick could never entertain a doubt on the matter.

As Charlotte died, Nicholls sprawled across the bed in a convulsion of grief, sobbing loudly. Patrick stood upright with dry eyes. Then, completely under control, he quietly turned and left the room, leaving Martha and Tabitha Brown wondering at his hardness of feeling. After her sister had closed Charlotte's eyes, Tabitha left the room, followed by Martha, leaving the shattered husband alone with his beloved. Thinking that Patrick had gone down to his study, Tabitha opened his bedroom door and then stopped abruptly. Patrick was kneeling by his bed in an attitude of prayer and crying in agonized tones, "My poor Charlotte! My dear Charlotte!" As Tabitha would later admit: "I understood Mr Brontë better then: I never understood him before."

There in his bedroom he could permit his control to give way. In privacy he could bow to sorrow. As he knelt there alone, Patrick had reached the end of his long road of grief. Nothing could hurt him any more now.

On Wednesday, 4th April 1855, they again opened the little gate of the dead, and carried Charlotte through, past the grave of the faithful Tabby, to join her sisters. Behind, came her old father and her young husband, then Martha and Tabitha Brown. Next came Ellen Nussey and Margaret Wooler, Nancy Garrs, now Mrs Wainwright, John Brown and his wife and one member of almost every family in Haworth. The old custom of "bidding" a large number of people to the funeral was adopted, and every member of a family hoped to be the person to attend the service. The funeral procession, both through the churchyard and down the lane, was the largest seen there for many years.

The outside world knew not that Charlotte was dead. Mrs Gaskell was indeed invited to the funeral but did not come. It was not "Currer Bell" they were burying, nor was it Charlotte Brontë, nor yet Mrs Nicholls; it was "t'parson's Charlotte", and Haworth said good-bye with a poignant thought for the aged clergyman who survived. The funeral was conducted by the Rev. Sutcliffe Sowden, who had married her only such a short time before.

Charlotte Nicholls	Haworth	April 4th	38	Sutcliffe Sowden Off. Minister

When all was over and those who had come to pay their last heartfelt respects had departed, the three who were left in Haworth Parsonage went to their respective rooms: Martha to the kitchen, Nicholls to the dining-room, and Patrick Brontë to his parlour. There he saw the Irish mountains, the lanes of Essex, the pistols out at Rawfolds Mill, the ruins of Kirkstall Abbey, the sunlit garden of Kipping House, his first glimpse of Haworth, and seven dearly beloved faces. Patrick sat long without moving; even tears could not efface or wash away such nostalgic visions. Then with a long sigh he braced himself, blew his nose, and decided he must have some kind of loving companion to share his loneliness. Nicholls would certainly not suffice. He would get himself another dog!

CHAPTER 28

Mrs Gaskell

PATRICK soon kept to his resolution regarding a new pet. Only a little over a week after Charlotte's funeral he entered in his notebook: "On April 13th 1855, I bought from Mr Summerscale, 'Cato', then only a year and a half old—for £3-0-0. He is two thirds a Newfoundland dog and one third a retriever—his Mother belonged to Mr Ferrand . . . He greatly admired him. P.B." Meanwhile there were several letters of condolence to answer and both he and Nicholls were kept fairly busy. Patrick wrote to Mrs Gaskell and George Smith.

To Mrs E. C. Gaskell. 17 Cumberland Terrace, Regents Park, London.

Haworth, near Keighley. April 5th, 1855.

My Dear Madam,

I thank you for your kind sympathy. My daughter is indeed, dead, and the solemn truth presses upon her worthy and affectionate husband, and me, with great and, it may be, with unusual weight. But others also have or shall have their sorrows, and we feel our own the most. The marriage that took place seem'd to hold forth long and bright prospects of happiness, but in the inscrutable providence of God, all our hopes have ended in disappointment, and our joy, in mourning. May we resign to the Will of the Most High. After three months of sickness, a tranquil death closed the scene—but our loss, we trust, is her gain. But why should I trouble you longer with our sorrows?—"The heart knoweth its own bitterness"—and we ought to bear with fortitude our own grievances and not to bring others into our sufferings. With my very respectful regards to Mr. Gaskell and your family, I remain, My dear Madam,

Yours respectfully and truly, P. Bronte.

P.S. Excuse this brief scrawl—I am not fit at present to write much—nor to write satisfactorily.

Years later the Right Rev. Bishop Welldon would say of that letter: "There is something of stoicism as well as of Christianity in the bereaved father's calm and stern submission to the Almighty will."

To George Smith, Patrick wrote:

Haworth, near Keighley—Yorkshire. April 20th, 1855.
My Dear Sir,

I thank you for your kind sympathy. Having heard my dear daughter speak so much about you, and your family, your letter seemed to be one from an old friend. Her husband's sorrow and mine, is indeed very great. We mourn the loss of one whose like we hope not ever to see again, and, as you justly state, we do not mourn alone. That you may never experimently know sorrow such as ours, and that when trouble does come you may receive due aid from Heaven, is the sincere wish and ardent prayer of—

Yours very respectfully and truly, P. Brontë.

Three days after Charlotte's burial, the Rev. Dr Cartman came over from Skipton to stay a night at the parsonage and on the following morning, Sunday, 8th April, he conducted the funeral service. The sorrowing heads in Haworth Church all turned towards Patrick, sitting so erect, as Dr Cartman took for his text, "And all wept, and bewailed her: but he said, Weep not; she is not dead, but sleepeth" (Luke viii: 52).

From henceforth, there was seldom an occasion for Patrick, wearing his green eye-shade, to pace up and down his room muttering aloud to himself as he memorized his sermons by heart (as he was heard to do by more than one visitor to the parsonage). Nicholls carried out the bulk of the church duties, whilst Patrick now preached only about once a month. Yet when he did so he was as vigorous as ever.

Even now, Patrick's troubles were not over. Only a few weeks after Charlotte's death, Martha Brown, completely exhausted by her labours, became seriously ill. As with old Tabby, there was now no possibility of nursing her at the parsonage, and as at this same time John Brown's health suddenly collapsed Martha could not easily be nursed at her home. She was sent to Leeds for rest and treatment whilst her sister, Eliza, temporarily took her place at Haworth Parsonage. Patrick writes to her:

To Miss Martha Brown, Mrs Drans Alms Houses, 37—Harrison St. Leeds

Haworth, Nr Keighley June 9th 1855.

I am glad, Martha—that, notwithstanding you do not seem to get much better, you have not got worse—and I think that it will be best for you to come home at the time you mention—Eliza says she can stay

PLATE 29 *Patrick Brontë in old age*   PLATE 30 *Dr Wilson*

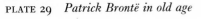

PLATE 31 *Facsimile of the end of Patrick Brontë's letter to William Campbell*

PLATE 32   *Nancy Garrs*

PLATE 33   *Martha Brown*

here till you get well—and are able to do the work of the house, as usual—Should Mr Nunnelly, deem it necessary, to give you any instructions, you can abide by them here. I am quite satisfied with Eliza's proceedings, she is very steady, and does her work very well. I will tell Mr Nicholls, that you were very much pleased with, and thankful for his calling to see you—Both He, and I, are very desirous of your recovery—and, for this, you must use the best means, and pray to God, for his blessing, and then, and then, only, all things will be well with you, in regard to this life, and that which is to come—All your Family, except your Father, are well—He is not worse, than when you last saw him—but he is not much better. The warm weather may do him some good—but his case is dangerous.

Your Mother—Eliza, and all your Family, send their love to you—
I remain, Your Wellwisher, P. Brontë.

Should you want any money, I will send it to you.

Mercifully, Martha soon recovered, yet her homecoming was a sad one: her father was dying. Just over four months after Charlotte's death Patrick lost his faithful sexton. John Brown died on Friday, 10th August 1855, at the age of fifty-one.

The dust from his work as a stonemason had damaged his lungs. He had been sexton for twenty years, and was succeeded in that position by his younger brother, William. For Patrick it was the severing of an affectionate link with his errant son, and his heart was the sadder for that. Patrick sat with Martha and Mrs Mary Brown in the Brontë pew as Mr Nicholls conducted the service.

John Brown, – Haworth – Augt: 13th – 51 yrs – A. B. Nicholls, Curate.

Reference has been made, on two occasions, to Patrick's little brown leather notebook. Let us glance over his shoulder as he sits writing in it, towards the evening of his life.

"Always, when necessary, get a receipt—and keep the last one only —or pay before witnesses, and make a memorandum. When this is filled, put it into the trunk with the others—and procure a new memorandum Book. I will never write across the line, or in the margin, of this book . . . I shall not write in this book anything of much consequence . . . but what is in some way connected with pecuniary matters—very necessary—lest—as formerly, it should become very troublesome, and inconvenient. . . ." Then follows an entry showing that, after obtaining Cato, Patrick got another dog. "I bought Plato, from Mr Summerscale, in the middle of 1855—for £3-0-0. Plato, is a breed from a Newfound-

land bitch and a water spanniel [*sic*] . . . B. . . . on Sept: 19th 1854, I
ordered the Daily *Times*—second hand at £1-3-0 a quarter, to be paid
beforehand to Mr Henry Chasserean—Newsman, 97 High St. Camden
Town, 7 houses from the Post Office—London . . . On Sept 18th 1854,
I sent to E. J. Mitchell Esq, Treasurer, Bradford Yorkshire, £2-10-0
for the Jews Society of which, £2-5-0 was got by the collection and the
remainder was my own yearly subscription. . . ." Then follows an exact
repeat of the newspaper order save that payment is to be made to Mrs
Charlotte Chasserean—"Paid on Sept. 18th 1857 . . . 1845. Assessed
taxes—I formerly paid only £2-6-7 half-yearly—In 1845 I had to pay
for three windows more, all of which I have, and for hairpowder, and
dogs (by way of surcharge, £3-14-4 to Mr Wm Garnett.) The next
half-year-will be only £2-15-5½ . . . Paid to Mr Ogden April 1848
£3-11-6. . . . 1845 Rateable value of my House £7-13-5. Gross estimate
£9-4-1. B. In Sept 1847—I got the well cleaned by a pump—and two
men—for five shillings—The water was tinged yellow by eight tin
cans, in a state of decomposition—It had not been cleaned for twenty
years, before. B. [1847 was too late, alas—any damage from this source
had been done.] On July 14th 1848 received from the Rev. P. Brontë for
painting all his windows, doors, gates, water-spout, and water tub—
£0-18-0 (Signed) John Hudson. Paid 2/- more in 1852 for the front
part." Then follows "Martha Brown's account" which continues to
intrude throughout the pages of the notebook. The entries are so
numerous in extent that only a few can be given, as an indication of
Martha's wage. "Paid her till Jan. 18th 1846 at the rate of 2/3 per week
—29/3. From that time forward to give her 2/6 a week. . . . Paid till
18 Oct 1846—£1-12-6. . . . To add—as a present 2/6 quarterly—making
it £1-15-0 a qr. Optimum erit decere nihil to the ch-dr. This will be
£7-0-0 a year. Some have £8 or £9. [It must be remembered that, by
the end of 1846, Martha was only eighteen. When Charlotte died, she
was twenty-seven.] . . . I owed her a quarter's wages on April 18th
1849—which amounted to £1-15-0—she refused to take this at the time
[Anne was gravely ill]—wishing it to be put off until July the 18th 1849
when I shall owe her £3-10-0. Besides this she placed in my hands
£2-15-0 making together £6-5-0. B. All this I paid, and 10/- over—all
settled Oct 18th 1849. . . . Jan 18th 1851—I paid Martha 5s for this
quarter, the rest remains in my hands. All paid—soon afterwards.
Assessed Taxes Paid to Mr Whalley Esq. £11-6-0 on May 5th 1851 . . .
In 1850, and 1851 I got the rooms painted and stained, for just about
£4-0-0 and from what I have seen—they ought to do—for, at the least,
till 1860 B. On Sunday, Oct. 26th 1851—collected 10s and sent this sum
under seal, to the Treasurer of the Society for the propagation of the

Gospel, in foreign parts, 79-Pall Mall, London. on Sun. 2nd. Nov: 1851 I preached and made a collection amounting to £1-2-9½ and sent it to William Masterman Harris Esq . . . Bank, Bradford—Yorkshire. I will never flag the garden walks—since Charlotte and Martha—discernunt est, it would cost £5—looking worse and be more slippery in frost—require washing and produce weeds between the joinings. B. 1851. For 1851—the whole of the dues—after the deductions were made was £10-5-6—half of which was £5-2-9 and sent to the Vicar of Bradford. I have (agreeably to advice) given up all thoughts of breaking the gables, in order to improve the chimney vents—as the expense and trouble would be too great and blowers at only 5/- each will do as well or better—The other would cost ten or twenty pounds or perhaps more besides the dust & confusion—1852. My house was valued in 1851—at £10-13-0 formerly it was valued at about £7-0-0 or nearly. For the assessed taxes I paid to Mr. Ogden, April 29th 1852, £1-8-3½. This was for half a year and included the dogs and hair powder. There is no window tax now, and as my house is rated below £20—I am not subject to—duty. In Oct. 1852, I paid Mr. Williams £2-16-7, the whole of the year's taxes. Received from the Rev. P. Brontë on July 19th 1852 £1-1-0, for painting all his windows, gates, doors, water spouts and water tubs. To suffice for two years. John Hudson." We now revert to "Martha Brown's account". "Paid Oct. 18th 1852 the quarter's wages —£1-15-0 and 5s over . . . a parasol and shawl. I have raised Martha's wages to £8-0-0 a year . . . Grant of £100 made for one year by the C.P.A. Society in November 1852—To last till March 1853—their letter in my desk. Another grant till March 1854. . . . In March 10th 1855, agreed with John Brown for leave to hang up the clothes for drying in his field—for 2s a year. March 1855. Clock and watch cleaned for 2s6d. In June 1857, Humphrey Wood painted all the outside of the windows of the house and all the doors, posts & etc. for £1-1-0. For the gas acct, *vide* the receipt. The Recs for 1847, 1848, and 1849 are put up together in the upper part of my trunk. B. On April the 18th 1855 [immediately after Charlotte's death], I raised Martha Brown's wages to £9-0-0 a year . . . Paid Brooks Booth of Morton Banks, Nr. Bingley, in the presence of Martha Brown, £1-5-0, for 45 stones . . . of potatoes, Oct. 21st 1858. P.B. Martha Brown's wages is now ten pounds a year to be paid quarterly. The next quarter's payment will be on Jany. 18th 1859. Jany 18th, 1859 paid £2-10-0. . . . Jany 18th 1861—paid Martha [this was entered, as may be supposed, in a very shaky hand]. . . ." The last entry, in the now feeble handwriting, is an interesting one in that it shows that at the time of Patrick's death, Eliza Brown had been permanently employed at the parsonage to help her sister Martha:

". . . February 1st 1861. Eliza Brown hired at £10. a year." The hiring of Eliza, for all that it is entered on page 3 of the notebook, was the last time Patrick Brontë wrote in it. The book could then be laid next to the others in the upper part of the trunk.

As there has been much mention of Martha Brown in the notebook, it will be best to give here two short notes that Patrick wrote out for her.

Haworth. July 18th 1856.

The money contained in this little Box, consists of sums, given by me, to Martha Brown, at different times, for her faithful services to me, and my children. And this money, I wished her to keep ready for a time of need—

P. Brontë A.B. Incumbent of Haworth—Yorkshire.

The second note reads :

Certain drawings by my children that were given to my daughter Anne, and left in her box, I have given to my servant, Martha Brown, as fond momentos [sic],—reserving to myself any of these which I might claim for any particular purpose. If I should not claim them, they will be entirely at her disposal.

P. Brontë A.B. Incumbent of Haworth, Yorkshire.

Nor was Martha forgotten in Patrick's will, as will be seen later. For her part, Martha was devoted to her master and took a great interest in his writings in addition to those of his daughters. When in 1859 Abraham Holroyd reprinted *The Cottage in the Wood* as a sixteen-page pamphlet (published by M. Nelson and A. Holroyd of Bradford) she ordered several copies.

Haworth Parsonage, Augt. 10th, 1859.

To A. Holroyd Esq. Westgate, Bradford.

Dear Sir,

I hope you will forgive my not writing to you sooner, the reason is I have been very buisey [sic] preserving fruit. I have duly received eight numbers of the "Cottage in the Wood", for which I return you my thanks. I have given one with the cover on to Mr Bronte—he sends you his respects—and thinks that for the price they are neatly got up.

I remain, Yours respectfully, Martha Brown.

Having examined the notebook, we now turn to a small Bible bound in old calf, Jeremiah to Malachi only, which Patrick possessed. It gives a clue to some of the texts that were his favourites, and used by him when composing his sermons. It is twice inscribed with his name, "P. Brontë, Incumbent of Haworth" and again with the addition "A.B."

Against the passage, "Then said I, oh Lord God! behold, I cannot speak; for I am a child," Patrick wrote: "1834. The lessons taught to man by nature." Many dates are inserted throughout the Bible and occasionally some pencilled or inked comments of religious reflections. One that more than merits attention is the comment Patrick scribbled inside the back page: "respecting Solomon's final victory & etc. *vide* II Samuel VII & 14 and 15", which read: "I will be his father, and he shall be my son. If he commit iniquity, I will chasen him with the rod of men, and with the stripes of the children of men: But my mercy shall not depart away from him, as I took *it* from Saul, whom I put away before thee."

In the centre of the Bible are eight pages of plain paper tied with black ribbon, on which Patrick had written a number of texts for his sermons. These include the following: "The first General Epistle of St. John. The second chapter, & the 16th & 17th verses. 'For all that is in the world, the lust of the flesh, the lust of the eyes, and the pride of life, is not of the Father, but is of the world. And the world passeth away, and the lust thereof, but he that doeth the will of God, abideth forever.' " Next follows: "Job, the V ch. the 6 and 7 verses: 'Although affliction cometh not forth of the dust, neither doth trouble spring out of the ground; yet man is born unto trouble, as the sparks fly upward.' " Then is written: "The Certainty of trouble and the principal cause of it. The source of consolation under it, and the way to obtain it." The 3rd verse of the 24th chapter of the Book of Proverbs is next quoted: "Through wisdom is an house builded; and by understanding it is established." "The 7th ch. of the Gospel acc^g to St. Matthew, the 13 & 14 verses: 'Enter ye in at the strait gate: for wide *is* the gate, and broad *is* the way, that leadeth to destruction, and many there be which go in thereat: Because strait *is* the gate, and narrow *is* the way, which leadeth unto life, and few there be that find it.' " (This is the Biblical text; Patrick has stressed the word "strait" the first time it is used.) Patrick ends with Colossians, the 3rd chapter, 1st and 2nd verses: ". . . set your affections on things above, not on things on the earth," and "the 1st Epistle General of St. John, the 2nd chapter and the 4th and 5th verses: 'He that saith I know him (Patrick adds, "i.e. Christ"), and keepeth not his commandments, is a liar, and the truth is not in him. But whoso keepeth his word, in him [verily] is the love of God perfected: hereby know we that we are in him.' "

Patrick also owned *The New Family Receipt Book—containing One*

Thousand Truly Valuable Receipts, 1824. He marked on the flyleaf those that interested him—"How to destroy rats . . . cure damp walls . . . preserve eggs fresh . . . making varnishes". Another possession was "An Earnest Address to the Working Classes of Old England, on the aims and objects of the religious and political parties of the day. By a Poor Man" ; and Patrick found that "This work is just and Excellent, in all its parts . . . 1837." Among other works in Patrick's library were two volumes of *System of Anatomy*, 1783, *Historical Grammar*, 1771, *Gospel according to St Matthew*, Revelations, *Gospel according to St Matthew*, Apocalypsis, Oxford University Prayer and Psalter, *Gardens and Menagerie*, Dryden's *Works of Virgil*, George Allen's *Life of Sir Walter Scott*, 1834, *Poems of Ossian*, *A System of Materia Medica and Pharmacy*, Sir Humphrey Davy's *Elements of Chemical Philosophy*, *The Lay of the Last Minstrel*, and the Works of Lord Byron.

Patrick often ordered his books from John Greenwood. Several notes survive, dated between 1850 and 1859 : "To Mr. John Greenwood, Bookseller. Please to order the following. P. Brontè . . . Adventures of the Lion Hunter, of South Africa . . . three copies of a letter to the Archbishop of Canterbury on certain alterations which are required in the Liturgy and offices of the Church of England . . . South's hints on emergencies or House hold surgery . . . The Act for Amending the Laws concerning the Burial of the Dead in England, beyond the Metropolis . . . The Numbers of the Month, or Literary and Critical Journal—the number I want is in Vol 3 second Augt 1858, containing notice of Currer Bell."

Towards the end of his life, when his eyes were again dim, he received a Psalter in large print inscribed : "Will the Reverend P. Brontë honor a young friend so far as to accept and make use of this large type Psalter, which is accompanied by every good wish for the present season, and the New Year. Christmas Eve 1857."

Patrick sometimes gave books to his parishioners, particularly to those in need of spiritual comfort. A copy of "Songs in the Night—By Susanna Harrison, a young woman, under heavy afflictions" was given "To Hannah Jackson, with Mr Bronte's kind regards and prayers for temporal and eternal Interest."

Before quitting Patrick's beloved books, mention should be made of his copy of *Chambers' Miscellany of Useful and Entertaining Tracts*, published in Edinburgh in 1845. Volume three contains a Life of Nelson and on page 30 is the following reference to Lady Hamilton : "the infamous woman who had been the only disgrace of his life". In pencil, the word "infamous" is crossed through and at the bottom of the page is written : "Was Emma Hamilton worse than yourself, poor hypocrite ?" This apostrophe has often been ascribed to Patrick Brontë, but whilst it could be one of Branwell's varying scripts, it is unlike the writing of any member of the family.

After the Brontë sisters became famous, many recipients preserved the letters written by Patrick. As a result much of his correspondence towards the end of his life has survived.

Firstly, a letter to Henry Garrs, the brother of Patrick's former servants Nancy and Sarah, written in answer to a note of sympathy sent on the first anniversary of Charlotte's death. It is still edged thickly in black :

To Mr. Henry Garrs. Milton Lane. Sheffield.

Dear Sir,   Haworth, Nr. Keighley. April 2nd 1856.

I thank you for your friendly and able letter—your lines are pathetic and good, and I might say much upon them—but my grief is so deep and lasting, that I cannot long dwell on my sad privation—I try to look to God, for consolation, and pray that he will give me grace, and strength equal to my day—and resignation to his will—That He may direct you and your family, and bless and prosper you, in reference to *both the worlds*, is the sincere wish and prayer, of yours, truly,   P. Brontë.

Henry Garrs had ambitions to be a poet. He had sent some of his poems to Charlotte for her criticism in 1854, and the "lines" referred to by Patrick were simple verses in praise of Charlotte, enclosed in his letter.

Next, another letter to George Smith ; it makes mention of Charlotte's biography :

To George Smith.

Dear Sir,   Haworth, near Keighley. March 30th 1857.

I thank you and Mrs Gaskell for the biographical books you have sent me. I have read them with a high degree of melancholy interest, and consider them amongst the ablest, most interesting, and best works of the kind. Mrs Gaskell, though moving in what was to her a new line —a somewhat critical matter—has done herself great credit by this biographical work, which I doubt not will place her higher in literary fame, even than she stood before. Notwithstanding that I have formed my own opinion, from which the critics cannot shake me, I am curious to know what they may say. I will thank you, therefore, to send me two or three newspapers containing criticisms on the biography, and I will remit the price of them to you in letter stamps.

I remain, dear Sir, yours respectfully and truly, P. Brontë.

It is more than a little to Patrick's credit that in his first perusal of his daughter's Life he was so busy re-living with his children that he barely noticed the attacks on himself it contained; but the world would soon point them out to him.

Again he writes to Smith:

Sept: 4th 1857.

My Dear Sir,

I thank you for the books, which I have just received—Mr. Nicholls also sends his thanks for those you have given to him. As far as I have gone through the third edition of the *Memoir* I am much pleased with it—I hope it will give general satisfaction. Should you see any reviews worth notice, be so kind as to let me have them, as I am rather anxious to know what the sage critics may deem it expedient in their wisdom to say. I hope, that by this time, Mrs Smith has fully recovered her health —your anxiety on her account must be very great. Mr. Nicholls joins me in kind and respectful regards.

Yours very respectfully and truly, P. Brontë.

The next letter is a nostalgic one, addressed to Elizabeth Nunn, the wife of his old University friend who had been curate at Shrewsbury when Patrick was at Wellington. Indeed his quarrel with Nunn had been over the latter's decision to marry this lady.

To Mrs. Nunn, near Eye, Suffolk.

Haworth, near Keighley. February 1st, 1858.

My Dear Madam,

I thank you for your kind offer of the excellent newspaper you have mentioned, but there is no necessity of sending to me, since, owing to the newspapers I take, and the various institutions in the village, I can see the *Record*, or any other I may choose, daily. And truly in this changeable and ever-changing world, this state of our probation, we clergymen ought to read and know what is passing, and to discern the signs of the times, so that we may be able to speak a word in season to the people committed to our charge. I have forgotten the age of my dear old friend Mr Nunn—will you be so kind as to mention it when you next write. I am now in the eighty-first year of my age—I think he must be six or seven years younger; but it appears that his bodily strength has considerably failed him, and that it is now his duty not to exert himself, as formerly, but to be a little cautious, so that by Divine aid his useful life may be spared long for the benefit of the flock of our blessed Lord and Saviour. I preach once every Sabbath afternoon, but I cannot do more. Mr. Nicholls joins me in kind regards.

I remain, My dear Madam, yours in the best of bonds, P. Brontë.

There is something touching in Patrick's pride in his age, and in his strength superior to that of his old friend.

Some three days after writing to Mrs Nunn, Patrick and Nicholls received an invitation to attend a local party.

Haworth, February 4th, 1858.

Dear Sir,—I thank you and Mrs —— for your kind invitation, but I never go out at night, nor indeed by day, to any parties. Mr. Nicholls will, however, do himself the pleasure of visiting you at the time specified. I remain, yours respectfully and truly, P. Brontë.

By this time, Patrick was being inundated with requests to send various mementoes and souvenirs of his daughters, especially Charlotte. Any sample of her handwriting was in particular demand and the harassed and grief-stricken father was quite overwhelmed with letters. A few letters that Charlotte had sent him were taken out of the bundle and sacrificed, Patrick cutting them into small fragments so as to lose as few precious letters as possible, and to please as many "admirers" as he could. The practice of splitting up the Brontës' letters and selling them for profit would later succeed Patrick's more honourable spoliation. The following letter is a pathetic one: a sign of the vulgarity to come.

To Franklin Bacheller, Lyn, Mass: U.S.A.

Haworth, Near Keighley, England. December 22nd, 1858. Dear Sir,

Owing to the many demands upon me, I can send you only a small piece of my dear Charlotte's handwriting, which is herewith enclosed. I remain, dear Sir, Very respectfully yours, P. Brontë.

Attached to this short letter was the fragment of the beginning of a letter from Charlotte to her father: "Dear Papa; I left . . . having settled all. . . ."

In June 1859 Patrick wrote to his niece Elizabeth Jane Kingston (mentioned in Aunt Branwell's will). ". . . I had a letter from my Uncle Brontë . . . he says he was in his 83rd year, but, though feeble, was still able to preach once on Sunday, and sometimes to take occasional duty;

his son-in-law, Mr. Nicholls, will continue with him. He says strangers still continue to call, but he converses little with them, but keeps himself as quiet as he can. . . .''

Again Patrick writes to Mrs Nunn:

To Mrs. Nunn, Rectory, near Eye. Suffolk.

Haworth, near Keighley, October 26th, 1859.

My Dear Madam,

I thank you for the picture of the Rectory—it is *well* executed, and shows a very respectable and convenient building, which is, I hope and believe, only the *earnest* and forerunner of *"that* House, not made with hands, eternal in the Heavens". But large and commodious as your house, is, I think it has no room for a third person as a lodger, who would probably be a discordant string that would spoil your domestic harmony. You enquired whether your parcels and letters cost me anything—they all come free, and I pay for all I send to you. The newspaper account of the idle and ostentatious pageantry got up in the church, where the gospel was once faithfully preached, grieves me. But, my dear Madam, a bad spirit, some call it the spirit of the age (I fear it might rather be called the spirit of revolution, vanity, scepticism, and Romish idolatry), this ominous spirit of the age is actuating numbers; and the young, thoughtless, and vain, have looked upon, loved, and greedily embraced the delusion. But Christ, who conquers death and hell, will give his followers the victory, and make all things work together for good to those who enlist in his service, and fight the good fight of Faith, in his name, and by his wisdom and power. All things work together for good to those who love God—Yes, for good, in reference to *both* the worlds. I hope that you will be able to read this miserable scrawl—my sight is very scanty, and the day is dim. Mr Nicholls joins me in kind regards to you, and my dear old friend. Yours very truly, in the best of bonds,   P. Brontë.

I have posted for you a picture of my house and church.

It is pleasant to reflect that this was probably the first of those pictures of "my house" ever sent out from Haworth. Since that day how many hundreds of thousands of pictures of the parsonage, and of the old church too, have left that moorland village and found a home in all parts of the world! John Nunn, the last surviving friend of early days, was not destined to outlive Patrick either. He died aged seventy-eight at Thorndon Rectory, Suffolk, on 15th April 1861 from "Congestion of the Lungs"—only seven weeks before Patrick.

Three days later Patrick wrote again to Mr Rand, then living at Ipswich :

To Mr Rand, Ipswich.

Haworth, Nr. Keighley. Oct : 29th, 1859.

Dear Sir,

I am much pleased to learn, that through divine mercy, you are again able to see. I know what it is to be unable to behold the light of the Sun, and again, to see his beams. You have had your trials, and I have had mine—May the Lord sanctify them, and make them tend to our happiness in time and eternity ! Give my kind regards to Mrs Rand, Mrs Bacon, and your son—I remain, yours very truly   P. Brontë.

Mercifully, Charlotte's prayer that her father's sight would remain with him until the end was answered. He could see but dimly during the last years of his life, but he never became completely blind. That was the *only* threatened disaster of his life that never materialized !

The last time Patrick appears to have written to George Smith was in March 1860.

To George Smith

Haworth, near Keighley. March 26th, 1860.

My Dear Sir,

Though writing is to me now something of a task, I cannot avoid sending you a few lines, to thank you for sending me the magazines, and for your gentlemanly conduct towards my daughter in all your transactions with her, from first to last. All the numbers of the magazines were good—the last especially attracted my attention and excited my admiration. The "Last Sketch" took full possession of my mind. [Thackeray's tribute to Charlotte Brontë, being the Introduction to her fragment "Emma", published in the *Cornhill Magazine*, Vol. I, 1860.] Mr Thackeray, in his remarks in it, has excelled even himself—he has written multum in parvo, dignissima cedro. And what he has written does honour both to his head and heart—thank him kindly both in Mr. Nicholls's name and mine. Amongst the various articles that have been written in reference to my family and me, it has pleased some of the writers, for want of more important matter, to set up an ideal target for me as a mark to shoot at. In their practice a few have drawn the long bow with a vengeance, and made declensions very ridiculously wide—others have used the surer rifle and come nearer the mark—but all have proved that there is still space left for improvement, both in theory and practice. Had I but half Mr. Thackeray's talents in giving a photographic likeness of human nature, I might have selected, and might yet select, a choice number of these practising volunteers, and, whether they like it or not, give their portraits to the curious public. If organless spirits see as we see, and feel as we feel, in this material clogging world, my daughter Charlotte's spirit will receive additional happiness on scanning the remarks of her Ancient Favourite. In the last letter I received from you, you mentioned that Mrs. Smith was in delicate health—I hope that she is now well. I need scarcely request you to excuse all faults in this hasty scrawl, since a man in his eighty-fourth year generally lets his age plead his apology.

I remain, my dear Sir, Yours very respectfully and truly, P. Brontë.

How one wishes that Patrick had possessed "half Mr Thackeray's talents" and had himself answered all the slanderous attacks made against him at that time and continued ever since. There is no certain evidence that Charlotte's "Ancient Favourite" ever met Patrick, although it is known that Thackeray wrote to him near the time of his visit to Bradford on 9th December 1856 to lecture on "The Four Georges".

The mention of "a photographic likeness" in Patrick's letter is a reminder that it was in this year of 1860 that he had his photograph taken two or three times—those famous pictures that show only too clearly his stock rising almost to the mouth. They were taken by James Barraclough, assistant to Edwin Feather, who was postmaster at Haworth and also kept a jeweller's shop at the top of Kirkgate. Barraclough, using the old wet-plate process, was to pride himself until the end of his days on having taken Mr Brontë's photograph, although, as he later admitted, it was done under vigorous protests from Nicholls. The curate, who had certainly also been photographed by Barraclough, was fearful that the picture of Patrick would be sold commercially.

To end the letters of Patrick Brontë, we give his correspondence with Mrs Gaskell, mostly written in connection with her biography of Charlotte.

That such a book should be written was originally the idea of Ellen Nussey. Only some nine weeks after Charlotte's death, she wrote to Nicholls: "June 6th, 1855 . . . I have been much hurt and pained by the perusal of an article in *Sharpe* for this month . . . will you suffer the article to pass current without any refutations ? . . . Should not her aged father be defended from the reproach the writer coarsely attempts to bring upon him ? I wish Mrs Gaskell, who is every way capable, would undertake a reply, and would give a sound castigation to the writer.

Her personal acquaintance with Haworth, the Parsonage, and its inmates, fits her for the task . . . will you ask Mrs Gaskell to undertake this just and honourable defence ? I think she would do it gladly. . . ." A defence of Charlotte certainly, but if only poor Ellen had known of the virulent rubbish about Patrick that Mrs Gaskell was writing to her friends ! Nicholls was, from the first, against the idea of a biography of his late wife : he abhorred publicity above all things. Besides, Mrs Gaskell was a Unitarian, which was gall to his Puseyite principles. He ended his reply to Ellen with : "the remarks concerning Mr Brontë excited in him only amusement—indeed, I have not seen him laugh as much for some months as he did while I was reading the article to him. We are both well in health, but lonely and desolate. . . ." But Arthur Nicholls was wrongly interpreting that laugh of Patrick's : he missed entirely its hollow ring. More attacks came upon the old clergyman's head, more misrepresentations of Charlotte, and strange rumours about Emily !

That decided Patrick. With great determination, backed with the threat of another towering rage, he wore down his curate's opposition and it was agreed between them that Mrs Gaskell should be approached in the matter. On 16th June 1855 Patrick sent her the following letter :

My Dear Madam,

Finding that a great many scribblers, as well as some clever and truthful writers, have published articles in newspapers and tracts—respecting my dear daughter Charlotte, since her death—and seeing that many things that have been stated are true, but more false—and having reason to think that some may venture to write her life who will be ill qualified for the undertaking, I can see no better plan under the circumstances than to apply to some established Author to write a brief account of her life—and to make some remarks on her works. You seem to me to be the best qualified for doing what I wish should be done. If, therefore, you will be so kind as to publish a long, or short, account of her life and works, just as you may deem expedient and proper—Mr. Nicholls and I will give you such information as you may require. I should expect and request that you would affix your name, so that the work might obtain a wide circulation, and be handed down to the latest times. Whatever profits might arise from the sale would, of course, belong to you. Mr. Nicholls approves of the step I have taken, and could my daughter speak from the tomb I feel certain she would laud our choice. Give my respectful regards to Mr. Gaskell and your family, and believe me, my dear Madam,

Yours very respectfully and truly, P. Brontè.

Writing from her home, Plymouth Grove, Manchester, Mrs Gaskell immediately accepted the task (indeed she had already privately sounded George Smith on such a project) and Patrick wrote to her again supplying some general details concerning his life and those of his family.

June 20th, 1855.

My Dear Madam,

Since, at Mr Nicholls request and mine, you have kindly consented to give a brief account of my daughter Charlotte's life, I will state a few facts which, as her biographer, you might wish to know. For the gratification of those who might be desirous of knowing anything of me —I will, in as few words as I can, gratify their curiosity. My father's name was Hugh Bronte. He was a native of the south of Ireland, and was left an orphan at an early age. It was said that he was of ancient family—whether this was, or was not so, I never gave myself the trouble to enquire, since his lot in life as well as mine, depended, under providence, not on family descent but our own exertions. He came to the north of Ireland, and made an early, but suitable marriage.

His pecuniary means were small—but, renting a few acres of land, he and my mother, by dint of application and industry, managed to bring up a family of ten children in a respectable manner. I shew'd an early fondness for books, and continued at school for several years. At the age of sixteen—knowing that my father could afford me no pecuniary aid—I began to think of doing something for myself. I therefore opened a public school—and in this line I continued five or six years. I was then a tutor in a gentleman's family—from which situation I removed to Cambridge, and enter'd St. John's College. After nearly four years' residence, I took the Degree of Bachelor of Arts—and was soon after ordained to a Curacy in the south of England. Having officiated in two Curacies in the south, I came to Yorkshire. I was soon presented to the small Living of Hartshead, in the parish of Dewsbury—by my good Vicar—here I remained for five years. The next five years I had the Living of Thornton, in the parish of Bradford, in the county of York. From this I came to Haworth—in the said parish, where I have continued as Incumbent during thirty-five years. Whilst at Hartshead I became acquainted with Miss Branwell, a native of Cornwall. In due time we were married. In Hartshead, two children were born to us— Maria and Elizabeth. In Thornton, Charlotte, Patrick Branwell, Emily Jane, and Anne were born—thus, in all, we had one son and five daughters. In Haworth my family afflictions began. After a happy union of nine years, and only one year's residence, my dear wife died—and left me with the care of six small children. Soon after, my wife's sister came, and afforded me her assistance for twenty years.

My daughters went early to school—those that were old enough went first to a good school in Wakefield. Charlotte, Emily Jane and Anne went to a school in Dewsbury, conducted by Miss Wooler, a clever, decent, and motherly woman. Maria, Elizabeth, Charlotte and Emily Jane went to Cowan Bridge, near Kir[k]by Lonsdale. At the school there, Maria and Elizabeth contracted a consumption, and came home, where they died within six weeks of each other, Maria in the eleventh, and Elizabeth in the tenth year of their age. Maria had a powerfully intellectual mind—Elizabeth had good solid sense. Charlotte and Emily Jane went afterwards to Brussels, and stopp'd some years there to finish their education. Anne, in the meantime, acted as a governess in a clergyman's family. Charlotte was also a governess for some time. On the death of their aunt, my children came home and remained with me till they died—all after they were of full age. My son died first—he was a young man of varied and brilliant talents—but these he marr'd by living too freely, which brought on a decline that shortened his days. Nearly in the same year, my daughters Emily Jane and Anne died, of consumption, and in this year in which I write my daughter Charlotte has died and left her affectionate husband and me to lament her great and irreparable loss. She was married, with my full consent, to the Revd Arthur Bell Nicholls, a graduate of the Dublin University. He had been my Clerical Assistant for eight years. Their union was congenial and happy, but alas! it was short. In about nine months after their marriage, death separated them—thus adding another proof to the precarious tenure by which we hold all our earthly joys. Emily and Anne, under the fictitious names of Acton and Ellis Bell, wrote several works which, though clever in their kind, never reach'd the great celebrity of those works written by Charlotte, under the assum'd name of Currer Bell. During the illness and deaths of her brother and sisters, Charlotte had a hard task to perform. She watch'd over them with a mother's kindness and care, and spent sleepless nights and weary days without one word of complaint, and only regretting that she was not able to do more for them in their seasons of distress. I never knew one less selfish than she was, or more disposed to suffer herself, to save others from suffering. When my daughters were at home they read their manuscripts to each other and gave their candid opinions of what was written. I never interfer'd with them at these times—I judged it best to throw them upon their own responsibility—Besides, a clergyman, bordering upon the age of eighty years, was likely to be too cold and severe a critic of the efforts of buoyant and youthful genius. Hence it came to pass that I never saw their works till they appear'd in print. From these few facts here mentioned—you can select, choose, or reject as you please—on future opportunities I may be able to give you further information, accordingly as you may require it— and may do it better than at present, whilst I am labouring under so great a weight of sorrow.

I remain, My dear Madam, Yours very respectfully and truly,

Patrick Brontè.

P.S. Your kind consent has given Mr. Nicholls and me great pleasure— it has broken in like a ray of light on our gloomy solitude. We shall have great pleasure to see you here, whenever you may choose—But you will see a sad change.

You will be so kind as to let us know a few days before your arrival.

Attached to this letter was a separate sheet containing some brief notes on the dates of various events in the Brontë family's life. They are not included here, as being too repetitious and because, writing so many years after most of the events recorded, as well as under the double handicap of grief and old age, Patrick made many errors. Indeed there are several such in his letters to Mrs Gaskell. Although, of course, it was Charlotte's life that was the popular interest, it is to be noticed that, knowing well her intense hatred of publicity, Patrick played down Emily's talents and existence at this moment.

Mrs Gaskell came to Haworth on Monday, 23rd July, with her friend Catherine Winkworth. She could see at once that Patrick was eager to have his daughter's life published and that Nicholls was not. "His feeling was against its being written, but he yielded to Mr. Brontë's impetuous wish . . . Mr. Nicholls was far more aware of the kind of particulars which people would look for, and saw how they had snatched at every gossiping account of her . . . Mr. Brontë not perceiving the full extent of the great interest in her personal history felt by strangers. . . ." Mrs Gaskell summed up her visit, however, as "a most peaceful visit. Both Mr Brontë and Mr Nicholls cried sadly. I like Mr. Nicholls." There was a warning bell for Patrick in those last words ! As Mrs Gaskell was leaving, Patrick followed her out to the garden door, and she has recorded his parting words : "No quailing, Mrs Gaskell. No drawing back."

Nicholls then informed Ellen Nussey that the biography was under way. ". . . I confess that the course most consonant with my own feelings would be to take no steps in the matter, but I do not think it right to offer any opposition to Mr Brontë's wishes. We have the same object in view, but should differ in our mode of proceeding. Mr Brontë has not been very well—Excitement on Sunday (our rush-bearing) and Mrs Gaskell's visit yesterday have been rather much for him. . . ."

On the day following Mrs Gaskell's visit to Haworth, Patrick sent her another letter.

July 24th, 1855.

My Dear Madam,

As I well know there will be difficulty, for want of adventure and incident, in writing a brief account of my daughter Charlotte's life, I will here state some things respecting the development of her intellectual powers. But here a difficulty meets me in the very commencement, since she was from a child, prone to say very little about herself and averse from making any display of what she knew. However, in her childish days, she often gave proofs of intelligence and quickness, so that the servants often said that they never saw such a clever little child, and that they were obliged to be on their guard in regard to what they said, and did, before her. Yet she and the servants always lived on good terms with each other. When mere children, as soon as they could read and write, Charlotte and her brother and sisters used to invent and act little plays of their own, in which the Duke of Wellington, my daughter Charlotte's hero, was sure to come off the conquering hero—when a dispute would not infrequently arise amongst them regarding the comparative merits of him, Bonaparte, Hannibal and Caesar. When the argument got warm and rose to its height, as their mother was then dead, I had sometimes to come in as arbitrator and settle the dispute according to the best of my judgment. Generally, in the management of these concerns, I frequently thought I discovered signs of rising talent which I had seldom, or never before, seen in any of their age. As they had few opportunities of being in learned and polished society, in their retired country situation, they formed a little society amongst themselves—with which they seem'd contented and happy. After they got older, and had been at different good schools, the same habits and ways of proceeding were carried out by them, during the vacations and at other opportunities, only then, their compositions and plots were more matur'd and had less of romance and more of taste and judgment. They often walked out together, in company with a favourite dog, and express'd themselves greatly pleas'd with the beautiful irregularity of uncultivated nature. Sometimes, Charlotte walk'd out alone, and when she return'd home her countenance seem'd lighted up with delighted contemplation. She was an ardent admirer of the sublime and beautiful—it often seem'd to me, however, that the sublime was the greater favourite. I have heard her speak with pleasure of the glittering ripple of the sea waves in the quiet moonlight, and with rapture with her view of the swelling billows, when with hollow sound, they rushed into the caverns of the rocky shore. The above is a mere outline of the life of my happy little family till deaths came in fearfully rapid succession, till my daughter Charlotte was left alone.

At the different schools she was at, she always distinguished herself —and generally got the highest reward. She was an excellent wife and daughter—a kind mistress, very charitable to the poor, and liberal according to her means, and generally beloved by all—and most by those who knew her best.

On some future opportunity I may give you a little more information. Mr. Nicholls joins me in very respectful regards. I remain, My dear Madam,

Yours very truly, P. Brontë.

Six days later Patrick wrote again. The first part of the letter gives some more dates, most of which are hopelessly wrong: for instance, he mentions that after the deaths of his two eldest children, "I left Emily and Charlotte at the school, where they remained a year and then came home,"—whereas, of course, as the school records clearly show, he removed them hastily the day after Elizabeth came home, a dying child. The letter, dated 30th July 1855, continues: ". . . Sometimes, also, they wrote little works of fiction they call'd miniature novels. All these things they did of their own accord—and evidently took great pleasure in their employment. Charlotte got the principal part of her knowledge of the Duke of Wellington from the newspapers, and what she heard in company—and of the other Heroes, from Ancient History —she was a general admirer of all works of genius, but I cannot say what books she admired most. The most favourable opportunities she had for contemplating ocean scenery consisted in her visits to the coasts of Scarborough and Filey, and in her voyages between London and Ostend, as well as during the first month of her marriage, when she made a delightful excursion to Ireland. I have heard her speak with rapture of the sea-views from the bold, rocky coasts of that Kingdom. The most exquisite combinations of the sublime and the beautiful, she witness'd in her visits to the Lakes of Cumberland and the far-fam'd lake of Killarney. . . ." Then follows the description of the questioning of his children under cover of a mask, which has already been quoted in full. The letter then concludes, ". . . As my eyes cannot bear close attention, you will kindly excuse the many and great faults of this hasty scrawl. Mr. Nicholls joins me in the kindest and most respectful regards.

> "I remain, My dear Madam, Yours very truly, P. Brontè."

Meanwhile Mrs Gaskell had been making outside enquiries regarding Patrick, and word of this reached the parsonage. He was at once extremely wrathful.

My Dear Madam,   Augt. 27th, 1855.

I have heard, indirectly, that it has been reported that I was opposed on my entrance into this Living—and that my salary was withheld from me for two years, and that this was mentioned to a Clergyman by a lady who was engaged in writing the life of "Currer Bell". As there is misunderstanding here, I wish to say that I never met with any opposition and never had any part of my salary kept from me—but on the contrary, have always received from the inhabitants and patrons, friendly and kindly treatment. The mistake arose, I imagine, from the following circumstance: This Living has for its patrons the Vicar of Bradford and certain Trustees. My predecessor took the Living with the consent of the Vicar of Bradford but in opposition to the Trustees—in consequence of which he was so opposed, that after only three weeks' possession he was compel'd to resign—and I was appointed with the consent of all parties.

The people here generally are poor, but whether rich or poor, they have always been not only civil to me and mine but friendly when an opportunity offered of shewing their disposition. On a solemn occasion I saw this clearly exhibited. My children, generally, and my dear daughter Charlotte, in particular, were both kind, liberal, and affable with the inhabitants. A thorough sense of this proceeding was not wanting on the death of each of them—and when the last death took place, when my dear Charlotte was no more—both rich and poor throughout the village, and the neighbourhood, both publicly and privately, gave sure proofs of genuine sorrow. The poor have often been accused of ingratitude—I think wrongfully. There was no instance of this when my dear Charlotte died. A case or two I might mention as an illustration of what I say. One moral and amicable girl, who had been deceived and deserted by a deceitful man, who had promised her marriage—when she heard of my daughter's hopeless illness, without our knowing it at the time—she spent a week of sleepless distress, and ever since deeply mourns her loss; and all this because my daughter had kindly sympathised with her in her distress, and given her good advice and helped her in her time of need, and enabled her to get on till she made a prudent marriage with a worthier man. Another case I would speak of, which is only one amongst many—a poor blind girl, who received an annual donation from my daughter, after her death required to be led four miles to be at my daughter's funeral, over which she wept many tears of gratitude and sorrow.

In her acts of kindness my dear daughter was, as I thought, often rather impulsive. Two or three winters ago a poor man fell on the ice and broke his thigh—and had to be carried home to his comfortless cottage, where he had a wife with twins, and six other small children. My daughter, having heard of their situation, sent the servant to see how they were—on her return she made a very eloquent and pathetic report. My daughter, being touched, got up directly and sent them a sovereign, to their great astonishment—and pleasure—for which they have ever afterwards been grateful. Though I could not help being pleased with this act—though hardly in accordance with my daughter's means—I observed to her that women were often impulsive in deeds of charity. She jocularly replied, "In deeds of charity men reason much and do little—women reason little and do much, and I will act the woman still."

As writing is to me here no easy task, and I am obliged to get it over as hastily as I can—you will kindly excuse all faults. Mr. Nicholls joins me in the most respectful regards.

I remain, My dear Madam, Yours very truly, P. Brontë.

So it was that Elizabeth Gaskell worked away at her biography of Charlotte Brontë, whose husband was soothed and pacified now the task had begun; and Patrick found it "a ray of light on our gloomy solitude". Had he only known what Mrs Gaskell was writing of himself, of the cruel and absurd accusations she was committing to paper, then he would have realized that even this flower of soothing consolation in his old age would have for him a nettle in its centre. Meanwhile the months passed, but Mrs Gaskell did not come to Haworth again. She appointed a local man to enquire into any matter considered of sufficient interest and accepted his evidence as being the strict truth. John Greenwood, who had been the first to inform Mrs Gaskell of Charlotte's death, was also questioned by her. Indeed both she and Harriet Martineau corresponded with him, but from the deep affection for Patrick so clearly shown in his diary and other notes, they would be able to extract little poison from him. On 24th December 1855, Nicholls informs Ellen : "We have neither heard nor seen anything of Mrs Gaskell . . . If Mrs Gaskell wishes to see Mrs Brontë's letters and will communicate that wish to Mr Brontë I dare . . ." The rest of the sentence is lost.

Patrick next wrote to Mrs Gaskell on 23rd January 1856:

My Dear Madam,

You will find herewith a letter and verses which I have received from a lady with whom I have no acquaintance. You will exercise your own judgment in reference to them, and all other concerns connected with the arduous and responsible task you have kindly undertaken. Mr. Nicholls and I often think of what you have so obligingly entered on, of what the public will expect from you on whatever subject you may write, and of the few facts and incidents you have of a biographical nature. We so frequently talk over and meditate on these things, that we are forced, at last, to solve the difficulty by saying that you must draw largely on the resources of your own mind. My daughter had that to do in no small degree, in the works which she gave to the world—She had not seen much of the world—she thought more about it and, most of all, with critical acumen and a careful attention to the operations of nature, she endeavour'd to discover the truth and to present it to her readers, as far as she was able, in the most attractive form and colours. I often think, that if you would write a running critique on her *works* as well as her *life* it would be highly popular, and render your task easier, by an accession of subject matter. But I must have done—an oppressive sadness comes over my heart, when I reflect that my dear daughter is forever gone. Remember me very respectfully to Mr. Gaskell and your family. Mr. Nicholls joins me in very kind and respectful regards. I remain, My dear Madam,

Very truly yours, P. Brontë.

Patrick was quite obviously burning with curiosity regarding the biography. At the same time he was most anxious that Charlotte's books should be fully dealt with, as her private life appeared to him to lack romance and incident.

On Sunday, 4th May 1856—National Thanksgiving Day on the conclusion of the war with Russia—the Rev. William Gaskell (husband of Charlotte's biographer) preached a sermon in Cross Street Chapel, Manchester (the Gaskells were Unitarians), in which he dwelt on the ethics of making peace with an enemy. In July of that year he sent a copy of his address to Patrick.

The Revd W. Gaskell, M.A. Manchester

Revd and Dear Sir,   Haworth, near Keighley. July 23rd, 1856.

I thank you for your sermon, which I have read carefully over with pleasure and, I trust, with profit. The principles and practices which it so ably advocates are perfectly in accordance with my own on the great subjects of peace and war—and it exposes in their sad consequences the sophistical arguments of an ignorant or knavish class of men who, if their doctrines were to be followed out to their ultimate results, would establish the tyranny of the wicked over the righteous, destroy all safety for honour and honesty, introduce a chaos of licentiousness, and banish liberty of conscience and political liberty from the world.

We often wonder here, how Mrs Gaskell is getting on with her mournful but interesting task. Mr. Nicholls joins me in the kindest and most respectful regards to you, Mrs Gaskell, and your family.

I remain, Rev^d and Dear Sir, Very truly yours, P. Brontë.

It was at this point that Mrs Gaskell went to Brussels, and Madame Heger refused point-blank to see her. However, Constantin Heger received her and was very charming.

In September 1856 Mrs Gaskell again called at Haworth Parsonage, this time with Sir James Kay-Shuttleworth. She referred to his presence thus: "He had not the slightest delicacy or scruple: and asked for an immense number of things, literally taking no refusal."

Mrs Gaskell was finding Nicholls now reticent to produce more letters and other material in his possession. Hearing that she was going to Haworth, Ellen writes: ". . . I think you may win him by your own heartiness in the work—at any rate you will Mr. B., and for a quiet life Mr N. will have to yield where Mr B. is urgent and impatient. . . ."

On 8th September 1856 Mrs Gaskell was already making emendations respecting her portrait of Patrick: ". . . in fact I had to re-write about 40 pages. They give a much pleasanter though hardly less *queer* notion of the old father. . . ."

In October, as the book neared its end, a pamphlet appeared, containing many false statements about Patrick and his family.

Novr 3rd 1856.

My Dear Madam,

At the same time that this letter will be posted, there will also be posted a pamphlet which I wish you to see, and which is, like some other articles and pamphlets in regard to my children and me, a strange compound of truth and error. Where the writer talks about my marriage he is in many respects entirely wrong. I was never in Penzance, or in Cornwall, the native town and county of my wife—I saw her only in Yorkshire. She was then of full age and so was I. Her parents were dead, and with respect to our intended union we had none to consult—

we exercised our own judgment, and none ever express'd any dis-satisfaction with our marriage. After we were married we resided in Hartshead, in this county, for two years, and afterwards in Thornton, where Charlotte was born—which is only about six miles from where I now live.

In a moderate competency my wife and I lived in as much happiness as can be expected in this world—for nine years. At the end of this time, alas! she died, which occasioned great sorrow of heart to me, and was an irreparable loss, both to me and my children. She was an excellent wife and mother, and a highly respected member of society—her sound sense, her affectionate disposition, and delicate tact and taste you would discover in the letters which I entrusted to your perusal. The book-making gentry whose little works I have seen, appear to make me a somewhat extraordinary and eccentrick [*sic*] personage—I have no great objection to this, admitting they can make a penny by it. But the truth of the matter is—that I am, in some respects, a kindred likeness to the father of Margaret, in "North and South"—peaceable, feeling, sometimes thoughtful—and generally well-meaning. Yet unlike him in one thing—by occasionally getting into a satirical vein—when I am disposed to dissect and analyze human character and human nature, studying closely its simples and compounds, like a curious surgeon. And, being in early life, thrown on my own resources—and consequently obliged, under Providence, to depend on my own judgment and exertions, I may not be so ready as some are, to be a follower of any man, or a worshipper of convention-alities or forms, which may possibly, to superficial observers, acquire me the character of a little eccentricity. Thus freely have I spoken to you—in order that, in your work, you may insert such facts as may counteract any false statements that have been made, or might be made, respecting me or mine.

From what has already transpired, I think you will see the prudence of our choice, and request in reference to your undertaking to write the life of "Currer Bell". We begin now to long for seeing your work in print—and doubt not you will see the propriety of shewing your manuscript to none, except Mr. Gaskell, your family, and the publisher and compositor. Much harm has often been done by an opposite line of conduct—Authors have been fetter'd, bias'd, and made to appear in other lights than their own. Genius has often been crush'd and fame mar'd by officious critics and familiar friends.

Remember me respectfully to Mr. Gaskell and your family—Mr. Nicholls joins me in kind and respectful regards. Be so kind as to let me hear from you after you have received this. You will kindly excuse this miserable scrawl—written with a bad pen, deficient sight, and in some haste. I remain, My dear Madam,

Respectfully and truly, P. Brontè.

On Saturday, 7th February 1857, Mrs Gaskell was finished with her task: "I have to-day finished my Life of Miss Brontë, and next week we set out for Rome. . . ."

The Life of Charlotte Brontë was published, in two volumes, on Wednesday, 25th March 1857. Of its true greatness there has never been any doubt; and it is because of its brilliant portrayal of Charlotte that the errors committed in dealing with the setting of her life and other members of her family have for so long been considered as unimportant.

At first all went well. The book was at once in great demand and after three weeks the second edition was issued. Patrick read it in great excitement and realized that the work was a masterpiece, that it presented a wonderfully sympathetic portrait of Charlotte. He decided, therefore, to deal gently with the adverse, and often offensive, statements concerning himself. He wrote to Mrs Gaskell on 2nd April 1857.

My Dear Madam,

I thank you for the Books you have sent me containing the Memoir of my Daughter—I have perused them, with a degree of pleasure and pain, which can be known only to myself. As you will have the opinion of abler criticks [*sic*] than myself, I shall not say much in the way of criticism—I shall only make a few remarks in unison with the feelings of my heart. With a tenacity of purpose, usual with me in all cases of importance, I was fully determined that the Biography of my Daughter should, if possible, be written by one not unworthy of the undertaking. My mind first turned to you—and you kindly acceded to my wishes— had you refused I would have applied to the next best—and so on— and had all applications fail'd, as the last resource, though above eighty years of age, and feeble and unfit for the task, I would myself have written a short though inadequate memoir, rather than have left all to selfish, hostile or ignorant scribblers. But the work is now done, and done rightly, as I wish'd it to be, and in its completion, has afforded me more satisfaction than I have felt during many years of a life in which has been exemplified the saying that "man is born to trouble as the sparks fly upwards" [*sic*]. You have not only given a picture of my Dear daughter Charlotte, but of my Dear wife, and all my Dear children, and such a picture too as is full of truth and life.

The pictures of my brilliant and unhappy son, and his diabolical seducer, are masterpieces—indeed, all the pictures in the work have

vigorous, truthful, and delicate touches in them, which could have
been executed only by a skilful female hand. There are a few trifling
mistakes which, should it be deem'd necessary, may be corrected in the
second Edition. Mr Nicholls joins me in kind and respectful regards to
you, Mr Gaskell and your family. Wishing you greatest good in both
the worlds, I remain, My dear Madam,

Yours respectfully and truly, P. Brontë.

When this letter arrived at the Gaskells' home near Manchester,
Mrs Gaskell was still away in Italy, and it was opened and read by the
Rev. William Gaskell, who had already heard the distant rumblings of
an approaching storm over his wife's book. Now Mr Brontë was murmuring over a "few trifling mistakes" ! Mr Gaskell wrote to Patrick and
asked for details of these. Patrick replied on 7th April :

My dear Sir,

The principal mistake in the Memoir—which I wish to mention, is
that which states that I laid my Daughters under restriction with
regard to their diet, obliging them to live chiefly on vegetable food.
This I never did. After their Aunt's death, with regard to the household
affairs they had all their own way. Thinking their constitutions to be
delicate, the advice I repeatedly gave them was that they should wear
flannel, eat as much wholesome animal food as they could digest, take
air and exercise in moderation, and not devote too much time and attention
to study and composition. I should wish this to be mentioned in the
Second Edition. I am happy to find that the criticks [*sic*] are all speaking
well of the Memoir. Mr Nicholls joins me in kind and respectful
regards.
                     I remain, My Dear Sir, Yours faithfully, P. Brontë.

P.S. The Eccentrick Movements ascribed to me, at pages 51 and 52,
Vol. I—have no foundation in fact.

This was a tart answer from Patrick, who was now more conversant
with the poisonous remarks Mrs Gaskell had made respecting him in
the book. Nicholls was also smarting under a grievance, as it was implied
that he had not been quite the most sympathetic of husbands. The
"Eccentrick Movements" that brought forth a hot denial from Patrick
were, of course, the absurd tales of the slashing of his wife's gown, the
burning of the red shoes, the stuffing of the hearthrug up the chimney
and the sawing off of the backs of the chairs.

By the beginning of May 1857 the storm had burst. Mrs Robinson
(Lady Scott) was threatening a libel action, so were the friends of the

Rev. Carus Wilson of Cowan Bridge School fame. A son-in-law of Samuel Redhead was angry about Mrs Gaskell's description of the latter's expulsion from Haworth. "He gives another as true, in which I don't see any great difference," wrote Mrs Gaskell. There were protests from friends of the girl who had been seduced and who had been aided by Charlotte: the word "seduced" was altered to read "betrayed"; and, amidst other objections, the people of Haworth were, rightly, incensed at the descriptions of themselves and their moorland village. Mrs Gaskell, although not a Lancashire lass, lived at Manchester and was considered as an adherent of the hated Red Rose by those loyal supporters of the White. Ellen Nussey told Mrs Gaskell: "Some of the West Ridingers are very angry, and declare they are half a century in civilisation before some of the Lancashire folk, and that this neighbourhood is a paradise compared with some districts not far from Manchester." Well, there is certainly no denying that!! Even Mr Nicholls broke silence to send five letters to the *Halifax Guardian*, stoutly defending his wife's description of the harsh conditions at the Clergy Daughters' School at Cowan Bridge, and lashing the Calvinist founder with Puseyite relish.

A careful study of the many books for young readers written by Carus Wilson should serve to condemn the man. In addition, the *Lancaster Guardian* for December 1837 presents an abject glimpse of him.

He had charged the Board of Guardians, Kendal, with starving to death old Mary Cornthwaite, who had died in a fire at her home at Casterton. When the case was taken up, after frantic attempts by Carus Wilson to retract, it was easily proved that the old lady had ample food in her house, clothing, furniture and, indeed, 8s 6d in her pocket. There had also been £4 17s in Kirkby Lonsdale Savings Bank of which Wilson was a director.

"Mr Carus Wilson's case having thus completely failed, the Rev gentleman attempted to get rid of the case by a childish and contemptible shuffle. He said it might be a Mary Cornthwaite three hundred miles off that he alluded to. Mr Voules [the Assistant Commissioner of Westmorland] checked this trifling by handing this Christian Minister a Bible, and putting him on his oath. . . . He very reluctantly admitted the fact that it was Mary Cornthwaite to whom he had referred. After much prevarication, he was at last compelled to admit the blackness of the charge, and to sue for mercy. . . . Mr Wilson having *retracted every part of his statement*, and affixed his signature to the retraction, the inquiry closed."

The magistrate "expressed himself in terms of strong disapprobation of Mr Wilson's conduct" and the newspaper concludes : "The injury to the cause of religion, and particularly to the Established Church, from such conduct cannot well be overrated." No, it is not possible to remove from Carus Wilson the foul stigma of "Brocklehurst" which will adhere to his memory for ever.

But, alas, we must not follow up the great disputes that followed the publication of *The Life of Charlotte Brontë*. There are so many letters, so much argument, that we should never have done with them. It must suffice to mention that neither Patrick nor Nicholls caused Mrs Gaskell any additional trouble, although many of her stupid falsehoods against the former were omitted from subsequent editions, together with much that had to be withdrawn regarding Lady Scott, under threat of a libel action. Indeed, to avoid such an action Mrs Gaskell was forced to apologize on this latter head, in a letter to *The Times*, although in this instance she had been very near to the truth of the matter. Patrick Brontë had dreamed happily about the publication of his daughter's biography, yet when it came out he found himself bitterly abused. No action did he take, however, to defend himself—to his eternal credit. Indeed, he tried to persuade his friends not to jump to his defence in print ; and thus it is that his character is blackened to this day because of the untrue statements of Elizabeth Gaskell.

Of course Patrick was approached by Nancy Garrs (Mrs Wainwright) who, together with her sister, had been described by Mrs Gaskell as wasteful, and it was in the late summer of that year that Patrick wrote out for them the testimonial already quoted.

By the beginning of May 1857, all unsold copies of the biography were withdrawn from sale, only six or seven weeks after publication, and on the 26th Mrs Gaskell's solicitor wrote his full retraction of all statements made which "imputes to a widowed lady, referred to, but not named therein, any breach of her conjugal, or of her maternal, or of her social duties . . . which imputes to the lady in question a guilty intercourse with the late Branwell Brontë. . .". Patrick was relieved. For all his "diabolical seducer", it helped Branwell's memory. He presented Lady Scott's solicitor, Henry Newton, of Messrs Newton & Robinson, York, with ten volumes of Campbell's *Lives of the Lord Chancellors* (1856/7 edition) "in recognition of legal services rendered to Branwell Brontë".

Upon her return from Italy in June 1857, Mrs Gaskell truly found herself in what she described at the time as "a veritable hornets' nest".

In July, William Dearden of Bradford, a schoolmaster who had known Patrick for over thirty years, was stung into retaliation on behalf of his friend and wrote his long and admirable defence of Patrick in the *Halifax Examiner*. It was based on his own knowledge of Patrick, the evidence of the Garrs sisters and of Martha Brown, "who had gathered round his hearth for above a quarter of a century" and were "best acquainted with the domestic habits and conduct of the master of the house" (in contrast to the evidence of the temporary nurse). As for Patrick's not wishing for his children's companionship, Dearden wrote : "I remember having seen him more than once conversing kindly and affably with them in the studio of a clever artist who resided in Keighley ; and many others, both in that town and in Haworth, can bear testimony to the fact of his being often seen accompanied by his young family in his visits to friends, and in his rambles among the hills." Dearden's article was, however, written and published without the knowledge or consent of Patrick, who was rather annoyed when he heard of it. For all the attacks upon him she had made, he believed in Mrs Gaskell's integrity and was contented that whatever alterations were necessary would appear when the biography was again on sale. After the publication of this article, Patrick wrote the following letter to Mrs Gaskell, who was staying in Ambleside. It is dated 30th July 1857 :

My Dear Madam,

I thank you for your letter and those of others, which I have received from you this morning—their contents pleased me much. I may have been troublesome to you and your amiable daughter, but I was roused a little by the impertinent remarks of a set of penny-a-liner, hungry, pedantic, and generally ignorant reviewers—no one despises them and their productions more than I do—but the misfortune is that the multitude see not as we see, and not judging for themselves, are often misled by the false judgment of others. I do not deny that I am somewhat eccentrick. Had I been numbered amongst the calm, sedate, concentric men of the world, I should not have been as I now am, and I should in all probability never have had such children as mine have been. I have no objection whatever to your representing me as a little eccentrick, since you and other learned friends will have it so—only don't set me on in my fury to burning hearthrugs, sawing the backs of chairs, and tearing my wife's silk gowns—With respect to tearing my wife's silk gown, my dear little daughter must have been misinform'd— This you will be convinced of when I assure you that it was my repeated advice to my wife and children, to wear gowns and outward garments made *only of silk or wool*, as these were less inflammable than cotton or linen—on account of my wife and children all being near-sighted I had an eccentrick dread of accidents by fire.

I am much pleased with reading the opinions of those in your letters, and other eminent characters, respecting the "Memoir". Before I knew theirs, I had formed my own opinion, from which you know I am not easily shaken. And my opinion, and the reading World's opinion of the "Memoir", is that it is every way worthy of what one Great Woman should have written of Another, and that it ought to stand, and will stand, in the first rank of Biographies till the end of time. Some slips there have been, but they may be remedied. It is dangerous to give credence hastily to informants—some may tell the truth, whilst others, from various motives, may greedily invent and propagate falsehoods. I think that I have already stated to Miss Marianne Gaskell, that I never forbade my wife or children, or servants, the use of animal food.

The error committed on this head was unfortunate, as Mr [Carus] Wilson and his party, most uncharitably, turn'd it to the advantage of their hollow cause. I am not in the least offended at your telling me that I have faults—I have many—and, being a Daughter of Eve, I doubt not that you also have some. Let us both try to be wiser and better as Time recedes and Eternity advances.

Begging that you will kindly excuse this hasty scrawl, I remain, My Dear Madam, Yours very respectfully and truly,

Patrick Brontè.

What a thousand pities that this gallant, kind and charming letter has not been made more widely known; perhaps then the distorted image of Patrick Brontë would have been swept away and something of the true figure have emerged.

Meanwhile, in this month of July, Arthur Nicholls was stoutly defending his wife's description of Cowan Bridge School, as depicted in the Lowood of *Jane Eyre* in a series of letters to the *Halifax Guardian*. There was a move to obtain Patrick's signature to sustain the argument, but he was not going to be dragged into this dispute. He wrote to the editor, who had approached him, as follows:

July 22nd 1857.

Dear Sir,

I thank you for your polite note. As it may be the wisest plan, to drop the controversy—I do not wish to affix my name—I remain Dear Sir,

Yours respectfully, P. Brontë.

In this month also, on 8th July, Francis Leyland, Branwell's friend, visited Patrick at Haworth, and found him quite upset at the passages concerning himself in the *Memoir*. Leyland has recorded that Patrick told him : "I did not know that I had an enemy in the world, much less one who would traduce me before my death, till Mrs Gaskell's *Life of Charlotte* appeared. Everything in that book which relates to my conduct to my family is either false or distorted. I never did commit such acts as are there ascribed to me." When pressed, later, to explain the word "enemy", he replied, "false informants and hostile critics". Leyland explained that Patrick was quite aware that village scandal in general and information from the discarded nurse in particular had been swallowed whole by Mrs Gaskell. The nurse, according to Leyland, was dismissed after Patrick had detected her in proceedings that fully merited such dismissal. With the double purpose of explaining her dismissal and injuring Patrick she had invented many of the ludicrous incidents that appeared about him in Mrs Gaskell's book.

During July and August Mrs Gaskell was back at her work, preparing the revised, third edition of the biography. Many alterations had to be made and in the aggregate the contents of ten pages were removed. George Smith informed Patrick of the corrections which were to be made in regard to himself, before the issue of the new edition. Patrick wrote to Mrs Gaskell at once :

My Dear Madam,   Augt : 20th, 1857.

I have received from Mr Smith, this morning, a letter in reference to the third Edition of the "Memoir"—what he says gives me great satisfaction, both in regard to Charlotte and myself ; what is stated in the "Memoir" is of vast moment, in consequence of its effect throughout the world, till the latest times. I may just mention, by the way, that an article in reference to the "Memoir"—by Mr Dearden of Bradford, has lately appeared in the "Bradford Observer", and abstracts from it in some of the country newspapers—and that with this article, I had nothing whatever to do. I knew nothing of it till I saw it in print, and was much displeased when I saw it there. Though hard pressed by some ruthless critics, as well as Mr Wilson and his party [here he refers to the son of the founder of the school at Cowan Bridge], I held both my tongue and my pen, believing that you were a friend to my daughter Charlotte, and feeling confident that whatever you found to be mistakes you would willingly correct in the third edition. With my kind and respectful regards to Mr. Gaskell and you, not forgetting my fair correspondent, I remain, My dear Madam,

Yours truly, Patrick Brontë.

The "fair correspondent" was Mrs Gaskell's daughter, Marianne, who had replied to Patrick's last letter on her mother's behalf, she having found it quite unanswerable and pleading illness. Hence Patrick's remark to Dearden that "Mrs. Gaskell was unwell and not able to write", and his first learning of the corrections about himself in the third edition, from George Smith. Patrick was now greatly perturbed at the manner in which his friend's article was being quoted in newspapers throughout the West Riding. He wished Mrs Gaskell to have peace of mind as she completed the third edition. Her reply to his letter showed only too plainly that she was in depressed spirits, and in another letter written at this time she says, "I did so try to tell the truth—I weighed every line with my whole power and heart. . . ."

That of course was true, but it was her *misfortune* to be misled by false informants ; it was her *fault* that she made no attempt to corroborate such information. Her letter sounded so despondent that Patrick wrote again to try to cheer her.

Augt: 24th, 1857

Dear Madam,

I sincerely thank you for your very kind letter, which I have received this morning. As you must be nearly overwhelmed with letters, and oppress'd with answering them, I should not have troubled you with this of mine, were it not that I think it may divert your attention from considerations which may disturb you more than is necessary. Why should you disturb yourself concerning what has been, is, and ever will be the lot of eminent writers ? But here, as in other cases, as according to the old adage, "the more cost the more honour".—Above three thousand years since, Solomon said, "He that increaseth knowledge, increaseth sorrow—much study is the [*sic*] weariness of the flesh."— So you may find it, and so my Daughter Charlotte found it—and so thousands have found it in times past, and so thousands may find it till the end of the world, should this sinful, perverse world last so long as to produce so many Authors, like you and my daughter Charlotte. You have had, and will have much praise, with a little blame. Then drink the mix'd cup, with thankfulness to the great physician of souls— it will be far more salutary to you in the end, and even in the beginning, than if it were all unmix'd sweetness. But I am forgetting to whom I am writing in this line—and so I must conclude a most ill-written, incoherent scrawl.

We have many visitors weekly—Amongst the rest, the Duke of Devonshire has call'd, and stopp'd with us about an hour.—Excuse all faults, and believe me, very sincerely and truly yours,

Patrick Brontë.

There is something infinitely touching in the old man of eighty
swallowing the abuse that had been hurled at his head and attempting
to encourage the younger person on her way. It was following this brief
visit that the Duke of Devonshire sent to the parsonage a large present
of game for Patrick, whose calm nobility had greatly impressed him. It
will be remembered that the latter referred to this visit from His Grace
in his letter to Sir Joseph Paxton, given earlier in this volume. The
Cavendish family, descended from the de Keighleys, were patrons of
Keighley Church. The sixth Duke of Devonshire died a few months
after this gift of game to his old Cambridge friend.

Harriet Martineau now entered the arena with an article in which
she says: ". . . a third edition never can set right the mistakes caused by
a first. . . ." William Dearden read the article, found some slighting
references to Patrick in it, and rushed over to Haworth Parsonage.
Patrick again wrote to Mrs. Gaskell.

Augt: 31st, 1857.

My Dear Madam,

Owing to circumstances, I deem it necessary to trouble you once
more with a few lines. Miss Martineau has lately published a short
article which, from what it express'd or implied in it, seems to me to be
rather equivocal. Mr. Dearden who, without my knowledge, also wrote,
excited by what Miss Martineau has written, call'd on me to make
enquiries. I told him that I had taken the liberty of writing to you, and
that I had spoken in the highest terms of the "Memoir", mentioning,
however, that there were a few statements respecting myself that were
erroneous, and which I wish to have omitted in the Third Edition,
which was all I expected and desired, and all that could be now safely or
prudently done—and that you had obligingly promised to omit them—
and that, consequently, I was anxious that no more should be either
said or written in this case respecting either you or me. I, moreover,
distinctly informed him that I never said or wrote anything to Miss
Martineau, him, or any other, intimating in the remotest degree that I
considered you an enemy; that I fully believed you were a friend to my
Daughter as she was to you, and that you were no enemy to me; and
that when I did speak of an enemy, I alluded only to false and malignant
informants, and a few prejudiced, ruthless, and unjust critics who, like
soldiers of fortune, make their bread by the sword of destruction.—
As Mr. Dearden seems inclined to write in answer to Miss Martineau,
and I know not what, in their wisdom, they may say, I have thought it
right to make these few remarks which, if they should serve no other
purpose, will at least give satisfaction to myself. My real or pretended

friends seem, in their gossiping skill, to have combined to paint me not
as a single, but a double Janus, looking, and smiling or frowning, with
my four faces, in opposite directions, as may best suit my own selfish
convenience. They would please me better by minding their own affairs
and letting mine alone.

From different parts of this variegated world, we have, in this place,
daily many strangers who, from various motives, pay a visit to the
Church and neighbourhood, and would, if we would let them, pay a
gossiping visit to us, in our proper persons. However, we can admit
only a select few. These things, with others, tend to revive those fond
but sad remembrances, which require no such stimulants, since my
spirits without them are sufficiently low. My kind regards to Mr. Gaskell
and your Family, I remain, My dear Madam, Yours respectfully and
truly,
                                            Patrick Brontè.

At the same time Patrick sent a strongly worded letter to Dearden
down in Bradford.

Mr. W. Dearden. Bradford.
                        Haworth, Nr. Keighley. August 31st, 1857.
Dear Sir,
I trouble you with a few lines merely to state that I wish nothing
more should be written against Mrs Gaskell, in regard to the "Memoir".
She has already encountered very severe trials, which generally pass to
the lot of celebrated authors. She has promised to omit, in the third
edition, the erroneous statement respecting me, which is all I can now
reasonably expect or desire, as no more, I think, can be safely or
prudently done. As for myself, I wish to live in unnoticed and quiet
retirement, setting my mind on things above in heaven, and not on
things on the earth beneath, and performing my duty to the utmost of
my power ; esteeming myself after all but an unprofitable servant, and
resting my hopes for salvation on the all-prevailing merit of the Saviour
of a lost world, and considering that the passing affairs of this life—
which too much occupy the attention of passing mortal man—are but
dust and ashes, when compared with the concerns of eternity. I remain,
Dear ["Sir" omitted],
                                Yours respectfully, P. Brontë.

P.S. I never thought otherwise of Mrs Gaskell, than that she was a
friend of my daughter and no enemy to me. In alluding to enemies I
meant false informants and hostile critics.

34

As those last words are the same as those quoted by Leyland, it is all too obvious that several gentlemen in Bradford were getting their heads together and discussing the Brontë affair at great length.

As Mrs Gaskell worked on, some of Patrick's recent kindnesses towards her touched her heart. She wrote to George Smith: ". . . I only hope Mr Brontë won't be over-worried. Hitherto he has acted like a 'brick'. (I hope you understand slang?). . ."

The third edition of *The Life of Charlotte Brontë* was issued at the beginning of September 1857, and those references to Patrick which have been mentioned were all omitted. Patrick was at once supplied with a copy of the new version.

My Dear Madam,
Sept: 9th, 1857.

Though my opinion may be worth little, I wish to say that I have look'd over the third Edition of the "Memoir", and that it gives me full satisfaction in all its parts and bearings, and that I ardently wish it may go down, without alteration, augmentation, or diminution, to the latest posterity. With the work as it now stands, all reasonable persons must be satisfied, since in it there is much to praise and little, or nothing, to blame. It has, I think, arrived at a degree of perfection which was scarcely attainable in a first and second Edition. I hope that I may conclude that after a storm there will now be a calm, and that there will be no fault-finders—unless someone like Miss Martineau should arise, determined to be hostile, and put the worst construction on the best intentions, both in words and actions. Notwithstanding Miss Martineau's strange and unhappy illusions, which mystify and bewilder her Atheistical brain, I had thought she was a Woman who would not, knowingly or willingly, injure the memory of anyone, especially that of the dead, who were unable to defend themselves. For such wrongs, infidelity will afford but poor relief—The prospect only of blank and eternal annihilation will give but little support to feeble humanity in the season of sorrow, or an accusing conscience can ever remonstrate with those who believe that there is no God.

With very kind regards to Mr. Gaskell and your Family, I remain, My Dear Madam, Yours respectfully and truly,
Patrick Brontë.

The publication of this third edition and Patrick's letter expressing his approval brought to a close the correspondence between himself and Mrs Gaskell concerning it. His attitude throughout the entire dispute had been courteous, dignified, sensible and gentlemanly. Whilst the smaller minds and unafflicted hearts contended among themselves, the last of the Brontës maintained the fine tradition of the family he had bred. It was not so very long, of course, before all the offending passages were reintroduced, and they remain to this day.

On 25th January 1858 Dr Edward White Benson—cousin to Charlotte's pupils in 1839, the Sidgwicks of Stone Gappe, Lothersdale—later Archbishop of Canterbury, visited Haworth Parsonage. He recorded his visit, from which the following is an extract. "Mrs Gaskell was very hasty and inaccurate in the steps she took to gain information, and never consulted Mr Nicholls or old Mr Brontë, as the latter himself told me. They never saw the book . . . till it was in print. He lamented much the 'many unfounded things pertaining to our neighbours' which was therein related, and though he said there were also 'many ridiculous anecdotes about himself which never had any existence except in some curious imaginations', this did not seem to move him. He seemed too old and too composed to mind it. . . . Mr Brontë thought the third edition more truthful, but he said 'Vulgar readers would always prefer the 1st'. . . ."

To a visiting Methodist minister Patrick remarked: "Mrs Gaskell is a novelist, you know, and we must allow her a little romance, eh? It's quite in her line. But the book is substantially true, sir, for all that. There are some queer things in it, to be sure—there are some about myself, for instance—but the book is substantially true. . . ."

Towards the end of June 1859 word would reach Patrick and Mrs Gaskell that Lady (Lydia) Scott, who had plagued them both in differing ways, had died on the 19th of that month aged fifty-nine. Later that year, on 30th December, there died in London Patrick's other old "enemy", the Rev. William Carus Wilson, aged sixty-eight. Doubtless Patrick attempted some Christian forgiveness for both.

Over three years after his letter of thanks to Mrs Gaskell for the third edition of the biography, Patrick received from her a portrait, believed to be that of her husband. Patrick's brief reply is the last of his letters that we have, although, as will be seen, he wrote again to Mrs Gaskell after this:

To Mrs. Gaskell. Manchester.

Haworth, Nr. Keighley. Oct. 2nd, 1860.
My Dear Madam,
I thank you for the very interesting portrait—The Head is intellectual and noble, and gives outward symptoms of inward greatness. Remember me with kindly and respectful regards to Mr. Gaskell and all your Family,
I remain, Dear Madam, Yours respectfully and truly, P. Brontë.

Thus, through the pen of Elizabeth Gaskell the world learned something of the Brontës, but by no means all. The secret of their genius remained locked away in the fastness of those beautiful moors. For Patrick her biography was, of course, a disaster: his name remains tarnished to this day.

What must have been his feelings when he read in the *New York Times* shortly after the biography appeared, the following lines: ". . . Here for the rest of their lives dwelt the family of this moody, wretched parson—a man who like a mad dog ought to have been shot, or like a victim of its bite, smothered between two feather beds. Society is far too tolerant of these domestic hyenas, who are perpetual glooms upon their households . . . a few months after their removal to Haworth, this poor persecuted woman died, a victim to the dogged, gloomy asceticism of this believer in the Thirty-nine Articles." All this because of the old familiar stories of furniture sawing, rug burning, gown slashing, and so on. Haworth of course is, as always, pictured as a bog inhabited by savages. Patrick's pain and Ellen Nussey's anger when they read this were considerable. Indeed, Ellen's dislike of Mrs Gaskell's book and the harm it had done became quite intense at this time. (Although, to present all aspects fairly, it must be admitted that in her confused old age she turned on Patrick, "that old villain" as she described him to Sir T. Wemyss Reid in November 1876; but then poor Ellen turned on practically everybody connected with the Brontë story before the end. Her mind became clouded and, sadly, three of her family were certified.) As for the people of Haworth, they have never forgiven Mrs Gaskell to this day, and there is no reason at all why they ever should.

It was during this period of the late 1850s that William Scruton first visited Haworth. It was a fine summer's day. "I had the privilege (for I accounted it no less) of seeing a tall, venerable-looking old man, with hair as white as snow, and a face full of intelligence and benevolence, enter the old church, walk down the aisle, mount the three-decker pulpit (for it was the Sabbath), and preach what was then known as 'the afternoon sermon'. This was the Rev. Patrick Brontë. His appearance, to say the least, could not fail to inspire feelings of reverence. . . ."

R. Spence Hardy, the Wesleyan minister, frequently came up to Haworth from Keighley at this time to collect material for his book, "William Grimshaw, Incumbent of Haworth"; he met Patrick several times and described him as ". . . an ardent and intelligent Irishman, who had seen the eagle strike its talons into the sacred lamb near his own parsonage . . . who still lives in that silent dwelling, the picture of a fine old man ; hoary and roseate as the mountain-snow when crimsoned by the setting sun".

Finally, there are the memories of the Rev. Canon Bardsley, one time Vicar of Huddersfield, who in 1899 recalled a visit he had made with his father to Haworth Parsonage after Charlotte's death. ". . . As I returned with my father to Keighley, he told me how distressed he had been to see the tears in the eyes of old Mr. Brontë while he spoke of the aspersions on his domestic character, and the exaggerated statements with reference to the eccentricities of his daily life. . . ." But Charlotte's name was shining forth ; her life was there for the world to respect and admire ; and that, after all, was what Patrick had really wanted.

CHAPTER 29

Death

SHORTLY after writing his letter to Mrs Gaskell on 2nd October 1860, thanking her for the portrait, Patrick was forced to take to his bed. He was now very feeble and it had been many months since he had ventured farther than the church. He was nearly eighty-four and knew that his long life was at last drawing to a close. Until this autumn of 1860 he had still enjoyed walking round the little parsonage garden; at such times, if Nicholls was from home, he would leave his newspaper open on his table with a message written across it to inform Martha that he was only out in the garden if she wanted him. This used to amuse her, as it was very easy to see him from any of the front windows, there being few trees or bushes that could quite hide him from view. He had until July still managed to preach the occasional sermon, leaving Nicholls to conduct the rest of the service. (Patrick's last funeral service was taken on 26th October 1858.) One of his very last texts was, "I had rather be a doorkeeper in the house of my God, than to dwell in the tents of wickedness." During this summer of 1860, Patrick, with Nicholls's assistance, mounted Grimshaw's famous pulpit for the last time, and appropriately announced "Ecclesiastes, the twelfth chapter and the thirteenth verse. 'Let us hear the conclusion of the whole matter: Fear God, and keep his commandments: for this *is* the whole *duty* of man.' " Then, after his sermon, he walked slowly past the flags that covered his family, past the pew where only Martha sat, and slowly left Haworth Church. But the long-awaited reunion was near at hand now. When he next entered his church the burden of sorrow would have been lifted from him.

Towards the end of his life, Patrick, whilst remaining a loyal servant of the Established Church, was so disturbed by what he considered the shallow pretensions of such Puseyite clerics as Collins and, later, Nicholls, that he returned very close to Methodism, that religion which in his youth had given him so much material assistance and spiritual inspiration. Indeed Patrick had to ponder the Evangelicals' problem. It had been essential to Methodism that John Wesley and his followers should leave the Church, and equally important to the Church of England that Charles Simeon should influence the remaining enthusiasts including Patrick and his friends from leaving also, in order to maintain a vital Evangelical wing in the Establishment. But Patrick lived long enough to witness the grave weakening to Evangelicalism by these double divisions of its strength.

On Tuesday, 7th August 1860, *The Times* recorded the following, under the heading "The Father of Charlotte Bronte".

"The *Halifax Courier* has the following paragraph : Age and infirmity have at length so far prevailed, that the Rev. P. Brontë has been compelled to cease from active duty. He preached his last sermon in Haworth Church on Sunday the 21st [22nd] ult. We believe that the Rev. Mr Nicholl [*sic*], husband of Charlotte Brontë (Currer Bell), will become the incumbent of Haworth."

Both the *Halifax Courier* and the London *Times* presumed too much in that last sentence ; but, like many a Vicar of Bradford before them, they reckoned not with the Haworth Church Land Trustees. Indeed it is not even appreciated today that there would have been no Grimshaw, no Brontë at Haworth but for this body and the world would have whistled in vain for such an evangelical revival in West Yorkshire, and for masterpieces like *Wuthering Heights* and *Shirley*.

On Thursday, 25th October 1860, Mrs Gaskell wrote (from Gargrave, Yorkshire) and asked Patrick if she might call, bringing with her her second daughter, Margaret Emily, known as Meta. Patrick, although confined to bed at that time, sent a note to say he would be most pleased to receive them. That Meta Gaskell was quite fascinated by Patrick is only too obvious from the most interesting account of her visit written to a friend on the following Saturday. ". . . What I want really to tell you about, is a visit which Mama and I paid to old Mr. Brontë to-day. We were talking about him on Thursday, and I was expressing a great wish to see him, out of which conversation sprung a plan for my going alone to call on him—Mama saying that she fancied he would not like to see her ; because so many reviews, letters in newspapers, etc ; which she knew had reached him, had dwelt on the way in which, while pretending to have been his daughter's friend, she had held up his character to ridicule, etc. etc. But, however, at length it seemed better that she'd go to [*sic*] ; to brave his displeasure if there were any, and to please him by the attention if there were none. So she wrote on Thursday evening to ask him if we might go. This she did, thinking that then, if he really had any objection to seeing her, it would give him the opportunity of preventing our visit. However, this morning there came a few tremulous, feeble lines to say he should be glad to see us ; and we scuttled through our breakfast and caught an 8.40 train, which took us to Keighley, and then we got a fly that brought us to Haworth by about 11.15.'Martha', such a blooming, bright, clean young woman, gave us a hearty welcome ; and took us into the parlour (Miss B.'s sitting-room), where we waited for about ¼ of an hour ; when she came to fetch us to Mr. B.—Mama had no idea he was confined to bed, as he is now—we were taken into his bedroom ; where everything was delicately clean and white, and there he was sitting propped up in bed in a clean nightgown, with a clean towel laid just for his hands to play upon—looking Oh ! very different from the stiff scarred face above the white walls of cravat in the photograph—he had a short soft white growth of beard on his chin ; and such a gentle, quiet, sweet, half-pitiful expression on his mouth, a good deal of soft white hair, and spectacles on. He shook hands with us, and we sat down, and then said how glad he was to see Mama—and she said how she had hesitated about coming,—feeling as if he might now have unpleasant associations with her—which never seemed to have entered into his head—then he asked her how, since he last saw her, she had passed through this weary and varied world—in a sort of half grandiloquent style—and then interrupting himself he said 'but first tell me how is that young lady, whose friend went to the Massacres in India ?' I thought he meant the Ewarts, or something, and was quite surprised (besides other things) when Mama pointed to me, and said I was here, and then he prosecuted his inquiries about the engagement, and its breaking off [Meta Gaskell's engagement to an officer, which had been broken off] ; and then turned round and told me that he hoped I would forget the past ; and would hope—that we ought all to live on hope.—Then he told Mama how many, many applications he had for bits of Miss B's handwriting,—how he had to cut up her letters into strips of a line each.—He talked of her as simply 'Charlotte' without any hesitation—He said to Mama—'As I told you in my first letter, the *Memoir* is a book which will hand your name down to posterity,' and that there was only one fault he had to find with it ; might he speak out openly before me ? Mama told him he might, and we both sat expecting some allusion to the Lady S[cott]'s past—but what he said was that the statement that he had not allowed his children to have meat till they were (a certain age) had been quoted by either Mr. Carus Wilson, or his defenders, as more likely to have been the cause of their delicacy than the fare they subsequently had at Cowan's Bridge. Now—this statement was a mistake. His children had always been allowed meat ; but he said he had chosen not to defend himself at the expense of proving Mama inaccurate : and so giving a handle to those who accused her of mis-statements—I wish I could remember more of what he said.

"He very soon turned the conversation to politics : asked Mama whether she thought the English ought to interfere in Italian affairs at present, or wait till the Italians asked for help; and seemed very much pleased when she said she thought we ought to hold back for the present. 'You see we agree in politics as in everything else.' He had been *very* much pleased with Thackeray's notice in the *Cornhill*—he thought it showed 'heart, but Thackeray was an odd man, a very odd man.' He alluded to his own 'eccentricity' with a certain pride; and his 'independence', too, of other people's opinion; not but what he valued the opinion of good people—Mama said: 'Yes—I was just telling my daughter as we came up the hill, that I thought you had always done what you thought right.'—'And so I have,' he said, 'and I appeal to God.' There was something very solemn in the way he said it; and in him altogether —None of the sternness I had fancied—Mama said something about our not staying too long to tire him and that we were going, for me to make a sketch; and he said, 'There are certain circumstances, you see,' looking very knowing, 'which make it desirable that when you leave in 5 minutes or so, we should shake hands—and I give your daughter free leave to make a sketch, or do anything *outside* the house. Do you understand Latin? Mrs Gaskell does at any rate, well, *Verbum sap.*, a word to the wise,' and then he chuckled very much; the gist of it was, as Mama saw, and I guessed, that he feared Mr. Nicholls's return from the school—and we were to be safely out of the house before that. Mama is telling Mr. Shaen all about the sexton. Just before leaving Haworth we went to call on John Greenwood; and whilst Mama was talking to him, his wife volunteered to me how she disliked Mr N., as they all seemed to do—(The sexton [William Brown] said, 'Aye, Mester Brontë and Mr Nicholls live together still *ever near* but *ever separate*', and he told us how when the fresh monument was put up in the church [to the memory of Mrs Brontë and the six children—there being no space for Charlotte's name on the original], Mr N. made him take the old tablet-stone, and with a hammer break it into small pieces, which he then bade, and saw, him bury 4 ft. deep in the garden: for fear any one should get hold of a piece for a relic). Well—Mrs Greenwood had a puny, precocious little lad clinging to her dress, about 17m$\frac{1}{2}$ old [he was born on 12th March 1859]—so of course I asked its name, and she said, 'Brontë, Miss. Eh, Mr Nicholls was angry a' that.' He heard they were going to give it the name; and said in Mr B's hearing that he wouldn't christen the child, whereupon Mr. B. sent word by Martha of his determination to the Greenwoods, to spare them the annoyance of a direct refusal, so they kept the child unchristened till it was 6 months old when it became so ailing that they thought it wouldn't live; and Mr. B. hearing of this, sent for it (as far as I understood) to his own bedroom (it is a year since his health began to fail) and christened it there ; having the Register-book for baptisms, and writing down its name with his own hand. [14th November 1859.] It was years since he had christened a child. Of course the next baby Mr. N. condescended to christen, he went to write its name down, and there saw Mr B.'s registration of the christening of little Brontë Greenwood. Mrs. G. said that there and then he strode straight back to the Parsonage, and up into Mr B's bedroom ; and 'So I see you have christened your namesake.' And Mr B. got out of it by saying that he had done it to save Mr N. from the terrible scrape in which he would have found himself, had the child died unchristened, etc. But this is a specimen of Mr N's sullen, obstinate rooted objection to any reverence being paid to Miss B. one might almost say at any rate to people caring to remember her as an authoress. . . ." [Brontë Greenwood thrived and flourished in the United States of America.]

Mrs Gaskell also relates her visit to Haworth in a letter to W. S. Williams of Smith, Elder & Co. dated 20th December 1860. ". . . About six weeks ago I paid a visit to Mr Brontë, and sat for about an hour with him. He is completely confined to bed now, but talks hopefully of leaving it again when the summer comes round. I am afraid that it will not be leaving it as he plans, poor old man ! He is touchingly softened by illness ; but still talks in his pompous way, and mingles moral remarks and somewhat stale sentiments with his conversation on ordinary subjects. Mr Nicholls seems to keep him rather *in terrorem. He* is more unpopular in the village than ever ; and seems to have even a greater aversion than formerly to any strangers visiting his wife's grave ; or, indeed, to any reverence paid to her memory, even by those who knew and loved her for her own sake. . . ." Then follows the story of the christening of little Brontë Greenwood in exactly the same terms as those used by Meta.

Even at this stage there is an air of flippancy in Mrs Gaskell's mention of Patrick that destroys one's resolution to forgive her. Well might she have hesitated before making that final visit. Yet had she known her man, as she once claimed she did, then she would have guessed that all was forgiven and forgotten. Indeed, the only remark Patrick was heard to make in these later years was, "Mrs Gaskell has made us all appear as bad as she possibly could", but he was thinking of the people of Haworth, not himself.

Patrick, anxious his servants should possess copies of his daughters' works, gave Martha *Wuthering Heights, Villette*, the first edition of *The Tenant of Wildfell Hall*, and *Shirley*, as well as his own *Cottage Poems. Shirley* was inscribed : "A Gift to Martha Brown, by the

Revd P. Brontë A.M. Min^r of Haworth, July 15th 1858". Tabitha Brown was given a first edition of *The Life of Charlotte Brontë* in October 1858 (for all that it contained), Martha receiving her copy from Mrs Gaskell.

As for Arthur Nicholls, he was indeed becoming extremely unpopular again and the trustees were already murmuring against him. Soon they would act decisively once more, as will be seen in the next chapter.

As 1860 neared its end, Patrick rallied a little, gaining strength from the crisp, frosty weather; but as the New Year came in, he grew suddenly much weaker and, after only a week or two of being downstairs, was forced to remain in bed, never to quit it again. Martha Brown nursed her old master with unstinted devotion as the months passed and he became weaker and weaker. His bronchitis became chronic and his dyspepsia troubled him after even the lightest nourishment. January, February, March, April and May came and went, and as the summer sun shone brightly on the village and moors, and still it was always Nicholls who appeared, the people knew they had already bade farewell to their old parson, who had lived and worked and suffered amongst them for so many years.

Those first days of June 1861 were hot, almost sultry days, and in his bedroom Patrick was murmuring to himself as his mind wandered. What did he see in his imagination as he lay there dying? Was there the preacher galloping along the lanes of Ireland, were there the hills of Mourne blue against the afternoon sun? Did he walk again the cloistered calm of Cambridge, and with Mary Burder across the Essex meadows? There, surely, was the Wrekin, with stout Morgan and Nunn toiling up its slopes. There also must be Robin Tweed to bark a welcome; and a frightened half-witted face as a poor youth was drowning in the Calder : Patrick stirred in his bed with the effort of rescue and Martha smoothed down his sheets. Then Patrick was back at Dewsbury again, hurling bullies across the road and brandishing his shillelagh over the heads of astonished bell-ringers. He saw dimly the little old church of St Peter's at Hartshead and thought he heard the faint clink of spades as the Luddites secretly buried their dead by night. There was the soft enchantment of Woodhouse Grove and he saw through his tears the beloved face of his sweet Maria ; they were walking together by Kirkstall Abbey and in the scented Calverley Woods. He would write his next book soon and fill it with poems about Maria. He was sure he could write a beautiful poem, like Anne or Charlotte or . . . Patrick's thoughts were at once moved into the garden of Kipping House and there were all his children playing happily around him, only they were not children, but grown up and strange-looking ; and there was Elizabeth Firth talking to someone who looked like Fennell. . . . Martha moved her chair slightly and Patrick's waking dreams took a new shape. He could see and hear Stephen Taylor shouting from the top deck of his own pulpit, "We won't have you—we will have you—we, the Trustees, alone can decide !"

Then he saw Maria again, but she was dead ; so was his little mother, his dearest Maria ; and Elizabeth, and Branwell was not there to grieve, he was no doubt out at the Bull again drinking himself stupid— he must go and fetch him home ! Martha's gentle hands pushed him back on to the pillow as he tried to rise. She knew nothing of his wanderings until she saw his hand caressing the air beside him and she knew that it was old Keeper he was stroking. Patrick's mind was now all confusion : Emily must be home soon, it was getting dark and she was out on the moors, Branwell was drunk and raving again—what had he done to deserve such a son ?—Oh ! his dear little Anne would die, let Charlotte say what she will, he knew the signs, the doctor said he might save his sight but he must have the operation ; Oh, where was Emily ?—Poor old Tabby, she really was past all heavy work but he must keep her ; where had that scoundrel Nicholls taken his Charlotte, where was he hiding her ?—Let Mrs Gaskell and the world say what they liked, he *did* allow them all to eat meat, plenty of meat. Ah ! here at last was Emily with that light of eternity in her eyes. He was quite still now, and Martha left him gently sleeping ; in that last peaceful dream he saw the now radiant faces of all those he had buried, William Weightman, the old people, and the newborn babes. Perhaps he also saw a vision of things beyond the telling of man, a vision that showed him that the God he had served so faithfully, and for so long, was not unmindful of His humble servant at this, the moment of death.

Patrick Brontë died on the afternoon of Friday, 7th June 1861, in his eighty-fifth year. For some hours before the end he was seized with convulsions and, leaving Eliza Brown in the kitchen, Martha and Nicholls remained with him until the end. It was just after two o'clock (the hour when his beloved daughters Emily and Anne had died) that he fell back on his pillow at peace, and there was only the sound of his grandfather clock on the stairs, ticking away steadily, as Martha Brown and Arthur Nicholls gazed at each other in silence over his corpse. It would be a very long time before the people of Haworth could get used to the idea that there were no Brontës left to live in the old grey parsonage behind the Church. With the death of Patrick Brontë there passed away not only the last of that famous family but the final direct link with the great evangelical revival of the eighteenth century.

The certified cause of death was: "Chronic bronchitis; dyspepsia; convulsions, duration nine hours." Ellen Nussey was away in the Isle of Wight and wrote to inquire how Patrick had died. She received the following answer from Nicholls, which she afterwards termed "an ungracious reply":

Haworth Parsonage, June 18th 1861.

Dear Madam,

I have little information to communicate on the subject of your note. Mr. Brontë had been confined to his bed for several months, on Friday morning he was seized with convulsions and died in the course of the afternoon. I am, Dear Madam, Yours very truly,

A. B. Nicholls.

Patrick's will was proved on 28th June 1861 at Wakefield.

"In Her Majesty's Court of Probate: Wakefield District Registry. Probate of the Will of The Reverend Patrick Brontë deceased. Dated 28th June, 1861.

"Being of sound mind and judgment, in the name of God the Father, Son and Holy Ghost, I Patrick Brontë B.A. Incumbent of Haworth in the Parish of Bradford and County of York make this my last Will and Testament—I leave Forty Pounds to be equally divided amongst all my Brothers and Sisters to whom I gave considerable sums in times past—And I direct the same sum of Forty pounds to be sent for distribution to Mr Hugh Brontë, Ballinasceaugh, near Loughbrickland, Ireland. I leave Thirty pounds to my servant Martha Brown as a token of regard for long and faithful services to me and my children. To my beloved and esteemed Son in Law The Revd Arthur Bell Nicholls B.A. I leave and bequeath the residue of my Personal Estate of every description, which I shall be possessed of at my death for his own absolute benefit, and I make him my sole Executor and I revoke all former and other Wills. In witness whereof I, the said Patrick Brontë have to this my last Will contained in this sheet of paper set my hand this twentieth day of June, one thousand eight hundred and fifty-five— Patrick Brontë—

"Signed and acknowledged by the said Patrick Brontë as his Will in the presence of us present at the same time and who in his presence and in the presence of each other have hereunto subscribed our names as witnesses—Joseph Redman—Eliza Brown."

The administration paper shows that the estate was "sworn under £1500, and that the Testator died on the seventh day of June, 1861 . . . personal estate etc. etc. to the Reverend Arthur Bell Nicholls, Clerk, the sole executor."

Many obituary notices appeared. Like all such they glossed over the dark facts believed true and stressed only what was considered good. Only those who had known him found a true echo. *The Times* for Monday, 10th June 1861, had "Death of the Rev. Patrick Brontë, B.A.—On Friday afternoon last the Rev. Patrick Brontë, B.A., incumbent of the village of Haworth, in the West Riding of Yorkshire, died at his parsonage. The deceased was father of Charlotte, Anne, and Emily Jane Brontë, the authoresses originally well-known as Currer, Acton, and Ellis Bell. He was born on St. Patrick's-day 1777, and consequently was 84 years of age. His health had been declining for a considerable length of time, and for some hours prior to his death he was unable to articulate.

"Mr Brontë was himself an author, having at different periods written and published two small volumes of poems, chiefly on homely and rural subjects, and two prose compositions, one a tale of Irish life, and the other a pleasing little narrative entitled the 'Cottage in the Wood; or the Art of becoming Rich and Happy.' He was highly respected by the people among whom he lived. . . ."

The *Illustrated London News* under the heading "Obituary of Eminent Persons" recounts the main events of his life (with many errors) and concludes—"Literature was the solace and recreation of Mr Brontë's leisure; and several volumes of poems and tales were published by him. He was universally esteemed by the people among whom he lived, and his death is deeply lamented." This, at least, is true, for the older generation in Haworth today still tell of their grandparents' deep love for "Parson Pat".

In the *Bradfordian* for 1st September 1861, was a long notice, ". . . When Mr Bronte entered on the duties of his office [at Haworth], . . . the appearance of a really good man, and a true Christian produced no small excitement amongst them. . . ." Then followed several extracts from his poems. ". . . these books written by their father, first incited the little Brontes to attempt composition themselves; thus laying the foundation of their present world-wide fame. . . . But my task would be incomplete, were I to make no attempt to clear away some of the aspersions which have been thrown on his good name, in the life of his daughter Charlotte, by Mrs Gaskell. These aspersions were published in the first and second editions of that work, but were silently withdrawn in the third; a tacit acknowledgment that they were false. But the slander poison had gone forth, and not long since we heard that true Poet Gerrald [*sic*] Massey, in a lecture delivered in our Mechanics' Institute, retail the same untruths to the audience. I will, however, state that after he had visited the old minister at Haworth, he resolved that in future he would use every effort when he lectured on Charlotte

Bronte, to disabuse the public mind of the errors I have referred to. . . . Now that he has gone, let us never hear again these foul charges, but in future let his name be ever mentioned with respect, and his memory cherished by all."

The funeral was on Wednesday, 12th June 1861. The mourning card read: "In memory of Rev. Patrick Bronte, B.A. Incumbent of Haworth, who died June VII, MDCCCLXI, aged LXXXIV years." Some time previously an Order in Council had closed most of the old part of the churchyard against future burials; and the precincts of the church itself came under this closure, save that Patrick was allowed to be buried with his family. He was the last that could be interred within the church. Having ascertained that there was no objection to this from the Secretary of State, Nicholls had everything arranged for the funeral.

Just before noon they opened the little gate of the dead for the last time. Soon it would be walled up, for there were no Brontës left to be carried through on their way to glory. The Brontë family vault was opened for the last time also, to receive its senior member. After this there would be no more burials in St Michael's Church. The closing of the gate and the tomb marked the end of the real Brontë story. Haworth was still and silent that day. The village was thronged with mourners: a vast multitude waited in the churchyard to see the last journey of the parson who had served them for over forty-one years. The chief mourners were Mr Nicholls, Martha and Eliza Brown, Mrs Brown, and Nancy Wainwright, who came over from Bradford to bid adieu to her old master.

The *Bradford Review* recorded: "Great numbers of people had collected in the churchyard, and a few minutes before noon the corpse was brought out through the eastern gate of the garden leading into the churchyard. The Rev. Dr Burnet, Vicar of Bradford, read the funeral service, and led the way into the church, and the following clergymen were the bearers of the coffin: The Rev. Dr Cartman of Skipton; Rev. Mr Sowden of Hebden Bridge; the Incumbents of Cullingworth, Oakworth, Morton, Oxenhope [Mr Grant], and St John's, Ingrow [the Rev. William Mayne, then married to Fennell's daughter, Mary]. The chief mourners were the Rev. Arthur Bell Nicholls, son-in-law of the deceased; Martha Brown, the housekeeper; and her sister; Mrs Brown, and Mrs Wainwright. There were several gentlemen followed the corpse whom we did not know [the trustees]. All the shops in Haworth were closed, and the people filled every pew, and the aisles in the church, and many shed tears during the impressive reading of the service for the burial of the dead, by the vicar. The body of Mr Brontë was laid within the altar rails, by the side of his daughter

Charlotte. He is the last that can be interred inside of Haworth Church. On the coffin was this inscription: 'Patrick Brontë, died June 7th, 1861, aged 84 years'."

After the service was over and the coffin had been lowered into the vault, the mourners slowly filed from the church. Dr Burnet signed the registers: "Patrick Brontè—Haworth—June 12th—84—J. Burnet LL.D. Vicar." Then he followed the last of the congregation out into the sunlight. Thus they left Patrick sleeping amidst the ashes of genius.

CHAPTER 30

St Michael's

ALTHOUGH Dr Burnet was anxious that Arthur Nicholls should succeed to the living of Haworth—indeed he was rash enough to promise it to him—the people of Haworth in general, and the trustees in particular, were heartily sick of him. Indeed, they had only waited for their old parson's death before taking immediate steps to rid themselves of their moody curate. The excuse was not lacking, and as soon as Patrick was buried, the trustees informed the Vicar of Bradford that his choice of successor was wholly unacceptable to them. Once again the Ancient Charter of Queen Elizabeth the First's time, and the power it gave the people of Haworth, was brought into play.

The ready-made excuse the Haworth Church Land Trustees invoked for driving Nicholls down the hill (although in a less robust fashion than that used against Samuel Redhead) concerned their late chairman, Michael Heaton. This gentleman, one of the Heatons of Ponden House, lived at Royd House. Some months before Patrick's death, he died and his heir called at the parsonage to ask that representation be made so that Michael Heaton could be buried with his late wife in the family grave. Patrick, who was too feeble to take the funeral service, advised him to apply to Nicholls. The latter advised that, as that part of the churchyard was now closed for burials, nothing could be done in the matter ; whereupon the Heatons applied to the Secretary of State and leave was granted from Whitehall on 7th March 1860. As Patrick could not, and Nicholls would not, conduct the service, Grant came over from Oxenhope to bury Michael Heaton, who was laid next to his wife.

This naturally incensed the trustees against Nicholls more than ever, and when they learned that the latter had written to the Secretary of State in regard to his father-in-law's burial in the church, which had also come under the closure, they considered his inaction in the case of their late Chairman sufficient reason to rid themselves of an unpopular and unwanted cleric. Despite the strong recommendations of Dr Burnet, the trustees refused to consider Nicholls as their new incumbent. Once again they had exercised their powers under that famous Elizabethan Charter !

Shortly afterwards, Arthur Nicholls, who had waited so patiently for the living of Haworth and who had kept his promise to Charlotte that he would remain with her father until the end, went slowly down Kirkgate with all his belongings (including those many precious Brontë manuscripts); and there was not one who was sorry to see him go! Yet an obligation to Patrick was kept also, for Plato went with him to a happy home. The love Nicholls bore all the parsonage dogs was not the least trait in his favour.

Bitterly disappointed at his further frustration in the church, Nicholls returned to Ireland, where he soon afterwards resigned his clerical Orders to become a farmer and, in so doing, perhaps showed more of his true character than he had ever openly revealed whilst in the church. On 25th August 1864 he married again—his cousin, Mary Bell.

On 5th November 1861 Nicholls wrote to a clerical friend: "Hill House Banagher . . . There are extensive repairs going on at the Parsonage, I understand—I dare say I shall scarcely know it when I see it, but it will not be the same to me. I am busy farming in a very small way; we have two cows, a heifer & a calf. It affords me some little employment . . . the Rheumatism is still troublesome."

Yet to John Greenwood, Nicholls, for all his refusal to baptize his son, remained the last link with the Brontës. This, allied to the fact that Martha Brown was now with Nicholls in Ireland, prompted the kind stationer to write to the man who had wrecked his ecclesiastical career, first for Charlotte's sake and finally by his own stupid stubbornness. Nicholls answered thus:

Banagher—Kings Co. Ireland.

Dear Sir,
Nov. 25—1861.

Many thanks for your long and interesting letter on the sayings and doings at Haworth—I sincerely trust that you may not be subjected to any further annoyance from the proceedings of the persons you mention —It would be more creditable to them to let bygones be bygones and set themselves to restore peace and harmony to the parish—as far as I am concerned I have benefited very much by the change—My health is much better than it has been for some time—Martha also is stronger than she was, so that on the whole I am quite satisfied with the turn matters took, tho' I should rather not have got such an insight into the dispositions of some of my former neighbours—I have also to thank you for the prospectus of the photographic views of the locality about Haworth—I shall be glad to have some of them when I visit Hth next year as I hope to do. Believe me very truly yrs

A. B. Nicholls

The new incumbent of Haworth was the Reverend John Wade, M.A., a native of Bradford. In many respects a worthy cleric, Wade had one weakness, a great inferiority complex in having to follow the father of such a famous family, and he earned for himself the soubriquet, "the envious Wade". He it was who added the wing to the north side of the parsonage (1872), and under his incumbency the old church was pulled down. Yet as against this, it was while Wade was at Haworth that the village gained its independence from Bradford. "By an Order in Council dated 30th August 1864, this Church of St. Michael, Haworth, which hitherto had served as a Chapel of Ease to the Parish Church of Bradford with the status of a Parochial Chapelry, had a lawful and separate district assigned to it, constituting it a District Chapelry, to become a new Parish on the avoidance of the Vicarage of Bradford, the Rev^d Dr John Burnet, the present Vicar of Bradford. The assigned district comprehends that part of the Parish of Bradford called the Township of Haworth to the exclusion of the two hamlets of Far and Near Oxenhope already assigned to the Church of St. Mary at Uppertown. John Wade being then the Incumbent and George Merrall and William Wood the Churchwardens of the said Church."

Again we find that : '. . . Whereas it has been made to appear to us that certain tithes, or rent-charges in lieu thereof, arising within the District Chapelry of St. Michael, Haworth, in the county of York in the Diocese of Ripon, belong to the Incumbent of the Church of such district chapelry : now, we, the said Ecclesiastical Commissioners for England, acting in pursuance of the 'District Church Tithes Act 1865', do hereby declare that from and after the time of the publication of these presents in the London Gazette, pursuant to the provisions of the same Act, the said Church of the district chapelry of St. Michael, Haworth, aforesaid, shall be and be deemed to be a Rectory . . . this twenty-fifth day of July, in the year one thousand eight hundred and sixty seven."

As a result of this the tithes and rent-charges mentioned were purchased of Thomas Dixon, Bradford, the lay improprietor, by the Rev. John Wade and were conveyed to him and his successors in the benefice. In consequence of this restoration of tithes, Haworth Church became a rectory on the date of publication of the aforementioned, 6th August 1867, and Wade was the first rector. Finally, "In the month of November 1864, the graveyard of this Church of St. Michael, Haworth, was planted with trees."

The thorny questions, "Why was the old Haworth Church demolished in 1879 ?" and "Was the Brontës' tomb disturbed at that time ?" are still asked.

The storm of protest that arose when the danger of demolition was known and the many arguments that took place in the national press were considerable, but we must content ourselves by giving some extracts from the Minutes of a meeting held in Haworth on Wednesday evening, 28th May 1879, when the matter was thoroughly discussed, and a promise made that the Brontë grave would not be disturbed. We add two letters showing that the promise then made was kept, one by C. E. Wade, son of the rector responsible for the demolition, the other by the late M. H. Merrall, whose family have long associations with Haworth Church.

"The Chairman [Col. Barras] in opening the proceedings, read letters of apology which he had received from Mr. W. B. Ferrand J.P. the Lord of the Manor, and Mr Isaac Holden J.P. Oakworth House, who were unable to attend the meeting, but wrote sympathising with its objects [against demolition]. He afterwards stated that with regard to the remark of the rector that his duty was to keep a house of God, and not to keep a show-place for strangers, he wished to point out that the Queen kept two chapels, Wolsey and St. George's, at Windsor ; Dean Stanley kept Westminster Abbey, and the Bishop of London kept St. Paul's Cathedral, and allowed people to look through them as show places, so that the Vicar could not be far wrong in following such good examples.

"Mr. Empsall, the president of the Bradford Antiquarian Society, addressed the meeting at considerable length as to the history of the Church, and the desirability of preserving such ancient buildings. He stated that this was the only ancient church which existed in that part of the Riding, whilst other parts of the county had many of them, and which no one dared to interfere with. Concluding, he proposed : 'That, considering the early antiquity of Haworth Church, it is the opinion of this meeting that the said church ought not to be destroyed, and that every effort be made to preserve it by judicious restoration or enlargement.' Mr Wm. Greenwood, an old resident in the neighbour-hood, seconded the motion. Mr G. S. Taylor, whose grandfather had been a churchwarden for between 20 and 30 years, his father [Stephen Taylor] for the same period, and who had himself been churchwarden at the same time Mr Brontë was incumbent, deprecated the object of the meeting. He himself had been compelled to give up worshipping at the church because he could not obtain a sitting, above ten years ago, and he believed that anyone who constantly attended the church would not want it to be kept up. He mentioned that Mr. Michael Merrall had offered to give £5,000 for the erection of a new church—an offer which he felt sure they would not again have the chance of taking, and he urged upon them to accept it. They had had no offer similar to that of Mr Merrall from any person who had joined in the agitation. The agitators had gone much too far in their reproaches; neither Mr Wade nor Mr. Merrall was one-twentieth part as worthy of blame as they had been represented to be. It was not an insult to the memory of Charlotte Brontë but the highest honour that this proposal should have been made. (Applause.) How could Mr. Merrall have shown greater respect to her memory than by volunteering his money? He had seen the plans of the new church, and he was perfectly satisfied that the graves of her and her family, and indeed of any person to whom a monument had been raised in the church, would not be interfered with at all. Promises had been made which had fully satisfied Mr. Nicholls, the only living representative of the Brontë family, that all care would be taken of their remains. If Mr Wade had intended to destroy all traces of the Brontë family in connection with the building, would he not have begun long ago? When he made the alterations to the parsonage he did not destroy the part associated with Charlotte Brontë, but did nothing more than add a new wing. It had been said that another site would be offered; but who was to build the church if the site was to be given? (a Voice: 'The Antiquarians') The rebuilding of the church without the steeple would cost £5000, and probably the finished building would cost £10,000. Did they prefer before a new building, the present church with its square inconvenient pews? He moved as an amendment— 'That this meeting expresses entire confidence in the course which Mr Wade may adopt in regard to the offer received from Mr. Merrall for the rebuilding of Haworth Church.' Mr. S. Waite seconded the amendment. Dr. Maffey, of Bradford, who had at first some difficulty in obtaining a hearing, emphatically disclaimed on the part of the Antiquarian Society any intention of throwing dirt at Mr. Wade. The correspondence which had gone on in the papers had pained the Antiquarians as much as it must have done anyone in Haworth. He considered that the main question had been overlooked. The people of Haworth would like to have their old church left where it is, provided they might have it made comfortable. That was perfectly possible (a Voice: 'It's a lie', and disorder.) Going into the question of the age of the church, he said it was a church of Henry VII's time, and was built before 1500, the part now said to be tumbling down having only been erected 150 or 200 years. If the church were restored in keeping with its original form, as many architects could restore it, it would be one of the most beautiful churches in the West Riding. He spoke at length on the structure of the building, pointing out that many parts of it were of great antiquity. The principal structural alterations were made in 1755, during the time of the Rev. Wm. Grimshaw, when the aisle was widened, the galleries were added on three sides, and other alterations were made. With regard to accommodation, were the galleries now taken out, and the floor space filled with modern pews, there would be quite as many sittings, and he had been assured by a competent architect that of the oak boarding there was quite sufficient for the purpose. The members of the Historical Society had several times been asked where the money to do the alterations was to come from ? He could assure the Haworth people that there would be money in abundance; and it would not involve more than a fourth of the expenditure to restore the church which would be required to rebuild it. He asked them to carry the resolution moved by Mr Empsall. He would remind them that every parishioner, Dissenter or Churchman, had a perfect right to be heard before the Consistory Court at Ripon, and either to ask that the church should be left to them as at present, or that it should be restored. (Applause)

"The original resolution was carried by a large majority. It was resolved, on the motion of Mr. Cudworth, Secretary of the Bradford Antiquarian Society, that copies of the foregoing resolution should be forwarded to the Lord Bishop of Ripon, the Rector of Haworth, and Mr. Michael Merrall."

On Thursday, 19th June 1879, a Consistory Court was held in the nave of Ripon Cathedral and all objections to the request for the demolition of Haworth Church were fully considered. Alas, however, the old place was doomed. A Faculty was granted allowing the work to proceed.

Happily, the old tower was spared and stands with the new church today, still notched with Patrick's bullets. The last service in the old church was held on Sunday, 14th September 1879, to a more than crowded congregation.

Here are the two letters in connection with the Brontës' tomb.

39, Regent's Park Road, London W.1

Dear Sir,

Thanks for your letter received this morning. As regards the Brontë grave, I can assure you that you were quite right in assuming that the remains were left in the vault at the time of rebuilding. As you observe, no authorisation was either asked for or given by the Faculty to deal therewith. The Brontë grave was in no way interfered with and the remains were left as they were placed at their funerals.

Over their graves, as over the others, was laid a thick layer of concrete (how necessary, those who knew the Old Church will remember) upon which the present Edifice stands. I will repeat as emphatically as I can, on the authority of my Father, spoken scores of times in my hearing, that undisturbed in their original burial place that gifted family were left. Above them is now the protective covering of concrete, and unless some mighty convulsion (or a new Faculty) shatters them, there they will lie for ever.

Yours truly, C. E. Wade.

But no concrete holds down their immortal souls: they are free, like the moorland winds.

Law House—Haworth.
Dear Rector,
Thanks for sending me Mr Wade's letter, which I now enclose. It seems to furnish quite conclusive proof that the Brontë vault was not disturbed. As regards the "thick layer of concrete" which was laid on the old graves, I am sure it would be necessary. I can well remember the vault-like smell of the old church.

Very truly yours, M. H. Merrall.

The story ends with the great kindness shown to Martha Brown by Nicholls. Once her enemy, he became her friend, inviting her to Ireland many times and writing frequent letters to her in Yorkshire. Martha's first visit was in 1862, after she had worked for Dr Ingham of Haworth for some months. In August of that year, leaving Martha as servant at Hill House, Banagher, Nicholls revisited Haworth, staying with Grant and calling on Mrs Brown and Tabitha. Martha came back at the year's end. On 12th December 1863 Nicholls informs her ". . . Plato is very well—He was getting very thin; so I made them give him some dinner. . . ."

On 7th September 1864: "We were married on Augt 25th and arrived here the following day [Upper Bangor, North Wales]."

Again he writes to Martha: ". . . I don't think Jemmy Whitham would be a good match for you—you must be careful how you commit yourself in that way. . . ." 25th March 1865: ". . . I was glad to hear that you had so far recovered as to be able to return to Dr. Ingham's . . . I should like something more to do than I have here. . . ." 24th August 1865: ". . . I am really very sorry that I can't comply with your request to send one of the small magazines for Mrs. Greenwood. I got one to enclose to you: but when I looked at the handwriting I could not bring myself to part with it—I have not anything else that I could send you. . . ." 8th May 1866: "Dear Martha . . . Poor Plato died about a fortnight ago; he had become very helpless, wasted away like Keeper. . . ."

On several occasions Nicholls sent Martha a money order for £1 or £2. In September Martha prepared for another visit to Ireland. Nicholls notified her that "The steamer will leave the *Clarence Dock*, Liverpool. . . ." She remained for more than a year. Nicholls continues, 16th January 1868: ". . . Edwin Feather has not returned the Photograph—Mrs. Nicholls is uneasy about it. . . ." 2nd March 1868: ". . . I hope you have got your Manchester money . . . I think either Mr. Bronte or I tried to have it paid in Keighley & failed. I trust Mr. Wade may be more successful. . . ." 27th April 1868: ". . . We shall be all pleased to see you in Autumn & hope that you will settle to stay with us. I don't think that there is any necessity for you to be working when your health is not good, and you know that your Mistress & Master would not have wished you to do so; neither would I. . . ." 17th July 1868: ". . . I hope you will soon be able to come to us . . . I can't see that there is any necessity for you to go on working when you can have a comfortable home with us. . . ."

Martha stayed for another year at Banagher and further visits were paid at the end of 1870, in 1876 and 1878. Between these visits she had lived for some years with her sister Ann Binns at Saltaire (between Keighley and Bradford) from whose husband, Benjamin, Nicholls ordered black and white tweeds.

But after her last journey to Ireland Martha came back to Haworth to be near the rest of her family and lived the last year of her life in Stubbing Lane at the foot of the hill, surrounded by Brontë souvenirs. She never married, and maintained to the last that, at the parsonage, she had never been treated "like a housegirl, but as one of the family" and that "a kinder man could not be than Mr. Brontë". She died on Monday, 19th January 1880, in her fifty-second year, almost immediately after the destruction of the old church. She is buried with her parents just outside the south wall of the parsonage garden not very far from her "rival" Tabby.

From Ireland Nicholls wrote to Robert Ratcliffe (husband of Martha's sister Tabitha):

Jany 20th 1880

Dear Sir,

Herewith I send to you as one of the Executors the following documents.

Viz. Will of Martha Brown

1. Certificate for £100 Great Western Guaranteed Stock.

2. Certificate for £50 Great Eastern Railway 5 per ct Stock

3. Certificate for £48 North Eastern Railway Consols —

B. Binns and you will kindly sign the receipt for same and return it to me —

We were greatly distressed by the news of Martha's death. Yrs. very truly

A.B. Nicholls.

If there was not one spiritual word in all those letters, it mattered little, for the former curate had become the kindly farmer.

As for the rest of those surviving links with Patrick, the story can soon be told.

John Greenwood did not long outlive the last of the family he admired so greatly. He died on 25th March 1863 aged fifty-six.

Mrs Gaskell died on 12th November 1865, only some four years after Patrick.

Margaret Wooler lived to be ninety-three, dying on 3rd June 1885 ; whilst Ellen Nussey died on 26th November 1897, aged eighty.

Arthur Bell Nicholls died at Banagher, King's County, Ireland, on Monday, 2nd December 1906, in his eighty-eighth year. His second wife died on 27th February 1915.

Martha Brown's sister Tabitha (Mrs Ratcliffe) had lived until 30th November 1910.

But one cannot help wondering what became of Cato. Did he go to Ireland with Nicholls and Plato or find a new master in Haworth ? Let us hope he lived to enjoy a kind home and a happy life, for he was one of the last two living creatures to love Patrick, and to be beloved by him.

Valedictory

IN GIVING the long life-story of Patrick Brontë the intention has been to show not only his famous family but also those friends and acquaintances amongst whom his days were spent. We have attempted to picture him against the historical background of his time, and to bring to life the village and people of Haworth who have been so sadly neglected in Brontë biographies. The family at the parsonage has always been depicted as a solitary one, having no contact with people outside, and Patrick in particular as having arrived in the place where he would spend half his life without previous friendships.

Can it be doubted that to call Patrick Brontë "a man of sorrow" is fully justified, when one reads the sad shape of his existence? Besides losing all his beloved family, he survived his most faithful old servant, his favourite pets and nearly all his friends. His son, in whom he had such great hopes, proved a trial and a disgrace to him, a shame which would be revealed to the eager world. All his mature life Patrick was to be in fear of complete blindness; and, finally, when in old age he derived such a joy of anticipation in the publication of his daughter Charlotte's biography, he was to find that in it he was sullied and abused by the most absurd accusations.

When he died there was no one to remember what he had done. His own modesty in his letters to Mrs Gaskell had not made easy such a discovery, and the Unitarian novelist and the Puseyite curate were hardly the people to understand or sympathize. So, with only Martha's devotion remaining, Patrick had outlived his age. The old ways were outmoded, the old language no longer spoken, the old fervour gone.

Who was there left to speak for him as his name was attacked by those who knew nothing of what he had been? Palmerston, the only surviving acquaintance from earlier days, was a busy Prime Minister.

Yet Patrick could die triumphant. The Evangelical foothold in the Church was maintained: indeed Palmerston was openly encouraging the appointment of Evangelicals as Bishops; the Wesleyans remained strong and free; his own earthly ministry was faithfully done and his daughter Emily would lead a host as yet unborn to see "by faith through nature to nature's God".

Letters written by or to the Brontës, as well as other material, are still coming to light as the years pass. Further facts about Patrick Brontë will yet be learned. Meanwhile we have followed his long and faithful journey and, we hope, cleared some of the entanglements of ignorance and falsehood which, for over a century, have obscured that path.

We have tried to show him as a youth, an undergraduate, curate, lover, author, husband, father and clergyman of the Church of England. We have also attempted to deal with his interest in military matters, politics, science, medicine, and the law, and to tell of his great love for and kindness to children and animals. As we said at the beginning, Patrick Brontë was no hero, nor yet the dark villain he has been painted. Perhaps there is no hero or heroine in the Brontë story (who could choose between Anne's patient courage, Charlotte's brave energy, or Emily's gigantic strength when on her beloved moors ?). Perhaps there is no complete villain either (the brutal Uncle Burder ? Carus Wilson, the harsh Calvinistic cleric ? the wicked Lydia Robinson ? the weak, degenerate Branwell ? or the gloomy Nicholls ?—all have their avid detractors).

When all is said and done, however, the real abiding strength of Patrick's life, the only consolation that enabled him to face his continual sorrows as bravely as he did, was his quite unshakable faith in the ultimate mercy of God. Never once did his trust in Christ waver as blow after blow rained down on his unbowed head. From the ever-lasting hills, too, he derived courage, fortitude, and tranquillity of mind—as a young lad from the Mourne mountains, and then, later, from those wild, beautiful, heathery moors that surround Haworth on every side and look down upon that old church tower, under the shadow of which, for over forty-one years, the incumbent was the Reverend Patrick Brontë.

ACKNOWLEDGEMENTS

THE authors wish to express their gratitude to all those clergymen whose churches and chapels are listed in the Sources of Evidence and who are too numerous to mention here.

Our thanks go also to the commissioners, trustees, registries, societies (both clerical and literary), universities, public libraries, museums, record offices, private companies, colleges, schools, etc., also listed there, and to many individuals as well, for their permission to examine and use letters and documents in their possession.

We are especially grateful to the late Frederick A. T. Mossman (former diocesan Registrar for Bradford); Geoffrey Beard, F.L.A. (former Secretary to the Brontë Society); Miss Frances Branwell of Penzance; the late Eleanor Stanton of Haworth (niece of Martha Brown and daughter of Tabitha Ratcliffe); the Rev. Archie Bradford; Mary Preston and Arthur Hartley of Haworth; and Mrs F. G. Sutcliffe.

We owe a great debt to Winifred Gérin, who besides constant practical assistance placed her vast knowledge of the Brontës, and especially of Charlotte, Branwell and Anne, entirely at our disposal.

But our greatest sense of acknowledgement is to Patrick Brontë himself; we merely had to find and follow that long path he trod so courageously in life.

List of Sources

ORIGINAL LETTERS AND DOCUMENTS

Patrick Brontë's ordination testimonials: Lambeth Palace Library (Fulham Palace Papers Box No. 32).

The Archbishop's Registers: York.

Letters of Patrick Brontë and Henry Heap; nomination papers, Testimonials, etc.: Benefice Papers, Diocesan Records, The Borthwick Institute of Historical Research, York.

Brontë probate papers: York Probate Records, The Borthwick Institute of Historical Research, York.

Letters of Patrick Brontë: The Church Commissioners, London.

The Bishop's Act Books: Bishop of London's Registry, Westminster.

The Bishop's Registers: Diocesan Registry, Salisbury, Wiltshire.

Registers, documents, etc.: Diocesan Registry, Bradford, Yorkshire.

The Episcopal Registers: Diocese of St David's, The National Library of Wales.

Letters of Patrick Brontë, A. B. Nicholls, J. B. Grant, S. Sowden, W. Cartman, Dr Burnet, and documents: The Archives, The Society for the Propagation of the Gospel, London S.W.1.

Details of grant for Rev Wm. Weightman: The Minute Books, The Church Pastoral-Aid Society, London E.C.4.

Letters of Patrick Brontë and official documents: In the possession of the Haworth Church Land Trustees.

Registers, minute books, documents, memorials and tombstones of the following churches and chapels: Drumballyroney Church, Co. Down; Holy Trinity, Cambridge; St Mary Magdalene, Wethersfield, Essex; Wethersfield Congregational Church, Wethersfield, Essex; St Peter's, Colchester, Essex; St Peter's, Glenfield, Leicestershire; St Mary's, Broughton Astley, Leicestershire; St Chad's, Shrewsbury, Shropshire; St Mary's Shrewsbury, Shropshire; All Saints, Wellington, Shropshire; All Saints, Thorndon, Suffolk; St Cynog, Boughrood, Radnorshire; St Michael's, Madeley, Shropshire; St James's, Slaithwaite, Yorkshire; All Saints, Dewsbury, Yorkshire; St Peter's, Hartshead, Yorkshire; St John the Evangelist, Bierley, Yorkshire; Christ Church, Liversedge, Yorkshire; St John the Evangelist, Dewsbury Moor, Yorkshire; St Peter's, Birstall, Yorkshire; St Madron, Penzance, Cornwall; St Mary's, Penzance, Cornwall; St Oswald's, Guiseley, Yorkshire; the former Christ Church, Bradford, Yorkshire; The Old Bell Chapel, Thornton, Yorkshire; St James's, Thornton, Yorkshire; Kipping Chapel, Thornton, Yorkshire; St Peter's (Bradford Cathedral), Yorkshire; St Paul's, Cross Stone, Yorkshire; St Mary's, Todmorden, Yorkshire; St John the Evangelist, Great Horton, Bradford, Yorkshire; St Wilfred's, Calverley, Yorkshire; St Mary's, Luddenden, Yorkshire; St Peter's Huddersfield, Yorkshire; St Michael and All Angels, Haworth, Yorkshire; West Lane Methodist Church, Haworth, Yorkshire; West Lane Baptist Church, Haworth, Yorkshire; Hall Green Strict Baptist Chapel, Haworth, Yorkshire; St Mary the Virgin, Oxenhope, Yorkshire; Stanbury Church, Yorkshire; Christ Church, Oakworth, Yorkshire; St Andrew's, Keighley, Yorkshire; Temple Street Methodist Church, Keighley, Yorkshire; St John the Evangelist, Ingrow-cum-Hainworth, Yorkshire; St Mary the Virgin, Gomersal, Yorkshire; Christ Church, Sowerby Bridge, Yorkshire; St John the Baptist, Tunstall, Lancashire; Christ Church, Colne, Lancashire; St Lawrence's, Appleby, Westmorland; The United Anglican Church, Brussels; St Mary the Virgin, Westmill, Hertfordshire; All Saints, Bingley, Yorkshire; Holy Trinity, Skipton-in-Craven, Yorkshire; Holy Trinity, Little Ouseburn, Yorkshire; St Mary's, Scarborough, Yorkshire; Christ Church, Scarborough, Yorkshire; Christ Church, Woodhouse, Huddersfield, Yorkshire; All Saints, Hulcott, Buckinghamshire; St Mary's, Kirk Smeaton, Yorkshire.

Letters of Patrick Brontë—his diaries, notebooks, sermons, first editions of his works, books, personal effects and other material belonging to him; letters, documents, and material relating to his children and others: Belonging to the Brontë Society at the Brontë Parsonage Museum, Haworth.

Letters, documents, books of the Brown family; old voting registers, old street maps, diaries, etc.: Belonging to the people of Haworth.

Letters, diary and documents of John Greenwood: Belonging to Mrs Mary Preston, Haworth, Yorkshire.

Letters and documents: Belonging to the Authors.

Letters, copies of deeds, etc.: Belonging to the Ashley Library, Department of Rare MSS., British Museum.

Details of Wm Morgan's son: The Records, The Middle Temple, London.

Copies of Marriage and Death Certificates: From the General Registry Office, Somerset House, London.

Letters of Patrick Brontë and others, documents etc.: The General Board of Health (Ministry of Health Papers, 1839) At Ministry of Works, London.

Letters of Patrick Brontë: War Office Records (Ordnance Office), Public Record Office.

The Registers: St John's College, Cambridge.

The Registers: Trinity College, Dublin.

Letter of Patrick Brontë to Rev. Wm Campbell: Department of Rare Books, Princeton University, U.S.A.

Books and manuscripts: Berg Collection, New York Public Library, U.S.A.

Elizabeth Firth's Diaries, 1812–25, 1829: Sheffield University Library, Yorkshire.

Letters of Patrick Brontë to the Gaskells: The Christie Library, Manchester University.

Letter of Patrick Brontë to Revd Wm Gaskell: Central Library, Manchester.

Letters of Branwell Brontë, documents, etc.: The Brotherton Library, University of Leeds.

Details of Patrick Brontë's stay in Brussels: Registre des Etrangers pour l'Année 1842—aux Archives de la Ville de Bruxelles.

Letters of Patrick Brontë, A. B. Nicholls, and Wm Scoresby: The Heaton Collection, Cartwright Memorial Hall, Bradford.

The Eyton Collection (6656002): The Archives, Salop Record Office.

Documents and relics at Oakwell Hall, Birstall, Yorkshire: The Oakwell Hall Estate Committee.

The Registers: Woodhouse Grove School, Apperley Bridge, Bradford, Yorkshire.

The Registers: Casterton School, Carnforth, Kirkby Lonsdale, Westmorland.

The Registers: Harrow School.

Documents relating to Patrick Brontë: Yorkshire Bank Ltd, Keighley, Yorkshire.

The Records: Undercliffe Cemetery, Bradford, Yorkshire.

Patrick Brontë's Will: District Probate Registry, Wakefield, Yorkshire.

A Survey with Maps of Lands Lying within the counties of York and Lancaster Belonging to Richard Emmott, Esq.—R. Lang and T. Addison, (1769): Documents of Rawdon Estate.

PERIODICALS, NEWSPAPERS, ETC.

Newspapers, periodicals, etc.: Preserved in the British Museum Newspaper Library, Colindale, London N.W.9.

Brontë Society Transactions: Fourteen volumes, 72 parts—1895–1962.

The Arminian/Wesleyan Methodist Magazine: 1798–1812.

Pigot's Yorkshire Directory: 1841, 1848.

Indicateur Belge: 1840.

Leeds Mercury: November 10th, 1810; August 10th, 1811; April 18th, 1812; April 25th, 1812; May 16th, 1812; September 1824 (various dates).

Leeds Mercury Supplement: March 25th, 1893.

Morning Chronicle: July 25th, 1811.

'A Day at Haworth': *The Todmorden and Hebden Bridge Historical Almanack*, 1880.

'Thornton Old Chapel': W. E. Preston, *The Bradford Antiquary*, vol. 6— Bradford, 1921.

The Bookman: October, 1904.

Scribner's Monthly Magazine, May, 1871: Ellen Nussey: 'Reminiscences of Charlotte Bronte'.

The Pastoral Visitor, August 1816 (Bradford): Review of *The Cottage in the Wood* by the Rev. William Morgan.

The Cottage Magazine (edited by Rev. John Buckworth): January 1812 and 1813, November 1816, June 1817, January 1825.

Halifax Guardian (1857): May 23rd, June 6th, June 13th, July 4th, July 11th, July 18th, August 1st, August 8th.

Halifax Examiner: July 1857.

Lancaster Guardian: December 1837.

Cornhill Magazine: vol. 1, 1860.

Armagh Guardian: August 16th, 1957.
Bradfordian: October 1860–December 1861, Abraham Holroyd, Bradford, 1862.
Bradford Observer: February 17th, 1894, and May 15th, 1895.
Yorkshire Observer: November 22nd, 1934.
Yorkshire Post: September 12th, 1894.
Shrewsbury Gazeteer: December 15th, 1809.
The Keighley News: April 3rd, 1886.
The Nelson Gazette: June 7th, 1938.
The Times: February 27th, 1837, August 7th, 1860, June 10th, 1861.
Leeds Intelligencer: September 16th, 1824; January 15th and 29th, 1829; February 5th, 1829; May 6th, 1830; February 25th, 1837.
Illustrated London News: June 22nd, 1861.
London Gazette: August 6th, 1867.
'Eminent Men and Popular Books': An extract from *The Times* of April 25th, 1857 (Routledge, Warne, & Routledge, 1860).
Brontë Files: Compiled by William Scruton (Bradford, 1894).
The Sphere: August 23rd and 30th, 1913.
Report to the General Board of Health on the Sanitary Condition of Haworth, 1850: Benjamin Herschel Babbage, 1850.
Manor Rolls of Haworth: Bradford Antiquarian Society.
The Grimshaw Family: Rev. Frank Baker, B.A., B.D. (Halifax Antiquarian Society, November 3rd, 1945).

WORKS BY THE REV^D PATRICK BRONTË AND HIS FAMILY

The Rev. Patrick Brontë's Collected Works: Edited by J. Horsfall Turner, T. Harrison & Sons, Bingley, 1898.
Winter-Evening Thoughts, P. Brontë, B.A. (Anon.): Longman, Hurst, Rees & Orme, London, and John Hurst, Wakefield, 1810.
Cottage Poems: Rev. Patrick Brontë, B.A., P. K. Holden, Halifax, 1811.
The Rural Minstrel: Rev. Patrick Brontë, A.B., P. K. Holden, Halifax, 1813.
The Cottage in the Wood: Rev. Patrick Brontë, A.B., T. Inkersley, Bradford, 1815.
The Maid of Killarney: Rev. Patrick Brontë, A.B. (Anon.), Baldwin, Cradock, & Joy, London, 1818.
The Phenomenon: Rev. Patrick Brontë, A.B., T. Inkersley, Bradford, 1824.
A Sermon Preached in the Church of Haworth, in reference to an Earthquake: Rev. Patrick Brontë, A.B., T. Inkersley, Bradford, 1824.
The Signs of the Times: P. Bronte, A.B., R. Aked, Keighley, 1835.
A Brief Treatise on the Best Time and Mode of Baptism: P. Bronte, A.B., R. Aked, Keighley, 1836.
A Funeral Sermon for the Late Rev. William Weightman, M.A.: Rev. Patrick Brontê, A.B., J. U. Walker, Halifax, 1842.
'On Halley's Comet in 1835': P. Bronte, *The Bradfordian,* August 1861.
'On Conversion': Rev. Patrick Brontë, *The Pastoral Visitor,* 1815.
Letter from 'Sydney': Rev. Patrick Brontë, *Leeds Mercury,* December 15th, 1810.

'Cremation': Patrick Brontë, *Leeds Mercury*, March 16th, 1844.
Wuthering Heights: Emily Brontë, Smith, Elder & Co., 1893 and Oxford
University Press, 1955.
Jane Eyre, Shirley, Villette, and *The Professor:* Charlotte Brontë, separate
volumes, Smith, Elder & Co., 1893.
Emma—A Fragment: Charlotte Brontë, *Cornhill Magazine,* vol. 1, 1860.
The Twelve Adventurers and Other Stories: Charlotte Brontë, Hodder &
Stoughton, 1925.
Agnes Grey and *The Tenant of Wildfell Hall:* Anne Brontë, separate volumes,
Smith, Elder & Co., 1893.
Poems by Currer, Ellis and Acton Bell: Aylott & Jones, London, 1846.
The Complete Poems of Emily Jane Brontë: Edited by C. W. Hatfield, Oxford
University Press, 3rd edition, 1952.
The Poems of Emily Jane Brontë and Anne Brontë: Edited by T. J. Wise and
J. A. Symington, The Shakespeare Head Press, Oxford, 1934.
*The Miscellaneous and Unpublished Writings of Charlotte and Patrick Branwell
Brontë* (vol. 2): Edited by T. J. Wise and J. A. Symington, The Shakespeare
Head Press, Oxford, 1938.

OTHER PUBLISHED WORKS

THEOLOGICAL, HISTORICAL AND SOCIAL

The Journal of the Rev. John Wesley, A.M. (4 vols.): J. M. Dent & Co.
Letters of John Wesley: Standard edition.
The Life of Wesley: Robert Southey, 3rd edition, Longman, Brown, Green
& Longmans, 1846.
The Life of John Wesley: John Telford, published by Charles H. Kelly.
The Life of the Rev. Charles Wesley, M.A. (2 vols.): Thomas Jackson, John
Mason, City Road, London, 1841.
History of Wesleyan Methodism (3 vols.): George Smith; vols. 1 and 2:
Longman, Brown, Green, Longmans, & Roberts, London, 1857, 1858;
vol. 3: Longman, Green, Longmans, & Roberts, 1861.
A New History of Methodism (2 vols.): W. J. Townsend, D.D., H. B. Workman,
M.A., D.Lit., George Eayrs, F.R.Hist.S., Hodder & Stoughton, 1909.
The Rev. Oliver Heywood, B.A. 1630–1702. His Autobiography, Diaries and etc.
(4 vols.): edited J. Horsfall Turner, vols. 1 and 2, A. B. Bayes, Brighouse,
1882 and [*sic*] 1881; vols. 3 and 4, T. Harrison, Bingley, 1883 and 1885.
The Life of Oliver Heywood: Rev. Joseph Hunter, F.S.A., Longman, Brown,
Green, & Longmans, 1842.
The Autobiography of Joseph Lister: edited by Thomas Wright, M.A., John
Russell Smith, London, 1842.
Biographia Evangelica (vol. 4): Rev. Erasmus Middleton, W. Justins, London,
1786.
History of Methodism in Ireland (3 vols.): C. H. Crookshank, M.A., vol. 1,
R. S. Allen, Son & Allen, Belfast, 1885; vols. 2 and 3, T. Woolmer, London,
1886 and 1888.

Memoirs of the Life of the Rev. Charles Simeon, M.A.: Rev. William Carus, M.A., Hatchard and Son, London; MacMillan, Barclay, & Macmillan, Cambridge: 1847.

Simeon and Church Order, A Study of the Origins of the Evangelical Revival in Cambridge in the Eighteenth Century: Charles Smyth, Cambridge University Press, 1940.

Henry Martyn: George Smith, C.I.E., LL.D., The Religious Tract Society, London, 1892.

Fathers of the Victorians: Ford K. Brown, Cambridge University Press, 1961.

Wilberforce: R. Coupland, Oxford, 1923.

The Life of Wm. Wilberforce (5 vols.): Robert Isaac Wilberforce, M.A., and Samuel Wilberforce, M.A., 2nd edition John Murray, 1839.

The Life of the Rev. John Fletcher: Joseph Benson, R. Lomas, City Road, London, 1806.

The Life of Mrs Mary Fletcher: Compiled by Henry Moore, 3rd edition, Thos. Cordeux, London, 1818.

John and Mary Fletcher: Rev. T. Alexander Seed, published by Charles H. Kelly.

The Parish Priest: Pourtrayed in the Life, Character, and Ministry, of the Rev. John Crosse, A.M.: Rev. William Morgan, B.D., Rivingtons, & Hatchard & Son, London, 1841.

A History of the Parish of St John, Bierley: Wilfrid Hiles, Wm. Byles & Sons, Bradford.

Memorials of Calverley Parish Church: Rev. Henry Stapleton, M.A., Richard Jackson, Leeds.

The Life and Times of Selina Countess of Huntingdon (2 vols.): By a Member of the Houses of Shirley and Hastings [Aaron Crossley Hobart Seymour], William Edward Painter, London, 1840.

A Short History of Woodhouse Grove School. 1812–1912: H. Walton Starkey, W. N. Sharpe Ltd, Bradford, 1912.

Woodhouse Grove School Memorials and Reminiscences: J. T. Slugg, F.R.A.S., T. Woolmer, London, 1885.

The History and Architecture of Dewsbury Parish Church: W. E. Gundill, O.B.E., J.P., Hon.F.R.P.S.

The Church of St Oswald, Guiseley: Alan Dobson, M.A., LL.B., and R. G. Rawnsley.

Methodist Heroes in the Great Haworth Round: J. W. Laycock, Wadsworth & Co., The Rydal Press, Keighley, 1909.

Memoirs of the Life of the Rev. William Grimshaw, A.B.: Rev. John Newton, John Greenwood, Haworth, 1854.

The Life and Writings of the Late Rev. Wm. Grimshaw, A.B., Minister of Haworth: Willian Myles, 2nd edition, Thomas Cordeux, City Road, London, 1813.

William Grimshaw, Incumbent of Haworth, 1742–63: R. Spence Hardy, John Mason, City Road, 1861.

Grimshaw of Haworth—A Study in Eighteenth Century Evangelicalism: George G. Cragg, M.A., The Canterbury Press, 1947.

Answer to a Sermon lately published against the Methodists by the Rev. Geo. White, 1749: Rev. William Grimshaw.

Methodist Good Companions: G. Elsie Harrison, B.A., The Epworth Press, 1935.

Funeral Sermon and Memoir: Rev. Henry Venn, G. Wright, Leedes [*sic*] 1763.

The Life and A Selection from the Letters of the Late Rev. Henry Venn, M.A.: edited by the Rev. Henry Venn, B.D., 6th edition, John Hatchard & Son, 1839.

Notes on the Old Haworth Registers: Rev. T. W. Story, M.A., A. E. Hall, Haworth Printing Works, 1909.

The Registers of Hartshead: The Yorkshire Parish Registers Society, 1903.

Those Two Hundred Years (1748–1948), West Lane Baptist Church, Haworth: Alec Charlton, Pastor, & G. H. Richards, 1948.

Baptism Without Controversy: 'Peter Pontifex' (Rev. Moses Saunders), R. Aked, Keighley, 1936.

The Life of Jabez Bunting, D.D. (2 vols.): By his son, Thomas Percival Bunting, vol. 1, Longman, Brown, Green, Longmans, & Roberts, 1859; vol. 2, T. Woolmer, London, 1887.

Jabez Bunting: A Great Methodist Leader: Rev. J. H. Rigg, Charles H. Kelly.

John Newton: Bernard Martin, Heinemann, 1950.

Memoirs: Charles Hulbert, privately printed, 1852.

The University of Cambridge in the 18th Century: D. A. Winstanley, M.A., Cambridge University Press, 1922.

A History of the University of Cambridge, its Colleges, Halls and Public Buildings: Rudolph Akermann, 1815.

Akermann's Cambridge: Reginald Ross Williamson, Penguin Books, 1951.

Alumni Cantabrigiensis: Compiled by J. C. Venn, Cambridge University Press, 1940.

The Life and Work of Sir James Kay-Shuttleworth: Frank Smith, John Murray, 1923.

The Remains of Henry Kirke: Robert Southey, Longman, Hurst Rees, Orme & Brown, 1823.

The Homes and Haunts of Henry Kirk White: John T. Godfrey and James Ward, Simpkin Marshall, Hamilton, Kent & Co. Ltd, 1908.

Paxton and the Bachelor Duke: Violet R. Markham, C.H., Hodder & Stoughton Ltd, 1935.

The Prelude: William Wordsworth.

English Social History: G. M. Trevelyan, Longmans, Green, 1944.

Victorian England. Portrait of an Age: G. M. Young, Oxford University Press, 2nd edition, 1957.

Novels of the Eighteen-Forties: Kathleen Tillotson, Oxford University Press, 1961.

Palmerston: W. Baring Pemberton, The Batchworth Press, 1954.

TOPOGRAPHICAL

The History of Huddersfield and the Vicinity: D. F. E. Sykes, LL.B., The Advertiser Press Ltd, Huddersfield, 1898. *Ben o' Bill's, the Luddite:* D. F. E. Sykes, LL.B., and Geo Henry Walker, Simpkin, Marshall, Hamilton, Kent, & Co. Ltd, London. Also Huddersfield, 1898.

The Risings of the Luddites: Frank Peel, T. W. Senior, Heckmondwike, 1880.
Yorkshire Anthology: J. Horsfall Turner, T. Harrison & Sons, Bingley, 1901.
The Poets of Keighley, Bingley, Haworth: Edited by Chas. F. Forshaw, W. W. Morgan, London, 2nd edition, 1893.
A Man of the Moors: Halliwell Sutcliffe, T. Fisher Unwin Ltd, 1897.
Concerning Todmorden Parish: C. G. Ramshaw, Fredk. Lee & Co., Todmorden, 1911.
The History and Topography of Bradford: John James, Longman, Brown, Green & Longmans & Charles Stanfield, Bradford, 1841.
Round about Bradford: William Cudworth, Thos. Brear, Bradford, 1876.
Pen and Pencil Pictures of Old Bradford: William Scruton, Thos Brear & Co. Ltd, Bradford, 1889.
Rambles Round Horton: Wm Cudworth, Thos Brear & Co. Ltd, Bradford, 1886.
History of the Ancient Parish of Guiseley: Philemon Slater, Hamilton, Adams & Co., London, 1880.
Keighley, Past and Present: Robert Holmes, Arthur Hall, Virtue & Co., London, 1858.
Keighley, Past and Present: Wm Keighley, A. Hey, Keighley, 1879.
Ancient Bingley: J. Horsfall Turner, Thos Harrison & Sons, Bingley, 1897.
Chronicles and Stories of Bingley and District: Harry Speight, 4th edition, Elliot Stock, London, 1904.
Brontë Moors and Villages, from Thornton to Haworth: Elizabeth Southwart and T. Mackenzie, John Lane The Bodley Head Ltd, 1923.
By Moor and Fell in West Yorkshire: Halliwell Sutcliffe, T. Fisher Unwin, 1899.
A Spring-Time Saunter Round and About Brontë-land: Whitely Turner, The Halifax Courier Ltd, Halifax, 1913.
Haworth—Home of the Brontës: John Lock, 2nd edition, H. Petty, Haworth, Yorkshire, 1961.

BRONTË BIOGRAPHIES

The Brontës: Their Lives, Friendships, and Correspondence (4 vols.): Edited by T. J. Wise and J. A. Symington, The Shakespeare Head Press, Oxford, 1932.
Charlotte Brontë and Her Circle: Clement K. Shorter, Hodder & Stoughton, 1896.
The Brontës and Their Circle: Clement Shorter, J. M. Dent & Sons, Ltd, 1914.
The Brontës. Life and Letters, (2 vols.): Clement Shorter, Hodder & Stoughton, 1908.
Charlotte Brontë and Her Sisters: Clement K. Shorter, Hodder & Stoughton, 2nd revised edition, 1906.
The Life of Charlotte Brontë: Mrs Gaskell, Smith, Elder & Co., 1893, and No. 318 Everyman's Library, J. M. Dent & Sons Ltd, 1946.
Elizabeth Gaskell: Her Life and Work: A. B. Hopkins, John Lehmann, 1952.
The Brontës in Ireland: Rev. W. Wright, D.D., Hodder & Stoughton, 1893.

The Brontës—Fact and Fiction: Angus M. MacKay, B.A., Service & Paton, 1897.
In the Footsteps of the Brontës: Mrs Ellis H. Chadwick, Sir Isaac Pitman & Sons Ltd, 1914.
Life of Charlotte Brontë: Augustine Birrell, Walter Scott, 1887.
Charlotte Brontë: T. Wemyss Reid, Macmillan & Co., 1877.
The Father of the Brontës—His Life and Work at Dewsbury and Hartshead: W. W. Yates, Fred. R. Spark & Son, Leeds, 1897.
The Brontë Country: Its Topography, Antiquities and History: J. A. Erskine Stuart, Longmans, Green & Co., 1888.
Thornton and The Brontës: William Scruton, John Dale & Co. Ltd, Bradford, 1898.
Haworth—Past and Present: A History of Haworth, Stanbury and Oxenhope: J. Horsfall Turner, J. S. Jowett, Brighouse, 1879.
A Brontë Moorland Village and Its People: A History of Stanbury: Joseph Craven, The Rydal Press, Keighley, 1907.
Pictures of the Past: Francis H. Grundy, Griffith & Farran, 1879.
The Brontë Family, with Special Reference to Patrick Branwell Brontë (2 vols.): Francis A. Leyland, Hurst & Blackett, 1886.
Emily Brontë: A. Mary F. Robinson, W. H. Allen & Co., 1883.
Emily Brontë: Charles Simpson, Country Life Ltd, 1929.
Emily Brontë—Expérience Spirituelle et Création Poétique: Jacques Blondel, Presses Universitaires de France, 1955.
The Three Brontës: May Sinclair, Hutchinson & Co., 1912.
Charlotte Brontë 1816–1916. A Centenary Memorial: Edited by Butler Wood, T. Fisher Unwin Ltd, 1917.
The Brontës' Web of Childhood: Fannie Elizabeth Ratchford, Columbia University Press, New York, 1941.
Gondal's Queen: Fannie E. Ratchford, University of Texas Press, Austin, 1955.
A Census of Brontë MSS in the United States: Mildred G. Christian, reprinted from the *Trollopian*, Berkeley, California, 1947–8.
In the Steps of the Brontës: Ernest Raymond, Rich & Cowan, 1948.
Haworth Parsonage—A Study of Wesley and the Brontës: G. Elsie Harrison, B.A., The Epworth Press, 1937.
The Clue to the Brontës: G. Elsie Harrison, Methuen & Co. Ltd, 1948.
The Father of the Brontës: Annette B. Hopkins, Johns Hopkins University Press, Baltimore, 1958.
Ann Brontë: Winifred Gérin, Thomas Nelson & Sons Ltd, Edinburgh, 1959.
Branwell Brontë: Winifred Gérin, Thomas Nelson & Sons Ltd, Edinburgh, 1961.

Index